The IBM Personal Computer™ From the Inside Out

Revised Edition

The IBM
Personal Computer™
From the Inside Out

Revised Edition

Murray Sargent III and **Richard L. Shoemaker**
The University of Arizona

Addison-Wesley Publishing Company, Inc.
Reading, Massachusetts • Menlo Park, California • New York
Don Mills, Ontario • Wokingham, England • Amsterdam • Bonn
Sydney • Singapore • Tokyo • Madrid • San Juan

This book was prepared in camera-ready form using the PS Technical Word Processor running on IBM PC computers with Diablo daisy-wheel printers. Your corrections and suggestions are welcome: please send them to the authors at the Optical Sciences Center, The University of Arizona, Tucson, AZ 85721.

Library of Congress Cataloging-in-Publication Data

Sargent, Murray.
   The IBM personal computer from the inside out.

   Includes bibliographies and index.
   1. IBM Personal Computer. 2. IBM Personal Computer--
Programming. 3. Assembler language (Computer program
language) I. Shoemaker, Richard L. II. Title.
QA76.8.I2594S27 1986   004.165   86-17321
ISBN 0-201-06918-0

Copyright © 1986, 1984 by Addison-Wesley Publishing Company, Inc.
Published simultaneously in Canada

Many of the designations used by manufacturers and sellers to distinguish their products are claimed as trademarks. Where these designations appear in the book and the authors were aware of a trademark claim, the designations have been printed with initial capital letters – for example, IBM Personal Computer.

Printed in the United States of America

10 11 12 13 14 - MW - 9594939291
Tenth printing, January 1991

To our wives,
Helga and Marianna

Contents

Preface

This book provides an in-depth explanation of the IBM PC and PC AT's hardware and software. As the title indicates, both the inner workings of these computers and their interactions with the external world are discussed. The emphasis is on fundamentals, with thorough discussions of both assembly language and computer hardware. The book starts out by covering elementary topics such as binary arithmetic and basic concepts of machine and assembly language. However, the level advances quickly, leading up to discussions of how to extend or modify the operating system to suit your special needs, how to interface assembly language subroutines to programs written in a high-level language, how to write macros, and how to use the 8087. Similarly, the hardware discussions start with explanations of diode and transistor operation, and lead up to detailed explanations of how the PC and PC AT's internal circuitry works and of how you can interface these computers to many different types of devices.

The book also gives a perspective on how the IBM PC and the IBM AT relate to other microcomputers and to mainframe computers. The IBM PC is an excellent, reliable computer for word processing, for controlling and monitoring devices in the home or laboratory, for accounting, for moderate-sized data-base management, for games, and for many other tasks. But it's not the ideal machine for everything and everybody. Just as this book is best read by people with some prior knowledge of computers, the IBM PC can most effectively be operated by people with a little computer knowledge. In this sense, the IBM PC is not as user friendly as Apple's Macintosh with its mouse/icon-driven software. Nonetheless, the IBM PC is a relatively easy to use and powerful computer that enjoys unprecedented hardware and software support from the microcomputer industry.

In fact, the IBM PC has become so popular that it defines a standard that is conformed to by a host of other manufacturers. On the one hand, such a standard is good, since standardized hardware and software allow you to interchange programs and data with others and to build on a large, strong pyramid of hardware and software contributions. On the other hand, standardization can discourage the free-wheeling atmosphere that made the microcomputer market so technologically innovative in the first place. With this in mind, our descriptions of the IBM PC and PC AT reveal both their good points and their limitations.

While other books are available that present many of the topics included here, our book is unique in having sufficient depth and breadth to show in detail how all the various hardware and software pieces of the PC and PC AT fit together. Noteworthy features include discussions of many advanced assembly-language techiques pertinent to the PC or any other 8088-based computer, detailed discussions of the PC's hardware based on schematic diagrams, explanations of how you can interface the IBM PC to many different types of devices, and a discussion of how you can construct and debug your own interfaces. Major programs presented in the book include several interrupt handlers, an example of an installable device driver, and two keyboard redefinition programs.

This book is useful for anyone who wants a basic understanding of how the IBM PC and other computers work, and for anyone who wants to develop hardware or software extensions for the IBM PC (or PC AT). The book can also be used as a textbook or as a reference on PC hardware and software. We use it at the University of Arizona as the basis for a one-semester course on microcomputer interfacing.

It's a pleasure to thank Martha Stockton for her expert editorial help and for the final printing of the camera-ready manuscript. We also thank Allen Shoemaker and Jerry Van Wesep for their helpful comments on the manuscript, Michael Aronson and Chris Koliopoulos for the benefit of their insights and their knowledge of the IBM PC, and David Glasco for help in understanding the PC keyboard. Finally we thank our wives, who, against their better judgment, permitted us to write yet another book and continue to tolerate our computer mistresses.

Tucson, Arizona   Murray Sargent III
June 1986   Richard L. Shoemaker

1
Introduction to a Supermicro

IBM is IBM is IBM.
—with apologies to Gertrude Stein

A year before IBM announced its now famous personal computer, we concluded that IBM would never make it in the microcomputer market. Our reasons were based on IBM's previous approaches and seemed inescapable:

1. IBM would write its own software.
2. IBM would charge too much.
3. IBM couldn't think small enough.
4. IBM would use a processor no one outside IBM had ever heard of.
5. IBM would discourage anyone from competing with them.

We were wrong on all five counts. Whatever blow to our egos this might have struck was almost immediately overshadowed by the excitement and delight generated by what IBM had wrought. Suddenly the microcomputer world, up to then dominated by a hobbyist mentality, had grown up, with the professional and hobbyist alike benefiting greatly.

First of all, IBM chose not to write the software, except for some support routines. Instead, IBM representatives traveled around the nation studying what the microcomputer industry had to offer, and then selected a set of programs and hardware components to use for their personal computer (PC). Only a few of the component pieces of the PC were designed by IBM.   IBM's crucial contribution was to organize the basic computer concepts and quality control well known in the world of their bigger machines and apply them to the microcomputer.

We had predicted that IBM would use an abridged version of their OS 360, the famous (or perhaps infamous) operating system of larger IBM systems, which suffers from being too big and very hard to use.   Such a system could never survive in the microcomputer market, where many users are novices and user friendliness is required.   But IBM didn't produce a small OS 360; they adopted a disk operating system from Microsoft, a leading developer of microcomputer software.   This operating system was MSDOS 1.0, primitive by current MSDOS standards, but a very effective upgrade from the earlier pioneering microcomputer disk operating system, CP/M-80. Furthermore, IBM sold it for an extremely low price.

Nor did they charge too much for the complete computer.   In fact, for relatively superior hardware, although admittedly accompanied by very little software at the time, they charged only a little more than the popular Tandy TRS-80 Model III and Apple II computers.   They sold their PC through mass outlets such as Computerland and Sears Computer Stores and have since expanded their retail outlets to many other stores that satisfy their requirements of customer support.   They did not employ the time-honored IBM method of the business-suited, persuasive salesman who boasts substantial knowledge of the machine.   Such sales people earn high salaries not available from the small profit margin offered by the IBM PC.   A disadvantage here was that the non-IBM sales people for the IBM PC often did not know a great deal about the computer they were selling, and this infuriated some customers.   However, the public is becoming ever more knowledgeable about computers (in part by reading this book!) and many would prefer to spend less, even at the cost of not having help from IBM's very capable sales force.

In designing the PC, IBM didn't have to think small—they simply put a big machine into a small box!   Instead of being limited to the 65,536-byte (64K) memories used at the time by Apple and Tandy, IBM used a processor that accesses 1,048,576 bytes (1 megabyte), 16 times as much.   Believe it or not, that still is not enough memory for an increasing number of applications, but it provided major relief from the memory squeeze in microcomputers of the 1970s.   In 1983, IBM further increased the PC's capabilities with the introduction of the IBM PC-XT, which features a built-in 10-megabyte hard disk drive, and in August 1984, IBM introduced the IBM PC AT.

We were wrong about IBM's choice of microprocessors too.   IBM used a well-known processor developed by someone else, the 16-bit Intel 8086, or rather its 8-bit data bus version, the 8088.   Thanks to the IBM PC, this has now become the most popular 16-bit processor in the microcomputer world, with quantities of software written and being written for it.   The 8088 lacks the elegance and power of the Motorola 68000 or the National Semiconductor 16032, both of which have 32-bit internal registers.   But it was thoroughly debugged and reliable at the time of the choice, with more software than any other 16-bit microprocessor. The 8088 is noticeably easier to program than the 8085, Z80, and 6502 8-bit processors used in earlier microcomputers, and it gives users access to a one-megabyte address space. It also has powerful bigger brothers: the upward-compatible 80286 used in the IBM PC AT and the gorgeous 32-bit 80386. This upward growth path gives 8088 assembly language routines a longer lifetime.

As a fifth and final surprise, IBM not only didn't discourage competition, but they helped it, by publishing an excellent technical reference manual on the PC giving the schematics of the hardware and the software listings of crucial interface routines. Madness? On the contrary! The result of all this was, in social terms, a revolution. In physics, one would describe what happened as a phase transition. Just as little magnetic domains inside a large magnetizable substance initially point in random directions, but then suddenly all line up facing the same direction when the temperature is reduced, more than ever before people are following the standards that IBM has created. Hundreds of small companies, some of whom have now grown quite large, make IBM PC compatible boards of excellent quality. Myriad groups are producing software for the IBM PC, and many companies are making IBM PC lookalikes. In short, if you work with a small computer today, it behooves you either to use an IBM PC, or to use an IBM PC compatible computer. You can then become part of this huge, unforeseen world of microcomputing, thereby taking advantage of the work of many others and saying yourself from reinventing the wheel. Synergy is a phenomenon in which the whole is larger than the sum of the parts. That's what has happened in the IBM PC world. It's true that IBM isn't making all the money being made in the PC world. But because so many people are involved, IBM is making far more money than it would have if our five suppositions had proved to be true. Curiously enough, while IBM emulated Apple Computer's Apple II open-box philosophy, Apple followed several of our five suppositions with its Macintosh for about two years and this almost ruined the company.

There is, of course, another reason for IBM's success, namely that IBM is IBM is IBM. Many people buy IBM because IBM is *the* computer company. Although we would claim that that reason isn't always valid, people acting on that reason alone reach the same conclusion as those who know: IBM has packed a great deal into a little box and has pulled the entire industry up onto a higher plateau.

A basic IBM characteristic has been to place primary emphasis on reliability and secondary emphasis on innovation. For example, the original PC's used 16-kilobit RAM chips, with the 64-kilobit chips already available, and used the small but certainly reliable Tandon 100-1 drives (single-sided, double-density, 48 tracks per inch), only later switching to the double-sided Tandon 100-2 drives for 320 kilobytes. The Tandon 100-4's with over 700 kilobytes were soon available, but were ignored.

With this in mind, we were once again astonished and delighted when, in August 1984, IBM announced its PC AT, a microcomputer so innovative that in spite of the detailed *Technical Reference*, no one managed to "clone" it for almost one year! Equipped with the relatively elegant full 16-bit Intel 80286 microprocessor giving a 2.5X boost in speed and potentially 1 gigabyte per task of virtual memory, the AT came with a quiet, speedy 20-megabyte CMI hard disk, provision for much larger drives, access to a full 16-megabyte real address space, a bigger box with a 192-watt power supply, eight full-length larger slots, a 1.2-megabyte floppy disk drive, and a surprising degree of compatibility with the PC. Tremendously excited, we violated our time-honored policy of never buying a new piece of equipment until it had been out for six months (one of us had waited a full year to buy the original PC). Sure enough, that same one of us had to replace his CMI drive three times within the first year warranty period, and some software was initially incompatible, but we just smiled. The AT easily doubled our productivity and we were very thankful that IBM had had the courage to step out in front.

All this is not to say that IBM is infallible. Its PC*jr*, discussed at length in the first edition of this book, was too underpowered for the price and time to succeed, the PC color/graphics video adaptor was an inferior piece of engineering, IBM PC memory cards have always been way behind the competition, and IBM still hasn't included a reset switch.

This book is dedicated to spilling the beans on the PC and the PC AT. How and why are IBM's choices good or bad for microcomputer applications? How can you go beyond the standards set by IBM and achieve even more powerful, exciting results? How can you program the PC or PC AT in its native machine language? How can you tailor the basic system to suit your needs in word processing, process control, telecommunications, business, games, or whatever? How can you develop new boards for special needs? And how can you use this knowledge to save money when buying a PC or PC AT and accessories for them?

At the outset, we wish to emphasize that some knowledge of computer hardware or software is a prerequisite to understanding this book. For example, the reader should have a knowledge of BASIC or some other computer language. If you don't have any computer background, we recommend that you first read one or more introductory books on the IBM PC and spend some time programming the PC in a high-level language like BASIC. With such a background, it should be possible by reading this book both to control the IBM PC and to have it control whatever you want. We have had many exhilarating experiences in working with the IBM PC, and we hope this book passes on some of these experiences to you.

The remainder of this chapter gives an overview of the hardware and software choices made by IBM for its first personal computers and explains more concretely why the PC is useful in so many different applications.

1-1. Overview of the IBM PC Hardware

The Boca Raton division of IBM put together the IBM PC in 13 months, announcing their achievement on August 12, 1981. To do this, the people involved didn't have time to design a computer from scratch. Some of the key members of the project were avid microcomputer hobbyists and had developed an excellent feel for what was then available on the microcomputer marketplace. Furthermore, they also knew what big mainframe computers could do, and asked themselves what big-machine features could be incorporated into a microcomputer costing about $3000. Some of the original ideas have fallen by the wayside. For example, we have never seen an IBM PC that used the cassette recorder facility for mass storage. The floppy-disk drive has become a much more convenient storage device for a very reasonable price. To a lesser degree, the original color/graphics display option was overshadowed by the beautiful higher-resolution monochrome display. But a remarkable number of the choices made were right on. In particular, *not* building the video circuitry into the system board was an excellent decision since it allows users with varying tastes to suit their needs and budgets.

IBM's willingness to purchase components from elsewhere in the industry is typified by the PC's floppy-disk drives bought from Tandon. It's well known that IBM invented the floppy disk, so why would they purchase drives from outside? Simply because it was a field-proven, less expensive, and immediate solution. Similarly, the much higher capacity hard-disk drives known as Winchester drives were invented by IBM, but they often buy these from outside as well.

Now let's take a quick tour through the inside of the IBM PC. Don't worry if you don't understand all the technical jargon introduced here. Everything is explained in detail in later chapters.

Opening up the PC cabinet, we admire the well-designed and reliable main computer board shown in Fig. 1-1, with its five expansion board slots (eight on the hard-disk based XT version) into which additional boards can be plugged. On the main board, up to 262,144 bytes (65,536 bytes on PC's made before May 1983) of parity-checked random access memory (RAM) sit in front of 40,960 bytes of read-only memory (ROM). The ROM contains a nice BASIC interpreter and special routines to interface to the standard input/output devices (keyboard, screen, disk, cassette, timer, serial communications, parallel printers, and so on). Next to the ROM chips are three hard-working support chips.

First, the 8253 counter/timer chip signals the microprocessor to indicate that one more tick of the clock has occurred. This allows the microcomputer to maintain the time of day and the date if the power is left on. One very useful big-machine improvement of the PC over earlier microcomputers is that the times and dates of file creation are recorded on the diskettes along with the files themselves. This allows you and special utility programs to know which of two files having the same name is the most

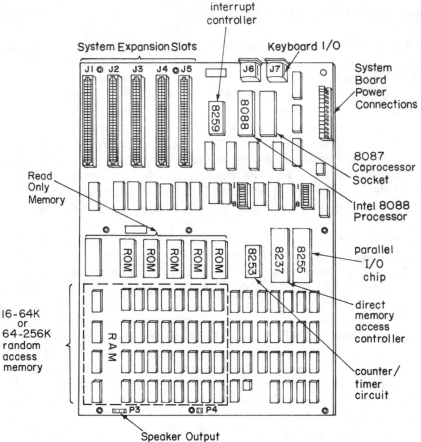

Fig. 1—1. Layout of the IBM PC main system board.

recent and to know if the latest versions of your subroutines have been compiled. The 8253 also produces signals that drive the little speaker in the left front corner of the PC so that it can beep at you or play music.

Next to the counter/timer chip, we discover the 8237 direct memory access (DMA) chip, which allows devices like the disk-drive controller to transfer data directly to and from the computer memory, without using the microprocessor. Hence the microprocessor can be busy with something else while these data transfers take place. In addition, one of the four DMA channels teams up with one of the three counter/timer channels to refresh the dynamic RAM's memory, a simple solution to a famous problem. This refresh technique also works for any additional memory on expansion boards plugged into one of the five sockets.

Finally, next to the DMA chip sits the 8255 parallel port circuit. This chip reads the system board switches to determine how much memory you have installed in the PC, as well as the number of disk drives and type of display screen that are present. The 8255 also reads the data coming in from the keyboard.

Moving on back next to the expansion board slots, we find an 8259A eight-channel interrupt controller integrated circuit, which is a handy invention neglected by most earlier microcomputers. This is the circuit that allows various devices to tap the microprocessor on the shoulder, announcing that they need attention. For example, the keyboard interrupts the microprocessor in this fashion whenever you type a character.

Finally we reach the 8088 microprocessor at the rear of the main board. The 8088 has eight 16-bit arithmetic registers, all of which can add, subtract, and, or, exclusive or, move data to and from memory, and perform various other operations. In addition to these general purpose uses, each of these registers has special features that greatly enhance the power of the instruction set. By allocating special features to different registers, the 8088 designers allow programmers to create programs that are quite byte-efficient.

Next to the 8088 is an empty socket into which you can place an 8087 floating-point coprocessor. This is a fascinating beast that can take the square root of an 80-bit floating-point number in only 36 microseconds, more than 1000 times faster than the TRS-80 and Apple II computers! With this IC (integrated circuit) and the FORTRAN 77 compilers that support it, the IBM PC with a hard disk is a respectable calculating machine, noticeably more powerful than the multimillion-dollar IBM 7094, which was the mainstay of a whole computer generation in the early 1960s.

To the right of these processors, we find a large metal box that encloses a sophisticated switching power supply. This supply provides the main board with power and each of the expansion slots with up to 1 ampere apiece. If it senses a glitch in the incoming powerline voltage, it crowbars the current to zero, thereby protecting the computer circuitry (but unfortunately erasing any data in memory).

Moving back left to the expansion board slots, we typically find plugged into them a disk controller board for the two floppy-disk drives, a video board to drive the CRT display, and perhaps a RAM memory board with an RS232 serial port, a parallel port, and a digital clock with battery backup. Such combination serial/parallel clock/calendar and memory boards are made by many companies that support the IBM PC. Upon your booting up the system (turning the power on and inserting a diskette), the PC knows the time and date (unlike many big computers).

In front of the cabinet, we see the beautiful IBM PC keyboard, which has attracted a great deal of attention, both pro and con. We are pro, and say why in Sec. 8-1. In particular, this keyboard is entirely "soft"; that is, you can make any key do anything. Any key can be a shift key, a function key, an "A", or whatever; the choice is up to you, the programmer. It also allows the computer to know how long a key is pressed, so you can play music or games with it. With regard to the music, a speaker attached to one of the counter/timer channels allows you to play tunes with finely graduated pitch but at a single (or two at best) volume level. This is far from hi-fi, but it does add fun and spirit to the programming world. Appendix C illustrates this with an assembly-language program that turns the IBM PC into a piano of sorts.

Looking at the display, we probably see well-designed upper- and lower-case green letters with descenders and serifs. Alternatively, we might see characters in color/graphics with 640 x 350 resolution. The monochrome long-persistence display has 720 points horizontally and 350 points vertically, and is refreshed 50 times per second. Its character generator ROM contains 253 characters, allowing the display of both English and foreign alphabets as well as single- and double-lined boxes. The computer system board and disk drives, the keyboard, and the display are all housed in attractive burled beige cabinets that are equally at home in Fortune 500 executive offices or your home den.

Chapter 11 outlines some of the large amount of outside-vendor hardware available for the PC. Here we just note that it is extensive, providing high-resolution graphics, complete lines of laboratory interface boards, expansion chassis, asynchronous and synchronous serial communications, modem boards, many RAM boards including a versatile bank-switching variety known as the Expanded Memory Specification (EMS), hard-disk systems, and other processor boards, including those with Z80's, 68020's, 8086's, 80286's, 80386's, and 16032's. It's fair to say that, in terms of industry support, the PC has easily surpassed all other microcomputer markets and has also become the ideal hobbyist computer. The only problem for the hobbyist is that there is such a variety of commercially available boards that one is hard pressed to think of something new to build.

1-2. Overview of the IBM PC Software

Without good software, you can throw the hardware out. Many excellent machines have fallen by the wayside because too few programmers got excited enough about them to teach them the desired tricks. The IBM PC is an exception. When the IBM PC first came out, the disk operating system (DOS) was offered for a mere $40 along with promises that Digital Research's CP/M-86 and Microsoft's XENIX, a UNIX-like system, would follow soon. A nice disk BASIC accompanied the DOS, substantially extending the power of the cassette BASIC contained in ROM. Very little other software was available, and what was available typically was flawed with bugs. Many people said, 'The IBM's a pretty machine, but there's no software. If you want a good selection of software, buy an Apple.' Not us! Although we predicted before we saw the PC that IBM wouldn't make it in the microcomputer field, we certainly didn't afterward.

The situation changed rapidly. The IBM rapidly outdistanced the 8-bit microcomputers not only in raw power and size, but also in software. Many word processors are available, at least one of which has capabilities not even found on the big machines. Many financial spreadsheet programs including Lotus 1-2-3 run on the IBM, along with a host of other financial programs and data-base programs. At least four full FORTRAN 77 compilers are available with in-line instruction support for the 8087 number cruncher, making the PC a very competitive scientific and engineering machine. Pascal and COBOL are each represented by at least three compilers, and the C language is honored by over 15 compilers at last count. FORTH, too, has several versions, along with various other languages. The Microsoft Macro Assembler, which we treat quite extensively in this book, is fast and has great power.

In short, the PC is a logical, reasonably priced choice for many computer applications: for word processing, laboratory control, medium-scale number crunching, smart terminal use, teaching, much business computing, and small-scale data-base management. With the advent of effective networking, the PC could be an excellent choice for large-scale data-base management as well. With its built-in console, the PC is actually superior to larger computers in many situations because there is no serial communications link to the terminal to slow down screen response. This is particularly true in screen editing, where a time-shared large computer has difficulty filling up the screen at 1000 characters per second, a snail's pace compared to the refresh rates of 10,000 cps achieved by several PC editing programs. The importance of high-speed refresh is that the screen can be rewritten essentially instantly, reducing the user fatigue that results from excessive screen motion.

1-3. The Nature of This Book

This book describes the various hardware and software parts of the IBM PC and PC AT, showing how they fit together in the original design and how they can be used in new ways for special applications. The software portion of the book applies equally to both computers, since they are almost completely software compatible. The hardware discussions present the standard PC hardware first, and then indicate where the PC AT's hardware differs from the PC. An attractive feature of both computers is that they can be easily extended in hardware and software to satisfy uses far beyond running simple BASIC programs and games. On the hardware side, the expansion capabilities allow for easy additions to the hardware, while on the software side, the DOS concepts of a "resident routine" and an "installable device driver" allow easy run-time and/or permanent modification of the operating system, such as adding your own keyboard, screen, and other input/output drivers.

Briefly, the book starts by explaining assembly language and shows how to modify the programs that run the hardware to suit particular needs better. Then it describes the basic hardware that makes the PC (both the standard PC and PC AT) tick, and describes additions to this hardware that allow the PC to control external processes. The final chapters show how to connect the PC to other computers and to mass storage devices, and review the wide assortment of available hardware and software. Thus the reader learns how to control the PC and to use the PC to control devices.

More specifically, Chap. 2 introduces the basic concepts and terminology of machine and assembly language in terms of the 8088 microprocessor's instruction set, and shows you how a modern computer works internally as it does its basic operations. The principles are illustrated with simple programs that can be entered and run using the DOS DEBUG program or more easily with Scroll Systems' SST assembly language debugger/interpreter. Chapter 3 then discusses assembly language and the 8088 instruction set in greater detail along with how to use the various instructions effectively in commonly encountered situations. It also shows you how to use the Microsoft Macro Assembler to write simple programs.

Chapter 4 goes on to treat more advanced topics, including how to structure large, complex assembly language programs and how to find errors in them, how to use macros and conditional assemblies, how to write assembly language subroutines for programs written in various high-level languages, how to write your own driver programs for any device attached to the computer, how to control disk files from assembly language, and how to program the 8087 numeric coprocessor.

With this software foundation in place, Chap. 5 introduces basic microelectronics, including the diode, the transistor, simple logic gates (AND, OR, XOR, and others), buffers, flip-flops, latches, clock circuits, shift registers, counters, and multiplexers, all of which are essential in building a microcomputer like the IBM PC or in designing custom PC interfaces. These thoughts are extended by Chap. 6, which describes the hardware inside the PC and PC AT computer boxes, including the major "smart" integrated circuits, such as the 8088 microprocessor itself, and the expansion input/output (I/O) channels. It also describes some features of the 80286 protected virtual address mode and shows how to switch between this mode and the 8086 real address mode.

Chapter 7 discusses the very important concepts of interrupts and direct memory access, both of which are used extensively in the running of the PC. Ways to modify and extend this usage are discussed and are illustrated in Chap. 8 by a keyboard routine that allows you to define the keys any way you like. In addition, Chap. 8 shows how the PC's remarkable keyboard and video displays work and discusses the four video display options for the PC and PC AT in some detail.

At this point, the basic IBM PC has been covered, except for the disk drives.

Leaving the disk drives to Chap. 11, Chap. 9 discusses simple devices that can be plugged into a PC, such as parallel ports, switches and relays, AC power devices, stepper motor controllers, analog-to-digital converters, and digital-to-analog converters. Two noise-reduction techniques, signal averaging and lock-in detection, are defined and implemented on the IBM PC using a simple combination of hardware and software. Waveform generation and recognition, speech processing using a CODEC, and computer music are discussed. The techniques of this chapter allow you to monitor and control a laboratory, a home or building, and other environments.

Chapter 10 explains "standard" parallel and serial communications and how to use them on the PC. These techniques allow the exchange of programs, data, or other information back and forth between two computers. Serial communications are also used extensively to hook up peripheral devices to a PC. In addition, computer networks, printer spoolers, modems, and other carrier media are discussed. Software is presented that completely bypasses the system routines for special situations that unfortunately arise all too often. The chapter also discusses the IEEE 488 Interface Bus, which is useful for laboratory control, and the SCSI bus, which is popular for interfacing hard disks, tape backups, and other block I/O devices.

Chapter 11 discusses mass storage devices such as floppy disks and hard disks, their formats, idiosyncrasies, and uses. It gives an overview of representative boards available for the IBM PC, along with a discussion of the two Expanded Memory Specifications, which allow the PC to access up to 8 megabytes of RAM with surprising ease. References are given to more extensive literature and relevant periodicals. In a similar spirit, the chapter discusses representative software available for the PC. This includes compilers, interpreters, linkers, word processors, spread-sheet programs, and other programming aids. The disk operating system DOS (essentially Microsoft's MSDOS) is discussed briefly with mention of multitasking front ends like Microsoft's Windows and IBM's TopView and with some comparison to UNIX. Finally, the chapter discusses computer hierarchies, revealing where the IBM PC and PC AT fit in the overall scheme of computing.

Chapter 12 shows you how to design, construct, and debug your own interfaces, using a wire-wrapped serial/parallel board as an example project. Although a great variety of interfaces are commercially available for the PC, the hands-on experience of building your own can provide valuable understanding and experience with computer hardware and can occasionally save you money. In addition, when that special situation comes up that can't be handled by a commercial product, you'll have the ability to build it yourself.

References

The primary references for the IBM PC are IBM's own publications, which are available from all authorized dealers. In addition to the *Guide to Operations* and *BASIC* manuals that come with the computer, you will find the following manuals to be useful:

> *Disk Operating System* (Version 2.0 or later)
> *Technical Reference*
> *Macro Assembler*
> *Options and Adapters Technical Reference, Vols. 1-3*

We strongly recommend that you obtain all of these manuals.

Other books that cover many of the same topics discussed here are:

D. J. Bradley, 1984, *Assembly Language Programming for the IBM Personal Computer*, Prentice-Hall, Englewood Cliffs, NJ. Provides excellent in-depth discussions of assembly language programming using the IBM Macro Assembler.

D. C. Willen and J. I. Krantz, 1983, *8088 Assembler Language Programming: The IBM PC*, Howard W. Sams and Company, Indianapolis, IN. Contains introductory discussions of assembly language, use of the IBM Macro Assembler, and the hardware of the PC. Their presentations are good but brief.

P. Norton, 1983, *Inside the IBM PC*, Robert J. Brady Company, Bowie, MD. Describes the PC hardware and system software. Especially good coverage of floppy disks and disk files. Uses some assembly language but does not teach the subject.

Much useful information, plus news, software reviews, and tutorial articles can be found in computer magazines. Magazines dedicated to the IBM PC include:

PC Tech Journal
PC Magazine
PC World

In addition, *BYTE* magazine, although not dedicated solely to the IBM PC, is a top quality, technically oriented magazine that is very much worth reading.

2
Introduction to Assembly Language

> It [Babbage's Analytical Engine] has no
> pretensions whatever to originate anything. But it
> can do whatever we know how to order it to
> perform.
> —Ada Augusta, Countess of Lovelace, 1844

Assembly language is a human-readable form of the machine language used by computers to run programs. Discussing it before discussing computer hardware helps to reveal how the computer works and why computer hardware is built the way it is. Assembly language gives you the ability to make a computer do literally anything it is physically capable of doing. This kind of power is often essential if you want to write programs to control the IBM PC's input and output (I/O) devices, to add new I/O interfaces, and in general to perform tasks outside the scope of high-level languages like BASIC and Pascal. A hardware interface without the necessary software (computer program) to drive it is totally useless.

We begin this chapter by discussing the advantages and disadvantages of assembly language compared to high level languages. We hope to convince you that assembly language is worth the effort required to learn it before we launch into a discussion (Secs. 2-2 and 2-3) of how numbers and text are stored in a computer, along with some other basic computer concepts and terminology. You get a chance to play around with signed and unsigned binary numbers, learn how to count in hexadecimal, and find out what ASCII, BCD, and floating-point numbers are. Section 2-4 then presents a simple paper and pencil model of a computer. The idea is to get you to build up a

13

good mental model of how a computer operates, so that you know how a computer program is executed from the computer's point of view. Once you've got a solid understanding of this model, an understanding of assembly language and computer interfacing follows in a fairly straightforward fashion. Without a good mental model of a computer, most of the remainder of this book would seem like gibberish.

Section 2-5 clarifies the distinction between assembly language and machine language. The 8088 register set is introduced in Sec. 2-6, followed by a discussion (Sec. 2-7) of how the IBM PC keeps track of one million memory locations. Finally, Sec. 2-8 presents several short, simple assembly language programs for you to trace through and play around with on your own computer. Remember, the fastest way to learn anything new is to get in there and try things out on your own.

2-1. Why Use Assembly Language?

If you have never worked with assembly language before, you may wonder why we don't just use BASIC, since BASIC is the one computer language that almost everyone knows. There are several reasons for our choice. First, as we've already pointed out, learning assembly language leads to a fairly detailed mental model of how the computer operates. You can't write I/O programs or do computer interfacing except in cookbook fashion without this understanding. Second, assembly language programs can provide you with a lot more speed and power than BASIC.

The increase in speed of program execution is tremendous, with assembly programs often running hundreds of times faster than BASIC programs. The reason for this is that each line of assembly language corresponds to a single instruction that can be directly executed by the computer in about 1 microsecond (one-millionth of a second). By contrast, each line of a BASIC program must be translated into assembly language by another program called the BASIC interpreter. (For the moment we speak as if assembly language and machine language are identical. The distinctions between the two are discussed in Sec. 2-5.) This translation is done as the BASIC program is being run, and it typically takes thousands of microseconds to execute each line of BASIC. Although a line of BASIC typically does a lot more than a line of assembly code, the time required for the translation and the somewhat inefficient code that is produced result in very slow execution speeds. Of course, there are other high-level languages, such as FORTRAN, that have the translation done before the program is run and thus execute much more rapidly (these are called compiled languages). However, no high-level language gives you full control over the machine, or the fundamental knowledge of what is happening while the program is running.

The following simple example illustrates the difference between assembly language and a high-level language. Suppose you wanted an electronics shop to build you a power supply for a piece of equipment. One way to do this would be to give them a detailed step-by-step list of instructions and circuit diagrams describing exactly how to build the supply. This would be equivalent to giving the computer an assembly language program. However, you could also just give them a brief description of the power supply's specifications, i.e., the voltages and currents required, along with a book on power supply design. This is analogous to giving the computer a BASIC program. Both methods would (we hope) produce a power supply. The second method would be easier and quicker for you to write up, but it would take the shop longer to complete the task of building the supply. Most important, with the second method you wouldn't know exactly what was inside the power supply, since the shop designed it, not you. With the first method you *would* know. The same is true for assembly language compared to a high-level language. Working with assembly language gives the benefit of knowing exactly what the computer is doing. When you use a high-level language, you only know what results are produced, not how they are obtained. This lack of knowledge may prevent you from exterminating various software/hardware bugs.

In addition to letting you know exactly what is going on when a program is run, assembly language also gives you considerably more power over the computer than you have using BASIC. When an assembly language program is executed (run), it literally takes over complete control of the machine. An assembly program can direct the computer to do absolutely anything that is within the physical capability of the machine's hardware. With BASIC, the interpreter program always retains ultimate control and attempts to keep the user from doing anything it considers unreasonable. Of course, the added power of assembly language also has its dangers. It's all too easy to have an assembly language program failure that erases both the program itself and the operating system from memory! There's nothing much you can do after such a program crash than to turn off the computer, and, after you've calmed down and stopped swearing, to turn it back on again and start over. Although this kind of problem is very rare with BASIC, it's an all too common occurrence with assembly language. Nonetheless, the power of assembly language is very useful. You can easily write programs that directly control all kinds of I/O devices, and arrange to have these control programs left in memory even after the assembly program has finished and you've gone on to something else. This kind of thing simply can't be done with BASIC.

2-2. Bits, Bytes, Hex, and All That Jazz

In order to understand how a computer operates, you first need to master some terminology and concepts regarding numbers and how they are represented within the computer. Inside the central processing unit (CPU), which is the brain of the computer, numbers are held and processed in registers. A register is just a set of flip-flops (usually eight or sixteen of them) whose contents are read or written simultaneously as a single group. A flip-flop is an electronic device that can store one of two voltage levels: either a low voltage (typically about 0.5 volts) which the computer regards as being a "0", or a high voltage (typically about 3.5 volts) which the computer regards as being a "1". Thus a register can store a group of eight 0's and 1's if it's made of eight flip-flops, and a group of sixteen 0's and 1's if it's made of sixteen flip-flops. Each of the 0's or 1's is called a *bit* (the word is a contraction of "binary digit"). A group of 16 bits is called a *word* on a 16-bit computer like the IBM PC. A group of 8 bits, or half a word, is called a *byte* on all computers. The originator of this term must have been hungry when he coined it! Logically enough, a group of 4 bits is called a *nibble*. A group of bits taken together form a binary number, just as the group of digits, 6, 7, and 8, taken together form the ordinary decimal number, 678.

The CPU inside the IBM PC is made by Intel, and is called an 8088. It contains both registers that are one byte wide and registers that are one word wide. For example, the 8088 contains a 16-bit register called the AX register. It consists of 16 flip-flops and thus can hold a 16-digit binary number; in other words, any one of the 65,536 binary numbers between 0000000000000000 and 1111111111111111. If this confuses you, recall that with ordinary decimal numbers, the position of each digit in the number is significant. In the number 179, the 9 represents nine 1's, the 7 represents seven 10's, and the 1 represents one 100. Thus starting from the rightmost digit in the number, the value of each digit position increases by a factor of 10 as you go to the left. The same thing is true for binary numbers, except that the value of each digit increases by a factor of 2 as you go to the left. Thus the number 179 in decimal would be 10110011 in binary (one 1, one 2, zero 4's, zero 8's, one 16, one 32, zero 64's, and one 128). Counting in binary goes like this: 0, 1, 10, 11, 100, 101, 110, 111, 1000, 1001, ... To get a feel for binary numbers, try a few conversions back and forth between decimal and binary. The numbers 24, 63, and 100 in decimal should be 11000, 111111, and 1100100 in binary.

Occasionally you'll need to pick out specific bits in a register, and to do this you will need some way to name each bit. The standard convention is to number each bit starting from the right with bit 0. Figure 2-1 illustrates this. For an 8-bit register, bit 7 is called the high-order or most significant bit (it's the $2^7 = 128$'s position). Bit 15 is the high-order bit for a 16-bit register. Bit 0 is the low order or least significant bit for both 8- and 16-bit registers.

Computer memory is like a set of thousands of registers, except that memory is physically located outside the CPU. In the IBM PC, the memory is organized in bytes; that is, each memory location is a set of eight flip-flops. As a result, each individual memory location can hold any of the 256 binary numbers between 00000000 and 11111111. The amount of memory one has is usually given in kilobytes (often written Kbytes or just K), and

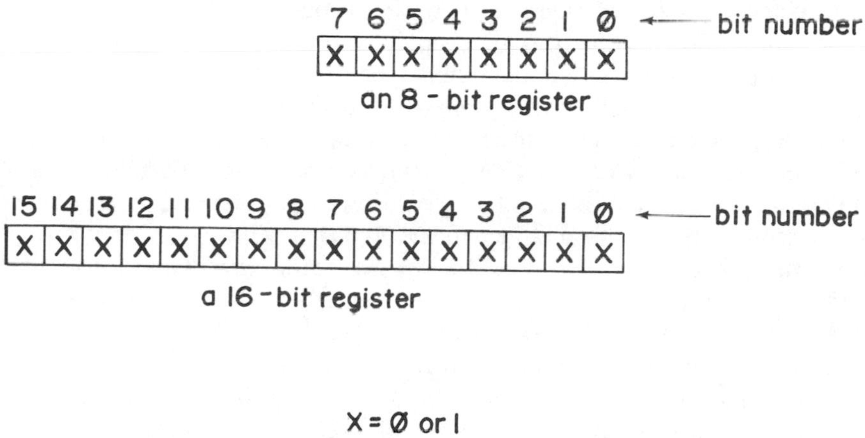

```
       7 6 5 4 3 2 1 0  ←——— bit number
      ┌─┬─┬─┬─┬─┬─┬─┬─┐
      │X│X│X│X│X│X│X│X│
      └─┴─┴─┴─┴─┴─┴─┴─┘
        an 8 - bit register
```

```
  15 14 13 12 11 10 9 8 7 6 5 4 3 2 1 0  ←——— bit number
 ┌─┬─┬─┬─┬─┬─┬─┬─┬─┬─┬─┬─┬─┬─┬─┬─┐
 │X│X│X│X│X│X│X│X│X│X│X│X│X│X│X│X│
 └─┴─┴─┴─┴─┴─┴─┴─┴─┴─┴─┴─┴─┴─┴─┴─┘
        a 16-bit register
```

X = 0 or 1

Fig. 2-1. Naming the bits in 8- and 16-bit registers.

1 kilobyte is 1024 memory locations. Thus if a computer is said to have 64K of memory, that means it has 64*1024 = 65,536 memory locations.

From this discussion, it might seem that only positive integers can be contained or manipulated in registers or memory. This is not the case, however. With the appropriate conventions, any kind of number can be represented in computer memory and in the registers. The most commonly encountered need is to represent negative integers. This is done using what is called *two's complement notation*. The two's complement of a binary number is defined as the number obtained by changing all the 1's in the number to 0's, all the 0's to 1's, and then adding 1 to the result. Hence the two's complement of 011 is 101, and of 10011000 is 01101000. It may be tempting to regard this convention as just another plot to confuse beginners, but it's really not. It turns out to be the simplest way to allow for proper addition and subtraction of both positive and negative numbers.

To see how it works, suppose we have just a 4-bit register (we're using one of those cheap, 99 cent computer chips). The first requirement is that 0 and minus zero ought to be the same number. The two's complement of 0000 is 1111 + 1 = 0000. Notice that when there's a carry out of the high order bit it is simply lost because the register only holds 4 bits. It's this feature that allows everything to work properly. The two's complement of 0001 is 1111, so 1111 is minus 1. Similarly, the two's complement of 0010 is 1110, which is minus 2. If there's any justice here, two plus minus two should be zero. Let's try. 0010 + 1110 = 0000 plus a carry out of the high order bit which is ignored. It works! Also, two plus minus one is 0010 + 1111 = 0001 as it should be. In fact, the two's complement convention gives proper arithmetic results for all positive and negative integers. It also works for any size register, be it nibble, byte, or word. Try a few 4-bit examples for yourself. Note that the negative numbers start with 1111 (-1) and go to 1000 (-8). They all have in common the fact that their high-order bit is 1.

The price paid for allowing signed binary numbers in two's complement form is a reduction in the range of allowable positive integers. With an 8-bit register, an unsigned binary number can be in the range 0 to 11111111 (255 decimal). A signed binary number, however, cannot be bigger than 01111111 (127 decimal) because the next higher number is 10000000, and all signed binary numbers whose high-order bit is 1 are negative numbers. Thus 10000000 binary is -128 decimal. Similarly, signed 16-bit binary numbers are restricted to the range +32,767 to -32,768.

As can be seen from these examples, it's rather awkward for us humans to write out binary numbers, and even more awkward to do arithmetic with them. Unfortunately, it's also awkward to try to describe computer operations using only decimal numbers. The main problem is that a lot of important information about a binary number is lost when it is written in decimal. For example, does the binary equivalent of 32,760 have all zeros in its low byte (the rightmost 8 bits)? Do the binary equivalents of 87 and 91 differ in only 1 bit position? These questions can be answered only by converting from decimal to binary, which as you've no doubt noticed if you tried some examples, is slow and tedious.

Fortunately, there is another number system that is easier to write and read than binary, retains much of the structure of binary numbers, and is very easy to convert to binary and back. This is the hexadecimal (base 16) number system. Decimal notation has 10 unique digit symbols, 0 through 9. In hexadecimal 16 unique symbols are needed. The standard convention is to use 0 through 9 plus the first 6 letters of the alphabet, A through F. Thus one counts 0, 1, 2, ..., 8, 9, A, B, C, D, E, F, 10, 11, ..., 1F, 20, ... The use of letters to represent numbers causes a few problems, but it's the standard notation.

Conversion between binary and hexadecimal is very easy. It relies on the fact that there are exactly sixteen 4-bit binary numbers, 0000 through 1111. Thus any group of 4 bits converts to exactly one hexadecimal digit. To convert any arbitrary binary number to hexadecimal, divide it up into groups of 4 bits starting from the right. If the number of bits is not a multiple of 4, just add zeros on the left of the binary number until it is. The conversion of each group of 4 bits can then be done by inspection. We strongly recommend learning the hexadecimal names of the 16 combinations of 4 bits. To get going, just remember that the leftmost bit in the group has a value of 8, the next has a value of 4, the next a value of 2, and the rightmost bit a value of 1. For example, 1011 is 8 + 2 + 1 = B. By the same process, a hexadecimal number can easily be converted to binary, digit by digit. To convert the hexadecimal number D (which is 13 in decimal), just note that it can be written as 8 + 4 + 1, which is 1110 in binary.

Hexadecimal notation is used extensively throughout the rest of this book. In cases where confusion can arise as to whether a number such as 17 is decimal or hexadecimal, we write an "H" after the number to indicate that it's hexadecimal. Thus we write 17 hexadecimal as 17H. Another possible confusion is whether CH is a number or a register name. Consequently we start all numbers with a decimal digit. Instead of CH, we write 0CH.

Doing arithmetic in hexadecimal notation takes a bit of time to learn. Fortunately, one usually needs only addition and subtraction, and these are fairly easily mastered. If you don't want to make the effort, you can always use the "H" command of the IBM DEBUG program. This calculates the sum and difference of any two hexadecimal numbers for you. You'll also find it useful to be able to count backward in hexadecimal so that you can count with signed binary numbers. For example, 0FF, 0FE, 0FD are the hexadecimal equivalents of the 8-bit signed binary numbers -1, -2 , and -3.

There are always occasions where you need to convert from hexadecimal to decimal and vice versa. There is no really easy way to do this (unless you write a little computer program to do it or have a programmer's calculator). A hexadecimal-to-decimal conversion table is a very useful aid. A nice form of this table is given in Appendix B. There are a few conversions that are worth memorizing, namely that 100H is 256 decimal, 1000H is 4096 decimal (often referred to as 4K), and 10000H is 65,536 decimal (64K).

If this discussion still sounds like Greek to you, you may want to consult Osborne and Bunnell's book, which is listed in the references at the end of this chapter. Extensive discussions of number systems and binary arithmetic are given there at a very elementary level.

2-3. How Numbers and Letters Are Stored in a Computer

You have just seen how positive integer numbers can be stored in the computer as binary numbers, and how both positive and negative integers can be stored as signed binary numbers using two's complement notation. At this point you might be wondering how the computer knows whether the number 0FE in an 8-bit register is the unsigned number 254 decimal or the signed number -2. The answer is that the computer doesn't know and doesn't care! The computer just operates as it's told to on binary numbers. How they are interpreted and what operations are done is up to you, the programmer. Hence you can let the binary numbers in the computer mean anything that you wish. All that's required is that the operations you do on them be appropriate for the interpretion you give to them.

In light of this, it shouldn't be surprising that there are other ways of using binary numbers to represent numerical quantities and even letters. Let's look quickly at three widely used representations: ASCII code for numbers and letters, BCD numbers, and floating point numbers.

ASCII is the acronym for American Standard Code for Information Interchange. In ASCII, the letters of the alphabet (both capital letters and lower case), the decimal digits 0 through 9, and various punctuation symbols, are each assigned a unique 7-bit binary number. The complete set of 128 ASCII codes is given in Appendix A. Since computer memory handles only 8-bit quantities, an extra bit set to 0 is added as the high-order bit when ASCII is stored in the computer. Thus if you want to store the string of letters "THIS IS TEXT" in computer memory, you store the sequence of hexadecimal numbers "54 48 49 53 20 49 53 20 54 45 58 54" in memory. Thus text is stored in computer memory using 1 byte of memory per letter. Similarly, the decimal number 689 would be stored in memory as 3 bytes, "36H 38H 39H" using ASCII. If you look at the ASCII table, you will also notice that the ASCII codes 0 through 1FH are assigned as control codes. The computer uses these codes to tell I/O devices like printers or display screens to do operations like "start a new page" or "back up one space". You will see lots of examples of ASCII code later in the book.

In the IBM PC there is also an additional set of 128 extended ASCII codes that are used to represent a variety of other symbols like foreign alphabets and graphics characters. These extended codes are not part of the ASCII standard. The definitions of these extended ASCII codes can be found in the IBM PC *Technical Reference* manual.

Another way of representing numbers in a computer is to use *BCD*, which is short for *binary coded decimal*. In BCD, one uses 4 bits to represent each decimal digit 0 through 9, with 0 = 0000, 1 = 0001, ..., and 9 = 1001. The remaining 4-bit codes 1010 through 1111 (corresponding to hexadecimal digits A through F) have no meaning and are not allowed. In the computer two BCD digits are packed into each byte. Thus the decimal number 689 would be stored in memory as 2 bytes, 06 89, using BCD.

The most flexible number representation of all is to store numbers as floating-point numbers. This method allows the computer to handle both very large and very small numbers, and is based on so-called scientific notation, which is commonly used by scientists and engineers. The idea is to represent a number as a product of a mantissa and an exponent. For example, to represent the decimal number 1,749,000, you write 1.749×10^6. To represent the decimal number 0.0000314, you write 3.14×10^{-5}. The mantissa is a number between 1 and 10, and gives the significant digits in the number, and the exponent tells you where to place the decimal point. Thus in the first example above, the mantissa is 1.749 and the exponent is 6, which tells you that you should move the decimal point in 1.749 six places to the right to obtain the number in its ordinary form.

The same thing can be done with binary numbers. Any binary number can be written in the form $(+/-)1.BBBBBB \times 2^{(+/-)EE}$, where the B's and E's are 1's or 0's. In a single-precision floating-point number, 24 bits are used for the mantissa, including 1 bit for the sign, and 8 bits (including a sign) are used for the exponent. This allows numbers between 10^{38} and 10^{-38} to be represented with about 6 to 8 decimal digits of accuracy. If more range or accuracy is needed, a double-precision floating-point number can be used that allocates 53 bits for the mantissa and 11 bits for the exponent, giving a range of 10^{308} to 10^{-308} and an accuracy of about 13 to

16 decimal digits. Unfortunately, the exact format used for floating-point numbers varies from one computer to another and sometimes even from one computer language to another! There is now an IEEE floating-point standard, however, and most microcomputer software conforms to it. Floating-point number formats are discussed in more detail in Sec. 4-8.

You've just seen that there are a variety of ways to represent a given number in the computer. Which method is used depends on the situation. If you must be able to handle the largest range of number values, floating-point numbers are the only reasonable choice. However, it is very difficult to write assembly language programs that handle floating point numbers properly. The 8087 numeric data processor chip discussed in Sec. 4-8 takes much of the burden off the programmer, and standard packages of floating-point subroutines are available, but in general, you are much better off using a high-level language like BASIC or Pascal if you need to handle floating-point numbers in a given application. You can always combine high-level language programs with assembly language subroutines using the techniques presented in Sec. 4-5 to get the best of both worlds.

ASCII is nearly always used for text, but only rarely for numbers if any arithmetic has to be done with them. The 8088 CPU in the IBM PC has several special instructions that facilitate doing arithmetic with ASCII numbers (see Sec. 3-11), but it's still fairly complex to do.

The BCD representation is often used in business applications since it provides a relatively easy way to do exact arithmetic with very large integers. Since such numbers often represent dollars, you don't want to have round-off errors and you also want to be able to handle amounts larger than $65,535! The 8087 numeric data processor can do arithmetic with BCD numbers of up to 20 digits.

For handling input and output from I/O devices, signed or unsigned binary integers are by far the most convenient. Binary arithmetic is relatively simple and straightforward, and the computer's instruction set is optimized to handle binary arithmetic. While numbers often enter and leave the computer through I/O devices as ASCII, we typically convert them into binary immediately, operate on the binary numbers, and then convert them back to ASCII before outputting them.

2-4. A Paper-and-Pencil Computer

You're now ready to start building a mental model of how a computer works. A good way to start is to imagine a sort of paper-and-pencil computer that you can use to visualize what goes on inside a real computer. The two most essential parts of a computer are a central processor unit (CPU) and memory. The CPU contains a set of registers that can do arithmetic and logical operations (setting bits to 0 or 1, shifting them right or left, etc.) on numbers contained in them. Memory is like a whole set of registers, with each memory location having its own unique address.

Fig. 2–2. A do–it–yourself paper–and–pencil computer.

The paper-and-pencil model for memory is a set of mailboxes or pigeon-holes. Each mailbox is distinguished from all others by its address, which you can imagine to be a number written on the outside of each box. The mailboxes are numbered sequentially, 0, 1, 2, ..., so that any mailbox in the set can easily be found. Each mailbox can contain a single number inside it, which you should imagine to be written on a slip of paper and placed in the box.

The CPU consists of a person at a desk in front of the mailboxes. On the desk are small boxes that represent the CPU's internal registers. Each one can contain a number written on a slip of paper just like the memory mailboxes. Suppose that there are just two registers, labeled AL and IP, respectively. AL is an 8-bit register, while IP is a 16-bit register. The control circuitry for the CPU is represented by the person, who has a pencil and a pad of small slips of paper. He also has a small book containing a list of all the allowed operations the CPU can perform along with a numeric code for each operation. The human CPU can read what's in any memory address or register by just looking at what is written on the slip of paper inside and can write a new value in an address or register by writing the desired value on a new slip of paper and replacing the old slip of paper with the new one. Figure 2-2 illustrates the layout of the paper-and-pencil computer. As you'll see, the human control unit's job is very simple and repetitious, so here's a situation where a person can (and usually is!) replaced by a machine.

Now look at how this "computer" executes a simple program that adds 8 to the number stored in the mailbox whose address is 200 (or, more succinctly, the number in address 200). A simple program that does this is

```
MOV    AL,8
ADD    [200],AL
```

These instructions are essentially written in assembly language, although as explained in Chap. 3 you have to give the mailbox at address 200 a formal name when using the IBM Macro Assembler program. You can write the program exactly as shown here with the handy DEBUG program, which is used in Sec. 2-8. You can also add 8 to address 200 with a single instruction as discussed in Chap. 3, but the form just described has pedagogical advantages.

There are several standard conventions for 8088 assembly language being used here. First, the form of the assembly language statements is *action   destination,source*, i.e., the action to be performed is given first (e.g., MOV), then the destination where the result is to placed is written, followed by the source from which the data is to be obtained. The destination and source are separated by a comma. For MOV AL,8, the 8 in the instruction is moved into the AL register. Second, a number in square brackets means that you should interpret what's inside the brackets as a memory address and use the *contents* of that address as the source or destination data. Hence ADD [200],AL adds the contents of AL to the contents of location 200. The format of assembly language statements is discussed in more detail in Sec. 3-1.

How does the computer run a program like the one just given? The first question that comes up is: Where does the program go, and in what form? There is no special place in the computer to store programs, and even if there was, the computer isn't able to read English. The solution is ingeniously simple. Each instruction is represented by one or more numbers. These numbers serve as codes for the instructions. The encoded program is then just a string of binary numbers that is stored in the memory mailboxes. Note that the program is stored in the same memory as the data you want the program to manipulate. There is no visible distinction between a program stored in memory and data stored in memory (though the two are normally stored in separate areas of memory). When encoded as numbers, our little example program looks like:

```
B0 08
00 06 00 02
```

The number corresponding to an instruction is called the *op code* for that instruction. Here and throughout the rest of this section all numbers are hexadecimal.   The binary equivalents of these hexadecimal numbers are stored in order in a sequential set of mailboxes. If the program is stored starting at address 0, for example, address 0 would contain the number B0, address 1 would contain 08, address 2 would contain 00, address 3 would contain 06, address 4 would contain 00, and address 5 would contain 02.

To run this program, the CPU must somehow have the address of the first instruction placed in the IP register. We discuss how this can be done shortly. For the moment just assume that the program starts at address 0 and that the IP register contains 0 also. The paper and pencil computer can now be started up.

Execution begins with the CPU fetching (reading) the contents of the address to which the IP register is pointing. That is, it looks at the number contained in IP (which is 0 here) and then looks in the mailbox whose address is this number (mailbox 0). Inside mailbox 0 it finds a B0, which it reads (imagine that it gets copied onto a sheet of scratch paper). As soon as it reads the B0, it immediately increments IP; that is, 1 is added to IP. The process just described is called an *instruction fetch cycle*. The contents of IP are assumed to contain a memory address, the contents of this address are read by the CPU, and IP is incremented. Figure 2-3 illustrates what happens in an instruction fetch cycle. This cycle is repeated every time that the computer executes an instruction, so it's very important that you understand what happens. Make sure you distinguish between an address and the contents of that address, and between a register and the contents of that register.

Having fetched the first byte of an instruction, the CPU is now ready to execute it. To do this it checks a little internal table to see what the instruction requires it to do. In the paper-and-pencil model, this corresponds to looking in the small op code book sitting on the desk. In the example program, the instruction fetched was a B0. The internal table tells the CPU that B0 means to move an 8-bit value into AL and that this value is contained in the next byte of the program. Fetching the contents of address 1 (which is a 08), the CPU moves the value 8 into AL. It is then ready to fetch, decode, and execute the second instruction of the program. Fetching the op code 00 from address 2, the CPU knows it has to add a byte value in a register to some memory location. To find out which register and memory location to use, it fetches the next program byte (at address 3), which is a 06. This byte tells it that the contents of AL must be added to the memory location specified by the following two bytes, 00 and 02. These bytes are fetched by the CPU and combined to form the 16-bit address 0200. Note that the first address byte read is assumed to be the least significant (rightmost) byte of the word. This convention is always used by the 8088 CPU whenever a 16-bit word is stored in memory. It may seem backwards, but that's the way it's done, not only on the 8088, but also on many other computers such as the 8080 and the Z80.

We have now finished describing the execution of two instructions. Every instruction that the computer executes is done in roughly the same

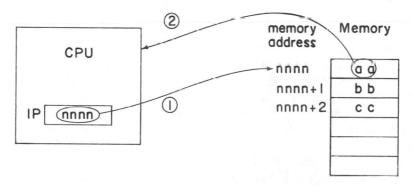

1. The CPU selects a memory address nnnn to read by using the contents of the IP register.

2. The contents of memory address nnnn, i.e. "a a", are then read by the CPU.

3. The IP register is incremented to nnnn + 1.

Fig. 2–3. An instruction fetch cycle.

way. The computer always begins by fetching the instruction from memory. It determines what the instruction means, and if required, fetches one or more additional bytes of the program to obtain any further information needed to complete the instruction. Notice that IP always contains the address of the next byte in the program because it is always incremented immediately after each byte is fetched from memory. Once the instruction fetch cycle and any additional memory reads are complete, the CPU completes the execution of the requested operation. The amazing thing about a real computer is that it takes only about one millionth of a second to do all of this!

At this point you should have a good grasp of how a computer executes a program. If you're still a little unsure, try actually setting up the paper-and-pencil computer and execute the program just presented yourself. In Sec. 2-8 we show how to enter and follow the execution of simple programs on the PC with a special type of program called a debugger.

Although we've described in some detail how a computer executes a program, several questions still remain unanswered. First, how does a computer get started; that is, what happens when the power is first turned on? The answer is that at power-on, IP is set to a fixed value by internal hardware inside the CPU, and the CPU then starts to execute whatever program is at that address. The program located at that address is usually contained in a special type of memory chip called a ROM (see Sec. 6-2). This program is permanently etched in the chip and cannot be altered or erased except by replacing the chip. In the IBM PC, the 8088 CPU starts to execute the program in ROM, and this program tells the computer to load in a much more elaborate program from the floppy disk called a disk operating system (DOS), provided the system has a disk drive attached. The procedure of having a small program load in a much more complicated one is called *bootstrapping* or *booting up the system*. The terminology comes from the old phrase "lifting yourself by your own bootstraps." The DOS program controls the screen and keyboard and permits other programs to be loaded into memory at your command.

When a program such as the two-instruction example just discussed is stored into memory by the DOS, the DOS keeps track of where it stored it, and then places the beginning address in the IP register. The instruction that places a new value in IP is called a *jump instruction*, since the program execution suddenly jumps to a new place in memory when the value in IP is changed. Once the jump instruction is executed, the little program starts to execute.

A second question is what happens at the end of the program? Does the computer stop operating or what? The answer is that the program is incomplete. If the program were loaded as given, the computer would execute the MOV and ADD instructions. The IP would then be pointing to the next location in memory, and the CPU would fetch whatever was there. But what's in memory there may not be an instruction! It's just some random number that happened to be there when power was turned on or a number that was left there by a previous program. The results of having the computer fetch random numbers and interpret them as instructions are often quite bizarre and unpredictable. Typically all of memory quickly gets garbage written into it (remember the computer executes hundreds of thousands of instructions per second), and the computer stops responding to anything. This is called having the computer *crash*.

The way to avoid producing a crash at the end of a program is very simple. The proper jump instruction is placed in memory after the last instruction of the program. This instruction loads the IP with the address of an entry point (the first instruction of a program or a section of a program) to the DOS. In this way the computer immediately goes back to running the operating system program as soon as it finishes a user program.

2-5. Machine Language versus Assembly Language

One point that needs to be clarified before going on is the relationship between machine language and assembly language. As you've seen, when the computer executes a program, it reads a list of binary numbers in memory, and interprets them as instructions. To make the numbers easier to read, they are normally writen in hexadecimal. The list of numbers, whether in binary or hexadecimal, is called a *machine language program*. The hexadecimal listing of the little program discussed in the previous section is an example of machine language.

Although programs can be written directly in machine language, the process leaves a lot to be desired. After deciding what instructions you want the computer to execute, you have to look up the numeric code corresponding to each instruction. The resulting list of hexadecimal numbers can then be entered into computer memory and executed. If you wish, you can actually try this using a debugger program (see Sec. 2-8). The "E" command allows you to enter the op codes into memory, and the program can then be executed using the "G" or "T" commands. This whole process is slow and tedious since the op codes for each instruction must be calculated using a reference book such as Intel's *iAPX 88 Book*. There are about 134 distinct instructions, and most of these can use any one of 24 memory addressing mode variations or any one of 16 different CPU registers for both the source and the destination. Thus a single instruction can have up to 1024 variations, and the total number of distinct op codes is many tens of thousands. What's worse, if a mistake is found (and one almost always is) that requires the addition or deletion of instructions in the middle of the program, much of the program has to be re-entered into memory, and the codes for some instructions (jumps and calls) have to be recalculated. An equally severe problem is the lack of documentation. A machine language program is virtually unreadable when you go back to look at it even a short time after you've written it. This makes it extremely difficult to modify or improve a previously written program.

Almost all the problems just described can be eliminated by using assembly language instead of machine language. Assembly language is essentially a human-readable form of machine language. Recall the little program discussed in the previous section:

```
B0 08           MOV    AL,08
00 06 00 02     ADD    [200],AL
```

The machine language program is on the left, while the equivalent assembly language program is on the right. The assembly language is obviously far easier to read and understand. Since it's really a shorthand description of the computer operations to be performed, assembly code can be written down directly, without having to look up anything.

An obvious problem with assembly language is that something has to be done to allow the computer to read it. This job is accomplished by having the computer run a special program called an assembler. The assembler reads your assembly language program and translates each assembly language statement into binary machine language. This process is fairly fast, requiring only seconds for a program of average size. Also, unlike humans, the computer doesn't make mistakes when doing the translation. The Microsoft (or the IBM) Macro Assembler is the standard assembler program available for an IBM PC running PC DOS. In the following two chapters we discuss its operation and capabilities in considerable detail.

The DEBUG program included on the IBM DOS disk or any of the other debuggers discussed in Sec. 2-8 also have miniassemblers built into them that can be used to enter, run, and save small assembly language programs. Although not suitable for writing substantial assembly language programs, the debugger assemblers are much simpler and easier to learn than the Macro Assembler. In the last section of this chapter we present some short programs that you should try out for yourself using a debugger program. This will give you a feel for what assembly language is all about. First, though, let's take a quick look at the registers available in the 8088 CPU, the chip that is the heart of the IBM PC.

2-6. The 8088 Register Set

For the purposes of assembly language programming, the 8088 can be looked at as simply a set of registers whose contents can be modified in various ways by assembly language instructions. Figure 2-4 shows the complete set of 8088 registers. As can be seen, the 8088 has a total of fourteen 16-bit registers. They can be divided into four different functional groups as shown in the figure. Many of the registers have special functions when used with certain instructions, although they can also be used as general purpose registers. If you don't understand everything in this section on first reading, don't be alarmed. The various special register uses are discussed in detail in the next chapter as the instruction set is presented. This is just a brief preview.

The most important register group is the data registers, as these are the most flexible and most often used. They are unique in that each of the four can be used either as a single 16-bit register or as a pair of 8-bit registers. For example, we could fill the 16-bit AX register with the number 0008 using the MOV AX,8 instruction. The same number could also be put in the register using two instructions, MOV AH,0 and MOV AL,8. The "H" and "L" in AH and AL stand for the "High" and "Low" bytes of the 16-bit AX register. It's your choice whether you want to use the data registers as 8-bit registers, 16-bit registers, or any mixture of the two. This flexibility is especially convenient when handling ASCII characters and small integers.

The data registers behave identically for most instructions, but there are some differences. First of all, many instructions execute faster and/or have a shorter machine language instruction when the AX (or AL) register is used. Also, the AX (or AL) register is used for all input/output instructions. The AX register is often referred to as the *accumulator*, because in early computers, this register was the only register where arithmetic could be done and where arithmetic results could be accumulated. In the 8088, arithmetic operations can be done in all registers except the segment registers and the IP and flags registers.

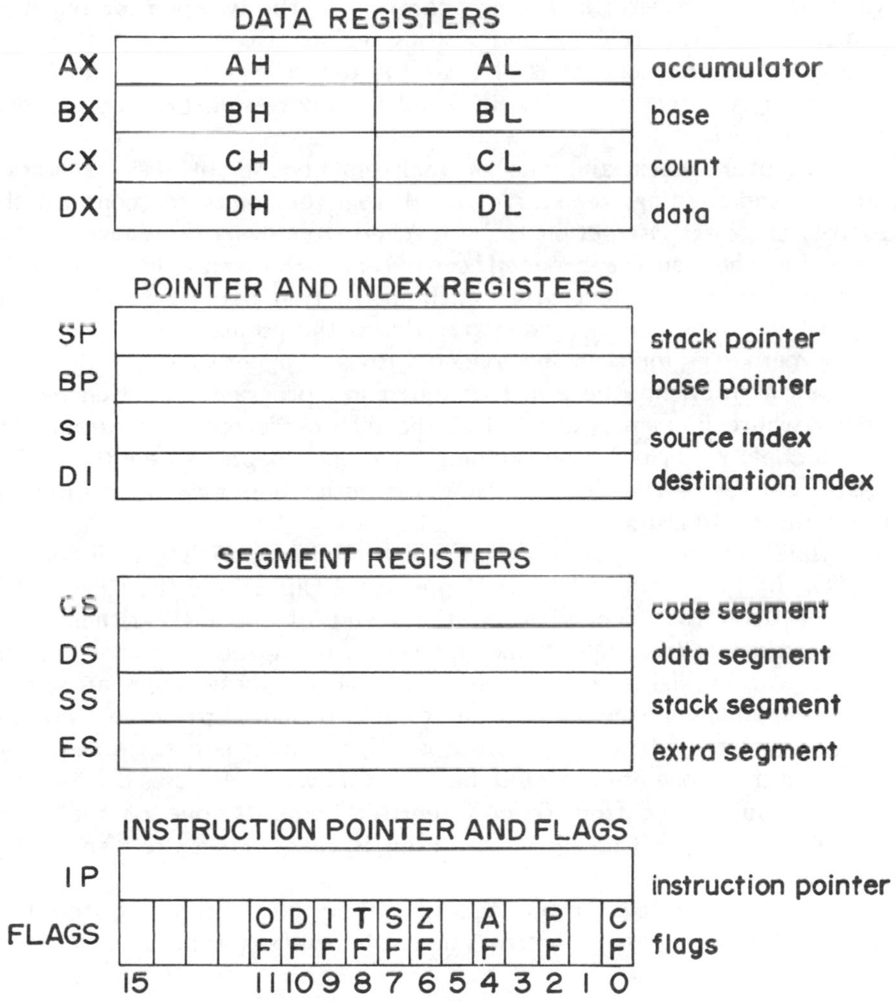

DATA REGISTERS

AX	A H	A L	accumulator
BX	B H	B L	base
CX	C H	C L	count
DX	D H	D L	data

POINTER AND INDEX REGISTERS

SP		stack pointer
BP		base pointer
SI		source index
DI		destination index

SEGMENT REGISTERS

CS		code segment
DS		data segment
SS		stack segment
ES		extra segment

INSTRUCTION POINTER AND FLAGS

IP		instruction pointer

FLAGS | | | | | O F | D F | I F | T F | S F | Z F | | A F | | P F | | C F | flags

15   11 10 9 8 7 6 5 4 3 2 1 0

Fig. 2–4. The 8088 register set.

The BX register has a special use in addressing memory, as discussed in Sec. 3-4, where the memory addressing modes are presented in detail. It's sometimes called the *base register*. The CX register is often used as a counter to contain a "count" value for certain repetitive instructions. For example, there is a LOOP instruction that works like BASIC's FOR...NEXT loop. The number of times the loop is repeated is determined by the value in CX. The DX, or *data register*, has only one special use, and that is to contain the I/O port address for input and output instructions.

The pointer and index register group consists of four 16-bit registers; the base pointer (BP) register, the stack pointer (SP) register, the source index (SI) register and the destination index (DI) register. These registers cannot be accessed in 8-bit pieces, but they can be used if desired for general purpose arithmetic and logic operations. The two pointer registers are typically used for reading and writing values from a data structure called a *stack*. This concept is discussed in detail in Sec. 3-5. Similarly, the two index registers are primarily used for addressing memory, as discussed in Sec. 3-4.

An absolutely essential group of registers consists of the instruction pointer (IP) and the flags register. The IP register points to (contains the address of) the next instruction to be fetched from memory as discussed in Sec. 2-4 for the paper-and-pencil computer. The value in IP may be changed in two ways. Just after each instruction byte is fetched from memory, IP is always incremented by 1. This is the normal way IP changes. The other method is for IP to be loaded with a completely new value by a jump or call instruction. These instructions allow program execution to skip around anywhere in memory. It's like the difference between turning the pages of a book one by one, and skipping from one chapter to another. The IP register cannot be changed by a MOV instruction and it cannot be used as a general purpose register.

The flags register is not a normal register. Instead it's a collection of *flag bits*, or *flags* for short. A flag is just a flip-flop in the CPU that is set to 1 or reset to 0 depending on the result of the last arithmetic or logical operation. You might think of them as being the computer equivalent of the warning lights on your car's dashboard. These lights are either on or off, depending on the state of your car. If the oil pressure drops too low, a light goes on. If the oil pressure is OK, the light is off. An example of computer flag operation would be the following: If the BX register contents are subtracted from the AX register contents, one of the flags, called the zero flag, will be set if the result is zero. Flags are discussed in detail in Sec. 3-7.

Finally, there are four 16-bit registers called the segment registers that enable the 8088 to address its entire 1 megabyte memory space.

2-7. The Segment Registers

To understand how the segment registers are used, you have to understand how the 8088 addresses memory. Unlike the previous generation of 8-bit microprocessors such as the 6502, the Z80, and the 6809, which all could access only 64K of memory, the 8088 can directly access 1 megabyte of memory. This is very handy, since memory has become so inexpensive. We cannot imagine running on machines with less than 128K, if that little! However, there's a price to be paid for this capability. As you've seen, the 8088 registers, and in particular the IP, are only 16 bits wide. This means that only $2^{16} = 65,536$ different memory locations can be accessed by the IP register. How then can the 8088 address a megabyte of memory?

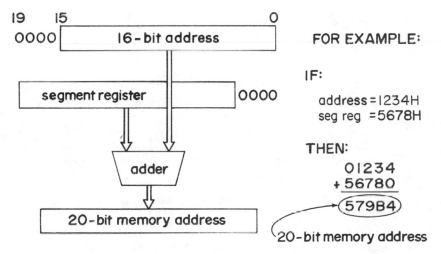

Fig. 2-5. How memory addresses are formed by the 8088.

The answer is that whenever the 8088 sends out a memory address, it is always a 20-bit address formed from the sum of a segment register and one of the other registers (or in some cases a 16-bit address contained in the instruction or memory). The sum is done in the following way: The segment register contents are shifted left 4 bits (by one hexadecimal digit) and then are added to the contents of the other register. For example, when an instruction is fetched from memory, the address is the sum of the IP and the code segment register, CS. Figure 2-5 illustrates the process by which a memory address is formed. If IP contains 0100H and CS contains 0200H, the memory address sent out by the CPU would be 02100H. The formation of a 20-bit address is automatically done by hardware in the 8088 and is not under the programmer's control. To refer to such an address concisely, we often write it as CS:IP, so that in the example just given, CS:IP = 200:100. The DEBUG program always displays addresses in this format.

The fact that two registers have to be added to obtain a 20-bit address may seem somewhat awkward, and in certain cases it is. Newer microprocessors such as the Motorola 68000 and the National 16000 have 32-bit-wide internal registers and hence can directly address many megabytes of memory. At the time the 8088 was designed, microprocessors of this complexity were not yet feasible. On the other hand, there is a disadvantage to having 32-bit registers, namely that programs on such machines require a lot more memory than they do on the 8088. A Pascal compiler currently available for the 68000 requires a minimum of 512 kilobytes of memory!

All memory accesses by the 8088 are done with 20-bit addresses. When data is moved to or from memory with the MOV instruction, a 20-bit address is formed using the data segment (DS) register. For example, the instruction MOV AL,[100] moves data into AL from location 100 plus DS shifted

IP – added to CS always

SP – added to SS always

BP – added to SS   these segment register assignments

all other – added to DS   can be changed with a segment
registers   override prefix

EXCEPTION: DI is always added to ES for string
primitive instructions

Fig. 2–6. Default segment register assignments.

left 4 bits. There is also a stack segment register (SS), which is added to
the pointer registers SP or BP to obtain an address. Finally there is the
extra segment (ES) register, which is primarily used together with DI to
form a 20-bit address for certain "string primitive" operations (see Sec.
3-10). Figure 2-6 shows the default segment register assignments for the
8088. The use of segment override prefixes to change the default assignments is discussed in Sec. 3-12.

The picture of memory that emerges from all this is as follows: Each
segment register points to the beginning address of a 64K block of memory
(called a *segment*) located within a one-megabyte memory space, and this
64-kilobyte segment can start at any address that is a multiple of 16
(because of the 4-bit left shift used to form a 20-bit address). Figure 2-7
shows how a map of memory would look for one set of values in the segment
registers. The memory segments pointed to by the CS, DS, SS, and ES registers can totally or partially overlap, or they can point to totally different
areas of memory. There are no restrictions.

Fortunately, 95% of the time, you'll be able simply to ignore the fact
that such things as segment registers exist. The reason for this is that the
operating system initializes the segment register values for you when it
loads your program into memory for execution. Hence, unless your program
and data amount to more than 64 kilobytes (and few assembly language
programs even approach this size), you can simply think of all your addresses
as being 16 bits. The segment registers just provide a fixed offset into the
memory address space. This also means that whatever other programs are
stored in memory below your program (the operating system, special I/O
drivers, "RAM disks", etc.) do not change your 16-bit addresses; they only
change the segment registers. This relocation capability proves to be very
useful.

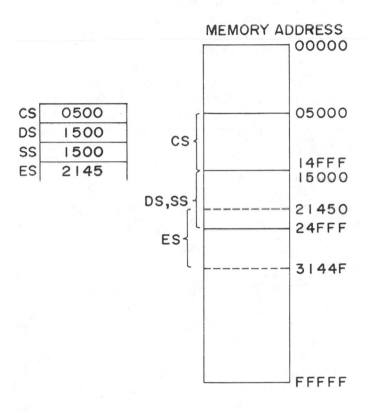

Fig. 2-7. An example of how memory segments are addressed using the segment registers.

2-8. Some Simple Assembly Language Examples

One of the best ways to get a firm grasp of the ideas presented in this chapter and to learn some new things besides, is to try out some examples of assembly language programming for yourself.   In this section you'll find some suitable programs for doing this.   Try to enter and run these examples using the DEBUG program that comes with IBM DOS.

DEBUG is an example of a type of program called a *debugger*.   This name comes from the fact that errors in a computer program are called *bugs*.   Hence debuggers are programs that assist you in finding and removing bugs.   The DEBUG program does this by allowing you to enter, change, and trace the operation of your programs.   Programs can be entered under DEBUG using machine language or, with DOS 2.0 and later versions, using assembly language.

Before you try the examples you should understand how DEBUG displays memory addresses. Addresses are shown in the form XXXX:YYYY, where XXXX and YYYY are 16-bit hexadecimal numbers. This represents a 20-bit memory address that is the sum of XXXX0 and YYYY. Thus DEBUG gives addresses in the same way that addresses are formed in the 8088, namely by summing a left-shifted segment register value and a second 16-bit quantity (see Sec. 2-7). The tricky thing about giving addresses this way is that the same address can be written in many different ways. For example, the memory address 12345 can be written as 1234:0005, or as 1230:0045, or as 1233:0015, etc. This takes a little getting used to, but causes few problems once you get the hang of it.

Let's start out by looking again at the example program discussed in Sec. 2-4:

```
XXXX:0100   B0 08         MOV   AL,8       ;Move an 8 into AL
XXXX:0102   00 06 00 02   ADD   [200],AL   ;Add AL to contents of
                                           ; memory location 200
```

Here the program addresses appear in the leftmost column, followed by the machine language, and finally the assembly language. To aid in explaining how the program works, comments have also been added after the assembly language instructions. The beginning of each comment is marked by a semi-colon. Comments are ignored by the computer, so there is no point in entering them when DEBUG is being used. The segment portion of the address is left as XXXX here because this value varies from one IBM PC to another depending on the equipment installed in the PC and the version of the operating system being used. The segment value will automatically be chosen for you when DEBUG is loaded and will remain fixed unless you change it. Thus if you want to enter this program in machine language, just type E100(enter) where (enter) denotes pressing the ENTER key, and then type B0 08 00 06 ... Alternatively, to enter the program in assembly language, type A100(enter) and then type MOV AL,8(enter), ADD [200],AL(enter). DEBUG will automatically translate the assembly language to machine language and enter the machine language into memory.

Once you've entered the program into memory, you can look at it again using U100(enter), which will translate the machine language back into assembly language and display it on the screen. You can look at the machine language or the numbers contained in memory locations alone with the "D" command.

To see how the program executes, first type R(enter). This will display the current register contents on the screen. The IP should contain 100, so that it's pointing at the first instruction of the program. Now use the "T" command to single step through the program, watching what each instruction does. Section 2-4 describes the action that is performed by each instruction. After each step, the register contents are displayed along with the instruction that will be executed when you do the next single step (not the instruction that just was executed). To start the program over again, use the "R" command as described in the DOS manual to set IP back to 100 again. You can examine the contents of location XXXX:200 at any time using the "D" command. You might also be interested to know that the action taken by this entire little program can be done using only one instruction, namely ADD BYTE PTR [200],8. Try it! We wrote it as two simpler instructions for illustrative purposes only. You are probably asking yourself why the "BYTE PTR" is there. PTR stands for *pointer*, and the words BYTE PTR mean that [200] points to a byte in memory. It's there to tell DEBUG to assemble the code for adding 8 to the byte contained in location 200, rather than to the 16-bit word contained in locations 200 and 201. To add 8 to a word starting at 200, we'd enter ADD WORD PTR [200],8.

Now let's look at a slightly more complex program which calculates the sum of the integers 1 through 10. Here it is:

```
XXXX:0100   B9 01 00   MOV   CX,1    ;1 is first integer to be added
XXXX:0103   B8 00 00   MOV   AX,0    ;Initialize the sum to zero
XXXX:0106   01 C8      ADD   AX,CX   ;Add an integer to the sum
XXXX:0108   41         INC   CX      ;Increment the integer by 1
XXXX:0109   83 F9 0A   CMP   CX,0A   ;Is new integer greater than 10?
XXXX:010C   76 F8      JBE   106     ;Jump back to address 106 if not
XXXX:010E   90         NOP           ;At this point sum will be in AX
```

The operation of the first three instructions here should be self-evident by now, and the INC instruction is a shorthand way to add 1 to something. The compare (CMP) and jump-if-below-or-equal (JBE) instructions work together. CMP CX,0A compares the contents of CX with the number 0A. The result of the comparison is stored in the flags, and used by the JBE instruction. If the number in CX was below (less than) or equal to 0A, then the JBE 106 instruction puts a 106 into IP so that the next instruction to be executed is ADD AX,CX. If CX was greater than 0A, the JBE 106 instruction does nothing, and the next instruction to be executed is NOP. The two instructions are the assembly language equivalent of the BASIC statement "IF CX<=10 THEN GOTO 106". The NOP instruction is a do nothing instruction; it stands for *no operation*. We've put it at the end of the program just to have a place to refer to as the end of the program.

You can single step through this program with the "T" command, or you can just execute it to find the sum by using the "G" command. If IP is set to 100, just type G10E(enter). The program will then execute until it reaches address 10E, and then will stop and display the registers. Don't just type G(enter), or the 8088 will attempt to execute the contents of the uninitialized memory locations following the program as instructions, and will probably crash.

Now let's recode this program with a new twist to it. We shorten the program by doing the addition in reverse order, so that it now looks like:

```
XXXX:0100   B9 0A 00    MOV    CX,0A    ;10 is first integer to be added
XXXX:0103   B8 00 00    MOV    AX,0     ;Initialize the sum to zero
XXXX:0106   01 C8       ADD    AX CX    ;Add an integer to the sum
XXXX:0108   E2 FC       LOOP   106      ;Decrement CX, loop if CX not 0
XXXX:010A   90          NOP             ;At this point the sum is in AX
```

We've eliminated two instructions by using the LOOP instruction. This instruction performs three operations in one instruction. It decrements CX (subtracts 1 from it), compares CX with 0, and then jumps to address 106 if CX is not zero. It's rather like BASIC's FOR...NEXT loop with CX serving as the counter variable. Doing the additions starting with 10 allows us to use this powerful instruction and reduce the length of the program. A general principle is at work here, namely that whenever you need to increase the speed or reduce the size of a critical program section, look for ways of redoing the logic in a fashion that takes advantage of the 8088 instruction set's strengths.

If you look at the machine language for this program and the previous one, you'll see that the JBE and LOOP instructions don't contain the address 106 where the program execution is supposed to jump to. Instead, they contain a signed 8-bit binary number as the second byte of the instruction, which gives the displacement that must be added to the current value of the IP to reach the desired address. Check this out for yourself to see that it works. The reason for doing things this way is that it makes the machine code *relocatable*, meaning that you can move the program so that it starts at a different memory address and it will still run correctly. This is a very valuable feature to have in a computer. A second reason is that a target address can be given in a single byte. Of course this greatly restricts the range of conditional jumps (in contrast to the earlier 8080 and Z80 microprocessors).

Next let's look at a program that produces some visible results, namely one that prints the word "HELLO" on the screen:

```
XXXX:0100   BB 20 01    MOV    BX,120   ;Point BX at string to output
XXXX:0103   B9 05 00    MOV    CX,5     ;CX has # of chars to output
XXXX:0106   8A 17       MOV    DL,[BX]  ;Get a character
XXXX:0108   B4 06       MOV    AH,6     ;Call DOS function 6
XXXX:010A   CD 21       INT    21
XXXX:010C   43          INC    BX       ;Point BX at next character
XXXX:010D   E2 F7       LOOP   106      ;Loop back till 5 chars done
XXXX:010F   90          NOP

XXXX:0120   48 45 4C 4C 4F                ;ASCII string to output
```

To enter the ASCII string at the end of the program, use DEBUG's "E" command. Then run the program by typing "G10F(enter)". You should see the word "HELLO" appear on the screen.

This program introduces two new concepts. First, we see a new way to move a value from memory into a register. The MOV DL,[BX] instruction moves the contents of the memory location whose address is contained in BX into DL. Think of BX as playing the role of a pointer, which points to the memory location where the desired data is. The advantage of using this rather than using MOV DL,[120] is that you can point to another memory location by just changing the contents of BX, and thus reuse the MOV DL,[BX] instruction inside a program loop.

The second new idea is that of a *DOS function call*. The disk operating system contains a number of functions (which are just small programs) that handle input and output for the keyboard, the CRT screen, the printer, and the disk drives. With IBM DOS, you can use these DOS functions yourself by means of the software interrupt instruction (INT). The INT instruction works as follows: The number following INT is used by the 8088 to find an address in a table in low memory of the IBM PC, and program execution jumps to the address found in that table when an INT is executed. When the function call ends (with an IRET instruction), program execution resumes at the next instruction following the INT. Thus the INT instruction works rather like BASIC's GOSUB instruction. We have a great deal more to say about INT later in the book, since it provides a very powerful method of controlling I/O devices. In fact we'll show you how to write your own function calls, which can replace the DOS calls and handle your I/O devices in any way you desire.

One particular interrupt, namely INT 21, is used to reach the I/O functions present in IBM DOS. Which function is executed depends on the number present in AH when the INT 21 is executed. Appendix D of the IBM *DOS* manual describes the various function calls available. In the program above, the DOS function call used is function 6, direct console I/O. When this function is called via INT 21, the DL register must contain the character that you want written on the screen. Hence the little program above loads ASCII characters from memory locations 120 through 124 into DL and does an INT 21 each time.

One word of caution about using the "T" command to trace program execution through an INT instruction. If you do this, you'll find yourself single stepping through the DOS function call program, and this program is very long. You may find it educational to look at this code, but be prepared to single step for a very long time. If you get tired of single stepping and use the G command—for example, "G10C(enter)"—to get out of the function call routine, you may find that the computer doesn't return properly to your program. This is a bug in the current version of DEBUG; perhaps it will be fixed in later versions. The best procedure for single stepping through programs containing an INT is to use the "T" command until you reach the INT instruction, and then to use the "G" command to get to the next instruction following INT. In the example above, use "T" to get to address 10A, then type "G10C(enter)" to get past the function call.

DOS function calls can also be used to read values in from the keyboard. Here's a little example that reads the keyboard and then simply prints what's typed on the screen:

```
XXXX:0100  B4  06       MOV   AH,06    ;Set up for DOS function call 6
XXXX:0102  B2  FF       MOV   DL,FF    ;set DL=FF for keyboard input
XXXX:0104  CD  21       INT   21       ;Check the keyboard
XXXX:0106  74  FC       JZ    104      ;Check again if zero flag set
XXXX:0108  88  C2       MOV   DL,AL    ;Else move character into DL
XXXX:010A  CD  21       INT   21       ;And output to screen
XXXX:010C  EB  F4       JMP   102      ;Loop back for more input
```

Here we use another feature of DOS function call 6, namely that if DL contains the value FF when the INT is executed, the DOS program will look at the keyboard input and see if a character was typed. If one has been typed, it returns to your program with the character in AL; otherwise it returns AL=0 and sets the zero flag. The instruction jump-if-zero (JZ) jumps back to the INT again if no character was typed, so that the program hangs in a little loop repeatedly executing INT 21 until a character is typed. When one is typed, it's printed on the screen and then the program goes back to look at the keyboard again.

The pair of instructions INT 21 and JZ 104 are a nice example of what's called a *polling loop*. This is one popular method of slowing down the computer so that it can receive input data that comes in at a much slower rate than the computer is capable of receiving. You simply have the computer hang in a little loop, waiting for some signal that indicates that new input data is available. To get some idea of the speed at which the computer receives data, you might ponder the fact that the computer executes the polling loop in the preceding program several hundred times during the time it takes you to depress a single key on the keyboard.

As a final example, consider a program that takes the binary number in AL and prints it on the screen. This is done by converting the number into two hexadecimal digits, and then translating each hexadecimal digit into ASCII:

```
XXXX:0100  88  C6       MOV   DH,AL    ;Save copy of number in DH
XXXX:0102  D0  E8       SHR   AL,1     ;Shift high nibble into low
XXXX:0104  D0  E8       SHR   AL,1
XXXX:0106  D0  E8       SHR   AL,1
XXXX:0108  D0  E8       SHR   AL,1
XXXX:010A  E8  08  00   CALL  115      ;Convert to ASCII & print
XXXX:010D  88  F0       MOV   AL,DH    ;Move number into DL again
XXXX:010F  24  0F       AND   AL,0F    ;Zero out high nibble
XXXX:0111  E8  01  00   CALL  115      ;Convert to ASCII & print
```

```
XXXX:0114   90              NOP                 ;End of main program

XXXX:0115   04  30          ADD     AL,30       ;Add 30H to convert to ASCII
XXXX:0117   3C  39          CMP     AL,39       ;Is digit between 0 and 9?
XXXX:0119   76  02          JBE     11D         ;Conversion complete if so
XXXX:011B   04  07          ADD     AL,7        ;Add 7 more if digit is A-F
XXXX:011D   88  C2          MOV     DL,AL       ;Print character in DL
XXXX:011F   B4  06          MOV     AH,6
XXXX:0121   CD  21          INT     21
XXXX:0123   C3              RET                 ;End of subroutine
```

As you can see, simply printing out an 8-bit binary number in hexadecimal on the screen takes a bit of effort. The number is split up into two nibbles (4-bit chunks). The high-order nibble is treated first by shifting it 4 bits to the right (with SHR, the shift right instruction) so that it occupies the position originally held by the low-order nibble. The SHR instruction also moves zeros into the high-order bits. We then do the conversion of this nibble to ASCII by calling a subroutine. A CALL instruction works just like the GOSUB instruction in BASIC. Program execution transfers to the start of the subroutine (address 115) and continues until a return (RET) instruction is encountered. Program execution then transfers back to the instruction following the CALL. As in BASIC, whenever a piece of code occurs more than once in a program, you should consider making it into a subroutine. The resulting program not only is shorter, but is also easier to understand.

If you look at the ASCII table in Appendix A, you can see why the conversion to ASCII is done the way it is. The ASCII code for 0 is 30H, the code for 1 is 31H, and so on. However, there's a gap of seven characters between an ASCII "9" and an ASCII "A", so we must add an additional 7 if the hex digit is between A and F.

To treat the low-order nibble, the program first zeros out the high-order nibble. This is conveniently done with an AND DL,0F instruction, which sets all bits in DL to zero that are zero in the number 0F. The number is then converted to ASCII by calling the subroutine at 116 again.

One point often misunderstood by beginners is the fact that when you do a single step in a program using DEBUG, there is a great deal more going on than meets the eye. It's easy to think that when you type "T", the 8088 just executes one instruction, shows you the register contents, and sits there doing nothing until you type something else. When you type "T", you actually initiate the execution of a very substantial program. First the 8088 looks up in a memory table the values that were supposed to be in the registers at this point in your program. Then it loads up all the registers, executes the instruction, and saves all the register values in memory again. These values are converted to ASCII and printed on the screen as in the preceding program, and finally DEBUG goes into a loop as in the keyboard echo program example, looking at the keyboard waiting for a character to be typed. Thus the appearance of single stepping through a program is actually a clever illusion.

The examples presented in this section should give you an idea of what assembly language programming with the 8088 is like. In the next chapter the entire 8088 instruction set is examined in detail. At first glance it looks very complicated, but after you've worked with it for a while you'll find that most of the instructions fall into a few logically related groups and are fairly straightforward to learn.

References

A. Osborne and D. Bunnell, 1982, *An Introduction to Microcomputers: Volume 0 - The Beginners Book*, Osborne/McGraw-Hill, Berkeley, CA. This book contains excellent discussions of how computers work, binary arithmetic, and computer logic operations.

Disk Operating System, Version 2.0, IBM Corporation. The DOS manual contains the official reference manual for the DEBUG program.

3
Assembly Language Programming

The trouble with computers is that they do what you tell them to do, not what you want them to do.
—a frustrated programmer

For writing short and simple assembly language programs, debuggers are fast and easy to use. However, they have some severe drawbacks that make them unacceptable for use as a general purpose assembly language tool. You can't edit your assembly language source program in DEBUG or conveniently save it on disk. An equally serious problem is that you can't refer to memory locations or numbers symbolically (except for SST, which has a built-in assembly language interpreter). This capability is essential whenever programs need to be modified or relocated, and it also greatly enhances their readability. To see what is meant, consider again the program example from Sec. 2-8:

```
0100    MOV    CX,0A                MOV    CX,TEN
0103    MOV    AX,0                 MOV    AX,0
0106    ADD    AX,CX         NEXT:  ADD    AX,CX
0108    LOOP   106                  LOOP   NEXT
```

The left-hand version shows the program the way it would appear using a debugger, while the right-hand version is the way the program might appear using a full-fledged assembler. If anything is added to or deleted from the debugger version, the LOOP 106 statement has to be changed also, because the ADD statement, which is the place the program is supposed to jump to, will move to a new address. In a complex program with many jumps, this becomes intolerable. There's no debugger equivalent of BASIC's RENUM statement. In the right-hand version the target of the jump is just called "NEXT", and the programmer doesn't have to worry about what memory address this corresponds to. Program changes can be made freely without having to change previously written code. In addition, the right-hand version is considerably more descriptive and easier to read.

In the rest of this book we assume you're going to be using an assembler, in particular the standard Microsoft Macro Assembler. IBM's Macro Assembler is nearly identical to Microsoft's, but at this writing it's more expensive and doesn't include a number of useful utility programs such as the SYMDEB debugger. The discussions in this chapter are applicable to either assembler. The Macro Assembler offers such features as the ability to write separately assembled program modules, to create subroutines for use with high level languages, and to use macros to extend the instruction set or simplify the coding of repetitive program sections. The penalty for these advantages is additional complexity. To write and run an assembly language program, you have to create the program as a disk file using your favorite editor, then run the assembler to translate the assembly code into machine language, and finally run the LINK program to transform the assembler output into an executable file in the format expected by the operating system. Despite these drawbacks, using an assembler is the only practical way to do serious assembly language programming.

This chapter begins by discussing the program format that the Macro Assembler expects for assembly language programs. This should enable you to sucessfully assemble some programming examples for yourself and to learn by doing. The bulk of the chapter is then devoted to a detailed discussion of the IBM PC's instruction set at the assembly language level. While the chapter is by no means a reference manual for assembly language programming on the IBM PC, it is intended to make it as easy as possible to get started in assembly language.

3-1. Format of Assembly Language Statements

Each line of an assembly language program must follow a fixed, relatively simple format or layout, so the assembler can properly interpret what you want it to do. Each line of assembly code is divided into four areas or fields as shown in Fig. 3-1. Each field can have arbitrary length and is separated from the next field by one or more blanks (spaces) or tabs. Any or all of these fields may be omitted or left blank. This may sound confusing in the abstract, so consider this line of assembly code:

```
FILL:   MOV    CX,78              ;let CX be a counter
```

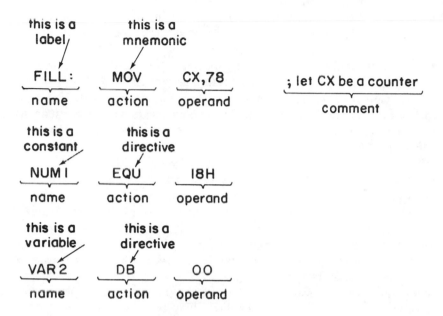

Fig. 3–1. The format of assembly language statements.

The first field is the *name field*. In this example it contains a label, FILL. The assembler knows that FILL is a label from the fact that it ends with a colon. The label is used to give a symbolic name to the address where the instruction MOV CX,78 is stored. Labels are used in front of any instruction that you want to refer to somewhere else in the program. For example, you could write JMP FILL somewhere else in the program (a jump, JMP, is the assembly language equivalent of BASIC's GOTO statement). When executed, this would cause the computer to jump to the address FILL and execute the MOV CX,78 instruction there. The name field can be left blank if desired, and in fact it is left blank for most assembly language statements.

The second field is the *action field*. The word in this field tells the assembler what action is to be performed. In the example, this field contains the word MOV, which tells the computer to move some data. A computer instruction contained in this field is called a *mnemonic* (pronounced "neh-mon'-ik," from the Greek word meaning "an aid to the memory"). Instead of a computer instruction, the field can also contain an assembler directive, which is an instruction for the assembler, rather than a part of the computer program. You'll see examples of this later.

The third field is the *operand field*. The expression contained in this field gives the assembler any further data it needs to take the requested action. In the example, this field contains two operands, CX and 78. This tells the assembler that the data source is the number 78, and that the destination for this data is the CX register. Thus the number 78 is to be moved into CX. When two operands are present they must be separated by a comma with no intervening spaces. A given mnemonic can require 0, 1, or 2 operands. For example, the RET instruction (the equivalent of BASIC's RETURN statement) requires no operands.

The final field is the *comment field*. This field must always begin with a semicolon. Whenever the assembler encounters a ";", it regards everything that follows it on the line as being a comment (the assembly equivalent of BASIC's REM statement). Comments are only present to help human beings understand what is being done by the program. The assembler simply ignores them. Despite the fact that comments are not strictly necessary, you should use them liberally. The first time you try to understand an uncommented assembly language program that you've written three months earlier, you will instantly acquire a strong appreciation for the importance of comments! Comments should not be trivial recapitulations of what the instruction means, but rather why the instruction is being used. To comment MOV AL,8 with the comment ";AL=8" is redundant. Instead say why you want AL to equal 8. For pedagogical reasons, we occasionally do use redundant comments in this chapter.

Some lines of an assembly language program do not contain computer instructions. Instead they contain directives to the assembler. Here are some examples:

```
TITLE   TEST PROGRAM
PAGE    60,96
        END

NUM1    EQU     18H

VAR1    DW      1234H
VAR2    DB      00
```

Here, TITLE, PAGE, END, EQU, DW, and DB are assembler directives, often called *pseudo ops*. The assembler determines whether a line in a program is a computer instruction or an assembler directive by looking at the first word on the line. If it ends with a colon, it's a label for a program location. If it's one of the 8088 mnemonics (like MOV or JMP), the line is a computer instruction. If it's not a label or a mnemonic, the assembler checks to see if it's one of the legal directives (like TITLE or PAGE). If it's one of these reserved words, the rest of the line is interpreted as required by the directive.

For example, the TITLE directive says to print everything that follows it on the line as the title line or heading on every page of the assembly language listing. This listing is a printout that shows both the assembly source code and the machine language produced by the assembler. The PAGE directive says that the two numbers that follow on the line are to be used as the number of lines per page and the maximum number of characters per line in the assembly language listing. The END directive tells the assembler that the end of the program has been reached.

The final possibility is that the first word on the line is not a label, a mnemonic, or a directive. The assembler then interprets the word as a name and looks at the second word on the line to see what kind of name it is. In the examples above, NUM1, VAR1, and VAR2 are names. The EQU (read this as "equals") directive means that the name preceding EQU is a constant whose value is the number following EQU. Thus in the example above, NUM1 will simply be interpreted as the number 18H everywhere it appears in the program.

The DW (define word) directive means that the name preceding it is a variable, and that the assembler should reserve a word (2 bytes) of memory for this variable. In addition the assembler will initially fill that word of memory with the value following the DW. Thus VAR1 is a variable whose initial value is 1234H. Any other part of the program can refer to this word of memory by simply using the name VAR1. The DB (define byte) directive is like DW except that only 1 byte is reserved for the variable in memory. In the example, VAR2 is a 1-byte variable whose initial value is 00.

Be sure you can distinguish between variables, constants, and labels. The assembler keeps track of which is which, and treats them very differently. Just remember that variables are defined using DB or DW assembler directives and are names for memory locations whose contents can be changed by your program. Constants are defined using the EQU directive and are simply names for numbers. A label is defined as a name ending with a colon and specifies a memory address for a computer instruction.

3-2. Model Layout for an Assembly Language Program

A number of assembler directives must be included in even the simplest assembly language program for it to assemble correctly. This section presents a model program whose form can be used for many assembly language programs and which shows why the various items in the program are needed. Additional items must be included for more complex situations like those discussed in Chap. 4, but this simple model takes you a long way.

Figure 3-2 shows the layout required of a simple assembly program for the Microsoft/IBM Macro Assembler. As can be seen, there's a lot of code present considering that the actual program body is only three lines long! What are all the extra statements for? Well, let's take a look. The first line, which gives the title of the program, is mainly for your information. It's good practice to start every program with a title since it can remind you of what the program is all about. The line must begin with the reserved word "TITLE", or the assembler will give an error message. If the line is present, the assembler prints it as a heading on every page of the program listing it produces.

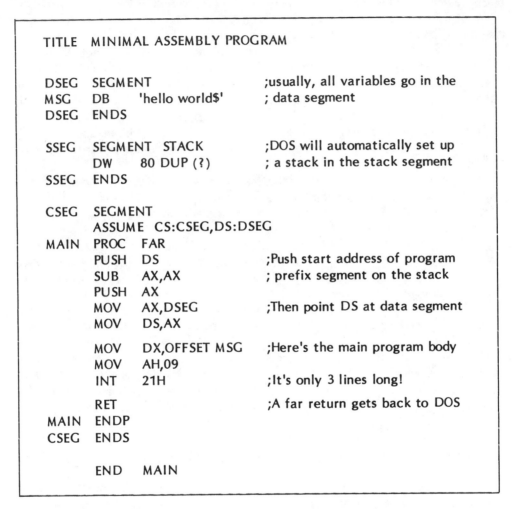

```
TITLE   MINIMAL ASSEMBLY PROGRAM


DSEG    SEGMENT                     ;usually, all variables go in the
MSG     DB      'hello world$'      ; data segment
DSEG    ENDS


SSEG    SEGMENT  STACK              ;DOS will automatically set up
        DW      80 DUP (?)          ; a stack in the stack segment
SSEG    ENDS


CSEG    SEGMENT
        ASSUME  CS:CSEG,DS:DSEG
MAIN    PROC    FAR
        PUSH    DS                  ;Push start address of program
        SUB     AX,AX               ; prefix segment on the stack
        PUSH    AX
        MOV     AX,DSEG             ;Then point DS at data segment
        MOV     DS,AX

        MOV     DX,OFFSET MSG       ;Here's the main program body
        MOV     AH,09
        INT     21H                 ;It's only 3 lines long!

        RET                         ;A far return gets back to DOS
MAIN    ENDP
CSEG    ENDS


        END     MAIN
```

Fig. 3-2. Model layout for simple assembly language programs.

The program body is divided into three sections, each of which is called a *program segment*. Segments begin with a segment name followed by the reserved word "SEGMENT" and end with a line in which the segment name is repeated and is followed by the reserved word "ENDS" (end segment). A segment is simply a block of machine code or data that can be addressed by a single value contained in one of the segment registers (see Sec. 2-7). The "ASSUME" statement following the declaration of CSEG tells the assembler which segment you want each segment register to point to. Thus in the program above, we want the CS register to point to CSEG, since this segment contains the program, and CS plus IP must always point to the next instruction to be executed. We want DS to point to the segment where the variables are stored, since the 8088 normally assumes that variables are reached through DS unless explicitly told otherwise by a segment override (see Sec. 3-11). Note, however, that the ASSUME does *not* actually point DS at DSEG; it only tells the assembler to assume that your code will point DS there. In this program, the assembler doesn't have to be told to assume anything for ES since this register isn't being used for anything. If you do use ES to access any variables, you'll have to properly initialize ES and give an ASSUME value for it also. Finally, the assembler does not have to be given an ASSUME value for SS because DOS automatically points SS at the STACK segment.

The stack segment, which we have called SSEG, deserves a little extra comment. For the segment containing the stack, you need to follow the SEGMENT directive with the word "STACK". This tells the assembler that SSEG contains the stack. When the program is loaded into memory for execution, the DOS will automatically set the registers SS:SP so that they point to the end of the stack segment. For the contents of the stack segment we've put "DW 80 DUP (?)". This tells the assembler to reserve 80 words of memory (80 DUP means to duplicate the DW 80 times), but not to worry about what values are in those locations (that's what the "(?)" means).

The program code is contained in the code segment, which we have called CSEG. The code here is written as a single subroutine, which the Macro Assembler calls a *procedure*. We explain why the main program is written as a subroutine below; for now just accept it as necessary. The subroutine (procedure) must begin with a line giving the procedure name ("MAIN" in the example) followed by the reserved word "PROC" followed by the word "FAR". The end of the subroutine is denoted by a line that repeats the subroutine name followed by the reserved word "ENDP" (for end procedure). The reason the term "procedure" is used is that the Macro Assembler's authors at Microsoft were Pascal enthusiasts, who wanted to make assembly language programs look like Pascal. Thus, early versions of the Macro Assembler were written in Pascal and were very slow.

The last line of every program must be an END statement. Following the END on the same line you must put the name of the procedure where you want program execution to begin. This tells the assembler how DOS should set the initial value of IP for program execution to begin.

To use this model layout for your own programs, just replace the three lines of code MOV DX,OFFSET MSG; MOV AH,09; and INT 21H with your own program and replace the line MSG DB 'hello world$' with any variables or data that you need for your program. Then let 'er rip! More precisely, you'll write your assembly language program using your editor (which is not EDLIN, we hope!), and save it on disk as a file. Suppose you've named the file containing your program "MYPROG.ASM". Then you enter "MASM MYPROG;" (the assembler is called MASM) to assemble the program and store the machine language produced on disk as the file "MYPROG.OBJ". Next you must run the linker program by entering "LINK MYPROG;". The LINK program takes the machine code and converts it into a form that can be loaded and executed from DOS. It does this by adding a block of code known as a *header* in front of the machine code. This header tells the DOS how to initialize the segment registers before transferring control to the program and how to relocate the program—that is, how to modify any instructions that depend on exactly where in memory the program segments are loaded by DOS. The LINK program produces a disk file called "MYPROG.EXE", which can be run from DOS by just entering "MYPROG".

Finally, let's see why the model program is written as a subroutine and what the first few lines of the code are for. What we're trying to do is to arrange things so that when the last line of the program is executed, the computer will jump back into DOS and wait for further commands. This would seem to be a simple thing: just end with a jump instruction. Unfortunately the place the DOS expects the computer to jump to is DS:0, where DS is the contents of the DS register when execution of the program begins, and the assembler doesn't allow you simply to jump to an absolute location in memory. So, how to get to DS:0? The simplest way is to push the address DS:0 onto the stack, and then return to it (see Sec. 3-5 for an explanation of how the stack works). Thus the first three lines of the program code push the contents of DS on the stack and then push a 0000 onto the stack. The last line of the program is a far return (RET) instruction. The assembler knows it is supposed to be a far return in which both CS and IP are changed, because of the word "FAR", which we put after the reserved word PROC. The far return instruction takes the last word put on the stack and sticks it in IP, and takes the next-to-last word and sticks it in CS, so that CS:IP now points to DS:0, the proper DOS entry point. Try assembling the model program, and then trace through it using DEBUG if you're still not clear about what is happening.

In lines 4 and 5 of the program, the DS register is changed so that it points to DSEG. This must be done in order to reach any variables contained in the DSEG segment (recall that DS is initialized to point at the DOS entry point as discussed above). Once you've loaded up DS (and ES if you're using it), you can usually forget about the segment registers in the rest of your program. When the program is loaded into memory, the DOS takes care of both initializing SS:SP to point to the stack segment and initializing CS:IP to point to the start of the program, so there is normally no need to initialize the CS or SS segment registers.

3-3. Data Movement Instructions

The remainder of this chapter presents a detailed look at the 8088 instruction set. The first type of instruction to be discussed is one you've already encountered: the MOV instruction. The form of this instruction is "MOV destination,source". All 8088 instructions use this slightly backwards notation, in which the source of the data (the place the CPU is getting the data from) is given last. This takes a little getting used to, but it's the standard notation for the 8088 as well as many of the other microprocessors available today. Thinking of MOV as being "MOVTO" may help. A closely related instruction to MOV is the exchange instruction, "XCHG destination, source". This interchanges the contents of any two registers or of a register and a memory location. With XCHG, both operands are destinations and sources.

Table 3-1 summarizes the forms of the data movement instructions. Note that data can be moved between any register and any other register or memory location, but not between two memory locations. Doing the latter requires two MOV instructions such as MOV AL,mem1 followed by MOV mem2,AL. A value can also be loaded directly into any register or memory location as shown by the third form of the MOV instruction in Table 3-1. A direct memory-to-memory move can be done in one instruction using the string primitive instruction MOVS discussed in Sec. 3-10. We discuss the MOV instruction in more detail, and with many examples, in the next section. There the various possibilities for the meaning of the "mem" operand are presented.

Data Movement Instructions

MOV	reg,reg/mem	XCHG	reg,reg/mem
MOV	reg/mem,reg		
MOV	reg/mem,num		
LEA	reg16,mem		
XLAT			

Input/Output Instructions

| IN | ac,port | OUT | port,ac |
| IN | ac,DX | OUT | DX,ac |

where "ac" is AX or AL, and "port" is an I/O port address

Table 3-1. Data movement and I/O instructions. See Table 3-2 for an explanation of the "reg", "reg/mem", and "num" operands.

A special purpose data movement instruction that occasionally comes in handy is the XLAT (translate) instruction. This instruction replaces the value in AL with a new value taken from a list or table of values in memory. The instruction assumes that the BX register points to the beginning of this table—that is, BX contains the address of the first entry in the table. The value in AL determines which item in the table is used. For example, if AL contains the value 3, then the third item in the table pointed to by BX will be placed in AL by the XLAT instruction. Obviously there must be as many items in the table as the number of expected values in AL.   Thus if any value is allowed in AL, the table must be 256 bytes long.

The most frequent use for the XLAT instruction is to translate values from one type of encoding scheme to another.   An example is the translation of a 4-bit binary number to an ASCII encoded hexadecimal digit.   If the 4-bit number is in AL, this can be done with a table and two instructions:

```
        MOV     BX,OFFSET TABLE
        XLAT
        ...
TABLE   DB      '0123456789ABCDEF'
```

Doing this job without the XLAT instruction requires you to add 30H to AL if the digit is 0-9, and 37H if it is A-F as shown in the last example of Sec. 2-8.   Nevertheless, the program of Sec. 2-8 uses fewer (8 versus 20) bytes.

The final type of data movement instruction is the LEA (load effective address) instruction.   To understand this instruction, you need to understand the 8088's addressing modes.   This topic and a discussion of the LEA instruction are taken up in the next section.

IN (input) and OUT (output) instructions are a special type of data movement instruction that reads data in from an input port or sends it to an output port.   Input ports and output ports are special hardware circuits used by the computer to communicate with external devices.   A discussion of how they can be built occupies a large portion of the rest of this book.   From a programming point of view they are simply a special type of memory location that can be accessed only by means of the IN and OUT instructions. It is possible (but highly unlikely!) to have up to 65,536 different I/O (input and/or output) devices attached to your IBM PC since the I/O port addresses are 16-bit numbers.   Actually, most I/O devices require more than one I/O port to control them, because they are typically interfaced via a smart, programmable I/O controller chip.   For example, the disk drive controller chip and the video display controller chip in your IBM PC require two I/O ports apiece through which data is passed back and forth to the CPU.

A point sometimes overlooked is that the CPU doesn't care whether or not an I/O port address is connected to anything.   It quite happily writes data to any of its 65,536 output ports whether or not any devices are connected to them, and it reads in garbage from any of its 65,536 input ports regardless of whether input devices are present.

There are two types of IN instructions.   The first type has the form IN AL,DX.   What this instruction does is to place in AL the data available at the input port address contained in DX.   Suppose, for example, that DX contains the number 03F5, which is the port address of the floppy-disk controller's data register in the IBM PC.   Executing the instruction IN AL,DX would then load the contents of that data register into AL.   Notice that the

IN instruction is not general purpose the way the MOV instruction is. The destination can only be AL (or AX), and the port address must be contained in DX. An instruction such as IN BL,CX is not allowed. The form IN AX,DX is allowed, but it's not immediately obvious what it does because the IBM PC has only an 8-bit data bus for use by I/O devices. If you were to use IN AX,DX in your program (a practice we do *not* recommend, as it can cause problems with some I/O devices, especially when the code is run on an 80286), the result is equivalent to executing the code:

```
INC   DX
IN    AL,DX
MOV   AH,AL
DEC   DX
IN    AL,DX
```

The second type of IN instruction is more limited. It has the form IN AL,port where "port" is an input port address (a number) between 0 and FF. Thus it can only access the lowest 256 input ports. On earlier microcomputers this seemed to suffice, but on the IBM PC, the system board has reserved all the lowest 256 ports.

The output instructions have the same allowed forms as the input instructions and work in the same way except that the value in AL is sent (written) to the port. For example, we can use either OUT 37,AL or MOV DX,37 plus OUT DX,AL to send the contents of AL to output port 37. The contents of AL are left unchanged by an OUT instruction.

3-4. Addressing Modes

Now take a look at what *mem* means in Table 3-1. Mem is a memory address, but the 8088 provides many ways of specifying a memory address. In fact there are twenty-four distinct possibilities. Fortunately, most of these are variations on just a few basic types (called *addressing modes*). Nonetheless, learning about addressing modes and how to utilize them effectively is one of the more difficult aspects of assembly language. Thus let us try to proceed carefully and with many examples.

To begin with, in assembly language you can't refer to memory by an explicit address as was done in the example programs in Sec. 2-8. The reason you can't is that absolute addresses are usually not known at the time the program is written. The computer determines the actual addresses at the time the program is loaded into memory for execution. Also, there is no need for a programmer to keep track of absolute addresses. You simply use symbolic names for all memory locations you want to use and let the assembler worry about keeping track of all the details.

Suppose, for example, you want to write a simple game program in which a human player plays Tic Tac Toe against the computer. In writing this program, you need to keep track of various things such as the current state of the Tic Tac Toe board (where the X's and O's are) and how many games the player has won, lost, and drawn. You also want to store various messages that the computer can print on the screen. In assembly language, this data storage area might be implemented as follows:

```
BOARD   DB      00,00,00
        DB      00,00,00
        DB      00,00,00
WON     DB      00
LOST    DB      00
MSG1    DB      'You win'
MSG2    DB      'You lose'
```

As discussed in Sec. 3-1, the names in the leftmost column are called variables. The reason is that the most common use for symbolically named memory locations is to store values that can vary during the execution of the program. For example, "WON" is a variable that holds the current number of games won by the human player.

Recall that the mnemonic DB in the action field stands for "define byte." It means that the number(s) that appear on the remainder of the line are to be stored in memory, allowing one byte per number. Several 1-byte numbers can be defined in a single DB directive by writing the numbers after the DB and separating them by commas as done in the variable BOARD above. Only numbers between 0 and 0FFH can be stored in 1 byte, so the range of allowable numbers is limited. If you want to have a variable with a larger range of allowable values, you can use the DW (define word) mnemonic, which stores the value following it as a 2-byte value in memory and hence can handle numbers up to 0FFFFH. Floating-point numbers such as 89.73 can also be stored in memory (see Sec. 4-8).

Once you have defined a variable, you no longer need to worry about its address. Just refer to it anywhere else in the program by its name. When the assembler encounters a DB, the number(s) following it will be assigned sequential memory locations, starting at the first available memory address. Suppose, for example, that when the variable BOARD was encountered, the next unused address was 1020H. The data area would then appear as follows:

```
1020  00 00 00                  BOARD   DB      00,00,00
1023  00 00 00                          DB      00,00,00
1026  00 00 00                          DB      00,00,00
1029  00                        WON     DB      00
102A  00                        LOST    DB      00
102B  00                        DRAWN   DB      00
102C  59 4F 55 20 57 49 4E      MSG1    DB      'You win'
1033  59 4F 55 20 4C 4F 53 45   MSG2    DB      'You lose'
```

The left-hand column gives the starting address corresponding to each assembly language statement, and the numbers to the right of the address are the values that are stored starting at that address. Note that MSG1 and MSG2 are handled in a special way. When the assembler sees quote marks following a DB, it treats everything between the quotes as a string literal. That is, it stores the ASCII code value for each character in the string in memory (see Sec. 2-3). BASIC stores strings this way also.

Now that you know what variables are and how they're stored in memory, we can get to the heart of the addressing-mode discussion. Suppose that in the Tic Tac Toe game program, you've calculated the number of games won and put the result in the AL register. You can then store this number in the variable WON using MOV WON,AL. This assembly language statement means, "Place the contents of AL into memory location WON." Similarly, MOV AL,LOST places the contents of memory location LOST into AL.

Technically, the addressing mode being used here is called *direct addressing* because the address of the data source or destination is given directly in the machine language instruction. MOV WON,AL is identical to MOV [1029],AL if the variable WON is at location 1029. You might think that MOV [WON],AL should be equivalent to MOV [1029],AL, but it's not. In fact, MOV [WON],AL isn't a legal assembly language statement, and the assembler won't accept it. The way to think about the situation is that the assembler treats registers and variables on an equal footing. Whenever you write the name of the register or variable, you always mean "use the contents of" that variable or register. Thus MOV AL,3 moves a 3 into register AL, and similarly MOV WON,3 moves a 3 into the variable WON. Being able to treat variables like registers is very useful, because it effectively gives you a CPU with an unlimited number of registers. The only difference is that instructions referencing variables take a little longer to execute, and you cannot use MOV WON,LOST—that is, direct memory to memory moves are not allowed.

You can also make more complex expressions from variables and numbers. For example, MOV AL,BOARD+3 moves the contents of memory location 1023 into AL. When the assembler encounters these arithmetic expressions, it looks up the 16-bit address of the variable name that appears and then does any indicated arithmetic to yield a single 16-bit effective address. The contents of this effective address are then used as the source or destination for the instruction.

In some situations you may want to load an address itself into a register instead of the contents of an address. To tell the assembler you want to do this, you use the reserved word "OFFSET". For example, the statement MOV DX,OFFSET WON would put the number 1029 into DX. You'll get into big trouble if you don't clearly understand this distinction. MOV CX,BOARD and MOV CX,OFFSET BOARD mean two entirely different things. The reason the term OFFSET is used is that a 16-bit address is an offset (a displacement) from the start of a 64K segment of memory whose origin is determined by a segment register. The expression "OFFSET variablename" is just a symbolic way of specifying a number. Thus the instruction MOV CX,OFFSET BOARD causes machine code for the instruction MOV CX,1020 to be generated. Both instructions simply move a number into a register. This kind of instruction is an example of what is often called the *immediate* addressing mode. There is also an alternative to using MOV reg,OFFSET variablename, and that's the LEA (load effective address) instruction discussed at the end of this section.

In addition to the direct and immediate addressing modes just discussed, there is one other very powerful type of addressing mode available for the 8088. This mode is called *indirect* or *indexed* addressing. In the simplest form of this mode, a register contains the address whose contents are to be used as the source or destination. For example, suppose the BX register contains the number 1029. Then the instruction MOV AL,[BX] would put the contents of memory location 1029 (the value of the variable WON in the example) into AL. The square brackets around BX in the instruction MOV AL,[BX] tell the assembler that the source of the data to be moved is not the contents of the BX register, but rather the contents of the address contained in BX. This is why an instruction like MOV AL,[BX] is called indirect addressing. The operand given is a register, but the data to be moved are not the contents of the register.

Indirect addressing can be used with only four registers: BX, BP, SI, and DI. It can also be used for either the source or destination operand (but not both). Thus MOV CX,[SI], MOV [DI],BX, and MOV [BX],AL are all valid instructions.

In some cases of indirect addressing you must specify the size (byte or word) of the destination. It's obvious that the destination is a 16-bit word if the instruction is MOV [BX],AX, since the source is a 16-bit register. However, what should the assembler do with MOV [BX],3? There's no way for the assembler to know whether BX is pointing to an 8-bit or a 16-bit quantity. To resolve this situation, the assembler provides the keywords BYTE PTR (byte pointer) and WORD PTR (word pointer). These are placed in front of the destination so that the assembler knows whether you want to move 8 or 16 bits. Thus MOV WORD PTR [BX],3 would move the 16-bit quantity 0003 into locations [BX] and [BX]+1, while MOV BYTE PTR [BX],3 would just move the 8-bit quantity 03 into location [BX]. In general, any time it's not clear whether an 8- or 16-bit quantity is being referred to, you must use BYTE PTR or WORD PTR to specify what you mean. You can also use these keywords to override the normal definition. For example, MOV WON,3 normally specifies an 8-bit move because the variable WON was defined as an 8-bit variable. However, you can store the 16-bit quantity 1234 in WON and WON+1 by using MOV WORD PTR WON,1234.

More complicated forms of indirect or indexed addressing add numbers or variable addresses to the quantity [reg]. For example, MOV AL,[BX]+5 and MOV [BX]+BOARD,AL are valid instructions. Note that, in the latter example, the *address* of BOARD is added to [BX], not the contents of the variable BOARD, as would be the case for an instruction like MOV BOARD,AL. The usage is clarified in the two other equivalent ways of expressing the quantity [reg]+disp, namely [reg+disp] and disp[reg]. Thus MOV [BX]+BOARD,AL and MOV [BX+BOARD],AL and MOV BOARD[BX],AL all represent the same instruction and cause the assembler to generate the same machine code. Which form you use is a matter of personal preference.

The key thing to remember is that the assembler always looks at the operand and performs whatever operations are indicated in order to come up with an *effective address*. The contents of this effective address are the data to be moved. Fig. 3-3 shows schematically how this type of indirect addressing mode works. If BX contains 8000, MOV AL,[BX+3] transfers the contents of 8000 + 3 = 8003 into AL. Similarly, if BX contains 0A, MOV [BX+BOARD],AL moves the contents of AL into the address 0A + 1020 = 102A (since the address of BOARD is 1020). You can also use both a number and a variable address together; for example, MOV [SI+3+WON],CL.

Execution of a MOV AX,[BX] + 3 instruction causes the following actions:

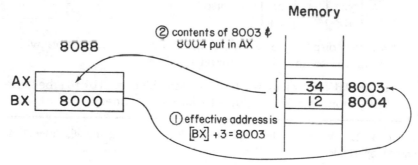

After the instruction has executed: AX contains 1234.

Fig. 3-3. Execution of a MOV instruction using indirect addressing.

The final type of indirect addressing is to use the sum of the contents of two registers as an effective address. For example, MOV AX,[BX+SI] is a valid instruction which tells the CPU to form an effective address from the sum of the contents of BX and SI, and then to move the contents of that effective address into AX. With this method of addressing memory, you are restricted to using BX or BP for the first component of the sum, and SI or DI for the second component; that is, MOV AL,[SI+DI] is not allowed.

All of the memory addressing possibilities discussed are summarized in Table 3-2. As can be seen in the table, an effective address can be built up using any or all of the following: [BX or BP], and/or [SI or DI], and/or any expression that yields an 8- or 16-bit number. Thus the general structure is fairly simple, even though there are many possible variations.

1. "num" is an 8- or 16-bit number, or more generally, any expression that evaluates to an 8-bit or 16-bit value.

2. "reg/mem" means "reg" or "mem".

3. "reg" is any one of the following registers:

   AX SI AH AL
   BX DI BH BL
   CX BP CH CL
   DX SP DH DL

   "reg16" is any one of the 16-bit registers shown in the first two columns.

4. "mem" is an EFFECTIVE ADDRESS given by any combination of entries from the following columns:

$$\begin{bmatrix} BX \\ or \\ BP \end{bmatrix} + \begin{bmatrix} SI \\ or \\ DI \end{bmatrix} + disp$$

   where "disp" is a variable name or any expression which evaluates to an 8-bit or 16-bit number.

   EXCEPTION: mem = [BP] is assembled as [BP+0] because [BP] alone is not an allowed addressing mode.

Table 3-2. Allowed values for "reg", "reg16", "reg/mem", "mem", and "num" operands.

At this point you may be wondering what use the more complicated addressing modes have. The answer is that they're very handy for dealing with various forms of structured data such as arrays and records.

Suppose you have a one-dimensional array having 10 elements: a list of 10 values stored one after the other in memory. To be concrete, let each array element be the number of Tic Tac Toe games won by one of 10 different players. Also, let the initial address of the array, where the number of games won by player number 0 is stored, be named PLAYER. You can now easily get the number of games won by player number n by just moving n into SI and using an instruction like MOV AL,PLAYER[SI]. This notation is much like that of a subscripted variable in high-level languages and provides a very simple and logical way of accessing array elements. For example, suppose you want to print out a list of how many games each player has won. This can be done using a little loop (the assembly language equivalent of BASIC's FOR...NEXT loop) as follows:

```
        MOV   CX,0A              ;CX is loop counter
        MOV   SI,0               ;SI is player number
NEXT:   MOV   AL,PLAYER[SI]      ;Get # games won by a player
        ...
        ... (code to print the value in AL goes here)
        ...
        INC   SI                 ;Increment player number
        LOOP  NEXT               ;Repeat loop CX times
```

The instruction INC SI increases the value in the SI register by 1, and the LOOP NEXT causes all the instructions between NEXT: and LOOP NEXT to be repeated 0A times (the number contained in CX).

The situation where two registers are used for indirect addressing is very handy for dealing with two-dimensional arrays. For example, there was a nine-element array called BOARD in the hypothetical Tic Tac Toe program. Each element corresponds to one of the squares of the Tic Tac Toe board, and the value of the element indicates whether an X, an O, or nothing is currently in that square. In this case it's convenient to think of the elements of BOARD as a two-dimensional array with board positions given by row and column number. For convenience, let row 0, column 0 be the square in the upper left corner. The center square would then be row,column = 1,1. To address any square on the board you could put the row number in BX and the column number multiplied by 3 in SI, and use MOV BOARD[BX+SE],AL to put the contents of AL into a given board position.

Another good use for [BX+SI] would be to access items in an array of records. An example might be a set of student records, with each student's record having the student's name in a 30-byte field, grade level in a 2-byte field, and current classes being taken in six 8-byte fields. If RECORD is the address of the start of the student records and you wanted to find out how many students were in a certain grade level, you could let SI point to the grade level field within a record (let SI = 31), and let BX point to the start of each student's record (BX must be a multiple of 30 + 2 + 6*8 = 80). The grade level of each student could then be picked out and placed in AX using MOV AX,[BX+SI+RECORD]. You could certainly do this job with a simpler addressing mode, but it's far easier for you or someone else to come back later and understand what's being done when the addressing method just described is used. Writing clear and understandable programs is a skill you should develop early and use consistently.

If you're going to do much assembly language work with records and fields within records, you should learn to use the Macro Asembler's STRUC and RECORD directives, which can make programming with these data structures considerably easier and clearer.

Occasionally you will want to load the effective address itself into a register instead of the contents of the effective address. For this situation, the 8088 designers included the LEA (load effective address) instruction. For example, if you want to load the address of the variable RECORD into register BX, you can use LEA BX,RECORD. In this simple situation, you could also have done this with MOV BX,OFFSET RECORD. The two methods do the same thing, athough the latter technique uses one less byte. The usefulness of the LEA instruction becomes apparent only when a more complex effective address must be loaded into a register. For example, suppose you wanted to load the effective address [BX+SI]+RECORD into BX for later use. The single instruction LEA BX,[BX+SI]+RECORD accomplishes this, whereas otherwise you would have had to perform an ADD BX,SI followed by an ADD BX,OFFSET RECORD to do the same thing. This technique can also be used in general to add two registers and a constant, even if they have nothing to do with addresses.

3-5. Jumps, Calls, and Stacks

If all a computer could do were to execute a single list of instructions with no possibility of modifying its actions based on previous results, it would be of very limited usefulness. All modern computers, including the 8088, have an extensive set of control transfer instructions. Most of these are conditional control transfers in which the decision to jump to a new place in the program is based on a set of special control bits called the flags. These flags and the conditional jumps that rely on them are discussed in Sec. 3-7. First, however, consider two very useful unconditional control transfer instructions, the JMP (jump) and the CALL. Table 3-3 summarizes the allowed forms of these instructions.

A JMP instruction is the simplest type of control transfer. It works just like BASIC's GOTO statement. When written as "JMP address", the instruction causes the CPU to put the given address into the IP so that the next instruction to be executed is the one at that address and not the instruction that follows the JMP. The address is usually given in the form of a label (a name terminated by a colon) that begins the line of assembly code you want to jump to. For example, if you want to jump to a place labeled THERE, simply write JMP THERE. A common use for the JMP instruction is to terminate a subsection of the program and cause the CPU to jump back to an entry point in the main program.

A more sophisticated form of the JMP instruction is "JMP reg/mem". In this case the jump is to the address contained either in a register or in a memory location. For example, if the BX register contains 1234, then JMP BX causes program execution to jump to the instruction at address 1234. This form of the JMP instruction is very useful for making multiway jumps (the equivalent of BASIC's ON...GOTO statement). The multiway jump is typically implemented with a *jump table*. The following example demonstrates how to execute one of four subprograms, PROG0, PROG1, PROG2, or PROG3, depending on whether the BX register contains 0, 1, 2, or 3:

Unconditional Control Transfer Instructions

```
    CALL    label               RET
    CALL    reg/mem             RET     nn

    JMP     label
    JMP     reg/mem
```

where "label" is a program label, and nn is a 16-bit number

Stack Instructions

```
    PUSH    reg16/mem           POP     reg16/mem
    PUSHF                       POPF
```

Interrupt Instructions

```
    INT     n                   IRET
    INTO

    CLI
    STI
```

where n is an 8-bit number

Table 3-3. Unconditional control transfer, stack, and interrupt instructions. See Table 3-2 for an explanation of the "reg", "reg16", "reg/mem", and "mem" operands.

```
    CMP    BX,4              ;Be sure BX is in range
    JNC    ERROR
    SHL    BX,1              ;Convert to word offset
    MOV    BX,TABLE[BX]      ;Index into table, get subprogram addr
    JMP    BX

TABLE DW   PROG0
      DW   PROG1
      DW   PROG2
      DW   PROG3
```

Obviously this technique can be extended to jump to any number of subprograms. Just make the table longer.

A second extremely important type of control transfer is the CALL instruction. This is the assembly language equivalent of BASIC's GOSUB statement, and it works as follows: Suppose the CPU encounters CALL SUBPROG, where SUBPROG is the starting address of a subroutine (this is just a piece of the program or a subprogram) you want the CPU to execute. It executes this instruction by first saving the current contents of IP (recall that IP contains the address of the next instruction—the one immediately following the CALL) in a memory area called the stack. It then sticks the address of SUBPROG into IP so that the subroutine is the next thing to be executed. The subroutine must end with a RET (return) instruction. When this instruction is executed, the CPU retrieves the previously saved address of the instruction following the CALL, and puts it into IP. Thus a CALL instruction simply causes the computer to go execute a subprogram and then return to the main program at the instruction immediately following the CALL.

The CALL works the same way that BASIC's GOSUB...RETURN works, but it provides considerably better documentation than standard BASIC. With GOSUB, only the form "GOSUB statementnumber" is allowed, which tells you nothing about what function the subroutine is supposed to perform. In assembly language the CALL is usually followed by a symbolic name (a label), which, if chosen carefully, can remind the reader of the subroutine's purpose. A second powerful feature of the assembly language CALL is that the form "CALL mem/reg" is allowed. The reg/mem operand works the same way for a CALL as described previously for JMP mem/reg. This form of the CALL can be used in a fashion similar to BASIC's ON...GOSUB statement; that is, it can be used to call different subroutines depending on the contents of a register or memory location.

In addition to knowing operationally how a simple CALL works, it's important for more advanced techniques to have a good understanding of the data structure called the *stack*. Recall that the CPU saves the current IP contents on the stack when a CALL is executed. But what is the stack? A stack is simply an area of memory (which can be located anywhere) where a list of data items is stored consecutively. The distinguishing feature of the stack is the way the list is ordered and maintained. Technically speaking, it is a LIFO (last in, first out) buffer. The nontechnical analogy is a stack of plates in a restaurant (in fact, this idea is where the stack gets its name). Imagine that each plate corresponds to a memory location and that the only allowed operations are to write something on a new plate and put it on top of the stack, or to take the top plate off the stack and read what's written on it. You now have a good mental model of how the stack works.

Two operations, PUSH and POP, correspond to the reading and writing of plates. PUSH reg16, where reg16 is a 16-bit register, takes the contents of the indicated register and writes it in the memory location that is currently the top of the stack. A CALL instruction does the equivalent of a PUSH IP automatically. The SP (stack pointer) register keeps track of where in memory the top of the stack is located. The address contained in this register is normally the location of the top of the stack. When PUSH AX is executed, SP is automatically decremented by 2, and then the contents of

AX are put in the memory location pointed to by SP. Thus SP again points to the new top of stack. Since SP is decremented, the top of stack is always the lowest numbered memory address in the stack. The SP is decremented by 2 because 16 bits (2 bytes) are always stored by a PUSH. You can't do PUSH AL! Figure 3-4 shows schematically how a PUSH operation affects the stack. In addition to PUSH reg16, the form PUSH mem (e.g., PUSH WON where WON is a variable name) is also allowed.

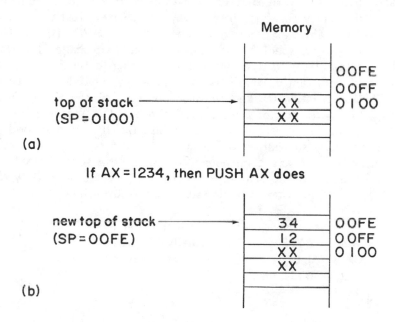

Fig. 3-4. How a stack operates. (a) The initial condition of the stack. (b) The stack after a PUSH operation.

The opposite of a PUSH is, quite naturally, a POP. The instruction POP AX reads 2 bytes from the top of the stack and stores them in AX. The SP is also incremented by 2 so that SP now points to the new top of stack. Just as for the PUSH instruction, the forms POP mem and POP reg16, where reg16 is a 16-bit register, are both allowed.

The PUSH and POP instructions are often useful for temporarily storing register contents. Suppose we have a number in CX that we need later on in the program. Before that, though, we want to use CX temporarily for something else. This is easily done using:

```
PUSH   CX
...
...       (other instructions that use CX)
...
POP    CX
```

Just make sure that a POP is always executed at some point after you do a PUSH! Otherwise your machine will crash in a horrible manner referred to as a *stack crash*. Fortunately, this is not quite as dire as a stock crash!

The PUSHF instruction pushes the contents of the flag register onto the stack, and POPF pops the word on top of the stack back into the flag register. The primary use for this instruction is to allow you to save the original state of the flags (see Sec. 3-7) during some operation that changes them, and then to restore that original state. It can also be used as a clever way to modify the flags in any way you desire. Just use PUSHF, POP AX, change AX in any way desired, and then do a PUSH AX, POPF. Normally you'll use the various special instructions available to change the flags, but this technique can be used to do absolutely anything to the flags.

The stack is exactly what's needed to allow nested subroutine calls. When a CALL instruction is executed, the contents of the IP are automatically pushed onto the top of the stack. When a RET instruction is executed, the 2 bytes on top of the stack are popped into the IP. If a second CALL is encountered in the subroutine before the RET occurs, another 2 bytes are pushed onto the stack and then popped off when the second CALL's RET is executed. The top of stack is now exactly the address needed by the first CALL's RET. The following example uses nested subroutines:

```
PRINTB:   MOV    AL,BH        ;Get high order byte
          CALL   PBYTE        ;Print both nibbles
          MOV    AL,BL        ;Then print low order byte
          CALL   PBYTE
          RET

PBYTE:    PUSH   AX           ;Save a copy of AL
          MOV    CL,4         ;Shift AL right 4 bits
          SHR    AL,CL
          CALL   PRINT        ;Print hex digit
          POP    AX           ;Restore original AL
          CALL   PRINT        ;Print second hex digit
          RET
```

PRINTB is a subroutine that prints out the contents of BX as four hexadecimal digits. To accomplish this, PRINTB calls PBYTE, which prints out the contents of AL as two hexadecimal digits. PBYTE in turn calls PRINT (not shown here), which prints out the single hexadecimal digit that is in the low-order nibble of AL. As illustrated in this example, the nesting doesn't have to stop at two levels deep. Any subroutine can contain one or more calls to other subroutines, which can in turn call more subroutines, and so on, ad infinitum. The only limitation is the amount of memory space you've reserved for the stack.

The return instruction that ends a subroutine can optionally be followed by a number. This number is added to the stack pointer immediately after the return address is popped off the stack. The purpose of this option is so that you can push values or addresses that you want to pass to the subroutine onto the stack just before you make a CALL and then discard them from the stack with a RET nn. This technique is used to pass variables back and forth between assembly language routines and high-level language programs. This important and powerful feature is discussed further in Sec. 4-5.

Finally, you should realize that the stack is a considerably more powerful structure than you might guess on first encountering it. High-level languages make extensive use of the stack, and often use multiple stacks in memory. There's no problem in doing this as long as you make sure to load the appropriate stack pointer value before working with each stack. In fact, you can use the stack to do almost everything that you usually do in the CPU registers. Several high-level languages, of which FORTH is the best-known example, use stacks for almost all their operations.

3-6. Software Interrupts

An instruction closely related to the CALL instruction is the INT (software interrupt) instruction. It is basically a special type of indirect call. The execution of an INT nn instruction causes the following sequence of events: The flags register, the CS register, and then the IP register are pushed on the stack. IP and CS are then loaded with the contents of the two words at the absolute memory addresses 0:nn*4 and 0:nn*4+2, respectively. Thus program execution jumps to the address contained in these two absolute memory locations. The idea here is that the lowest 400H memory locations (addresses 0:0 through 0:3FFH) are assumed to contain starting addresses of subroutines that you may want to execute; that is, low memory is assumed to be set up as a big jump table. Each group of four locations contains the offset and segment address of a subroutine as shown in Fig. 3-5, and is called an interrupt vector.

The subroutines jumped to by an INT instruction differ from normal subroutines reached by a CALL only in that they must end with an IRET (return from interrupt instruction). The IRET restores CS, IP, and the flags in the proper order, whereas a RET instruction only restores IP, or IP and CS (in the case of a far return, see Sec. 3-12).

You may be wondering why this funny type of call instruction was included in the 8088 instruction set, and why it's called a software interrupt. The reason has to do with the existence of something called a *hardware interrupt*. Hardware interrupts are a very important method for handling communications to and from peripheral devices (see Sec. 6-4 and Chap. 7 for details). A hardware interrupt occurs when an external device such as a disk drive or a keyboard sends a signal to the 8088 on a special line called the interrupt request line. The 8088 responds by stopping whatever it's currently doing (i.e., it's interrupted, just as you can be interrupted in what you're doing by a phone call), and jumping to a subroutine

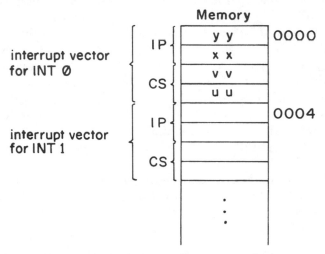

Fig. 3–5. Structure of the interrupt vector area in low memory. The starting address of the interrupt handler for INT 0 is CS:IP = **uuvv:xxyy.**

that handles the data going to or coming from the device. Which subroutine is jumped to is determined by a number n, which is passed to the 8088 on the data lines. The number n is used to find the subroutine in the same way as described above for the INT n instruction. Thus the INT n instruction provides a way to simulate a hardware interrupt in software.

One use for software interrupts is to provide an easy way to execute and debug the subroutines used for hardware interrupts. However, a far more common use of the INT instruction is to provide a way for user programs to access routines within the operating system and I/O device drivers (subroutines that control I/O devices such as keyboards, printers, video screens, and disk drives). We saw some examples of this in Sec. 2-8. The reason an INT is used to call system routines instead of a simple CALL is that it is a much more flexible method of communication. Suppose we used direct calls to the operating system. This requires that we give the exact starting address of the subroutine with any CALL we use. Now IBM comes along with a new revision of the operating system, in which all the operating system subroutines are at new addresses. The result is that all of the programs we bought or wrote that used operating system calls don't work anymore! They have to be rewritten with the correct subroutine addresses put in. This situation is quite unacceptable. It's also unnecessary, because the INT instruction gives a way to call the operating system without knowing subroutine addresses. You simply use INT's for operating system calls and let the operating system fill in the interrupt vector table at 0-3FF with the appropriate addresses when power is turned on.

A wonderful fringe benefit of controlling I/O devices and making operating system calls in this way is that you, the user, can also take over any I/O device you want, and do whatever you like with it. All that must be

done is to change the appropriate address in the Interrupt vector table.
Table 3-4 gives a memory map showing the currently assigned interrupt
vectors and the device or function each controls. Many of these interrupt
vectors point to device handlers in the built-in ROM memory of the PC. The
source code for these handlers can be found in IBM's *Technical Reference*
manual for the PC along with the protocol expected by the
various device drivers. We discuss in detail how to take over interrupt
vectors in Sec. 4-6.

INTERRUPT	FUNCTION
0	Divide by zero
1	Single step
2	Non-maskable interrupt (NMI)
3	Break point instruction
4	Overflow
5	Print screen
6,7	Reserved
8	Time of day hardware interrupt (18.2/sec.)
9	Keyboard hardware interrupt
A	Reserved
B,C	Serial communications hardware interrupts
D	Fixed disk hardware interrupt
E	Diskette hardware interrupt
F	Printer hardware interrupt
10	Video I/O call
11	Equipment check call
12	Memory check call
13	Diskette I/O call
14	RS232 I/O call
15	Cassette I/O call
16	Keyboard I/O call
17	Printer I/O call
18	ROM basic entry code
19	Boot strap loader
1A	Time of day call
1B	Get control on keyboard break
1C	Get control on timer interrupt
1D	Pointer to video initialization table
1E	Pointer to diskette parameter table
1F	Pointer to graphics character generator
20	DOS program terminate
21	DOS function call
22	DOS terminate address
23	DOS CTRL-BRK exit address
24	DOS fatal error vector
25	DOS absolute disk read
26	DOS absolute disk write
27	DOS terminate, fix in storage
28-3F	Reserved for DOS
40-5F	Reserved
60-67	Reserved for user software interrupts
68-7F	[not used]
80-85	Reserved by BASIC
86-F0	Used by BASIC interpreter while running
F1-FF	[not used]

Table 3-4. Interrupt vector assignments in the IBM PC.

One other special interrupt instruction is the conditional interrupt INTO (interrupt on overflow), which causes a software interrupt if the previous operation has set the overflow flag. This interrupt is useful in connection with signed arithmetic operations (see next section).

Finally, there are two instructions that clear or set a flag (a bit inside the CPU) called the interrupt flag (IF). CLI (clear interrupts) clears the interrupt flag (makes it zero), and STI (set interrupts) sets the interrupt flag. This flag is used in connection with hardware interrupts. If the IF flag is set, interrupt requests from external devices will be recognized and handled as prevously described. However, if the IF flag is cleared, hardware interrupts will be ignored until the flag is set back to 1 again. The execution of software interrupts is not affected by the IF flag. To remember whether STI enables or disables the CPU's response to interrupts, you might think of STI as meaning "Start interrupts" and CLI as meaning "Cut off interrupts." The reason for having this capability is that certain operations are time critical and cannot afford to be interrupted by anything else until they're done. When this situation occurs, you simply execute a CLI at the beginning of the critical section of code and then execute an STI at the end. Since the subroutines jumped to via interrupts are often time critical, the 8088 designers had the INT instruction automatically clear the interrupt flag. IBM PC hardware interrupt subroutines typically are not time-critical, and start with an STI instruction to reenable interrupts. If you do not do this, the IRET instruction will restore interrupts after a hardware interrupt.

3-7. Conditional Jumps and Flags

The jumps and calls described in Sec. 3-5 cause the program execution to branch to another place in the program every time they're encountered. Often, however, you want to do a jump or not do a jump, depending on what's happened previously in the program. The 8088 provides this capability with a set of conditional jumps. With these instructions, a jump is performed or not depending on the state of one or more flag bits. For example, the instruction JC THERE causes the program execution to jump to the location labeled THERE, if the carry flag is set to 1. If the carry flag is 0, no action is taken and the instruction immediately following JC THERE is executed.

Obviously you need a clear idea of how the flags work in order to use conditional jumps effectively, so let's take a closer look at them. As mentioned in Sec. 2-6, the flags are somewhat analogous to the idiot lights on a car's dashboard. They are indicators of the current state of the CPU that has resulted from previous operations. For example, if the CPU executes the instruction ADD AL,5 (add 5 to the AL register), several flags will be set to 1 or reset to 0, depending on the result of the addition. The zero flag will be set if the addition gives zero in AL. Otherwise it will be reset. The carry flag will be set if the addition produces a number greater than FF in

AL. If not, the carry will be reset. Hence during the execution of the ADD instruction, the flags are altered to reflect the result of the addition. Instructions following the ADD can test the flags and use them to make decisions that depend on the result of the addition. If ADD AL,5 was followed by JZ THERE, the jump would be taken only if AL+5 was zero.

There is a total of nine different flags. Each is a single bit in a register called the flag register. If desired, this register can be saved on the stack and restored using the instructions PUSHF and POPF. In all other respects, however, each flag behaves like an independent entity, and the flag register cannot be manipulated like the other general purpose registers. Nine flags is a large number of flags to learn about and keep track of. Fortunately, three of these are very special purpose, and only two of the remaining six are important for 95% of the computer programs you'll encounter.

The three special purpose flags are the interrupt flag, the direction flag, and the trap flag. The *interrupt flag* (IF) indicates whether interrupts are enabled or disabled. Interrupts and this flag are discussed in Sec. 3-6. The *direction flag* (DF) is used only in conjunction with the string primitive instructions discussed in Sec. 3-10. The *trap flag* (TF) allows diagnostic programs such as DEBUG to single step the CPU. When set, the TF flag causes an interrupt to occur after each instruction of a program is executed. With the proper interrupt service routine, one can watch the 8088 single step through a program.

The remaining six flags are used in connection with arithmetic and logical operations. Arithmetic operations consist of the usual addition, subtraction, multiplication, and division, plus increment, decrement, and negate. These operations are discussed in detail in Sec. 3-8. Logical operations consist of AND, OR, XOR, NOT, plus various shift and rotate instructions and the TEST instruction. The logical operations are discussed in detail in Sec. 3-9. The six flags are as follows:

CF - the carry flag. If an arithmetic operation produces a result that exceeds the capacity of the register, the carry flag is set (to set means to set to 1; to reset means to clear or to reset to 0). More precisely, a carry out of the high-order bit of the result, or a borrow into the high-order bit, sets the carry flag. Otherwise CF is cleared. The carry flag can also be changed by shift and rotate instructions, and is conveniently set, cleared, and complemented by the STC, CLC, and CMC instructions, respectively.

ZF - the zero flag. If an arithmetic or logical operation produces a result of zero, the zero flag is set. Otherwise ZF is cleared.

SF - the sign flag. If an arithmetic or logical operation produces a result whose high-order bit is a 1, the sign flag is set. Otherwise SF is cleared. Recall from Sec. 2-2 that a negative binary number in two's complement form has the high-order bit set.

PF - the parity flag. If an arithmetic or logical operation produces a result whose low-order 8 bits contain an even number of 1's, the parity flag is set. Otherwise PF is cleared.

OF - the overflow flag. If an arithmetic operation produces a result that exceeds the capacity of the register when the result is interpreted as a signed number, the overflow flag is set. Otherwise OF is reset. More precisely, OF is set if there is a carry into the high-order bit of the result but not a carry out, or a carry out of the high-order bit but not a carry in.

AF - the auxiliary carry flag. If an arithmetic operation produces a result in which a carry or a borrow occurs in or out of the low-order 4 bits, the auxiliary carry flag is set. Otherwise AF is reset. This flag is used almost exclusively for operations involving BCD or decimal arithmetic.

Of these six flags, the carry flag and the zero flag are by far the most important. You will use these two all the time to control loops and program branches via the conditional jumps. You'll encounter the sign flag when signed binary arithmetic is being done, but otherwise will seldom use it. You'll rarely encounter the PF, OF, and AF flags unless you're writing a floating-point arithmetic package.

You will find examples of uses for the carry and zero flags below, where conditional jumps are discussed. Although conditional jumps represent the most common use for flags, they can also be used as single-bit registers to indicate, for example, the presence of an error condition in a subroutine. The carry flag is often used this way because there are three special instructions that can manipulate just this flag. The three instructions are STC (set the carry flag to 1); CLC (clear the carry flag to 0); and CMC (complement the carry flag—that is, change it to 1 if it's 0, or to 0 if it's 1). The following subroutine illustrates the use of the carry flag to indicate whether or not a period has been typed on the keyboard:

```
PERIOD:   CALL   CONIN      ;Get a character from the keyboard
          CMP    AL,'.'     ;Compare it with a period
          JNE    ISNT       ;Skip ahead if no match
          RET               ;Return with CF clear if match
ISNT:     STC               ;Return with CF set if no match
          RET
```

This subroutine calls a console input routine that gets a character from the keyboard and returns it in AL. The value in AL (which is the ASCII code for the character) is then compared to the ASCII code for a period. If the two codes are equal, the zero flag is set, the carry flag is cleared, and the JNE (jump if not equal) instruction causes no action. If the codes don't match, the zero flag is cleared, and the jump to ISNT is taken. The carry flag is then set before the return to the program that called PERIOD is taken. The net result is that the main program finds the carry flag set if a period wasn't typed and cleared if it was.

Looking at the subroutine just given, you probably noticed that we seemed to assume that some instructions don't affect the flags. This is exactly right. The designers of the 8088 instruction set have been very careful in choosing which instructions affect the flags and which do not. Learning which is which is something you'll have to do in order to write assembly language programs. Fortunately, most of what you need to know can be summarized in just two generalizations:

1. The flags are never changed by data movement instructions (see Table 3-1) or by control transfer instructions (see Tables 3-2 and 3-5).

2. The flags are changed by arithmetic and logical instructions (see Tables 3-6 and 3-7).

The first generalization has no exceptions. The second has one exception (the NOT instruction) and several partial exceptions, since only some of the six arithmetic flags are changed by a number of arithmetic and logical instructions. For example, the increment and decrement instructions do not affect the carry flag. The exceptions are mostly reasonable ones, so you'll find after a while that you don't often need to check to see whether an instruction changes a particular flag. When you do need to check, refer to a reference manual on the 8088 such as the *iAPX 88 Book*.

Let's now turn our attention to the conditional jumps, where you really need to make use of the flags. Looking at Table 3-5, you'll see that there are two sets of conditional jumps, one for unsigned numbers and one for signed numbers, plus several LOOP instructions, and a few special purpose conditional jumps.

The first set of conditional jumps is meant for use with unsigned (positive only) binary numbers. They have the following meanings:

JA	(jump if above)		
JAE	(jump if above or equal)	or	JNC (jump if no carry)
JE	(jump if equal)	or	JZ (jump if zero)
JNE	(jump if not equal)	or	JNZ (jump if not zero)
JBE	(jump if below or equal)		
JB	(jump if below)	or	JC (jump if carry)

The mnemonics given in the second column are synonyms (that is, another way of writing the same instruction) for the corresponding jumps in the first column. If you write them as shown in the second column, the jumps refer directly to the state of the zero or carry flags, whereas the form in the first

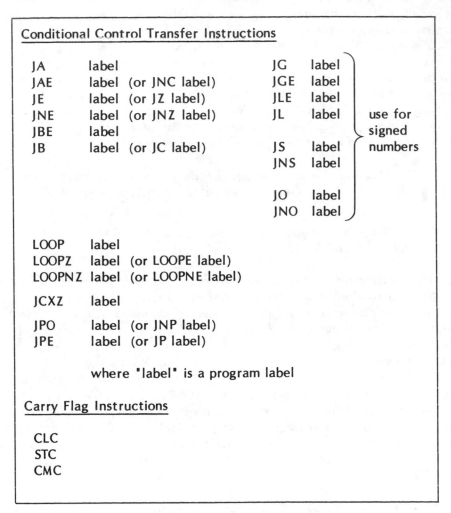

Table 3—5. Conditional control transfer and carry flag instructions.

column implies that two quantities are being compared to see if the jump will take place. Both ways of writing the jumps are useful.

The first form of the jump is intended for use when the CMP (compare) instruction is used before the jump to compare the magnitude of two quantities. For example, suppose you want to jump to subprogram 1 if the contents of BX are less than 8, to subprogram 2 if they equal 8, and to subprogram 3 otherwise. This can be done using

```
CMP    BX,8          ;Compare BX to 8
JB     PROG1         ;Go to PROG1 if <8
JE     PROG2         ;Go to PROG2 if =8
JMP    PROG3         ;Else go to PROG3
```

Together, the compare and jump instructions are the equivalent of BASIC's IF...GOTO statement. Notice that when the condition specified in a conditional jump is not met, the CPU simply ignores that jump instruction and continues on to the next instruction.

When the JA, JAE,...,JB forms of the conditional jump instruction are used, it's not so obvious how the flags are being used to decide on whether to jump. Writing the preceding program as

```
CMP    BX,8
JC     PROG1
JZ     PROG2
JMP    PROG3
```

makes it clear how the jumps are using the flags. However, the original form, using JB and JE, is more readable and consequently should be used following a compare. To understand how the program works when written using JC and JZ, you need to know how the compare instruction sets the flags. What CMP does is to subtract the source (8) from the destination (BX) and set the flags accordingly. However, the result of the subtraction is thrown away and the source and destination are left unchanged. If BX is less than 8, the subtraction requires a borrow into the high-order bit and hence sets the carry flag. If BX equals 8, the subtraction gives zero and sets the zero flag.

Notice that there is no synonym for the JA or JBE instructions because they rely on a combination of two flags. Jump if above (JA) is true if the destination in a previous compare instruction is greater than the source so that both the carry and zero flags are 0. Jump if below or equal (JBE) is true if the destination is less than or equal to the source so that either the carry flag or the zero flag is set.

If you want to jump or not depending on whether a single number is zero, you can use the OR instruction to set the flags properly. For example, suppose you want to jump if the number in AX is zero, and you haven't just done an arithmetic operation so the flags are not set. To do this, just use

```
OR     AX,AX
JZ     ITSZERO
```

The instruction OR AX,AX does a logical OR of each bit in AX with itself (see Sec. 3-9). This leaves AX unchanged but sets the zero and sign flags according to the number in AX and clears the carry flag.

The forms JC, JNC, JZ, and JNZ are preferable following any logical or arithmetic instructions other than a compare. For example, here is a trivial program that adds the integers 1 through 9:

```
        MOV   BL,9
        MOV   AL,0
NEXT:   ADD   AL,BL
        DEC   BL
        JNZ   NEXT
```

The JNZ instruction causes the loop (a loop is just a backward jump to a previous point in the program) to be repeated until BL is decremented to zero. This kind of loop, where some quantity is decremented to zero, is so common that the 8088 designers provided a special instruction tailored for just this situation. This is the LOOP instruction, which acts as a DEC and JNZ combined into a single instruction. Using this, the addition program becomes

```
        MOV   CX,9
        MOV   AX,0
NEXT:   ADD   AX,CX
        LOOP  NEXT
```

We had to switch to using the CX register because the LOOP instruction works with CX only. Another unique feature of LOOP is that unlike DEC and JNZ, the LOOP instruction does not change any flags. LOOP looks directly at the CX register to see if it's zero. This can be very useful in loops where the flags are being used to keep track of other things.

There are also two other less used variations of the LOOP instruction, loop-if-zero (LOOPZ) and loop-if-not-zero (LOOPNZ). LOOPZ decrements CX and jumps to the operand address if CX is not zero *and* the zero flag is set. Use this instruction whenever you want to do something repeatedly while two quantities remain equal, up to a maximum of n times. This is readily done by moving n into CX and using LOOPZ. Similarly, LOOPNZ decrements CX, and jumps to the operand address if CX is not zero *and* the zero flag is cleared. In many cases, the situations where you would want to use these instructions can be handled more efficiently with the string primitive instructions CMPS or SCAS, discussed in Sec. 3-10.

A handy instruction often used along with the LOOP instruction is the jump-if-CX-zero (JCXZ) instruction. JCXZ jumps only if CX is zero. At first glance this may not look very useful, but it's invaluable in one common situation. Suppose you want to repeat some action a number of times using the LOOP instruction, and the initial value in the CX register is a number that depends on the result of a previous calculation. This is no problem unless that initial value happens to be zero. Then, instead of repeating the action zero times, which is what you want, the LOOP instruction decrements CX from zero to 0FFFFH, sees that it's not zero, and loops back 65,536 times! You can eliminate this problem by using a JCXZ at the beginning of the loop:

```
     ....                        ;Some program that initializes CX goes
                                 here
     ....
     JCXZ    DONE
NEXT: ....                       ;The body of the loop goes here
     ....
     LOOP    NEXT
DONE: ....                       ;The program continues on here
```

If CX equals zero initially, the program loop between NEXT and DONE will not be executed.

An annoying limitation on all the jump-on-condition instructions is that the range of the jump is limited to 127 bytes forward in the program or 128 bytes backward. If you try to use a conditional jump to a location farther away than this, the assembler gives an error message. The limitation is a result of the fact that conditional jump instructions indicate the address to jump to as only an 8-bit signed displacement.

What if you need a conditional jump to go farther than 128 bytes? You're then forced to reverse the sense of the logic and skip around an unconditional jump. For example, suppose you want to do JZ FARAWAY, where the location FARAWAY is more than 128 bytes distant. The solution is to use

```
     JNZ    SKIP
     JMP    FARAWAY
SKIP:   (put next instruction here)
```

This is annoying and clutters up programs, but nothing can be done about it! The older 8085 and Z80 microprocessors do have conditional jumps with 16-bit addresses. If you're familiar with those processors, this flaw is especially annoying.

Now we come to the second set of jumps shown in Table 3-5. These conditional jumps are to be used only with signed binary numbers (see Sec. 2-2). Their meanings are:

JG (jump if greater)
JGE (jump if greater or equal)
JLE (jump if less or equal)
JL (jump if less)
JS (jump if sign)
JNS (jump if not sign)
JO (jump if overflow)
JNO (jump if not overflow)

JG, JGE, JLE, and JL are the analogs for signed binary numbers of JA, JAE, JBE, and JB for unsigned binary numbers. It's important to use each kind of jump with the appropriate kind of number because they depend on different flags and can give entirely different results. JB causes a jump if the carry flag is set, but JL causes a jump if the sign flag does not equal the overflow flag. An example of the kind of trouble you can get into by using the signed number jumps on unsigned numbers is this piece of code:

```
CMP    AL,BL
JG     BIGGER
```

You want to jump to BIGGER if AL is a larger unsigned binary number than BL. This code works properly if AL is 20H and BL is 1FH; but it gives the opposite of the result you expect if AL is 80H and BL is 7FH, because the JG instruction treats 80H as a negative signed binary number (-128 decimal), which is smaller than 7FH (127 decimal).

The instructions JS and JNS are used to jump if the sign flag is set or not set. You can use these instructions to jump when a number is positive or negative, provided you set the flags first using an OR instruction.

When an operation produces a signed number result that exceeds the register capacity, the overflow flag is set. For example, suppose AL contains the signed number 70H and you do an ADD AL,20H. You get 90H in AL as the result, which is the negative signed integer -112 decimal. Usually you'll want to take some special action when this kind of erroneous result occurs, and this can be done using a jump-if-overflow (JO) or jump-if-not-overflow (JNO) instruction.

Finally, there are two seldom used jump instructions, jump-if-parity-odd (JPO), and jump-if-parity-even (JPE). These two instructions jump or not depending on the state of the parity flag. The parity flag (PF) is set if the result of some operation generates a result having an even number of "1" bits in it. If there is an odd number of 1's in the result, PF is cleared. You might use these instructions in a program to control a serial communications port. When a byte of data is sent to a serial port, a parity bit is sometimes sent in addition to the byte. This parity bit works just like the parity flag. It's set if the byte contains an even number of 1's. The program running the serial port can check this bit to see if it matches the parity of the received byte, and jump to an error routine if it doesn't.

3-8. Arithmetic Instructions

The 8088 has a fairly powerful set of arithmetic instructions, which are summarized in Table 3-6. The most basic instructions in this class are the ADD (addition) and SUB (subtraction) operations. These instructions support the full range of addressing modes for operands, just as described earlier for the MOV instruction (see Sec. 3-4). ADD and SUB can be done equally well on either 8-bit or 16-bit quantities. For example, ADD BL,CH adds CH to BL, leaving the result in BL, while SUB SI,1234 subtracts the

```
Arithmetic Instructions

     ADD    reg,reg/mem        ADC    reg,reg/mem
     ADD    mem,reg            ADC    mem,reg
     ADD    reg/mem,num        ADC    reg/mem,num

     SUB    reg,reg/mem        SBB    reg,reg/mem
     SUB    mem,reg            SBB    mem,reg
     SUB    reg/mem,num        SBB    reg/mem,num

     CMP    reg,reg/mem
     CMP    mem,reg
     CMP    reg/mem,num

     INC    reg/mem            DEC    reg/mem

     NEG    reg/mem

     MUL    reg/mem            IMUL   reg/mem  ⎫
     DIV    reg/mem            IDIV   reg/mem  ⎬  use for
                                              ⎪  signed
                               CBW            ⎪  numbers
                               CWD            ⎭
```

Table 3–6. Arithmetic instructions. See Table 3–2 for an explanation of the "reg", "reg/mem", and "num" operands.

number 1234 from SI, leaving the result in SI. The destination for the result can be any register or memory location. This capability allows you to directly manipulate numbers stored in memory without having to move them into a register, do the arithmetic, and then store them back in memory. Hence if WON is the location where the number of Tic Tac Toe games you've won is stored, you can dramatically increase your score with the simple instruction ADD WON,100. In this regard, the 8088 is considerably more powerful than the previous generation of microprocessors such as the 8005, Z80, and 6502, where the result of arithmetic operations typically had to end up in the accumulator.

Since the operand lengths are fixed at either 8 or 16 bits, the result of an arithmetic operation can exceed the register or memory location capacity. For example, if AX = 0F910H and the instruction ADD AX,800H is executed, the sum, 10110H, is too large to fit in 16 bits. In this case, the CPU sets the carry flag, and only the least significant 16 bits (0110H) are left in AX. You must decide what you want to do when a result like this occurs. If the numbers being added are being interpreted as signed binary numbers, you have to be even more careful since any sum of two positive

16-bit numbers that exceeds 7FFFH will be incorrect. Similar care must be exercised when using subtraction. If AL = 20H and BL = 36H, the operation SUB AL,BL sets the carry flag to indicate that a borrow into the high order bit has occurred, and the number EAH (which is -16H in two's complement form) is left in AL. This result is correct if the numbers are being interpreted as signed binary numbers, but not otherwise.

The moral is that when dealing with arithmetic operations, you must either know in advance that only an appropriate range of numbers will be encountered as arithmetic operands or make explicit tests for erroneous results in the program. For unsigned numbers, you can do this by checking the carry flag and using a JC (jump on carry) instruction to jump to an error-handling routine. For signed numbers, check the overflow flag and use a JO (jump on overflow) instruction. An alternative is to use the special instruction INTO (interrupt if overflow), which causes an interrupt if the overflow flag is set. The advantage of using INTO is that you don't have to write a separate overflow error-handling routine for every program where it's needed. There can just be a single overflow handler that stays resident in the machine.

The SUB instruction is in some sense superfluous since one number can always be subtracted from another by adding its two's complement as described in Sec. 2-2. In fact, there's even an arithmetic operation that produces the two's complement of any number for you. Its called NEG reg/mem, and it forms the negative of any 8- or 16-bit binary number. Thus NEG BX followed by ADD AX,BX produces the same result as SUB AX,BX. Using SUB is of course faster and clearer, so NEG is used only to change the sign of a number. One glitch to watch out for is the case where you try to NEG the number 80H (-128 decimal) or 8000H. In this case the 8088 leaves the number unchanged and sets the overflow flag to indicate that something's wrong, because positive signed integers only go up to a maximum of 7FH (+127 decimal) or 7FFFH.

The ADC (add with carry) and SBC (subtract with borrow) operations are primarily intended to facilitate multiword or multibyte arithmetic. The ADC instruction forms the sum of two operands *plus* the carry flag. Thus if the carry flag was set to one by a previous operation, an extra "1" is added into the result. This is just what's needed to do, for example, the addition of two 64-bit numbers stored in memory at locations OP1 and OP2:

```
SUM64:   CLC                          ;Start with CY flag = 0
         MOV     SI,OFFSET OP2         ;Point to start of both numbers
         MOV     DI,OFFSET OP1
         MOV     CX,4                  ;Must add 4 16-bit words
NXTWRD:  MOV     AX,[SI]               ;Get a piece of OP2
         ADC     [DI],AX               ;Add it to OP1 along with CY
         ADD     SI,2                  ;Advance pointers
         ADD     DI,2
         LOOP    NXTWRD                ;Loop back for more
```

This code adds OP2 to OP1, leaving the result in OP1, and assumes that OP1 and OP2 are stored in the usual reverse order, with least significant byte first, most significant byte last. Similarly, SBB op1,op2 performs the operation op1 - op2 - CY, thus propagating a borrow from one word to another in multiword subtraction operations.

An extremely useful instruction closely related to SUB is the CMP (compare) instruction. This instruction subtracts the source from the destination, sets the flags appropriately to indicate borrow, overflow, and so on, and then throws away the result, leaving the source and destination operands unchanged. To put it simply, CMP op1,op2 compares op2 to op1 and indicates via the flags whether op1 is bigger (CY=1, Z=0), equal (CY=0, Z=1), or smaller (CY=0, Z=0) than op2. As discussed in the previous section, the primary use of this instruction is for making decisions based on comparisons of two quantities. For example, if AL contains the ASCII code for some letter you've typed on the keyboard, the code

```
        CMP    AL,'a'      ;Do nothing if character is less than "a"
        JB     DONE
        CMP    AL,'z'      ;Or if it's greater than "z"
        JA     DONE
        SUB    AL,20H      ;Change to upper case if between "a" and "z"
DONE: ...
```

converts the letter to upper case (to a capital letter) if it was originally a lower case letter. The assembler interprets 'a' and 'z' as being just the numbers 61H and 7AH, respectively—as the ASCII codes for the letters "a" and "z" (see Appendix A).

Two other very common arithmetic instructions are increment (INC) and decrement (DEC). These add or subtract "1" from any register or memory location. Their primary use is in counting operations where you want to keep track of how many times you've done something. Thus the instruction INC LOST, where LOST is some memory location, allows you to keep track of how many Tic Tac Toe games your opponent has lost to you. Just execute this instruction each time he loses a game (or more often if you're inclined to cheat!). Since ADD op1,1 and SUB op1,1 can accomplish the same thing as INC op1 and DEC op1, you might wonder why these special instructions have been provided. The answer is that the increment and decrement operations are so common that the 8088 designers wanted them to have short op codes and to execute as quickly as possible. Adding one to a register via ADD reg,1 requires a 3-byte op code and takes nearly 1 microsecond (4 clock cycles) to execute, while INC reg requires only a 1-byte op code and executes twice as fast.

The next set of 8088 arithmetic instructions are the multiply (MUL and IMUL) and divide (DIV and IDIV) instructions. These instructions provide the 8088 with the capability to multiply and divide 8-bit and 16-bit signed and unsigned binary numbers.

MUL does multiplication of two unsigned 8-bit numbers or two unsigned 16-bit numbers. In the 8-bit case, one of the numbers is an 8-bit register or a byte in memory while the other number is assumed to be in AL. Hence the instruction has only one operand, MUL op1. The other operand, AL, is implied, and the result of the multiplication is returned in AX. Similarly, if one operand is a 16-bit register or a word in memory, the other is assumed to be in AX, and the result of the operation is returned in DX (most significant 16 bits) and AX (least significant 16 bits). Figure 3-6 shows schematically the register usage for the 8- and 16-bit multiply instructions. IMUL works the same way as MUL but treats the operands as signed binary numbers, so that a number with the high-bit set is treated as a negative number.

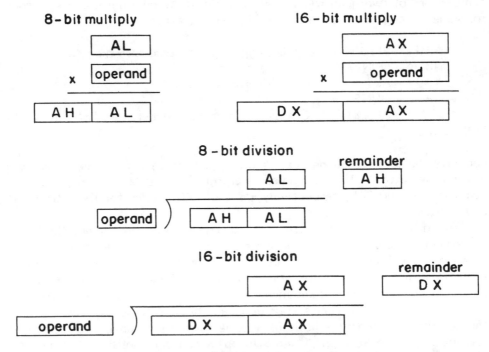

Fig. 3-6. Register usage in 8088 multiplication and division instructions.

Often you'll encounter situations where multiplication by a small integer (say between 2 and 20) is needed. If computation speed doesn't matter, the MUL or IMUL instruction does just fine. However, it requires on the order of 70 to 150 clock cycles to execute the instruction, depending on the operand size and addressing mode used. Much quicker multiplication for small integers can be done by using shifts and additions or subtractions. The trick here is to observe that shifting a binary number left by 1 bit multiplies it by 2 (just as shifting a decimal number left by one digit multiplies it by 10). Shifts are discussed in detail in Sec. 3-9, but for now all you need to know is that a left shift moves all bits of a binary number one position to the left, with a zero being placed in the least significant bit position, and the most significant bit being thrown away. To multiply a binary number by 8, just do three left shifts. To multiply a number in AX by 10, add the result of the first shift to that of the last:

```
MULT10:  SHL   AX,1           ;Multiply by 2
         MOV   CX,AX          ;Save this in CX
         SHL   AX,1
         SHL   AX,1           ;Now we have 8*AX
         ADD   AX,CX          ;Add in 2*AX
```

If you don't know the maximum size of the number you are starting with in AX, you'll have to check to see that no overflow has occurred.

DIV and IDIV operate in a manner analogous to MUL and IMUL. The dividend (the number being divided) is assumed to be in AX for division by a value in an 8-bit register or byte in memory. When dividing by a 16-bit value, the dividend is assumed to be a 32-bit value contained in DX (most significant word) and AX (least significant word). The quotient is returned as an integer in AL (AX for division by an 16-bit value), plus a remainder in AH (DX for 16-bit division). Figure 3-6 shows the register usage for division in pictorial form. When dividing AX by an 8-bit number, be sure to remember that the answer is only in AL. AH contains the remainder. (That error has cost one of us several hours!) If the quotient exceeds 256, you have to divide AX by a 16-bit quantity, first setting DX to 0.

Division is a relatively slow process, taking 80 to 180 clock cycles, so it's a good idea to avoid them if high computing speed is needed. In general, however, the 8088 DIV instruction is considerably faster than a division done by a software subroutine. One obvious exception is the case where a division by any power of 2 is needed. Here you should always use right shifts of the number. For division by other small integers, the choices aren't very attractive, although you may be able to do such divisions somewhat faster by making an initial guess that you know to be too low (or too high), and then incrementing (or decrementing) the guess until the guess multiplied by the divisor becomes larger than the dividend. For example, to divide AX by 3, make an initial guess of $(AX/4) + (AX/16)$. This initial guess is within about 6% of AX/3 and is always below or equal to the correct answer.

If the value of the divisor is not known before the division is done, you should always test it to make sure it's not zero. Attempting to perform a DIV or IDIV with a divisor of zero causes an INT 0 to be executed automatically (see Sec. 3-6 for an explanation of interrupts). This will bring the execution of your program to a quick and possibly painful halt. The exact behavior depends on the interrupt service routine pointed to by memory locations 0 through 3.

Finally consider two instructions that are most often used with the IDIV instruction, namely, CBW (convert byte to word) and CWD (convert word to double-word). The need for CBW arises because the shortest dividend for a signed number division is a 16-bit word in AX. Thus if you have a byte-length value that must be divided by some other number, you have to move the value into AL and then convert it from a byte in AL to a word in AX. CBW does this last operation for you. It examines the byte in AL and sets AH to either 00 or 0FFH depending on the high-order bit (the sign bit) of the value in AL. CWD works in the same way, except that it converts the word in AX to a double-length word in DX:AX. DX is set to either zero or 0FFFFH depending on the sign bit of the value in AX. You need this instruction if you want to divide a signed value in AX by a 16-bit number, since IDIV then requires the dividend to be a 32-bit value. As an example, suppose you want to divide a signed value in SI by a signed value in CX. This could be done as follows:

```
MOV    AX,SI              ;Move dividend into AX
CWD                       ;Convert to double word in DX:AX
IDIV   CX                 ;Divide by the value in CX
```

The result is in AX, and you need to remember that the CWD instruction clobbers DX. You can also use CBW or CWD any time you want to convert a signed byte or word into a word or double word. Just make sure you don't use them on unsigned values!

3-9. Logic Instructions

The 8088 has a nice selection of logic instructions that can perform operations in software that are analogous to the logical operations performed by the hardware gates discussed in Chap. 5. Table 3-7 summarizes this class of instructions. Consider first the three instructions AND, OR, and XOR, which are direct analogs of the elementary two-input gates (see Sec. 5-2).

The instructions AND, OR, and XOR perform the logical operations of ANDing, ORing, and XORing two binary numbers together. The AND and OR logical operations are very simple, and correspond to our intuitive notions of what such operations should do. The result of ANDing two bits together is a binary "1" only if the first bit is a 1 and the second bit is a 1. Thus 1 AND 1 = 1, 1 AND 0 = 0, and 0 AND 0 = 0. The result of ORing two bits together is a 1 if either the first bit is a 1 or the second bit is a 1, or both are 1's. Thus 1 OR 1 = 1, 1 OR 0 = 1, and 0 OR 0 = 0. The XOR (eXclusive OR) logical operation gives a result that depends only on whether the two bits are the same or different. The XOR of two bits is a 0 if the two bits are the same and is a 1 if the two bits are different. Thus 1 XOR 1 = 0, 1 XOR 0 = 1, and 0 XOR 0 = 0. Figure 3-7 summarizes the way these three logical operations work. While they may look rather trivial, we'll see that they can actually do some very useful things.

Logic Instructions

AND	reg,reg/mem		TEST	reg,reg/mem
AND	mem,reg		TEST	mem,reg
AND	reg/mem,num		TEST	reg/mem,num
OR	reg,reg/mem			
OR	mem,reg			
OR	reg/mem,num			
XOR	reg,reg/mem			
XOR	mem,reg			
XOR	reg/mem,num			
NOT	reg/mem			
SHR	reg/mem,1		SHL	reg/mem,1
SHR	reg/mem,CL		SHL	reg/mem,CL
SAR	reg/mem,1		SAL	reg,mem,1
SAR	reg/mem,CL		SAL	reg/mem,CL
ROR	reg/mem,1		ROL	reg/mem,1
ROR	reg/mem,CL		ROL	reg/mem,CL
RCR	reg/mem,1		RCL	reg/mem,1
RCR	reg/mem,CL		RCL	reg/mem,CL

Table 3-7. Logic instructions. See Table 3-2 for an explanation of the "reg", "reg/mem", and "num" operands.

AND	OR	XOR
$0 \cdot 0 = 0$	$0 + 0 = 0$	$0 \oplus 0 = 0$
$0 \cdot 1 = 0$	$0 + 1 = 1$	$0 \oplus 1 = 1$
$1 \cdot 0 = 0$	$1 + 0 = 1$	$1 \oplus 0 = 1$
$1 \cdot 1 = 1$	$1 + 1 = 1$	$1 \oplus 1 = 0$

Fig. 3-7. Results of the three basic logical operations on two binary digits. The standard notations " $\cdot$ ", "+", and " $\oplus$ " for AND, OR, and XOR are used.

The AND instruction ANDs two 8-bit or 16-bit quantities together. For example, if AL contains 0C3H and BL contains 46H, the instruction AND AL,BL does an AND operation of bit 0 of AL with bit 0 of BL, bit 1 of AL with bit 1 of BL, ..., and bit 7 of AL with bit 7 of BL. In other words, each bit in AL is ANDed with the corresponding bit in BL. The technical description of this operation is that the AND instruction performs the bit-wise logical AND of its two operands. In the example just given, the result of ANDing 0C3H with 46H is a 42H, which is left in AL after the instruction has executed. Notice that the result has all its bits set to zero except in the bit positions (bits 6 and 1) where both operands have bits set to one. In bit positions where only one or neither of the operands have bits set to one, the result has a zero.

The most common use for an AND instruction is to mask off (set to zero) selected bits in some value. For example, suppose you want to see what number is set in the three least significant bits of a value in AL, regardless of what is contained in the other bits. AND AL,7 does this since 7 = 00000111 in binary. Thus bits 0, 1, and 2 in AL remain unchanged. This kind of situation often arises when reading in switch settings from a parallel input port. In the IBM PC, for example, there is an eight-position DIP switch on the system board. Positions 5 and 6 on this switch indicate the type of display (monochrome or color/graphics) that is present. The computer can then determine the type of display present with the following code:

```
IN      AL,SWITCH       ;Read in switch settings as 1's or 0's
AND     AL,30H          ;Throw away all but bits 4 and 5
CMP     AL,30H          ;If both bits set, it's monochrome
JE      MONOCROME
```

The OR instruction works just like the AND instruction, except that the corresponding bits in the two operands are ORed together. For example, if AL contains 0C3H and BL contains 46H, the instruction OR AL,BL leaves a 0C7H in AL. The most common use for an OR instruction is to set selected bits in some value. Thus it can be used to do the opposite of the AND instruction, which clears selected bits. To set bits 6 and 7 of the value in some memory location called MEMVAL, just use OR MEMVAL,0C0H. This sets bits 6 and 7 in MEMVAL and leaves all the other bits untouched.

The XOR instruction also works like the AND instruction, but the corresponding bits in the two operands are XORed together. Using the same example as before, suppose that AL contains 0C3H and BL contains 46H. Then the instruction XOR AL,BL leaves an 85H in AL. One of the most common uses of the XOR is to toggle selected bits in some value—that is, the selected bits are set to 1 if they're 0 and to 0 if they're 1. Thus to toggle all the bits in MEMVAL, you can use XOR MEMVAL,0FFH. Where a bit in MEMVAL is 1, it is set to 0 because the bits in both operands are the same, and where a bit in MEMVAL is 0, it is set to 1 because the bits in the two operands are different. A second common use for the XOR is to set values to zero. For example, XOR AX,AX zeroes AX. MOV AX,0 does the same thing but requires one more byte of code and takes longer to execute. However, MOV does not affect any flags, and XOR affects most, in particular clearing CF and setting ZF. The XOR operation is used extensively in bit-mapped video displays (see Sec. 8-3) to erase images (by XORing an image with itself) or to blink them (by repeated XORs).

The three instructions just described allow you to manipulate individual bits within an 8- or 16-bit value. Set them with OR, clear them with AND, or change them with XOR. One other very useful instruction for working with individual bits in a register or memory location is the TEST instruction. TEST does an AND of two operands, sets the flags according to the result of the operation, and then throws away the result, leaving the original operands unchanged. You can think of TEST as a kind of compare (CMP) instruction that compares individual bits instead of numbers.

Most often, TEST is used to pick out an individual bit in a register or memory location to see if it is 1 or 0. For example, one way to check if a signed 8-bit binary number in DH is positive or negative would be to execute the instruction TEST DH,80H. If the number in DH is positive, so that the most significant bit in DH is 0, then TEST DH,80H will set the zero flag but won't change DH. A common situation where TEST is used is when we want to check a bit from an input port and wait until it goes low. This is done with the code:

```
        MOV    DX,STATUS_PORT  ;Point DX at status port
HANG:   IN     AL,DX           ;Input from the port
        TEST   AL,1            ;Is bit 0 still high?
        JNZ    HANG            ;Keep on checking if so
LOW:    ......                 ;Get here only when bit 0 goes low
```

All the rest of the logic instructions are shift and rotate instructions. These shift all the bits in a register or memory location either right or left. The actions performed by each instruction are shown in Fig. 3-8. Look first at the two shift instructions SHL (shift logical left) and SHR (shift logical right). SHL AX,1 shifts each bit in AX one position to the left. The most significant bit of AX is shifted out of AX and placed in the carry flag, and a zero is shifted into the least significant bit position. This action effectively multiplies the number in AX by 2, as discussed in Sec. 3-8. A variation of this instruction allows you to shift left several bits at a time with one instruction as follows:

```
        MOV    CL,n            ;Put number of bit positions to shift in CL
        SHL    AX,CL           ;Shift AX left nn bits
```

This is equivalent to executing the SHL AX,1 instruction n times. The contents of CL are not affected by the SHL AX,CL instruction.

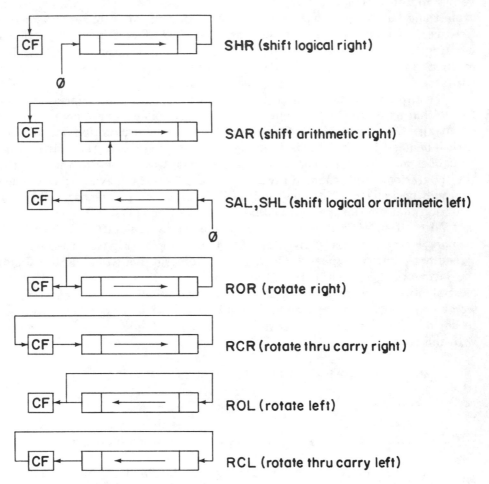

Fig. 3-8. Operations performed by the shift and rotate instructions.

The SHR instruction works in a similar manner to SHL except that all bits are shifted to the right with the least significant bit going into the carry flag and a 0 going into the most significant bit position. It has the effect of dividing an unsigned binary number by 2.

Another pair of shift instructions is SAR (shift arithmetic right) and SAL (shift arithmetic left). The SAR instruction works just like SHR except that instead of putting a 0 in the most significant bit, the SAR instruction puts a 1 in the most significant position if a 1 was originally there. Otherwise a 0 is placed in the most significant position. The reason for having such an instruction is that it allows signed binary numbers to be divided by 2 (recall that a negative binary number always has a 1 as its most significant bit). The SAL instruction is included only for symmetry. It does a multiply by two for signed binary numbers, but a multiply is the same for signed or unsigned binary numbers. Hence the SAL instruction is identical to the SHL instruction and they both have the same machine language op code.

The instructions ROR (rotate right) and ROL (rotate left) move bits around in a circular fashion. More precisely, an instruction like ROR AX,1 shifts the bits in AX to the right by one bit position, except that the least significant bit is moved back around into the most significant bit position. In addition, the least significant bit is copied into the carry flag. If you were to execute the instruction MOV CL,16 followed by ROR AX,CL, the AX register would remain totally unchanged. The chief value of this instruction is that it allows you to rearrange the bits in a byte or word without irretrievably destroying the original information. For example, executing four ROR AL,1 instructions swaps the high and low nibbles in a byte.

The ROL instruction is the inverse of the ROR instruction. ROL rotates bits to the left and can exactly undo the effect of a previous ROR. Executing ROR MEMVAL,1 followed by ROL MEMVAL,1 leaves the word or byte in memory location MEMVAL unchanged. The carry flag is affected, however, since the most significant bit is copied into CF by the ROL instruction.

The final two logic instructions are RCR (rotate through carry right) and RCL (rotate through carry left). These instructions operate like ROR and ROL except that the carry flag acts like an extra bit tacked onto the left of the most significant bit in the byte or word being rotated (see Fig. 3-8). The primary use for these instructions is in doing right or left shifts on multiple word quantities. For example, to do a logical right shift on a 32-bit integer LONGINT in memory you can use

```
SHR    LONGINT+2,1    ;Shift high word of LONGINT one bit right
RCR    LONGINT,1      ;Then rotate low word with carry from
                      ; previous shift going into MSB
```

3-10. String Primitive Instructions

One of the most powerful instruction groups in the 8088 is the string primitive group. These instructions (summarized in Table 3-8) allow you to rapidly move blocks of data from one place to another or to compare two blocks of data. String primitive operations are so called because they provide the basic (or primitive) instructions that you can combine to perform complicated operations on strings of data. In this context a string just means a block of data contained in consecutive memory addresses. Consider first the data movement capability.

The *move string instructions* (MOVSB to move a byte at a time, and MOVSW to move a word at a time) move data from one place in memory to another. The instructions assume that the SI register is pointing at the source (the place you want to move from), and that the DI register is pointing at the destination (the place you want to move to). For example, suppose you want to move one word of data from a memory location called

```
String Primitive Instructions

      MOVSB                    CMPSB
      MOVSW                    CMPSW

      LODSB                    SCASB
      LODSW                    SCASW

      STOSB
      STOSW


Prefixes for String Primitives

      REP
      REPE   (or REPZ)
      REPNE  (or REPNZ)

Direction Flag Instructions

      CLD
      STD
```

Table 3-8. String primitives and related instructions.

SOURCE to a location called DEST. Then the code

```
    MOV    SI,OFFSET SOURCE
    MOV    DI,OFFSET DEST
    MOVSW
```

does the trick. Notice that you must load SI and DI with OFFSET SOURCE and OFFSET DEST (recall that OFFSET means "address of") because we want to point them at the address of SOURCE and DEST, not load them with the values in SOURCE and DEST. Alternatively, you could use LEA instructions instead of MOV instructions to load the source and destination addresses.

What the MOVS instruction (either MOVSB or MOVSW) does is really the operation MOVS [DI],[SI]. However, the operands are totally superfluous here because SI must always contain the source and DI must always contain the destination. In fact, that's where the SI and DI registers get their names. SI is the source index register, and DI is the destination index register. Thus the assembler does not need any operands to be given with the MOVS instruction. It does need to know whether a word or a byte is to be moved, however, and hence the suffix "B" or "W" is required.

Another feature of the MOVS instruction, and indeed of all the string primitive instructions, is that the source and destination can be in different segments, allowing data transfers between memory locations more than 64 kilobytes apart. The source address for all string primitives is always DS:SI, and the destination address is always ES:DI (see Sec. 2-7 and Sec. 3-12). Often the ES and DS segment registers are set to the same segment address at the beginning of a program, so the segment registers can be ignored. We assume this is the case in the rest of this section.

At this point you may be wondering why the MOVS instruction is so great. After all, you could just as well use MOV AX,SOURCE followed by MOV DEST,AX to move the word of data in the preceding example, and this method would execute even faster! The answer is that MOVS does more than just move the data. If the direction flag is cleared (see below), it also automatically increments both SI and DI (by 1 for MOVSB and by 2 for MOVSW), so that SI and DI are both pointing at the next word or byte in memory. The idea is that MOVS is intended to be used when you want to move more than one word or byte. Furthermore, the MOVS instruction can be used with a prefix called REP, which causes the move instruction to be executed n times, where n is the value in the CX register. Thus,

```
        CLD                     ;Clear the direction flag
        LEA     SI,SOURCE       ;Point at source & destination
        LEA     DI,DEST
        MOV     CX,20H          ;Move 20H bytes
REP     MOVSB
```

moves 20H bytes of data starting at location SOURCE into 20H bytes starting at location DEST. This is a very fast way to move blocks of data around. Note that the REP prefix causes CX to be decremented each time MOVSB is executed. The single instruction REP MOVSB is equivalent to the entire group of instructions

```
LOOP:   MOV     AL,[SI]
        MOV     [DI],AL
        INC     SI
        INC     DI
        LOOP    LOOP
```

but REP MOVSB executes far faster. Also, unlike the LOOP instruction, if CX = 0, REP executes MOVSB zero times.

As stated previously, the MOVS instruction automatically increments SI and DI if something called the direction flag (DF) was cleared. This flag, mentioned briefly in Sec. 3-7, is used only by the string primitive instructions. Its purpose is to allow the user to have SI and DI either incremented or decremented by the string primitive instructions. There are two instructions that affect DF, namely CLD (which clears DF) and STD (which sets DF). If the direction flag is set by STD, then SI and DI are decremented when a string primitive is executed. If DF is cleared by CLD, then SI and DI are incremented when a string primitive is executed.

Having the increment/decrement choice is very useful when you want to move a block of memory to another area that partially overlaps the original area. Suppose, for example, that you want to move the 100H words starting at location START to a new location that is only one word higher in memory. In this situation you must move the last of the 100H words first, and work your way downward in memory using

```
STD                        ;Decrement SI & DI in string move
LEA     SI,START+100H      ;Point to end of old & new blocks
LEA     DI,START+102H
MOV     CX,100H            ;Move 100H words
REP     MOVSW
```

If you had started at the beginning of the block and worked upward, the values transferred first would overwrite the values to be transferred later. On the other hand, if you want to move a memory block to an overlapping location lower in memory, you need to do a CLD and work from the beginning of the block upward. Since overlapping moves are not that common, it's often useful to simply execute a CLD at the beginning of a program and then just assume that SI and DI are incremented in all string operations. If a decrement is needed, do an STD followed by the string operation, and then immediately execute a CLD.

Another string primitive instruction is the *store string instruction* (STOS). STOSW moves the value contained in AX into the word in memory pointed to by DI and then increments (or decrements if DF is set) DI by 2. STOSB moves the value contained in AL into the memory byte pointed to by DI and then increments (or decrements) DI by 1. The SI register is left unchanged. This instruction is very handy if you want to fill some area of memory with a constant value. Just load the desired value into AL or AX and use REP STOS to produce as many copies of the value as you wish.

The *load string instruction* (LODS) is the inverse of STOS. LODSW moves the memory word pointed to by SI into AX and then increments (or decrements) SI by 2. LODSB moves the memory byte pointed to by SI into AL and then increments (or decrements) SI by 1. By itself, this instruction makes little sense, since there is no point in moving a string of values into AX with each new value overwriting the previous one. The primary reason for having LODS and STOS is to make it easy for you to build up complex string operations in which values are loaded into AL or AX from memory, transformed in some way, and then stored somewhere else in memory. For example, here is a program that takes the absolute value of 20H signed 8-bit integers, which are stored starting at location NUM:

```
CLD
LEA     SI,NUM      ;Point SI & DI to start of table
MOV     DI,SI
MOV     CX,20H      ;Transform 20H values
```

```
NEXT:    LODSB                     ;Get a signed number
         TEST    AL,80H            ;Is it positive? (bit 7 = 0 if positive)
         JZ      POSTIV            ;Skip ahead if so
         NEG                       ;Else make it positive
POSTIV:  STOSB                     ;Store the transformed number
         LOOP    NEXT
```

The final two string primitive instructions are string compare operations. The *compare string* (CMPS) instruction is used to compare two
strings in memory to see if they are the same or not. The *scan string*
(SCAS) instruction is used to look for a particular value in a single string.
These are very powerful instructions, but a bit of thought is required to use
that power fully. Look first at CMPS.

The CMPSB instruction compares the byte pointed to by SI with the byte
pointed to by DI, and sets the flags according to whether [SI] is greater
than, equal to, or less than [DI]. The two bytes being compared are left
unchanged by the CMPSB instruction, but SI and DI are both incremented
(or decremented if DF is set). The comparison is done by subtracting the
byte pointed to by DI from the byte pointed to by SI (that is, by calculating
[SI] - [DI]), setting the flags accordingly, and then throwing away the
result. Note that the subtraction is source minus destination, rather than
the destination minus source convention that is used with the CMP instruction. It's unclear why the 8088 designers did this. CMPSW works just like
CMPSB except that two words in memory are compared instead of two
bytes, and SI and DI are incremented (or decremented) by 2.

Two prefixes can be used with the CMPS instruction: *repeat while
equal* (REPE) and *repeat while not equal* (REPNE). The Macro Assembler also recognizes REPZ (repeat while zero) and REPNZ (repeat while
not zero) as being synonyms of REPE and REPNE, respectively. The prefixes
cause the CMPS instruction to be repeated a maximum of n times, where n is
the number contained in the CX register. The CX register is decremented
each time the CMPS instruction is executed. With REPE, the repetition quits
when CX is decremented to zero *or* when the two bytes (or words) being
compared are different, whichever happens first. With REPNE, the repetition quits when CX is decremented to zero *or* when the two bytes or words
being compared are the same. Thus you can compare two strings and either
find the first place where the strings differ or find the first place where
they match.

Consider an example to clarify all this. Suppose you have two
programs, PROG1 and PROG2, stored in memory, and you want to see if
these two programs are identical. Assume also that PROG1 is 4321H bytes
long. You can easily do the comparison with the following subroutine:

```
COMP: CLD
      LEA    SI,PROG1              ;Point to start of both programs
      LEA    DI,PROG2
```

```
        MOV    CX,4321H            ;Compare bytes till they don't match
        REPE   CMPSB               ; or till end of PROG1 reached
        RET
```

This subroutine returns with CX = 0 if the two programs match, and CX > 0 if they don't. Furthermore, OFFSET PROG1 + (4321H - CX) is the address of the first byte in PROG1 where the two programs differ.

  The other string compare primitive is SCAS. SCASB compares the byte in memory pointed to by DI with the byte in AL, sets the flags accordingly, and increments (or decrements) DI. Thus while CMPSB compares corresponding bytes of two strings in memory, SCASB compares the bytes in a single string with a fixed value in AL. The comparison is done by subtracting the memory byte from the byte in AL; that is, the operation AL − [DI] is performed, but AL and [DI] are left unchanged. Only the flags are changed. SCASW does the same thing as SCASB, except that a comparison is between a word in memory and AX.

  Just as with CMPS, SCAS can take either REPE or REPNE as a prefix. For example, suppose you have a string of text in memory (recall that text is stored in memory as a sequence of bytes, with each byte containing the ASCII code for the letter). If you want to find the first occurrence of some letter, say the letter "E", in the string, you can use

```
STRING  DB     'THIS IS TEXT'      ;The assembler converts each letter
                                   ; between the quotes to ASCII code

        CLD
        LEA    DI,STRING           ;Point to start of text string
        MOV    AL,'E'              ;Look for an "E"
        MOV    CX,0CH              ;String contains 12 bytes
        MOV    BX,CX               ;Save string length in BX
REPNE   SCASB                      ;Loop till match found or CX=0
        SUB    BX,CX               ;Calculate (string length)-CX
                                   ; to find position of "E" in string
```

This code finds the position in the string where an "E" first occurs and places it in the BX register. In the present example, BX will contain 9.

  The use of SCAS and CMPS together provides a very powerful facility for finding patterns in a string of numbers, or equivalently for finding particular words in a string of text (recognizing the words in a string of text is called *parsing a text string*). The procedure is to use REPNE SCAS to find the first number in the string that matches the pattern, and then to use REPE CMPS to see if the rest of the pattern matches. If it doesn't match, go back to REPNE SCAS and scan further in the string.

3-11. Miscellaneous Instructions

All the the major 8088 instruction groups have been discussed in previous sections. The few instructions left that haven't been covered are listed in Table 3-9.

BCD and ASCII Adjust Instructions

    DAA   AAA
    DAS   AAS
                                AAM
                                AAD

Other Miscellaneous Instructions

    NOP

    HLT

    SAHF
    LAHF

    ESC   opcode,mem
    WAIT
    LOCK

Table 3-9. BCD and ASCII adjust instructions and miscellaneous other instructions. See Table 3-2 for an explanation of the "mem" operand. "opcode" is a byte that specifies the coprocessor instruction to be executed (see text).

The DAA (decimal adjust for addition) and DAS (decimal adjust for subtraction) instructions allow you to do simple arithmetic directly on BCD (binary coded decimal) numbers. As discussed in Sec. 2-3, BCD numbers are stored with 2 digits in each byte, each digit being a number in the range 0 through 9. If you add 2 bytes, each containing a 2-digit BCD number, the result will not necessarily be a correct BCD number, since the ADD instruction assumes the bytes contain simple binary numbers. The DAA instruction changes the result so that it's correct when interpreted as a pair of BCD digits. For example, suppose you have the BCD number 36 in AL, and you want to add the BCD number 27 to it. A simple ADD AL,27H gives the result AL = 5DH, which is not correct for a BCD addition. Instead use the pair of instructions

```
ADD     AL,27H
DAA
```

which leaves the correct result of 63 in AL. The DAA instruction operates only on a number in AL, changing it into a valid BCD number. It does this by examining the auxiliary carry flag setting (see Sec. 3-7) produced by the previous ADD and the value contained in AL. *The 8086/8088 Primer* (Morse 1982) explains in detail exactly how this is done.

The DAS instruction operates exactly like DAA, except that it adjusts the result of a subtraction to be the correct BCD result. There are no instructions for doing a decimal adjust after a multiplication or division operation. If you want to do such operations on BCD numbers, you have to either convert the numbers to binary, do the operations, and then convert them back to BCD, or use the 8087 numeric coprocessor chip (see Sec. 4-8). If you've put an 8087 into your machine, the latter approach is very attractive because the 8087 can do the full range of arithmetic operations on multi-digit BCD numbers up to twenty digits in length.

The 8088 designers also included a set of four adjust instructions for numbers stored as ASCII digits. Actually the instructions operate on unpacked BCD numbers—that is, numbers stored with only one digit in the range 0 through 9 contained in each byte (in contrast to the packed BCD numbers discussed previously, where two digits are stored per byte). To convert ASCII to unpacked BCD, just subtract 30H so that the high nibble of the byte is 0. The AAA (ASCII adjust for addition) and AAS (ASCII adjust for subtraction) instructions are used with unpacked BCD numbers just as the DAA and DAS instructions are used with packed BCD numbers. In addition, there are AAM (ASCII adjust for multiplication) and AAD (ASCII adjust for division) instructions, which can be used with multiplication and division operations. The exact way in which these instructions are used can become complicated if operations on multidigit unpacked BCD numbers are performed. The ASCII adjust instructions are seldom used. Typically it's much easier to just convert ASCII to binary and then do binary arithmetic. If you're interested in using the ASCII adjust instructions, consult *The 8086/8088 Primer* (Morse 1982), which has an excellent in-depth discussion of how to use these instructions.

The next instruction in Table 3-9 is the NOP (no operation) instruction. Although the name seems to imply that this instruction does nothing, that's only approximately true. Actually, a NOP has a 1-byte op code, takes three clock cycles to execute, and exchanges AX with AX. Its function is to use up 1 byte of memory and/or to waste some execution time. Neither of these functions may sound very useful, but sometimes they are. The most common use of NOP's is when you're trying to find errors using DEBUG. Suppose you have an instruction or two in the middle of a program that you suspect to be causing a problem. You can temporarily eliminate those instructions by using the "E" command to enter NOP's in place of the program bytes occupied by the questionable instructions. Since a NOP is only 1 byte long (the op code is 90H), you can enter exactly the right number of NOP's to eliminate any computer instruction. NOP's can also be inserted to lengthen the time required to execute a program loop. If you look at the machine code produced by the assembler, you'll sometimes find that NOP's have been inserted following certain instructions, such as the JMP instruction. The assembler does this because on its first pass through a program it sometimes doesn't know whether a short JMP (2 bytes) or a long JMP (3 bytes) can be used. Thus it reserves 3 bytes for the instruction and then later puts in a short JMP plus a NOP if it can.

The HLT (halt) instruction is another seemingly useless instruction that actually can be very handy. It causes the 8088 to halt, to stop executing instructions. After executing a HLT, the 8088 just sits there doing nothing until either a pulse is sent to the RESET line (see Sec. 6-1) or an interrupt occurs. It's the latter situation where HLT comes in handy. Suppose you come to a point in a program where you require some input from an external device and that device is interrupt driven—that is, the device causes a hardware interrupt to occur when it has new data for the CPU (see Sec. 6-4 for a discussion of hardware interrupts). The easiest way to handle this situation is to put a HLT in the program so that the 8088 just stops until the interrupt occurs. When it does, the interrupt service routine is executed and the CPU returns to the instruction following the HLT and begins to execute instructions normally again.

The SAHF (store AH into flags) instruction moves the contents of AH into the low byte of the flags register. The LAHF (load AH from flags) does the reverse; it moves the contents of the low byte of the flags register into AH. These two instructions are provided only for compatibility with Intel's earlier 8080/8085 CPU's. In particular, they allow you to emulate the 8080/8085 instructions PUSH AF and POP AF with the 8088 instruction pairs LAHF, PUSH AX and POP AX, SAHF. With the inclusion of these two instructions, the 8088 instruction set can be used as a superset of the 8080's or 8085's instruction set. Hence programs written for the 8080 or 8085 can easily be translated into 8088 assembly language. Note that such translations are not optimal, because they fail to take advantage of the 8088's more powerful instruction set. Nevertheless, they may be as good as the code produced by compilers for the 8088, since people worked so hard at optimizing code for the smaller 8080 processor. Unless you're doing such a translation, you'll have no need for these two instructions.

Finally, three instructions, ESC (escape), WAIT, and LOCK, are used to synchronize operations when multiple processors are present. Two multiple processor situations are of interest for the IBM PC.

The first is the case where another CPU card (another 8088 or some other CPU such as a Motorola 68000) is added in one of the expansion slots of the PC. Although you are not likely to be writing the basic software drivers for such a system, it may be enlightening to see how such situations can be handled. Also, the LOCK instruction prefix doesn't make sense unless you understand the problem that makes it necessary.

When a second CPU is added, the two independent CPU's are both capable of addressing memory, using the disks, or writing to the screen at any time. Clearly disaster ensues if both CPU's try to use any of these resources simultaneously. The standard way to solve this problem is to dedicate a few memory locations to serve as semaphores. A *semaphore* is just a memory location containing a flag bit that is set if either CPU is using a particular resource. When the CPU is finished using the resource, it clears the flag bit again. Thus the semaphore is like a railroad semaphore signal that permits only one train to travel a given section of railroad track at a time. If a CPU wants to use a certain resource, say a given block of memory containing variables shared by both CPU's, it first looks at the semaphore to see if it's set. If it is, the CPU just sits in a program loop looking repeatedly at the semaphore until it sees that the semaphore has been cleared. Then the CPU sets the semaphore itself, does whatever it wants to do with the resource, and clears the semaphore when it's finished. This sounds simple, but it's not. Suppose you check the semaphore and set it as follows:

```
BUSY: TEST   SEMPHR,80H    ;Is the semaphore set by the other CPU?
      JNZ    BUSY          ;Hang in a loop if it is
      MOV    SEMPHR,80H    ;Else set the semaphore
      ...                  ;Then go ahead and use the resource
```

This code doesn't always do what you want it to. Suppose CPU 1 executes the TEST instruction here and sees that the semaphore is clear. Thus it falls through the loop, executes the MOV SEMPHR,80H, and starts using the resource. But suppose that CPU 2 also executes a TEST SEMPHR,80H between the time CPU 1 executed its TEST and its MOV instruction. CPU 2 will then think that the resource is free and also attempt to use it.

The only way to make the semaphores work properly is to have a single, indivisible instruction that both tests and sets the semaphore. This works because memory hardware prevents two processors from accessing a given memory location at exactly the same time. What you have to prevent is doing the test and set with more than one memory access. If two memory accesses are required to test and set, the other processor can always sneak in between the test and the set and foul things up. An instruction that seems to do the job is XCHG reg,mem. Here's how it works:

```
BUSY: MOV    AL,80H        ;Prepare to set semaphore if not set already
      XCHG   AL,SEMPHR     ;Set semaphore & get previous value in AL
      OR     AL,AL
      JNZ    BUSY          ;If previous value was nonzero, hang in loop
      ...                  ;Else go ahead & use the resource
```

This looks good except for one problem. The XCHG instruction actually requires two memory accesses to execute even though it's a single instruction. Thus we still seem to be in trouble. Here is where the 8088 designers came to the rescue by providing the LOCK instruction prefix. When LOCK is put in front of an instruction, the 8088 responds by sending out a signal on a

CPU pin called $\overline{LOCK}$. The $\overline{LOCK}$ signal remains active for the complete duration of a single instruction. If the hardware is properly wired up, memory accesses by another processor are prevented while $\overline{LOCK}$ is active (see Sec. 6-1). Thus you can modify the preceding code by writing the XCHG instruction as LOCK XCHG AL,SEMPHR and everything will work fine.

A second type of multiple CPU situation is one that you're much more likely to encounter with the IBM PC: the use of a coprocessor. A coprocessor is a slave CPU that can handle certain specialized tasks more efficiently than the 8088 can. Intel makes two coprocessors for the 8088, the 8089 I/O processor and the 8087 numeric data processor. The 8089 provides intelligent input/ouput and DMA transfers (see Sec. 6-4), which can be useful in certain specialized situations. However, the IBM PC already has a different built-in DMA controller chip and in general the 8089 is a seldom used chip, so we say nothing more about it here. The 8087 is another story. It provides a tremendous increase in speed for mathematical computations, and there is an empty socket in the IBM PC right next to the 8088 that is all wired up for the 8087. You can just plug the 8087 right in.

The 8087 is connected to the same address and data lines as the 8088 CPU, and can be thought of as a sort of CPU assistant. The 8087 watches the instructions being executed by the 8088, but does nothing unless it sees an ESC (escape) instruction. The 8087 recognizes ESC as an instruction that the 8088 needs assistance to execute. ESC is not a single instruction, but rather a class of 2-byte instructions that begin with the byte 11011XXX, where the X's can be either 0 or 1. Some of the ESC instructions involve memory references, and some do not. If no memory reference is involved, the 8088 CPU simply ignores the ESC and the 8087 executes the instruction all by itself. When the CPU encounters an ESC instruction that involves a memory reference, however, it calculates the effective address specified in the instruction, places this address on the bus, and initiates a memory read cycle. The 8087 then takes over, reads the data coming in from memory, and finishes executing the rest of the instruction. Meanwhile the CPU can either go on with the next instruction or wait for the 8087 to finish its job. If it needs to wait until the 8087 is finished, the escape instruction is followed by a WAIT instruction. A WAIT causes the CPU to just sit and do nothing until the 8087 sends it a signal saying it's finished executing an instruction. A WAIT instruction is also normally inserted before an ESC to make sure that the 8087 is finished with whatever it was doing previously before it's given a new task. Thus the ESC and WAIT instruction pair allow the 8088 to work effectively in synchronism with a coprocessor.

The 2-byte machine code for the ESC instruction has the form 11011XXX modXXXr/m, where the X's can be either 0 or 1. Here 'mod' and 'r/m' are 2-bit and 3-bit fields, respectively, which specify the addressing mode to be used. If the 'mod' bits are 11, the instruction doesn't involve a memory reference, and the machine code for the ESC instruction could be placed directly in the program using a DB directive. Thus the instruction to initialize the 8087, called FINIT, could be written as

   DB 0DBH,0E3H

In cases where the ESC instruction involves a memory reference, the assembler allows you to write an escape instruction as

   ESC opcode,mem

where "mem" has the usual meaning as given in Table 3-2, and "opcode" is a byte whose lower 6 bits specify the bits labeled X in the machine code for ESC given above. These opcode bits determine which 8087 instruction is being specified. In practice, however, there is no need to ever enter ESC codes into your programs. The assembler recognizes the 8087 op codes such as FINIT, and automatically produces the appropriate ESC machine codes, preceded by a WAIT instruction. The use of the 8087 coprocessor and how to write programs for it are discussed in detail in Sec. 4-8.

3-12. Segment Register Instructions

The segment registers have been ignored until now in the discussion of 8088 instructions. When you're doing your own programming, you will also be able to ignore the segment registers most of the time. However, as shown in Sec. 3-2, you can't ignore them at the beginning of a program where you have to set up a proper return to the operating system. You also can't ignore them if you're writing more sophisticated programs such as video screen handling programs, large programs that must be split into many modules, or resident interrupt handlers. These more advanced techniques are the subject of the next chapter.

Before looking at the options available for manipulating the segment registers, recall how the segment registers are normally used. This subject is briefly introduced in Sec. 2-7, where a figure listing the default segment register assignments is given. As can be seen there, the normal situation is really fairly simple:

1. Addresses pointed to by IP are always relative to CS, which means the program being executed must be in the CS segment.

2. Addresses pointed to by SP are always relative to SS, which means the stack is always in the SS segment.

3. Addresses pointed to with addressing modes involving the BP register are relative to SS.

4. Addresses pointed to with all other addressing modes are relative to DS. Thus variables are normally located in the data segment.

5. For the string primitive instructions, the source address is relative to DS and the destination address is relative to ES.

Table 3-10 shows all the instructions that involve the segment registers (except for the INT instructions discussed in Sec. 3-6).

```
Instructions Involving Segment Registers

    MOV     segreg*,reg/mem
    MOV     reg/mem,segreg

    PUSH    segreg
    POP     segreg*

    LDS     reg16,mem
    LES     reg16,mem

    where   "segreg" is one of CS, DS, SS, ES
            "segreg*" is one of DS, SS, ES


Segment Override Prefix

    segreg:

Intersegment Control Transfer

    JMP     faraddr
    JMP     ddmem

    CALL    faraddr                 RET
    CALL    ddmem                   RET     n

    where   "faraddr" is a program label in another segment
            "ddmem" is a double word variable
            "n" is a 16-bit number
```

Table 3-10. Instructions involving the segment registers. See Table 3-2 for an explanation of the "reg", "reg16", and "mem" operands.

The most straightforward way to change a segment register is just to move a new value into it. As can be seen from the table, however, the MOV instruction's operands are somewhat restricted when a segment register is involved. First of all, MOV CS,reg/mem is not allowed, as this would, in effect, cause a jump to a new segment without any change in IP (the next instruction to be executed is always given by CS:IP). There's no legitimate use for such an instruction, so the 8088 designers did not allow it. The other two major restrictions are that you can't move an immediate value into a segment register, and you can't move the contents of one segment register directly into another. To do these tasks, you normally use another register for intermediate storage. For example, to move the contents of CS into DS, use

```
MOV    AX,CS
MOV    DS,AX
```

Since you can PUSH and POP the segment registers, an alternative is to use PUSH CS followed by POP DS. Note that POP CS is not allowed for the same reason that MOV CS,reg/mem isn't. Also, since the stack is always pointed to by SS:SP, be very careful if you do a POP SS!

Two special data movement instructions involving the segment registers are also available; LDS (load pointer using DS) and LES (load pointer using ES). LDS allows you to load values into any 16-bit register *and* the DS register with a single instruction. The source of these two 16-bit values is the memory location specified by the second operand (this location can be specified using any of the 8088's addressing modes). For example, the instruction LDS SI,DWORD PTR [BX] loads SI with the contents of the memory locations pointed to by DS:BX and DS:BX+1, and then loads DS with the contents of memory locations DS:BX+2 and DS:BX+3. The instruction LES SI,DWORD PTR [BX] does the same thing except that the ES register is loaded instead of the DS register. The words "DWORD PTR" in the operand are necessary to tell the assembler that BX is a pointer to a double word (4 byte) value.

The most common use for LDS and LES is in connection with the string primitive instructions. The instruction MOVSB moves a byte from the memory location pointed to by DS:SI to the location pointed to by ES:DI. Thus you need to load the DS:SI and ES:DI register pairs before the MOVSB instruction is executed, and this can be done quite efficiently by the LDS and LES instructions.

Sometimes you want to access memory using a segment register other than the one given by the default assignments described earlier in this section. This can be done using a *segment override prefix*. This prefix is just the name of the segment register you want to use followed by a colon and placed just before the memory operand involved. For example, if you want to load a variable that is in a segment pointed to by ES:BX, you can use MOV AX,ES:[BX] to load the variable into AX. The segment override prefixes CS:, SS:, DS:, or ES: can be used with any of the 8088's addressing modes. Here are some examples:

```
MOV    CL,DS:[BP]+3    ;Load CL with the contents of DS:BP+3
                       ; instead of the normal SS:BP+3
MOV    BH,ES:VARBL     ;Load BH with the contents of the memory
                       ; location VARBL which is located in
                       ; the segment pointed to by ES
MOV    DI,SS:[BX+SI]   ;Load DI with the contents of SS:(BX+SI)
                       ; instead of the normal DS:(BX+SI)
```

```
       MOV    AX,CS:[SI]        ;Load AX with the contents of CS:SI
                                ; instead of the normal DS:SI
```

A useful application of an override prefix is in the construction of a multiway jump with the jump table located in the code segment:

```
ENTRY:  SHL    BX,1
        JMP    CS:[BX]+TABLE
TABLE   DW     PROG0
        DW     PROG1
        DW     PROG2
```

This little piece of code assumes that BX contains the value 0, 1, or 2 when the instruction SHL BX,1 is executed. The SHL instruction multiplies the value in BX by 2 and the JMP instruction then produces a jump to PROG0, PROG1, or PROG2.

Finally, there is a set of intersegment jump and call instructions, also known as *far jumps* and *far calls*. These enable you to jump to any location in the 8088's megabyte memory address space or to call a subroutine located anywhere in memory.

The far jump (JMP) instruction works just like the intrasegment (near) jump instruction discussed in Sec. 3-5, except that both the CS segment register and the IP register are loaded with a new value instead of just the IP. As with a near jump, two forms are possible. In a direct jump, the operand is a program label, and its segment and offset within the segment are loaded into CS and IP respectively. In an indirect jump, the operand is a memory address. Four bytes must be stored in memory starting at this address. The first two bytes are loaded into IP and the next two are loaded into CS.

The far call (CALL) works in an analogous fashion. Both direct and indirect calls can be made, and in both cases CS and IP are loaded with new values, and the old CS and IP values are saved on the stack (IP is pushed first, then CS). There is a corresponding far return (RET) instruction that pops both CS and IP off the stack.

There is one obvious problem with the far jump, call, and return instructions, however. They use the same mnemonics that are used for near jumps, calls, and returns! How can the programmer or the assembler tell which is which? The answer is that the assembler assumes that a near jump or call instruction will be used unless the context makes it clear that a far instruction is needed or the programmer explicitly specifies the operand as being in a different segment. The following example may help to clarify how this works:

```
SEG1      SEGMENT
FARSUB    PROC   FAR
          ...
FARSUB    ENDP
SEG1      ENDS

SEG2      SEGMENT
MAIN      PROC   FAR
          CALL   NRSUB2        ;This is a near call
          JMP    NRSUB1        ;This is a near jump
          CALL   FARSUB        ;This is a far call
          CALL   FAR PTR FSUB2 ;This is a far call to a forward reference
          JMP    FARSUB        ;This is a far jump
          JMP    FAR PTR FSUB2 ;This is a far jump to a forward reference
BACK:     RET                  ;This is a far return
MAIN      ENDP

NRSUB1    PROC   NEAR
          JMP    BACK          ;This is a near jump
NRSUB1    ENDP

NRSUB2:   ...
          RET                  ;This is a near return
SEG2      ENDS

SEG3      SEGMENT
FSUB2     PROC FAR
          ...
FSUB2     ENDP
SEG3      ENDS
```

You see a main program, which is itself written as a subroutine as explained in Sec. 3-2, plus four other "procedures." A procedure is just a block of code that begins with a line containing the reserved word PROC, and ends with a line containing the reserved word ENDP. A procedure is often a subroutine, but it doesn't have to be. From the assembler's point of view, every computer program is just a collection of procedures. Procedures can be either NEAR or FAR. FAR procedures are accessed from other procedures by far (intersegment) CALL's or JMP's. NEAR procedures are accessed from other procedures by near (intrasegment) CALL's or JMP's. Since the default is a NEAR procedure, it need not be declared at all, as illustrated by NRSUB2. We prefer this form since it's simpler and shorter.

Whether to call a procedure NEAR or FAR depends on the situation. In simple programs you make the main program body a FAR procedure as discussed in Sec. 3-2 and make all other subroutines NEAR procedures. In some of the more complex situations discussed in the next chapter, several FAR procedures may exist within a program.

As the assembler makes its first pass through the program code, and encounters JMP or CALL instructions, it tries to decide whether the near or far variety should be used by noting whether the procedure being called is NEAR or FAR. It can do this unambiguously unless a forward JMP or CALL is encountered, that is, a JMP or CALL to a label that is farther ahead in the code. In this case, it assumes the instruction is NEAR unless you specify otherwise by placing FAR PTR in front of the operand. If this assumption turns out to be false, an error message will be generated.

The rules for RET instructions are very simple. If a RET instruction is within a FAR procedure, a far return is always generated. If the RET is within a NEAR procedure, a near return is generated.

For indirect jumps and calls you have to specify to the assembler if a FAR instruction is needed since the assembler can't tell from an instruction like JMP [SI] where you're headed. Since the default is NEAR, the assembler always assumes JMP [SI] is a near jump. If you want a far jump, you must specify JMP FAR [SI].

References

iAPX 88 Book, 1981, Intel Corporation, Santa Clara, CA. This is the authoritative reference on the 8088 instruction set and electrical characteristics, published by the chip's manufacturer.

S. P. Morse, 1982, *The 8086/8088 Primer*, Hayden Book Company, Rochelle Park, NJ. Written by one of the 8088's designers, this book has an excellent discussion of the 8088 instruction set from a machine language point of view.

L. Scanlon, 1983, *IBM PC Assembly Language*, Robert J. Brady Company, Bowie, MD. Good introductory discussion of assembly language and the use of the IBM Macro Assembler.

D. Willen and J. Krantz, 1983, *8088 Assembler Language Programming: The IBM PC*, Howard W. Sams and Company, Indianapolis, IN. Introductory discussions of assembly language, use of the IBM Macro Assembler, and the hardware of the PC. Presentations are good but brief.

D. J. Bradley, 1984, *Assembly Language Programming for the IBM Personal Computer*, Prentice-Hall, Englewood Cliffs, NJ. Provides excellent in-depth discussion of assembly language programming using the IBM Macro Assembler.

4
Advanced Assembly Language Techniques

Inside every large program, there is a small program struggling to get out.
— C. A. R. Hoare

For small and relatively straightforward programming projects, the program model presented in Sec. 3-2 is adequate. There are other occasions, however, when specialized and/or more sophisticated types of programs are necessary. In this chapter we discuss several program types and programming techniques that fall into this category. In particular, we provide answers to the following questions:

1. How can programs be written to handle multiple code or data segments in memory?

2. How can large programs be split up into several pieces or modules each of which can be separately edited and assembled?

3. When the programs you've written don't work, what techniques can be used to find the errors in them?

4. If several versions of a program are needed for different applications or hardware configurations, how can they be simultaneously updated or maintained?

5. What are macros, and when should they be used?

6. How can programs that are mixtures of a high-level language and assembly language be written so that you can take advantage of the best features of both?

7. How can control programs for new I/O devices be added to the operating system or replace the ones currently provided for existing I/O devices?

8. How can the .COM files needed for I/O drivers and extensions to DOS be created?

9. How can disk files be loaded, executed, read, and/or written from an assembly language program?

10. How can the 8087 numeric data processor be used to do high-speed mathematical or graphics computations?

In the sections that follow, all of these topics are discussed in some depth. One important area not discussed as a separate topic is proper programming and documentation techniques (although good examples to imitate are given). If you're going to pursue computer programming seriously, you should read some of the many books that discuss such topics as structured programming, top-down design, and the importance of good documentation for program maintenance.

4-1. Multisegment Programs

This section examines how to create multisegment programs—programs that access more than one data or code segment. In the program model presented in Sec. 3-2, you were concerned only with the segment registers at the beginning of the program where a proper return to DOS was set up. There are occasions, however, when you'll need to manipulate the segment registers in the body of your program. The most common situation where this occurs is when you want to directly access a fixed memory area such as the video memory at 0B0000H or the interrupt vectors at 0. Another example is when you must deal with a very large amount of data (more than 64K). In these cases you need to set the segment registers in your program and make sure they're always pointing at the proper area of memory.

The basic structure of a multiple segment program is very simple. Each segment begins with a SEGMENT declaration and ends with an ENDS statement. For example, a data segment might be defined as

```
DSEG   SEGMENT
       ...
DSEG   ENDS
```

The simple model program of Sec. 3-2 had three segments defined: a data segment where program variables were stored, a code segment for the actual program code, and a stack segment for the program's stack. Unless you're writing separately assembled program modules, a situation discussed in the next section, it's rare to need more than one data or code segment in a single program. You can use more if you want, but as you'll see shortly, accessing multiple segments can be tricky, and should be avoided if possible.

The most common reason to have multiple segments is in order to access fixed locations in memory. There are several fixed address areas in memory that you're most likely to use: the interrupt vectors in locations 0:0 through 0:3FF, a system RAM area at locations 40:0 through 40:1FF, the code in ROM at locations 0F400:0 through 0FFFF:F, and the memory-mapped video areas starting at locations 0B000:0 (monochrome display) and 0B800:0 (color/graphics display).

To access fixed locations, it's simplest to just specify the address needed directly. For example, to load AX with the contents of memory location 40:10, you can just load DS with the segment value 40, and then write MOV AX,[10]. Although this can be done, it's poor programming practice because the program then contains no clear documentation of the segment and offset of the location or what it's used for.

The clearest way to specify and document the use of a fixed memory location is to use the "SEGMENT AT" statement to create a dummy segment that lists the variable names and offset addresses you want to use. A segment that begins with SEGMENT AT is not actually loaded in memory. It's just a template or model the assembler uses to generate the proper machine code. Thus to access location 40:10, write

```
SYS_DATA     SEGMENT AT 40H
             ORG      10H
EQUIP_FLAG   DW       ?
SYS_DATA     ENDS
```

This tells the assembler that there is a 16-bit variable called EQUIP_FLAG located at an offset address of 10H within a segment that starts at 40:0. You can now read the value of EQUIP_FLAG with

```
        ASSUME   DS:SYS_DATA
        MOV      AX,SYS_DATA
        MOV      DS,AX
        MOV      AX,EQUIP_FLAG
```

Note that DS must be loaded with the proper segment value before accessing EQUIP_FLAG, and an ASSUME statement for DS is needed. Note that the ASSUME doesn't change the DS register value; it just tells the assembler to look in the segment SYS_DATA for any variables that are subsequently accessed using DS. It's a good idea to put an ASSUME in your program any time you change a segment register value. This alerts you (and others) to the fact that a different area of memory is now being accessed. If a variable is being accessed by name in the new segment, the assembler requires the ASSUME statement. Otherwise it's optional. The ASSUME statement is discussed further in Sec. 4-2.

Similarly, if you want to call or jump to an absolute location in the ROM BIOS (see the IBM PC *Technical Reference* manual for a listing of the ROM BIOS source code) you can use the same segment template technique. For example, write

```
ROM          SEGMENT AT 0F000H
             ORG     0E05BH
RESET        LABEL   FAR
ROM          ENDS
```

and then use JMP RESET in the program to jump to location 0F000:0E05B. A jump to the particular location in this example causes the computer to reset itself just as if the power had been turned off and then back on. In general it's a poor idea to jump directly into the ROM code, since IBM reserves the right to change the ROM contents in new versions of the PC (and has done so several times). However, in some situations it can be quite useful.

Yet another example of the segment template technique can be found in Sec. 4-6, where the purpose is to access the program segment prefix that is automatically placed at the beginning of every program by the linker.

A second way to access variables at fixed offsets in another segment is just to define the variable's offset address with an EQU statement and then use indirect addressing. For example, instead of using the template method, you could access the variable EQUIP_FLAG as follows:

```
SYS_DATA     EQU     40H          ;DOS data segment
EQUIP_FLAG   EQU     10H

             MOV     AX,SYS_DATA
             MOV     DS,AX
             MOV     BX,0
             MOV     AX,[BX+EQUIP_FLAG]
```

This technique is also illustrated in App. D, where it's used to access data in a memory block whose starting address is passed to the subroutine in ES:BX.

When changing segment register values in your program, double check that the segment registers are pointing at the proper segment *every* time you access memory. A slip up here is a very common cause of program errors. As an example, consider a new version of the model program of Sec. 3-2 that writes directly to the screen instead of using INT 21 as was done previously. Writing the screen RAM directly is essential to achieve the instant screen response characteristic of high-performance editors. For details on how the memory-mapped video screen works, see Sec. 8-3. For now, all you need to know is that you can make letters appear on the screen by writing ASCII characters into the even-numbered memory addresses starting at location 0B000:0000 (assuming a monochrome display). Here's the new version of the program:

```
          MOV    SI,OFFSET MSG
          SUB    DI,DI
          MOV    AX,0B000H
          MOV    DS,AX
          MOV    AH,7                ;Use ordinary screen attributes
NEXT:     LODSB
          CMP    AL,'$'
          JZ     DONE
          STOSW
          JMP    NEXT
DONE:     ...
```

Unfortunately, this program won't work because LODSB accesses DS:SI, and we've pointed DS at 0B000H rather than at the data segment where the string MSG is. To make the program work, we must change MOV DS,AX to MOV ES,AX. In this way DS remains pointing at the data segment where MSG is located, and ES points to the video RAM area at 0B000H.

The foregoing example illustrates a good way to access data in two different segments of memory. Use DS to point at one segment and ES to point at the other. For all instructions other than the string primitives, you must use a segment override to access the data in the segment that ES points to (see Sec. 3-12 for the default segment register assignments). If you need to access more than two data segments in memory, you'll have to switch DS back and forth between the segments and be very careful.

Unless you have a very good reason and know exactly what you're doing, don't fool around with SS. If you change SS, you lose your current stack, which typically leads to disaster. Occasionally you may need to change SS in order to set up a local stack for some subroutine or interrupt handler. To do this you must save SS:SP for the original stack, set up the new stack, and then restore the original stack before a return to DOS or the main program is done. Here's an example of how to set up a new stack:

```
          MOV    SPSAVE,SP
          MOV    SSSAVE,SS
          MOV    AX,NEWSS
          CLI
          MOV    SS,AX
          MOV    SP,NEWSP
          STI
```

The old value of SS:SP is saved in two 16-bit memory locations, SPSAV and SSSAV, so the original stack can be restored later. Before SS and SP are changed, interrupts are disabled, since an interrupt occurring between the MOV SS and MOV SP instructions would try to push values onto a nonexistent stack with disastrous results. Actually, on current 8088's (but not on chips manufactured before 1983) you should be able to get away without the CLI and STI instructions, because the 8088 is supposed to automatically refuse to accept an interrupt during the instruction immediately following a MOV SS,reg instruction. However, we usually choose to be conservative and leave the CLI in, just to make sure.

4-2. Program Modules

A powerful feature of the Macro Assembler and linker is that they can handle programs that are broken up into several modules or pieces. Each module can be written, edited, and assembled separately. Then the modules can be linked together by the linker to create a single executable program. If you want to change something, you only have to edit and reassemble one of the modules, not the entire program. This capability can be a lifesaver if you have to write large programs, since they can then be broken up into smaller pieces. It also encourages you to write modular programs, which is a good programming practice in any event. Having separately assembled program modules is also very useful if you need to write several different programs that utilize large portions of identical code. If you like, you can build up libraries of program modules, each of which is a subroutine or a collection of subroutines, and then make use of them as needed in other programs. In other words, using program modules allows you to create your own custom set of software tools. You can also link in modules created by compilation of higher-level languages.

If the program module needs no data segment, or uses only its own local data segment, creating program modules is very simple and straightforward. Consider a program divided into two modules: a main program module, and a module containing the two subroutines SUB1 and SUB2. The main program is written in the same form as the programs discussed in previous sections, with normal code, data, and stack segments. To use subroutines in the other module, just write CALL SUB1 or CALL SUB2 as if they were part of the main program module. However, you must somehow flag the subroutine names so that the assembler knows they are located in another module. This is done by putting the following at the beginning of the program:

```
EXTRN     SUB1:NEAR,SUB2:NEAR
```

Also, instead of starting the code segment with CSEG SEGMENT, we write:

```
CSEG      SEGMENT  PUBLIC
```

What do these two statements tell the assembler? The EXTERN statement says that the program labels SUB1 and SUB2 are external; they are not in the current program. Following each label with :NEAR tells the assembler that although the labels are in another module, the linker will be told to load them in the same segment as the present code segment. Hence the assembler generates a near call when CALL SUB1 is encountered. The modifiers to the CSEG SEGMENT declaration are passed to the linker by the assembler. The word PUBLIC tells the linker to concatenate all program segments beginning with CSEG SEGMENT PUBLIC together into one physical segment in memory—that is, in a single block of code that can be addressed by a single value of CS.

The program module containing SUB1 and SUB2 is written as follows:

```
        PUBLIC     SUB1,SUB2

CSEG    SEGMENT PUBLIC
        ASSUME     CS:CSEG
SUB1:   ...
        RET
SUB2:   ...
        RET
CSEG    ENDS
        END
```

Here the labels SUB1 and SUB2 are declared to be PUBLIC. This causes the assembler to flag the addresses of these labels so that the linker can find them and fill in the proper call addresses in the main program module. Since the subroutines are declared to be NEAR in the main program, the subroutines must be placed in a segment that has also been declared PUBLIC, and whose name is CSEG, the same name that was given to the main program segment. This ensures that the linker will combine the subroutines with the main program in the same physical segment of memory.

An alternative way to do things would be to declare the subroutines as

```
        EXTRN      SUB1:FAR,SUB2:FAR
```

in the main program. The assembler then generates far calls, and you don't have to declare the segments to be PUBLIC. You can also name the segments anything you want. However, you must declare SUB1 and SUB2 to be FAR procedures. It's entirely up to you whether you want to use this method or the previous one using near calls. Near calls are quicker and shorter, but far calls are better if you're making a library of subroutines to be used with several different programs.

The NEAR calls and jumps allow us to have a byte-efficient small (16-bit) address displacement for the majority of calls and jumps, while the FAR jumps and calls provide the ability to manipulate data anywhere in the megabyte address space. The penalty is having to worry about segment registers. Any program module can have its own local data segment(s) without causing any problems. The drawback is that you have to keep changing DS to make it point to the proper local data area. For example, suppose SUB1 needed to access a variable VAR1. You could include this by writing

```
DSUB   SEGMENT
VAR1   DW        ?
DSUB   ENDS
```

Then to load AX with the value of VAR1, you would have to write

```
PUSH     DS
MOV      AX,DSUB
MOV      DS,AX
ASSUME   DS:DSUB
MOV      AX,VAR1
POP      DS
```

This is a lot of code just to get the value of one variable. If the same data segment were used for both modules, you could set DS to point there once and for all at the beginning of the program, and then just do MOV AX,VAR1 to access VAR1 from subroutine SUB1.

There are at least three ways to handle a data segment that is shared among two or more program modules. Each has its own advantages and drawbacks. One method is to put all the variables needed by all modules in a single large data segment within one of the modules. Then, when another module needs to access some of the variables, it declares them as external. Going back to the example, suppose VAR1 had been defined to be a variable in a data segment called DAT within the main program and declared PUBLIC. Then to access it from SUB1, you would make the following declaration at the beginning of the module containing SUB1:

```
DAT    SEGMENT PUBLIC
       EXTRN VAR1:WORD
DAT    ENDS
```

This tells the assembler that VAR1 is in another module within a segment called DAT. You also need an ASSUME DS:DAT within SUB1 (ASSUME statements are discussed in more detail below). This method works very well, and is quite simple and straightforward. If you have global variables (a global variable is one that is accessed by two or more modules), you must use either this method or one to be presented next. The main drawback to declaring variables as external is that, if you want to add a variable to a module, you need to edit and change two files: the module that uses the variable and the module that contains the data segment for all modules.

An alternative method, best suited for cases with many global variables, is to declare a COMMON data segment. Here you write

```
DAT    SEGMENT  COMMON
VAR1   DW     ?
       •••
DAT    ENDS
```

where DAT contains all the variables used in all the modules. The best way to access this COMMON data segment is to put it in a file of its own, say DAT.ASM, and then to include it in every module needing to access it by inserting the statement

```
INCLUDE      DAT.ASM
```

near the beginning of each module. The "INCLUDE filename" statement causes a copy of the entire source code file called "filename" to be inserted into the program at the point where the INCLUDE statement is encountered. Declaring a segment to be COMMON causes it to be placed at the same address in memory with all other COMMON segments having the same segment name. It is possible to place the DAT segment explicitly in each module without using the INCLUDE statement, but then any changes lead to error-prone re-editing of all the different copies of DAT. Throughout the history of computing this problem has been one of the worst sources of program bugs. *Moral*: Always INCLUDE a single copy of the common block, be it in assembly language, FORTRAN, PL/I, C, or you name it!

A final method of handling the variables present in different program modules is to have a single data segment, say DSEG, which is formed by concatenating pieces of DSEG that are present in each module. In other words, DSEG can be formed in the same way that a single code segment is formed from the various program modules. In each module you declare

```
DSEG  SEGMENT  PUBLIC
      •••
DSEG  ENDS
```

and place whatever variables you need for a particular module in that piece of DSEG.

To conclude this section, it might be useful to discuss some of the assembler directives associated with modular and/or multisegment programs. These are often confusing to the programmer who is trying to write such programs for the first time. In particular, let's look at the ASSUME directive, the various modifiers associated with the SEGMENT declaration, and the GROUP directive.

The ASSUME directive tells the assembler which segments you want to point the various segment registers at. Suppose you had a program with a data segment DSEG, a stack segment SSEG, and a code segment CSEG. Then at the beginning of the actual program code you could put

ASSUME   CS:CSEG,DS:DSEG,SS:SSEG,ES:NOTHING

However, you do not really need to specify an assumed segment for every segment register. Normally the statement

ASSUME   CS:CSEG,DS:DSEG

works equally well. The reason is that the assignments given in an ASSUME statement are used by the assembler only when a variable or label is accessed by name in the program. In other words, the ASSUME statement tells the assembler where to look to find a variable or program label. Since you normally will not access named variables through the SS register, it's rare that you need to specify an ASSUME value for it. Also, the ASSUME value 'segreg:NOTHING' is ignored by the assembler. It's simply a comment to the programmer that can be included or not.

An ASSUME value for CS normally must be present, however, because almost all programs have labels that are used as the destination for JMP or CALL instructions. Similarly, you normally will have variables in a data segment that are accessed by name, and an ASSUME value for DS is necessary to reach these variables using the DS register (unless you explicitly include a segment override prefix for every variable access).

When people begin using the macro assembler, they are often puzzled about why an ASSUME statement is necessary. After all, the assembler can tell from the source code which segment(s) the variables and labels are in. Why tell it again? The reason is that the ASSUME statement serves at least two purposes. First, remember that bad segment register values cause *hor*rible er*rors* (abbreviated *horrors*!). The ASSUME statement attempts to reduce the likelihood of these horrors by providing an error message whenever the programmer tries to access variables in two or more different segments with the same segment register. For example, if you had a program with segment DSEG1 containing VAR1 and DSEG2 containing VAR2, then writing

```
MOV       AX,VAR1
...
MOV       BX,VAR2
```

would produce an error message. To eliminate the error message you must write

```
ASSUME    DS:DSEG1
...
MOV       AX,VAR1
```

```
...
ASSUME    DS:DSEG2
...
MOV       AX,VAR2
```

Note, however, that the code generated here would still be incorrect (in spite of the absence of error messages) unless you had actually set DS to DSEG1 and DSEG2 respectively. An easy way to remember this fact is to recall that the ASSUME statement just tells the assembler to *assume* that you've set the segment registers properly; it does *not* do it for you. Thus in the example you must write something like

```
ASSUME    DS:DSEG1
MOV       AX,SEG DSEG1
MOV       DS,AX
MOV       AX,VAR1
...
ASSUME    DS:DSEG2
MOV       AX,SEG DSEG2
MOV       DS,AX
MOV       AX,VAR2
```

to generate correct code. Since forgetting to set segment registers properly in multisegment programs is one of the leading causes of program errors, requiring you to use an ASSUME statement isn't all bad.

The ASSUME statement can also provide an automatic segment override for accessing a variable. This is most useful when you want to access variables using a segment register other than DS. In this case an ASSUME can set things up so that you don't have to include a segment override prefix every time you access variables this way. Look again at the example where VAR1 is in DSEG1 and VAR2 is in DSEG2, and suppose you want to access VAR1 using DS, and VAR2 using ES. You can do this by writing

```
ASSUME    DS:DSEG1,ES:DSEG2
...                        ;Code to point DS & ES at DSEG1 & DSEG2
...                        ; must be included here
MOV       AX,VAR1
MOV       BX,VAR2
```

Notice that you did not have to write the last instruction as MOV BX,ES:VAR2, as would be required if you hadn't used ASSUME ES:DSEG2.

Next consider another often confusing assembler directive, the SEGMENT declaration. The general form of this directive is

segname SEGMENT align combine 'class'

All of the modifiers except segname are optional. The segment name "segname" is used to identify each of the various segments of your program, and can be any legal name that you want.

The "align" modifier is easy to understand. It specifies whether the segment begins on the next free byte, word, paragraph, or page (256-byte boundary). If you don't specify an align type, which is the normal situation, the assembler defaults to paragraph; that is, the segment begins at the next free address that is evenly divisible by 10H.

The "combine" modifiers PUBLIC, COMMON, and AT have already been discussed. There is also a STACK combine type that tells the assembler that the segment is to contain the stack. Unlike the situation for the DS and ES segments, the linker sets SS:SP to the end of the stack segment before control is passed to the program. Thus you don't have to worry about setting up SS:SP in your program code.

The "class" modifier provides you with a way to group segments together when your program is linked into an executable file. In the absence of class names, the linker orders the segments in the order in which they appear in the source file. Thus if your source file contains data, stack, and code segments in that order, called DSEG, SSEG, and CSEG, respectively, then DSEG would be loaded in first (at the lowest memory address), SSEG second, and CSEG third. If you had two or more program modules, the order would be the order in which the segments appear in each module, except that, if you have in a later module a segment that has been declared PUBLIC and that has the same segname as an earlier segment, it will be loaded together with the earlier segment as discussed previously.

Class names provide a way to change this default ordering scheme. All segments of the same class name are always grouped together, and the ordering of the segment classes depends on the ordering of the first appearance of each class within the modules. Note that you can make up any class names you want, and that they must always be enclosed in single quotes.

To see how all this works, suppose you have two modules containing the following segment declarations:

```
module 1:    BSEG    SEGMENT 'DATA'
             SSEG    SEGMENT STACK
             ZSEG    SEGMENT
             CSEG    SEGMENT PUBLIC 'CODE'

module 2:    AAA     SEGMENT 'DATA'
             CSEG    SEGMENT PUBLIC 'CODE'
             ASEG    SEGMENT
             ZZZ     SEGMENT 'ZZZ'
```

When the two modules are assembled and linked together, the segments are loaded into memory in the following order:

segname	class
BSEG	DATA
AAA	DATA
SSEG	
ZSEG	
ASEG	
CSEG	CODE
ZZZ	ZZZ

Note that all members of each class are grouped together regardless of which module the segment appeared in. Note also that the linker treats all segments with no class name as being members of a single class. Since BSEG, SSEG, and CSEG are the first members of the data, no name, and code classes to appear, the class order is determined by the order of appearance of these three segment names. The ZZZ segment is in the last module to be linked, and the class name used has not appeared before. Meeting these two conditions ensures that the ZZZ segment will be the last segment of the program. In later sections we encounter situations where it's very useful to be able to know which segment is the last segment to be loaded and hence which segment marks the end of the memory used by the program.

Although the ordering and grouping of segments is all done in a logical fashion, it can become complex to figure out if you have many modules and segments. If you have a program where the ordering of segments is crucial, it's best to check how the linker is arranging the segments by requesting that a .MAP file be generated by the linker. The section of the IBM *DOS* manual describing LINK tells how to do this.

Like the class names that can be added to SEGMENT declarations, the GROUP directive is mainly a convenience to give enhanced flexibility for programmers writing code that uses multiple data segments. What the GROUP directive does is to collect a number of data segments together within a single physical 64K segment in memory. You can then use the group name instead of the individual segment names to refer to any variable within the segments that have been grouped together. Thus the result of using GROUP is typically the same as giving all the data segments the same segname and declaring them PUBLIC. In addition, COMMON segments can be included in a GROUP. You then use "ASSUME DS:groupname" to tell the assembler that DS is pointing at the group as a whole. The linker then adds in the appropriate offsets to access the variables in the different segments in the group. Note that if you use the OFFSET operator for a member of a group, the offset relative to that member is returned. To get the offset relative to the group origin, use "OFFSET groupname:" in place of OFFSET alone. Now isn't that clear as mud?! Try it out using your debugger to see just what surprises the assembler and linker come up with. You'll probably succeed in being surprised almost every time!

4-3. Debugging Techniques

You've written your program and now you're going to run it for the first time. You hear the program load and you wait expectantly for some output, but nothing happens! The screen goes blank, the keyboard doesn't work any more, and the computer just sits there like a lump of lead. Aside from uttering something unpublishable, all you can do is turn the machine off, turn it back on again, and sit there wondering what to do next.

Unfortunately, this scenario is a not uncommon occurrence in writing assembly language programs. The intent of this section is to present some ideas about what to do next. After some general comments about debugging strategies, we present a variety of more specific suggestions.

The basic strategy is very simple: Divide and conquer! While an entire program typically represents a formidably complex piece of logic, it's built up out of simpler pieces, any one of which is easier to grasp than the entire program. But, how easy or hard it is to divide a program into separate logical blocks depends on how you've written it. Ideally you should give some thought to potential debugging problems both before and during the writing of the program. An important motivation for writing well structured programs is to make the inevitable debugging chore easier.

Assuming you can divide your program into smaller pieces, you must still decide which piece(s) to look at. Sometimes this is evident from how far the computer gets through the program before it crashes, or the way in which it crashes. It's always a good idea to observe carefully the way in which a program dies, and then to ask, Where in the program would an error produce this behavior?

In many cases, however, you don't have a clue about where to look. The program dies instantly, and you've looked at a number of likely possibilities without finding the problem. Now what? Four different strategies are often effective:

1. If you've been thinking about the problem for some time, take a break and go do something else. You'll be amazed at how often the answer or at least a fresh approach to the problem will come to you while you're standing in the shower or are out mowing the lawn.

2. If you have a patient friend, sit him or her down and explain how the program works. Alternatively, sit down and explain out loud to your computer exactly how the program works. This may not do much for your reputation as a sane member of society but it can be very effective at uncovering errors.

3. Add diagnostic sections to the code. The maxim is "When in doubt, print more out." The diagnostic may be as simple as printing a message that says "ok up to here", or it may have to be much more complex. It all depends on the specific program and what you want to learn about its current state. Note that you can easily obtain

snapshots of the state of your computer while it's running your program by using a debugger as described later in this section.

4. Sometimes the best approach is to simplify your program by creating a new test version in which all but a few key features have been deleted. Then get this skeletal program to run. When it's working properly, you can start adding in more pieces of the original program until everything is working.

Many of you are undoubtedly reading this section only because you currently have a program that doesn't work, and you need some ideas about how to find the problem. However, for those few wise and prudent souls who don't currently have a nonworking program and are reading this ahead of time, there are a few thoughts to keep in mind when you begin writing a program. The rest of you will have to bear with us for a bit. We'll get back to your problems shortly.

First of all, for fairly complex programs it's a good idea to employ the last debugging strategy listed above right from the start. Write the simplest possible skeletal program first, get it running correctly, and then add more pieces in several steps. To keep the initial version simple, you can often make good use of dummy subroutines. These consist of a single RET or perhaps a few instructions that simply load fake results into registers or memory and then return.

Another approach is useful when the program involves a very complex algorithm that you may not be sure you understand. In this case it may be wise to program the algorithm first in interpretive BASIC. The advantage is that you can try the program, change it, and then try it again very rapidly. Because assembly language is complex to write and because you have to edit, assemble, and link each time a change is made, assembly language is not the best choice to use for developing new algorithms.

Turning now from general debugging strategies to some more specific details, how do you actually go about finding errors in a program? You have two basic tools at your disposal: your brain and a debugger.

Consider first a purely mental, but nonetheless effective, technique. The idea here is to reexamine your code critically at some later time after you've written it. Check through the program by mentally stepping through the code, making sure each instruction is doing what you intended it to do. Look especially at program loops and conditional jumps. Here are some of the most common problems to check for and some examples of how they are typically caused:

1. Using inverted logic in conditional jumps. For example, you wrote JC when you needed to jump if the carry flag was clear.

2. Using the wrong addressing mode. For example, you wrote MOV AX,VAR when you meant MOV AX,OFFSET VAR.

3. PUSHing a value onto the stack and then forgetting to POP it off. Be especially careful about this in subroutines or if there are program branches between the PUSH and the POP. This usually leads to an inanimate keyboard—a complete crash.

4. Using a register temporarily to hold a value you need to use later, and then calling a subroutine that uses that register and hence destroys the value.

5. Forgetting to account for the case when a loop is entered with a loop counter value of 0. For example, you do a repetitive operation using the LOOP instruction, and CX = 0 on entry. The loop will then be repeated 65,536 times!

6. Assuming that a flag was set by an operation that doesn't affect that flag. For example, you wrote MOV AX,VAR followed by JZ THERE and expected the program to jump to THERE if VAR = 0.

7. Forgetting to initialize a register or memory location with the proper value. Be especially careful about segment registers.

8. Forgetting that the operands are ordered as "destination,source". For example, you wanted to subtract BX from AX and leave the result in AX, but you wrote SUB BX,AX. Typographical errors in which the operands are transposed are easy to make but hard to find.

9. Miscounting the number of iterations necessary to fill or move an area of memory. For example, to fill locations 1000—1003 requires 4 bytes, not 3.

10. Incrementing loop counters in the wrong place or not at all. Be especially careful if you have nested loops—loops inside of loops.

11. Forgetting to preserve all registers *and* flags in programs that handle hardware interrupts. Failure to do this results in a computer system that crashes for no apparent reason at random times!

12. Failing to provide enough stack space in your program. Interrupts and system calls can eat up a lot of bytes of stack space in a hurry. Some software interrupt routines recursively call themselves up to four times, and push all the registers onto the stack each time. If the stack overflows, it will wipe out part of your program or data and can produce some really strange results. 100H bytes of stack space is not too much. Periodically check your stack with the debugger to see how far down it has been pushed.

This list could be extended indefinitely, but the main point is this: It often pays to step mentally through the logic of your program after you've written it as well as while you're writing it.

Besides purely mental review of the code as a way to find errors, there is another very powerful aid at your disposal: a debugger program. This type of program is often the most effective method you can use to uncover errors. As discussed in Sec. 2-8, there are a number of different debuggers available, each with its own advantages. In this section we discuss debugging using the commands available in DEBUG. These same commands are supported by most other debuggers. After you've brought up the debugger and loaded a program to debug, the CS:IP register values displayed by the "R" (register display) command tell you where the program has been loaded in memory. If the program is a resident I/O driver that has already been loaded, just bring up your debugger with no filename and use the "S" (search) command to find where your program is located. Enter the machine code for the first couple of instructions from a program listing as the string of bytes to search for. Alternatively, if such a program takes over an interrupt vector, you can find it by displaying low memory.

You can use the "U" (unassemble) command at any time to list the assembly language code for your program on the screen. The best way to proceed in debugging is to employ a combination of the "G" (go) and "T" (trace) commands. The G command executes the program starting at the current value of CS:IP (as given by the R command) up to a specified end address (this is called setting a breakpoint). Typically you use G to execute the program up to some critical or suspicious section of code, and then use T to step through that area one instruction at a time. One situation where you have to be careful with this combination is in interrupt handlers. If you use the T command to trace into an interrupt and then try to use G to finish execution of the interrupt routine, most debuggers will not return properly from the interrupt. You should either use G to execute the entire interrupt handler, or if the interrupt handler is the program being debugged, use G both to enter the routine and to leave it, or use T all the way through it.

To find the section of code where you want to set a breakpoint, you have three choices. First, you can use the S command to search for the appropriate instruction. Unfortunately, unless you're using SST or Advanced Trace-86, the search command cannot accept assembly-language mnemonics, so you have to enter the machine language for the instruction as the argument for S. Second, you can use the U command to look through the assembly language text of the program. The last alternative is to have an assembly language listing made when the program is assembled, and to have the linker make a .MAP file to determine where a piece of code is.

Note that the G command works by replacing a byte of code with 0CCH, which is the machine code for an INT 3 instruction. This has several consequences. First, you can't use G to stop inside the code in the IBM PC's ROM's (although you can single-step into the ROM's). Second, you must make sure that the address that follows G (the address where the debugger is supposed to stop) is the address of the *first* byte of an instruction. Otherwise the results are totally unpredictable. Use the U command to find the proper address to stop at. Finally, if you specify an end address that's never reached, the substituted byte of 0CCH remains in your code. Keep this in mind if you try to save the program you've been debugging back onto disk.

In addition to G and T, you also need to use the "D" (display memory) command to look at data areas. When doing this, remember that 16-bit words are stored backwards in memory, with the low byte first and the high byte second. Also, double word memory addresses (segment plus offset) are stored as two 16-bit words with the offset first and the segment second.

Sometimes, in order to debug a particular section of code, you need to skip over an earlier piece of code without executing it. If you just want to skip one or two instructions (for example, a subroutine call), you can easily eliminate the instruction by using the "E" (enter new value) command to write over the instruction with the appropriate number of NOP's (recall that the machine code for NOP is 90H). Alternatively, you can use the G command to execute the program up to the beginning of the section you want to skip. Then change the IP register to point to the end of the section you want to skip and use G again to resume execution. You can also use the "G=addr,breakaddr" form to start at "addr" and stop at "breakaddr".

Once you find a bug, you can either leave the debugger and correct the source program, or try to fix the bug on the spot. Unless you're fairly sure that you know how to fix the bug and that it's the only mistake present, it is often wise to try to fix it on the spot and then test further. You can change an instruction or enter new ones with the "A" (assemble) command. When you change the code, be very careful that the new machine code generated is equal to or shorter than the old code; otherwise you'll overwrite a part of the program that you don't want to change. If you need to add more code into the middle of a program, you can use what's called a program *patch*. To do this, you replace one or more instructions with a jump (or a call) to an unused area of memory. If you've allocated a generous amount of memory to the stack, you can jump to the low memory end of the stack segment. There you put the instruction(s) you've replaced with the jump (or call) followed by any instructions you want to add to the program. Then end the patch with a jump (or a return) back to the main program.

4-4. Conditional Assemblies and Macros

The Macro Assembler has two capabilities that appreciably increase its power and flexibility: conditional assembly capability and macro definition capability.

Conditional assembly means that the assembler can be told to include or exclude certain parts of your assembly program, depending on the value of some constant or variable in the program. The primary use for conditional assemblies is when you have several versions of a program that are substantially the same but differ in a few portions. For example, suppose you have a program that sends its output to a printer. Sometimes you want to send the output to a dot matrix printer that is connected to the IBM PC via a parallel port and sometimes you want to send it to a Diablo daisy wheel printer that is connected via a serial port. Instead of having two separate versions of the program, you can handle both possibilities with a single program that has the output section of the program as a conditional assembly. The program would then look like this:

```
DIABLO      EQU      1     ;Set DIABLO=1 for output to serial port
            ...
IF DIABLO
            ...                ;Code to send output to serial port goes here
ELSE
            ...                ;Code to send output to parallel port goes here
ENDIF
            ...                ;Remainder of program
```

The assembler interprets this code by looking at the value of the symbol following the IF. If the value of the symbol is nonzero, everything following the IF statement is assembled until the ELSE statement is encountered, and everything between the ELSE and the ENDIF statement is ignored. If the value of the symbol following the IF is zero, then the block of code between the IF and the ELSE is ignored, and the block of code between the ELSE and the ENDIF is assembled. As shown here, the block of code between IF DIABLO and ELSE would be assembled into machine code, while the code between ELSE and ENDIF would be ignored because the symbol DIABLO was assigned the value 1.

The structure just shown allows you to assemble either of two blocks of code, but not both. To assemble the second block of code and not the first, simply change the defining statement for DIABLO to DIABLO EQU 0. To remember how the IF statement works, make the association TRUE=1 and FALSE=0. Then the statement IF ARG can be read as "if ARG is true, then assemble what follows".

The ELSE statement is optional. If you have only a single block of code that you want to either include or not, you can simply use

```
IF ARG
            ...
ENDIF
```

This block of code will be assembled if a prior EQU statement has defined ARG to be nonzero. It won't be assembled if ARG is set to zero.

By using one or more of the IF statement structures just shown, you can readily maintain two or more versions of a program in a single file. If you keep separate assembly language files for each version, it's all too easy to make updates or corrections to just one version and not the others. This soon results in a chaotic situation where you have no idea which version has had which corrections or additions made to it. If you use conditional assembly blocks in the program, you won't have this problem.

It's also useful to use conditionally assembled blocks that contain test or diagnostic code. Then include this code only during test runs, and reassemble the program without the diagnostic code in the final version.

One drawback to the use of conditional assemblies is that you need to edit the file to change which blocks of code you want included. The ideal way of implementing conditional assemblies is to allow the user to interactively specify which blocks of code are to be included while the assembly is taking place. Some assemblers support this feature, but at this writing, the Microsoft (or IBM) Macro Assembler unfortunately does not. One thing that can and should be done is to include statements telling which version of the program is being assembled. Otherwise it's too easy to forget which version the file is set up for and to assemble the wrong thing. To have the program tell you which version is being assembled, include a '%OUT textstring' statement in each conditional block. The %OUT directive causes the text string that follows it to be printed on the screen if the block of code it's in is being assembled. For example, writing

```
IF DIABLO
          %OUT  **serial version**
          ...                      ;Code to send output to serial port goes here
ENDIF
```

produces the message '**serial version**' on the screen during assembly only if DIABLO is nonzero, meaning that the serial port code block is being included in the assembly.

In addition to the simple IF ARG statement, several other variations of the IF statement can be used for conditional assemblies. These are described in the macro assembler manual. One of the more useful ones is IFDEF ARG, which causes the code following it to be assembled only if ARG is a symbol that has been defined elsewhere in the program.

Although conditional assemblies are handy for maintaining several versions of a program, they do tend to clutter up program listings and make them hard to read. Hence it's best to use them sparingly and to keep them as simple as possible. Don't get carried away with complicated constructions involving nested IF statements.

Another powerful Macro Assembler capability is *macros*. In its simplest form, a macro is just a convenient way of grouping together a sequence of instructions that can then be included anywhere in the program by typing in a single name. For example, suppose you have several places in a program where you need to save AX, BX, CX, and DX on the stack. Instead of writing the four PUSH instructions in each place, define a macro:

```
PUSHABCD  MACRO
          PUSH    AX
          PUSH    BX
          PUSH    CX
```

```
        PUSH    DX
        ENDM
```

Whenever you want to perform these PUSH's, simply include the line PUSHABCD in the program as if it were an ordinary op-code mnemonic. The assembler automatically inserts the machine code for the four PUSH instructions whenever it encounters PUSHABCD. Thus you can regard a macro as a single new macro instruction. The assembler just expands this macro instruction into several ordinary instructions whenever it sees it.

In general, to define a macro, you place its definition somewhere before the macro is used, preferably at the beginning of the program. A macro definition begins with the name of the macro followed by the reserved word "MACRO" and ends with the reserved word "ENDM" (end macro). Each subsequent occurrence of the macro name in the program then causes the macro name to be replaced with the code listed in the macro definition.

As described so far, macros may seem to be a convenience but not much more. In fact, they're considerably more powerful than that. First of all, the macro name can be followed by one or more dummy parameters that are used in the macro definition. When the macro is invoked in the program, the macro name is followed by the actual parameter values you want used in the macro definition. In this way, the macro can be adapted to a specific situation each time it's invoked in a program. Consider an example to clarify this notion. Suppose you want to move lots of different strings around within a single segment of memory. The most efficient way to do this is to use the MOVS instruction, but each time MOVS is executed, the CX, SI, and DI registers have to be loaded with the proper values (assume that ES and DS always contain the proper segment values). You can make writing the program considerably easier by defining the macro

```
MOVSTR      MACRO   SOURCE,DEST,LEN
            MOV     CX,LEN
            LEA     SI,SOURCE
            LEA     DI,DEST
REP         MOVSB
            ENDM
```

and placing it at the beginning of the program. Then when you want to move a 20-byte string from starting location BLOCK1 to BLOCK2, just write

```
        MOVSTR  BLOCK1,BLOCK2,20
```

and the assembler inserts the machine code corresponding to the instructions

```
            MOV     CX,20
            LEA     SI,BLOCK1
            LEA     DI,BLOCK2
REP         MOVSB
```

Note that BLOCK1 simply replaces every occurrence of SOURCE in the macro definition, BLOCK2 replaces DEST, and 20 replaces LEN. If you later want to move 16 bytes from BLOCK4 to BLOCK1, simply write

        MOVSTR   BLOCK4,BLOCK1,16

You can also go one step farther and use IF statements with dummy parameters as arguments inside the macro definition. In this case, you cause different instructions within the macro to be assembled, depending on the values of the parameters. An example where this might be useful is in defining a macro that sets bits in a status byte for some I/O device. That is, some I/O driver routine returns to its calling program the location of a byte in memory (the status byte) that has various bits set or cleared in it to indicate the current status or condition of the device. This can be done very conveniently using macros. Define

```
STATUS    MACRO      STATE,ERRCODE
          MOV        STATB,0          ;Start by clearing the status byte
IFIDN     <STATE>,<BUSY>
          OR         STATB,40H        ;Set bit 6 if device not ready
ENDIF
IFIDN     <ERRCODE>,<ERROR>
          OR         STATB,80H        ;Set bit 7 if error occurred
ENDIF
          ENDM
```

after you have defined the status byte with STATB DB 00 in a data segment at the start of the program. The way this macro works requires some explanation. The reserved word IFIDN (if identical) causes the assembly code starting on the next line (and up to the next ENDIF) to be assembled if the two strings in angle brackets following IFIDN are identical. Note that the angle brackets enclosing the strings must really be present.

You can now set the status byte later in the program using a macro instruction that is almost self-documenting. To set the status byte to indicate that the device is ready for new data and that there were no errors, write

        STATUS   READY,NOERR

When the assembler encounters this macro it produces the machine code for MOV STATB,0. On the other hand, if an error occurred, you would jump to an error-handling section of the I/O driver and place the macro instruction

        STATUS   READY,ERROR

there. When the assembler encounters this it produces the machine code for

```
MOV     STATB,0
OR      STATB,80H
```

because the second parameter, ERROR, matches the string in angle brackets following the second IFIDN.

There are a number of IF statement variations available for use within macros as well as more complex operators such as REPT (repeat) that allow you to do complicated conditional assemblies within a macro definition if you so desire. If you want to get into this, read the macro assembler manual for descriptions of the various operators and IF statement types available for use within macros.

How much use you make of macros is up to you. Some programmers like to use them a lot while others don't use them at all. We tend to use them rather sparingly. One potential trap to look out for when you do use macros has to do with flags. If a macro includes code that changes the flags, make sure you're aware of that fact each time you use the macro because it's not obvious whether or not a given macro affects the flags without studying its definition.

For many purposes, subroutines and macros are just two different ways of doing the same thing. Which technique you use depends on your aims. If you don't care about execution speed, the use of subroutines produces a shorter program (fewer bytes of machine code) because the subroutine code appears only once and is reached from other places in the program by a CALL. Since macros produce new in-line code each time they're invoked, they make the program longer, but they also execute faster since the time required for a subroutine CALL and RET is unnecessary. Another reason to use macros is to make a program more portable. When moving to a new machine, you just redefine the macros, rather than convert all the code.

If you're writing a number of programs that require similar code sequences, you might find it useful to create a *macro library*. This is just a source code file containing a bunch of macros. Whenever you want to use some or all of these macros, place the statement "INCLUDE filename" near the beginning of your program. The assembler then reads the file "filename" and treats it as part of the program.

Another powerful use for macros is to define new single computer instructions. In this way macros provide an extensible assembly language instruction set. For example, as discussed in Sec. 3-12, the assembler does not recognize different near and far RET's. You have to use what we call the "PROC crap" to tell the assembler which type of RET you want. If this annoys you sufficiently, you can fix it by defining new RET instructions:

```
RETF    MACRO
        DB      0CBH        ;This is the machine code for a far return
        ENDM
```

```
RETN    MACRO
        DB        0C3H        ;This is the machine code for a near return
        ENDM
```

Notice that a DB statement is used here to define the machine code for the new instruction. This is perfectly legal and it works!

4-5. Assembly Language Subroutines for High-Level Languages

One of the most useful additions to a programmer's bag of tricks is the ability to write programs in a mixture of a high-level language (such as C, Pascal, BASIC, or FORTRAN) and assembly language. The great advantage of high-level languages is the ease and speed with which complex programs can be written. The penalty in using these languages, however, is a significant loss in speed and flexibility. In some applications, particularly those involving real-time control of input/output devices, you may need all the speed you can get. Flexibility in handling I/O devices and in doing the associated data conversions can also be a problem with high-level languages. They can do certain standard operations well, but if you want to do something unorthodox, the language can fight you every step of the way. In these situations, it's useful to employ assembly language for certain parts of the program. Of course, you can always write the entire program in assembly language, but the programming is much faster and easier if you mix in just the amount of assembly language you need. This section shows you how to do that. A large number of different high-level languages exist, each with its own advantages and disadvantages (see Chap. 11 for a comparison of some of them). To keep the discussion in this section manageable, however, we restrict our attention here to the widely used Microsoft versions of three popular languages: Pascal, C, and FORTRAN, plus IBM's compiled and interpreted BASIC languages.

With only minor variations, all major high-level languages use the same basic technique to communicate with assembly language routines. You write the assembly language portion as one or more subroutines. These subroutines are then CALLed from the high-level language. Any values that you want the subroutine to know about (these are called *parameters*) are automatically placed on the stack by the high-level language and thereby passed to the subroutine. The CPU registers are used to pass a returned value back to the caller.

Consider first the use of assembly language subroutines with Microsoft Pascal. Suppose you want to implement the equivalent of BASIC's OUT statement in assembly language. This can be done by defining the output operation in the Pascal program to be an external procedure with two parameters; that is,

PROCEDURE outpt(VAR portnum,valu:integer); EXTERN;

> (*this statement defines outpt as an external
> procedure with 2 integer parameters*)

...

VAR portnum,valu:integer;

...

portnum:=200; valu:=36;

outpt(portnum,valu);   (*here the external procedure is invoked
                                   to send the value 36 to port 200*)

...

The assembly language routine is then written as

```
PUBLIC      OUTPT                     ;Allow the procedure OUTPT to be
                                      ; accessed by other programs
A_TEXT      SEGMENT  'CODE'
ASSUME      CS:A_TEXT
OUTPT       PROC   FAR                ;Must have FAR proc so a far RET is done
            PUSH   BP                 ;BP must not be changed
            MOV    BP,SP              ;Point BP at top of stack
            MOV    BX,[BP]+8          ;Get address of first param from stack
            MOV    DX,[BX]            ;And then get param itself
            MOV    BX,[BP]+6          ;Get address of second param from stack
            MOV    AX,[BX]            ;Then get param itself
            OUT    DX,AL              ;Do the output operation
            POP    BP
            RET    4                  ;Discard params from stack on return
OUTPT       ENDP
A_TEXT      ENDS
            END
```

This is a complete working subroutine that you can try for yourself. To use an assembly language subroutine like OUTPT.ASM with a high-level language, assemble it to produce an OBJ file and separately compile your high-level language program. Calling the latter HIGHPROG.PAS, run "LINK HIGHPROG+OUTPT,,HIGHPROG/M;". The /M option produces a map that allows you to use SST to trace execution starting at OUTPT. Methods for calling assembly subroutines from other languages besides Pascal are shown below. First, though, let's see why the subroutine is written the way it is.

The code segment is declared to be of class 'CODE'. This ensures that this segment will be grouped with the code generated by the high level language by the linker. The segment name can be anything, but names ending with _TEXT are the Microsoft convention. The routine is written as a FAR procedure. This is because the high-level language automatically does a far CALL, and hence a far return is needed to end the subroutine. The name of the procedure must also be declared as PUBLIC so that the LINK program can link it into the high-level language program. The first thing done in the routine is to get the parameters being passed to it from the high-level language. Here two parameters are being passed: the output port number and the value to be output. They're sitting on the stack just below the 32-bit return address. Unfortunately, they can't just be POPped off the stack because SP must remain pointing at the return address. Instead the routine loads SP into BP and accesses the parameters through BP. However, BP must be saved first, because high-level languages normally assume that DS, SS, and BP are preserved by external routines. The first parameter is now at [BP]+8 and the second is at [BP]+6, as can be seen in Fig. 4-1. BP here is called the *frame pointer*, and the group of quantities placed on the stack for use by the subroutine is called the *stack frame*. Note that what is passed on the stack in this example is not the parameter itself, but rather the *address* of the parameter. Thus the address is put in BX, and MOV reg,[BX] is used to get the parameter itself. This works properly because Pascal leaves DS pointing at the Pascal data area when the subroutine call is made. Finally, the routine does the output operation, restores BP, and returns. Pascal expects the parameters to be gone from the stack on return, so we do a RET 4 that discards 4 bytes from the stack.

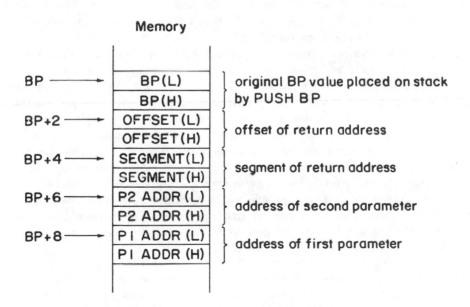

Fig. 4-1. Organization of the stack (that is, the stack frame) after a call from Pascal with two parameters and execution of PUSH BP and MOV BP,SP.

Here is a summary of the actions occurring in an assembly language call from Pascal:

1. The Pascal code pushes all parameters onto the stack in the order declared and then does a far CALL.

2. The assembly language subroutine reads the parameters from the stack and performs its actions. The only restriction on the subroutine is that it must preserve the BP, DS, and SS registers, and leave the direction flag cleared.

3. The subroutine must end with a far return that removes the entire stack frame. Typically that means doing POP BP and RET nn, where nn is equal to the number of bytes taken up by the parameters passed to the routine on the stack.

In the example above, the parameters were passed by a 16-bit address; that is, the offset address relative to DS was placed onto the stack. There are several other ways that parameters can be passed on the stack. These vary from language to language, so each language must be discussed in turn.

Pascal has the greatest variety of options for passing parameters. Parameters can be passed as either variables or values. To pass a parameter as a variable, the reserved word VAR is used in the procedure definition as was done in the preceding example. The *address* of the parameter is then passed onto the stack. If VAR is not used, the *value* of the parameter itself is passed. Thus if we had defined "outpt" as "PROCEDURE outpt(portnum,val:integer); EXTERN;", the values 200 and 36 would have been placed on the stack as 16-bit values in the example.

Passing the value seems more convenient, because you don't have to first get the address and then get the value. However, there are good reasons for passing parameters as VAR. First, most high-level languages other than Pascal allow parameters to be passed by address only. If you do this in Pascal also, you may be able to use your subroutine with other languages as well. Also, when you pass the parameter as VAR, you can change its value in your assembly language routine. This allows you to conveniently return new values to the high-level language. Finally, passing parameters as VAR means that the high-level language pushes a 2-byte address onto the stack for each parameter. If you pass a value parameter, the number of bytes pushed onto the stack depends on whether the parameters are integer or real, and this makes it easy to get confused when you're trying to access the parameters from assembly language.

The one parameter type that is handled differently is the character string—that is, ASCII text. As an example, suppose you have an assembly language subroutine called TEXT, which prints a message on the screen starting at any row and column. You can define this in Pascal as:

```
PROCEDURE text(VAR row,col:integer; VAR msg:lstring); EXTERN;
VAR row,column:integer;
    messag:lstring(80);
```

```
...
row:=12; column:=60;
messag:='It works';
text(row,column,messag);
...
```

The variable 'msg' is defined as an lstring type rather than a string type because lstrings allow the use of variable length strings. When an lstring variable is passed to an assembly language routine, the maximum length of the lstring (as specified when the particular lstring being passed was defined) is pushed onto the stack, followed by the address of the text string. Thus string variables take up four bytes on the stack. The assembly language routine to output the text might look like:

```
PUBLIC    TEXT
A_TEXT    SEGMENT  'CODE'
          ASSUME   CS:A_TEXT
TEXT      PROC     FAR
          PUSH     BP
          MOV      BP,SP           ;Point BP at top of stack
          MOV      SI,[BP]+6       ;Get address of lstring from stack
          MOV      CL,[SI]         ;Then get first byte = string length
          MOV      CH,0
          INC      SI              ;Point to first character in string
          MOV      BX,[BP]+0AH     ;Get address of column
          MOV      DX,[BX]
          MOV      BX,[BP]+0CH     ;Get address of row
          MOV      BX,[BX]
          MOV      DH,BL           ;Get row,column in DH,DL
          XOR      BX,BX           ;Use display page 0
          MOV      AH,2            ;Set cursor position
          INT      10H
NEXT:     LODSB                    ;Get a character
          MOV      AH,14           ;Write it on screen
          INT      10H
          LOOP     NEXT            ;Repeat till CX characters done
          POP      BP
          RET      8               ;Discard params from stack on return
TEXT      ENDP
A_TEXT    ENDS
          END
```

Notice that the first byte of an lstring is the number of characters in the lstring. The remaining bytes of the lstring are the characters themselves, one character per byte. The routine sets the cursor position and outputs the text to the screen using interrupt 10H, which is the IBM PC's low-level video I/O handler. This interrupt and the source code for it are described in the IBM PC *Technical Reference* manual.

Pascal also allows you to pass variables using a VARS specification in place of VAR. This causes Pascal to push 4 bytes per parameter onto the stack: the segment address and then the offset address. Normally there's no point in doing this since, on entry to the subroutine, DS already contains the segment address for all parameters (the default data area in the current version of Pascal is limited to 64K). The main use for VARS would be for compatibility with FORTRAN, which always passes 32-bit parameter addresses to subroutines.

Assembly language subroutines can also be Pascal functions. In this case Pascal expects the subroutine to return a value in a register. For example, if the function is supposed to return an integer value, that value must be in AX when the RET instruction in the assembly language subroutine is executed. In other respects, the assembly language program is written just like the subroutines discussed before. The register(s) used to return a value depends on the type of the Pascal variable. See your Pascal manual for details. To call an assembly language function from Pascal, simply declare the function EXTERN. Thus a function to return the value read from an input port could be written as

```
FUNCTION inpt(portnum:integer):integer; EXTERN;
...
VAR       result:integer;
...
result:=inpt(200);     (*read in a value from port 200*)
...
```

and use an assembly language routine

```
PUBLIC     INPT
A_TEXT     SEGMENT
           ASSUME     CS:A_TEXT
INPT       PROC       FAR
           PUSH       BP
           MOV        BP,SP          ;Point BP at top of stack
           MOV        DX,[BP]+6      ;Get parameter from stack
           IN         AL,DX          ;Do the input operation
           MOV        AH,00          ;Leave value in AX
           POP        BP
           RET        2
INPT       ENDP
A_TEXT     ENDS
           END
```

Here the input port number has been passed to the routine directly as a value parameter rather than by address.

Note that functions aren't really necessary because you can return values to Pascal by changing the value of a VAR parameter passed to an assembly language subroutine. However, using functions makes it more obvious that values are being returned, and thus it's often desirable to use them to make the program logic clearer and to be able to include them within arithmetic expressions.

Turning now to the use of assembly language with Microsoft C, we consider again the OUTPT subroutine. Calls to an external routine in C are done by just writing the routine's name with the arguments you want to pass to it. For example,

```
port = 200; valu = 36;
outpt(port,valu);
```

sends a 36 to port 200 if the C program this statement appears in is linked to an assembly language module containing:

```
PUBLIC      _OUTPT

A_TEXT      SEGMENT  'CODE'
            ASSUME CS:A_TEXT
_OUTPT      PROC     FAR           ;Must have FAR proc so a far RET is done
            PUSH     BP            ;BP must not be changed
            MOV      BP,SP         ;Point BP at top of stack
            MOV      DX,[BP+6]     ;Put 1st param on stack into DX
            MOV      AX,[BP+8]     ;Put 2nd param on stack into AX
            OUT      DX,AL         ;Do the output operation
            POP      BP            ;Restore BP
            RET                    ; and do a far return
_OUTPT      ENDP
A_TEXT      ENDS
```

Since the values themselves are passed in C, one can also just call the routine using "outpt(200,36);". As this routine illustrates, assembly language subroutines for C have some marked differences from those used with other high level languages:

1. Subroutine names must begin with an underscore.
2. Parameters are passed by value only, and are pushed on the stack in *reverse* order.
3. The subroutine must not pop the parameters off the stack before returning. This is done by the caller.

There are logical reasons for all of these differences. First, all assembly language subroutines used with C must begin with ' _ ' because when the Microsoft C compiler finds a call to a routine that is not a C routine, it automatically places an underscore in front of the name. Microsoft does this for compatibility with the UNIX operating system. Second, C allows parameters to be passed by value only, because this is the fastest and most efficient way of passing parameters. In C this is not a restriction because the address of a variable is easily passed to a subroutine by just passing a pointer to the variable.

Having the caller push parameters on the stack in reverse order and not allowing the subroutine to pop them off the stack before returning is a unique feature of the C language. This is actually an elegant way to do things because it leaves the first subroutine parameter at the top of the stack (below the return address). The subroutine doesn't even have to know in advance how many arguments have been passed to it! This provides a convenient mechanism for passing a variable number of parameters to a subroutine. For example, one can simply make a call in which the first parameter specifies how many other parameters are being passed in that particular invocation of the call.

The registers that must be preserved in a Microsoft C subroutine also differ from those for other languages. One must not change the segment registers, SI, DI, BP, or the direction flag. Actually, since SI and DI are used by C only for register variables, you can cheat and not save them if you are certain that your calling program will never use register variables.

In C, there is no distinction between subroutines and functions. Microsoft C assumes that a returned integer value will be in AX, and a returned pointer value will be in DX:AX.

Handling character strings in C is very simple. C strings are just a string of characters terminated by a byte containing 00. To pass a character string to an assembly language subroutine, one just passes a pointer to the first byte of the string.

Now let's turn to the use of assembly language subroutines with IBM's compiled BASIC (BASICA, IBM's interpreted BASIC, is considered later). In compiled BASIC you don't have any choice regarding how variables are passed. They are always passed by address (just as in Pascal when VAR is specified). Thus the subroutine OUTPT presented previously for Pascal works with compiled BASIC as it stands. To use the subroutine, just CALL it. For example, your BASIC program might contain

```
PORTNUM%=200: VALU%=36
CALL OUTPT(PORTNUM%,VALU%)
```

There is no need to declare OUTPT as an external routine because compiled BASIC assumes that all CALLs of this form are to external routines. Note that the variables PORTNUM and VALU have been specifically declared integer by ending them with a "%". We must make sure they are integers, because the assembly language routine assumes they are 2-byte integer values, whereas BASIC assumes that variables are 4-byte real numbers unless told otherwise by a DEFINT statement or a "%" appended to the variable name. Also, in both IBM compiled and interpreted BASIC, assembly language routines must preserve all segment registers, including ES.

Sad to say, strings are handled differently by the various high-level languages. Figure 4-2 shows the structure of strings for Pascal, interpreted BASIC, and compiled BASIC. Each string in compiled BASIC has a 4-byte *string descriptor* associated with it. The first two bytes of the string descriptor contain the length of the string, which allows strings up to 65536 bytes in length, and the second two bytes contain the starting address of the string (as an offset relative to DS). When a string parameter is passed on the stack to an assembly language subroutine, what's passed is the address of the string descriptor, not the address of the string. Thus the code

```
MOV     CL,[SI]         ;Then get first byte = string length
MOV     CH,00
INC     SI              ;Point to first character in string
```

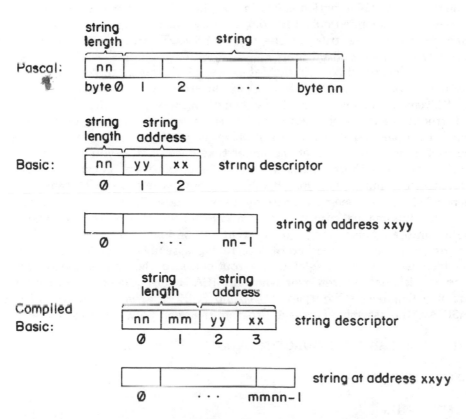

Fig. 4-2. The structure of string variables in Microsoft Pascal and IBM interpreted BASIC (BASICA) and compiled BASIC. FORTRAN and C use only simple character strings (see text).

which was contained in the Pascal version of the assembly routine TEXT, must be replaced with

```
MOV    CX,[SI]        ;Then get string length in CX
MOV    SI,[SI+2]      ;Put string address in SI
```

Also, the column and row variables must be picked up from [BP]+8 and [BP]+0AH, and the routine ended with RET 6, since BASIC string variables take up only 2 bytes on the stack, while Pascal lstrings take up 4 bytes. To pass a string variable to an assembly routine from compiled BASIC, you just pass the name of the string variable. Thus to call the TEXT routine, use CALL TEXT(X%,Y%,TXT$) where X% and Y% are integer variables and TXT$ is a string variable.

If you want to return a value to compiled BASIC from assembly language, the best way is simply to use a CALL in which the variable whose value you want to change is passed to the assembly routine. The assembly routine can then change the variable's value since it knows where it's stored in memory. A USR function exists in compiled BASIC, but it's very awkward to use and is supplied only for compatibility with interpreted BASIC. The same comment holds true for the CALL ABSOLUTE statement, which is also available in compiled BASIC.

We've described how to interface assembly language to compiled BASIC, but what about BASICA, IBM's BASIC interpreter? Because interpreted BASIC runs so slowly, assembly language routines can really be lifesavers. Unfortunately, it's more awkward to use assembly routines with BASICA than with compiled BASIC. The problem is getting BASICA to know where the routine is. You can't let the linker take care of it as you do in compiled BASIC. For very short programs, you can assemble them, get a listing of the machine code, put it into your BASIC program using a DATA statement, and then POKE it into memory byte by byte as described in the IBM *BASIC* manual. This manual also describes a complex way to make your assembly routine into a machine language file that can be loaded using BLOAD.

We prefer a third method of interfacing assembly language to BASICA. The idea is to attach the assembly routine(s) to the end of the operating system so it's not written over when BASICA is run. Suppose you have two assembly language subroutines, SUB1 and SUB2, that you want to call from BASICA. The assembly language program then can be written as follows:

```
TITLE    ASSEMBLY LANGUAGE SUBROUTINES FOR BASICA

PREFIX   SEGMENT AT 0
INT20    DB       ?
PREFIX   ENDS

A_TEXT   SEGMENT
         ASSUME   CS:A_TEXT,DS:PREFIX
```

```
ASUB    PROC    FAR
        JMP     SUB1            ;Start the program with a jump table
        JMP     SUB2


SUB1:   ...                     ;Subroutine SUB1 goes here
        RET


SUB2:   ...                     ;Subroutine SUB2 goes here
        RET
EOP:
ASUB    ENDP


SETUP   PROC    FAR
        PUSH    DS              ;Set up a return to DOS
        SUB     AX,AX
        PUSH    AX
        MOV     ES,AX           ;Set ES to start of memory
        MOV     AX,CS           ;Get segment of the start of this program
        MOV     BX,0180H        ; and poke it into location 0:180
        MOV     ES:[BX],AX
        MOV     INT20+1,27H     ;Change DOS return to INT 27H
        LEA     DX,EOP+100H     ;DX must contain program length
        RET
SETUP   ENDP
A_TEXT  ENDS

SSEG    SEGMENT STACK
        DW      80H DUP (?)
SSEG    ENDS

        END     SETUP
```

After the program is assembled and linked, it must be executed *before* you enter BASIC. What happens when this is done is the following: The END SETUP statement causes program execution to begin with the SETUP procedure. SETUP pokes the contents of CS into an absolute memory location, namely 0:180H. This is the location for interrupt vector 60H, which is the first of eight interrupt vectors reserved for user software interrupts. Thus it isn't used by either DOS or BASICA, and will remain a secure memory storage location that won't be written over by anyone else. The remainder of SETUP places an INT 27H in the program prefix and returns to DOS with DX set to the program length. This causes the program to remain in memory as described in Sec. 4-6.

Once the assembly subroutines are in memory, with the segment register value for the start of the program stored in location 0:180, BASICA can be run. In the BASIC program you can access the routines SUB1 and SUB2 by placing the following at the beginning of the program:

```
10 DEF SEG=0
20 DEF SEG=(PEEK(&H180)+PEEK(&H181)*&H100)
30 SUB1%=0: SUB2%=3
```

Lines 10 and 20 pick up the segment address that was placed there by the assembly language program. Line 30 then gives the offset addresses of the jumps to SUB1 and SUB2 that are at the beginning of the assembly program (each jump requires 3 bytes). The routines SUB1 and SUB2 can then be accessed with CALL SUB1% or CALL SUB2% statements as in compiled BASIC. When BASIC encounters a CALL statement, it interprets the variable name following the CALL as the offset address of the subroutine to be called. The last DEF SEG statement is used as the segment address. Since the offset address must be an integer, a "%" is appended to SUB1 and SUB2 in the example. This forces BASIC to read them as integer variables.

You may have noticed one potential disadvantage to the way the assembly program has been loaded for use with BASICA, namely that the assembly program stays in memory forever until power is turned off or the system is rebooted with Ctrl-Alt-Del. If your computer is short on memory, you might not like to have part of it permanently tied up this way. For most systems, though, the amount of memory lost is small enough that this is no problem. If you are using DOS 2.0, there's an alternative method that doesn't leave the program in memory after you exit from BASICA. The technique is to write an assembly program like the one just given, except that you replace the code that pokes an INT 27H into the prefix by code that loads and executes BASICA. The way to do this from assembly language is described in Sec. 4-7.

The structure of the assembly language subroutines SUB1 and SUB2 and the BASIC CALL statements used to access them are identical to the descriptions given for compiled BASIC: variables are always passed by address. Thus you can use the same routines for both interpreted and compiled BASIC. The one exception is routines involving strings. For some reason, BASIC's authors used slightly different string descriptors for compiled and interpreted BASIC, as shown in Fig. 4-2. Thus in the routine TEXT given earlier, you must replace

```
        INC     SI              ;Point to first character in string
```

by the code

```
        MOV     SI,[SI+1]       ;Load SI with string address
```

As for compiled BASIC, you also need to change the addresses for getting the column and row variables to [BP]+8 and [BP]+0AH and end with RET 6.

The call to the TEXT routine from interpreted BASIC is the same as in compiled BASIC. Just use CALL TEXT%(X%,Y%,TXT$).

Another common high-level language is FORTRAN. Microsoft's FORTRAN is very closely related to Pascal; in fact, the back end of the compiler is identical to Pascal's. Thus the discussion of variable passing and string structure presented for Pascal applies to FORTRAN as well, except that FORTRAN allows variables to be passed only as a segmented address, that is, in the same way as described for VARS in Pascal. Thus to call the routine OUTPT given earlier for Pascal you would write

```
INTEGER*2 PORTNUM,VAL
...
PORTNUM=200
VAL=36
CALL OUTPT(PORTNUM,VAL)
...
```

The assembly language routine would also have to be slightly changed. The two parameters have to be accessed from the stack at [BP]+6 and [BP]+0AH, and the routine must end with a RET 8. Here's how the body of the routine should look:

```
PUSH   BP                         ;BP must not be changed
MOV    BP,SP                      ;Point BP at top of stack
PUSH   DS                         ;Segment registers must be preserved
LDS    BX,DWORD PTR [BP]+0AH      ;Get address of first param
MOV    DX,[BX]                    ; and then get param itself
LDS    BX,DWORD PTR [BP]+6        ;Get address of second param
MOV    AX,[BX]                    ;Then get param itself
OUT    DX,AL                      ;Do the output operation
POP    DS
POP    BP
RET    8                          ;Discard params from stack on return
```

Notice that FORTRAN's 4-byte variable addresses are easily loaded using the LDS instruction, provided DS is restored before returning.

Assembly language routines can also be used as FORTRAN functions, returning values in the registers just as described for Pascal. Thus the INPT function given previously for Pascal could be accessed using

```
INTEGER*2 RESULT,PORTNUM
...
PORTNUM = 200
RESULT = INPT(PORTNUM)
```

provided the body of the INPT routine is changed to

```
PUSH    BP
MOV     BP,SP                       ;Point BP at top of stack
PUSH    DS
LDS     BX,DWORD PTR [BP]+6         ;Get parameter from stack
MOV     DX,[BX]
IN      AL,DX                       ;Do the input operation
MOV     AH,00                       ;Leave value in AX
POP     DS
POP     BP
RET     4
```

Although FORTRAN does not have built-in string manipulation functions, it does allow fixed length character variables. A variable defined as CHAR-ACTER*10 is just a memory area of 10 consecutive bytes. Such a character string is passed to an assembly language routine just like an ordinary variable; that is, a double word pointer to the address of the first byte of the character string is passed. A nice feature of Microsoft's FORTRAN and C (3.0 and later) is that they can be told to use each other's calling sequences so that you can mix subroutines from the two.

4-6. Adding New Operating System I/O Drivers

One of the great benefits of learning assembly language is that it gives you the ability to write custom routines for controlling any input/output devices you want, in exactly the way you want to do it, and with the maximum speed the computer can run. This section shows you what's involved in writing a *device driver*, which is a subroutine that controls all communications between the computer and the external device, and shows you how to install device drivers in the IBM PC so they're there when you want them.

The original philosophy of IBM PC DOS was to handle external devices by making each device driver an interrupt routine. You can wire up the device so that it causes a hardware interrupt whenever it needs to communicate with the computer (see Chap. 7), or you can communicate with it from your program by means of a software interrupt using the INT instruction (see Sec. 3-6). Later, starting with DOS 2.0, IBM added operating system support for *installable device drivers*. This type of device driver provides a uniform, relatively high level interface between any type of I/O device and the PC, and allows very sophisticated communications between the two. Both techniques are illustrated in this section. The older technique (presented first) can run under either DOS 1.1 or 2.0, but typically fails to support some of DOS 2.0's special features. Installable device drivers can be used only with DOS 2.0 and later versions.

Because considerable code is included in this discussion, we would like to make a small digression regarding the format of assembly language programs. In the discussion of assembly language so far, the assembly code has been printed in upper case in order to distinguish it from ordinary text. Traditionally assembly language was printed in upper case for a different reason, namely because printers and display screens couldn't handle lower case. In the 1970's, most computer systems acquired lower case capability, and more and more people wrote their programs with it. Since by now the reader knows the difference between assembly language and ordinary text, we too switch to lower case for our programs. The benefits are twofold: Lower case is easier to read because the characters have more variation, and up to 30% more characters (proportionally spaced) fit in the same space. The second benefit is particularly handy for assembly language, because it allows more room for comments to the right of the code. However, upper case will still be used for contrast when that helps to make things clearer.

Let's look first at the simpler interrupt routine approach to device drivers. This technique uses one of the 256 possible interrupts for the device we want to control. To implement the approach, a program is written that loads the device driver into memory, points the appropriate interrupt vector to the beginning of the device driver, and arranges to have the program left in memory as part of DOS when the program ends and returns to the operating system. Perhaps the simplest way to understand the mechanics of how all this is done is to look at an example.

Suppose you have a printer such as a Diablo daisy wheel printer which communicates with the computer via a serial port (see Secs. 10-2 and 10-3 for a discussion of serial communications). Unfortunately, DOS assumes that the printer is connected via a parallel port and thus has the device driver for the printer set up to handle a parallel printer connection rather than a serial printer. How can you remedy this situation? First look at the interrupt vector assignments for the PC shown in Table 3-4. This shows which interrupts have been assigned to various I/O devices by DOS. In addition, the ROM BIOS listing in the IBM *Technical Reference* manual gives the source code of the interrupt handlers for all standard devices. Looking through Table 3-4, you'll see that INT 17H is assigned as the printer I/O interrupt. What must be done is to replace this interrupt vector with a new one that points to a serial printer device driver. Here's a program to do this:

title SIMPLE SERIAL PRINTER DRIVER

;Serial port parameters

```
pnum    equ    0            ;Serial port card number
sdata   equ    03f8h        ;Serial port transmitter register
mctrl   equ    sdata+4      ;Modem control register
status  equ    sdata+5      ;Serial port line status register
uparm   equ    0e3h         ;Baud rate, word length, and parity
                            ; Here the port is set for 9600 baud,
```

```
                                   ; 8 bits, no parity
                                   ; (see BIOS listing for INT 14H in
                                   ; the technical reference manual)

prefix    segment at 0             ;Program prefix segment template
int20     db        ?
prefix    ends


sseg      segment stack 'data'
          dw        80h dup (?)
sseg      ends


cseg      segment
          assume    cs:cseg,ds:prefix


lister:   sti
          push      dx             ;Save registers used
          push      ax
          cmp       ah,0           ;Check function code in AH
          jz        print          ;Print char in AL if AH=0
          cmp       ah,1
          jz        init           ;Initialize serial port if AH=1
done:     pop       ax             ;If AH > 1, do nothing
          pop       dx
          mov       ah,90h         ;Force UART status to be OK
          iret


init:     mov       ax,uparm       ;Get UART parameters
          mov       dx,pnum        ;Get serial port card #
          int       14h            ;Initialize the UART
          mov       dx,mctrl       ;Set DTR and RTS low
          mov       al,3
          out       dx,al
          jmp       done           ;Clean up and return


print:    push      ax             ;Save output char
          mov       dx,sdata+4     ;Check xmitter status
print1:   in        ax,dx          ;Read in AL=mctl, AH=status
          xor       ax,2020h
          test      ax,2020h
          jnz       print1         ;Loop till xmitter clear and DSR true
          sub       dx,4           ;Then send char in AL
          pop       ax             ;Get char
          out       dx,al
          jmp       done
drvend:
```

```
setup    proc    far
         push    ds                    ;Set up a return to DOS
         sub     ax,ax
         push    ax
         lea     dx,lister+100h
         mov     al,17h                ;Set the printer I/O interrupt (INT 17H)
         mov     ah,25h                ; to DS:DX via DOS function call
         int     21h
         mov     ah,1                  ;Use the lister routine to initialize
         int     17h                   ; the serial port
         mov     int20+1,27h           ;Change normal return to INT 27H return
         mov     dx,offset drvend+100h ;Set DX:DS to end of program
         ret                           ; and jump to the INT 27H
setup    endp

cseg     ends
         end     setup
```

A little explanation is required to clarify how this program works. The part of the program that sets up and initializes the serial port device driver is the procedure SETUP. Because the program was ended with the statement END SETUP instead of a simple END statement, the linker produces a .EXE file in which execution starts with SETUP rather than at the start of the program. The procedure SETUP begins by setting up the usual return to DOS. Next the interrupt vector for INT 17H is changed to point to the beginning of the serial port driver—that is, to 'LISTER'—by using DOS function call 25H. To use this function call, you must place in AH the number of the interrupt vector to be changed, and you must point DS:DX to the beginning of the interrupt service routine. Here, the service routine is the device driver LISTER. Since LISTER is in the code segment, the straightforward way to set DS:DX is to use

```
         mov     ax,cs
         mov     ds,ax
         lea     dx,lister
```

However, it's easier to make use of the fact that, unless otherwise specified, .EXE files start with CS = DS + 10H. (Check it out for yourself with the DEBUG program.) Thus the offset of LISTER is 100H higher relative to DS than it is to CS, and we can just use LEA DX,LISTER+100H to get DS:DX to point at LISTER.

The final task that SETUP must perform is to ensure that the code for LISTER remains resident in memory and is not written over by other programs after execution returns to the operating system. There is an interrupt that does this job, namely INT 27H. The INT 27H instruction must be the last instruction of the program, and when executed, must have CS pointing to the program prefix segment of the program. You can read about the structure of the program prefix segment in the IBM *DOS* manual appendix entitled "DOS Control Blocks and Work Areas." The only thing you need to know about it here is that the first two bytes of the prefix segment contain an INT 20H instruction. DS:0 points to this instruction when the program starts, so the initial

```
push    ds
sub     ax,ax
push    ax
```

instructions in SETUP cause the RET instruction at the end of the program to produce a jump to the INT 20H instruction. The INT 20H then does the return to DOS. The SETUP routine subverts this sequence of events by changing the INT 20H instruction to an INT 27H. This action is done by the instruction MOV INT20+1,27H. To inform the assembler where the INT 20H is located, the template segment PREFIX is included in the program, with the variable INT20 at offset 0 in the segment.

Besides creating an INT 27H instruction, DS:DX must point to the last program address we want to save when the INT 27H is executed. To do this, OFFSET DRVEND+100H is loaded into DX. DRVEND is the last address plus 1 of the LISTER routine, but since DRVEND is in the code segment, the offset address produced by the assembler is relative to CS, not DS. This is fixed by adding 100H to the offset to get the proper ending address relative to DS (recall that DS = CS-10H). The code for the driver itself—everything from LISTER to DRVEND—can be understood by reading the section on serial communications (Sec. 10-2).

The program given here can be used as a model for any interrupt driver you want. Just change SETUP so that it takes over the interrupt vector you want, and replace the LISTER code with your own device driver. The main things you need to remember when writing the driver are that it should start with an STI instruction so that interrupts are reenabled (the 8088 turns interrupts off every time an interrupt occurs), and that it must end with an IRET instruction. Also, be sure that all registers are saved when the interrupt routine is executed since the standard convention is to always assume that interrupt service routines preserve all registers. Finally, if your device driver code requires a local data area, use an ORG statement to place your variables in the high end of the PREFIX segment (between offset addresses 5CH and 0FFH). If you simply set up a data segment DSEG, it will be loaded in memory above CSEG and written over by DOS.

If you're really concerned about the memory space used by the driver, you can have the SETUP code move the driver program down into the 100H byte program prefix area that the linker appends to the beginning of every program. Just don't move it down below location 5CH in the prefix, because DOS 2.0 uses that area. You can also convert your program from the normal .EXE file produced by the linker to a .COM file. This reduces the disk storage requirements for the driver program by several hundred bytes and also allows it to load faster. The conversion of .EXE files into .COM files is discussed later in this section.

If you want your device driver to be placed in memory whenever DOS is booted up, just place the file name of the driver program in an AUTOEXEC.BAT file as discussed in the "Batch Commands" section of the IBM *DOS* manual. For example, if the program just given were called SERIAL.EXE, then you would just place the name SERIAL in the file AUTOEXEC.BAT. If you don't want the driver to always be there, then run the program just before you need the device driver. Note, however, that once you've run the program, the driver stays there until you reboot the system. If you want a device driver to be present only temporarily, and then to disappear, look at Sec. 4-7, which shows how to write an assembly language program that can itself load in other programs.

As mentioned earlier, a second method of putting in new or modified device drivers was introduced in DOS 2.0, namely the installable device driver. The advantage of this newer method is that the interface between the driver and the operating system is at a higher level than the interrupt level and is therefore capable of being used in more sophisticated ways. The pros and cons of the installable device driver versus the interrupt takeover method are discussed after we've looked at how the installable device driver works.

First, however, let's consider briefly how you can produce .COM machine code files, because installable device drivers are required to be files of this type. It's not immediately obvious how to do this, since the current version of the linker (Version 2.0) takes the .OBJ files produced by the assembler and always converts them into files with an extension of .EXE. The solution is found in a utility program that comes with DOS called EXE2BIN. If you have a program called FILENAME.EXE, then entering "EXE2BIN FILENAME FILENAME.COM" converts that .EXE file into a .COM file. Read the "DOS Control Blocks and Work Areas" chapter of the IBM *DOS Technical Reference* manual for a description of the difference between the way .EXE and .COM files are handled.

Unfortunately, one hitch in this process is that unless the original .ASM file is written properly, you'll get back a message saying, "File cannot be converted", when EXE2BIN is run. Here are the rules for writing an assembly language program that can be converted into a .COM file:

1. Do not include a STACK segment.

2. Take all variables, tables, and so on, that you would normally put in a DATA segment, and move them into the CODE segment. In other words, you can't have any DATA segments.

3. Make sure that all of the references to the DS, ES, and SS registers in your ASSUME statement refer to the CODE segment. Thus, if your

code segment is called CSEG, you would write "ASSUME CS:CSEG,DS:CSEG,ES:CSEG,SS:CSEG".

4. Put an ORG 100H statement at the beginning of the code segment for a normal .COM file. For an installable device driver, however, this should be omitted.

5. Give the first instruction in the program a label, like "START", and then make sure that the last statement in the program is "END START". This, along with the ORG statement, tells the assembler how to initialize CS:IP when control is passed to the program.

6. Don't initialize DS, ES, or SS in your program. They're already pointing to the code segment when control is passed to the program.

7. If you assemble and link the program and then get an error message when EXE2BIN is run, reassemble the program and tell the assembler you want a .LST file to be produced. Then examine this .LST file to see if any machine code was generated which appears as "---- R". The dashes indicate that you've referenced something outside your CODE segment, and this isn't allowed in a .COM file.

8. When you run the LINK program, it will complain that no STACK segment was found. Ignore this error message.

If you follow these rules, you should be able to write assembly programs that are acceptable to EXE2BIN every time.

For an installable device driver, you don't need any setup procedure to attach the driver code to DOS. This is done automatically by DOS at boot time. Although this simplifies the program, it's compensated for by the rather complex format required of installable device drivers. The format of the driver is described in detail in the "Installable Device Drivers" chapter of the *DOS Technical Reference* manual. However, the overall structure is rather difficult to follow without a simple, concrete example to look at. Thus, let's rewrite the serial printer driver presented earlier in installable device driver form. Owing to its length, the program listing is given in Appendix D.

It's not our intention to give a complete, detailed description of all the installable device driver format options. Instead we want to supplement and help make comprehensible the material presented in the *DOS Technical Reference* manual. A good place to begin is to break the example program presented in Appendix D into more manageable pieces and then to look at why everything there has to be present. Every installable device driver must contain three major sections: a device header, a strategy routine, and a device interrupt handler. Here's an outline of the overall program organization:

A. DEVICE HEADER   contains a 5-item table describing the I/O device. The table items are:

    1. NEXT_DEV — address of device header for the next I/O device
    2. ATTRIBUTE — 16-bit device characteristics field
    3. STRATEGY — address of the device strategy routine
    4. INTERRUPT — address of the device interrupt handler
    5. DEV_NAME — device name or number of units (for block devices)

B. DEVICE STRATEGY — stores the address of the "device request header." The device request header is a data area containing all the information needed by the device interrupt handler to do a requested I/O operation.

C. DEVICE INTERRUPT HANDLER — contains the subroutines needed to carry out all the allowed operations of the I/O device. The interrupt handler determines what operation to perform and gets any other information needed for the operation from the device request header whose address was stored by the device strategy routine.

The driver must begin with the *device header*, which is an 18-byte table containing information that DOS needs to know about the device. The first item in the header is a double word (offset plus segment) called NEXT_DEV. To understand the purpose of this, you need to understand how DOS 2.0 keeps track of the various devices attached to the system.

The basic idea is that DOS 2.0 arranges all of its I/O drivers as a linked list. That is, the first 4 bytes of each driver are a pointer that gives the offset and segment address where the next I/O driver can be found in memory. The creation of this linked list is done when DOS is booted up. It looks into the special file CONFIG.SYS to see which user-written device drivers are present, and loads them in as the first items in the linked list. Then it adds its own standard device drivers to the end of the list. When you write the driver program, you must place a -1 (FFFF FFFF) in the NEXT_DEV pointer. DOS overwrites this value with the proper address when the driver is loaded.

You can see for yourself how this linked list works once you've booted up DOS with an installable device driver of your own. Just start up your debugger and search memory for your driver using the "S" command. When you've found it, look at the first 4 bytes of the driver. They contain the address of another device header. The first 4 bytes of this header are, in turn, the address of yet another device header, and so on. In this way you can track through and find the code for every device driver in the system, including all of the standard system devices!

The last four items in the device header contain information about the device driver. There is an attribute word (ATTRIBUTE) that tells DOS what kind of I/O device this driver is controlling. The *DOS Technical Reference* manual describes the meaning of the bits in ATTRIBUTE. In the example driver of Appendix D, only bit 15 is set to indicate that this is a character device, which means that it can accept information only one byte at a time. To keep the program simple, the example driver does not support IOCTL, so bit 14 is set to 0. Note also that, when IBM talks about standard input and output devices (bits 0 and 1 in ATTRIBUTE), they mean only the console keyboard and screen. Thus bits 0 and 1 are set only if you're replacing the console driver. DOS uses ATTRIBUTE to decide what kind of commands can and cannot be sent to the device. Following the attribute word are the beginning offset addresses of the other two major sections of the program: the strategy routine and the interrupt handler routine. This information tells DOS where to find the actual driver code.

The final item in the device header is an 8-byte area called DEV_NAME. If the driver is for a block device like a disk drive, the contents of this area are filled in by DOS, so its initial contents don't matter. For a character device, however, the name of the device must go here. The name must be a string of ASCII characters, with the name padded out to 8 bytes with blanks. The reason the name must be 8 bytes long is that DOS regards all character I/O devices as being equivalent to disk files. Hence it expects a standard 8-character file name (no .XXX extension is used) for each device. This way of doing things gives tremendous power and flexibility, as discussed later. The example program takes over the standard printer device. To do this the device name is given as 'PRN   ' (the 5 trailing blanks must be present) because PRN is the reserved device name for the main system printer (see Table 4-1). Whenever output is supposed to go to the printer, DOS scans through the linked list of device drivers looking for the name PRN (or its synonym LPT1). The first time DOS finds that name, it stops and sends the output to that device driver. Since user-defined device drivers are at the beginning of the linked list, they are always looked at first. Thus the standard PRN device driver in DOS is ignored if you name your device driver PRN.

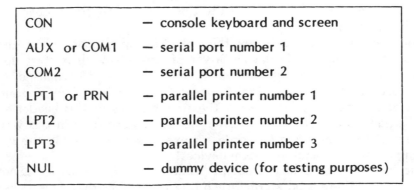

CON	— console keyboard and screen
AUX or COM1	— serial port number 1
COM2	— serial port number 2
LPT1 or PRN	— parallel printer number 1
LPT2	— parallel printer number 2
LPT3	— parallel printer number 3
NUL	— dummy device (for testing purposes)

Table 4-1. Reserved system device names.

The second main section of the driver is the *device strategy routine*. This is just a trivial 3-line subroutine that stores the contents of ES and BX in a local data area. Note that the RET here and in the following device interrupt handler must be far returns. To accomplish this, the entire device driver has been defined to be the FAR procedure SERIAL.

To understand the purpose of the device strategy routine, you need to consider how DOS executes an I/O operation through the device driver. Suppose DOS wants to output one or more characters to the printer. It first scans the linked list of device headers looking for the name PRN or LPT1. When it finds a header for a device of that name, it looks at the STRATEGY entry in the header to find the start address of the strategy routine. It then creates a data area called a request header, which contains all the information needed to do the output operation, including a code for the operation to be performed, the data to be output, and so on. The *DOS Technical Reference* manual discusses the request header format in detail. The point is that DOS now calls the strategy routine with ES:BX set so that they point to this request header data area. The strategy routine just stores the location of this request header and returns to DOS.

Next, DOS calls the third main section of the device driver program, the *device interrupt handler*. This piece of code looks at the information in the request header and uses it to do the actual output operation. At this point you're probably wondering why IBM has split up a simple I/O operation into two pieces, one subroutine that just sets up the information needed to do the I/O operation and another that uses that information to do the I/O. IBM doesn't say why they do this, but the reason may be that it facilitates I/O operations on devices that use hardware interrupts. In such cases, it's useful to be able to make requests to print information separately from actually doing the printing. The strategy routine of the printer device driver can then put these print requests in a queue (a list of operations to be done), and let the printer come in at its own speed via hardware interrupts to actually do the output. Note that the simple printer device driver being discussed here does not implement this idea. It only keeps a "queue" that holds one request at a time, and this print request is carried out under program control when DOS calls the device interrupt handler subroutine.

Now let's look at how the interrupt handler routine itself is written. First, note that although IBM terms this an interrupt handler, the routine is actually called by DOS, not entered via a hardware interrupt. Thus it's really just a subroutine. DOS assumes that the routine saves all registers, so they are all PUSHed onto the stack first. If the routine had made extensive use of the stack, a local stack would also have to be set up, as the DOS stack being used at entry is not all that large. Next the request header address that was stored by the strategy routine is picked up and the command code stored in that header is used to determine which operation has been requested. Refer to the *DOS Technical Reference* manual for the detailed structure of the request header.

Note that thirteen different commands are possible, although no one device ever implements all of them. For the unimplemented commands the routine just sets an error code in the request header's status word, restores all the registers, and does a far return. The rest of the code consists of the individual driver routines. In this simple printer driver, only three commands are implemented: initialization, output, and output status. The IBM *DOS* manual describes the structure of the request header for each of these commands and tells exactly what each command must do. Notice that to access data within the request header, the fixed offset of each data field within the header is defined as a constant at the beginning of the program, and that constant is then added to ES:BX to get the data. An alternative method would have been to use segment templates as described in Sec. 4-1. Also note that to reference local variables such as RH_SEG, a CS: segment override is necessary. This is because the program must end up as a .COM file, so the variables are in the code segment and you cannot count on any segment register other than CS to be pointing at this segment when DOS calls the device handler.

You should be able to use this sample program as a model for writing installable device drivers of your own. Your DOS diskette also contains the source code for an electronic disk device driver (VDISK.LST). This is a good example of a block I/O device driver. You can learn a lot about how disk drives are set up under DOS by studying this code.

To use an installable device driver from an assembly language program, you can just execute the appropriate DOS function call. For example, the printer driver just presented can be accessed using either function call 5 or function call 40H. The latter is preferable, as it has more flexibility. Both disk files and I/O devices are treated on an equal basis by function call 40H using the concept of a *handle*, which is just a numeric value assigned by DOS (the handle is 4 for the printer). File handles and the DOS function calls that use them are discussed in Sec. 4-7.

To end this section, let's compare the two methods discussed here for implementing device drivers. The interrupt takeover approach presented first is clearly the simpler method. Just write a routine to handle the device and point an interrupt vector at it. Doing this gives you device control at the lowest level of the operating system. Depending on what you want to do, this can be either good or bad. For simple device drivers like the printer driver, it's probably the best technique. The installable device driver approach, on the other hand, interfaces to the operating system at a considerably higher level. With this method, you can readily write drivers for nearly any kind of disklike storage device or write fancy I/O drivers that are dynamically reprogrammable. Such sophisticated drivers are better written as installable device drivers, even though they are more complex to write.

Another point in favor of the installable device driver approach to controlling I/O devices is that it allows you to take advantage of the operating system's full power. In particular, DOS treats installable device drivers exactly like files, as mentioned earlier. This allows you to use the I/O device in very powerful ways. For example, suppose (heaven forbid!) you wanted to attach a paper tape reader to the IBM PC. If you write the driver program for this device in installable form and name it OBSOLETE, then you can read a program on paper tape and store it in the PC as a disk file named PAPER.TPE by simply typing "COPY OBSOLETE: PAPER.TPE". In other words, you can refer to and manipulate your own custom I/O devices in the same ways that you handle disk files. This is a "big machine" concept that originated with the Bell Telephone Laboratory's UNIX operating system, and is the direction in which IBM is headed for future versions of DOS. Hence writing your routines in installable form may also allow you to take better advantage of future DOS enhancements.

4-7. Assembly Language Control of Disk Files

Occasionally you'll find it's very useful to be able to read in existing programs or data files from disk, and to be able to create new disk files and write data out to them. Some situations where you may want to do this include the following:

1. You want to run a program in a nonstandard environment. In other words, you want to use different I/O device drivers temporarily or alter the operating system in some way, run the program in this new environment, and then, before returning to the operating system, restore things to the way they were originally.

2. You want your assembly program to read or write data files on the disk.

3. You want to load another program (for example, a piece of commercial software), change that program in some way, and then execute it.

As you'll see, using disk files from assembly language is fairly straightforward, but it requires you first to obtain a good understanding of the structure of disk files and other associated concepts. The penalty for making a programming error is also very high: there's a good possibility of wiping out valuable disks. Thus in situations where you want to use a disk file from assembly language, it's wise to consider whether a simpler alternative can be used. In particular, using a mixture of assembly language and a high-level language often does the job. The high-level languages have debugged, relatively easy-to-use disk file handling utilities. Use them to do the disk accesses and then transfer control to your assembly language program via a CALL, as described in Sec. 4-5.

If you do want to write assembly language programs to access disk files, the first thing you need to do is to study carefully the "DOS Control Blocks and Work Areas" chapter in the *DOS Technical Reference* manual. In particular, you should understand how file control blocks and program prefix segments are structured and used. This understanding is invaluable in writing programs to handle disk files.

The next thing to do is to use DOS Version 2.0 or later. You can access disk files using DOS 1.1, but its capabilities are much more limited. Under DOS 1.1, you can load and execute only .COM files from assembly language, not .EXE files (see Sec. 4-6 for a description of how to create .COM files). Also, the DOS function calls available under DOS 1.1 are very limited and require you to construct your own file control blocks. This can be educational, but the programs end up being fairly complex. If you still want to write disk-accessing assembly programs under DOS 1.1, there is a step-by-step procedure given in one of the *DOS* manual appendixes for loading a .COM file from an assembly language program. Two items are left out of that procedure that you should know about, however. First, to create a new program prefix segment using DOS function call 26H, either your program must be a .COM file or you must make your .EXE file simulate a .COM file by making CS the same as DS. The latter is most easily done by pushing both DS and an offset onto the stack, and then doing a far RET. Also, the procedure doesn't say so, but you must zero out the record number fields in the file control block (bytes 32-36) before loading or using a file.

In the remainder of this section, it is assumed that you're using DOS 2.0 or a later version. It contains some powerful DOS function calls that make handling disk files from assembly language quite easy. Consider first the problem of loading and executing another file from an assembly language program. Here's an example that does this:

```
title     DOS 2.0 FILE LOADING & EXECUTION EXAMPLE


prefix    segment at 0              ;Program prefix segment template
          org      2ch
envseg    dw       ?
prefix    ends


;Parameter block. Pointed to by ES:BX before a program is loaded
dseg      segment public 'data'
pblock    dw       ?               ;Segment address of environment
          dw       80h
          dw       ?               ;Segment of pointer to command line
          dw       5Ch
          dw       ?               ;Segment of pointer to default FCB
          dw       6Ch
          dw       ?               ;Segment of pointer to 2nd default FCB
spsave    dw       ?               ;Storage area for SS:SP
sssave    dw       ?
filnam    db       'myprog.exe',0
```

```
errmsg    db          'File not found',0DH,0AH,'$'
msg1      db          'Program starting',0DH,0AH,'$'
msg2      db          'Program completed',0DH,0AH,'$'
dseg      ends


sseg      segment stack 'data'
          dw          80h dup (?)
sseg      ends


cseg      segment public 'code'
          assume      cs:cseg,ds:dseg
setup     proc        far
          cld                             ;All string moves go up
          push        ds                  ;Set up a return to DOS
          sub         ax,ax
          push        ax

          push        ds                  ;Print a "program starting" message
          mov         ax,dseg
          mov         ds,ax
          lea         dx,msg1
          mov         ah,9
          int         21h
          pop         ds

          assume      ds:prefix
          lea         bx,eop+10h          ;Get paragraph # of end of program
          mov         cl,4
          shr         bx,cl
          add         bx,cseg
          mov         ax,ds               ;Get paragraph # of program start
          sub         bx,ax               ;Difference is total program length
          mov         es,ax               ;Point ES at program prefix segment
          mov         ah,4ah              ;Shrink allocated memory to program size
          int         21h
          mov         bx,envseg           ;Get segment address of environment
          mov         dx,ds               ;Get program prefix segment address
          mov         ax,dseg             ;Point DS to local data area
          mov         ds,ax
          assume      ds:dseg
          lea         di,pblock           ;Fill in parameter block
          mov         [di],bx             ;With environment segment
          add         di,4
          mov         cx,3
filblk:   mov         [di],dx             ;And command line & FCB pointers
          add         di,4
          loop        filblk
```

```
          lea      bx,pblock        ;Point ES:BX at parameter block
          mov      ax,ds
          mov      es,ax
          lea      dx,filnam        ;Point DS:DX at file name
          mov      spsave,sp        ;Save stack location
          mov      sssave,ss
          mov      ax,4b00h         ;Load and execute new program
          int      21h

          mov      ax,dseg          ;Restore DS to local data area
          mov      ds,ax
          mov      ss,sssave        ;Then restore original stack
          mov      sp,spsave
          jnc      finish           ;Leave clean if CF not set on return
          lea      dx,errmsg        ;If CF set, print an error message
          mov      ah,9
          int      21h
          ret
finish:   lea      dx,msg2          ;Print a "program completed" message
          mov      ah,9
          int      21h
          ret                       ;And quit
setup     endp
eop       db       'end of program'
cseg      ends

          end      setup
```

The program begins by printing a message on the screen that says "Program starting". This little section of code would normally be replaced by code for whatever you wanted to do (for example, take over an interrupt, add a new I/O device driver, switch the display from text mode to graphics mode, and so on) before loading and executing another program on disk. Just make sure that DS and ES are preserved so that they're pointing at the program prefix segment when you're done.

The next section of code (starting at ASSUME DS:PREFIX) does the setup for loading a file from disk. What we need to find is the paragraph number of the end of the program. A paragraph is 16 bytes. Hence the paragraph number is the memory address divided by 16, in other words, the segment address. To get this, the end address of the current program is obtained by loading the offset address of eop + 10h. This is divided by 16 and added to the program segment address to give the paragraph number of the end of the program. The paragraph number of the program prefix segment is then subtracted from the program end paragraph number to get the total program length in paragraphs in the BX register. Making sure that ES points to the starting segment of the program (the program prefix), DOS function 1A is called to free all memory above the program. This is necessary because the DOS internally marks all of memory as being allocated to a program when it is loaded into memory.

Next, four quantities are initialized in a parameter block (PBLOCK) that's been set up in the data segment: the segment address of the environment string, a DWORD pointer (offset and segment) to a command line, and DWORD pointers to the two file control blocks (FCB's) in the original program prefix. If you're not familiar with these quantities, check the "DOS Control Blocks and Work Areas" chapter in the *DOS Technical Reference* manual. Since the default value of the environment is used here, the environment address is just picked up from the original program prefix (ENVSEG). Similarly, the program uses the original command line and the two default FCB's set up in the original program prefix, so pointers to them are stored in PBLOCK. Since the offsets of these three quantities in the program prefix are known in advance, they are fixed in the definition of PBLOCK, and only the segment address of the original program prefix needs to be filled in. Any of these quantities could be changed, if desired.

Now ES:BX is pointed to the beginning of the parameter block, and DS:DX is pointed to the name of the file to be loaded and executed. Unless the file name is preceded by a drive specification, the computer looks for the program on the default drive only. In the example, the program is named MYPROG.EXE. Change this to whatever file name you want to load. The file name is given as an "ASCIIZ" string, which is just an ASCII string followed by a byte of zero. Finally, the current value of SS:SP is saved in the data segment. Everything is now set up to load and execute the new program using DOS function call 4BH (set AH = 4BH and AL = 0). When this function call is executed, MYPROG.EXE is loaded into memory and executed.

When MYPROG.EXE has finished executing, control is automatically passed back to the next instruction in the program following the INT 21H (that is, to MOV AX,DSEG). Since *all* registers are destroyed by function call 4BH, the first action must be to restore DS so it points to the data area again, and then to reload the stack pointer. The program then finishes by printing out a "program completed" message. You can replace this code with any instructions you need to clean up, restore original interrupt vectors, and so on.

Notice that a JNC FINISH is done to get to the final section of code. This allows the program to handle the case where something goes wrong during the execution of DOS function call 4BH. If there is an error during the execution of the function call—for example, if the file to be loaded isn't on the disk—control is returned to the instruction following INT 21H with the carry flag set. In addition, AX is set equal to one of the error codes shown in Table 4-2. In the example program the error code isn't checked. Instead a "File not found" message is printed, since that's by far the most common error.

One limitation of this program is that you can't use it to load a program and modify it before execution, if that program itself relies on having a

CODE	CONDITION
1	Invalid function number
2	File not found
3	Path not found
4	Too many open files (no handles left)
5	Access denied
6	Invalid handle
7	Memory control blocks destroyed
8	Insufficient memory
9	Invalid memory block address
10	Invalid environment
11	Invalid format
12	Invalid access code
13	Invalid data
14	[not used]
15	Invalid drive was specified
16	Attempted to remove the current directory
17	Not same device
18	No more files

Table 4–2. Error Return Table. If a DOS function call is unsuccessful, the carry flag is set, and one of the error codes in this table is returned in AX.

program prefix segment present to load other disk files. The reason is that function call 4BH (with AL = 0) does the loading and execution together with no way to interrupt the process. You can load a program without executing it using function call 4BH with AL = 3. However, no program prefix segment is set up in this case. Thus you cannot load in BASICA.COM, modify it, and then begin execution of BASICA. In this situation you must first load in the file without executing it, make your changes to the file, write it back out to disk, and then reload and execute it.

A great many other disk operations can be done from assembly language using DOS function calls. DOS 1.1 provides a total of 48 function calls, 23 of which provide functions related to disk file handling. In general, these calls all work through file control blocks that you must set up and initialize yourself. DOS 2.0 provides an additional 40 function calls, 21 of which provide disk file handling functions. Many of these new calls provide the same functions as those available under DOS 1.1, but they are more powerful and considerably easier to use since you don't have to set up a file control block. Where duplicate functions exist, you should use the new functions rather than the old, unless you want to be able to run under both DOS versions.

The new DOS 2.0 disk file functions allow you to refer to disk files simply by a *file handle*. This concept works as follows: Whenever you create or open a file using DOS function calls 3C or 3D, you just pass DOS the name of the file as an ASCII string. It then does all the work of setting up the file control block for you, and returns a number to you in AX. This number is the file handle. To do any subsequent operations on this file, all you have to do is pass this number (the file handle) to the appropriate DOS function call. DOS keeps a table of the file handles for all open files, and uses this table to find and maintain the file control blocks for each file.

Actually, the file handle concept is even more powerful than just described because I/O devices (printers, screens, keyboards, and so on) also have a file handle associated with them and thus can be treated like disk files. This equivalence between devices and disk files was discussed in Sec. 4-6. One difference is that the file handles for the standard devices are preassigned, so they do not have to be opened or created to be used. Table 4-3 shows the preassigned file handles for devices.

HANDLE	DEVICE
0000	Standard input device (CON:) Input can be redirected
0001	Standard output device (CON:) Output can be redirected
0002	Standard error output device Output cannot be redirected
0003	Standard auxiliary device (COM1:)
0004	Standard printer device (PRN:)

Table 4-3. Preassigned file handles for I/O devices.

Space does not permit a description of all the function calls available. You can read about them in the *DOS Technical Reference* manual. Instead we end this section with examples of the two most common disk operations: writing to a disk file and reading from a disk file.

As an illustration of writing to a disk file, consider the following little program that creates a file called MYFILE.TXT on the disk, and then writes a sentence of ASCII text into the file:

```
title    WRITE FILE TO DISK

dseg    segment
bufr    db          'This is a really wonderful disk file'
filnam  db          'MYFILE.TXT',00
crerr   db          'Error: cannot create file',0DH,0AH,'$'
dseg    ends
```

```
sseg    segment stack               ;The DOS will automatically set up
        dw        80h dup (?)       ; a stack in the stack segment
sseg    ends


cseg    segment
        assume    cs:cseg,ds:dseg,ss:sseg
main    proc      far
        push      ds                ;Push start address of program prefix
        sub       ax,ax             ; segment on the stack
        push      ax

        mov       ax,dseg           ;Point DS:DX at file name in dseg
        mov       ds,ax
        lea       dx,filnam
        mov       cx,0              ;Make file attribute byte 0 (normal file)
        mov       ah,3ch            ;Create the file
        int       21h
        jc        error             ;Abort if there was a problem
        mov       bx,ax             ;Else store file handle in BX

        mov       cx,36             ;Write contents of BUFR to disk
        lea       dx,bufr
        mov       ah,40h
        int       21h

        mov       ah,3eh            ;Close the file
        int       21h
done:   ret                         ;This far return gets back to the DOS

error:  lea       dx,crerr          ;If error occurred during file creation
        mov       ah,9              ; print an error message
        int       21h
        ret
main    endp
cseg    ends


        end       main
```

The program begins by creating a file whose name is MYFILE.TXT. This is done by pointing DS:DX at the file name, putting the desired file attribute in CX, and calling DOS function 3CH. The file name must be an ASCIIZ string—that is, a string of ASCII characters ending with a byte of 00. If you wish, you can optionally precede the file name with a drive specification such as "A:". If no drive is specified, as is done in this example program, the current default drive is assumed. Also, if you're using a hard disk system with subdirectories, you must specify a path name in front of the file name just as you do to specify a file when you're in the operating system.

The file attribute byte is 00 for normal files, so it is set to 0 in the program. If you want to create a special type of file such as a read-only file, a system file, or a hidden file, you must change this value accordingly. The allowed values of the file attribute byte are discussed in the "DOS Disk Allocation" chapter of the *DOS Technical Reference* manual. DOS function call 43H can also be used to change the file attribute byte.

When the file is created by function call 3CH, it's automatically opened for either reading or writing, and the file handle is returned in AX. If no other disk files are open, you normally get a file handle of 5 (handles 0 through 4 are assigned to the standard I/O devices as shown in Table 4-3).

Immediately after the function call that creates the file, the program checks the carry flag and jumps to an error routine if it is set. You should always make this check immediately after the DOS function call that creates or opens a file. When an error occurs during a DOS file handling call, it returns with the carry flag set and an error code in AX (see Table 4-2). If you simply ignore the error and continue, you'll be using the error code as the file handle! This is likely to produce behavior that is at best unpredictable, and at worst disastrous.

The error routine used in the example is very minimal. It simply announces that an error has occurred and quits. A more sophisticated routine would examine AX to find out what kind of error it was and then send the appropriate message and/or take other appropriate recovery actions.

The next section of code writes the contents of BUFR into the newly created file. All that's required to do this is to point DS:DX at the beginning address of BUFR, put the number of bytes to write in CX, and have the file handle in BX. DOS function call 40H then takes care of everything else. Although it has not been done in the skeletal routine here, you should also follow all disk write function calls with a check for errors and an appropriate error handling routine. This is especially important if the data being written to disk is valuable or not easily replaceable. In a good file-handling assembly program, at least half the code should probably be devoted to error handling.

The program ends by closing the file with a call to DOS function 3EH. All that needs to be done here is put the file handle in BX and make the call. It's vital that the file be explicitly closed with this call before the program ends; otherwise you'll lose some or all of the data. The reason is that when you write to a disk file with DOS function 40H, the data is first written into a 512-byte buffer (the size of one disk sector) in memory. Only when a full 512 bytes have been written into the buffer is the data actually written onto the disk. This speeds up disk operations tremendously, but unless you've written an exact multiple of 512 bytes, part of the disk file remains in memory until a close file command is executed.

The reverse process of writing a disk file is reading from a disk file. Suppose you want to read in 9 bytes from the file created with the previous program, starting with the seventeenth byte in the file. The same program structure can be used as in the previous program, except that the body of the procedure MAIN must be replaced with:

```
push    ds
sub     ax,ax
push    ax

mov     ax,dseg            ;Point DS:DX at file name in data segment
mov     ds,ax
lea     dx,filnam
mov     ax,3d00h           ;Open the file for reading
int     21h
jc      error
mov     bx,ax              ;And store file handle in BX
mov     cx,0               ;Move file pointer to location 17 in file
mov     dx,17
mov     ax,4200H
int     21h
lea     dx,bufr            ;Read 9 bytes from file into BUFR
mov     cx,9
mov     ah,3fh
int     21h

mov     ah,3eh             ;Close the file
int     21h
mov     ah,9               ;Print the contents of BUFR on the screen
int     21h
ret
```

This code assumes that BUFR has been redefined to be a blank memory area that ends with a "$" (so we can use function call 9 to write it on the screen). Thus the variable BUFR in DSEG would be written as

```
bufr    db      80 dup (' '),'$'
```

The program works in much the same way as the previous one for writing files. The file is opened with function call 3DH. It does not need to be created because it already exists. The next task is to read in 9 bytes from the file, starting with byte 17. This is done by making use of another DOS file-handling concept, the *file read/write pointer*. This is a pointer into the file that is maintained by DOS and that is automatically incremented whenever a byte is read from or written to the file. The pointer is set to the first byte in the file whenever a file is opened or created. It can also be manipulated using DOS function call 42H. To use function 42H, you simply specify the file handle in BX and the offset you want the pointer to move to in CX:DX (the use of a 32-bit value allows manipulation of files larger than 64K). This offset can be relative to the start of the file, the current pointer position in the file, or the end of the file (as specified in AL). In the example program, AL is set to 0 on entry so that the offset is relative to the start of the file.

With the file pointer moved to byte 17, DOS call 3FH can be used to read 9 bytes from the file into memory starting at location BUFR. The file is then closed and the contents of BUFR written out to the screen so that you can see what's been read in from the file. The same general sequence used here to read from the middle of a file can also be used to modify an existing file or append new data onto the end of a file. Just replace the read function call with a write function call.

It should be obvious by now that manipulating files from assembly language under DOS 2.0 is really fairly simple once you understand the concepts involved. As mentioned previously, a great many other function calls are available for manipulating disk files in addition to the ones discussed here. Spend some time reading the "DOS Interrupts and Function Calls" chapter in the *DOS Technical Reference* manual to acquaint yourself with them. With their aid, you can do almost anything you want in assembly language. Probably the hardest part of writing such programs is providing a proper set of error-handling routines.

4-8. Using the 8087 Numeric Data Processor

One of the smartest decisions made by the IBM PC's designers was to include an empty socket wired up for the 8087 numeric data processor. This very powerful chip can speed up operations on floating-point and multi-digit BCD numbers by factors of 10 to 100 or more, depending on what's being done. For example, it calculates an 80-bit floating-point square root in 36 microseconds, competitive with machines much larger. In addition to scientists and engineers, business people also love it because it handles integers up to 18 digits in length, big enough for the U.S. national debt for quite a few years even with totally rampant inflation! You can buy the 8087 from a number of companies, stick it into the empty socket, and be up and running. Of course no speed improvements occur unless the software takes advantage of the 8087's presence.

To thoroughly describe all aspects of the 8087's operation would require an entire book, so all we do here is give a basic understanding of how the chip works, what its capabilities are, and what it's like to program it. For a complete technical description of the 8087, refer to the *iAPX 86,88 User's Manual* published by Intel.

The hardware of the 8087 is treated in Sec. 6-4, where we present a discussion of the signals present on the 8087's pins and how these allow it to remain synchronized with the 8088. On the software side of things, the basic method by which the 8087 recognizes instructions intended for it is given in Sec. 3-11. Here we discuss the 8087 further from a programmer's point of view.

To the programmer, the 8087 looks like an additional set of registers available inside the CPU. Figure 4-3 shows this register set. The heart of the chip is a set of eight 80-bit floating-point registers, R1—R8. The speed of the 8087 is due to the fact that one can do a wide variety of arithmetic operations (including square roots, exponentials, and trigonometric functions), on 80-bit numbers in these registers with single instructions. Associated with each register is a 2-bit tag field that indicates whether the register is empty (11), contains a valid number (00), contains zero (01), or contains an erroneous result (10). The last case would occur if an operation like a divide by zero was done. There is also a control register that determines the operating mode of the 8087, and a status word analogous to the 8088's flag register. Finally there are operand and instruction pointers that contain the current instruction, instruction address, and memory operand address. The contents of these registers are used by exception handlers (interrupt routines that decide what to do after an error has occurred).

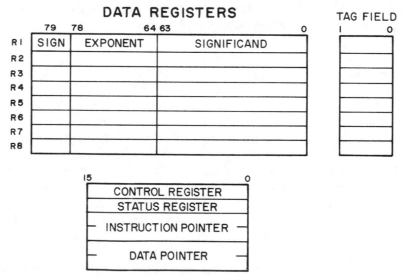

Fig. 4—3. The 8087 register set. Reprinted by permission of Intel Corporation, copyright 1983.

The 8087 recognizes three different classes of numbers: binary integers, packed decimal integers, and binary real (floating-point) numbers. Furthermore, the binary integers and the binary reals can each be in three different formats, resulting in seven different possible types of numbers. These seven types of numbers and their range of allowed values are shown in Fig. 4-4 and Table 4-4. The three integer types are just two's complement binary numbers of varying length, and the packed decimal type is just a string of BCD digits (see Sec. 2-3) preceded by a sign bit. The structure of a real number is more complicated. The basic idea is that the number is expressed in scientific notation as a product of a significand and an exponent. To see

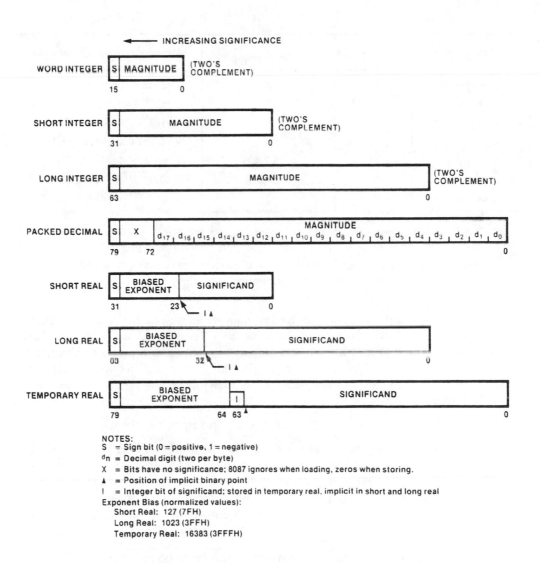

NOTES:
S = Sign bit (0 = positive, 1 = negative)
d_n = Decimal digit (two per byte)
X = Bits have no significance; 8087 ignores when loading, zeros when storing.
▲ = Position of implicit binary point
I = Integer bit of significand; stored in temporary real, implicit in short and long real
Exponent Bias (normalized values):
    Short Real: 127 (7FH)
    Long Real: 1023 (3FFH)
    Temporary Real: 16383 (3FFFH)

Fig. 4–4. Data formats for the seven number types handled by the 8087. Reprinted by permission of Intel Corporation, copyright 1983.

how this works, consider how the number 197.625 is converted into a binary number in short real format. To do the conversion, you start by separately converting the integer and fractional portions of the number to binary. Thus 197 = 0C5H = 11000101 is the integer portion, and the fractional part is .625 = .101 in binary. To do the conversion of the fractional part, use is made of the fact that each digit in a binary fraction has a decimal value of 2^{-n}; that is, .1 in binary = 1/2, .01 in binary = 1/4, .001 = 1/8, .0001 = 1/16, etc. Thus

197.625 decimal = 11000101.101 binary

Data Type	Bits	Significant Digits (Decimal)	Approximate Range (Decimal)
Word integer	16	4	$-32{,}768 \leqslant X \leqslant +32{,}767$
Short integer	32	9	$-2 \times 10^9 \leqslant X \leqslant +2 \times 10^9$
Long integer	64	18	$-9 \times 10^{18} \leqslant X \leqslant +9 \times 10^{18}$
Packed decimal	80	18	$-99...99 \leqslant X \leqslant +99...99$ (18 digits)
Short real	32	6-7	$8.43 \times 10^{-37} \leqslant |X| \leqslant 3.37 \times 10^{38}$
Long real	64	15-16	$4.19 \times 10^{-307} \leqslant |X| \leqslant 1.67 \times 10^{308}$
Temporary real	80	19	$3.4 \times 10^{-4932} \leqslant |X| \leqslant 1.2 \times 10^{4932}$

Table 4–4. Range and precision of the seven number types handled by the 8087. The short real and long real data types correspond to what are often called single precision and double precision data types. Reprinted by permission of Intel Corporation, copyright 1983.

Next you need to write the binary number in scientific notation—that is, as a number of the form 1.XXXXXXX x 2^n. To do this, note that if the binary point (the "." in a binary real number) is moved one place to the left, the number is divided by 2. So take the 11000101.101, move the binary point seven places to the left, and then multiply it by 2^7 to regain the original number. Thus

$$11000101.101 = 1.1000101101 \times 2^7 \text{ in scientific notation}$$

To put this into the standard IEEE format you also need to bias the exponent by adding 7FH = 127 decimal to it. Hence in the example, the exponent is 7 + 7FH = 86H or 10000110 binary. Also, the 1 to the left of the binary point is not explicitly included in the IEEE format number (since it never changes, its presence is simply assumed), so the significand is just .1000101101. Hence the complete short real number for 197.625 is

0	10000110	1000 1011 0100 0000 0000 0000
sign	exponent	significand

The use of a biased exponent (an exponent with a constant added to it) may seem strange, but it has the advantage of speeding up the comparison of two real numbers to see which is larger (because all biased exponents are positive numbers).

Any of the seven number types can be loaded from memory into an 8087 register, or stored into memory from an 8087 register. However, it is important to realize that the 8087 does all its internal calculations on temporary real numbers. All other types are automatically converted into temporary real when they are loaded into an 8087 register, and converted back to the specified number type when they are stored into memory from an 8087 register. Thus all internal operations are on 80-bit floating-point numbers. However, four integer arithmetic operations are possible: integer add, subtract, multiply, and divide. If one of these four operations is done on two floating-point numbers in the 8087 that both represent integers, and the result is also an integer (it's not an operation like 4 divided by 3), then an exact integer result (in floating-point format) is produced. This greatly facilitates things like financial or bookkeeping calculations, where round-off errors are not tolerable.

When the 8087 stores a number in memory, it is broken up into byte-wide pieces and then stored in the usual "backward" format, least significant byte first. Figure 4-5 shows how the various number types are stored.

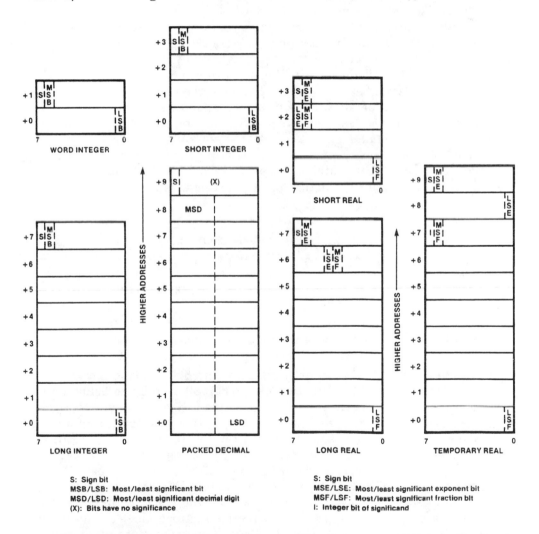

S: Sign bit
MSB/LSB: Most/least significant bit
MSD/LSD: Most/least significant decimal digit
(X): Bits have no significance

S: Sign bit
MSE/LSE: Most/least significant exponent bit
MSF/LSF: Most/least significant fraction bit
I: Integer bit of significand

Fig. 4-5. How the seven number types handled by the 8087 are stored in memory. Reprinted by permission of Intel Corporation, copyright 1983.

We postpone a discussion of the full 8087 instruction set until later in this section, and concentrate for the moment on how the 8087 does simple arithmetic operations. Let's look first at the floating-point registers, R1—R8. These registers are used in large part like a stack rather than a simple set of registers. For example, you can't load a number from memory into register R3. You can only load (push) a number in memory onto the current top of the eight-register stack. Which register corresponds to the current stack top depends on the operations that have been done previously. Similarly, to store a number back into memory from the 8087, it must be the top element of the stack, and many arithmetic operations work only on the top stack element. A concise way to describe R1—R8 is to say that they can be used like the register stack in a Hewlett-Packard hand calculator.

However, unlike a Hewlett-Packard calculator, the 8087 instruction set also includes a substantial number of conventional register operations. For example, you can interchange the contents of any two registers in the stack. Also, the four elementary arithmetic operations can be done with the source and destination being any two registers in the stack.

This combination of allowing both stacklike and registerlike operations may seem confusing at first, but in practice it works fairly smoothly and efficiently. The main problem is keeping track of which number is where in the stack. For example, suppose you have three real numbers AA, BB, and CC, and you want to calculate the quantity RESULT = (AA*BB)/CC. One way to do this is to use the floating-point registers as a classical stack:

```
TITLE   8087 TEST 1
        FINIT                ;Initialize 8087 & clear all registers
        FLD      AA          ;Load AA from memory onto 8087 register stack
(a)     FLD      BB          ;Then load BB
(b)     FMUL                 ;Multiply BB by AA and pop the register stack
(c)     FLD      CC          ;Now load CC onto 8087 register stack
(d)     FDIV                 ;Divide (AA*BB) by CC & pop the stack
        FST      RESULT      ;Store the stack top element into RAM
```

Here we use the standard Intel mnemonics for the 8087 instructions. These all begin with the letter "F" (for floating-point) followed by an abbreviation for the operation to be performed. Thus FLD loads a number into the 8087, while FST stores a number back into memory. If a mnemonic ends with a "P", it means that the stack is popped after the operation is performed. The machine codes for these instructions are variations of the ESC instruction plus a WAIT instruction as discussed in Sec. 3-11 (see also below). To see what's going on in the 8087 registers during the program just given, refer to Fig. 4-6. Here the contents of the 8087 registers are shown at four points in the program corresponding to the instructions labeled (a) through (d) in the listing above. Note that the figure shows the state of the registers *after* the labeled instruction has executed; for example, the section of

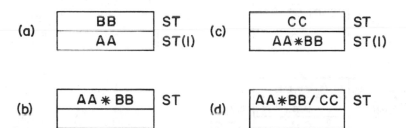

Fig. 4–6. The 8087 register stack during execution of 8087 test program 1.

the figure labeled (b) shows the state of the 8087 after the multiply operation FMULP has been done.

You've no doubt noticed that the registers in Fig. 4-6 are labeled ST, ST(1), ST(2), etc., instead of R1, R2, R3, etc. The reason is that the 8087 instructions access registers relative to the top of the stack only (ST stands for stack top). The register names R1—R8 are meaningless, since the stack top could be any of the registers R1—R8. Thus in 8087 instructions, registers are always referred to relative to ST, the register that is the current stack top. For example, ST(1) means the register immediately below ST, ST(2) is the second register below ST, and so on.

Using the 8087 as illustrated in the previous program requires keeping careful track of the stack since it's always being popped and pushed. An alternative method that makes it easier to keep track of what's going on is to load all the numbers onto the 8087 register stack at the beginning, and then to treat the 8087 as if it had a normal set of fixed registers. In this case the current stack top register (ST) acts like the accumulator register in a conventional CPU. Arithmetic operations are mostly done with ST holding one of the operands and ST being the destination for the result. With this technique the program looks like:

```
TITLE   8087 TEST 2
        FINIT                   ;Initialize 8087 & clear floating-point registers
        FLD     CC              ;Load all three numbers into 8087
        FLD     BB              ; so that AA is in stack top (ST)
(a)     FLD     AA
(b)     FMUL                    ;Multiply ST (AA) by BB
(c)     FDIV                    ;Divide ST by CC
        FST     RESULT          ;Store the result
```

Figure 4-7 shows the state of the 8087 registers after each of the three instructions labeled (a)—(c) is performed. We recommend using the 8087 in this manner when possible, because it's clearer where variables are located

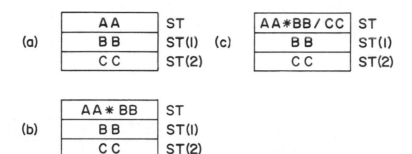

Fig. 4–7. The 8087 register stack during execution of 8087 test program 2.

in the stack. Note that the calculation of (AA*BB)/CC can be done even more simply by using numbers in memory as operands for arithmetic operations:

```
FINIT
FLD      AA          ;Load AA into 8087
FMUL     BB          ;Multiply by BB
FDIV     CC          ;Divide by CC
FST      RESULT      ;Store the result
```

In these examples, the FST RESULT instruction doesn't pop the 8087 stack, and hence this stack has one more value than when it started. If you don't need this value since it's stored in RAM, use the FSTP instruction instead. The third program has the advantage that it uses only one stack location, has fewer instructions, and runs faster. In general it's worthwhile to use the stack to store intermediate results since they then have the full 80-bit precision. On the other hand, try not to push unnecessary values onto the stack, since you may run out. If you do push the stack beyond its eight registers, it stores a special sticky code (you can use SST to examine this and other special codes) in the overrun positions instead of a numeric value. If you discover one of these values, you know that somewhere an error has occurred. A basic moral is to use rigorous stack rules: when a calculation is finished, the stack should be empty. A subroutine should never return with more stack values pushed than will be used by the calling routine(s).

To get around sloppy stack usage and other possible exceptions, you can include a FINIT instruction at the start of your code as in the examples above. For extended calculations, this is inefficient. A better method is to set a flag signaling the presence of the 8087 and initialize it for your program only then. Subsequent calls to 8087 subroutines should check this flag. A simple subroutine to initialize and flag the presence of the 8087 is as follows:

```
ists07     dw         0ffh

chk87:     fninit                ;Try to initialize the 8087 or 80287
           mov        cx,64h     ;Wait long enough to let it finish
chk872:    loop       chk872     ; (if it's there)
           fnstsw     ists87     ;Store status word
           ret
```

If the 8087 is there, it will clear the low byte of ists87, since the low byte of its status word consists of exception flags. These flags are cleared by the initialization instruction fninit. Hence the low byte of ists87 becomes a flag as to the presence of the 8087: if 0, an 8087 (or 80287) must be there to have stored it; if 0ffh, it's not there. Note that the "n" following the f in fninit and fnstsw tells the assembler not to insert a wait instruction before executing the instruction. If it did and no 8087 were there to release the CPU test line, the CPU would wait until you flipped the big red switch down and up, i.e., crash!

In general, the assembler inserts a wait instruction before the 8087 instruction to synchronize the 8088 and 8087. Since the 8088 and 8087 execute in parallel, the 8088 need only compute the absolute address for the 8087 and then it can go on to something else. If it gets to code that needs the 8087, it runs into an FWAIT instruction, forcing it to wait until the 8087 has finished with its last instruction. For the most part, the 80287 doesn't need this technique, since it has a hardwired busy line that causes the 80286 to wait when necessary. However, if you write code without the FWAIT's, plan on running that code on an 80286-based (or later) machine only. For all cases, you still need the FWAIT if the CPU needs to read RAM written by the 8087/80287, such as for interrogating status flags.

Microsoft and Intel high-level languages typically create EXE files that decide at run time whether to use 8087 instructions. These files have INT 34H to INT 3DH instructions followed by suitable bytes instead of the FWAIT/ESC n op codes that start 8087 instructions. The runtime initialization code sets up these interrupt vectors to point to handlers that emulate the 8087 instructions if the 8087 is absent. If an 8087 is present, INT 34H to INT 3BH are set up to point to a very simple interrupt handler that decrements the return address by 2 (pointing back to the INT instruction), and then subtracts 5c32H from the INT instruction; that is, it changes the calling program code on the fly! This converts the INT instruction into an FWAIT followed by the appropriate ESC code to yield the desired 8087 instruction. As the program runs, it converts itself into a native 8087 routine with essentially no loss in run speed. INT 3CH and INT 3DH are used to handle segment overrides and waits before returning from a subroutine.

To give a useful in-depth example of how to use the 8087, we explain how to compute the common trigonometric functions sine, cosine, and tangent. Although these functions are computed directly on the 80387, they require extra effort on the 8087 and 80287. We first give two useful subroutines, then summarize most of the 8087 instructions in greater detail, and finally give the code for the trigonometric functions themselves.

As on a Hewlett-Packard calculator, we use the letter x to refer to the input top-of-stack value st, and y for the input next-to-top-of-stack st(1). In this notation, a routine that is handy in the computation of trigonometric functions is RTX2T2, which returns st = the length of the hypotenuse of a right triangle with sides x and y, and leaves y in place (at st(1)). In the comment field, we describe the stack values relevant to the calculation after the corresponding instruction executes:

```
rtx2y2:   fmul    st,st(0)    ;st = x*x, st(1) = y
          fld     st(1)       ;st = y, st(1) = x*x, st(2) = y
          fmul    st,st(0)    ;st = y*y, st(1) = x*x, st(2) = y
          fadd                ;st = x*x + y*y, st(1) = y
          fsqrt               ;st = sqrt(x*x+y*y), st(1) = y
          ret
```

Try this routine out using the SST debugger/interpreter. Load up the 8087 registers using the sn= commands, and single-step the instructions forward and backward to see precisely what they do.

Another routine that is handy for the trigonometric functions is a Set Sign Plus routine SSP that returns with CF = 1 if st is less than 0. This routine illustrates how the 8087 flags can be transferred to the CPU's flags for conditional branching:

```
stat87    dw      ?

ssp:      ftst                ;x < 0?
          fstsw   stat87      ;Store 8087 status word
          fwait               ;Make CPU wait for 8087 to finish storing
          mov     ah,byte ptr stat87+1
          sahf                ;Set CF if < 0, set ZF if = 0
          fabs                ;Return st = abs(st)
ssp9:     ret
```

Now that you've seen some examples of how the 8087 can be used, a broader look at its overall capabilities is in order. Tables 4-5 and 4-6 summarize the complete instruction set of the 8087. Typical execution times for arithmetic instructions with an 8087 operating at 5 MHz on single precision real numbers are also shown.

Looking first at the basic arithmetic operations (Table 4-5), we see that several varieties of the add, subtract, multiply, and divide operations are available. Since these operations are the most common ones, the 8087 provides maximum flexibility in choosing where the source and destination

Addition		
FADD	add real	17µs
FADDP	add real & pop	18µs
FIADD	integer add	24µs

Subtraction		
FSUB	subtract real	17µs
FSUBP	subtract real & pop	18µs
FISUB	integer subtract	25µs
FSUBR	subtract real reversed	17µs
FSUBRP	subtract real reversed & pop	18µs
FISUBR	integer subtract reversed	25µs

Multiplication		
FMUL	multiply real	19µs
FMULP	multiply real & pop	20µs
FIMUL	integer multiply	27µs

Division		
FDIV	divide real	40µs
FDIVP	divide real & pop	41µs
FIDIV	integer divide	47µs
FDIVR	divide real reversed	40µs
FDIVRP	divide real reversed & pop	41µs
FIDIVR	integer divide reversed	47µs

Other Operations		
FSQRT	square root	37µs
FSCALE	scale	7µs
FPREM	partial remainder	25µs
FRNDINT	round to integer	9µs
FXTRACT	extract exponent & significand	10µs
FABS	absolute value	3µs
FCHS	change sign	3µs

Trancendentals		
FPTAN	partial tangent	90µs
FPATAN	partial arctangent	130µs
F2XM1	2^X-1	100µs
FYL2X	$Y \cdot \log_2 X$	190µs
FYL2XP1	$Y \cdot \log_2 (X+1)$	170µs

Load Constant		
FLDZ	load +0.0	3µs
FLD1	load +1.0	4µs
FLDPI	load π	4µs
FLDL2T	load $\log_2 10$	4µs
FLDL2E	load $\log_2 e$	4µs
FLDLG2	load $\log_{10} 2$	4µs
FLDLN2	load $\log_e 2$	4µs

Compare or Test		
FCOM	compare real	9µs
FCOMP	compare real and pop	9µs
FCOMPP	compare real and pop twice	10µs
FICOM	integer compare	17µs
FICOMP	integer compare and pop	17µs
FTST	test	8µs
FXAM	examine	3µs

Table 4-5. The 8087's arithmetic, transcendental, load constant, and comparison instructions. Approximate execution times for a 5-MHz 8087 are also shown.

operands are. Note that the execution times for these operations are on the order of 20 microseconds; that is, the 8087's throughput is about 0.05 MFLOPS (1 MFLOPS = 1 million floating-point operations per second). This is about 100 times faster than floating-point software for the 8088. Since instructions other than floating point are required to run, you usually don't pick up a factor of 100 in run speed, but speeds four to ten times faster are commonplace.

Several other arithmetic operations are also available to do rapid multiplication or division by powers of two (FSCALE), modulo arithmetic (FPREM), rounding of real numbers to integers (FRNDINT), and square roots (FSQRT).

All these operations work only on ST, the top element of the stack. Note the speed of the square root operation. It's faster than a simple division! This means that algorithms involving square roots are highly desirable.

Another group of instructions allows you to conveniently load constants into ST. Many of these involve logarithms because of the method used to do exponentiation on the 8087 (see below).

The transcendental functions available are limited to just a few basic functions. For example, the only trigonometric functions available are tangent (FPTAN) and arctangent (FPATAN). FPTAN is called a partial tangent because it returns two numbers, X and Y. To get the actual tangent you must then divide Y by X. One reason the 8087 uses this peculiar mode of operation is that it facilitates the calculation of the sine and cosine. Recall that for a right triangle with two sides X and Y and hypotenuse R = SQRT(X^2+Y^2), we have tan θ = Y/X, sin θ = Y/R, and cos θ = X/R. Hence to calculate sines and cosines, just calculate FPTAN(θ) to get X and Y, and then use the appropriate formula. However, it would have been preferable for the 8087 designers to include the sine and cosine functions directly since they are so common in many fields. One other limitation on these functions is that the angle θ must be less than $\pi/4$. The modulo division instruction FPREM is used to reduce all angles to a value in this range, and it stores a remainder in 3 bits of the 8087's status word register that determine which octant the original angle θ was in.

With a bit of logic, a routine called TRIG can be written that returns x and y for an arbitrary angle. This is the method used by the floating point calculator built into the SST debugger. We recommend that you go through these functions even if you don't need trig routines, since a number of 8087 features are used and explained. In terms of TRIG, the tangent, sine, and cosine are given by

```
ftan:    call      trig         ;Get st = x, st(1) = y given input angle st
         fdiv                   ;st = y/x = tan(input st)
         ret


fsin:    call      trig         ;Get st = x, st(1) = y for input angle st
fsin2:   call      rtx2y2       ;Get st = sqrt(x*x+y*y), st(1) = y
         fdiv                   ;st = y/sqrt(x*x+y*y)
         ret


fcos:    call      trig         ;Get st = x, st(1) = y for input angle st
         fxch                   ;st = y, st(1) = x
         jmp       fsin2
```

An advantage of this seemingly roundabout calculation is that computing all three trig functions can take only slightly more time than computing any one. In particular calculating the complex function exp(ia) is virtually as fast as calculating cos(a) or sin(a) alone. For example, the complex exponential of the angle st is given by

```
cexp:   call    trig        ;Return st = cos(st), sin(st)
        fld     st(1)       ;st = y, x, y
        call    rtx2y2      ;st = sqrt(x**2 + y**2), x, y
        fdiv    st(2),st
        fdiv
        ret
```

We still have to give TRIG, which calculates st = x and st(1) = y for an arbitrary input angle st given the built-in function fptan, which works only in the first octant. TRIG assumes the input is in radians. We have

```
minus2  dw      -2          ;Used for calculating pi/4
xzero   dw      1,-1,1,-1,0, 0,-1, 1        ;X values on octant bounda-
                                             ries
yzero   dw      0, 0,1,-1,1,-1, 1,-1        ; (not in octant order)
xyset   dw      trig7,xy5,xy2,xy6,xy3,xy7,xy4,xy8

trig:   push    bx
        call    ssp         ;Set st sign plus
        pushf               ;Save CF (=1 for negative)
        fild    minus2      ;Calculate pi/4
        fldpi
        fscale              ;st = pi/4
        fstp    st(1)       ;dump -2
        fxch                ;st = x; st(1) = pi/4

trig2:  fprem               ;Take st modulo pi/4 and report octant in
        fstsw   stat87      ; 8087 status. Be sure fprem finished by
        fwait               ; checking the 8087 status
        mov     ah,byte ptr stat87+1
        sahf                ;ah = status bits
        jp      trig2       ;Tests 8087 c2

        ftst                ;See if remainder is exactly 0 (c3 = 1, c0
                                = 0)
        fstsw   stat87
        mov     bl,ah       ;Compute octant index while waiting for
                                fstsw
        and     bx,3        ;bx will not be in octant order, but is 1
                                to 1
        test    ah,40       ;c3 = 0?
        jz      trig3
```

```
          add       bl,4            ;No
trig3:    shl       bx,1            ;Convert to word index

          fwait                     ;Be sure 8087 is finished storing
          and       byte ptr stat87+1,41
          cmp       byte ptr stat87+1,40     ;al = 0 iff remainder = 0
          jnz       trig4

          fstp      st              ;Remainder = 0. Pop it
          fstp      st              ; and pi/4
          fild      yzero[bx]       ;Load x y for octant
          fild      xzero[bx]
          jmp       short trig7     ;Done

trig4:    test      ah,2            ;Even octant?
          jnz       trig5
          fstp      st(1)           ;Yes. Get rid of pi/4
          jmp       trig6

trig5:    fsubp     st(1),st        ;Odd octant, compute st = pi/4 - st
trig6:    fptan                     ;Get the "partial tangent"
          jmp       xyset[bx]       ;Go translate to correct octant

;XYn - routines to convert fptan x y to correct octant x y

xy8:      fxch                      ; x -y (this stuff needed a flow chart!)
xy7:      fchs                      ; y -x
xy2:      fxch                      ; y  x
          jmp       short trig7
xy5:      fxch                      ;-x -y
xy6:      fchs                      ;-y -x
xy3:      fxch                      ;-y  x
xy4:      fchs                      ;-x  y

trig7:    popf                      ;Change sign on entry?
          jnc       trig8
          fxch                      ;Yes. Change y back
          fchs
          fxch
trig8:    pop       bx
          ret
```

Similarly the 8087 only has a "partial arctangent" from which to derive the arc trig functions. Converting to the general case is somewhat easier than for the TRIG case, but requires a similar mentality.

Exponentials are also done somewhat indirectly. The function 2^X can be calculated directly using F2XM1. To calculate other exponential functions such as 10^X, you can make use of the general formula

$$Y^X = 2^{X\log_2 Y}$$

and take advantage of the fact that the constant $\log_2 10$ can be loaded with the single instruction FLDL2T. Specifically we have the routines (built into SST's 8087 floating-point calculator)

```
;FYTX - return st = y**st

fytx:      fyl2x                        ;st = y * log base 2 of X
           jmp          short f2x

;F10X - return st = 10**st

f10x:      fldl2t                       ;Push log base 2 of 10
           jmp          short fexp2

;FEXP - return st = exp(st)

flde:      fld1                         ;FLDE - push e
fexp:      fldl2e                       ;Push log base 2 of e
fexp2:     fmul

;F2X - return st = 2**st

f2x:       call         ssp             ;Set sign plus
           pushf
f2x1:      fld          st              ;Dup x
           mov          al,4            ;Round Control bits = round down
           call         fround
           fsub         st(1),st
           fxch                         ;st = x - fix(x), st(1) = fix(x)
           fld          half
           fxch                         ;st = x - fix(x), st(1) = 1/2
           fprem                        ;st has x - fix(x) or x - fix(x) - 1/2
           fstsw        stat87          ;c1 = 1 if 1/2 subtracted
           fstp         st(1)           ;Get rid of 1/2
           f2xm1                        ;st = 2**(st) - 1
           fld1
           fadd
           test         byte ptr stat87+1,2
           jz           f2x2
           fld1                         ;x - fix(x) - 1/2, so multiply by sqrt(2)
```

```
          fadd       st,st(0)      ;st = 2
          fsqrt                    ;st = sqrt(2)
          fmul
f2x2:     fscale                   ;Put back integer portion
          fstp       st(1)         ;Get rid of fix(st)
          popf
          jnc        finv9
finv:     fld1                     ;Return st = 1/st.  2 8087 stack locations
                                   used.
          fdivrp     st(1),st
finv9:    ret


;FROUND - round st according to bit pattern al


fround:   push       bx
          fstcw      ctrl87        ;Save 8087 control word
          fwait
          xchg       bx,ax
          mov        ax,ctrl87
          and        ax,0f3ff      ;Clear out RC bits
          or         ah,bl         ;RC = round down
          xchg       ax,ctrl87
          fldcw      ctrl87        ;Set to round down
          frndint                  ;st = fix(x)
          mov        ctrl87,ax     ;Restore control word
          fldcw      ctrl87        ;Return to normal
          pop        bx
          ret
```

     The next group of instructions is a set of comparison instructions that compare two real numbers or two integers. The result of the comparison (greater than, less than, or equal to) is stored in two flag bits of the 8087's status word. The main purpose of these instructions is to allow programs to jump conditionally depending on the result of a floating-point calculation. You use these by executing one of the comparison instructions followed by an FSTSW instruction that stores the status word in memory. You then use normal 8088 instructions to examine the appropriate status word bits and make the appropriate program jump.

     Finally, there is a group of data transfer instructions and a group of processor control instructions (Table 4-6). Note that data transfers between the 8087 and memory involve only the register at the top of the stack. You have to use an additional register exchange instruction FXCH ST,ST(i) to load or store any other register. The processor control instructions largely provide control of the way errors are handled, saving and restoring the 8087's registers, and 8087 initialization.

Real Data Transfers	
FLD	load real
FST	store real
FSTP	store real and pop
FXCH	exchange registers

Integer Data Transfers	
FILD	integer load
FIST	integer store
FISTP	integer store and pop

BCD Data Transfers	
FBLD	BCD load
FBSTP	BCD store and pop

Processor Control	
FINIT	initialize 8087
FDISI	disable 8087 interrupts
FENI	enable 8087 interrupts
FLDCW	load control word
FSTCW	store control word
FSTSW	store status word
FCLEX	clear exceptions
FSTENV	store environment
FLDENV	load environment
FSAVE	save state
FRSTOR	restore state
FINCSTP	increment stack pointer
FDECSTP	decrement stack pointer
FFREE	free register
FNOP	no operation
FWAIT	CPU wait

Table 4—6. The 8087's data transfer and processor control instructions.

Overall the 8087 instruction set is flexible and well designed. The register stack concept is fairly efficient although it takes some skill to program effectively. One aspect of the 8087 that's not so nice is the relatively long time it takes to do a context switch—that is, the time required to save the state of the 8087 in memory and then load it up with a new set of values (94 bytes have to be saved, requiring about 43 microseconds). The 80286 CPU has hardware task switching facilities to get around this problem. On a task switch (protected mode only), the 80287 status is *not* saved. Should the 80287 be required by the new task, the 80286 executes an INT 7 (Processor Extension Not Available), which should save the current 80287 state and initialize it for the new task. In this way, the 80287 state is saved only if the 80287 is needed.

In other respects the 8087 is ideally designed for number-crunching calculations. A bugaboo that often arises in complicated calculations is loss of accuracy from an accumulation of round-off errors. The 8087 deals with this problem in two ways. First, it uses very precise 80-bit numbers for all calculations so that highly accurate results can be obtained even when a number of bits are lost through round-off errors. Second, in cases where the extent of round-off errors must be known, the 8087 allows a determination of their magnitude. Two bits in the 8087's control register determine how the rounding of numbers is done in each calculation, and these bits can be set by the programmer using the load control word (FLDCW) instruction. By doing all calculations twice, once with the 8087 set to always round upward, and once with the 8087 set to always round downward, the user can determine upper and lower bounds for the round-off error in a calculation.

Another problem in doing calculations that the 8087 handles beautifully is the problem of what to do when the result of a calculation is invalid. This occurs in cases such as division by zero, the use of an uninitialized memory location thought to contain a real number, an attempt to take the square root of a negative number, or the generation of a result too large to be represented. These situations inevitably arise, and you want the computer to handle them without either crashing the computer or, worse, having the calculation continue without any indication to the user that the results are garbage.

The 8087 deals with erroneous results in several ways. First, the 8087 sets one of six flags in the status word to indicate what kind of error has occurred. It then checks to see if the interrupt enable bit in the control word is zero. If not, the 8087 interrupts are said to be "masked" and no interrupt request is generated. In this case the 8087 generates a "special" number value. Special number values all have biased exponents of 111...11, that is, all ones. Two special number values are used to represent plus and minus infinity, and a third value is used to represent an indefinite result (for example, the logarithm of a negative number). The special value is placed into the appropriate 8087 register as the result of the calculation, and the 8087 continues on with the next instruction. However, the special number value gets propagated through subsequent calculations so that at the end you still have an infinity or an indefinite result. Furthermore, the error flags in the status word are "sticky bits," which means that once a flag is set, it cannot be cleared except by executing the special instruction FCLEX (clear exceptions) or reinitializing the 8087 with FINIT. Thus at the end of a calculation you can either check the status word to see if an error has occurred, or look at the result stored in memory to see if it's a special number type (for binary integers the only special number available is the largest negative number, 100...00).

Another alternative is for you to unmask 8087 interrupts by clearing the interrupt enable bit and the associated exception mask in the control word when the 8087 is initialized, and opening switch 2 of SW1 on the IBM PC system board. In this case the 8087 proceeds as above by setting a flag in the status word and generating a special number value as the result. However, it then generates an interrupt request on its INT line before proceeding to the next instruction. This allows you to write your own exception handlers if you want to. In the IBM PC, the INT line is connected to the 8088's NMI line (see Sec. 6-1) so that an INT 2 is generated. Be sure to take over this interrupt and allow for RAM parity check errors, which also cause NMI interrupts. (The standard parity check error response can be found in the ROM BIOS listing given in IBM's *Technical Reference* manual.)

The beauty of the 8087's error responses is that they give the user great flexibility. If you don't want to think about errors at all, you can just ignore them, and the computer won't crash. The next step is simply to examine the status word at the end of a calculation, and to throw out the result if an error flag is set. Finally, if you really want to get in there and take control, you can unmask the 8087's interrupts and handle each error individually in any way you choose.

References

D. J. Bradley, 1984, *Assembly Language Programming for the IBM Personal Computer*, Prentice-Hall, Englewood Cliffs, NJ. Provides excellent in-depth discussions of assembly language programming using the IBM Macro Assembler. Also contains a fine chapter on the 8087.

L. Scanlon, 1983, *IBM PC Assembly Language*, Robert J. Brady Company, Bowie, MD. Good introductory discussion of assembly language and the use of the IBM Macro Assembler.

D. Willen and J. Krantz, 1983, *8088 Assembler Language Programming: The IBM PC*, Howard W. Sams and Company, Indianapolis, IN. Introductory discussions of assembly language, use of the IBM Macro Assembler, and the hardware of the PC. Presentations are good but very brief.

Intel Corporation, 1981, *iAPX 86,88 User's Manual*, Intel Corporation, Santa Clara, CA. This manual contains a 109-page chapter on the 8087, and is the authoritative source for information about the 8087 chip. This book is a must if you're going to work seriously with the 8087.

R. Startz, 1983, *8087 Applications and Programming for the IBM PC and other PCs*, Robert J. Brady Company, Bowie, MD. This book is devoted entirely to the 8087 and contains a detailed discussion of the 8087 instruction set and its use in assembly language programming.

T. Field, 1983, "The IBM PC and the Intel 8087 Coprocessor," *BYTE* magazine, Vol. 8, No. 8, p. 331. This article provides macro definitions for all the 8087 instructions and a discussion of floating-point number format conversions.

J. E. Roskos, 1984, "Writing Device Drivers for MS-DOS 2.0 Using Tandon TM100-4 Drives", *BYTE* magazine, Vol. 9, No. 2, p. 370. Provides a clear description of how to write and debug a device driver for block I/O devices.

G. Young, 1980, *Digital Electronics: A Hands-On Learning Approach*, Hayden Book Company, Rochelle Park, NJ. This book is a good self-teaching guide to digital electronics, with many practical construction hints and a chapter on troubleshooting.

5
Introduction to
Digital Circuitry

*Any sufficiently advanced technology is
indistinguishable from magic.*
—A. C. Clarke

Unless you have a background in electrical engineering or solid state physics, you may think it's beyond your ability to comprehend how the electrical circuitry in a digital computer works. Actually, the basic building blocks from which computers are constructed are quite simple and easy to understand. Computers are complicated primarily because they contain so many of these building blocks. In this chapter we explain the basic digital logic circuits, showing you how they're made, what their properties are, and how they're used.

Even if you're never going to build any digital circuitry or computer interfaces yourself, you'll find that knowing the basics of what's going on electrically inside the machine is very useful when you're trying to decide which add-on card or computer peripheral to buy. In addition, if you ever plan to write or modify software drivers for devices like a printer or a serial link, you'll find that an understanding of how digital circuitry works is essential.

The key element in understanding how a computer's hardware works is to use the appropriate level of abstraction for the piece of circuitry being considered. If you want to understand how a simple logic gate works, it may be appropriate to consider how the transistors making up the gate behave. But if you want to understand how a one-shot or a shift register works, it's much more useful to consider their operation in terms of the logic gates from which they're constructed, not in terms of the individual transistors inside them. Once you know how a few of the logic gates work inside, it's no longer necessary to look at every logic gate in detail. You know they all operate in roughly the same way, and you can just use them as your basic elements. Similarly, once you understand how a few basic counters and registers work, you can understand how a more complex large-scale integrated circuit like an asynchronous serial port works in terms of counters and registers.

We adopt this point of view here, and start by explaining the elementary facts you need to know about diodes and transistors (and no more!), then show how logic gates are made from transistors, how more complex circuits are built up from elementary logic gates, and so on.

5-1. Diodes and Transistors

A diode is one of the neatest inventions to come along and a beautiful example of certain effects in semiconductor physics. However, for most purposes, you don't need to understand the semiconductor physics going on inside; you can just treat a diode like a black (or maybe translucent) box with certain properties. The basic thing you need to know about it is that it's a tiny electrical device that passes current in only one direction, as shown in Fig. 5-1. It's usually made from two tiny pieces of silicon contacted together. One piece has been chemically treated so it has an excess of mobile electrons (electrons that are relatively free to move about) and is called n-type silicon (electrons have a negative charge and the "n" stands for negative). The other piece is treated to produce a deficiency of mobile electrons and is called p-type silicon (the "p" stands for positive).

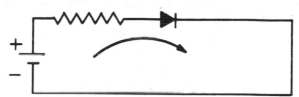

Fig. 5-1. Diode passes current from + to –. A resistor is needed to limit the current flowing through the diode.

Note that, by convention, current is said to flow from positive to negative, whereas in reality what is happening is that electrons are flowing from negative to positive. This unfortunate state of affairs is due to Benjamin Franklin, who picked the current convention before the existence of electrons was known. He had two equally plausible possibilities to pick from but chose the wrong one (Murphy's law strikes again!). Actually, in semiconductor physics, the absence of an electron, a "hole" in the electron sea, moves around and has a positive charge. So perhaps Ben had the forth-coming microelectronics revolution in mind.

When the two pieces of silicon are put together, a potential barrier (voltage drop) forms at the junction between the two pieces that allows electrons to flow from the n-type material into the p-type, but prevents them from flowing in the reverse direction from p into n. Thus when a voltage is applied to the diode that makes the p-type end more positive than the n-type end, electrons can flow from n into p and hence a current flows through the diode. But if the n-type end is made more positive, the poten-tial barrier prevents electrons from flowing from p into n and hence no current flows through the diode. Think of the barrier as a step. The elec-trons can easily roll off the top of the step and go down, but they cannot do the reverse and roll up. From now on, to avoid further confusion, we just talk about current and ignore what the electrons are doing whenever possible.

As shown in Fig. 5-1, the electrical symbol for a diode resembles an arrow pointing in the direction that current can flow through it. The p-type end of the diode is called the anode, and the n-type end is called the cathode. To use the diode, you can't just hook up a power supply such as a battery across it and let current flow through it. If you do, a tremendous surge of current will pass through and probably blow the diode up. The problem is that when the diode is forward biased—that is, when the anode is at a more positive voltage than the cathode—the diode looks like a short circuit plus a fixed voltage drop of about 0.7 volt (this drop is due to the internal potential barrier at the p-n junction). To prevent too much current from flowing, you need to put a resistor in series with the diode, as shown in Fig. 5-1.

The diode's behavior can be more precisely represented by an I-V curve (a plot of the current, I, versus the voltage, V), as shown in Fig. 5-2. Notice that the current is very nonlinear, and becomes tremendous if a

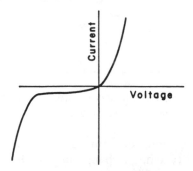

Fig. 5-2. An I-V curve for a diode. A large current flows when the voltage difference across the diode is positive, or when it's negative and exceeds the breakdown voltage.

positive voltage difference across the diode exceeds 0.7 volt. For a negative voltage difference, almost no current flows unless the voltage exceeds the so-called *breakdown voltage*. A negative voltage of this value causes an internal short in the diode, and it can destroy the device if too much current flows. Note that the diode's behavior is very different from that of a resistor. A resistor would give a straight line on the I-V curve since it obeys Ohm's law, $V = IR$, where R is the resistance. The typical diodes used for logic and display can handle 10 to 20 milliamperes (mA) of current easily, so for a 5-volt supply, a 330-ohm series resistor limits the current through the diode to a reasonable value [Ohm's law gives $V/R = (5 - 0.7)/330 = 13$ mA].

One of the most useful types of diodes is an LED (a light emitting diode), which produces light when it's forward biased so that a current passes through it. Most LED's produce a distinctive red color, although they can also be obtained in amber and green. The red indicator lights seen on computer disk drives and the red seven-segment displays on hand calculators are all LED's. Note that even when properly current-limited, LED's should not be pushed into reverse breakdown, since this diminishes their light output over time. A reverse direction diode in parallel with the LED can prevent this from happening.

As a simple experiment, connect an LED in series with a 330-ohm resistor to a 5-volt supply and see how light is emitted for one orientation of the diode, and not emitted for the other. This little circuit makes a convenient probe for logic circuits (see Fig. 5-3). If the LED cathode is touched to some point in a circuit, the LED lights up if the voltage at that point is less than about a volt or two. The LED remains dark if the voltage is greater than this value. What you've got here is a one-bit binary digital voltmeter!

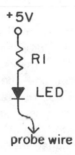

Fig. 5-3. LED logic indicator circuit.

In addition to LED's, there are logic diodes such as the 1N4148 or its equivalent, the 1N914 (reminds one of a Porsche!). These are used simply to ensure that the current in some circuit can flow in only one direction. There are also much heftier diodes, which are used to make the DC power supplies needed for computers and other electronic equipment. They take the alternating-polarity 110 volts that comes out of the sockets in your wall and convert it to a unidirectional DC voltage.

Although diodes are clearly very useful, an even more important related device is the transistor. The simplest description of a transistor is that it's a pair of diodes hooked back to back so they share a common end. More precisely, it consists of either two n-type regions separated by a thin p-type region (this is called an NPN transistor), or two p-type regions separated by a thin n-type region (a PNP transistor). The two n-type regions (p-type for a PNP) are actually not quite identical; one is called the collector and the other the emitter, as shown in Fig. 5-4. The central p-type region (n-type for a PNP) is called the base. This device doesn't sound very exciting, but such an arrangement has an amazing property. When you forward bias the transistor's base-to-emitter p-n junction so that current flows through that little p-n diode, a much larger current can flow through the entire transistor from the collector to the emitter. If you turn off the little base-emitter current, the collector-emitter current is completely turned off, and the transistor is said to be *cut off*. Thus the transistor is an amplifier: a small base-emitter current controls a larger collector-emitter current.

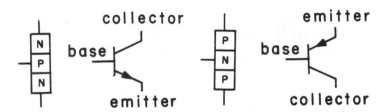

Fig. 5–4. Diagrams of NPN and PNP transistors.

Over a certain range of small base-emitter currents, the collector-emitter current is linearly proportional to the input base-emitter current so that the transistor faithfully amplifies small currents into larger ones. This is the way transistors are used in radios and hi-fi amplifiers. For larger base-emitter currents, however, the transistor acts as if there is nearly a short circuit between the collector and the emitter, and the transistor is said to be in *saturation*. In all but the fastest computers, transistors are used in a very simple fashion. They are simply switched back and forth between cut-off and saturation, and hence just act as switches to turn a current on or off and thereby to change an output voltage from low to high. Consider the simple circuit shown in Fig. 5-5. If the input voltage is held at zero volts, the p-n base-emitter junction has no current flowing through it and thus no current flows from collector to emitter. As a result, there is no voltage drop across resistor R (the drop is $V = IR$, but $I = 0$), and the output voltage is +5 volts. If we raise the input voltage to any value between about +2 and +5 volts, however, a base-emitter current flows, and this in turn allows a collector-emitter current to flow. If the base resistor R_b is chosen to be a value around 1000 ohms, then the base-emitter current is

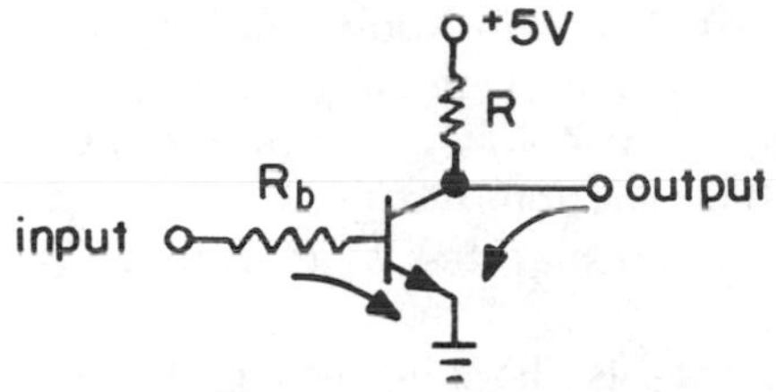

Fig. 5-5. An NPN transistor used as a switch. A positive voltage on the base turns on the transistor and pulls the output low (to about 0.5 volt). If the positive input voltage is removed, the transistor is turned off and the output is high (+5 volts).

large enough to saturate the transistor so that it looks almost as if there is a short circuit between the collector and the emitter. A current then flows through resistor R, and the output voltage is pulled down nearly to ground (it's typically at about 0.5 volt because the transistor still has a small resistance of a few ohms between collector and emitter).

In short, for digital applications, the transistor is simply a current-controlled switch. The PNP transistor works in the same way as the NPN transistor except that the base has to have a negative voltage with respect to the emitter in order to turn on the transistor. There are basic principles of semiconductor physics behind all of this, but for this discussion, all you have to know about transistors is this simple switching behavior.

5-2. TTL Gates—AND, NAND, OR, NOR, XOR

Before we show how transistors can be used to build digital logic gates, let us first take a look at what a TTL logic gate is. An excellent source of additional information on this subject is Lancaster's *TTL Cookbook* (see especially Chaps. 1 and 2).

TTL is an acronym for transistor-transistor logic. You will see the reason for this name in the next section. A logic gate is just something with inputs and outputs that performs a logic function. If you've already learned about the 8080's logic instructions (see Sec. 3-9), you'll find it easy to get on board with TTL. This logic family (a group of parts that can all be connected to each other) puts into hardware what you often do in programming. TTL gates use a DC 5-volt power supply regulated to within 5% (+ or - 0.25 volt), and are housed in DIP's (dual inline packages) having 14, 16, 18, 20, 22, or 24 pins arranged in two parallel rows. The ground pin is usually the last in the first row (for example, pin 7 of a 14-pin DIP), and the 5-volt power pin is the highest numbered pin (pin 14 on the 14-pin DIP). This is not always the case, though (for example, the 7490), so beware! A DIP package is often referred to as an IC, short for integrated circuit. TTL gates are identified by part numbers that have the form 74XX, where the XX is a number that tells which gate you're talking about. The inputs and outputs of TTL gates are either high (a voltage typically between 3 and 5 volts) or low (typically 0 to 0.7 volt). These voltages are abbreviated by H and L, respectively. The function of a TTL gate is typically given by a table called a truth table that enumerates what outputs (H's or L's) result for given inputs (H's or L's).

The simplest logic gate is the 7404 hex inverter, which comes with six inverters in a single DIP package, as pictured in Fig. 5-6. Inverters could also be called NOT gates since that's the logical function they perform. What's shown here is the standard logic symbol for each inverter (a triangle with a small circle on the output end) superimposed on an outline drawing of the DIP package. Each inverter converts an H into an L and an L into an H, as seen in the trivial truth table.

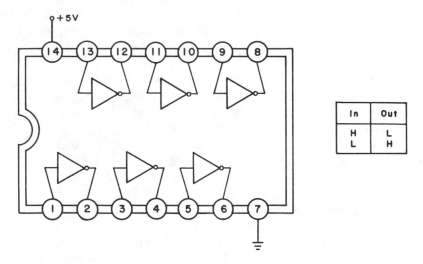

In	Out
H	L
L	H

Fig. 5-6. 7404 TTL hex inverter and its truth table. It's called a "hex" inverter because there are six inverters in the package.

Another logic gate is the 7408 AND gate, which has four gates per package. This gate and its truth table are pictured in Fig. 5-7. If both inputs are H, the output is H. If either input or both are L, the output is L. A useful variation of the AND gate is the 7400 NAND gate shown in Fig. 5-8. This gate simply adds an inverter to the output of an AND gate (the N in NAND stands for NOT). Thus if both inputs are H, the output is L, while if either or both inputs are L, the output is H. Notice that the NAND gate logic symbol differs from the AND gate symbol only by the addition of a small circle on the output. In logic diagrams the small circle universally stands for inversion of an output (or sometimes of an input).

The 7432 OR gate is pictured in Fig. 5-9. If either input is H, the output is H. If both inputs are L, the output is L. Notice the difference in

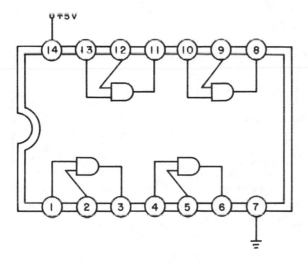

In 1	In 2	Out
L	L	L
L	H	L
H	L	L
H	H	H

Fig. 5–7. 7408 quad 2–input AND gate and its truth table.

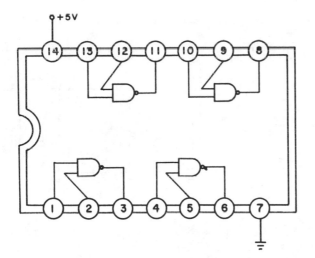

In 1	In 2	Out
L	L	H
L	H	H
H	L	H
H	H	L

Fig. 5–8. 7400 quad 2–input NAND gate and its truth table.

the shape of the logic symbols for the OR gate and the AND gate. The OR gate also has a popular NOR version, the 7402 shown in Fig. 5-10.

An important point to note is that exchanging H and L in the preceding descriptions exchanges the functions of the AND and the OR. Said another way, a positive logic AND is a negative logic OR. Negative logic here just means that the meanings of H and L have been reversed. This fact is very useful in reducing the number of IC's (DIP packages) required in a design, and typically the logic flow switches back and forth between negative and positive logic. This makes understanding the circuit diagrams a bit harder, but the result is cheaper and more compact.

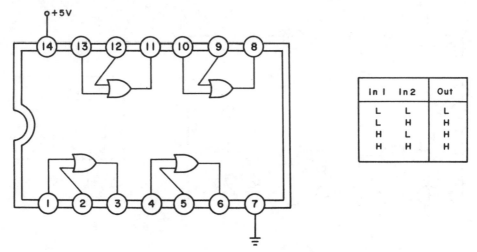

In I	In 2	Out
L	L	L
L	H	H
H	L	H
H	H	H

Fig. 5–9. 7432 quad 2–input OR gate and its truth table.

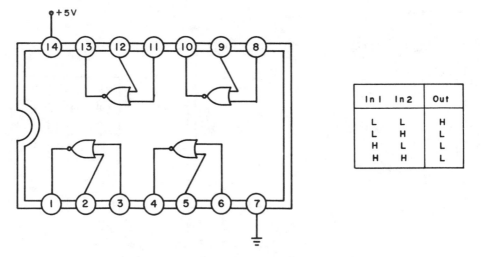

In I	In 2	Out
L	L	H
L	H	L
H	L	L
H	H	L

Fig. 5–10. 7402 quad 2–input NOR gate and its truth table.

The final elementary logic gate is the 7486 XOR (exclusive OR) gate shown in Fig. 5-11. Its output is H if the inputs are different and L if they are the same. Note that the XOR gate can be made into an inverter by simply connecting one of the inputs to +5 volts. Similarly, the NAND and NOR gates can be used as inverters if desired by tying both NAND or NOR inputs together. This often allows you to reduce the IC count in a circuit, as extra gates may be used in place of adding another 7404 inverter. Having a few extra gates left over in a design is not that bad, since they may be handy if custom modifications become called for.

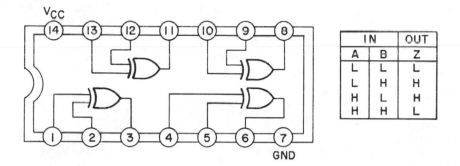

IN		OUT
A	B	Z
L	L	L
L	H	H
H	L	H
H	H	L

Fig. 5-11. 7486 quad 2-input XOR gate and its truth table.

You've now seen all the elementary logic gate functions. As you've no doubt noticed, these gates perform in hardware the same logic operations NOT, AND, OR, and XOR that the 8088 CPU performs in software. Also, just as useful programs are made from combinations of instructions, so combinations of these elementary gates can be built up to perform all kinds of useful functions.

5-3. TTL Input/Output Characteristics

Now that you know what logic gates are, let's examine how they are built from the basic transistors discussed in Sec. 5-1. Figure 5-12 shows a schematic of the internal circuitry of a single NAND gate in a 7400 IC. As you can see, it's a fairly simple circuit, containing just four transistors. The input transistor Q1 looks a little strange because it has two emitters, but

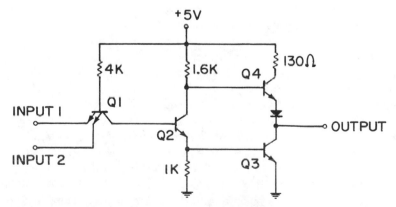

Fig. 5-12. Circuit diagram for a TTL NAND gate. The resistor values are given in kilohms (kΩ, or sometimes just K).

there is nothing mysterious about this. The base region of the transistor is just contacted to two n-type emitter regions instead of one, and each has its own wire connected to it.

To see how the gate works, suppose that both inputs either are not connected or are pulled high by being connected to a voltage source of 3 to 5 volts. In this situation there is not enough base-emitter current flowing in transistor Q1 to turn it on. Instead, the base-collector junction is forward biased by the voltage at the base of Q1, and this base-collector current turns on transistor Q2. When Q2 is turned on, a base-emitter current can flow through Q3 also, so it's turned on. At the same time, Q4 is turned off, because the current through Q2 and hence through the base-emitter of Q3 causes the base of Q4 to be held at a voltage of about 1 volt. This is not sufficient to turn Q4 on, because the emitter of Q4 is at a voltage of about 1.2 volts (there is a 0.5-volt drop across Q3 plus a 0.7-volt drop across the diode between Q4 and Q3). Thus Q4 is turned off, Q3 is turned on, and the voltage at the output is low, about 0.5 volt.

Now suppose that either or both of the inputs are connected to ground or are pulled low by being connected to a source that holds the input voltage between 0 and 0.5 volt. When this occurs, the Q1 base-emitter junction is turned on and hence current can no longer flow into the base of Q2. As a result, Q2 turns off. This causes Q3 to turn off, because no base-emitter current can flow, and at the same time causes Q4 to turn on, because now its base is connected to 5 volts through the 1.6-kΩ resistor. Thus Q3 is off, Q4 is on, and the output is held somewhere between 3 and 5 volts.

To summarize, the output of this gate is high (3 to 5 volts) if either or both inputs are low (0 to 0.5 volt). If both inputs are high, the output is low. Thus the gate performs the logical function of a NAND gate as can be seen from the truth table in Fig. 5-8. Now that you've seen how a NAND gate works inside, there's not much point in examining how other gates work internally because they're simply variations on this basic design. For example, if you take away the second emitter on Q1, the gate becomes an inverter. If you add an inverting stage to the NAND gate, you get an AND gate. What is really important to understand are the characteristics of the input and output circuitry of the gate.

Figure 5-13 shows standard TTL input and output circuits. The diode on the input circuit is there for protection against power surges or negative input voltages. In the previous discussion, holding an input at a voltage between 0 and 0.5 volt was said to pull the input low. This is only half the story, though, since to hold an input at that voltage requires current to flow out of the input transistor's base-emitter diode. In particular, to persuade a TTL input to be low, the output of a gate connected to it must be able to sink 1.6 mA; that is, 1.6 mA must flow into it. For this reason, TTL is called current-sinking logic. If you connect the totem pole output of a gate (it's called that because the two transistors are stacked on top of each other) to another gate's input, the totem pole output is easily able to sink 1.6 mA

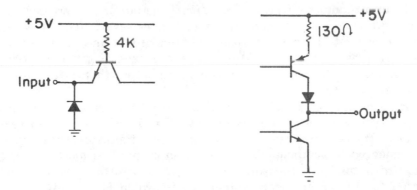

Fig. 5–13. Typical TTL input and output circuits. The standard output circuit shown here is called a totem pole output.

when it's low because the lower transistor is turned on and thus can conduct a fair amount of current.

On the other hand, to persuade a TTL input to be high takes almost no effort at all. In fact, an unconnected TTL input goes high all by itself, although you shouldn't count on this, because noise spikes can cause a floating input to go low momentarily. When the high totem pole output of a gate is connected to a TTL input, it pulls the input up solidly, and in fact a high totem pole output can "source" current (provide an output current) because the upper transistor is turned on.

The upshot of all this is that TTL gates can be connected directly to each other, outputs to inputs. This makes it very easy to connect gates to one another to build up complex functions. In fact, the name TTL comes from this. When you connect an output to an input, you connect output transistors directly to input transistors, hence the name transistor-transistor logic.

There are a couple of potential problems when TTL gates are hooked together that you should be aware of. First, if you connect too many other inputs to a single output, it has to sink more current than it can handle. The specification is that a low TTL output can sink ten TTL inputs. Also, never connect two TTL outputs together. If one goes high and the other goes low, you will have effectively shorted the 5-volt power supply to ground. Typically the output transistors are sturdy enough that a brief output short won't hurt anything, but your circuit certainly won't do what you want it to do. The second problem is that, if you use a TTL output to drive an LED, you should always sink current with standard TTL (point the LED diode toward the TTL output pin) and not source it (point the diode away from the pin), since the current-sourcing capability of the upper totem pole output transistor is about ten times smaller than the current-sinking capabilities of the lower totem pole transistor.

What has been described so far are standard TTL inputs and outputs. So what is nonstandard? Lots. In particular, many IC's in the 7400 series take higher input or output voltages for special applications, and certain so-called bus driver IC's (which can drive signals over several feet of wire) can sink larger amounts of current than the standard 16 mA, and can source large currents as well. In addition there are several different types of output circuits besides the standard totem pole output that we'd like to look at in a bit more detail.

First, a number of TTL IC's are available with *open-collector* outputs. This type of output circuit is shown in Fig. 5-14. As you can see, the output circuitry here consists of just a single NPN transistor whose collector is not connected to anything! To use such an output you must connect the collector to a *pull-up* resistor. This is just a resistor that has one end connected to the power supply voltage as shown in Fig. 5-14. With the pull-up resistor connected, the output can swing between 0.5 volt and the power supply voltage, depending on whether the output transistor is turned on or off. The neat thing about this kind of output is that several of them can be connected together. If any one of the outputs feels like sinking current, it can; you get a free n-gate negative logic OR by just connecting a bunch of open-collector outputs together. In the old days (or now too, if you're using old backplanes such as those on the Data General Eclipse and Nova computers, or Digital Equipment Corporation's old PDP 11 series of computers), the open collectors were used to drive the bus lines that connected the various computer boards to each other. The lines are all high until some selected board sticks some lows on the bus. The idea is that only one board drives the bus at a time, although that is a logical, rather than a physical, restriction. Newer computer systems use tristate outputs, as explained next. The open collector is also valuable for sinking currents through loads requiring higher voltages. For example, the 7406 open-collector inverter can withstand being pulled up to 30 volts.

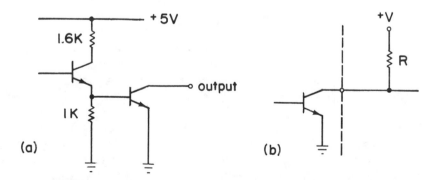

Fig. 5–14. (a) An open-collector TTL output. Note that no current-sourcing PNP transistor is present. (b) An open-collector output connected to an external pull-up resistor.

Modern computer systems rely heavily on a type of TTL output known as a *tristate output*. These devices have three output states. If you're not familiar with them, you're probably wondering what on earth we are talking about. We've been saying that logic gates have just two output levels, low and high, and now we're introducing something with three output states? Fortunately the answer to this puzzle is very simple. The third output state is a disconnected, or high impedance, state. The existence of this disconnected state allows you to wire several tristate TTL outputs together, something that is a no-no for standard TTL totem pole outputs.

A tristate output works by having an additional enable line present as shown in Fig. 5-15. If the enable line is high, the output is effectively disconnected from the outside world, and if the enable line is pulled low, the output is a normal TTL high or low voltage level. The shorthand way to describe this situation is to say that the enable line is *active low*. Logic gates called *buffers* commonly have tristate outputs. Buffers simply transmit the logic level present at the input to the output. A high input gives a high output, and a low input gives a low output. With tristate outputs, many outputs can be connected together as with open-collector systems, but substantially less power is involved. The only catch is that the logic driving the enable signals must allow only one of the gates connected together to be enabled at any one time, or there will be a fight. This style of output is very valuable for computer systems, which by their very natures have many devices all wanting to talk to the microprocessor.

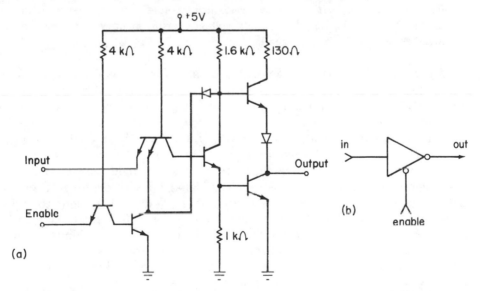

Fig. 5-15. (a) Circuit diagram for a tristate TTL inverter. (b) Logic symbol for a tristate inverter. The small circle on the enable line indicates that it's active when low.

In addition to the standard TTL input, there is also a Schmitt trigger input. To see how it works, consider a simple logic gate like a 7404 inverter. A plot of the output voltage versus the input voltage for this gate, which has a normal TTL input, is shown in Fig. 5-16a. As the input voltage is raised from zero, the output stays high. However, when the input voltage hits about 1.4 volts, the output switches sharply from high to low. Similarly, as the input voltage is lowered from 5 volts, the output stays low until 1.4 volts is reached, at which point the output switches suddenly to high.

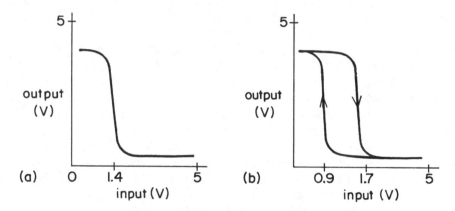

Fig. 5–16. (a) Output voltage versus input voltage for an inverter with a standard TTL input. (b) Output voltage versus input voltage for an inverter with a Schmitt trigger input.

Figure 5-16b shows the same type of plot for a Schmitt trigger input. In this case the point at which the output changes state depends upon the current state of the output. If the output is high, it doesn't go low until the input voltage is raised above 1.7 volts. However, if the output is low, it won't go high until the input falls below 0.9 volt. The technical term for this type of behavior is *hysteresis*. Having a Schmitt trigger input becomes very useful when you have to deal with logic signals that have noise superimposed on them. As a noisy signal goes through the transition region around 1.4 volts, the noise can cause a standard TTL input to switch back and forth from high to low several times when only a single high to low change was desired. The hysteresis in the Schmitt trigger input prevents this. Schmitt trigger inputs are also very useful for making clean square waves from slowly varying signals—for example, for making a nice 60-Hz square wave out of the powerline sine wave.

A good example of an IC with a Schmitt trigger input is the 7414 hex inverter shown in Fig. 5-17. Several very useful IC's incorporate both Schmitt trigger inputs and tristate outputs. One example is the 74LS244 octal tristate buffer shown in Fig. 5-18. We explain below what the "LS" in this part number means. The Schmitt trigger gives good noise immunity on

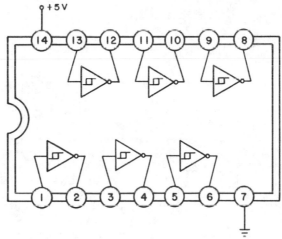

Fig. 5–17. 7414 hex Schmitt trigger inverter. The presence of a Schmitt trigger input is shown by placing a little hysteresis curve inside the logic symbol for the device.

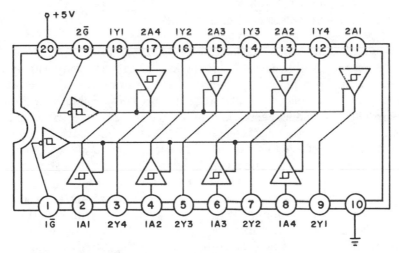

Fig. 5–18. 74LS244 octal tristate buffer. It has Schmitt trigger inputs and can both source and sink considerable current. The Schmitt trigger hysteresis is about 0.4 volt, half that of the 7414.

the input, while the outputs can sink 40 mA and source 10 mA, enough to drive an LED directly. Another useful tristate buffer is the bidirectional 74LS245 shown in Fig. 5-19. This IC is particularly handy for driving and reading an 8-bit bidirectional data bus (a set of eight wires on which logic signals travel in two directions, both into and out from a microprocessor).

In addition to the standard 74XX series of logic gates, which include literally hundreds of different parts, there are other families of TTL logic gates that have different power requirements, switching speeds, and/or

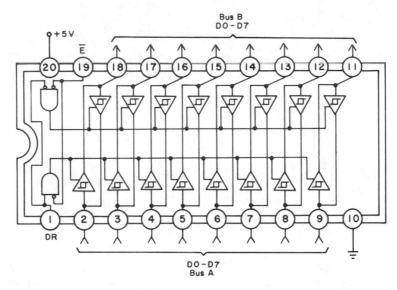

Fig. 5–19. 74LS245 octal bidirectional tristate buffer with Schmitt-trigger inputs (about 0.4 volt hysteresis). This IC is very useful for driving microcomputer bidirectional data lines.

output drive capabilities. The most important by far is the 74LSXX series, where "LS" stands for low-power Schottky. The LS family is pin for pin compatible with the original 74XX series, requires one-fifth the power (only 0.4 mA is needed to pull an input low), and has comparable switching times (on the order of 20 nanoseconds). An LS output can typically drive up to five standard TTL inputs. For complete TTL part specifications, consult any of the TTL data books published by the various semiconductor manufacturers. One of these books is a necessary part of any digital designer's library. In general, you should use LS rather than standard TTL, to reduce power consumption. Also, unused LS inputs can be tied directly to the 5-volt supply, whereas with standard TTL this may cause trouble (the military practice is to use a 1-kΩ pull-up resistor). Currently, in fact, LS is the de facto standard logic family, and the original 74XX family is obsolete.

In using either standard or LS TTL, an output can drive ten inputs of the same family. However, LS can typically drive only five standard TTL inputs, bus drivers like the 74LS244 excepted. When in doubt, consult a TTL data book.

There are a number of other logic families as well. One that is worth mentioning is the 74CXX series. The "C" stands for CMOS (complementary metal oxide semiconductor). These circuits require phenomenally low power by TTL standards and don't require accurate power supplies (typically, anything between 3 and 15 volts does fine). However, they switch substantially more slowly than TTL, can be damaged by static electricity, and have considerably less drive power. A newer version of this family, 74HCTXX, has faster switching speeds and can be intermixed with TTL parts.

To end this section, a few remarks on power supplies are perhaps in order. First, if you're wiring up your own circuits, it's good practice to connect a 0.1-µF capacitor (µF is the standard abbreviation for microfarad) between the 5-volt supply and ground near every second TTL package. When a TTL gate switches, it draws a burst of current, which can wreak havoc with other IC's unless there are enough of these so-called decoupling or bypass capacitors distributed around the circuit. A related principle is that there should be a bypass capacitor connecting a path of no more than 3 inches between the power and ground pins of a given IC. If you find a board on which this principle is badly violated, it may not work reliably.

Another handy thing to know is that you can get a 1-ampere, 5-volt power supply for TTL circuits very simply by using a 7805 three-terminal IC. Figure 5-20 shows the schematic of a power supply for TTL circuitry built with this part. The transformer reduces the voltage of the 110-volt alternating current coming out of your wall socket to about 12 volts, and the diodes convert this 12 volts AC into a steady DC current. The 7805 then reduces this to a precise, constant 5 volts, regardless of the load on the output. You should mount the 7805 on a heat sink, as it gets quite hot. The 7805 is just one member of a family of 78XX positive-voltage regulators. A corresponding 79XX family of negative-voltage regulators also exists.

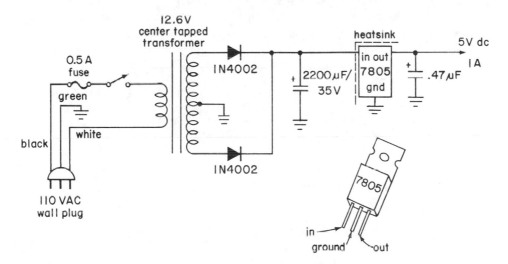

Fig. 5-20. A regulated 5-volt power supply for TTL circuits.

Voltage regulators are based on special diodes, called Zener diodes, which have precise reverse-biased breakdown voltages (see Fig. 5-2 for an illustration of breakdown voltage). These diodes can be used directly for power supplies with small current requirements. Connect one in series with a current-limiting resistor against the current flow, opposite to the arrangement in Fig. 5-1. The Zener-diode-resistor combination then provides a precise voltage if the current drawn is sufficiently small. A series Zener diode can also be used as a precise voltage drop device. For example, pointing a 3-volt Zener toward a regulated +15 volts gives a regulated +12 volts, provided the current flow is within the Zener's rating.

5-4. Flip-Flops

No, flip-flops aren't to wear. Rather, they are one of the most important building blocks in digital electronics. Some people think everything is black or white, no grays. Such an attitude is binary: on or off. A flip-flop is the way to store such a state of mind. It's a device that stores two states: on or off, high or low. In short, it's a one-bit memory. Figure 5-21 shows one way to make a flip-flop out of two 7400 NAND gates. When you ground the left terminal, the output goes low since both inputs to the right gate go high. Conversely, grounding the right terminal causes the output to go high. Leaving the switch in the middle leaves the output the way it was last. This interesting fact allows the circuit of Fig. 5-21 to function as a *bounceless switch*. When you close the mechanical switch, it bounces up and down several times before settling down to stay. But that first bounce grounds an input and is sufficient to switch the output regardless of further bounces on the contact. Note also that a TTL pulse going from high to low and back can be used to flip the flip-flop as well as a switch. So this circuit can be used by other electronic circuits as well as by human beings.

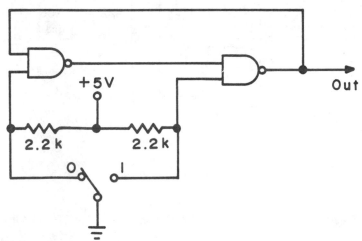

Fig. 5-21. A set—reset flip—flop made out of 7400 gates. This circuit debounces a switch or can be driven by TTL pulses instead of a switch.

You may not have much use for people with binary opinions, but virtually everything in computers is built on binary information. By grouping together the outputs of many flip-flops, we can make arbitrarily fine gradations of gray. A prime example is a register, such as those found in the

8088 CPU. As mentioned in Chap. 2, a 16-bit register is just a set of 16 flip-flops and can contain any one of 65,536 different numbers. The flip-flop is also used extensively to indicate the status of a device. When a keyboard wants to tell the computer it has a character, or when a 60-Hz clock wants to signal the next tick, it sets a flip-flop that either interrupts the computer (see Chap. 7) or is polled (looked at) by the computer periodically. Suffice it to say that flip-flops are indispensable to the whole arena of computer operation.

Although the circuit in Fig. 5-21 is very instructive and is even used occasionally in digital circuitry, a much more common and useful flip-flop is the edge-triggered D flip-flop of Fig. 5-22. This circuit comes two per package in the 7474. This type of flip-flop has an input called D, two outputs Q and $\overline{Q}$ ($\overline{Q}$ is the inverted value of Q), additional set and clear inputs, and a clock input. If the set line is pulled low and the clear (Cr) line is high, Q goes high regardless of what the other input signals do. If the clear line is pulled low and the set line is high, Q goes low no matter what. These inputs are analogous to the switch positions in Fig. 5-21. Ground one input and the flip-flop is forced into one state. Ground the other and the flip-flop goes into the other state. The active level—that is, the do-something level—of these inputs is low, so they're called active-low inputs. In addition, we have the D Input and the clock. The standard mode of operation is to have the clear and set inputs high (not active), so that a transition of the clock input from low to high (called a positive edge) *clocks* the value of D into Q and the inverse of D into $\overline{Q}$. The clock transition is required; D can do anything it wants to, but nothing happens to Q and $\overline{Q}$ until a positive edge occurs on the clock line.

The D-type flip-flop can be used in several ways. One way is as a memory element. Q and $\overline{Q}$ tell whatever is connected to them what value was clocked in. If you want to turn on an LED from your computer to

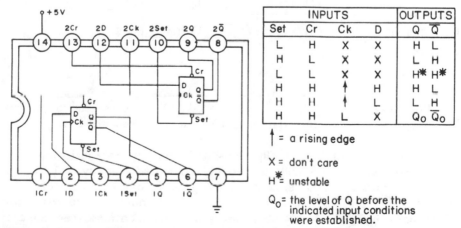

	INPUTS			OUTPUTS	
Set	Cr	Ck	D	Q	$\overline{Q}$
L	H	X	X	H	L
H	L	X	X	L	H
L	L	X	X	H*	H*
H	H	↑	H	H	L
H	H	↑	L	L	H
H	H	L	X	Q_0	$\overline{Q}_0$

↑ = a rising edge

X = don't care

H* = unstable

Q_0 = the level of Q before the indicated input conditions were established.

Fig. 5-22. 7474 D-type positive-edge triggered flip-flop and its truth table. It has a clocked mode as well as set/reset capability.

signal that an event has occurred, you can connect a data line from the computer to the D input of the flip-flop and then have the computer send a pulse on another line to the clock input. When the clock pulse goes from low to high, the state of the data line is clocked into the flip-flop and appears at the Q output. Often you want to use eight flip-flops at a time because the 8088 has eight data lines. The 74LS374 answers this need with eight flip-flops in a single 20-pin DIP package as shown in Fig. 5-23. The chip is called an octal latch because data are *latched* (stored) into all eight flip-flops at once by a single clock line. This is very useful for outputting a byte of data from your computer. What you do with the outputs is up to you. The IBM PC parallel printer port uses the 74LS374 for the data output. As you will see in Sec. 9-1, a low bit can easily turn on 20 amperes at 277 volts! (admittedly with the help of a relay or two). Now maybe you start to see why this micro stuff can feed nascent hungers for power! The 74LS373 is the same as the 74LS374, except that the clock line is replaced by a special enable line. While low, this latch passes the data level values straight through, just like a 74LS244 buffer. When the enable line goes high, the input values are latched, maintaining these values for the outputs until the enable returns low. This combination of modes gives the 74LS373 the name *transparent latch*. It's used to demultiplex the address-data lines for the 8088 microprocessor, as discussed in Sec. 6-1.

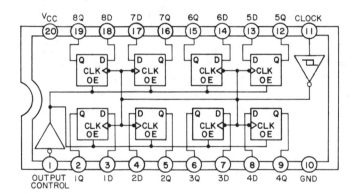

OUTPUT CONTROL	CLOCK	D	OUTPUT
L	↑	H	H
L	↑	L	L
L	L	X	Q_0
H	X	X	Z

Fig. 5-23. The 74LS374 clocked octal latch. A very useful IC for computer output, with tristate output control and substantial drive power.

Large arrays of D-type flip-flops with appropriate addressing circuitry are placed on a single chip to provide computer memory. This type of memory is called *static* in contrast to *dynamic* memory, which is substantially cheaper and less power hungry (it requires only one transistor per bit of memory instead of six), but has some complications (see Sec. 6-2). Dynamic memory stores the bits as charges on capacitors and hence does not use flip-flops.

The 7474-style flip-flop is also used to signal the computer that something has happened. Suppose you want to have your computer read every character you type even if it's off thinking about some calculation and ignoring the keyboard. Section 7-1 shows how a keyboard ships a pulse down the line that clocks a high (D gets tied to 5 volts for this) into Q and a low into $\overline{Q}$. The $\overline{Q}$ is used to pull the computer's interrupt line low (see Fig. 7-1), causing the computer to save its current state, and, assuming you've programmed correctly, branch to a keyboard input routine that saves the character. To prevent getting interrupted again for the same character, the computer signal that reads the character in is also used to force the flip-flop's clear line low, causing $\overline{Q}$ to go high again. Since the pulse from the keyboard has only one positive edge, all's done for that character. At first it seems like magic, but it's really just plain logic! The IBM PC uses a circuit very similar to the one shown in Fig. 7-1 to produce an interrupt every time you press a key on the keyboard.

Still another use for the D flip-flop is to divide a clock frequency (suppose it's a square wave) by two. You just connect $\overline{Q}$ to D, put the original frequency f into the clock input, and get f/2 at the Q output. This procedure is generalized in the form of counters such as the 74193, which we examine in Sec. 5-6.

5-5. Clocks

Next let's look at what makes the whole show tick: the clock. If your computer seems dead, really dead (not just off in some inexplicable loop), either the power's off or the clock's stopped. Clocks in a computer produce square waves that are used to run digital circuits just as a conductor's beat runs an orchestra. No clock, no music. The reason for clocks in complicated digital circuitry is to get rid of "race" conditions that occur when various gates change their output states at their own rates. With a clock, all gates do something at the same time and then settle down. The next tick causes the next step to happen. It's the settling down that's so important. Immediately after a gate changes its output level, the output voltage can fluctuate briefly up and down, and what ultimately (after 50 to 100 nanoseconds) becomes an H might have been an L for a few nanoseconds. So clocks are essential. The computer clock in the IBM PC ticks 4.77 million times a second. The PC uses its own dedicated clock chip, but you can also build clocks of your own, as shown in Fig. 5-24. Another clock, which is sometimes used to tell computers the time of day, is illustrated in Fig. 5-25. This clock is derived from the powerline frequency of 60 Hz. The diode chops off the negative-going portion of the sine wave, the capacitor averages out any high-frequency glitches, and the Schmitt trigger inverter cleans everything up into a square wave with edges that rise in less than 40 nanoseconds. Such a clock can be used to drive a D flip-flop that divides by 2 and interrupts the computer 30 times a second. The PC already

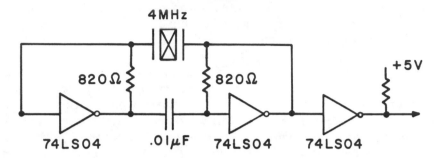

Fig. 5–24. A commonly used crystal oscillator clock circuit. The use of a crystal provides an extremely precise, unvarying output frequency.

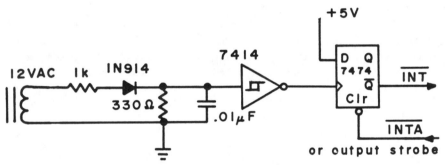

Fig. 5–25. A 60–Hz clock derived from the 110–volt powerline. It's useful for giving computers a real time clock (the everyday kind rather than the sub–microsecond kind).

has a built-in clock made from an 8253 timer/counter chip (see Sec. 6-4), which interrupts the computer 18.2 times a second.

A very popular and versatile clock chip is the CMOS 555 timer diagrammed in Fig. 5-26. This IC can use a 4- to 15-volt power supply, and its output can source or sink well over 100 mA. With a 5-volt supply, the 555 uses only 3 mA and is TTL compatible. The output value is determined by the voltages on two comparator inputs called the trigger (pin 2) and the threshold (pin 6). When the voltage on the threshold goes above 2/3 of the supply voltage V, the output goes low and an open-collector discharge transistor turns on, shorting pin 7 to ground. When the voltage on the trigger is less than 1/3 V, the output goes high and the discharge transistor turns off. Appropriate choices of resistors and capacitors can give nonsymmetric square waves at the output (see Fig. 5-27) or one-shots (Sec. 5-7).

The square wave configuration of Fig. 5-27 charges the capacitor C through $R_1 + R_2$ until the threshold voltage exceeds 2/3 V. It then discharges C through R_2 alone until the trigger voltage is less than 1/3 V. While C is charging, the output is high; while C is discharging, the output is low. The charge time is $0.693(R_1 + R_2)C$. The discharge time is $0.693R_2C$.

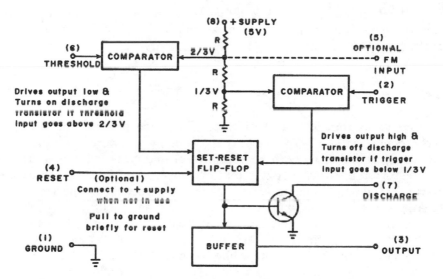

Fig. 5–26. Diagram explaining 555 timer IC. Appropriate choices of resistors and a capacitor can produce square waves (see Fig. 5–27) or one–shots (see Sec. 5–7).

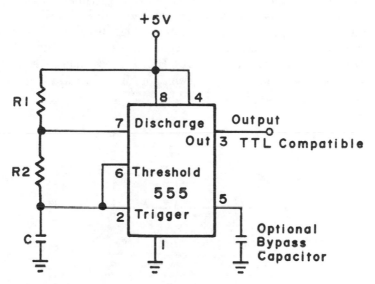

Fig. 5–27. The 555 timer IC wired as an asymmetric square wave generator.

The oscillation period is the sum of these times, yielding a frequency of $1.44/[(R_1 + 2R_2)C]$. The recommended maximum total resistance is 3.3 megohms; the minimum is 1 kilohm. The maximum capacitance is limited by the capacitor's leakage; the minimum is 500 picofarads. For noncritical oscillation frequencies less than 200 kHz, the 555 makes an excellent choice.   Lancaster's *TTL Cookbook* describes numerous interesting applications, ranging from temperature measurement to a music attack-decay generator.

5-6. Counters

As shown in Sec. 5-4, a D flip-flop can divide by 2.   Since two flip-flops are contained in a 7474, a 7474 can divide by 4.   More generally if you combine four D flip-flops with appropriate set and clear logic, you can construct the 74193 up/down counter pictured in Fig. 5-28.   Now since computers are so good at calculating in general and counting in particular, you might ask, why should we be concerned with such an elaborate IC?   Why not just input whatever is changing and count it with a program?   Two situations come to mind.   First, computers are slower than counters.   The 74193 can count 35 million times a second, while a typical microprocessor can count only about 100,000 times a second.   So if you have a rapid count to record, you can prescale the count using a TTL counter and then read the counter's contents at a slower rate, adding up the result using the computer.   Even if the count rate is within the computer's capability, you may not want to tie the computer up too much.   Counting something 30 times a second is no big deal, but counting 10,000 times a second requires a significant amount of execution time.   In Sec. 6-4, we discuss the Intel 8253 counter/timer circuit, which has three counters (or timers) in one package.   These counters can count at rates up to several MHz, and communicate directly with the microprocessor without any intervening gates.   For now, let's discuss the substantially faster, although less flexible, 74193.

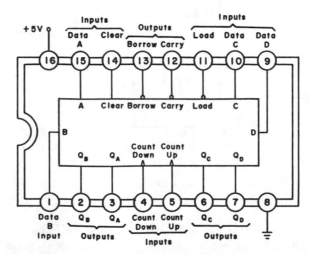

Fig. 5-28.   74193 synchronous up/down counter.   It can be used to divide by any number from 2 to 16.

If you raise the clear input, all four outputs are cleared. If you pull the load input low, the values on the A, B, C, and D input lines are loaded into their respective flip-flops. If you toggle the up count input, the Q_A output divides by 2, the Q_B by 4, the Q_C by 8, and the Q_D by 16. This is a binary counting process such that 15 positive edges on the up counter line leave all four outputs equal to 1 (high), if they started with 0's. Thus the 74193 is a divide-by-16 counter. At any given time, the number of counts registered (modulo 16) is given by the binary number formed by the four outputs. By connecting various outputs to the load line and choosing various load values, you can divide by numbers smaller than 16. For example, if A, B, and C are low and D is high, and you connect Q_D to the load line, you get a divide-by-8 counter since every time Q_D goes low the binary number 1000 (=8) is loaded in as a starter. Can you make a divide-by-2? By 3? By any number from 2 to 16? Yes! But they don't all have a symmetric square wave for an output. If you can tolerate an additional divide-by-2, a 7474 following the last stage yields a symmetric output. Figure 5-29 shows a timing diagram that illustrates the behavior of a 74193. This kind of diagram is well worth understanding, since many sophisticated LSI circuits like the 8088 microprocessor work only if you pay attention to their timing diagrams (more in Sec 6-2). As shown in Fig. 5-29, the 74193 can count down as well as up and can be cascaded using the carry output. This last characteristic means that the divide-by-16 (or whatever) output can be connected to the count input of another IC to continue the division process. Two 74193's can thus divide by any number from 2 to 256. In computer applications, these counters are for high speed. For lower speed

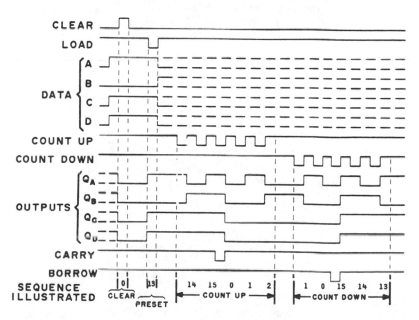

Fig. 5-29. An example timing diagram for a 74193 up/down counter.

counting, you're better off with a programmable counter such as the Intel 8253 discussed in Sec. 6-4.

5-7. One-Shots and Shift Registers

Two other common TTL IC's are one-shots and shift registers.

As the name implies, the one-shot (more properly known as a monostable multivibrator) produces a single pulse of controllable length when triggered by an input pulse. A very popular one-shot is the 74121 monostable multivibrator shown in Fig. 5-30. The length of the output pulse is linearly proportional to the product of the R and C attached to the 74121. The 74121 ignores all but the leading edge of input pulses. When its output shot is over, it's ready to listen again to the input. Another chip, the 74123, houses two *retriggerable* one-shots. These have the property that, so long as pulses arrive before the one shot is finished, the one-shot continues to be restarted (retriggered). It's like keeping a balloon up in the air. If you keep hitting it upward, it never falls to the ground. The retriggerability is handy for pulsed burglar alarm systems. You can also get two 74121-style one-shots in a single package with the 74221. The popular 555 IC discussed in Sec. 5-5 as a square-wave generator can also be used as a one-shot, by replacing R_2 in Fig. 5-27 by a wire and using pin 2 as an active low input. The IBM PC game adapter board uses the 558 quad version of the 555 in this one-shot mode to measure the resistances of the joystick potentiometers, and hence to measure the shaft position (see Sec. 9-5). Unless fast response time or retriggerability is needed, the 555 is the best one-shot choice. See Lancaster's *TTL Cookbook* for a detailed discussion of one-shots and multivibrators.

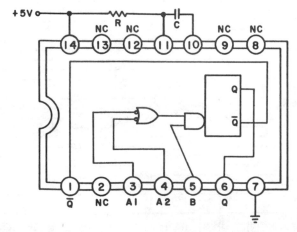

Fig. 5-30. 74121 one-shot IC. Unless a one-shot is in progress, Q is low and Q̄ is high. An input pulse edge that causes the (A1|A2)&B logic value to be true starts the one-shot (Q goes high).

Shift registers, as the name implies, are used to shift bits around one at a time. They come in many forms. A typical shift register, the 74165, latches an 8-bit input word much as the 74LS374 does. But instead of all bits being available at once as outputs, they are shifted out a single output pin, with one bit coming out for each positive edge of the shift clock. This is called parallel-to-serial conversion, and is used extensively in serial communications between computers and terminals or between one computer and another computer. A corresponding serial-to-parallel shift register, the 74164, has a single input and eight parallel outputs. Both kinds of shift register are combined with additional circuitry in the LSI circuits known as UART's for serial communications (see Sec. 10-2). The shift register is also useful for generating precise clocked one-shots. Once again, we refer the interested reader to the *TTL Cookbook* for further discussion.

5-8. Multiplexers and Demultiplexers

Two very useful types of circuit are multiplexers (also called data selectors) and demultiplexers (also called data distributors or decoders). These logic circuits are the TTL analogs of the many-to-one and one-to-many mechanical switches shown in Fig. 5-31. They can also be used in many other ways, as will be shown below.

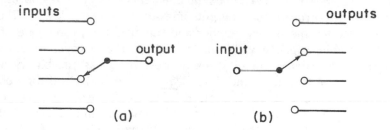

Fig. 5-31. Example of (a) a mechanical multiplexer and (b) a mechanical demultiplexer.

Consider first the demultiplexer. A demultiplexer has as its basic function the task of routing a digital logic signal (a string of highs and lows) on a single input line to any one of several different output lines. The 74LS138 shown in Fig. 5-32 is used here as a typical demultiplexer since it's very heavily used in the IBM PC. To use this chip as a standard demultiplexer, you tie pin 5 to ground and pin 6 to +5 volts. The input signal is then sent to the G2A enable line. This signal is routed through by the chip to one and only one of the output lines. All other outputs remain fixed at a high logic level. Which output line is selected depends on the 3-bit address present at the address lines A, B, and C. For example, if the address lines are all low, the output Y0 alone follows G2A.

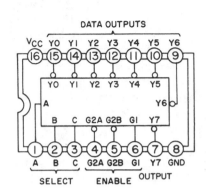

| INPUTS | | | | | OUTPUTS | | | | | | | |
| ENABLE | | SELECT | | | | | | | | | | |
G1	G2*	C	B	A	Y0	Y1	Y2	Y3	Y4	Y5	Y6	Y7
X	H	X	X	X	H	H	H	H	H	H	H	H
L	X	X	X	X	H	H	H	H	H	H	H	H
H	L	L	L	L	L	H	H	H	H	H	H	H
H	L	L	L	H	H	L	H	H	H	H	H	H
H	L	L	H	L	H	H	L	H	H	H	H	H
H	L	L	H	H	H	H	H	L	H	H	H	H
H	L	H	L	L	H	H	H	H	L	H	H	H
H	L	H	L	H	H	H	H	H	H	L	H	H
H	L	H	H	L	H	H	H	H	H	H	L	H
H	L	H	H	H	H	H	H	H	H	H	H	L

* G2 = G2A + G2B

H = high level, L = low level, X = irrelevant

Fig. 5–32. The 74LS138 decoder/demultiplexer and its truth table. Any one of eight outputs can be selected by placing the appropriate 3–bit number on the address lines and satisfying the three enable lines.

A more common use of the 74LS138 is as a decoder. In this application the output lines are connected to chips or devices that you want to select when a certain address or combination of highs and lows is present on the input lines. The idea is that a binary number encoded on the address input lines causes the corresponding output line to be pulled low. Thus the 74LS138 has decoded the binary number and selected the proper one of eight lines. For example, suppose you want to enable the outputs of a 74LS244 tristate buffer only when a set of three address lines has the binary number 6 on it (address line A is low, and lines B and C are high) and the computer simultaneously sends out an active low READ signal. All we have to do is connect output Y6 of the 74LS138 to the enable line of the 74LS244, connect the address lines to the 74LS138's address inputs, tie G2B low and G1 high, and connect the READ signal to G2A. With this setup, the 244's output is enabled if and only if a 6 is present on the address lines and the READ signal is low. This method of using address decoding to select devices is the primary technique used by the IBM PC 8088 to communicate with the devices and chips around it. You'll see more examples of how this works in Sec. 6-2.

The fact that the 74LS138 has three enable lines instead of just one gives it considerable flexibility. You can enable the outputs with either an active high or an active low signal, or you can use two of the enables as additional address lines. If you look at the schematic diagrams for the IBM PC in IBM's *Technical Reference* manual, you'll see the 138 being used all over the system as an address decoder and for performing simple logic functions that are somewhat awkward to do with other elementary gates.

There are several other decoder/demultiplexer chips available besides the 74LS138. The 74155 (used on the PC's printer adapter) and the 74139 are dual 2-line to 1-line decoder/demultiplexers. They contain two de-multiplexers per package, each demultiplexer having four outputs that can be selected by two address lines. If you need to select one of a larger number of devices, you can either cascade two 74LS138's together (connect the high-order bit of the address lines to the G2B line of one 74LS138 and to the G1 line of the other), or you can use a 74154, which comes in a 24-pin package and is a 4-line to 16-line decoder/demultiplexer.

Now let's look at multiplexers, which do the opposite of demultiplexers; that is, they select one of several input signals and connect it to a single output line. Since they select which input signal is to be transmitted through the device, they are also called data selectors. An example of this kind of chip is the 74157 quad 2-line to 1-line multiplexer shown in Fig. 5-33. The operation of this device is quite simple. Suppose you have 4 bits of data coming from two different sources, and sometimes you want to send the data from one source to the microprocessor, while at other times you want to send the data from the other source. The 74157 is made to do exactly this job. The 4 data bits from the two sources are connected to the two sets of four input lines on the 74157, and the output is connected to the microprocessor's data bus (typically through a 74LS244 tristate buffer). When the microprocessor wants to read data from source 1, it just needs to pull the select line low. To read data from source 2, it sets the select line high. The remaining pin on the 74157 is a chip enable line. This is usually tied to ground so that the chip operates normally. If it's pulled high, the outputs are all low, regardless of the input data.

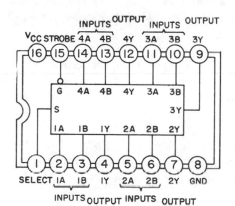

INPUTS				OUT
STROBE	SELECT	A	B	
H	X	X	X	L
L	L	L	X	L
L	L	H	X	H
L	H	X	L	L
L	H	X	H	H

H = high level, L = low level, X = irrelevant

Fig. 5-33. A 74157 quad 2-line to 1-line multiplexer and its truth table. It selects a 4-bit nibble from one of two sources and routes it to a set of 4 output lines.

One of the most common uses of a multiplexer is to make what is called *dual-ported memory* for video displays. This is used when you have an area of memory that can be either written into or read out by the CPU and also displayed on the screen by a video display controller chip. Accomplishing this requires that 2-line to 1-line multiplexers be put on the memory address lines so that sometimes the CPU can address the memory to read or write the data in it, and at other times the video display controller can read the memory contents and display them on the screen. For more detail on this type of circuitry, see Sec. 8-2. The 74158 is the same as a 74157 except with inverted output values. This multiplexer is used in the PC's dynamic RAM memory circuitry to select address lines alternately for the row and column lines (the bits are arranged in a square array). One can also use two 74LS244's to choose eight values from two input sources, but this technique requires a little more board space (it uses 20-pin IC's instead of 16-pin IC's).

As with the demultiplexers, there are several types of multiplexers available. These include several different 2-line to 1-line versions, as well as 4-, 8-, and 16-line to 1-line multiplexers. See one of the TTL data books for further details.

References

D. Lancaster, 1976, *TTL Cookbook*, Howard W. Sams & Co., New York. This is a classic book on TTL circuitry and its applications. Although somewhat dated, it still contains the best discussions available on TTL circuitry and how to use it.

Logic Databook, Vols. I and II, 1984, National Semiconductor Corp., Santa Clara, CA. These two volumes contain complete, detailed specifications for virtually all available TTL parts. Similar TTL data books are available from Motorola and Texas Instruments.

IBM PC Technical Reference, 1984, IBM Corporation, Boca Raton, FL. This manual contains authoritative descriptions of the PC's hardware, circuit diagrams for the IBM PC system board, and complete source code listings for the ROM BIOS routines.

IBM PC Options and Adapters Technical Reference, Vols. 1-3, 1984, IBM Corporation, Boca Raton, FL. This set of manuals contains complete schematics of all IBM-manufactured adapter boards for the PC.

P. Horowitz and W. Hill, 1980, *The Art of Electronics*, Cambridge University Press, New York. This is one of the best all around electronics reference books in existence. Although it's strongest in the area of analog electronic circuitry, it belongs on everyone's bookshelf.

6

The Inner Workings

At first it seems like magic, but it's really just plain logic!

In this chapter, we dissect the IBM PC and PC AT system boards, explaining what the major LSI (large-scale integration) integrated circuits do and how they use the logic circuits discussed in Chap. 5 to interface to the memory and to I/O devices. The discussions are presented initially for the PC, and each section ends with a subsection explaining any PC AT differences. You'll see that much of the discussion applies to both machines. A broad overview of the PC system board was given in Sec. 1-1. Here and in Chap. 7, we go into considerably more detail. The first question that comes to mind is "How does a 40-pin microprocessor control all the devices?" The Intel 8088 has fourteen 16-bit registers, but it has no additional memory on chip and no I/O ports. So how does it convince other IC's to provide it with the necessary memory and I/O ports? As usual, it's just plain logic.

Section 6-1 defines the 40 pins of the 8088/8086. Since the 40 pins for the 16-bit data bus 8086 and the 8-bit data bus 8088 microprocessors are so similar, we define both as we go along. Many of the 8086/8088's features are explained here, but the focus is on how they appear in the IBM PC. The main part of the section discusses the 8086 maximum configuration used in the PC, and the PC AT subsection discusses the 16-bit 80286 pinouts. The 8284 clock/reset IC and the 8288 bus controller IC are included in the discussion since these are required by an 8088 running in the maximum mode.

Section 6-2 shows how the 8088 reads and writes the microcomputer's memory locations and I/O ports, and it presents address maps showing where various devices are located in the IBM PC and PC AT. Section 6-3 gives an overview of the 8255 smart parallel port on the system board and shows how it reads the sense switches and the keyboard latch, enables parity checks, and so on. Section 6-4 discusses the remaining smart IC's on the system board, namely the 8253 counter/timer circuit, the 8259 interrupt controller, and the 8237 direct memory access (DMA) controller (the IBM PC AT has two 8259's and two 8237's). The interrupt controller's role is also discussed more completely in Chap. 7. Section 6-5 defines the lines on the IBM PC I/O channel bus, which connect to a set of five 62-pin connectors for expansion boards. These boards typically include a floppy-disk controller and a display and printer adapter. The section ends with a description of the IBM PC AT's 36-pin extended I/O channel connectors, which provide access to the full 80286 16-megabyte address space, to the 16-bit data bus, and to the additional DMA and interrupt request lines. Section 6-6 describes the AT's 80286 protected virtual address mode.

A major fringe benefit of understanding the PC system board is that you'll then understand the concepts common to all computer systems. Although some details vary, the basic principles are quite portable from machine to machine. Since our attention is focused on the IBM PC, which is a fairly complex microcomputer, the discussion is aimed at giving an overall understanding of the hardware and system software, rather than at showing how to design a microcomputer from scratch. The emphasis is on using the PC, not designing it. Our earlier Z80 book, *Interfacing Microcomputers to the Real World*, explains how to assemble and debug a simple microcomputer from the IC's, and a relatively ambitious construction project based on the 8088 has been presented by Steve Ciarcia (*BYTE*, November, 1982). Important references for this chapter are the IBM PC and PC AT *Technical Reference* manuals and the Intel *Component Data Catalog*. The *Technical Reference* manuals contain a wealth of description about the PC and PC AT, including complete schematics for each computer and source listings for the ROM BIOS routines. Intel's *Component Data Catalog* contains detailed discussions of all the Intel IC's in the PC. Intel also sells useful applications books, which are referenced at the end of this chapter.

6-1. The Forty Pins

As you can see in Fig. 6-1, 20 of the 8088's 40 pins have to do with addresses, namely, AD0—AD7, A8—A15, and A16/S3—A19/S6. To accommodate the many needs of a processor with only 40 pins, 12 of these 20 address lines have two different meanings, depending on what portion of a machine cycle (the sequence of actions taken by the 8088 to read or write a byte of

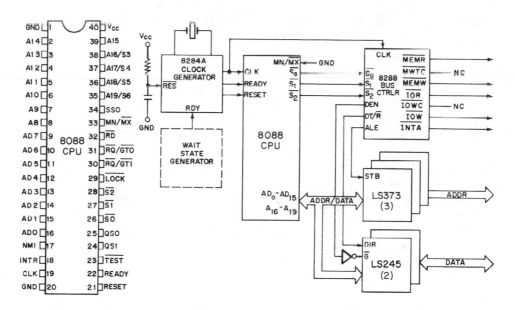

Fig. 6-1. The 8086/8088 pin configuration in maximum mode, together with its clock/reset circuit (8284) and bus controller (8288). The pins on the support circuits are named as used on the IBM PC.

data to memory or an I/O port) is active. Specifically, AD0—AD7 act as address lines at the start of a machine cycle, and then change to bidirectional data lines later on. This dual meaning depending on time is called time-multiplexing. The transparent octal latch 74LS373 discussed in Sec. 5-4 is used on the PC system board to latch the address line values during the initial portion of the machine cycle, thus freeing the lines for data transfers thereafter. The control signal that latches the address values is called ALE (address latch enable) and is generated by the 8288 bus controller circuit in response to a status signal sent by the 8088 as described in Sec. 6-2. When ALE goes from high to low, the address is stored in the 74LS373. You exclaim, "I thought you said the 8088 could do it all with 40 pins!?" Well, actually it needs a little help. Nevertheless, the lines of the 8088 have to be buffered anyhow to be able to drive so many circuits, and the use of a 74LS373 latch instead of a 74LS244 buffer increases neither the circuit board space nor the cost. The alternative of increasing the number of CPU pins *does* increase the required board space, so this time-multiplexing of the 8088's pins provides a nice saving.

Similarly, the A16/S3—A19/S6 lines have two meanings. Here S3—S6 refer to status signals that are not used by the PC. Just as for the AD lines, the PC uses two 74LS373's and the ALE line to latch the A16—A19 and A8—A15 address values. The demultiplexed A0—A19 lines are collectively referred to as the processor address bus, and specify 1 byte out of 1 megabyte ($2^{20} = 1,048,576$). A high on any line means a one, and a low means a zero.   A0—A15 are also used to specify the I/O port for I/O instructions.

Later in the machine cycle, the AD lines become bidirectional data lines—that is, the 8088 drives these lines when outputting a byte and reads them when inputting a byte.   Just as for the address lines, a high represents a one and a low is a zero.   In contrast to the 8088, the 8086 replaces the 8088's A8—A15 with AD8—AD15 and requires an additional 74LS373 for demultiplexing.   This gives the 8086 its 16 bidirectional data lines compared to the 8088's eight data lines.

Two of the unused status lines, S3 and S4, deserve special mention: they specify which of the four segment registers are being used to form the address.   These lines could be used to increase the memory size.   For example, the segment accessed with the ES register could have its own megabyte of RAM memory, which could be handy in specialized applications such as a large image-buffer RAM for laser printers.   However, to implement this you would have to modify the system board to decode S3 and S4, and unless the feature was added in a way that allows it to be disabled under software control, you wouldn't be able to use instructions like the string primitives, which require the ES register to access the same address space as the other segment registers.

Then there are the three essential lines, +5 volts, ground (two pins), and the clock.   The +5 volts and ground are distributed as conducting planes inside the system printed circuit board.   Such a board is called a "four-layer" printed circuit board, since it has the wiring between the chips on the top and bottom of the board plus two internal ground and power planes. The clock is an asymmetric square wave supplied by the 8284A clock generator circuit and is high only 33% of the cycle.   The 8088 does something every time the clock ticks (each period of the square wave), and if you stop the clock, you halt the 8088 in its tracks.   On the PC, the clock runs at 4.772727 MHz although the standard part is rated at 5 MHz.   The slower value is used because it equals 14.31818/3, where 14.31818 MHz is the dot clock frequency for the color/graphics display adapter board and 14.31818/4 is the color-burst frequency 3.579 MHz (see Sec. 8-2).   The division by 3 is used to give the 33% duty cycle.

Now we get to the *control bus*.   This set of lines allows the 8088 to control memory and I/O ports.   The control bus signals are generated by the 8288 bus controller circuit from the 8088 status lines S0—S2.   The 8288 has no intelligence of its own; it simply decodes the information present on the 8088's S0—S2 lines.   For example, if S0 and S2 are high and S1 is low, the 8288 pulls the $\overline{\text{MEMR}}$ line low.   All lines in the control bus are active low and go active only after the address bus has been latched by the 74LS373's. We use the bus line names given in the IBM PC *Technical Reference* manual's schematic diagrams, rather than the pinout (pin arrangement) names on the 8288.   MEMR (**mem**ory **r**ead) low means that the 8088 wants to read a byte from memory at the address present on the address bus; that is, it wants the memory to put a byte onto the data bus.   (Note that a signal with a bar over it (like $\overline{MEMR}$) means that the signal is active low; it does something when it's low.) Now if there's no memory out there at that address, the 8088 sees random junk since no pull-up resistors are used and nothing drives the data bus. Similarly, if the 8088 pulls $\overline{MEMW}$ (memory write) low, then it wants to write the byte it has placed on the data bus into the memory location specified on the address bus.

That takes care of referencing memory. To read and write I/O ports, the companion signals $\overline{IOR}$ and $\overline{IOW}$ are used instead of $\overline{MEMR}$ and $\overline{MEMW}$, respectively. In addition, only A0—A15 are used for I/O addresses, which means only 65536 ports can be addressed. You can see from this how an I/O device could be made to respond either like memory or like an I/O port; simply wire it up to respond either to the memory strobes $\overline{MEMR}$ and $\overline{MEMW}$ or to the I/O strobes $\overline{IOR}$ and $\overline{IOW}$. The advantages of making an I/O device act like memory include access to a more powerful instruction set and the fact that high-level languages, like PL/M and C, can then refer to I/O devices just the way they refer to memory (ordinarily they can't refer to I/O devices at all because they don't have the equivalent of BASIC's INP and OUT statements). The Victor 9000 computer, for example, uses PL/M with memory-mapped I/O to access most I/O devices. The 8088 itself doesn't know who's out there, and doesn't even care. With so much intelligence, it's amazing that it doesn't care! But today anyhow, computers are just automatons doing exactly what they're told to do without feelings.

If memory or I/O devices cannot respond as fast as the CPU is running, they must pull the I/O CH RDY line low. This signal is passed to the $\overline{RDY}$/WAIT line of the 8284 clock generator, which in turn pulls the READY line of the 8088 low at the proper point relative to the 8088's clock signal. Having the READY line low forces the 8088 to wait and do nothing until READY goes back high. The 8088 does this by inserting extra clock cycles into its machine cycle (see below) called *wait states*. During these wait states, the CPU does nothing but look at the READY line to see if it's returned high yet. The use of wait states is one powerful way to synchronize data flow between the processor and various devices that are not quite as fast as the CPU. The READY line should not be held low longer than 2.1 microseconds on the PC. The $\overline{TEST}$ line provides another synchronization technique. After executing a WAIT instruction, the processor waits until this line goes low. On the IBM PC, this line is connected to +5 volts through a pull-up resistor, so unless an 8087 numeric coprocessor is present, the PC will enter a useless infinite wait state (in other words, it will crash!) if you execute a WAIT instruction. Believe it or not, with the $\overline{MEMR}$, $\overline{MEMW}$, $\overline{IOR}$, $\overline{IOW}$, and I/O CH RDY, plus the address and data busses, you can do almost all of the interfacing you'll ever want to do.

When the CPU executes a program, it must read instructions from memory, using a memory read machine cycle. This machine cycle takes place as follows: The CPU reads data from memory by first putting the address on the address/data lines, having it latched, and then having $\overline{MEMR}$ go low as shown in the machine cycle timing diagram in Fig. 6-2. In this

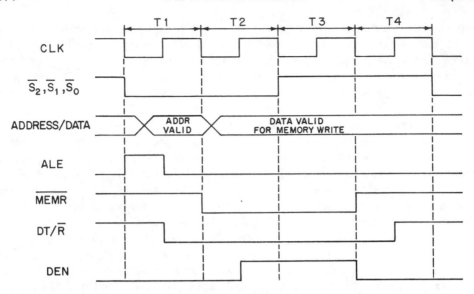

Fig. 6–2. Timing diagram for an 8088 machine cycle that does a memory read. The signals shown here (except for CLK and S0—S2) are those produced by the Intel 8288 bus controller.

figure, the top line shows the clock ticking away, T1, T2, T3, T4. The clock keeps everything synchronized and allows time delays so that all lines can settle to their correct levels. On the 4.77-MHz PC, the tick period is 210 nanoseconds. On the 8088, four clock periods are used for each machine cycle. In the middle of the T1 clock period, the ALE line goes low, latching the desired address values in the 74LS373's. At the same time, the DT/$\overline{\text{R}}$ (data transmit/receive) line goes low, causing the bidirectional 74LS245 data-line buffer to read the data lines (for a memory write machine cycle, the DT/$\overline{\text{R}}$ line would remain high). At the end of the T1 clock period, the $\overline{\text{MEMR}}$ line goes low, indicating to the memory chips that the processor wants to read a byte. In the middle of the T2 clock period, the DEN (data enable) line goes high to enable the 74LS245's tristated output onto the 8088's AD lines. Toward the end of T3, the READY line is sampled, and if READY is low, extra T states (clock ticks) called *wait states* are inserted so long as this line remains low. At the beginning of the T4 cycle (following any inserted wait cycles), the 8088 reads in the data from the AD lines.

A memory write machine cycle is almost the same as the read cycle, with $\overline{\text{MEMW}}$ going low instead of $\overline{\text{MEMR}}$. In addition, the DT/$\overline{\text{R}}$ line remains high, and the DEN line goes high at the beginning of the T2 period and goes back low in the middle of T4. I/O read and write machine cycles have the same timing diagrams as their memory counterparts, except that $\overline{\text{IOR}}$ and $\overline{\text{IOW}}$ play the roles of $\overline{\text{MEMR}}$ and $\overline{\text{MEMW}}$, respectively.

A special pin labeled MN/$\overline{\text{MX}}$ is grounded on the PC's 8088, specifying that the *maximum mode* is to be used. Connecting this pin to +5 volts puts the 8088 in *minimum mode*, which changes the definitions of certain pins to circumvent the need for the 8288 bus controller in smaller microcomputer applications. The IBM PC*jr* runs its 8088 in minimum mode. The primary limitation of this mode is that it cannot support coprocessors such as the 8087. Since the 8087 is powerful and inexpensive, this is a major disadvantage. Note that the $\overline{RD}$ line on pin 32 of the 8088 is superfluous in maximum mode, since the S0—S2 lines give that information to the 8288 controller. Hence the PC doesn't use this line. Similarly the PC doesn't use the $\overline{SSO}$ line, which remains permanently high in maximum mode.

On to the remaining pins. One of these, the interrupt line INTR, is so useful that we devote Secs. 7-1 and 7-2 to it. I/O devices can set this line high. If the 8088 has its interrupts enabled, having INTR go high will cause the 8088 to make an indirect CALL to an interrupt handler that can be located anywhere in memory. The calling procedure is like that used when a software interrupt is executed (see Sec. 3-6). The hardware actions that occur are as follows: When INTR goes high, the 8088 finishes executing its current instruction, and then pulls $\overline{S0}$, $\overline{S1}$, and $\overline{S2}$ all low to acknowledge the interrupt. This causes the 8088 bus controller to pull $\overline{INTA}$ (**interrupt acknowledge**) low and thereby asks the interrupting device to put a byte on the data bus specifying which of the 256 interrupt vectors in low memory (see Sec. 3-6) contains the desired interrupt handler address. The 8088 reads this interrupt vector and then jumps to the interrupt handler in the same manner used for the execution of a software interrupt instruction. The interrupt handler program must save whatever registers it needs to use, do its thing, restore the registers, and end with an IRET. On the PC and PC AT, the INTR line is controlled by an 8259 eight-level vectored interrupt circuit discussed more fully in Sec. 6-4. Section 7-2 illustrates the interrupt concept with a real-time clock implementation, and Sec. 7-3 shows you how the keyboard interrupts the processor.

Another interrupt line, NMI (**nonmaskable interrupt**), is available that uses interrupt vector 2. This interrupt line is particularly useful for handling disastrous situations such as power failure. The NMI line is positive edge triggered, in contrast to INTR, which is active high. The edge trigger is necessary because NMI is nonmaskable (cannot be disabled). On the PC and PC AT, extra circuitry is included to allow the NMI line to be disabled. See Sec. 6-5 for how to interrupt a program with an NMI button.

The RESET line is used to restart the system, typically when it has crashed or you've just turned the power on. When RESET goes high, the 8088 zeroes the DS, ES, SS, and IP registers and sets the code segment register CS to 0FFFFH. Hence computer memory should contain an initial startup routine that begins at address 0FFFF0H. A reset is like an interrupt, except for the register initializations and the fact that no return address is pushed onto the stack. Most computers have a switch connected to the RESET line to restart the system; however, the PC has the PWR GOOD signal from the power supply connected to it (this line is high if the power supply is operating properly). Hence if your machine has really crashed, a common

occurrence when you're debugging assembly language programs, you have to
turn the power off for a few seconds and then back on.   Bad news!
Hopefully IBM will add a reset switch someday. If the crash has left interrupts enabled and hasn't written over the interrupt vectors In low memory,
you can of course restart by pressing Ctrl-Alt-Del simultaneously. On the
PC*jr*, you can pull a program cartridge out and plug it back in to reset.

Earlier in this section you saw that the processor can be forced to wait
for slow devices by pulling its READY line low. This line is also used in the
IBM PC to implement a high-speed data-transfer method called *direct
memory access* (DMA).   In DMA, a kind of mini-CPU chip called a
DMA controller suspends the normal operation of the 8088 and takes over
the address, data, and control busses itself. It then does the requested data
transfer at rates up to 1.5 megabytes/second. It can do transfers at these
high rates because its hardware architecture is specialized for this purpose.
The PC uses some fairly intricate synchronization circuitry to ensure that
the 8237 DMA controller takes over the busses only at the end of a machine
cycle and only when the $\overline{\text{LOCK}}$ line is not active due to the execution of a
LOCK prefix.   When the DMA controller is active, it tristates the 8088
address/data/control buffers and, via the READY line output of the 8284
clock generator chip, causes the 8088 to insert wait states while the controller runs the address, data, and control busses.   For more discussion on
DMA, see Secs. 6-4 and 7-3. The IBM AT has two DMA controllers.

Another kind of processor "wait" involves the remaining pins, $\overline{\text{RQ}/\text{GT0}}$,
$\overline{\text{RQ}/\text{GT1}}$, QS0, and QS1. These lines coordinate the running of coprocessors
on the same bus as the 8088. Two basic kinds of coprocessors exist, those
that take over the bus and execute their own instruction streams, such as
other 8086/8088's and the 8089 I/O processor, and those that extend the
8086/8088 instruction set via ESC instructions, such as the 8087 numeric
coprocessor.   The 8087 coprocessor dramatically increases the execution
speed of numerical calculations.   Section 4-8 gives examples of programs
that call for the 8087 via ESC instructions.   Rather than duplicate the
addressing arithmetic in the 8087, the 8086/8088 supplies the initial address
via an ESC instruction along with the desired 6-bit 8087 opcode. The 8087
latches this address information and proceeds to load the required number of
bytes starting with that address. When the 8087 has the data it needs for a
given instruction, it can run simultaneously (in parallel) with the 8088. The
8087 needs to load as many as 10 bytes per operand and hence must gain
access to the CPU busses. It does this by driving the $\overline{\text{RQ}/\text{GT1}}$ line low for
one clock period. This pulse is called a *request* pulse. As soon as it can,
the 8088 responds on the same line with a similar low-level pulse, the
grant pulse, and then tristates its bus lines. After the 8087 has completed
its data transfers, it returns a *release* pulse, again on the same line, to let
the 8088 know that it can continue. Thus the $\overline{\text{RQ}/\text{GT1}}$ line is a bidirectional
handshake line, which allows a pair of processors to share the same CPU
busses.   The $\overline{\text{RQ}/\text{GT0}}$ line operates in the same manner but is not used in
the IBM PC.

The QS0 and QS1 pins tell whether the 8086/8088 is taking its next byte from its internal byte queue (see below), or from external memory. This information is used in combination with the $\overline{S0}$, $\overline{S1}$, and $\overline{S2}$ lines to let the 8087 recognize and decode ESC instructions.

Sometimes a critical instruction sequence is executed for which other processors must not intervene. Such a case is the setting of a *semaphore* flag in memory to signal that some processor is using a shared resource, such as a printer. To make sure that another processor doesn't gain access to this semaphore while the semaphore is being examined and updated, a special LOCK prefix can be executed as described in Sec. 3-11. This activates the $\overline{LOCK}$ line, which tells other processors to wait until the $\overline{LOCK}$ line goes back high.

That's all 40 pins. Although the 8088 has only its registers for memory and no I/O ports, the signals on these pins allow it to directly access 1 megabyte of RAM, 65536 input ports, and 65536 output ports. With a bit of imagination (perverse perhaps?), you see that the 8088 can rule the world! We've seen in this section that a number of the 40 pins are used to synchronize data transfers between the CPU and other devices. In particular, three important synchronization techniques were introduced: interrupts, DMA, and wait states.

One other synchronization technique should be mentioned here because it's an important part of the 8088's architecture, and that's the use of a FIFO (first-in, first out) buffer. Figure 6-3 illustrates how a FIFO works. It's just a temporary data storage area that is filled by one device and emptied by another in such a way that the first byte written into the FIFO is the first byte to be read out, the second byte in is the second byte out, and so on. Since the FIFO can contain a variable number of data bytes, the instantaneous rate at which data are written into the FIFO doesn't have to equal the rate at which data are read out (although over a longer period of time the rates must be equal or the FIFO will either overflow or be empty). FIFO's are useful for saving input/output data until the target device has time to process it. A good software example is the keyboard buffer discussed in Sec. 7-1, which allows you to type ahead of a program.

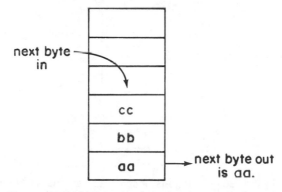

Fig. 6-3. How a FIFO (first-in, first-out) buffer works.

The 8088 has a 4-byte hardware FIFO inside it known as the instruction-fetch queue. Its purpose is to speed up program execution. This FIFO is constantly filled by a bus interface unit contained in the 8088 that picks up new bytes ahead of the instruction pointer, in anticipation of their use by the CPU. So long as the queue contains the next instruction code to be executed, the CPU doesn't have to wait to get the next instruction. However, jump instructions empty the queue, which then has to be refilled before the next instruction can be executed. Also, as discussed in Sec. 9-5, the instruction fetch rate of the bus interface unit is only 1.25 megabytes/second. Code that jumps around a lot thereby gets slowed down substantially relative to processors like the Z80, which has no queue but has an instruction fetch rate of about 2.5 megabytes/second.

Each of the synchronization techniques just discussed has its advantages and disadvantages, and several other synchronization techniques can also be used. All of these are discussed and compared in Sec. 7-3.

Intel 80286 Pins

The 16-bit 80286 microprocessor used in the IBM PC AT comes in a 68-pin package, five of which are not to be connected. The pins include 24 address lines for a 16-megabyte address space and 16 data lines (Fig. 6-4). By demultiplexing the address and data lines, somewhat faster execution is achieved. Status for reading/writing memory/IO ports along with interrupt acknowledge, halt, and shutdown is given by various combinations of the $\overline{S0}$, $\overline{S1}$, M/$\overline{IO}$, and COD/$\overline{INTA}$ control lines. The Bus High Enable line, $\overline{BHE}$, works together with the address line A0 to transfer words or bytes on the upper or lower byte of the data bus. Specifically, if both lines are low, a word is transferred. If $\overline{BHE}$ is low and A0 is high, a byte is transferred on

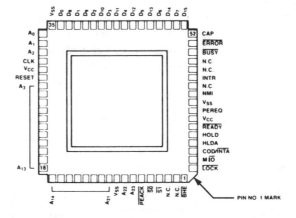

Fig. 6–4. The 80286 pinouts include all of the 8086 maximum mode signals.

pins D15—D8, while if $\overline{BHE}$ is high and A0 is low, a byte is transferred on pins D7—D0.   You can see that transferring a word to or from an odd address requires two memory accesses, compared to one for an even address.

The 80286 has three special lines to coordinate 80287 execution.   The PEREQ/$\overline{PEACK}$ (Processor Extension Operand Request and Acknowledge) line plays a role similar to the 8088's $\overline{RQ}/\overline{GT0}$ line, but provides 80286 memory management and protection capabilities.   The 80287 asserts the $\overline{BUSY}$ line to stop the 80286 on WAIT and most 80287 instructions until the 80287 has finished executing its current instruction.   This feature obviates the need to insert an FWAIT instruction before an 8087 instruction.   Note that if you want the 80286 to examine a value being stored by the 80287, you generally still need to use an FWAIT.   When the 80287 encounters an error and error interrupts are enabled, the 80287 asserts its $\overline{ERROR}$ line, which causes an IRQ 13 to occur on the AT.   Usually this line is connected directly to the 80286, which causes a processor extension interrupt (INT 16 or INT 10H).   On the AT, this would conflict with the standard software video interrupt.   Other 80286 interrupts (INT 5, 8—13) do conflict with Shift-PrtSc and with most of the standard 8259 interrupts, such as the time-of-day clock and keyboard.   The interrupt handlers can perform tests to figure out the cause of an interrupt.   In addition to the PEREQ and $\overline{BUSY}$ lines, the 80286 uses I/O ports 0F8H, 0FAH, and 0FCH to communicate with the 80287.

6-2. Interfacing Memory and I/O Ports

The 8088 would be useless without I/O devices and memory to converse with.   This section discusses general principles about how the 8088 reads and writes I/O devices and memory on the PC system board using the control, data, and address lines defined in Sec. 6-1.   A block diagram that provides an overview of the system board is shown in Fig. 6-5.   This section also summarizes the I/O and memory address allocations as used in the IBM PC and PC AT.   Two basic concepts are common to all I/O processes: latching the data and recognizing which device the CPU is addressing.

As was shown in the timing diagram of Fig. 6-2, the CPU spends only a very short time outputting or reading data.   If you want to light up some LED's with a particular pattern, you can't just connect them to the D0—D7 data lines.   For one thing, the 8088 outputs can't sink (or source) the required current.   But more important, the values on the data bus are constantly changing, since instructions as well as I/O data are continually passed back and forth on it.   So you have to catch the data byte destined for the LED's and hold it in some flip-flops.   This process is called *latching the data*, and an output port can be a simple latch (a collection of flip-flops) such as the 74LS374 (see Fig. 5-23).   Memory just consists of many latches, each of which responds only to its own address.   To input data, latching may not be required, because the input data may be stable for a long time compared to CPU machine cycle times.   If the data comes from

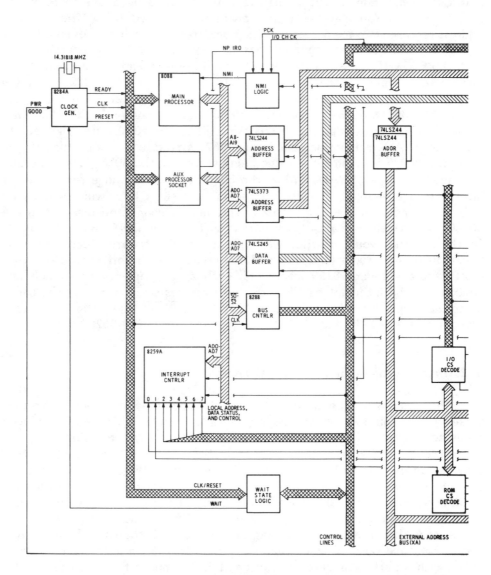

Fig. 6–5. Overview of the IBM PC system board. This page shows the 8088 with its address, data, and control buffers, and the 8259 interrupt controller.

a parallel keyboard, for example, the key remains pressed for at least several milliseconds, so if the CPU examines the keyboard often enough, the keyboard data doesn't have to be latched. For such data a simple tristate buffer such as the 74LS244 (see Fig. 5-18) is sufficient, along with some software to debounce the switches. On the IBM PC keyboard, the data is latched for other reasons, as described in Sec. 7-1.

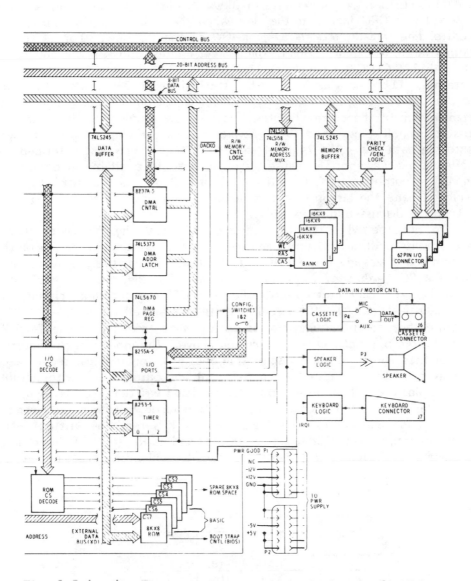

Fig. 6-5 (cont). This page shows the DMA circuits, the 64–kilobyte RAM (256–kilobyte on models since April 1983), the 40–kilobyte ROM, the counter/timer circuit, the I/O channel connectors, and the cassette, speaker, and keyboard interfaces. From the IBM PC *Technical Reference* manual, courtesy of IBM.

Second, a given I/O port or memory bank has to know that it, not some other device, is being addressed. This recognition process is called *address decoding* and involves making a comparison between the address lines and the I/O port number or memory address that the hardware designer has chosen. Furthermore, it requires the device to listen (for CPU output) or to respond (for CPU input) at the time when the CPU pulls the appropriate control line ($\overline{\text{MEMR}}$, $\overline{\text{MEMW}}$, $\overline{\text{IOR}}$, or $\overline{\text{IOW}}$ on the PC) low. For a 74LS374 output latch, the combination of the correct address and $\overline{\text{IOW}}$ low should set the 74LS374 CLOCK pin high, causing the 74LS374 to latch the byte on the data bus. LED's or whatever can be attached to the 74LS374's output pins as described in Chap. 5. Similarly, to input data from a 74LS244 buffer, the combination of the correct address and $\overline{\text{IOR}}$ low should pull the 74LS244's tristate enable pins 1 and 19 low, which causes the chip to place its byte onto the data bus. The 74LS374 and 74LS244 I/O ports just described are called *parallel* ports because all eight bits are available in parallel as inputs or outputs. An alternative type of I/O port is the *serial port*, which streams the bits in or out consecutively on single lines. This type of I/O port is discussed in Chap. 10.

To get the whole picture, consider the way the PC system board accesses its built-in I/O ports and memory. A functional diagram of the system board was given in Fig. 6-5, and detailed schematics are available in the IBM PC *Technical Reference* manual. Consider first the 8237 DMA controller, the 8259 interrupt controller, the 8253 counter/timer circuit, and the 8255 parallel I/O (PIO) circuit. These IC's are all called "smart" IC's, because they are programmable, as distinguished from the simple 74LS374 and 74LS244 parallel I/O ports discussed above. The individual characteristics of these smart IC's are discussed in Sec. 6-3; for now just regard each one as consisting of a set of parallel input and output ports with suitable control pins that allow these ports to be read and written (see Fig. 6-6). A particular port within a smart peripheral is read or written using a combination of internal and external logic. The port is read (or written) when both the peripheral's *chip-select* pin ($\overline{\text{CS}}$) and its $\overline{\text{RD}}$ (or $\overline{\text{WR}}$) pin are low. The port that is accessed within the chip is determined by the binary value

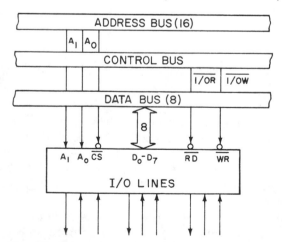

Fig. 6-6. General form of the bus interface for a smart peripheral IC, such as the 8255 PIO.

appearing on the peripheral's address pins. In Fig. 6-6, the A_0 and A_1 address lines are connected to the chip, allowing any one of four I/O ports within the chip to be accessed.

The appropriate external logic must be included to drive the peripheral's chip-select line low. In the IBM PC, the chip-select logic is typically carried out using the versatile 74LS138 3-line to 8-line decoder discussed in Sec. 5-8. When its three enable pins have the right values, this circuit pulls the one of eight output pins low that corresponds to the 3-bit value present on its address pins. The 74138 output pins are connected to the appropriate I/O device chip-select pins. As an example of this, Fig. 6-7 shows part of

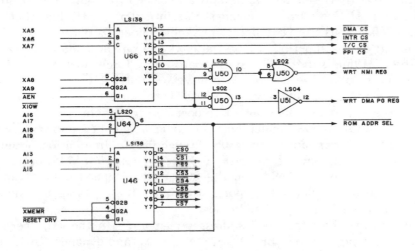

Fig. 6–7. The IBM PC system board I/O device and ROM decoding logic. Adapted from a diagram in IBM's *Technical Reference* manual. Courtesy of IBM.

the PC system board device decode logic. Consider the upper 74LS138. Coming into this IC are the address lines XA5 through XA9. The XAn lines are just the An lines (the 8088's address lines) latched by the 74LS373 address latches, and buffered in addition by 74LS244's for on-board use. The An lines have to drive the I/O channel boards as well, and conservative design calls for some extra buffering here. The PC uses XA0 through XA9 for I/O port addresses, and ignores XA10 through XA15. Hence any combination of bits on lines XA10 through XA15 will access the various ports specified by the lower address lines. This is called *redundant addressing*, and it saves some logic circuitry in cases where lots of I/O port values are available (the 8088 can address 65536 input ports and 65536 output ports!). The lines XA0 through XA4 are also ignored by the 74LS138, thus providing each IC selected by the 74LS138 with 32 on-chip port addresses.

For example, if XA5 through XA9 are all low and the address bus is enabled (AEN low), the 74LS138's Y0 pin goes low, selecting the 8237 DMA circuit. Any address between 00000 and 11111 = 31 decimal will thus select the 8237. However, the XA4 address line isn't used by the 8237, as it has only 16 I/O ports, so the addresses 0—15 and 16—31 are effectively the same. Similarly if XA5 is high and XA6 through XA9 are low, Y1 goes low, selecting the 8259 interrupt controller.

Consider the case when Y5 goes low, which occurs for ports 0A0 to 0BFH. If the buffered $\overline{\text{IOW}}$ line $\overline{\text{XIOW}}$ is also low (that is, an output instruction is being executed), this forces $\overline{\text{WRT NMI REG}}$ high. This line, in turn, clocks the XD7 (buffered D7) value into a 74LS74 flip-flop. The Q output of this flip is ANDed with the nonmaskable interrupt (NMI) line that goes into the 8088. Thus the NMI line is maskable under software control! If the Q output of the flip-flop is low, the NMI line on the 8088 can never go high. The NMI line is used for system-board and I/O-channel parity checks and 8087 interrupts. The use of Y5 to drive $\overline{\text{WRT NMI REG}}$ has considerable redundancy since outputting any of 80H—0FFH to ports 0A0H—0BFH enables NMI. On the AT, these values output to port 70H to disable NMI.

The 74LS138 has two select pins left unattached (Y6 and Y7), which correspond to I/O port addresses 0C0H through 0FFH. In addition, when the XA9 address line is low it enables a system-board 74LS245 buffer for reading. Hence no I/O devices in the PC's expansion board slots can use addresses with XA9 = 0 (that is, ports 0 through 1FF). Table 6-1 summarizes the available IBM PC I/O addresses.

Now consider how the 8088 addresses memory. In the PC, there are three different types of memory: ROM, static RAM, and dynamic RAM. ROM is an acronym for read only memory, and, as the name implies, the contents of ROM can be read, but you can't write anything into it. A ROM's memory contents are burned into the chip when it's manufactured and can never be altered. ROM is used in the PC to store permanent system programs like the built-in cassette BASIC. RAM (random access memory) is programmable memory; you can both write into it and read from it. Also, unlike ROM, RAM is volatile memory. When the power is turned off, the memory contents disappear. The difference between static and dynamic RAM is discussed later. One other useful type of memory is EPROM (erasable programmable read only memory). EPROM's provide permanent nonvolatile memory just like ROM, but instead of using factory-programmed EPROM's you can write programs into them yourself with special hardware called an EPROM programmer. We show later how these can be put into the PC to modify or expand the permanent system programs.

With that brief introduction to memory types, you are ready to consider an example of memory-address decoding. The simplest case is that for the built-in ROM lying in the uppermost 64K page of the 1-megabyte address space, that is, between 0F0000H and 0FFFFFH. Note first that the 74LS20 output in Fig. 6-7 goes low when this highest 64K is chosen (A16 through A19 are all high). This output is one of the three enable lines on the ROM

RANGE	DEVICE
	System Board
0—1F	8237 4-channel DMA controller
20—3F	8259 8-channel interrupt controller
40—5F	8253 3-channel counter/timer circuit
60—7F	8255 PIO (on AT, 8042 keyboard & NMI reset)
80—9F	DMA 64K page register (74LS612)
0A0—0BF	NMI reset (on AT, second 8259)
0C0—0DF	Second AT 8237 DMA controller
0E0—0FF	80287 math coprocessor interface
100—1FF	Unusable on PC, available on AT
	I/O Channel
1F0—1F8	AT fixed disk
200—20F	Game I/O adapter
210—217	Expansion unit
220—24F	Reserved
250—277	Not used
278—27F	Second parallel printer interface (LPT2)
280—2EF	Not used
2F0—2F7	Reserved
2F8—2FF	Second 8250 serial UART interface (COM2)
300—31F	Prototype card
320—32F	XT hard disk
330—377	Not used
378—37F	First parallel printer interface (LPT1)
380—38C	SDLC or secondary binary synchronous interface
390—39F	Not used
3A0—3AF	Primary binary synchronous
3B0—3BF	Monochrome display and first parallel printer
3C0—3CF	Reserved
3D0—3DF	Color/graphics display adaptor
3E0—3FF	Reserved
3F0—3F7	5-1/4" floppy disk drive controller
3F8—3FF	First 8250 serial UART interface (COM1)

Table 6–1. I/O port addresses used by standard devices in the IBM PC. Addresses in the 0—0FFH range have a number of equivalent values (redundant address decoding). The detailed port assignments and their meanings are given in the sections describing the circuits listed above (see book index for easy reference).

decoder circuit (the lower 74LS138 in Fig. 6-7). $\overline{XMEMR}$ is the other active low enable, since ROM is read-only, and the active-high enable is connected to the $\overline{RESET}$ $\overline{DRV}$ line (this line is high except in the rare case that RESET is low). Address lines A13, A14, and A15 are used to select one of the eight 74LS138 output lines $\overline{CS0}$—$\overline{CS7}$ that are used as chip-select lines for the 8-kilobyte 2364 ROM's (which are pin-for-pin compatible with the Motorola 68764 24-pin EPROM in Fig. 6-8, in case you want to change things). The standard PC has five 24-pin ROM sockets, while the hard-disk based PC-XT has two 28-pin sockets that can use 8K or 32K ROM's. On the PC, the 74LS138 ROM decoder's Y0 and Y1 lines, corresponding to addresses 0F0000H to 0F3FFFH, are ignored. The next 8 kilobytes are selected by Y2, cover addresses 0F4000H to 0F5FFFH, and select the empty ROM socket next to the edge of the system board. The next four ROM decoder output lines select the built-in 32-kilobyte cassette BASIC. The Y7 line selects the highest 8 kilobytes (0FE000H to 0FFFFFH), which contain the BIOS (basic I/O system) routines. The BIOS contains most of the I/O drivers used in the PC. You can write your own, of course, as described in Sec. 4-6, and this is sometimes necessary to handle special or new situations. Chapters 7, 8, and 10 discuss some of these cases. Thanks to the dynamic nature of the PC-DOS operating system, you almost never have to reprogram the ROM BIOS: routines loaded in RAM can easily overrule the ROM's.

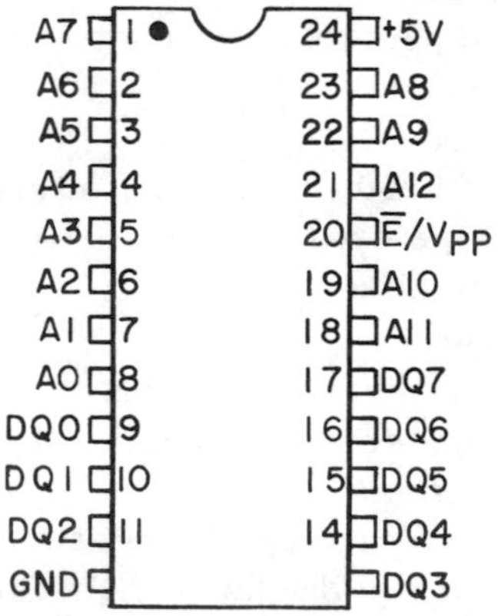

```
         A7 ⌑1 ●      24⌑ +5V
         A6 ⌑2        23⌑ A8
         A5 ⌑3        22⌑ A9
         A4 ⌑4        21⌑ A12
         A3 ⌑5        20⌑ E̅/Vpp
         A2 ⌑6        19⌑ A10
         A1 ⌑7        18⌑ A11
         A0 ⌑8        17⌑ DQ7
        DQ0 ⌑9        16⌑ DQ6
        DQ1 ⌑10       15⌑ DQ5
        DQ2 ⌑11       14⌑ DQ4
        GND ⌑              ⌑ DQ3
```

Fig. 6-8. The Motorola 68764 24-pin EPROM, which is pin-for-pin compatible with the 2364 ROM's used in the IBM PC. Other 8K EPROM's have 28 pins, unfortunately, so they can't be used in the PC.

If you want to use readily available 4-kilobyte 2732 EPROM's, you can, but the different pinout produces a gap in the middle of the EPROM's address space. For example, if you use the spare 0F4000 socket, the 2732 covers 0F4000—0F47FF and 0F5000—0F57FF. If you want to make the PC into a dedicated controller and don't need the ROM BASIC, you can replace the first BASIC ROM (at 0F6000) by your own EPROM. Then at power-on, the system will execute your ROM-based program provided the disk drives fail to respond (because no disk is inserted) or are missing.

Like the I/O devices, the 8 kilobyte 2364 ROM has a chip-select pin (pin 20). When selected by a low on pin 20, the 2364 outputs the byte stored at the address given by A0—A12 onto the eight tristate data lines. The 68764 EPROM pins are the same as those on the 2364 ROM except that pin 20 is also used to write the EPROM in *program mode*. This involves removing the EPROM and placing it in a socket wired up to special programming circuitry that can raise the voltage on pin 20 from 5 to 25 volts. Although you can program a single byte at a time and can set any bit to zero by reprogramming the byte containing it, you can't do the reverse. To set any zero bit to 1 you have to erase all the memory in the chip and start over. You can erase an EPROM by exposing the chip to a shortwave ultraviolet lamp through its transparent window for about 20 minutes. Electrically erasable programmable read-only memory (EEPROM) is becoming increasingly popular because it can be both erased and reprogrammed using only a 5-volt power supply. At this writing, it is still quite expensive, however. Note that the main reason for using ROM (or EPROM) instead of RAM is that ROM retains its memory when the power is turned off. Because ROM memory is present, the 8088 is able to find a program starting at the reset address 0FFFF0H when power is first turned on in the IBM PC.

The lowest fifteen 64-kilobyte "pages" of the megabyte address space are used for RAM. The decoding circuitry, while more complex, is similar to that used for ROM. The PC uses inexpensive dynamic RAM IC's (a dynamic RAM is often called a DRAM) for its programmable memory. Figure 6-9 shows the pinouts for the popular 16-kilobit 4116 DRAM's used on the early (pre-March 1983) PC system board, and for the equally popular 64-kilobit 4164 DRAM's used on current PC's and on all expansion boards that plug into the I/O channel. It's important to note that these DRAM chips are only 1 bit wide; you must have eight 4164's hooked up in parallel to have 64 kilobytes of memory. In contrast, the ROM's are byte-wide memory chips. Up to this point the only type of programmable memory we have discussed is static latches consisting of flip-flops, such as the 74LS373. This kind of

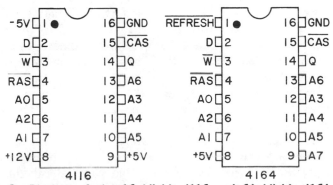

Fig. 6–9. Pinouts of the 16–kilobit 4116 and 64–kilobit 4164 dynamic RAM's currently used in many computers. The 256–kilobit RAM's are a better choice (their pin 1 is A8).

storage retains its stored values until either new data is written into memory or the power is turned off. The bits are either flipped or flopped! This design is easy to work with but requires about six transistors per bit of memory inside the chip. In contrast, dynamic memories require only one transistor per bit and hence use substantially less power and space. Essentially each bit cell is a sample-and-hold circuit (see Sec. 9-3) in which a capacitor is charged (for a 1) or discharged (for a 0).

The only problem in using DRAM is that the charge on the little memory capacitors leaks off, causing the memory to forget its values! To prevent this, the memory capacitors must be periodically recharged. This recharging operation is called *refresh*. To understand how refresh works, you need to know a bit more about the internal organization of a DRAM chip. The DRAM bits are organized into a square array of rows and columns. The DRAM read/write circuitry first places the row address on the DRAM address pins, and then a little later the column address. The row-column combination identifies a single bit in the array. Eight DRAM's accessed in parallel in this way remember a whole byte. Each time a DRAM is read, all bits in the corresponding row are refreshed; that is, the capacitors having a "1" are recharged. Some applications automatically ensure that at least one bit in every row is read every 2 milliseconds, the maximum rated time for reliable memory. Such a case occurs with the video refresh memory as discussed in Sec. 8-2. Normally, however, not all the DRAM rows in programmable memory will be read every 2 milliseconds, so some other mechanism must perform the refresh. In the IBM PC, a dedicated 8253 counter/timer channel causes an 8237 DMA channel to read an address in a new row every 15 microseconds, thereby keeping the DRAM's nicely refreshed both on the system board and on any I/O channel RAM boards. To prevent the 8088 from ever reading incorrect data, each PC DRAM bank includes a ninth DRAM, in which the parity ($\doteq$ 1 if the number of 1's in the byte is an even number, = 0 otherwise) of each byte is stored. When a byte is read, the parity is computed by the hardware and compared to the value in the ninth DRAM. If they differ, an NMI interrupt occurs, causing the PC to display a "PARITY CHECK" message, and the PC halts! Turn off the machine, wait 5 seconds, and turn it back on. It attests to the reliability of the DRAM's that such parity errors are quite rare. Sometimes a particularly bad program crash can also generate the parity check message, even though nothing is wrong with the memory.

One way to save money in buying a PC is to buy memory boards with only 64 kilobytes of DRAM's installed. Then you can buy the rest from a company advertising in the back of *BYTE* or *PC* magazine, and plug them in yourself. If you do this, be careful about static electricity when you handle the DRAM's, since a static discharge too small to be noticed by you can easily destroy a DRAM. Also be sure to plug the DRAM's in with pin 1 pointing in the same direction as the already installed DRAM's. See Sec. 12-2 for details on chip handling and finding pin 1 on an IC. After you've installed the DRAM, set the DIP switches on the system board to reflect the larger memory. Then when the IBM is turned on, it performs a quick memory check for you. That plus the built-in parity checking should report any memory problems.

Table 6-2 provides an overview of the 1-megabyte RAM assignments on the PC. The lowest kilobyte of memory is devoted to the 4-byte interrupt vectors discussed in Secs. 3-6 and 7-1. This is followed by 128 bytes of system RAM used by the ROM BIOS and 384 bytes used by BASIC, DOS, and certain other programs (see the IBM *Technical Reference* manual). The data in these areas can be used to determine the status of various devices. For example, you can determine if the display driver is in graphics or text mode, or see if the keyboard queue is empty. DOS loads itself in next, and it in turn loads all user programs just above itself. Essentially, you can use all RAM between the end of DOS and 9FFFFH (640 kilobytes) without problems. The 0A0000H page is used for EGA video graphics RAM (see Sec. 8-3), and monochrome video RAM area begins at 0B0000H and color/graphics RAM at 0B8000H. The 0C0000H and 0D0000H pages are checked by the ROM BIOS for expansion card ROM BIOS's, and can also be used for Intel/Lotus/Microsoft expanded memory specification (EMS; see Sec. 11-2). The 0E0000H page is reserved on the AT motherboard and the 0F0000H page is reserved for ROM as discussed previously. The 640K memory limit has become a real problem because of the proliferation of handy RAM-resident software, RAM disks, and generally greedy software. This limit is raised to 8 and 16 megabytes by the EMS and 80286 protected virtual address mode, respectively.

ADDRESS	FUNCTION
0—3FF	Interrupt vectors (see Table 3-4)
400—47F	ROM BIOS RAM (see *Tech. Ref.* App. A)
480—5FF	BASIC and special system function RAM
600—9FFFF	Program memory (usually not all installed)
0A0000—0AFFFF	EGA graphics mode video RAM
0B0000—0B7FFF	Monochrome video RAM
0B8000—0BFFFF	Color/graphics video RAM
0C0000—0CFFFF	I/O ROM BIOS's, EMS window
0D0000—0DFFFF	I/O ROM BIOS's, EMS window
0E0000—0EFFFF	Reserved on AT motherboard
0F0000—0F3FFF	Unused on PC, ROM BIOS on AT
0F4000—0F5FFF	PC spare ROM socket, ROM BIOS on AT
0F6000—0FDFFF	ROM BASIC
0FE000—0FFFFF	ROM BIOS

Table 6-2. Allocation of IBM PC 1-megabyte address space. In the standard PC, the 0C0000—0EFFFF area is reserved for ROM expansion with 0C8000—0CBFFF used for fixed disk control.

IBM PC AT System Board

Figure 6-10 shows the AT system board. It is based on the 16-bit 80286 microprocessor, which has advanced memory management and protection features, and improved instruction algorithms that result in about 2.5 times the speed of the PC (at a 6-MHz clock vs a 4.77-MHz PC). The board boasts doubled DMA and interrupt control, a battery-backed-up real-time clock and CMOS system configuration RAM, an enhanced keyboard controller (see p. 236), and eight I/O channels, six of which fully support the 80286 16-MB address space with 16-bit data transfers and secondary processor boards.

The board has two 8237A DMA controllers for a total of seven DMA channels. The second 8237A has three 16-bit channels (channels 5—7) that can transfer data between I/O devices and RAM up to 128 kilobytes at a time anywhere in the 16-megabyte address space. Its fourth channel (called channel 4) is used to cascade the 8-bit channels 0—3 of the first 8237A to the 80286. Unlike the PC, the AT does not use DMA channel 0 for DRAM refresh, thereby freeing up this 8-bit channel. The DMA controllers operate at 3 MHz on a 6-MHz AT, which is slower than the 4.77-MHz on the PC. There are also two 8259A interrupt controllers, with channel 2 of the first cascading the interrupts from the second. The extra controller handles interrupts from the AT real-time clock, the 80287, and the hard disk.

The battery-backed-up real-time clock is a welcome addition that automatically tells the computer the time and date. The MC146818 clock chip includes 64 bytes of CMOS RAM, 14 of which are used by the time/date functions. The remainder are reserved or are used for storing system configuration information. This eliminates the need for the motherboard dip switches, while providing better system descriptions.

A special "shutdown" byte of the CMOS RAM is used to tell the 80286 why a shutdown occurred, which allows software to switch from the 80286 protected virtual address mode back to the 8086 real address mode. The AT RAM disk and the SST debugger make use of this facility to switch back from protected mode. A round trip to and from protected mode takes about 400 microseconds on a 6-MHz AT, most of which is taken up by the switch back to real mode. For this, the 80286 is reset just as it would be if you turned the power off and back on, whereupon it "wakes up" in real mode and reads the shutdown byte, finding it has to return to a user program.

Some of the address decoding uses ROM's, which offer greater flexibility than the 74LS138's, such as duplicating the system ROM addresses 0F0000H and 0E0000H at 0FF0000H and 0FE0000H, respectively. The 0E0000H page is reserved for ROM on the system board. The port addresses 100H through 1FFH, which are inaccessible on the PC, are freed up for use in the I/O channels. One bizarre feature is the ability to gate address line 20, although lines 21 through 23 cannot be gated. There seems to be no purpose to this feature, and we have run without problems extensively with the gate on. Hence if you plan to use protected mode, turn the gate on and leave it on even if you switch back to real mode.

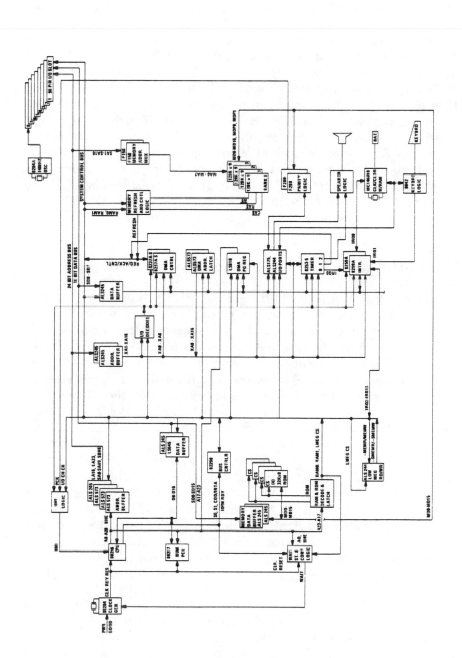

Fig. 6-10. IBM PC AT system board block diagram. From the IBM PC AT *Technical Reference.*

I/O and memory read/write strobes are generated by an 82288 controller chip. The system clock is generated by an 82284 clock circuit, and an 8284A is also included to generate a PC compatible 14-MHz clock and 8254 (like an 8253) counter/timer clocks. The motherboard has a socketed crystal whose frequency is divided by two for the system clock and by three for the 80287 clock. Hence a 12-MHz crystal gives 6 MHz and 4 MHz, respectively. Because a 4-MHz 80287 clock is slower than the standard PC 4.77-MHz 8087 clock, heavily 8087 bound code can actually run slower on the AT than on the PC. The crystal can be changed on most AT's to 16 MHz to get an 8-MHz machine with a 5.3-MHz 80287, or to 18 MHz for a 9-MHz machine with a 6-MHz 80287. Starting in 1986, AT's were delivered with a 16-MHz crystal. Some plug-in cards may no longer run reliably at this increased speed, and software drivers typically have to include extra instructions like JMP $+2 between IN's and OUT's to slow the 80286 down. Up to 1986, AT's had been delivered with 128-kilobyte piggyback DRAM's, and then IBM switched to 256-kilobit DRAM's (as had everyone else).

6-3. 8255 Smart Parallel I/O Circuit and System DIP Switches

The 8255 PPI (programmable peripheral interface), better known as a PIO (parallel I/O) chip, is the oldest smart peripheral chip in Intel's large family of microprocessor support circuits. This section gives an overview of the 8255, which is used on the PC for 16 lines of input and 8 lines of output. The 8255 is also used on the custom wire-wrap board whose design and construction are explained in Chap. 12. After describing the 8255, we summarize its uses on the PC system board and its replacement on the AT.

Because of its design and high sales volume over the years, the 8255 provides the lowest cost per bit of I/O of any parallel I/O circuit available: 24 bits for about $4.00. Three 74LS374's, for example, provide 24 pins of output, but cost a little more, have 60 pins, and need more board space than one 40-pin 8255. Furthermore there is considerable flexibility in how the 8255 pins are used: for input or output, with or without handshaking and interrupts, and so on. *Handshaking* is a technique in which signals are sent back and forth between two devices to synchronize the data flow between them. One device sends a signal that means "Did you get the data I sent?" and the other device sends back a signal that means "Yes, I got the data." That's handshaking. We discuss this important concept further in Secs. 10-1 and 10-2 as it applies to the Centronics printer interface and RS232 modem control. On the PC system board, 16 lines of the 8255 are used for input and 8 for output, with no handshaking or interrupts being used. Figure 6-11 is a block diagram of the 8255, which, like the generic smart peripheral of Fig. 6-6, has a microprocessor bus interface consisting of $\overline{RD}$, $\overline{WR}$, $\overline{CS}$, eight bidirectional data lines, and internal port address lines (A_0 and A_1). The chip implements three 8-bit ports, A, B, and C, each of which can be configured as an input port or an output port. Port A can also be configured as a

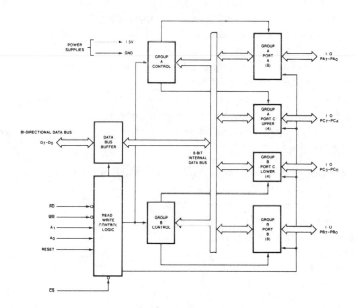

Fig. 6–11. Intel 8255 programmable peripheral interface diagram. Twenty–four pins can be used for input and/or output under program control. Some of these pins (those for port C) can also be used for handshaking and interrupt control.

bidirectional port using 5 lines of port C for handshaking. The bus interface lines also include a RESET line, which when high initializes all port pins to acts as inputs. This prevents any damage from occurring at power-on due to a pin acting as an output when the external circuitry wired to it expects the pin to act as an input.

The 8255 has four internal registers, three of which can be read as well as written. They are addressed by the 2-bit binary number on address lines A_1 and A_0. Specifically, $A_1A_0 = 00$ selects port A, $A_1A_0 = 01$ selects port B, $A_1A_0 = 10$ selects port C, and $A_1A_0 = 11$ selects the write-only control register. Hence for port A to be read, the lines A_1, A_0, $\overline{RD}$, and $\overline{CS}$ must all simultaneously go low, at which point the 8255 places the contents of Port A (whether configured as input or as output) on the data bus. The IBM PC's system board 8255 ports A, B, and C and the control register are located at I/O addresses 60H through 63H, respectively.

If 24 lines of input are needed, the 8255 requires no programming; the initial high value of the RESET line required by the 8086/8088 chooses this mode of operation. If some pins are to be used as output pins such as on the IBM PC system board, or if handshaking and interrupt capabilities are to be used, a byte of data called a *control word* must be sent to the control register ($A_1A_0 = 11$). The control register is used for four purposes: to select the direction of data flow through ports A, B, and C; to choose one of the three basic modes of operation for port A; to choose one of two modes for port B; and to set or reset single bits of port C. The IBM PC uses mode 0 (the "basic input/output" mode) for both ports A and B. This mode allows ports A and B to be used as either input or output ports, and port C to be split into two nibbles (4 bits apiece), each of which can be inputs or outputs. Mode 0 uses all 24 port pins as I/O; modes 1 and 2 use some of port C's pins for handshaking and interrupt control.

The 8 bits in the control word sent to the 8255's control register have the following meanings:

        bit 0 specifies the port C low nibble (C0—C3) direction
        bit 1 gives port B's direction
        bit 2 gives port B's mode (0 or 1)
        bit 3 gives the port C high nibble
        bit 4 gives port A's direction
        bits 6 and 5 give port A's mode (00 = mode 0, 01 = mode 1,
            10 = mode 2)
        bit 7 = 1

The 8255 control bits that choose the port I/O directions have the suggestive values of 1 for Input and 0 for Output. If bit 7 equals 0, the byte sent to the 8255 is not interpreted as a control word, but rather as a command to set or reset an individual bit in port C.

On the IBM PC, mode 0 is with ports A and C configured as input ports, and B as an output port. The desired control byte is thus 10011001, which is sent to the 8255 by executing

        MOV   AL,99H
        OUT   CMD_PORT,AL

where CMD_PORT = 63.

Mode 1 uses three port C lines for handshaking and interrupt control of port A. For input, a negative going pulse on line PC4 (bit 4 of port C) causes port A to latch the data on its input lines and to drive PC5 high as a "buffer full" message for the device connected to the input lines. PC5 goes back low when the CPU reads port A. This is a signal to the remote device that it can send another byte. Similarly, if port A interrupts are enabled by sending the proper control word to the 8255, PC3 also goes high when a byte is received. This signal can be used as an interrupt signal by connecting it to the 8259 interrupt controller discussed in the next section. This line also returns to a low value when port A is read. Port B functions similarly in mode 1 by using the three low pins of port C. Output using mode 1 occurs in a similar fashion. For a complete discussion of this and of mode 2, see Intel's *Component Data Catalog*. Note that mode 2 allows port A to be used as a bidirectional port with both handshaking and interrupt control by using five of port C's pins.

The primary advantages of smart parallel ports versus the dumb ones are that: (1) they can be dynamically programmed to be either input ports or output ports, (2) output ports can be read back in just like memory, (3) status information is provided, (4) fewer DIP pins are needed, and (5) handshaking and interrupt controls are available. Of course you can do all that with TTL circuits, but many ICs are required.

With all these advantages, you may ask, why would anyone ever use a dumb port? Well, that depends on your requirements. Dumb ports are typically made using 74LS244's and 74LS374's, which are bus drivers. They are far more rugged, source and sink much more current, and are less sensitive to noise at their inputs (due to their Schmitt trigger input circuitry) than the smart ports. The smart ones can also be destroyed by static electricity when they are handled. The dumb ones couldn't care less about static. So you may have to buffer the output of an 8255 with a 74LS244 anyhow! The PC system board is an excellent example of where the 8255 is the clear choice: low drive power and many I/O pins are needed.

IBM PC System-Board 8255 Usage

The PC 8255 input port A reads the system board DIP switch SW1 when PB7 output line is low and reads the keyboard input byte (see Sec. 8-1) when PB7 is high. The meanings of the SW1 switches are described in the IBM PC *Guide to Operations* under Options and specify the type of display monitor used, the number of disk drives, and the amount of memory on the system board. The instructions say to turn switch 2 of SW1 on. Turning this switch off allows the INT line of the 8087 numeric processor (if installed) to drive the 8088's NMI line (see the logic diagrams in the IBM PC *Technical Reference* manual). Unless you plan to write your own NMI interrupt handler allowing for 8087 interrupts, this switch should stay on. Typical 8087 support routines do not use interrupts.

Two bits of the high nibble of the IBM PC's 8255 input port C report RAM parity and I/O channel statuses to let the NMI handler know which one interrupted (or neither if the 8087 did it). The other two bits of the high nibble read cassette data input and the 8253 timer/counter channel 2 output line. The low nibble gives the binary value of the number of 32-kilobyte RAM banks in the I/O channel as set on the system board switch SW2. This allows the PC to know about up to eight 64-kilobyte banks (half a megabyte) in the I/O channel. Of course a program could also determine how much RAM there is, what displays are attached, how many disk drives there are, how much RAM is on the system board, and whether the 8087 is there. A cheaper and less confusing approach would have been for the IBM PC designers to eliminate the sense switches altogether and make the 8088 figure everything out with some simple code. The only advantage of the switches is that you can fool the power-on initialization routines into thinking there is less RAM than you actually have. This is convenient for bypassing some of the RAM check when the machine is turned on. With only

64 kilobytes of memory, this check is reasonably fast, but for half a megabyte it takes a long time. Note that except for the initialization routines, all other system programs and BIOS routines use the configuration information stored in the BIOS RAM area at 400H to 47FH as described in the ROM BIOS listings of the *Technical Reference* manual. Hence programs can change the configuration to suit their needs upon gaining control. This is handy for RAM emulation of a disk drive, which provides very high-speed disk response. For flexibility, your programs should *not* read the switches directly.

The PC 8255 output port B is used to enable (by setting PB0 = 1) 8253 timer/counter channel 2 to generate a square wave used for the speaker and the cassette outputs (see the 8253 discussion below and Sec. 9-5); to send programmed waveforms to the speaker (bit PB1, see Sec. 9-5); to read the low nibble of system board switch SW2 (by setting PB2 = 1); to turn the cassette motor off (by setting PB3 = 1); to enable RAM parity and the I/O channel status lines that are read by port C of the 8255 (by setting PB4 and PB5 = 0); to drive the keyboard clock line low (by setting PB6 = 0); and to choose between having port A read SW1 (when PB7 = 1) or the keyboard data (when PB7 = 0, normal mode).

IBM PC AT 8255 Counterpart

The AT extends the facilities provided by the 8255 in the ordinary PC by adding a CMOS RAM in place of the dip switches and replacing the 8255 by a smart 8042 keyboard controller. The 8042 is actually an Intel 8048-style single-chip microcomputer with custom ROM code on chip along with a CPU interface similar to the 8255. It is set up to carry on bidirectional data transfer with the AT keyboard, allowing the AT to control the lock indicator lights on the keyboard. As for the PC's 8255, the keyboard data port is 60H, and port 61H can be used for keyboard status and resetting the keyboard after a scan code has been received. Bits 0—3 of port 61H are latched by an 74LS175 with the same meanings as the PC's 8255 port B bits 0, 1, 4, and 5, respectively. Alternatively, I/O port 64H offers increased status and command capability and is used in the AT ROM BIOS routines.

In particular, writing port 64H with a 0D1H causes the next byte written to port 60H to be sent to an 8042 output latch with the following meanings: bit 0 low, reset 80286 (for shutdown back to real mode); bit 1 high, enable address line 20; bits 2 and 3, undefined; bit 4, output buffer full (connected to IRQ1); bit 5, input buffer full (input only); bit 6, keyboard clock (output); bit 7, keyboard data (output).

To read/write the CMOS RAM, output the desired CMOS RAM address to port 70H followed by the data byte IN or OUT to port 71H. For example, to return from 80286 protected mode (see Sec. 6-6) to the real address given by the double word at 40:67H, output 8FH to port 70H (which also disables NMI), 5 to port 71H, 0FEH (shutdown) to port 64H, and then execute HLT/JMP $-1 to really halt!

6-4. Interrupt Controller, Timer/Counter, DMA Controller

This section gives an overview of the three remaining smart I/O circuits on the IBM PC system board: the 8259A programmable interrupt controller, the 8253 programmable interval timer/counter, and the 8237 DMA controller. The roles of the interrupt and DMA controllers are discussed further in Chap. 7. The IBM PC AT system board has two 8259A's, two 8237A's, and an 8254, which is essentially the same as an 8253. The present section provides the reader with a broad view of the capabilities and operational modes of these chips. The uses of these smart circuits on the IBM PC and PC AT are explained with code illustrating how the circuits are programmed. For complete technical descriptions, consult the Intel *Component Data Catalog*.

Intel 8259A Programmable Interrupt Controller

Consider first the useful 8259A PIC (programmable interrupt controller), which is responsible for a crucial part of the smooth-running natures of the IBM PC and AT. This circuit is responsible for coordinating the interrupt requests that various hardware devices make. The interrupt concept is so important that Secs. 7-1 and 7-2 are devoted to it. For now, just think of the microprocessor as a busy executive. If a device is to get the executive's attention, it must talk first to the interrupt controller, which plays the role of the executive's secretary. The secretary decides which device has the highest priority and whether the executive is doing something that can be interrupted, and then buzzes the executive accordingly. This is a personification of what the 8259A diagrammed in Fig. 6-12 does. It handles eight active-high interrupt lines, labeled IRn, giving IR0 the highest priority and IR7 the lowest priority. The interrupt mask register in the 8259A is a byte whose nth bit *masks* the interrupt request from line IRn. That is, if bit n is nonzero, line IRn cannot cause an interrupt. When the 8259A authorizes an interrupt request, it raises the INT line on the 8088. If the 8088's interrupts are enabled (due to execution of an STI instruction), the 8088 acknowledges the interrupt by telling (via the S0—S2 lines) the 8288 bus controller to pull the INTA line low. On seeing this the 8259A places a 1-byte interrupt vector number on the data bus. This number identifies a 4-byte interrupt vector in the lowest kilobyte of RAM. More specifically, if the 8259A places the number nn on the bus, then the interrupt vector at absolute address 4*nn is used. In the 80286's protected virtual address mode, the interrupt vector at offset 8*nn in the Interrupt Descriptor Table (see Sec. 6-6) is used. The 8088 or 80286 then pushes its flags onto the stack and executes a far call to the address given by this interrupt vector. This is exactly the way the software INT nn instruction discussed in Sec. 3-6 works. The appropriate interrupt handler program (see Sec. 4-6) had better be present, or there'll be a crash! Thus a hardware interrupt is an

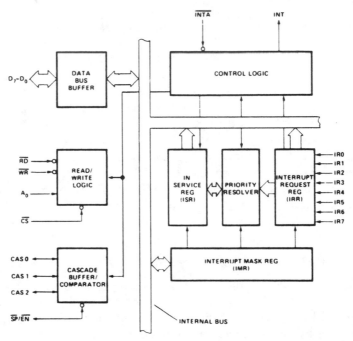

Fig. 6–12.   Block diagram of the Intel 8259A programmable interrupt controller, which coordinates the interrupt requests appearing on its eight interrupt request (IRn) lines.   Reprinted by permission of Intel Corporation, copyright 1983.

an asynchronous call to some location in memory.   Before discussing the software required to initialize the 8259A appropriately and to handle interrupt requests, let's look more carefully at the hardware.

As shown in Fig. 6-12, the 28-pin 8259A PIC is a smart peripheral of the form shown in Fig. 6-6.   That is, it has read, write, chip-select, data, and address lines.   In addition it has the eight interrupt lines discussed above, an INT output line that goes to the CPU's INT input, and an $\overline{\text{INTA}}$ input line used by the 8088 to request the interrupt vector byte.   The cascade lines CAS0, CAS1, and CAS2 are used to coordinate multiple 8259A's, and hence the AT's two sets of 8259A CAS lines are connected together.   The last pin, $\overline{\text{SP/EN}}$, goes low when the 8259A asserts the interrupt vector byte on its data bus.   On the PC this line is used to disable the 8088's 74LS245 data bus buffer, since the 8259A's data bus is connected directly to the 8088's ADn lines.

The 8259A has many modes of operation, as described in Intel's *Component Data Catalog*.   We discuss here only the popular mode used in the IBM PC and PC AT.   For this mode, three *initialization code words* (these are actually 3 bytes) must be sent to the 8259A.   This can be done using the code

```
mov    al,13h        ;Edge-triggered IRn, one 8259A, ICW4 needed
out    inta00,al     ;Send to first control port (20H)
mov    al,8          ;Use interrupt vectors 8—0FH for IR0 to IR7
out    inta01,al     ;Send to second control port (21H)
mov    al,9          ;ICW4: buffered mode, normal EOI, 8086
out    inta01,al
```

This sets up a single 8259A to respond to positive-going edges on the inter-rupt request lines (IRn), to use interrupt vectors 08 through 0FH (see Table 3-4 for interrupt vector assignments), to work with an 8086/8088 (rather than an 8080/8085), to drive $\overline{SP/EN}$ low when asserting the interrupt vector byte (buffered mode), and to reinitialize interrupts upon receipt of the EOI (end of interrupt) code. At this point the 8259A is ready to accept inter-rupt requests on all eight lines, and to raise its INT output accordingly.

Interrupts are then enabled on the 8088 by execution of the STI (set interrupt flag) instruction. Before the PC BIOS routines do this, they mask off (disable) five of the IRn lines. Specifically the instructions

```
mov    al,0bch       ;Enable disk (bit 6), keyboard (1),
out    inta01,al     ; and timer (0) interrupts
sti
```

are executed (after some initial testing of the 8259A is performed). When an interrupt occurs, further interrupts are disabled in the 8088, and the 8259A records but does not request further service until it receives an EOI code. Thus it is the responsibility of the interrupt handler programs to reenable interrupts by executing the sequence

```
sti
mov    al,20h        ;EOI command
out    inta00,al     ;Send to 8259A
```

For examples of timer and keyboard interrupt routines, see Secs. 7-1 and 8-1. You can set up your own interrupts on lines IR2—IR5 and IR7. These interrupt request lines are all available for for use by boards in the I/O channel (IR2 is used to cascade the AT's second 8259). Keep in mind, how-ever, that IBM has assigned (but not implemented) specific functions for all of these interrupt lines except IR2, which it simply lists as being reserved for future use (see interrupts 08—0F in Table 3-4). For example, IR7 is listed as being reserved for parallel printer interfaces, and IR4 for serial communications. More than one device can be attached to a given IRn line, in which case the software has to input a status byte from the relevant devices to find out which one wants service.

Intel 8253 Programmable Interval Timer

A smart peripheral that serves three important purposes on the IBM PC system board is the three-channel 8253 16-bit timer/counter circuit, diagrammed in Fig. 6-13. Each channel can be used to take an input clock signal having any frequency from 0 to 2 MHz and produce an output signal whose frequency is the input frequency divided by an arbitrary 16-bit number. On the PC, the input clock frequency for all three channels is 4.772727/4 = 1.1931817 MHz, derived from the system clock. The output from channel 0 is used to make the time-of-day clock tick, the output from channel 1 is used to tell the DMA controller on the IBM PC or the dedicated circuitry on the AT to refresh the dynamic RAM's, and the channel-2 output is used to send sound to the speaker (see Sec. 8-1 for "piano" keyboard) or cassette microphone input.

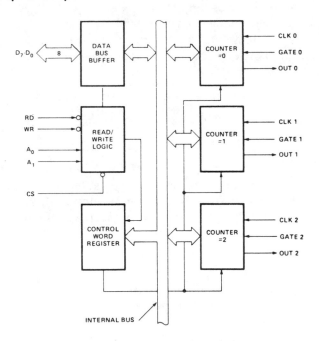

Fig. 6-13. Intel 8253 three-channel programmable interval timer used on the PC for its real-time clock, memory refresh, and "bell." Reprinted by permission of Intel Corporation, copyright 1983.

Just as in the 8255 PPI and 8259A PIC, the 24-pin 8253 has the usual control lines of the generic smart peripheral shown in Fig. 6-6. In addition, each channel has three special lines: a CLK input, a GATE input, and an OUTput. Although the IBM PC only uses the timer/counter's ability to create an output signal whose frequency is equal to that of the system clock divided by a programmable 16-bit number, the 8253 is capable of operating in other ways as well. Each channel can be programmed in one of six possible modes: 0, interrupt on terminal count; 1, programmable one-shot; 2, rate generator; 3, square-wave generator; 4, software-triggered strobe; and 5, hardware-triggered strobe. Briefly, setting mode 0 drives the OUT line low for the duration of a programmable number of pulses on the CLK input line, at which point OUT goes back high again. This can be used to interrupt the CPU after a specified time or as a program-initiated one-shot (compare with the 74LS121 hardware one-shot circuit of Sec. 5-7). Mode 1 yields a similar one-shot, except that the counting operation is started by reception of a rising GATE edge, rather than by a program command. Mode 2 is a divide-by-n counter, where n is a 16-bit number. The output waveform stays high for n input-clock periods and, at each countdown completion, goes low for one clock period. Thus the output is a very asymmetric waveform whose period is (input clock)/n. Mode 2 is used by channel 1 to drive the DMA DRAM refresh. Mode 3 offers a symmetric divide-by-n counter output that is a square wave whose high and low periods are equal. This mode is used by channels 0 and 2 for the time-of-day clock, speaker (bell), and cassette waveforms. Modes 4 and 5 are similar to modes 0 and 1, except that OUT remains high until the countdown completes, at which point OUT goes low for one input-clock period and returns high. Both GATE triggered modes (1 and 5) are retriggerable; that is, OUT remains in its count state (low for mode 1 and high for 5) for the full count after the last rising edge of GATE. For modes 0 and 2—4, a high GATE value enables counting. More detailed descriptions of the various modes are given in Intel's *Component Data Catalog*.

The programming of the three timer/counters can be illustrated by their respective uses in the IBM PC. The 8253 must be initialized by sending a mode control byte for each channel to the 8253's control word register. The bits in the mode control byte have the following meanings:

bit 0   = 0, count in binary
           = 1, count in BCD
bits 1—3   = mode number (a binary number between 000 to 101)
bits 4,5   = 00, latch current count for reading
           = 01, read/load low byte (no latching needed)
           = 10, read/load high byte (no latching needed)
           = 11, read/load low byte, then high byte
bits 6,7   = counter number (0, 1, or 2)

Sending a latch command (00 in bits 4 and 5) before reading both bytes of the 16-bit counter is desirable since otherwise the count can change in between reading the high byte of the counter and the low byte. On the PC, the three counters are programmed after power-up as follows:

```
timer   equ    40h           ;Port address of timer 0
cntrl   equ    43h           ;Port address of 8253 control word register
```

```
        mov     al,54h          ;Use mode 2 for timer 1; load a 1-byte
        out     cntrl,al        ; count value next
        mov     al,18           ;Load 16-bit count = 18 (1.19/18 = 66 kHz)
        out     timer+1,al      ; to start DMA refresh clock

        mov     al,36h          ;Use mode 3 for timer 0; load low byte next,
        out     cntrl,al        ; then high byte
        mov     al,0            ;Divide by "0" count, i.e., 65536, giving
        out     timer,al        ; about 18.2 time-of-day interrupts/second
        out     timer,al        ;Why doesn't the PC use 59659, giving 20 Hz?
                                ; See Sec. 9-5 for discussion
        mov     al,0b6h         ;Mode 3 for timer 2; load 2-byte count next
        out     cntrl3,al
        mov     ax,533h         ;Count value is 533H = 1331
        out     timer+2,al      ;Turn on 1193181/1331 = 896-Hz square wave
        mov     al,ah
        out     timer+2,al
```

To make the speaker beep using timer 2's square wave, the 8255's port B bits PB0 and PB1 must be set to 1 for the duration of the sound desired. For examples of waveform generation using the 8253, see Secs. 8-1 and 9-5.

Intel 8237 DMA Controller

We now come to the 8237 four-channel DMA (**d**irect **m**emory **a**ccess) controller chip, diagrammed in Fig. 6-14. This device is essentially a special-purpose microprocessor optimized for transferring blocks of data up to 64 kilobytes in length from one place in memory to another or between an I/O device and memory. Consider first transfers between an I/O device and memory. To input a byte of data, the 8088 has to hang in a little program loop waiting for a new byte of data to be ready, then read the byte from the input port into the AL register, and finally write AL out to some location in memory. In contrast, the DMA controller simply waits, doing nothing, until a signal indicating new data appears on its DREQ (**DMA req**uest) line. It then immediately sends a chip select signal to the I/O device via the DACK (DMA **ack**nowlege) strobe, causing the input port to place a byte on the data bus. Simultaneously it supplies a memory address and signals the destination to read it! The DMA process requires only 5 clock periods per byte transferred versus at least 29 clock periods for the CPU method—in other words, 1 microsecond instead of 6. The 8237 has four independent DMA channels, each capable of performing its own DMA transfers.

For I/O-to-memory transfers, $\overline{MEMW}$, $\overline{IOR}$, and the DACK line connected to the I/O device all become active simultaneously. Similarly for memory-to-I/O transfers, $\overline{MEMR}$, $\overline{IOW}$, and the appropriate DACK line become simultaneously active. Since there is also an address present, something must be done to prevent other I/O devices from responding to what looks like a port

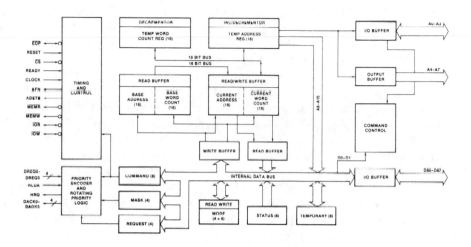

Fig. 6–14. Intel 8237A four–channel direct memory access controller. Used on the IBM PC for refreshing memory and disk data transfers. The IBM PC AT has two 8237A's, one for 8–bit transfers and one for 16–bit transfers. Reprinted by permission of Intel Corporation, copyright 1983.

address on the address lines along with an active I/O strobe. This is accomplished by the 8237's AEN (address **en**able) line, which is set high during a DMA transfer. All I/O device address decoders must examine the AEN line and prevent the I/O devices from being activated when AEN is high.

Memory-to-memory transfers require two 8237 DMA channels and sequential, rather than simultaneous, data transfer, since memory locations cannot be chip selected by a DACK line. Eight clock periods are required per byte transferred compared to the 17 periods required by the 8088's MOVS instruction. The 8237 uses DMA channel 0 for the source address and channel 1 for the destination address. A command bit is available that lets the source address increment, decrement, or stay constant. The latter is handy for writing a constant value into a block of memory up to 64 kilobytes long, although the STOS instruction is almost as fast (10 clock periods/byte). On the 8086/8088 systems, the major speed advantage of the DMA controller occurs for transfers between I/O and memory. In a special block transfer mode described below, successive bytes can be transferred in or out of memory using only two clock periods per byte (420 nanoseconds on the PC). Note that although the CPU doesn't have to think about DMA transfers while they take place, it does have to wait.

Examine the block diagram in Fig. 6-14 and you'll see that many of the pins resemble those of a CPU. As on the 8088 itself, the data bus is multiplexed with an address byte (the high address byte on the 8237). This must be latched by a 74LS373 when ADSTB goes high. In the 8237, unlike the

8088 CPU, the $\overline{\text{IOR}}$, $\overline{\text{IOW}}$, and the four lowest address bits are all bidirectional. They become output lines when the 8237 performs a DMA transfer. The rest of the time they are input lines, allowing the 8237 to act like a set of sixteen I/O ports. The four DREQn lines are inputs that can be attached to I/O devices that need DMA service. The corresponding DACKn output lines provide the I/O device chip selects. The 8237 sets HRQ high when it wants the CPU to tristate its address, data, and control signals so that the 8237 can use the address, data, and control busses itself. On the PC and AT, HRQ high puts the CPU into a wait state and tristates the buffers. The $\overline{\text{EOP}}$ line on the 8237 is bidirectional. When used as an output, $\overline{\text{EOP}}$ goes low when the terminal count is reached—that is, when the programmed number of bytes have been transferred. When used as an input, $\overline{\text{EOP}}$ can be pulled low by an external device to terminate any DMA operation in progress.

So far the capabilities of the 8237 have been described in general terms with an overview of its pin definitions. To understand how data transfers actually take place when appropriate programming is done, consider first the internal registers used to store memory addresses, block counts, modes, commands, and status. Each DMA channel has a 6-bit mode word and four 16-bit registers associated with it, namely a current address and count, and a base address and count. The base address (starting address) and count (the number of bytes to be transferred) are sent to the 8237 before a DMA operation takes place and automatically initialize the current address and count registers to the same values. After each byte is transferred during the DMA operation, the current address is incremented or decremented (depending on whether bit 5 of the channel's mode-word is 0 or 1), and the current count is decremented. Transfers continue until the current count decrements to 0 (the terminal count), or until the $\overline{\text{EOP}}$ pin is driven low by an external device. The base registers keep the initial values of the corresponding current registers so that when the current count decrements to 0 the current registers can be reloaded automatically if bit 4 of the channel's mode register is set to 1. Bits 3,2 of the mode register specify read (10) or write (01) transfers, and bits 7,6 specify one of four possible transfer modes: demand (00), single (01), block (10), and cascade (11). For transfer rates substantially less than 1 byte per machine cycle (4 clock periods) the single transfer mode is desirable. This transfers a single byte per activation of the channel DREQ line. For the DRAM refresh (every 72 clock periods) and floppy-disk transfers of 32 microseconds/byte on the IBM PC, the single transfer mode is used. The floppy-disk data rate is sufficiently slow that the 8088 could handle it using a program loop, but the time-of-day and keyboard interrupts would then have to be disabled. Hence the DMA method is preferable. The block transfer mode is used when the I/O device can operate nearly as fast as or faster than the DMA controller. If the I/O device is somewhat slower than the DMA controller, it can raise the 8237's READY line high, causing the 8237 to insert wait states just as the 8088 does. The initial byte transfer takes place in five clock periods, but subsequent transfers occur in three periods (630 nanoseconds on the PC). If the system bandwidth can handle it, a special two-clock-period mode is also available (420 nanoseconds on the PC).

There are three control registers on the 8237: a channel mask register allowing channels to be individually disabled, a channel request register allowing a program (instead of a DREQ line) to initiate a DMA request, and the basic command register. See the Intel *Component Data Catalog* for further details. Here we simply illustrate the use of the 8237 with several programming examples.

The PC uses DMA channel 0 for memory refresh. You saw previously that the 8253 timer/counter OUT1 line is set up to provide an active low pulse every 72 clock cycles (15 microseconds). This line clocks a 74LS74 flip-flop whose ouput drives the 8237's DREQ0 line, and the DACK0 line is wired up to clear this flip-flop. Hence DMA channel 0 is requested by the hardware to do something every 15 microseconds. The software sets up a memory read from 64K successive memory locations (128 bytes would satisfy the refresh requirements, but 64K is fine, too), with one location being read every 15 microseconds when DREQ0 goes high. Specifically, the code is

```
dma    equ  00
mov    al,0ffh       ;Set 16-bit count of 64K for RAM refresh
mov    dma+1,al      ;Store low byte of channel 0 count
mov    dma+1,al      ;Store high byte of count = 65535
mov    al,58h        ;Use single transfer mode for channel 0,
out    dma+11,al     ; increment, autoinitialize, and read
mov    al,0          ;Disable memory to memory transfer, enable
out    dma+8,al      ; 8237, normal timing, fixed priority,
                     ; DREQ active high, DACK active low
out    dma+10,al     ;Enable channel 0 DMA (unmask it)
```

The refresh operation causes the contents of some memory location to be asserted on the data bus, but no other device pays any attention because the AEN line is high. The DACK0 "chip select" resets the flip-flop that drove DREQ high, indicates a RAM refresh cycle (by turning on all memory chip RAS lines), and disables all memory chip CAS lines. This last action prevents using DMA channel 0 for anything but refresh. That's too bad since some superfast (2.4 megabytes/second) data transfers would be possible if the DACK0 circuitry didn't do this.

A nice example of using DMA for experiment control is a program that's used to output an arbitrary voltage waveform from a 12-bit DAC (digital-to-analog converter, see Sec. 9-2), without tying up the CPU. What's done in hardware is to connect DACK3 to the DAC's chip select line (so that DMA channel 3 will output data to the DAC), and to wire up a clock whose output is connected to DREQ3 (so that a new byte of data is requested from the DMA controller for every tick of the clock). A table of the 16-bit values that define the waveform is stored in a buffer area called WAVE. The following program then sets up DMA channel 3 to output the contents of WAVE, which is assumed to be in the same 64K memory page as the program:

```
dma       equ   0                    ;DMA port origin on IBM PC
dmapage   equ   80h                  ;DMA page register
dwavcnt   equ   2000h                ;Default waveform byte count (4096 words)

dmawav:   mov   al,5bh               ;Set DMA ch. 3 to single mode, read,
          out   dma+11,al            ; autoinitialize
          out   dma+12,al            ;Reset first/last flip-flop
          mov   ax,cs                ;Calc high order 4 bits of buffer area
          mov   cl,4
          rol   ax,cl
          out   dmapage+2,al         ;Store in ch. 3 64K DMA page
          and   al,0f0h
          add   ax,offset wave       ;Get page offset
          out   dma+6,al             ;Output waveform buffer start addr
          mov   al,ah
          out   dma+6,al
          mov   ax,dwavcnt
          mov   wavcnt,ax            ;Output DMA byte count
          out   dma+7,al
          mov   al,ah
          out   dma+7,al
          mov   al,3                 ;Unmask DMA ch. 3 (let 'er rip)
          out   dma+10,al
          ret

wavcnt    dw    dwavcnt              ;Waveform byte count
bfrptr    dw    0                    ;Waveform buffer pointer
          even
wave      dw    ?                    ;Waveform buffer area; values for
                                     ; DAC stored starting here
```

Note that the 8237 is capable of handling only one 64K memory "page" at a time. In fact, it doesn't even know that more than 64K of memory is in the system. To increase the DMA capability to a full megabyte (although admittedly retaining the 64K page-boundary problem), the PC uses a 74LS670 4-by-4 register file to store the four high-order address bits for each of the four DMA channels. This is the DMA page register DMAPAGE in the code above. A register file is like a latch, except that two independent sets of enable and address lines are present (one for read and one for write) so that read and write operations can be done simultaneously. The way the simple read decoding is set up on the PC's 74LS670, DMA channels 0 and 1 have the same page (I/O port address 83H in the DMA page register), which isn't a limitation since channel 0 can only be used for refresh (unless you want to make a couple of system board modifications).

The PC uses DMA channel 2 for floppy-disk transfers. These transfers are complicated by the fact that the transfers can cross 64K page boundaries. Hence the floppy-disk routine has to write the DMAPAGE register (at port address 81H) for channel 2 DMA operations to access the right memory address. See the ROM BIOS listings in the IBM PC *Technical Reference* manual for the complete resolution of this complication. Here we just consider setting up channel 2 to read in one sector (512 bytes) from the floppy disk into memory on the 64K page stored in DMAPAGE, starting at an offset within the page contained in BX. The code is

```
mov   al,46h        ;Ch. 2 single byte transfers.  Disk read
out   dma+11,al     ;Output mode byte (4AH for write disk)
out   dma+12,al     ;Reset first/last flip-flop
mov   al,bl         ;Output address offset on current DMAPAGE
out   dma+4,al
mov   al,bh
out   dma+4,al
mov   al,0          ;Output count = 512
out   dma+5,al
mov   al,2
out   dma+5,al
out   dma+10,al     ;Unmask ch. 2 and read the sector
```

On the AT, the second 8237A channels are numbered 4—7. Channel 4 is used to cascade the data from channels 0—3 and is not available for other uses. Channels 5—7 are general purpose 16-bit channels that operate on 128-kilobyte RAM boundaries. All channels can transfer data between RAM and I/O devices throughout the 80286's 16-megabyte address space. The AT has dedicated DRAM refresh circuitry, which frees up DMA channel 0 for general use. In fact, you can use channels 0 and 1 to block move data within one 64-kilobyte RAM area while the 80286 does something else. However, since the 80286 moves blocks faster and can work with 16 bits at a time, this is not particularly useful. In fact, the 80286 has string I/O instructions (rep insw and rep outsw) that transfer data between RAM and I/O faster than the 8237A's can, and the AT uses this feature to transfer 512-byte sectors to and from the hard disk controller.

6-5. The IBM PC I/O Channel Bus

The IBM PC system board needs a number of additional capabilities such as a video display controller, serial and parallel communications, and a floppy-disk controller before the computer system is really useful. The interface boards that implement these functions are plugged into the five-slot *I/O channel*. From a logical point of view, the I/O channel is simply a set of 62 signal lines that can be used to connect the PC to external devices not on the system board. Physically, the I/O channel is implemented by the five printed circuit board connectors (slots) in the left rear corner of the PC system board. Each of these slots is wired up to the same set of 62 I/O channel signal lines, so all slot positions are identical. In addition to the essential functions just mentioned, more memory, specialized I/O devices, battery-backed-up clock/date circuits, and many other functions can be plugged into these slots. The boards that fit in the slots have a maximum length of 12 inches and height of 4.5 inches, giving about 52 square inches of board space. The IBM PC XT has eight slots, three of which are "half-slots." Many boards are available for these smaller slots. This section defines the 62 I/O channel lines, and later chapters describe boards that use the I/O channel. For example, Chap. 12 describes how to build a wirewrap board that implements a serial port and three 8-bit parallel ports.

Figure 6-15 shows the I/O channel lines. All of the signal lines of the I/O channel have already been defined in this chapter except for T/C (DMA terminal count), OSC (14.31818-MHz high-frequency oscillator), and CLOCK (OSC/3 = 4.772727, the system clock). To find the relevant discussions for each line, please use the index (the functions of each line are also summarized in the IBM PC *Technical Reference* manual). Note that IBM uses -SIG rather than $\overline{\text{SIG}}$ to indicate that the line SIG is active-low.

IBM PC AT I/O Channel Bus

All eight slots of the AT I/O channel have the 62-pin connector shown in Fig. 6-15, and six slots have a 36-pin connector as well, which gives the extension to a full 16-bit data bus and a 24-bit address bus. On the AT, the address lines of Fig. 6-15 are renamed SA0 through SA19, the data lines are renamed SD0 through SD7, ALE is renamed BALE, pins B4 and B19 are named IRQ 9 and -REFRESH, respectively (IRQ 2 is used to cascade the second 8259A and DACK 0 is moved to the 36-pin connector of Fig. 6-16), -MEMW and -MEMR are renamed -SMEMW and -SMEMR, respectively, and the reserved line B8 has been called 0WS to allow high speed memories to run with "zero wait states". The S prefix can be thought of as meaning small, that is, valid for references to the small 1-megabyte memory space of the PC. Hence -SMEMR and -SMEMW are active only for memory references to the lowest megabyte of the 16-megabyte address space.

Figure 6-16 shows the 36-pin PC AT auxiliary I/O channel lines. Here -MEMR and -MEMW are the memory read/write strobes valid beyond the lowest megabyte. For example, reading an address like 1B0000H leaves -SMEMR high while pulsing -MEMR low. In this way, RAM cards like the video adapters don't have to decode the high-order four address bits, a feature essential for compatiblity with PC I/O channel cards. By pulling the -MEM CS16 and -I/O CS16 lines low, RAM and I/O cards can transfer data on the 16-bit data bus, rather than on the low byte alone. The -MASTER line allows an alternate processor to take over the system address, data, and control lines. Such a processor should not hold onto the bus for more than 15 microseconds, or loss of memory may result due to lack of refresh.

```
GND ----------- B1        A1 ----------- -I/O CH CK
RESET DRV -----             ----------- D7
+5 V ----------             ----------- D6
IRQ2 ----------             ----------- D5
-5 V ---------- B5        A5 ----------- D4
DRQ2 ----------             ----------- D3
-12 V ---------             ----------- D2
Reserved ------             ----------- D1
+12 V ---------             ----------- D0
GND ----------- B10      A10 ----------- I/O CH RDY
-MEMW ---------             ----------- AEN
-MEMR ---------             ----------- A19
-IOW ----------             ----------- A18
-IOR ----------             ----------- A17
-DACK3 -------- B15      A15 ----------- A16
DRQ3 ----------             ----------- A15
-DACK1 --------             ----------- A14
DRQ1 ----------             ----------- A13
-DACK0 --------             ----------- A12
CLOCK --------- B20      A20 ----------- A11
IRQ7 ----------             ----------- A10
IRQ6 ----------             ----------- A9
IRQ5 ----------             ----------- A8
IRQ4 ----------             ----------- A7
IRQ3 ---------- B25      A25 ----------- A6
-DACK2 --------             ----------- A5
T/C -----------             ----------- A4
ALE -----------             ----------- A3
+5 V ----------             ----------- A2
OSC ----------- B30      A30 ----------- A1
GND -----------             ----------- A0
```

Fig. 6–15. The IBM PC 62–pin I/O channel bus. It includes 20 address lines, eight bidirectional data lines, three DMA request and four DMA acknowledge lines, DMA I/O–decode disable (AEN), DMA terminal count (T/C), I/O channel ready (I/O CH RDY), I/O channel parity check (I/O CH CK), address latch enable (ALE), I/O and memory read and write strobes, five interrupt request lines, high frequency and system clocks, system RESET, and ±12 volts, ±5 volts, and ground.

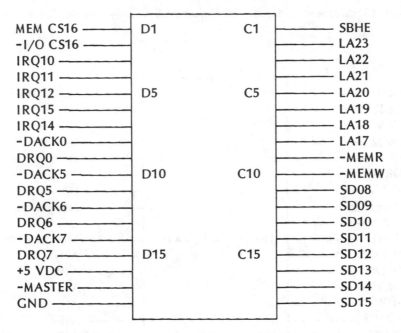

Fig. 6–16. IBM PC AT 36–pin auxiliary I/O channel bus. It includes the seven most significant address lines of the 16–megabyte address space, the eight high–byte data lines, the memory strobes to access RAM beyond the lowest megabyte, four DMA request/acknowledge pairs, five interrupt lines, an I/O and a RAM 16–bit data transfer line, byte–transfer–on–high–byte line, and a bus master request line. These lines give the AT full 16–bit data and 24–bit address capabilities, and allow an alternate processor (like an 80386) to take over.

6-6. AT Protected Virtual Address Mode

One of the powerful features of the IBM AT is its ability to switch back and forth between the Real Address Mode used by 8088/8086 programs and the Intel 80286 Protected Virtual Address Mode. The latter gives you access to the full 16 megabytes of physical memory, virtual addressing capability of 1 gigabyte per task, streamlined task switching, and substantially increased runtime protection. Since MSDOS programs (versions earlier than 5.0) generally cannot run unmodified in protected mode, you may find it handy to write custom routines that switch into this mode when needed and then switch back to real address mode for further processing. One example would be to manipulate a large data area up above the 1-megabyte real address limit. The built-in IBM AT INT 15h (AH = 87h) BIOS interrupt can be used to move blocks up to 64K to and from this extended memory, but it can be considerably more efficient to set up your program to manipulate that memory directly in protected mode. The INT 15h approach disables interrupts for as long as a millisecond (64K block move), which may not be tolerable.   Furthermore, use of this BIOS facility requires setting up some protected mode table entries, and once you've learned how to do that you might as well go the whole way.   This section describes some features of the 80286 protected virtual address mode and outlines how to switch between this mode and the 8086 real-address mode.   The discussion is far from a complete treatment of the protected mode (for this see the *iAPX 286 Programmer's Reference Manual*), but it offers a somewhat more elementary perspective and a number of insights missing in the manual.

The main problem with mixing protected-mode code with a basically real address system is that the segment values are interpreted differently. Instead of shifting the segment value left 4 bits and adding it to an offset to get a 20-bit absolute address (see Fig. 2-5), in protected mode, the segment value ANDed with 0FFF8H is used as an offset into one of two descriptor tables, the Global Descriptor Table (GDT) or the Local Descriptor Table. The latter streamlines a multitasking environment, but is beyond the scope of the present discussion.   The entries in these tables are called descriptors. They are 8 bytes long and specify the segment length up to 64 kilobytes, the segment absolute 24-bit address, and a special access byte.

It is possible to have a segment value, normally called a segment selector, that is identical in real- and virtual-address modes.   In particular the value 40H points at the BIOS RAM segment at absolute address 400H, and the GDT can be organized so that the entry at offset 40H also points at 400H.   This is very handy, since then BIOS routines such as the time-of-day and keyboard routines can run in either mode.   For the present discussion, the segment selectors are always multiples of 8.   Once you've learned how to handle these selectors, read about the others in the *iAPX 286 Programmer's Reference Manual*.

The GDT is a special segment in memory containing 8-byte descriptors of other segments.   It is itself defined by such a descriptor.   The descriptors have the form

Offset	Field
0	Length - 1 word
2	24-bit base address - 3 bytes
5	Access byte
6	Reserved word (= 0 for compatibility with the 80386)

Since the maximum segment length is 64K and each GDT entry is 8 bytes, there can be a maximum of 8192 GDT entries.   If each entry describes a 64K segment, this gives a maximum of 1/2 gigabyte of virtual memory defined by the GDT at any one time.   The first GDT entry is inaccessible and the second usually defines the GDT itself as a segment.   Other entries can define segments for the ROM BIOS code segment, the BIOS RAM data segments (40 and 50), a video segment, and user code and data segments. One possible layout reads

Offset	Segment
00	Null selector not accessible
08	GDT selector pointing to absolute address of null selector
10	CRT RAM segment
18	Interrupt descriptor table segment
20	ROM BIOS code segment
28	User stack segment
30	User code segment
38	User data segment
40	ROM BIOS RAM segment (coincides with real address value)
48	Extra segment
50	Extended BIOS RAM segment (coincides with real address value)

In addition, you should supply entries for any other segments you need. Code segments usually have an access byte 9BH, and data segments have 93H. Note that you can't write into a segment with a code access byte of 9BH, so if you must store into a code segment, define another segment with the access byte 93H pointing to the same area of RAM. Alternatively, you can change the code segment's access byte to 93H while writing into it, and then restore it to 9BH before trying to execute from it. You can't execute code in a segment with access byte 93H. Failure to follow these rules results in a General Protection error, abbreviated #GP in the 80286 manual. This exception automatically invokes interrupt vector 13 (0DH). You can load the GDT register (with the lgdt instruction) as soon as you have defined the table, and you must do so before switching into virtual mode.

Similarly you have to set up an Interrupt Descriptor Table (IDT), which is a segment having a minimum of 32 (20H) 8-byte entries. Many of these can point to an illegal-exception handler, but at the very least the keyboard (INT 9) has to have its own interrupt handler, and the clock (INT 8) is easy to set up. With the ROM BIOS code and RAM data segments defined in the GDT as above, the keyboard and clock interrupt vector descriptors can point to the ROM BIOS. The entries have the meaning: code offset, code segment selector, null byte, access byte (use 86H), and a null word. For example, with the GDT above, the ROM BIOS keyboard handler would be given by the four words: 0e987H, 20H, 8600H, 0.

To switch into protected mode, you enable address line 20 (see gate20 routine in IBM AT *Technical Reference*), clear interrupts, store the far address you want to return to in real mode in 40:[67], load the IDT pointer (with the lidt instruction), and unmask whatever hardware interrupts you have handlers for. If you have set up only the keyboard and clock, output 0fch to port 21h and 0ffh to port 0a1h. If you have an 80287, execute the fsetpm instruction. Then go for it! Execute

```
           mov     ax,1           ;Set PM bit
           lmsw    ax             ;Switch into protected mode
           jmp     30:virtmd      ;(May have to db/dw this instruction)
virtmd:    mov     ax,28
           mov     ss,ax          ;Set up stack segment
           sti                    ; (uses same sp as in real mode)
           mov     ax,38
           mov     ds,ax          ;Set up data segment
           ret                    ;Return in protected mode
```

To "shut down" the protected mode, follow the sequence in the last paragraph of Sec. 6-3. Your IDT exception handler entries should point to the shutdown routine, or better yet to a routine that saves information about the exception in RAM and then jumps to the shutdown routine. After being reset, the AT 80286 will return with all interrupts masked off to the address given by 40H:[67H]. This routine should set up the data and stack segments as need be, and unmask the keyboard, timer, and disk interrupts (output 0BCH to port 21H). The routine can then return to the caller that requested real mode, or to an appropriate error handler. To see this all in action, try the vm (virtual mode), γ (examine GDT), and rm (real mode) commands in the SST debugger.

References

IBM PC and AT *Technical Reference*s, 1983, IBM Corporation, Boca Raton, FL. These manuals contain authoritative descriptions of the PC's hardware, circuit diagrams for the entire IBM PC and some IBM manufactured adapter boards, and complete source code listings for the ROM BIOS routines.

Component Data Catalog, 1983, Intel Corporation, Santa Clara, CA. This book contains the technical specification sheets for all of Intel's integrated circuits. This book is essential if you're going to do any serious programming that utilizes any of the smart peripheral chips in the PC.

iAPX 88 Book, 1981, Intel Corporation, Santa Clara, CA. This book contains detailed descriptions of the 8088's 40 pins, the 8088 architecture, and the 8088 technical specifications.

iAPX 286 Programmer's Reference Manual, 1981, Intel Corporation, Santa Clara, CA. This book contains detailed descriptions of the 80286 and 80287.

L. C. Eggebrecht, *Interfacing to the IBM PC*, 1983, Howard W. Sams & Co., Indianapolis, IN.

7
Interrupts: Real-Time
Clock, Typing Ahead...

To type is human, to word process, divine!

A computer's purpose in life is to read, write, and manipulate data. While it's in the middle of processing data or waiting for some slow device to accept data, data from some other device may become available. If more than one piece of data comes in from that device, the first piece of data that came in is overwritten and the computer misses it altogether. This is a situation where the data transfer between two devices is not properly synchronized. A very valuable software/hardware method of avoiding this problem is the interrupt. When the data becomes available, the responsible device taps the CPU on the shoulder, asking it to drop everything long enough to process the data and then go back to what it was doing before. A prime example of this is the neglected keyboard. Your program is off in a loop somewhere; you'd like to stop it to see what's going on. Without interrupts, you'd have to restart the system, losing all information about where the machine has hung up. With keyboard interrupt capability and the proper interrupt handler, you can stop the program anywhere, look at the registers, stack, data, and so on, and then continue program execution just as if you'd never stopped it.

Just as when people are interrupted and have to remember what they were doing before the interrupt, the computer must remember what it was doing by saving the machine state (the registers and flags) at the time the interrupt occurred.   An interrupt can be regarded as an *asynchronous CALL*. Asynchronous, because it can happen at any time, and CALL because the return address (the current value of IP) and the flags are pushed onto the stack and a jump to some location occurs. The routine that is CALLed, the interrupt handler, then simply returns (by executing an IRET) when it has processed the data. It must also leave every register exactly as it was before the interrupt, so that the exact machine state present before the interrupt is restored.

Section 6-4 described how the Intel 8259 PIC (programmable interrupt controller) coordinates interrupt requests occurring on eight independent channels. This is an elegant method that is ideal for the IBM PC and PC AT because it's built into the system. This chapter discusses a more elementary approach that is both easier to understand fully and to implement in systems that have no interrupt controller and/or an insufficient number of interrupt lines available. The method is called *periodic polling* and is based on a single periodic interrupt driven by a square wave such as that sent by the 8253 timer/counter to the 8259A's IR0 input in the IBM PC. With a sufficiently fast clock frequency, software can *poll* (check the status of) all devices that might have data, without missing any data. Thus one interrupt line can serve many devices. We discuss this concept both in general and in the environment of the PC. In particular, when you interface new devices to the PC, they may need periodic attention. You must decide whether to give these devices one of the remaining five (eight on the AT) interrupt lines, or to poll them periodically.   Periodic polling is often the better solution.   In multitasking operating systems, periodic interrupts provide the basis for multitasking in time-shared computers.

Section 7-1 introduces the minimum hardware needed for a hardware interrupt in the absence of an interrupt controller, and considers a simple software scheme that takes advantage of such hardware to buffer keyboard input, so that you can type ahead of the system or stop execution of a running program and jump to a machine language monitor program for debugging purposes.

Section 7-2 presents a real-time clock scheme that can be used for periodic polling of slow devices. A program is presented that continuously displays the time of day on the IBM PC screen.

Section 7-3 summarizes and compares the ways in which data transfers between devices of differing speeds can be synchronized so that no data is lost. The techniques discussed are (1) dedicated polling, (2) interrupts, (3) periodic polling, (4) wait state insertion, (5) DMA, (6) dual-ported memory, and (7) FIFO buffers. Each has its place in computing, with relative advantages depending on the data rate, ease of programming, and cost.

7-1. Simple Interrupts and Keyboard Buffering

Figure 7-1 shows a keyboard interface that works with keyboards having ASCII code outputs and that could be made to work with the IBM PC's keyboard as well. It can be used either without interrupts in a polled mode where the computer loops until the keyboard status bit goes high, or in an interrupt-driven mode. In the polled mode the keyboard could be read using the following subroutine:

```
ci:     in      al,status       ;Read in status port bits
        test    al,1            ;Hang in a loop until bit 0 goes low
        jnz     ci
        in      al,keydata      ;Then read in the keyboard data
        ret
```

Here STATUS is the input port activated by the $\overline{I_0}$ strobe line, and KEYDATA is the port activated by the $\overline{I_1}$ line. Operation in the polled version requires very little code, but it either requires a dedicated CPU or takes a chance of missing characters.

In interrupt-driven mode, the keyboard works as follows. When a key is pressed, the keyboard generates a strobe pulse that clocks the 7474 flip-flop Q output high, thus setting INT high. When the 8088 sees this, it finishes

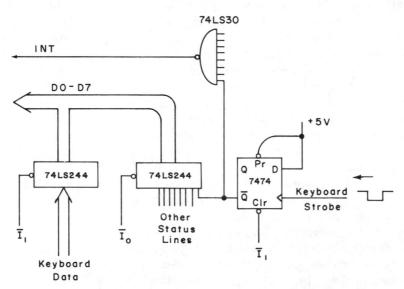

Fig. 7–1. Keyboard interface circuitry that permits either an interrupt or a polled mode of operation. Other devices can be added to this circuit by supplying additional 74LS244's for data input and connecting the device status lines to the $\overline{I_0}$ port and to the 74LS30. The $\overline{I_0}$ and $\overline{I_1}$ strobes are typically generated by a 74LS138 3-to-8 decoder used as shown in Fig. 6–7.

the instruction currently being executed and then responds to the interrupt by requesting a_byte telling the interrupt vector number. The request is made by pulling INTA (interrupt acknowledge) low. In a simple scheme, this could enable a 74LS244 onto the bus with its inputs wired to +5 V or ground so that some fixed number, say the number 8, is produced. This assigns interrupt vector 8 to the interrupt. At location 32 (20H) in memory, we must then have a 4-byte address for the keyboard interrupt routine, called CINT below. Up to seven additional lines (with associated flip-flops) could be connected to the INT line through the 74LS30. The computer determines which line caused the interrupt by checking the status bits connected to port I_0.

A minimal keyboard interrupt routine simply inputs and stores the interrupting character. Such a routine together with a CI (console input) routine to access the stored character is:

```
keyseg    segment
keychr    db        ?
keyseg    ends


cint:     push      ax              ;Be sure to save all registers used
          push      ds
          mov       ax,keyseg       ;Establish data segment addressability
          mov       ds,ax           ; used in interrupt routines
          assume    ds:keyseg
          in        al,data
          mov       keychr,al       ;Input and store character
          pop       ds
          pop       ax              ;Return to interrupted routine restoring
          iret                      ; flags (thus reenabling interrupts)


ci:       push      ds              ;Establish data segment addressability
          mov       ax,keyseg
          mov       ds,ax
          assume    ds:keyseg
          mov       al,0            ;Get potentially new character
          cmp       al,keychr       ;Wait for nonnull character
          jz        ci
          xchg      al,keychr       ;Clear keychr when character read in
          pop       ds
          ret                       ; and return with character
```

This CINT routine isn't particularly useful, but a small addition makes CINT *very* useful. Specifically, CINT should check to see if the interrupting character is some special character, for example, ©X (control X; press Ctrl key and X simultaneously). If ©X is found, the routine jumps to a handy monitor stored in memory or EPROM, which allows you to examine and change memory, read or write I/O ports, set breakpoints, and so on, and then to either resume program execution at the point where the ©X interrupted or do something else like jump back to the operating system.

Another limitation of the interrupt routine just presented is that, if more than one character is input before CI is called, only the last character is retrieved, and data can be lost. At the cost of some memory, you can remedy this lamentable situation by implementing a 128-byte FIFO buffer (see Sec. 6-1). The programs CONINT and CI given next keep track of what's in the buffer with two 1-byte pointers called C1 and C2, each of which indicates a position relative to BUFFER, the starting location of the buffer. The console interrupt handler CONINT uses C2 to determine where to put incoming data, while the console input routine CI uses C1 to determine where to retrieve data from the buffer. If C1 = C2, no new characters have been input. Hence C1 effectively chases C2 around the buffer. Since the high bit of both C1 and C2 is always set to 0, the buffer is a 128-byte *circular buffer*—that is, byte 0 follows byte 127. This is also called a circular FIFO and is a software emulation of the hardware FIFO. The IBM PC uses such a buffer with room for 16 entries (too few for touch-typing programmers). The circular-buffer technique is a powerful method for interfacing two devices having different data rates. The code we use requires that the buffer start on a 256-byte page boundary. With a few more bytes of code, the buffer could have arbitrary size and placement. Two routines are needed: CONINT, which stores a byte on interrupt, and CI, which gets the next character from the buffer. CI must be called regularly by whatever program is running in the computer.

```
bseg     segment page          ;Define data area
buffer   db      80h           ;128-byte buffer
c1       db      1             ;Trailing offset pointer
c2       db      1             ;Leading offset pointer
bseg     ends

cseg     segment
         assume  cs:cseg

conint:  push    ax            ;Console interrupt routine
         push    bx            ;Save the registers used
         push    ds            ;Establish data segment addressability
         mov     ax,bseg
         mov     ds,ax
         assume  ds:bseg
         in      al,data       ;Get byte, clear hardware interrupt
         lea     bx,buffer
         mov     bl,c2         ;Get leading pointer
         inc     bl
         and     bl,7fh        ;Modulo 128 buffer
```

```
               cmp      bl,c1            ;Caught up to trailing pointer?
               jz       conin1
               mov      c2,bl            ;No. Update pointer
               mov      [bx],al          ;Store it in buffer
conret:        pop      ds
               pop      bx               ;Restore registers. If 8259A PIC being used,
               pop      ax               ; need to include EOI command also
               iret                      ;Return to interrupted routine

conin1:        call     bell             ;Tell typer to wait
               jmp      conret           ;Ignore current character

ci:            push     ds               ;Console input routine
               mov      ax,bseg
               mov      ds,ax
               assume   ds:bseg
ci2:           mov      al,c2            ;Get leading (C2) buffer
               cmp      al,c1            ;If C1 = C2, nothing new
               jz       ci2              ;Loop till a byte bites

               push     bx               ;Caught one! Increment C1
               lea      bx,c1
               inc      byte ptr [bx]
               and      byte ptr [bx],7fh
               mov      bl,[bx]          ;Point at next byte in buffer
               sub      bh,bh
               mov      al,[bx]          ;Get next byte
               pop      bx
               pop      ds
               ret
cseg           ends
```

This routine prevents losing input characters unless 128 characters are typed before CI is called, which isn't likely. The buffering feature is very useful, but it's just the start. Now that characters are read asynchronously, special functions can occur. With a bit more code in CONINT, you could stop program execution with a ©S (control S) by hanging in a loop inside the interrupt routine (after executing an STI to reenable interrupts) and starting up again on receipt of a ©Q. This is handy when the computer outputs a document onto a CRT screen too fast. You can also arrange to have special character sequences restart your system or interrogate registers. You can asynchronously "poke" (store bytes) into memory or output to ports. You can also operate in a "line" mode for which CI gets characters only when a carriage return is received. This allows you to delete characters from the buffer so long as they're on the same input line.

Of course, the interrupt routine CONINT will not work on an IBM PC because the keyboard is interfaced to the computer somewhat differently than shown in Fig. 7-1, and it transmits key scan codes instead of ASCII characters. Hence the IBM PC routines corresponding to CONINT and CI (INT 9 and INT 16H, respectively) are more complicated. Section 8-1 and App. E discuss the PC's keyboard hardware and show how the IBM keyboard interrupt routine can be modified in various ways. The primary purpose of the discussion here is to show in a simple way how to handle an interrupt-driven device like a keyboard. You might want to enhance the ROM BIOS equivalent of the CI routine (INT 16H), however. INT 16H's 16-byte keyboard buffer is much too small, especially if you want room for deletions to compensate for typing errors.

As mentioned previously, several devices can drive Fig. 7-1's INT line high, causing an interrupt if interrupts are enabled. As soon as an interrupt occurs, interrupts are automatically disabled until an STI or an IRET is executed. By reading the status port enabled by $\overline{I}_0$, the computer can tell which port or ports have interrupted and then jump to the appropriate interrupt handler. This approach is simple and works on all sorts of computers. However, it treats all devices on an equal priority basis, which may not be adequate for more sophisticated applications. Devices with medium data rates (50 to 50,000 bytes/second) may require immediate attention to prevent loss of data. The next section shows how a fairly powerful computer system can be organized using only a single real-time clock interrupt. In this approach, the software sets the interrupt priorities.

7-2. Real-Time Clock Interrupt Scheme

Consider next how a computer can keep accurate time with a minimum of hardware and give interrupt capability to an arbitrary number of slow speed (data rates less than 60 bytes/second) devices. These might include a terminal, a modem talking over the telephone line at 30 bytes/second to a remote computer, and various keypads scattered around a house or lab. The basic method is to convert the 60-Hz line voltage into a square wave whose positive edges interrupt the computer 60 times each second. This single interrupt allows generation of the time of day and provides a frequent enough polling interval to check on the status of slow-speed devices. It also has better long-term accuracy than a crystal-controlled clock, since the power companies continually adjust the powerline frequency to keep the average value at exactly 60 Hz. In the absence of device action, the interrupt overhead is less than 3 milliseconds/second on the IBM PC, which is not noticeable to the user. The IBM PC BIOS time-of-day clock offers a similar facility by polling the routine pointed to by interrupt vector 01CH at an 18.2-Hz rate. We illustrate the use of this facility by a screen clock program and review how the 8253 programmable interval timer can be used to generate a real-time clock.

The hardware clock circuit used to generate 60-Hz interrupts was diagrammed in Fig. 5-25. The output of the clock should be connected to the clock input of a flip-flop wired up to INT in the same way as was shown In Fig. 7-1. The software is an extension of the console interrupt routines in Sec. 7-1. Suppose for now that only the keyboard is connected to the status byte (port $\overline{I}_0$ in Fig. 7-1). Up to seven other devices could be added with no increase in polling overhead. Then you can use the following code to divide down to 0.1-second intervals and poll the keyboard for action:

```
dseg      segment
pcount    db      0               ;Partial count
tenth     db      0               ;Tenths-of-a-second location
sec       db      0               ;Seconds location
min       db      0               ;Minutes location
hour      db      0               ;Hours location
cycle     db      9,59,59,23
dseg      ends


cseg      segment
          assume cs:cseg


clock:    push    ax              ;Save what we're about to clobber
          push    ds
          mov     ax,dseg
          mov     ds,ax
          assume ds:dseg
          in      al,status       ;Check status, clear interrupt
          inc     al              ;Anyone low?
          jz      clock1
          call    conint          ;If so, process the data
clock1:   mov     al,pcount       ;Load the partial count
          inc     al
          cmp     al,6            ;Down to 0.1 sec?
          jz      rtc             ;If so, go to clock routine (see below)
          mov     pcount,al       ;Update byte
          pop     ds
          pop     ax
          iret
```

Note that here the CONINT routine of Sec. 7-1 is called if any bit in the status port is low. If more devices are to be polled, the bits in STATUS must be examined and the appropriate interrupt handler for each low bit must be called.

Now let's look at a real-time clock (RTC) routine that divides from 0.1-second intervals down to seconds, minutes, and hours. It's easy to extend this to keep track of the date also. Furthermore, the RTC routine provides well-defined time intervals for processing very slow data, such as once-per-minute checks of temperature, humidity, wind velocity, or anything else you want to monitor. This minimal RTC routine can be easily extended to fairly complicated applications such as running a large mansion!

```
rtc:     push    bx                      ;Save additional registers
         push    si
         push    cx
         xor     al,al
         mov     pcount,al
         mov     cx,4                    ;Increment up to 4 time intervals
         lea     bx,tenth                ;Point to time interval array
         lea     si,cycle                ;Point to cycle array
rtclp:   mov     al,[bx]                 ;Get next time interval
         inc     al                      ;Increment it
         clc                             ;Clear CY for decimal arithmetic
         daa                             ;Use packed decimal format for
         mov     [bx],al                 ; easy display
         lodsb                           ;Complete cycle for this interval?
         cmp     al,[bx]
         jnc     rtcs                    ;If not, leave loop
         mov     byte ptr [bx],0         ;Yes.  Zero value and go on to next
         inc     bx
         inc     si
         loop    rtclp                   ;Do up to hours if necessary

;Real time clock routines.  BX points to the time interval being
;incremented.  SI points to the interval's maximum value.

rtcs:    cmp     cl,4                    ;This code executed every 0.1 second
         jz      rtcend                  ;Only 0.1 second incremented?
         nop                             ;This code executed every second
         cmp     cl,3
         jz      rtcend
         nop                             ;This code executed every minute
         cmp     cl,2
         jz      rtcend
         nop                             ;This code executed every hour
rtcend:  pop     cx                      ;Restore registers
         pop     si
         pop     bx
         pop     ds
         pop     ax
         iret
cseg     ends
```

You can inserts CALL's to any routines that you want executed every second, minute, or hour by replacing the NOP's with CALL's in the RTCS routine.

There are two potential problems with this simple, powerful method: (1) devices may have data rates in excess of 59 bytes/sec, and (2) some disk controllers insert so many wait states while waiting for disk data that clock counts are lost. The first problem can be solved by assigning individual interrupts to the higher-speed devices or by using a faster clock interrupt. The second problem can be solved by using DMA instead of polling with wait states or by incrementing the counters an estimated amount. In the IBM PC, the disk controller uses DMA as discussed in Sec. 6-4, and no timer counts are lost. The PC*jr* doesn't use DMA for disk transfers but avoids losing timer counts by employing an overflow counter (see end of Sec. 6-4). The PC*jr* does, however, lose any keyboard and serial I/O codes sent during disk transfers. The time-of-day clock can also be maintained by periodically updating it from a battery-backed-up clock circuit, such as those available on many multi-function boards for the PC and built into the AT's motherboard. This circuit is also handy at power-on, since the computer can then read the time and date rather than relying on you to type it in.

Instead of using a powerline frequency interrupt, you might prefer to use the 8253 programmable interval timer built into the IBM PC and PC AT. Channel 0 of the system 8253 divides its 1.193-MHz input frequency by 65536 to give interrupts roughly 18.2 times a second. For our purposes, it is better to program the 8253 to divide by 59659, which gives a 20-Hz interrupt almost as accurate as the system clock. With only minor modification, the countdown routines above can convert the 20-Hz interrupt to seconds, minutes, hours, and days. Two points emerge here: (1) 20 Hz is quite slow for periodic polling, so a divisor like 9861 (which produces an accurate 121-Hz interrupt) might be preferable, and (2) the IBM PC system TIME and DATE routines depend on an interrupt count (stored in locations 40:6CH— 70H) based on an 18.2-Hz interrupt rate. To make TIME and DATE work properly, either they must be changed or the routines just given must be modified to maintain the standard count.

To illustrate periodic polling, we show how the user clock interrupt (1CH) can be taken over to provide a display of the time of day in the upper right-hand corner of the video screen. The user clock interrupt is automatically called by the ROM BIOS time-of-day clock interrupt 18.2 times every second, and normally just points to an IRET instruction so that it does nothing. You can take it over to do anything you want. Here is how to make it contain a clock display:

```
data      segment at 40h
          org     6ch
timer_low         dw              ?
timer_high        dw              ?
data      ends

vidram    segment at 0b000h      ;Monochrome display RAM origin.  Use
          org     70*2           ; 0b800h for color/graphics adapter
```

```
clkcol    label    word               ;Starting vidram position for clock display
vidram    ends

cseg      segment
          assume cs:cseg,ds:data
          org      100h
start:    mov      dx,5ch             ;Set ds:dx to loc. 5ch in program prefix
          mov      al,1ch             ;Take over interrupt 1ch
          mov      ah,25h
          int      21h
          mov      di,dx              ;Move clock routine to 5ch in prefix
          mov      si,clkadr
          mov      cx,clklen
          rep      movsb
          mov      dx,di              ;End program but leave program resident
          int      27h

clock:    sti
          push     bx                 ;Save extra registers used
          push     cx                 ; (BIOS has already saved ax, dx, ds)
          mov      dx,timer_high      ;Calculate time (can't use nonreentrant DOS)
          mov      ax,timer_low
          shr      dx,1
          rcr      ax,1
          mov      bx,32772           ;65543 counts/hour. Approx by 2*32772
          div      bx                 ;Get hours
          xchg     ax,cx              ;Save 'em
          xchg     ax,dx              ;Get remainder
          xor      dx,dx
          shl      ax,1
          rcl      dx,1
          mov      bx,1092            ;Counts/minute
          div      bx
          push     ax                 ;Save 'em
          xchg     ax,dx
          mov      bl,18              ;Get seconds
          div      bl
          mov      dh,al

          assume ds:vidram
          mov      ax,vidram          ;Establish video RAM base address
          mov      ds,ax
          lea      bx,clkcol          ;Point at start of clock display
          call     blank
          call     blank
          xchg     ax,cx
```

```
            pop     cx
            call    disply          ;Display hours
            call    colon
            xchg    ax,cx
            call    disply          ;Display minutes
            call    colon
            mov     al,dh
            call    disply          ;Display seconds
            pop     cx
            pop     bx
            iret

disply:     cbw                     ;Display al at vidram = ds:[bx]
            mov     dl,10           ;Get ten's digit
            div     dl
            cmp     al,6
            jc      distor
            mov     ax,905h
distor:     call    vstore          ;Display it
            xchg    al,ah
vstore:     add     al,30h          ;Convert to ASCII
vstor1:     mov     [bx],al
            inc     bx
            mov     byte ptr [bx],7
            inc     bx
            ret
blank:      mov     al," "
            jmp     vstor1
colon:      mov     al,":"
            jmp     vstor1
clkend:
cseg        ends

clkadr      equ     (offset clock - offset start) + 100h
clklen      equ     offset clkend - offset clock
            end     start
```

This program should be assembled using MASM and EXE2BIN to produce a .COM file as described in Sec. 4-6. It will stay resident and produce a time display until you either reboot the system or turn the power off. Just run it, and bingo! you've got a clock up there to remind you that it's 2:00 AM and time to go to bed.

This clock routine illustrates the use of dual-ported video memory as well as interrupts: the program stores characters into the video RAM, and you also see on the screen what was stored. Dual-ported memory is simply RAM that can be accessed by two different data and address busses. In addition to the 8088's data and address busses, there's a second set of busses controlled by a CRT controller chip that reads the memory and displays its contents on the screen.   This approach is discussed in detail in Sec. 8-3. Dual-ported memory provides a very flexible, fast console display and is a great improvement over the relatively sluggish serial terminal.

7-3. Data Synchronization Techniques

To this point a variety of methods has been presented by which to syn-chronize the flow of data between two devices, namely: (1) dedicated polling, (2) interrupts, (3) periodic polling, (4) wait state insertion, (5) DMA, (6) dual-ported memory, and (7) FIFO buffers.   *Dedicated polling* was introduced in Sec. 7-1 and is discussed further in Chap. 10, where several "handshaking" schemes are introduced.   The TEST line coupled with the WAIT instruction provides a hardware polling example.   Hardware *inter-rupts* were introduced in Sec. 6-4 and some of their uses were illus-trated in Sec. 7-1.   Interrupts and polling are combined in *periodic polling* as discussed in Sec. 7-2.   These methods all work well for low to medium data rates.

For higher-speed operations (faster that 50 kilobytes/second), polling and interrupts are no longer feasible.   However, by designing your circuitry to insert *wait states* during an IN instruction, you can increase the data rate to about 130 kilobytes/second using a program loop like:

```
next:   in      al,dx
        stosb
        loop    next
```

Execution of the IN instruction is suspended while the READY line is high, as described in Sec. 6-1.   For even higher transfer rates, the *DMA con-troller* can be used to handle data rates up to 1.5 megabytes/second. This technique and its associated hardware were discussed in Sec. 6-4. *Dual-port memory* is discussed in Secs. 7-2 and 8-3.   It's also appropriate for high data rates since the transfer speed is limited only by the speed at which memory can be read and written.   FIFO buffers, discussed in Secs. 6-1 and 7-1, are used in conjunction with one of the other synchronization methods such as interrupts or dual-port memory.

This section compares some of these data synchronization techniques and gives an idea as to when each technique is the best.   The various methods are summarized in Table 7-1 along with typical maximum data rates.

In addition to sheer speed, ease of programming and expense are important considerations.   Both interrupt and DMA controllers add extra expense and some extra programming before their benefits are felt.   At least one kind of interrupt is very desirable, but for many small systems the

METHOD	MAXIMUM RATE	CPU OVERHEAD
Interrupts	50,000 bytes/sec	Part time (Sec. 7-1 CINT)
Polling		
Periodic	Clock rate (60 Hz)	Little (RTC in Sec. 7-2)
Dedicated	60,000 bytes/sec	Full time (CI in Sec. 7-1)
Wait states	180,000 bytes/sec	Full time (block I/O)
DMA	1.6 megabytes/sec	Little
Dual-port memory	Memory access rate	None, unless wait states used to resolve conflicts

Table 7–1. Overview of synchronization methods for data transfers between CPU and I/O devices. For arbitrarily slow devices all methods can be used, but periodic polling or interrupts are preferred. Maximum interrupt and polling data rates are based on a 4.77–MHz 8088 running the routines indicated in parentheses. FIFO's are not listed since they are used in conjunction with one of the other methods when that method is not fast enough to handle the transient peaks in the data transfer rate.

single real-time clock interrupt suffices to give many devices interrupt power without the cost and stack requirements of a multiple, prioritized interrupt system. Each time an interrupt occurs, the stack is pushed and popped, typically requiring about 30 bytes of memory and 60 microseconds. Hence nested multiple interrupts can require a larger stack allocation than many programs may provide (you should always allocate at least 128 bytes for a stack on the IBM PC), and the interrupt overhead can become appreciable. If the real-time clock interrupt can handle a number of potential interrupts through periodic polling, the pushes and pops are performed only once, saving memory and time. The IBM PC system is powerful enough that a multiple-level interrupt controller is justified, although it is not really necessary for the standard system. The PC typically uses only three interrupts, the real-time clock, the keyboard, and the disk. The keyboard could easily be polled by the real-time clock routine, since people cannot type 18 characters per second (or to be really conservative one could switch to 121 interrupts/second). The floppy-disk interrupt is also unnecessary the way it's currently programmed. A simple dedicated polling of the floppy-disk controller status register would be simpler (see subroutine J28 in the BIOS code for INT 13 in the IBM PC *Technical Reference* manual). So the 8259 PIC is somewhat a case of overkill, but for expansion purposes it's good to have it there. Also the modularity of the separate interrupt is appealing. You can code up an interrupt handler that is totally independent of anything else in the system and install it by making an end-but-stay-resident return to the system (see Sec. 4-6).

A clear case where extra interrupt levels are not desirable is the problem of monitoring a temperature in a regular, reliable way. This parameter varies very slowly, on the order of minutes. Here the real time clock routine of Sec. 7-2 is ideal. It can poll the temperature converter every 10 seconds and store the result. A burglar alarm system is another example. Polling the detectors with a 60-Hz interrupt is totally adequate. Similarly, serial terminals can be polled. Even 9600 baud (960 bytes/second) transmissions can be handled by a 1-millisecond real-time clock. So there's really no need to give each terminal on a time-shared system its own interrupt. Just poll them all quickly and IRET within 50 microseconds if nothing is there. The periodic polling adds about 5% overhead, which is actually less than the overhead for a multiple interrupt system if several terminals are active. If only our business organizations had so little overhead!

Printer spooling is also a good application for interrupts (or periodic polling). A dot matrix printer typically prints 200 or fewer characters/second, and daisy-wheel printers print only 20 to 55 characters/second. The computer can easily send out thousands of characters per second. A print spooler contains a FIFO like the keyboard FIFO of Sec. 7-1, only bigger. To start transmission, the spooler sends a character to the printer and enables the interrupt that occurs when the printer is ready for another character (more precise details are given in Chap. 10). Meanwhile the spooler buffers characters in the FIFO. Many special boards are available to do just that for the Apple, the TRS-80, and computers in general. On the IBM PC a simple interrupt-driven spooler routine suffices that uses the much larger and comparatively inexpensive 256K or 512K memory cards. Nevertheless, some companies sell special purpose spooler cards for the IBM PC! No further comment on them. With periodic polling, the real-time clock routine checks to see if more characters are in the buffer and if the printer is ready to accept them. If both answers are yes, a character is shipped.

More elegant spooling prints whole files from the disk. You command the computer to print a file, whereupon the spooler reads the first record from the file into a buffer. When this record has been transmitted under interrupt control, the spooler reads another record and so on until the complete file has been printed. DOS 2.0 includes such a facility. The print spooler is an example of a task, and the seemingly simultaneous running of multiple tasks (the program you're running, the print spooler, the keyboard routine, the real-time clock, and so forth) is called *multitasking*. Both multiple interrupts and periodic polling provide easy ways to run a simple multitasking system. More complex systems also use a real-time clock to pause the currently running task and let some other task have a chance. This approach is used in time-shared computers, where the multitasking algorithms take into account priorities and task resource requirements. This subject is well understood, and the reference at the end of this chapter can guide you further.

Priorities can be important, both to prevent loss of data and to ensure that some jobs get done immediately. High data rate tasks may have to run at higher priorities than low data rate tasks to prevent such loss. On the IBM PC, the interrupt handlers almost invariably reenable interrupts immediately upon being entered. This allows other interrupts to interrupt in turn. The interrupt rate is sufficiently slow that no problems are likely to occur. Should priorities become important in more complicated applications, the 8259 PIC can offer substantial help.

The use of the DMA controller in the IBM PC for the floppy-disk interface is a nice application of DMA where it apparently isn't needed. The data rate is 1 byte every 30 microseconds, which is easily handled by dedicated polling techniques, as countless microcomputers including the standard IBM PC*jr* can testify. However, the dedication must be complete: keyboard input and ticks of the real-time clock cannot be processed. This means that the clock typically runs slow, and whatever it's supposed to poll gets ignored. The DMA approach lets the microprocessor go on about its business, answering interrupt requests while it waits for a disk sector to be read or written. On the PC*jr*, the clock ticks are stored so that the time is kept accurately, but keyboard and serial-communications input is lost. DMA also allows greater throughput, since the processor isn't tied up waiting for the disk controller to handle each byte. The DMA controller can handle data rates up to 1.6 MHz. Such rates could be generated easily by various kinds of analog-to-digital converters (discussed in Sec. 9-3). A variety called a flash converter is even too fast for the DMA controller (up to 50 megabytes/second!), and must be handled using high-speed, dual-ported memory with a large word size.

In the screen time-of-day clock example given earlier, the dual-ported video RAM in the IBM PC is demonstrated. The 8088 can store into the video RAM, whereupon the screen image changes. The store operation is on the order of a few microseconds as distinguished from the millisecond required to send a character to a 9600-baud terminal. Hence the screen on the IBM can be updated over 10 times as fast as that on a terminal, so fast that it appears to the human eye to be instantaneous. The instantaneous screen is very desirable for screen editing since it reduces operator fatigue and allows one to concentrate on writing rather than on the computer. Dual-ported video memory is also called a *memory-mapped display* (see Sec. 8-3) and is quite common, being used in the TRS-80, Apple, Commodore Pet, Atari, Victor 9000, and a host of other personal computers. Note that many programs display characters on the screen by making operating system calls, rather than by writing into the video memory directly. Although this might sound more portable, that is, machine independent, it may not be: the memory-mapped video display is a very portable concept, whereas system call protocols vary greatly from one machine to another.

In summary, each of the data synchronization techniques has a valid niche in coordinating data transfers between devices of differing speeds. There is considerable overlap in their areas of applicability, so if economy is relevant, the desired microcomputer uses should be studied as a group. The IBM PC, in particular, has more raw synchronization power than current applications are using. But then, some Murphy's law must say that all available power will be quickly used up. Curiously enough, the speed of the 8088 limits the power of the PC much more substantially than the number of available DMA and interrupt channels.

References

D. Willen and J. Krantz, 1983, *8088 Assembler Language Programming: The IBM PC*, Howard W. Sams and Company, Indianapolis, IN. Introductory discussions of assembly language, use of the IBM Macro Assembler, and the hardware of the PC. Contains additional examples of keyboard and real-time clock programs.

Technical Reference, 1983, IBM Corporation, Boca Raton, FL. This manual contains descriptions and circuit diagrams of the IBM PC hardware plus complete assembly language listings of the ROM BIOS code.

Per Brinch Hansen, 1973, *Operating System Principles*, Prentice-Hall Inc., Englewood Cliffs, NJ. This is one of many computer science texts that describes techniques for implementing multitasking in computer operating systems.

8
Keyboard and Video Display

Everything should be made as simple as possible,
but not simpler.
  —Albert Einstein

An important part of a computer's makeup is its keyboard and video display. The user is constantly in either finger or eye contact with these components. Hence they both need to be agreeable and "ergonomic," that is, nicely engineered from a human point of view. The IBM PC incorporates the results of extensive studies along these lines, and has made some exciting advances. A detached keyboard and several video display options are offered.

The keyboard is a work of art, although the original placement of certain keys became sufficiently controversial that IBM and others now offer several alternatives, such as on the AT. Section 8-1 explains how the keyboard works, noting that it is as versatile as it is beautiful. For example, you can use it for playing music as shown by the "piano" program of App. C, or you can make any key act like any other, such as making the backslash key into a shift key, as shown in the keyboard redefinition program of App. E. Section 8-1 also describes another kind of input device that's becoming increasingly popular. This is the mouse, a gadget that fits into the palm of your hand and that you roll around on top of a desk. A special screen cursor follows the motion of the mouse as you move it. By pressing one of the buttons on the mouse, you instruct a program to choose options represented by words or pictures on the screen, to define blocks of text to operate on, or to identify points in a graphics design.

The rest of the chapter discusses video displays. With hindsight it's easy to conclude that one of the best decisions in the original PC design and those that have followed was in using plug-in cards for the video. User needs, tastes, and budgets vary substantially, and many options are available. Of the three main IBM display options, the monochrome display seems to be the most popular (although statistics are not readily available). This screen and its nongraphics adapter are sold by IBM dealers, but the heavily cloned monochrome graphics version by Hercules has become the standard. The screen has a long-persistence green phosphor, which reduces the eye fatigue produced by some black-and-white screens. The monochrome display's high resolution produces crisp, well-formed characters, arranged as 25 lines by 80 columns. Its character generator produces 253 different characters including the complete ASCII set, many foreign characters, a single- and double-line ruling set, and some game characters. The Hercules graphics standard gives 720 x 348 dots. Compatible good-looking green and amber monochrome displays are also available from several manufacturers.

The second IBM display option is the relatively low resolution color/graphics adapter (CGA), which is used with commerically available color TV's and video monitors. In text mode, 25 lines by 80 columns are offered, compatible with the monochrome display option but not nearly so easy to read. Graphics (in which each dot on the screen can be turned on or off independently of any other) is available with 200 x 640 dots in black and white, or 200 x 320 dots in four colors. The color/graphics card can reside in the machine at the same time as the monochrome card and is well supported by game programs. If you want to have color, however, you should get the more recent IBM Enhanced Graphics Adapter (EGA) option, or one of its many more efficient clones. The EGA offers better resolution at 640x350, with four planes for 16 colors per dot, a RAM character generator, and a host of other features.

Section 8-2 describes the basic concepts of computer video displays, how they work, how to evaluate them, and what signals are needed to drive them. Section 8-3 discusses the concepts of "memory-mapped" video displays, dual-ported memory, and hardware character generation. Four video display options for the IBM PC are also discussed, and illustrations of how they can be programmed and controlled are given.

8-1. The IBM PC Keyboard

One of the most striking features of the IBM PC is its beautiful streamlined keyboard. Slim, solid, artistic, and versatile, it sets a new standard in keyboard design. In this section, we study the IBM keyboard from the inside out and show how to take full advantage of its power. As this section shows, it's fairly easy to interface this keyboard using the standard serial communications techniques discussed in detail in Chap. 10. As with all other components for the IBM PC, the keyboard has been cloned, notably by Key Tronic, so you have more than one source for this kind of keyboard.

First we describe the keyboard and say why we feel it is superior to others. Then we show how to redefine the keyboard to suit special needs, such as entry of foreign-language and mathematical text or switching to the more efficient Dvorak keyboard layout. The simple program called KEYTRAN given in App. E is useful in extending the power of word processors. You can modify the program as desired to handle applications in which the key closure duration plays a role, such as for a musical keyboard, or to implement foreign-language keyboards. The codes used by the keyboard to represent key closures and breaks are also presented. The way the IBM PC system board decodes these codes is discussed next. Further discussion of the keyboard and how to interface it to other computers is given in an article by Glasco and Sargent (1983), and parts of this section are taken from that article. The article gives a keyboard-encoding algorithm that is more powerful than the ROM BIOS routine, and yet requires only one-third the number of bytes.

Solidly built and with an excellent key feel, the keyboard allows both flat and inclined placement on the table. It is equipped with a black coiled cable for remote connection, so that it can be moved around to suit the user's mood. The key choice includes the English letters, Arabic digits, complete ASCII punctuation characters, ten special function keys (labeled F1 to F10), three types of shift keys (Ctrl, Shift, and Alt), three shiftlock keys (CapsLock, NumLock, and ScrollLock), and fifteen "cursor/numeric keypad" keys. One key that's missing is a key labeled "HELP". Just what pressing a HELP key accomplishes depends on the software that reads the keyboard input, but user-friendly systems should support such a key. Much software for the IBM PC is standardizing on using F1 as the HELP key, since help is the first thing you need, so you might want to paste a little HELP label on it. The question mark is also often used for help.

There is a fair amount of controversy concerning the placement of the shift, backslash, carriage return, and delete keys. The choice deviates substantially from the standard that IBM itself established with the Selectric typewriter. The carriage return and delete keys are often thought to be a bit farther from standard positions than desired for high-use keys. The location of the backslash key (between the left shift and "Z" keys) is heavily lamented in the United States because touch typists are used to finding one large shift key that starts in the backslash position. One justification for the IBM PC choice is that it's symmetric: on the standard Selectric keyboard, the forward slash occupies the position between the right shift key and the period, so why not have the backslash between the "Z" and the left shift key? Furthermore, the right little finger has to move the same distance to reach its shift key as the left little finger does to reach its shift key on the IBM PC keyboard. However, the primary justification for IBM's choice is that it conforms to the European DIN standards, for which extensive ergonomic studies were made to determine the most comfortable way people can type. The backslash (or some other) character is often found between the left shift key and the English Z key on European keyboards, so Europeans feel this is quite natural. At any rate, after a few hours, the backslash no longer presents a problem for the touch typist (and it never did for anyone else). If this placement really bothers you, the KEYTRAN program in App. E shows how to change the keys to any order you desire! IBM also followed the DIN standards by labeling the backspace, tab, shift, and carriage return keys with various arrows, which is a bit confusing at first and presents typographical problems when one writes about these keys.

IBM listened, and the AT keyboard has Lock indicator lights, big Shift keys, and a big Enter key, which made many people happy. However, valuable real estate was lost. In particular, the all-important delete key was cut in half, which makes it significantly harder to hit, and the Esc key was moved to the number pad (you can move it back and use KEYTRAN to tell the software). On balance the AT keyboard seems to be a nice compromise. Then in 1986, IBM came out with a new keyboard, which separates the cursor and numeric keypads, a long requested feature. Unfortunately for most popular PC software, IBM interchanged the Ctrl and CapsLock keys. Fortunately IBM agreed to continue selling the older models.

Meanwhile a number of manufacturers, most notably Key Tronic, sell alternatives. Key Tronic's version of the IBM PC keyboard comes in a number of layouts all with Lock indicator lights and a softer feel than the "breakover feel" of the IBM keyboard. It is used often in PC compatibles, is less expensive, and is substantially quieter (you can type away unnoticed while listening to someone on the phone who doesn't seem to realize that you have many other things to do with your time!).

One superior feature of the IBM keyboard (and the Key Tronic clone) is that you can cause any key combination to create any code you want. To understand how this is done, you need to know the keyboard encoding scheme. This scheme mirrors the elegant look and feel of the keyboard, combining the flexibility of memory-mapped keyboards (such as the TRS-80's), with the reduced processor overhead of fully encoded keyboards such as those found on computer terminals. Specifically, the IBM PC keyboard contains an Intel 8048 microcomputer that sends out a serial bit code when a key makes contact, and a similar code (the same one but with the high bit set) when the contact is broken. If the key stays depressed for more than 0.5 second, the keyboard sends out the make code repetitively 10 times per second. Each key is treated identically at this level; any key could be a shift key, a number, or a special function key. Since the duration of a key closure can be determined from the time between make and break codes, you can also use the keyboard for playing music and simulating simple joysticks in addition to the usual typewriter applications. Meanwhile the main computer doesn't have to waste time monitoring and "debouncing" the keyboard. That's done by the dedicated 8048 microcomputer. The penalty paid for the completely general flexibility is that the main computer has to translate the make/break codes into standard ASCII. This overhead is relatively minor and well worth it.

DOS carries this flexibility to another level. You can run programs that define or redefine some capability in the system and leave it resident until the system is rebooted as discussed in Sec. 4-6. Furthermore, since DOS **auto**matically **exec**utes programs named in the AUTOEXEC.BAT file when it boots up, you can bring up a substantially modified operating system with very little effort. In particular, the keyboard codes are often intercepted by programs for specialized purposes. Borland's Sidekick is a popular example, and gives you an appointment calendar, an editor for jotting things down, and a phone manager, among other things. The SST debugger can also be resident, allowing you to interrupt whatever program is running to see an ASCII chart in various formats, access a floating-point calculator, change screen parameters, watch your program execute instruction by instruction, or figure out why a program has hung up somewhere, such as in trying to send characters to a printer that isn't turned on.

The KEYTRAN keyboard program in App. E provides a prototype of keyboard interrupt programs that take over the keyboard hardware interrupt (INT 9). The idea is to peek at the interrupting keyboard scan code along with the ROM BIOS shift status bits to decide if a particular keyboard combination is relevant. If it is, the routine processes the scan code, resets the interrupt hardware, and returns from interrupt. Otherwise, it jumps to the INT 9 handler active when KEYTRAN was run. KEYTRAN's tables would generally be extended for custom purposes. As it stands it provides both the efficient Dvorak and inefficient Qwerty keyboard translations (discussed shortly), Alt and Shift-Alt translations for the umlauted characters *aou* in German, and the ability to turn all translations on or off. Specifically, Ctrl-Alt-D turns on the Dvorak keyboard; Ctrl-Alt-Q returns to the usual Qwerty. Ctrl-Del disables all translations, and Ctrl-+ (from the numeric keypad) reenables them. The PS Technical Word processor used to typeset this book uses an expanded version of KEYTRAN that provides the Selectric symbol-ball characters on the Alt and Shift-Alt keys. Other combinations can generate codes for script or italics.

DOS 2.0 has a keycode translation capability that allows you to assign any character or string of characters to any of the codes generated by the ROM BIOS INT 9 interrupt handler. This approach can be very useful but is not as general as KEYTRAN. There's no way to assign values to codes that the standard INT 9 routine ignores, such as Shift-Alt codes or Ctrl-+. For large numbers of changes, KEYTRAN is also more convenient.

In the first translation of KEYTRAN, the keyboard layout is rearranged to produce the Dvorak keyboard. The Dvorak keyboard is an alternative to the standard *qwerty* keyboard layout, which C. L. Sholes designed in the 1870's to be purposely so awkward that typists couldn't type fast enough to jam the keys on the early mechanical typewriters! The Dvorak layout was proposed by Dr. A. Dvorak and his associates after carrying out extensive research on the relative frequency and sequences of letters. For example, the characters *aoeui* and *dhtns*, which occur more than 75% of the time in English text, are placed under the left- and right-hand standard positions, respectively, leading to very efficient keyboard entry. The standard lower-case Sholes and Dvorak layouts shown together look like

```
12345  67890-=        12345  67890]=
qwert  yuiop[         ',.py  fgcrl/
 asdfg  hjkl;'         aoeui  dhtns-
  zxcvb  nm,. /         ;qjkx  bmwvz
```

Typing Ctrl-Alt-D when using KEYTRAN switches to the appropriate table for defining the Dvorak keyboard layout. Typing Ctrl-Alt-Q returns to the qwerty mode, so you can switch back and forth literally at any time. If you like the Dvorak keyboard enough to abandon the qwerty layout, Key Tronic and Maxi Switch have IBM PC keyboards with Dvorak lettering, or you can change your IBM PC keyboard itself. Starting with the backslash key, use a screw driver to carefully pry the key caps off and then put them back on with the Dvorak ordering. Then use KEYTRAN to switch the codes to Dvorak. Why fight if you can switch?

Since the IBM PC keyboard doesn't have CapsLock and NumLock warning lights, you might want to extend KEYTRAN to display a reverse-video ↑ in the upper right-hand corner of the screen when CapsLock is on, and a reverse video # when NumLock is on. This feature is unnecessary on the AT since it has the corresponding indicator lights, but in any event when the Dvorak mode is enabled, it's nice to display a reverse-video d (CapsLock off) or D (CapsLock on). Furthermore such code should act in accord with the current video mode, writing to the appropriate screen RAM with the correct format. These details are taken care of in the SYMBOL.ASM program distributed with the PS word processor.

We see that a software definable keyboard is a major focal point in the PC, not only allowing you to specify many different characters for a variety of purposes, but also allowing you to switch from one task to another with a couple of key strokes. In a real sense, this gives the PC a multitasking capability that you might expect to need a multitasking operating system for. The advantage of the latter is its built-in ability to coordinate the tasks. A routine like KEYTRAN cannot blithely issue DOS interrupts, since DOS is generally not reentrant, and KEYTRAN may get control while a DOS program is running.

With this overview in mind, let's now consider the keyboard encoding scheme in detail. Figure 8-1 shows the decimal values of the key codes transmitted by the keyboard to the PC when a key closure is made (the make code). The corresponding code when the key closure is broken (the break code) is the same code plus 128. In binary, this corresponds to turning on bit 7 in the byte transmitted by the keyboard. Figure 8-2 shows in detail how a code is transmitted serially. When no code is being sent, the output remains low (0 volts). To indicate the start of a code, the keyboard

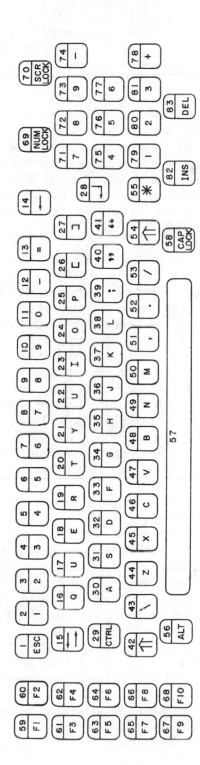

Fig. 8-1. Make codes, expressed in decimal. When a key contact is made, the keyboard transmits the corresponding code serially as an 8-bit binary number. The same code, but with the high bit set to 1, is sent when a contact is broken.

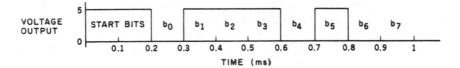

Fig. 8-2. Diagram illustrating the TTL-compatible serial stream generated by the IBM PC keyboard when a key is pressed. It shows the voltage output on pin 2 versus time starting when the key "C" (scan code 46 decimal, that is, 00101110 binary) is pressed. In the absence of transmission, the voltage level is 0. Two high (5-volt) "start bits" define the start of a code transmission. Eight bits follow, each lasting 0.1 millisecond, except for the last, which is slightly shorter. (Reprinted from Glasco and Sargent, 1983)

output goes high (5 volts) for 0.2 millisecond. The 8-bit code then follows, using 0.1 millisecond per bit, least significant bit (bit 0) first, break bit (bit 7) last. A 1 is represented by a high value, a 0 by a low value.

This serial encoding is similar to that used on standard serial terminals. For terminals, an LSI circuit called a UART or USART is typically used to translate a serially transmitted code into a byte of parallel data and vice versa (see Sec. 10-2). Specifically, the UART output stays high in the absence of character transmission (the opposite of the IBM PC keyboard). The start of a character is flagged by a low for a single bit (baud-rate) period. This contrasts with the IBM PC's two high periods. Bits are sent least significant bit first, optionally followed by a parity bit, and terminated by at least one high bit period. As on the IBM PC, ones are represented by high values, and zeros by low values. As discussed in Sec. 10-2, the serial stream from the keyboard can be read using a UART, provided one inverts the signal.

Other methods of reading the serial stream also come to mind. One can copy the circuit used in the IBM PC itself, since it's published along with the rest of the PC's schematics in the IBM PC *Technical Reference* manual. This manual is a must for working with the keyboard, and gives the internal schematic of the keyboard as well. Figure 8-3 shows this circuitry; the figure includes only those lines and integrated circuits that pertain to keyboard functions. The circuitry shown can be replaced by a UART at no increase in expense, and the UART can talk directly to the system microprocessor, without the intervening 8255 PIO.

The IBM circuit works as follows: The KBD CLK clock line from the keyboard is delayed two system clock periods (CLK = 4.77/2 MHz) and inverted by the pair of 74LS175 latches. This new clock line is used to shift the KBD DATA bits into the 74LS322 serial-parallel shift register. The shifts are clocked by the KBD CLK generated by the keyboard 8048 microprocessor. When 8 bits have been shifted in, the 74LS322 carry output is latched to provide an interrupt on the IRQ1 line. This calls the INT 9

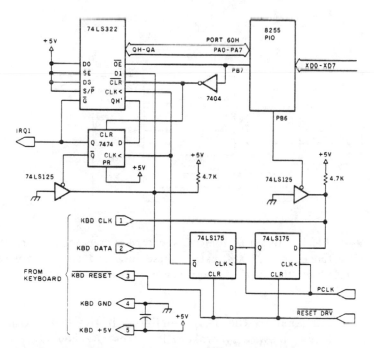

Fig. 8-3. IBM keyboard input interface. (Reprinted from Glasco and Sargent, 1983)

interrupt handler to read the character through port A of the 8255 parallel I/O circuit and to clear the interrupt. Port A is also used for reading the system board DIP switch SW1, depending on the value of port B's bit 7. Since both the keyboard 74LS322 and the sense switch 74LS244 have tristate outputs, they could have been connected directly to the system data bus, somewhat simplifying the programming and hardware.

Since the keyboard bit stream is quite simple, it could also be decoded directly using a single parallel port bit read by a program as described in Sec. 9-4 and in Glasco and Sargent (1983). The PC*jr* uses this method to decode its serial keyboard data stream. A disadvantage of this approach is that it requires dedicated CPU attention; to work correctly, no interrupts can occur during decoding. Internally the IBM PC keyboard generates its bit stream using an Intel 8048 single-chip microcomputer as diagrammed in Fig. 8-4. There, 5 output bits from the 8048 cause a data distributor circuit to pull one of 23 normally high lines to a low voltage. A particular key connects one of these lines to one of 4 interrogation lines that run to a data selector circuit read by the 8048. The 8048 scans the keyboard switch array by sinking the 23 lines one at a time and checking to see if any of the 4 interrogation lines is low. It does this continually. When it finds a closure, it waits a few milliseconds to let the key stop bouncing (when you press a key, it may make contact four or five times in rapid succession before making a firm contact). The 8048 then stores the make code in a

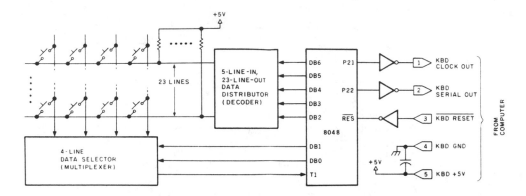

Fig. 8-4. Block diagram of IBM PC keyboard microprocessor circuit. The keys are arranged in a 23 x 4 matrix whose rows and columns are repeat-edly sampled by the 8048 microprocessor. (Reprinted from Glasco and Sargent, 1983)

buffer for transmission to the PC. Similarly, if the 8048 notices that a previously made key closure is broken, it stores the key code in question with bit 7 set (the break code). The codes are sent out serially as described above. The 8048 also autorepeats any key (except shift keys) that remains down for longer than 0.5 second. IBM calls this *typematic* key action. The circuit in Fig. 8-4 includes a clock out line used by the IBM PC inter-face in Fig. 8-3, and an input reset line. The reset line is toggled by the restart routines of the IBM PC, although it's not necessary.

The ROM BIOS keyboard routine in the PC stores the characters in a circular buffer 16 entries long, something like the buffer described in Sec. 7-1. It's too bad they didn't make the buffer longer, say 64 bytes, so you could type one or two command lines ahead while the computer was executing the current command. The entries in the keyboard buffer consist of two bytes for each character, with the low byte usually being the encoded character and the high byte being the keyboard scan code shown in Fig. 8-1. Special keys such as the function keys and numeric keypad keys typically have a 00 low byte, with the keyboard scan code in the high byte. The 'Keyboard Encoding and Usage' section of the *Technical Reference* manual gives a complete description of the keyboard codes.

INT 16H in the ROM BIOS retrieves the character codes from the 16-word buffer, returning the value in AX. Since the scan code is in AH, you can tell the difference between two keys that produce the same ASCII code, for example between BACKSPACE and control H. If AH = 0 on entry, INT 16H waits until a character from the keyboard is present in the buffer, and then reads that character, returning it in AX. If AH = 1 on entry, INT 16H returns with the zero flag set if no character is available, and with it reset if a character is available. In either case, AX contains the word pointed to by the trailing buffer pointer. Hence if ZF = 0, AX contains the word that the next AH = 0 INT 16H will return. This allows a subroutine at a low level to peek at the next character in the keyboard FIFO *and* let some higher level subroutine see that entry as well. This is particularly handy with command characters like control C. Be sure to test the zero flag to know if a character is waiting; merely checking AL may give you the character stored 16 entries earlier. Note also that when you use INT 16H with AH = 1, the buffer pointer is *not* adjusted. You must actually read the character using an INT 16H with AH = 0 to remove it from the buffer.

To illustrate just how flexible the keyboard is, a program is presented in App. C that turns the PC keyboard into a piano keyboard. (Well, something like a piano!) The sound is limited to the square-wave generator output discussed in Sec. 9-4 and heard through the tiny PC speaker, so it really doesn't sound much like a piano. But the tones generated are accurate to within 1 cent (a 100th of a half tone), and hence are accurate to well within the ability of a human being to perceive an error. The keys in the *asdfg* row play whole notes and the keys in the *qwerty* row play sharps and flats. The shift keys shift up an octave, while the Alt and CapsLock keys shift down an octave. The space bar toggles between half and full volume. Since the keyboard sends make and break codes, the program knows precisely how long a key is depressed. Hence the corresponding sound for the last key closure lasts as long as that key is depressed. Besides being fun, the program illustrates several important principles: how to take over and restore an interrupt, how the keyboard can be used for a very different application from what it was originally designed for, how tones of precise frequency can be generated using the 8253 clock/timer circuit, and how a high-frequency modulation of the square-wave output can cut the volume level in half. If you're intrigued, try the program out. Waveform generation is discussed further in Sec. 9-5.

The Mouse

The mouse was originally developed at the Xerox Research Laboratories in Palo Alto to be used on high-performance, bit-mapped graphics screens (see Sec. 8-2) where multiple applications are being displayed on the same screen. On a 25 x 80 text screen, you don't know exactly where the mouse is within the character cell, so the mouse screen cursor jumps up and down a line as you attempt to move it horizontally across the screen. With a bit-mapped screen, this problem is minimized, since you can see where the cursor is within the character cell. However, bit-mapping requires much more processor overhead and leads to slow response on the IBM PC. On the AT, the mouse is quite handy for controlling multitasking operating system front ends like Microsoft's Windows and Microsoft's Mondrian (a fast TopView look-alike). Heavily graphics-oriented programs like laser font editors and computer aided design programs like AutoDesk's AutoCad benefit substantially from having a mouse.

In general, regardless of machine speed, it's faster to use your ten fingers for almost all word processing operations than to use a mouse, even for typing mathematical equations. With the PS word processor, equations are typed in a linear format well suited to touch-typing special symbols and editing. Moving a mouse around the screen or using a digitization pad is about ten times slower. One exception to this is operations on blocks of text, the extremities of which can be conveniently defined with a mouse.

The Microsoft mouse is an example of what's currently available for the PC. It has two buttons on top of the mouse, and comes with a plug-in controller board that interrupts the computer using the 8259A IR2 line (or IR3, IR4, or IR5 if desired) whenever motion of the mouse or a button depression is detected. The package includes a program that takes over interrupt vector 33H, and gives user programs essentially complete control over mouse operations, including full interrupt capabilities. Most other mice for the PC have three buttons. Apple's Macintosh has only one button, but most people can master and benefit from having more.

Special Features of the AT Keyboard

Like the PC keyboard, the AT keyboard is controlled by an 8048 single-chip microcomputer, but unlike the PC the interface on the motherboard also has a dedicated 8042 single-chip microcomputer. This gives the AT keyboard some nice extra features, such as soft control of CapsLock, NumLock, and ScrollLock indicators, emulation of the PC keyboard scan codes, and a programmable autorepeat (also called typematic) rate.

Auto repeat is invoked when you hold a key down for more than a fraction of a second. On the PC, you have to hold the key down for 1/2 second before the auto repeat starts, and the repeat rate is fixed at ten characters per second. Particularly for moving cursor keys around in an editor, you may find this too slow. The following autort subroutine allows you to customize the delay and repeat rate to suit your tastes.

```
data     segment at 40H        ;ROM-BIOS RAM segment
         org     97H
kbflag2  db      ?             ;AT ROM-BIOS extra keyboard flag byte
data     ends

autort:  mov     bx,DATA       ;Enter with ah = autorepeat code.  Rate
         mov     ds,bx         ; increases monotonically with low 5 bits
         assume  ds:DATA       ; Delay increases with bit6 & bit5. Bit7=0

         mov     bh,0F3H       ;Send typematic rate/delay command
         call    keyout
         mov     bh,ah         ;Send desired code
         call    keyout
         mov     bh,0F4H       ;Enable keyboard
```

;KEYOUT - output bh to 8042 handling acknowledge and retries

```
keyout:   mov     bl,3              ;Maximum of three retries
keyou1:   cli
          and     kbflag2,0CFH      ;Kill acknowledge and resend bits
          sub     cx,cx
keyou2:   in      al,64H            ;Wait for last command to be accepted
          test    al,2              ;Input buffer empty?
          loopnz  keyou2            ;Fall through if keyboard out to lunch
          mov     al,bh             ;Send value. Should cause INT 9 setting
          out     60H,al            ; acknowledge or resend flag bit
          sti
          mov     cx,1A00H          ;Load count for 10 msec
keyou4:   test    kbflag2,10H       ;Acknowledge received?
          jnz     keyou9
          test    kbflag2,20H       ;No. Resend received?
          jnz     keyou5
          loop    keyou4            ;No
keyou5:   dec     bl                ;Decrement retry count
          jnz     keyou1
          or      kbflag2,80H       ;Signal transmit error
keyou9:   ret
```

You might want to make a COM file including this code in a routine that reads the rate and delay numbers from the file1 and file2 parameters on DOS command line, and reference it in your autoexec.bat file. In particular, the value ah = 0 gives a 0.25-second delay followed by a 30-cps repetition rate, which is the fastest option possible and the one we use. Just don't let you fingers rest on the keyboard! The standard option of 0.5-second delay followed by 10 cps is given by ah = 2CH. See the AT *Technical Reference* for other combinations and extensive discussions of the AT keyboard options.

Note in the code above that outputting a command code to the 8042 outputs, in turn, a command to the keyboard, which usually returns a special scan code of 0FAH called an "acknowledge" and might return the code 0FEH meaning "resend." Receipt of one of these scan codes causes an INT 9 to occur and leads the ROM-BIOS keyboard routine to set bit 4 or 5 of the byte at offset 97H in the ROM-BIOS RAM. After outputting a control byte, the keyout subroutine simply hangs waiting for one of these bits to be set by such an interrupt. This is an example of dedicated polling to synchronize data transfer as discussed in Chap. 7. Since the timing isn't critical, the polling loop is executed with interrupts enabled.

Figure 8-5 shows a block diagram of the 8042 keyboard interface on the AT system board. In addition to the keyboard interface, the circuit provides access to some system information and control of the 80286-reset and address-20 gate lines discussed in Secs. 6-2, 6-3, and 6-5.

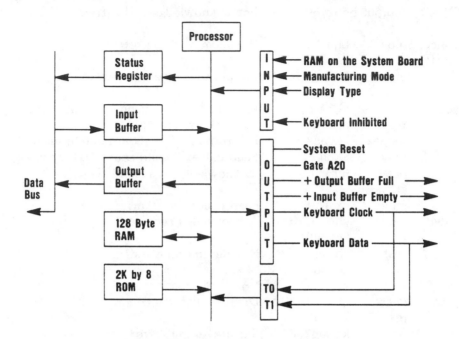

Fig. 8–5. Block diagram of 8042 single–chip microcontroller on AT motherboard.

8-2. How Video Displays Work

One of the most important devices a computer must interface to is a video display, such as a stand-alone video terminal. The interface is often done by connecting the terminal to the computer with a serial link as will be described in Chap. 10. However, substantially higher performance (more speed and flexibility) can be obtained with displays based in the microcomputer itself. Here an interface board containing part of the computer's memory generates the signals needed to directly drive a CRT (cathode ray tube) display. This latter approach is used in the IBM PC. In this section, we describe how video displays work and discuss the signals needed to drive them. The next section describes how several popular video boards for the PC work, and briefly discusses how they can be programmed.

The CRT displays discussed here are called *raster* displays, because the picture or text is produced on the display screen by a beam of electrons that repeatedly scans across the screen to form a uniform pattern of closely spaced horizontal lines (the raster), which covers the entire screen. The screen's surface is covered with a phosphor that glows when the electron beam hits it, so pictures are formed on the screen as the beam turns on and off while scanning across the screen face. Figures 8-6 and 8-7 show in more detail how this is done.

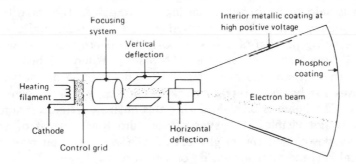

Fig. 8–6. Basic design of a CRT tube. The intensity of the electron beam coming from the cathode is controlled by the control grid, and the position where the beam strikes the phosphor–coated screen is determined by the voltages applied to the horizontal and vertical deflection plates.

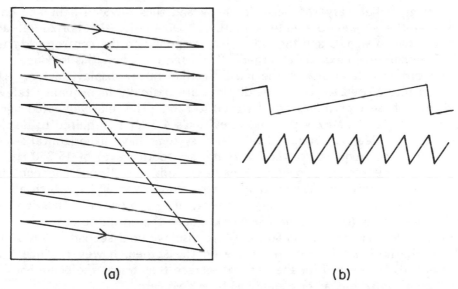

(a)   (b)

Fig. 8–7. (a) Raster scan pattern on the screen created by the sawtooth waves applied to the horizontal and vertical deflection plates. (b) Vertical and horizontal sweep sawtooth waves.

The horizontal sweep of the beam across the screen is created by a high-frequency sawtooth wave applied to the horizontal deflection plates. During the rising portion of the wave, the beam is swept from left to right across the screen, and during the more rapid falling portion, the beam re-traces back to the left side of the screen. During the retrace, a voltage is applied to the control grid that greatly reduces the beam intensity, so that the retraces (the dashed lines in Fig. 8-7) are not visible on the screen. The beam is said to be *blanked* during retraces. At the same time, a much lower frequency sawtooth is applied to the vertical deflection plates. During the rising portion of this sawtooth, the beam moves slowly down the screen while the horizontal sweeps take place. When the beam reaches the bottom of the screen, the more rapidly falling portion of the vertical sawtooth causes the beam to retrace back to the top of the screen as shown in Fig. 8-7a. The beam is blanked during this entire vertical retrace period, so it's normally not visible. However, if you turn the contrast of your display all the way down, and the brightness all the way up, you may be able see the vertical retrace lines appearing on the screen.

What's just been described is an electrostatically deflected CRT. Also common is magnetic deflection, where coils producing magnetic fields are used instead of plates producing electric fields. In magnetic deflection, it is the current through the coil that must be a sawtooth wave rather than the voltage. In other respects the two deflection methods are identical.

During the left-to-right horizontal sweeps, signals are applied to the control grid that vary the beam intensity and thus produce light and dark spots on the screen to create a picture. Obviously, the horizontal and vertical sweep signals and the video signals applied to the control grid must all be synchronized exactly together. You'll see later how this is done.

An ordinary television is the most familiar raster display device. The video monitors used for computer displays are basically high-quality television sets whose electronics are designed to handle the relatively wide signal bandwidths (10—20 MHz versus the television's 4.5 MHz) required to display small details clearly. Standard television systems have a horizontal sweep frequency (the frequency of the horizontal sawtooth wave) of 15,750 Hz, so each scan line requires about 53.5 microseconds plus 10 microseconds for the horizontal retrace. The vertical sweep frequency is 60 Hz, which allows 262.5 horizontal scan lines during one vertical sweep period. Thus it takes 16.7 milliseconds (one 60th of a second) to scan the entire screen area once (this is called one field), and 60 fields are displayed per second. Only about 245 of the horizontal lines are visible on the screen, however, since 1.25 milliseconds is required for the vertical retrace that brings the beam back to the top of the screen after a field has been completed.

In most computer displays, each field contains the entire picture or text being displayed. However, in standard broadcast television and some high resolution displays, two successive fields are required to make one complete picture or frame. The second field is shifted down by one-half line, so that its scan lines fall between the lines of the first field. This is called an *interlaced* picture and gives 525 lines of vertical resolution. One problem with an interlaced display is that small details on the screen appear to flicker on and off. This is because a phosphor spot on the screen glows for only a short time after it's lit up by the electron beam, and the full picture is refreshed (the process of redrawing the picture is called refreshing the screen) only 30 times per second. If many small, high-contrast details are present in the picture, this is not fast enough to fool your eyes into believing that a steady picture is being displayed. Broadcast television pictures have far less detail than a display of text on a computer screen, so the flicker is not objectionable there. In interlaced computer displays, the flicker problem is often solved by using a CRT with a green (P39) long-persistence phosphor. The P39 phosphor continues to glow for a much longer time after it's struck by an electron beam than the standard white (P4) phosphor.

Color video displays work the same way as monochrome displays except that three electron beams are used, and the screen, instead of being coated with a uniform coating of phosphor, is coated with a pattern of little circular or rectangular phosphor dots. One-third of the dots use a phosphor that glows red when hit by an electron beam, one-third use a phosphor that glows green, and the final third use a phosphor that glows blue. You can see this construction clearly if you look closely at a color television screen. Each of the three electron beams illuminates only the phosphor dots of one color, as shown in Fig. 8-8. If the red, green, and blue phosphor dots are equally illuminated, we perceive the result as the color white at normal viewing distance. By varying the relative intensities of the red, green, and blue electron beams, any color you want can be produced.

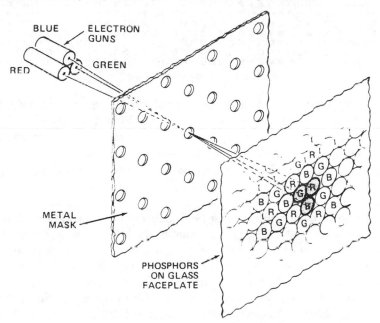

Fig. 8–8. Electron beam and screen geometry for a conventional color CRT. The metal shadow mask prevents the electron beam for one color from illuminating the phosphor dots for another color. Conrac Corporation.

Now let's look at how numbers and letters are drawn on a computer display and what implications this has for the construction of the display and the signals required to drive it. To draw letters, the electron beam is simply turned on and off as the beam is scanned, thereby producing a pattern of dots on the screen. Thus the characters are represented by a closely spaced dot pattern, drawn one raster line at a time as shown in Fig. 8-9. In this figure a 5x7 matrix of dots contains the letter; however, many other matrix sizes are also used.

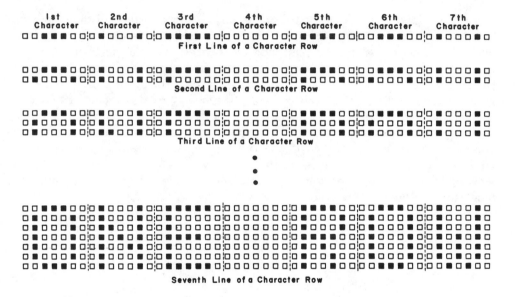

Fig. 8—9. Illustration of drawing a set of characters on a raster. Each character line consists of several raster lines. Here each letter is formed by a 5x7 dot matrix, and typically 10 raster lines are used per character line to allow for interline spacing and lower—case descenders such as on the letter "g". Reprinted by permission of Intel Corporation, copyright 1983.

The IBM PC monochrome display adapter (the interface board that drives IBM's monochrome display) produces its letters as a 7x9 dot matrix contained within a 9x14 character box to allow for descenders and for intercharacter and interline spacings as shown in Fig. 8-10. The monochrome display itself uses a higher than normal horizontal sweep frequency and a lower than normal 50-Hz vertical sweep frequency to give 350 raster lines. Because a long persistence phosphor is used, the 50-Hz refresh rate does not produce any visible flicker. The monochrome adapter produces 720 dots per horizontal raster line to obtain the 80 characters per line. Since these dots must be sent out during the 44 microseconds required to scan a single raster line, severe requirements are placed on the circuitry in the display and the adapter. One dot must be sent out every 61 nanoseconds (61×10^{-9} second),

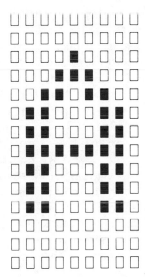

Fig. 8—10. The letter "A" as represented on the IBM monochrome display. Since each dot on the display is 1.5 times as high as it is wide, vertical lines are made two dots wide.

requiring a bandwidth of more than 16 MHz for the video amplifiers in the display. Because of the high bandwidth and nonstandard sweep rates, only IBM's monitor and other monitors (like the Amdek 310a amber monitor) that have been specifically designed to run with the monochrome adapter can be used.

The IBM enhanced color/graphics adapter (EGA) in its standard color mode has bandwidth requirements slightly less than those for the monochrome adapter because it uses an 8x14 character box. It requires a special RGB (short for red, green, blue) color monitor intended for use as a color display. RGB monitors contain three wideband amplifiers, one for each of the red, green, and blue electron guns, and typically have much higher bandwidth and smaller phosphor dot sizes than ordinary color television sets. The EGA requires a nonstandard RGB monitor compatible with the IBM enhanced color display to use its full capabilities. In particular, the monitor must be able to recognize the inverted polarity vertical sweep signal used by the adapter to indicate that it is operating in high resolution mode. When used with an ordinary RGB monitor, the EGA can only operate in a mode that emulates the older color/graphics adapter.

Even with a good wideband RGB color monitor, the quality of text displayed on a color screen is not as good as on the monochrome display. The problem is the inherent graininess of a color CRT, produced by the discrete phosphor dots on the screen (see Fig. 8-8). Each dot is about 0.1 millimeter in diameter for a high quality display, and three of them have to be illuminated to make a single white dot.

The IBM color/graphics display adapter can work with both standard RGB monitors and ordinary television sets. Like the other adapters, it produces a noninterlaced display. Letters are produced as a 7x7 matrix within an 8x8 character box, and there are 25 lines of characters with 40 or 80 letters per character line. This means that 320 or 640 dots are put on each horizontal raster line, and only 200 raster lines are used. The remaining 40 to 45 raster lines are unused. The justifications for using fewer lines are that an 8x8 matrix can be produced with simpler digital logic (since 8 is a power of 2), the 640x200 dots can be stored in 16K of memory, which is easily controlled by the Motorola 6845 CRT controller, and cheap television sets can be used. These sets typically overscan the screen boundaries to avoid problems with distortion in the corners and edges of the raster field.

When the color/graphics adapter is used with a normal television set, the display is limited to 40 characters per line because the bandwidth of the video amplifiers in a television set must be less than 4.5 MHz. Worse yet, colors other than white have a bandwidth of only about 1 MHz. These low bandwidths are required by the scheme used to transmit signals to a color television. You also need to buy a little box called a modulator to go between the adapter and the television set. To understand why this is so requires some additional discussion of display drive signals.

What signals need to be sent to a display to drive it? Obviously the video information telling where to light up dots on each raster line must be sent. Furthermore, this information must be synchronized exactly to the horizontal and vertical sweep of the display. To synchronize the sweeping electron beam to the video data, both coarse and fine adjustments are used. Coarse adjustments are made using the horizontal and vertical hold knobs on the monitor, which change the approximate oscillation frequencies of the beam sweep circuits. Fine adjustment is made by use of horizontal and vertical synchronization, or sync, signals, which are sent along with the video data by the device driving the display. Circuitry in the display forces the vertical and horizontal sawtooth wave oscillators to have exactly the same frequency and phase as the sync signals. Often these sync signals are combined with the dot stream itself to form a *composite video* signal as shown in Fig. 8-11. A bright spot is caused by a high signal (about 1.8 volts), a dark spot by an intermediate voltage (about 0.4 volt), and a sync signal by pulses of 0 volts. The horizontal sync signal is distinguished from the vertical sync signal by being a much shorter pulse. The brightness control on the display changes the on-off threshold of the dot data, while the contrast control changes the video signal gain. Circuitry in the display separates out the horizontal sync (a 15,750-Hz stream of negative-going 5-microsecond pulses), vertical sync (a 60-Hz stream of negative-going 190-microsecond pulses), and video portions of the composite video signal.

The composite video signal just described does not include color information. The composite video signal for a color display is more complex. In addition to the black-and-white composite video signal, color information is superimposed as a phase- and amplitude-modulated 3.579-MHz subcarrier.

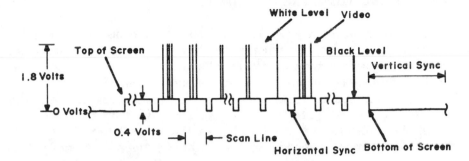

Fig. 8—11. Illustration of a standard composite video output.

The interested reader is referred to one of the many books on color television for a more detailed description.

No composite video signal is available from the IBM monochrome adapter. Instead, the two sync signals and the video signal are sent separately to the monochrome display. In addition, the video signal is divided into two pieces, a normal video signal and an intensify signal that produces brighter, boldface letters on the screen when it's on.

The IBM color/graphics adapter produces two separate outputs. One is the composite video signal described above. This signal is primarily meant for use with television sets or closed circuit television monitors. A television set cannot use composite video directly. Instead, it expects to receive a high-frequency carrier wave (for example, 61.25 MHz for channel 3), which has the composite video impressed upon it as an amplitude-modulated (AM) signal, since this is the way normal television signals are broadcast. Thus you must hook up a small box called a VHF modulator between the composite video output and the television. This device converts composite video into the proper AM signal.

The second output from the color/graphics adapter is a set of signals that can drive RGB monitors. These signals consist of separate vertical and horizontal sync signals, a total intensity signal, and separate red, green, and blue signals. The red, green, and blue signals are sent to the individual red, green, and blue electron guns via three wideband video amplifiers. The gain of these amplifiers is controlled by the intensity signal. Thus the color at a given place on the screen is determined by the ratio of the red, green, and blue voltages, while the brightness of the color there is set by the intensity signal.

The EGA has only an RGB output. In low-resolution mode, the signals are identical to the color/graphics adapter output, but in high-resolution mode the intensity signal is replaced by separate red, green, and blue intensity signals and the vertical sync signal polarity is inverted.

Having looked in some detail at how CRT displays and the video signals that drive them work, we now turn to a discussion of how the video signals are generated, and how the computer can control them.

8-3. Monochrome, Color, and Graphics Boards

In this section we show how memory-mapped video display boards like those used in the PC are constructed and how they can be programmed. Memory-mapped displays are far faster and more flexible than serial terminals. This difference is particularly noticeable in word-processing and high-resolution graphics applications, where a serial link proves to be rather slow. Some of the computer's memory space is used up by a memory-mapped display (IBM has reserved addresses 0A0000h—00BFFFFh, which is 128 Kbytes, for memory-mapped displays in the PC), but the PC has enough memory that this isn't yet a major problem. After discussing memory-mapped displays in general, we look in more detail at four popular display boards for the IBM PC: the IBM monochrome display adapter (IBM calls all its PC plug-in boards adapters), the Hercules Computer Technology monochrome graphics card, the IBM color/graphics display adapter, and the IBM enhanced graphics display adapter.

The basic idea of a memory-mapped display is very simple. Any computer terminal or video display has its own memory, which contains the information that determines which screen dots are turned on or off. In a terminal, this memory is contained within the terminal, whereas in a memory-mapped display this memory is part of the CPU's memory space. While this is a simple change, it makes a tremendous difference in the performance of the display. With a memory-mapped display, the information displayed can be changed as fast as the computer can write new information into memory (several hundred thousand bytes per second), while a terminal can receive new information only through its serial data link (typically at transmission rates of 960 bytes per second or less).

It may not seem useful to be able to change the screen so rapidly, but it is. When editing a document, you want to be able to move from one page (screenful) of text to another in a fraction of a second, so that you can flip from one page to another rapidly, just as you can rapidly flip through the pages of a book. Since an 80 character by 25 line screen holds 2000 characters, it typically takes over 2 seconds to change the screen on a terminal, which is too slow. You can turn book pages faster than that! When you insert text into a paragraph, words may be pushed beyond the right margin and have to wrap down to the next line. Unless this word wrap is instantaneous, the screen flickers, which causes fatigue and is distracting. The need for speed is even more apparent when graphics are being used. The IBM color/graphics display has 640 x 200 = 128,000 points in high-resolution mode. If 1 bit per point is used to store the information on the screen, it will take almost 17 seconds to rewrite the terminal's screen. Try doing animations at that speed!

In the preceding paragraph, we've hinted at the fact that there are actually two different types of memory-mapped displays: one type that handles text and another that handles graphics. The difference is in the way the information is stored in memory. In a graphics display, a value for every possible dot position on the screen is stored as one or more bits in memory, and the contents of this memory are directly read out to the video monitor 60 times per second. Such displays are often called *bit-mapped* displays since there's a one-to-one mapping between the bits in memory and the dots on the screen. The IBM color/graphics board works like this in its 640x200 high-resolution mode. In its lower resolution 320x200 mode, a 2-bit quantity is stored for each dot on the screen, with each 2-bit number corresponding to one of four possible colors for that point.

The *alphanumeric* type of memory-mapped display does not store an image of the screen in the refresh memory, but rather stores just the ASCII values of the characters for each character position on the screen. The ASCII values are then translated into dot patterns on the screen by a *character generator*. IBM's monochrome display adapter is an alphanumeric type of display. The other adapters discussed here have circuitry to support both alphanumeric and bit-mapped modes of operation.

One advantage of an alphanumeric display is that it requires considerably less memory. For example, only 2000 bytes of memory are needed for an 80 character by 25 line alphanumeric display (using one byte per character position), whereas 16 kilobytes are required for a 640x200 bit-mapped display (using one bit per dot on the screen). Actually, in the PC the difference isn't this great, because IBM's adapters use 2 bytes for each alphanumeric mode character. One byte contains the ASCII character itself, and the second byte contains an attribute that specifies whether the character is to be boldfaced, blinked, reverse video, or normal. A second advantage is that it's fast and easy for the CPU to change the screen. It has only to write out the ASCII character and perhaps an attribute byte if that also needs to be changed.

The big advantage of a bit-mapped display is its flexibility. You can draw both pictures and text on the screen. Furthermore, since text characters must be literally drawn dot-by-dot in the screen refresh memory, the character font is user definable. You can do anything you want. The drawbacks are that it takes fairly complex software to properly control the screen, and it takes a lot longer to redraw the screen than it does for an alphanumeric display.

Monochrome Display Adapter

To see in more detail how a memory-mapped display works, consider the operation of IBM's monochrome display adapter. A block diagram of this adapter is shown in Fig. 8-12. The heart of the display adapter is a Motorola 6845 CRT controller, a smart peripheral chip that provides all the timing and control signals for the video display. The on-board screen refresh RAM is *dual-port* memory. This means that it can be accessed by the CPU and the 6845 CRT controller, although not by both at the same time. Multiplexers (see Sec. 5-8) on the address lines determine which of the two can address the memory. The memory's data lines connect (via

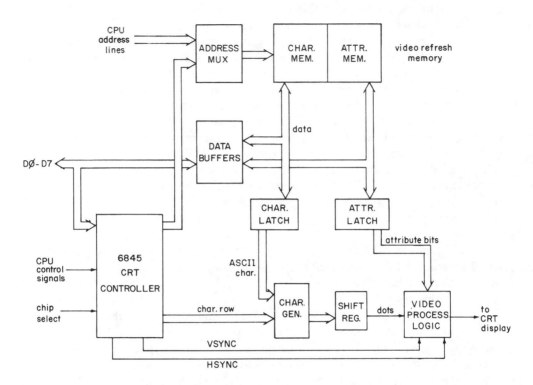

Fig. 8–12. Simplified block diagram of the monochrome display adapter. Both CPU and 6845 CRT controller have access to the 4K RAM video refresh memory. The contents of the RAM are translated into dot-matrix raster format by the character generator and shifted out serially in accord with appropriate timing signals.

buffers) both to the CPU data lines and to the circuitry that produces the video display. Thus the memory can output data to two different places (in other words, it has dual ports).

When the CPU is not accessing the refresh RAM, the operation of the board is as follows: The 6845 continually produces the proper horizontal and vertical sync pulses needed by the CRT display (see Fig. 8-11), and also reads out the contents of the refresh memory in between sync pulses to produce synchronized video data on the screen. Since the data in memory is ASCII characters, however, it must be translated into rows of dot patterns before being sent to the CRT. This translation is performed by a *character generator*, which is a ROM memory containing the dot patterns for each character. Eight of the ROM's address lines are connected to the data lines holding the ASCII character read from memory, and four address lines are connected to the output of a row counter in the CRT controller chip. The eight lines select the character pattern to be used, and the four lines select which row of the pattern to output. For example, if the character being sent on the eight lines is a 41H (an "A") and the row counter lines have a 5, then the character generator will output the 5th row of Fig. 8-10. The character generator output is loaded into a shift register (see Sec. 5-7), and the dots are shifted out one at a time to the CRT display. At the same time a character is read out of memory, its attribute bits are also read out and latched. These bits can modify the dot stream sent to the CRT to produce, for example, reverse video by inverting the dots. This modification is done in the video process logic.

When the CPU wants to write new information into memory, the address multiplexers and data buffers are switched by the CPU control signals so that the CPU address and data lines access the memory instead of the CRT controller. However, when this happens, a problem results. A CPU read or write takes 800 nanoseconds, but the CRT controller must send a new byte of data from memory to the character generator every 553 nanoseconds (the data rate to the screen is 1.8 megabytes/second!). If nothing special is done, this means that one row of at least two characters is lost whenever a CPU access is done. The effect is to produce black glitches on the screen when the CPU is reading or writing to the refresh memory. You may have seen this effect on the IBM PC color/graphics display. You don't see it on the monochrome display because IBM used fast static RAM memory on the monochrome adapter and built in some clever latches and timing circuitry that allow the CPU to read or write memory by sneaking in between the CRT controller's memory accesses.

Another unique feature of the monochrome adapter is a set of line-drawing and area-fill characters that give continuous lines and filled areas. This is unusual for a display with a 9 x 14 character box (see Fig. 8-10) because the character generator provides a row only eight dots wide. On most displays, a blank 9th dot is then inserted between characters. On the monochrome display there is circuitry that duplicates the 8th dot into the 9th dot position for characters whose ASCII codes are 0B0H through 0DFH (see the section entitled "Of Characters, Keystrokes, and Color" in the IBM PC *Technical Reference* manual).

The monochrome adapter also contains several curious features. First, although only a 4K ROM is required for the character generator, an 8K ROM was used. The other 4K contains the two fonts used on the lower resolution color/graphics display adapter. Jumper J1 on the monochrome board selects the other 4K, but also turns off the dot clock, so nothing appears on the screen. Provisions also exist in the circuitry for a light pen. However, a light pen cannot be used with the monochrome display because it uses a long-persistence P39 phosphor. Light pens work by having a little optical detector in the tip of the pen. This produces a short pulse when the flash of light occurs that's caused by the electron beam sweeping over that point in the raster. The time at which this pulse appears relative to the horizontal and vertical sync signals can be used by the CRT controller to determine the light pen position. With the P39 phosphor, however, the light flash lasts so long that the pulse cannot be used for accurate timing.   Finally, the video output circuitry has provisions for driving an RGB color display, as can be seen from the schematics in the IBM PC *Options and Adapters Technical Reference* manual.   At this writing, color displays are not readily available that accept the monochrome board's nonstandard vertical and horizontal sweep rates.   These features are probably either vestiges of features that were removed from the final design, or are features that have been included for compatibility with future products.

From a programmer's point of view, the monochrome adapter looks like four I/O ports and a 4K memory area starting at 0B0000H, as shown in Fig. 8-13.   The CRT control port has 3 bits that can be set by the user.   The high-resolution mode bit must always be on, and an output instruction to set this bit in the control port must be the first access made to the adapter after a reset.   Otherwise you'll hang up the computer in an infinite wait state!   The video enable bit turns the video output stream on and off.   By resetting this bit to zero, you can blank the entire screen instantaneously, and later turn it back on again by setting it back to 1.   Similarly, the blink enable bit allows you to enable or disable the blinking of characters. Issuing a 29H to this port gives normal operation.

The CRT status port can be read by the user and provides the state of two signals on bits 0 and 3: the horizontal sync signal and the stream of video dots going out to the display.   Neither of these signals is very useful. It's too bad that IBM didn't include the vertical sync signal as one of the status port bits as they did on the color/graphics adapter so that you could synchronize computer operations to the start of a new video frame.

The 6845 CRT controller has 18 programmable internal registers.   Programming them is a two-step process.   First you output the number of the register (0–17) you want to program into the 6845 index register, and then you output the data for that register into the 6845 data register.   This technique allows the 6845 to take up only 2 output ports instead of 18.   most of the 6845 registers are used to specify the number of display lines, the number of characters per line, and the timings of the vertical and horizontal sync signals.   You should not play around with these values, as programming the 6845 incorrectly can burn out the monochrome display!   Refer to the IBM PC *Options and Adapters Technical Reference* manual for the normal values of these registers and to the Motorola 6845 specification sheet for detailed explanations of each register's function.

There are four 6845 registers that you might want to play with.   Registers 0AH and 0BH determine the cursor start and end address, that is, on which raster line in a character the cursor starts and on which line it ends. The normal values are start = 0B and end = 0C, which gives a 2-line cursor underneath the character.   If you specify start = 0, end = 0C you get a big block cursor, which some people prefer.   The other two registers are registers 0EH and 0FH, which determine the position of the cursor on the screen. This position is a number between 0 and 1999, with number 0 being the character position in the upper left corner.   The most significant byte of the

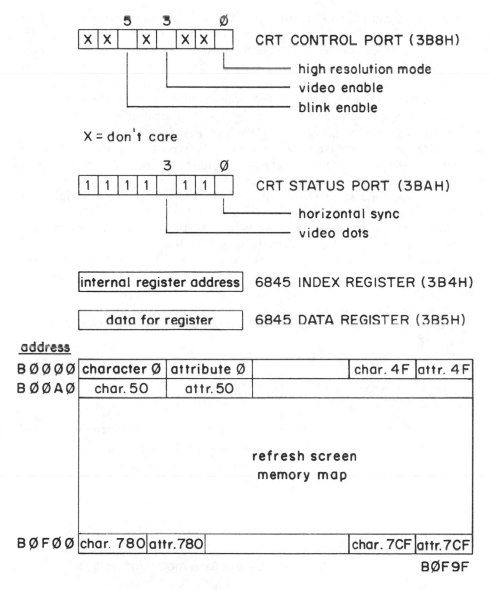

Fig. 8–13. I/O ports used by the IBM monochrome display adapter and the relationship of character positions on the screen to addresses in the video refresh memory.

number goes into 0E and the least significant byte into 0F. The cursor size and position can also be changed using the INT 10H video I/O calls described later. The cursor blink rate is fixed by hardware and cannot be changed.

Now let's see how characters can be placed directly in memory. As seen in Fig. 8-13, each character position on the screen corresponds to a 16-bit memory location. The first byte of the 16 bits is the ASCII character, and the second byte is the attribute. The refresh memory area starts at location 0B0000H. This is the memory address for the character in the upper left corner of the screen. Subsequent memory locations correspond to the rest of the character positions on the screen, in the order that you would read them. Thus the address of a given character is just 2*(80*rownum + colnum), where the row number (rownum) and column number (colnum) are assumed to begin with 0. For example, the third character on the second line (column number 2 of row number 1) would have an address 0B00A4H. The last character on the screen (lower right corner) is at address 0B0F9EH. Similarly, the attribute byte for each character is located at 2*(80*rownum + colnum)+1.

The allowed values for the attribute byte are summarized in Fig. 8-14. As can be seen, setting bit 7 in the attribute byte causes the character to blink, and setting bit 3 intensifies or highlights the character. Because of the method used by IBM to decode the attribute bits, underlining and reverse video are specified by a combination of 6 bits. Setting all 6 foreground-background bits to 0 causes the character not to be displayed. The normal value of the attribute byte is 7. This may seem like a strange way of defining the attribute byte, but IBM set up the monochrome adapter's attribute byte this way in order to be compatible with IBM's color/graphics

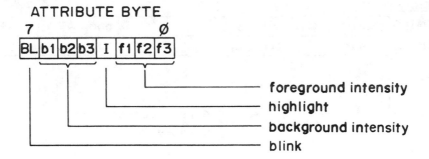

ATTRIBUTE BYTE

Only 4 combinations of the foreground and
background intensity bits are meaningful:

b1	b2	b3	f1	f2	f3	
0	0	0	0	0	0	non-display
0	0	0	0	0	1	underline
0	0	0	1	1	1	normal
1	1	1	0	0	0	reverse video

Fig. 8-14. Bit assignments for the monochrome display attribute byte.

and enhanced graphics adapters. In those adapters, the three foreground and three background bits are used to define text foreground and background colors.

With the information just given, you can write routines to control the screen directly in any way you desire. Playing around in DEBUG with some tiny programs that directly write the screen is a very educational experience and will make clear exactly how the attributes and screen addressing work. However, in normal programs, it's usually easier to make use of the large set of video screen subroutines that make up INT 10H. Table 8-1 shows the available functions. See the BIOS ROM source code in the IBM PC *Technical Reference* manual for a complete description of the calling sequence for each function—that is, which registers contain the parameters passed to the routines. Additional higher level screen functions are provided by the DOS function calls accessed through INT 21H.

FUNCTION NUMBER	INT 10H VIDEO ROUTINE
0	Set new graphics or text mode
1	Set cursor size
2	Set cursor position
3	Read cursor position
4	Read light pen position
5	Select active display page
6	Scroll display window up
7	Scroll display window down
8	Read character and attribute at cursor position
9	Write character and attribute at cursor position
10	Write character at cursor position
11	Set color palette
12	Write dot
13	Read dot
14	Write teletype (simulate a dumb printer)
15	Read current video state

Table 8-1. Screen handling functions available in INT 10H, the video I/O interrupt. The functions are accessed by executing an INT 10H with AH containing the function number shown.

In general, it's a good idea to use the INT 10H or INT 21H routines to write to the screen since they provide a well documented standard. If you really need high performance from the screen, however, you'll have to write your own routines, because the INT 10H routines are rather slow. This is a result of the general purpose way the routines were written. They push and pop all registers regardless of whether they're destroyed by the routine, they check each time to see whether the monochrome or color/graphics adapter is installed, and many of the routines recursively call other INT 10H functions during their execution. For example, function 14 of INT 10H pushes and pops the entire register set four times and checks low memory to see which adapter is installed four times in the course of outputting just one character on the screen! Because of this, programs like screen editors, which must rapidly manipulate the screen, generally write the screen directly without going through INT 10H. The clock display program in Sec. 7-2 is an example of such a program. One way to get good performance and still maintain portability is to write a program that takes over INT 10H and does things the way you want them done. We have used this technique very sucessfully in several programs.

Hercules Graphics Card

The IBM monochrome adapter and display provides beautiful crisp text, but it leaves your PC with no graphics capabilities. The Hercules Graphics Card from Hercules Computer Technology is a replacement for the monochrome adapter that eliminates this problem very nicely by providing both text and graphics. This card drives the standard IBM monochrome display, and in text mode (the default mode present at power-up) it behaves absolutely identically to IBM's monochrome adapter. It also has a built-in parallel printer port just like IBM's board. Everything said about the monochrome display adapter so far applies to the Hercules card also, except that two additional bits are defined in the CRT control port and there is an additional configuration switch port.

Setting bit 1 of the CRT control port (3B8h) switches the card into graphics mode. In this mode, the refresh memory contents are not sent to the character generator but are sent directly to a shift register so that they appear as video dots on the screen. Each memory bit that is set to 1 then appears as a bright dot on the screen, giving you a bit-mapped display. In its bit-mapped mode, the Hercules card provides 720x348 graphics, nearly double the number of dots available with IBM's color/graphics adapter. With this relatively high resolution, you can draw really first-class graphics, although obviously not in color. Furthermore, because there's 64K of memory on board, two graphics pages are provided, with the active page being selected by bit 7 of the CRT Control Port. You can display or write into each page independently of the other. The configuration switch port enables you to disable the second graphics page (which starts at 0B8000h). This allows the board to be used in the same computer with a color/graphics or enhanced graphics adapter.

The board comes with a modified BASICA program that allows you to use all of BASIC's nice graphics commands with the card. Another nice feature is that the character generator is a 2732 EPROM. This means that you can modify the character set and/or add new characters if you wish. The Hercules card has gained a tremendous amount of software support, and several different companies offer workalikes (clones) of it. As a result, it has become the de facto standard for monochrome IBM PC graphics.

An enhanced version of the graphics card called the Hercules Graphics Card Plus is also available. This works just like the original Hercules card in its basic text and graphics modes, and provides two additional text modes in which a RAM character generator is used; i.e., the bit patterns used to define text characters are stored in RAM memory instead of in ROM. This allows the use of user-defined characters in text mode. These characters can be defined in a character box that is either 8 or 9 pixels wide (the 9th pixel is handled just as it is on the IBM monochrome board) and 8 to 16 pixels high. With 8-pixel-wide characters, 90 columns of text can appear on the screen. The character bit patterns are stored in the on-board memory area above the 16 Kbytes required for text mode display memory. The RAM character generator modes (called RamFont modes) are controlled by three registers, which appear as additional 6845 CRT controller index registers. In the first RamFont mode, each character is specified by an 8-bit ASCII code along with an attribute byte just as in normal text mode. This provides you with 256 user-definable characters. The second RamFont mode uses 12 bits to specify the character code along with 4 bits to specify the attribute. This provides you with up to 3072 different user-definable characters. This large number of on-line characters is ideal for scientific and technical word processing, especially when combined with a laser printer for output.

Color/Graphics Display Adapter

IBM's original offering in the graphics display area was the color/graphics display adapter (CGA). Like the Hercules card, the CGA can operate either in text mode using a ROM character generator or in a bit-mapped graphics mode. Little need be said about the hardware of the board, since, in block diagram form at least, it looks very much like the monochrome card and uses the same 6845 CRT controller chip.

In 80 x 25 text mode, the CGA behaves much like the monochrome adapter. The refresh memory map is the same as shown in Fig. 8-13 except that the starting address is 0B8000H. The attribute byte is also organized in the same way as shown in Fig. 8-14, except that no underlining is possible. Also, the three foreground attribute bits f1—f3 and the three background attribute bits b1—b3 can be individually set or reset to obtain colored text on a colored background. See the IBM PC *Options and Adapters Technical Reference* manual for details on the colors available. Since the color/graphics adapter has 16K of memory on board, while a page of text requires only 4K, you can use four independent pages of text, any one of which can be displayed on the screen at any given time. The displayed text page is set by changing the memory start address used by the 6845 (internal registers 0C and 0D). This can be done conveniently with function call 5 of INT 10H (see Table 8-1). The color/graphics adapter can also be programmed to provide 40x25 text for use with ordinary television sets, which must be attached via a modulator as discussed in Sec. 8-2.

The two most noticeable characteristics of the color/graphics adapter's text relative to the monochrome adapter's text are the lower quality characters and the blinking of the screen when the display scrolls. The characters are in an 8x8 box instead of a 9x14 box, which reduces the readability considerably. The use of only one blank dot between characters is a severe problem, as it tends to make the characters run together. The blinking is due to the slower dynamic RAM that is used instead of the fast static RAM of the monochrome adapter. Thus the screen cannot be refreshed by the 6845 when reads or writes of the refresh RAM are being done by the CPU. When just one character is being written, a software loop polls the color/graphics card status register until the CPU sees the horizontal sync signal (bit 0) and then writes to the display during the retrace time between raster lines. When the display scrolls (everything moves up one line), however, the entire screen must be rewritten. To accomplish this at reasonable speed, the display is momentarily blanked while the screen is being rewritten. This produces the blinking.

The color/graphics adapter can be used in three different bit-mapped graphics modes: 160x100 with 16 colors, 320x200 with 4 colors, and 640x200 monochrome. By far the most common mode is 320x200, so we consider only that mode here. Figure 8-15 shows the relationship of pixel positions on the screen to addresses in the refresh memory. As can be seen, each 2 bits of a byte in memory describe the color of a pixel on the screen. The word *pixel* is an abbreviation of "picture element," and is just the technical name for a dot position on the screen. IBM likes to call a pixel a *pel*. The mapping of the four possible values for each 2-bit pixel into four different colors is determined by the setting of the color select register. If you look at the memory map in Fig. 8-15, you'll notice that the organization of memory is rather peculiar. Pixel values for all the even-numbered raster lines are stored in the first half of the 16K refresh memory, and pixel values for the odd-numbered lines are stored in the second half. This was done in order to simplify the hardware. However, it means that software routines that draw lines or other figures on the screen must be more complex.

IBM Enhanced Graphics Adapter

In the fall of 1984, IBM introduced a much improved successor to the original color/graphics adapter called the enhanced graphics adapter (EGA). This is a multipurpose board that can drive either a monochrome or a color monitor in both text and graphics modes. The original IBM EGA board was quite expensive, and required the addition of a piggyback memory module to utilize its full capabilities. However, in late 1985, Chips & Technologies produced a set of four custom VLSI chips that could be used to build a

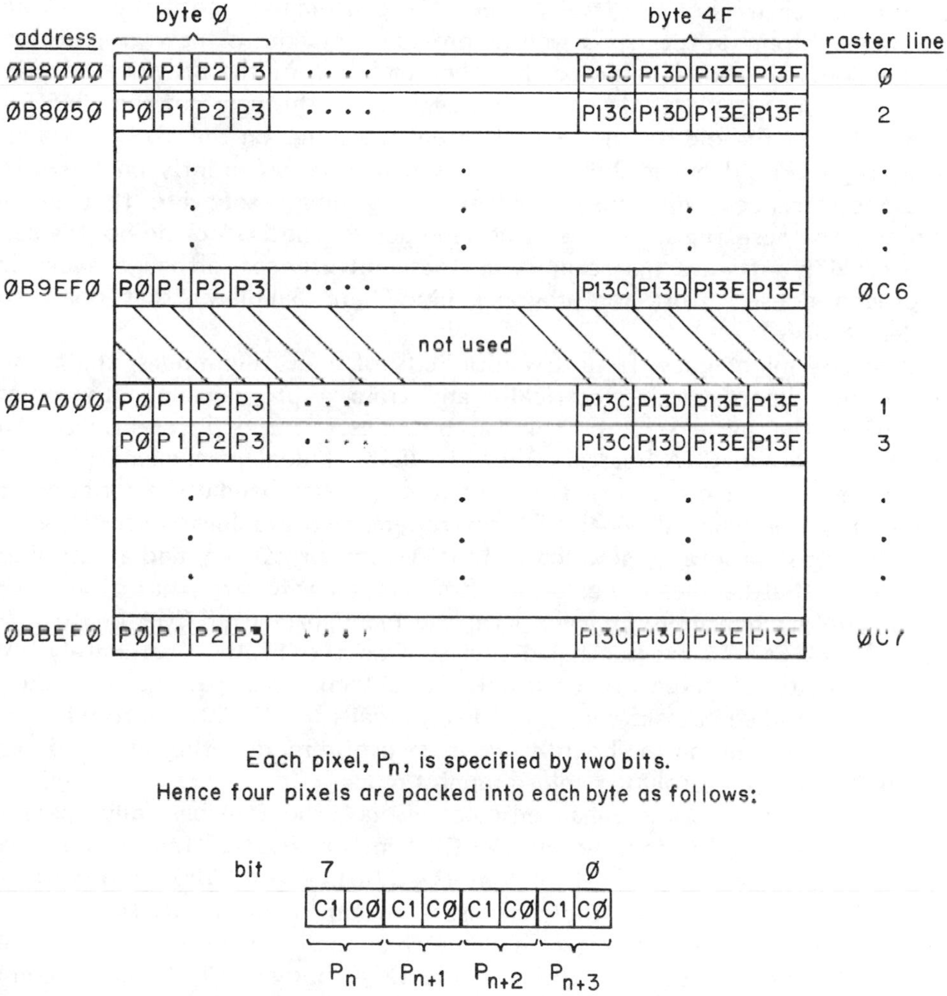

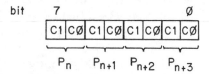

Each pixel, P_n, is specified by two bits.
Hence four pixels are packed into each byte as follows:

Fig. 8-15. Relationship of pixel (dot) positions on the screen to refresh memory addresses for the 320x200 bit-mapped graphics mode on the color/graphics adapter.

complete, inexpensive EGA on a single board. Many manufacturers took advantage of this to produce EGA workalikes (clones) at prices far below IBM's price. The popularity of these boards has made the EGA into the current de facto standard for IBM PC color graphics. In fact, at this writing, the clone EGA boards are preferable to the IBM version because they offer better downward compatibility with the old IBM CGA via special software, and they support a Hercules graphics card mode for monochrome graphics. IBM has tried to ignore the Hercules standard and provides only an incompatible monochrome graphics mode of 640x350.

A full discussion of the EGA's architecture and capabilities would require an entire book in itself. The EGA can emulate both the CGA and the monochrome adapters, as well as provide a number of new graphics and text modes. It should be noted that the emulation of the previous adapters is by no means perfect. In particular, registers 2 through 8 of the 6845 CRT controller on the old boards have different meanings on the EGA. In addition, registers 3d8h and 3d9h on the CGA behave differently on the EGA. These differences will cause problems for graphics software that writes directly to these registers. As mentioned above, the EGA clone boards usually provide software that can fix up these differences, although even this approach doesn't work for programs like Flight Simulator that don't run under DOS.

As one might guess from its multiplicity of operating modes, the EGA is a complex board, both electrically and from a programming standpoint. However, the basic structure of the board is not too different from the monochrome and CGA boards. There is 256K of dual-port memory, a CRT controller (which consists of two custom chips that handle the functions of the monochrome board's 6845 CRT controller), two graphics controller chips that handle character generation and bit stream formatting, and an attribute controller that handles the color palette. From a software point of view the board looks much more complex than the monochrome or CGA boards. In fact, there are 71 programmable registers on the EGA! Fortunately, the vast majority of these are used only for setting up a particular mode of operation, and such tasks can be handled by calls to INT 10. Here we focus our attention only on the board's two most useful modes: the text mode and the 640x350 high-resolution color graphics mode.

In text mode on an enhanced color display, the EGA basically operates like the monochrome adapter and the CGA in text mode. The memory map is as shown in Fig. 8-13, except that the 32K memory block used starts at 0B8000H (like the CGA). The characters appear within an 8x14 character box, and hence are much more readable than those on the CGA. Available text colors are the same as those on the CGA, namely 16 character colors and 16 character background colors (or 8 background colors and blinking characters).

The EGA text mode on an enhanced color display has two very useful additional features. First, the EGA uses its RAM memory to hold the bit patterns used to draw the text mode characters; i.e., it uses a RAM character generator instead of the ROM character generators used on the monochrome and CGA adapters. This allows the use of user-defined characters in text mode. You can define the bit patterns for up to 4 fonts of 256 characters each and store them in the EGA's memory, although only 2 fonts can be active at any one time. Two default fonts (the 8x14 EGA font and the 8x8 CGA font) are stored in a 16K video BIOS (basic I/O system) ROM on the EGA. At power-on, code in this BIOS downloads these fonts into the RAM character generator area, takes over the INT 10 video interrupt and points the vector to its own enhanced INT 10, and initializes the EGA.

The EGA BIOS provides support functions that make using your own fonts relatively easy. Here's an example of the code needed to do this:

```
font        segment                 ;this is a 14 row character font
            db      41*0e dup (01)
asc_41      db      0,0,0,0,0,76h,0dch,0d8h,0d8h,0dch,76h,0,0,0       ;alpha
            db      0,0,0,0,7ch,0c6h,0fch,0c6h,0c6h,0fch,0c0h,0c0h,40h,0
                            ;beta
            db      3d*0e dup (01)
font        ends

setup:      mov     bx,font         ;point es:bp at font table start
            mov     es,bx
            mov     bp,00
            mov     cx,80h          ;total number of chars in font
            mov     bh,14           ;number of bytes per char pattern
            mov     bl,01           ;load font into char gen #1
            mov     dx,00           ;char offset into font table
            mov     ax,1100h        ;function code to load user font
            int     10h
            mov     ax,1103h        ;function code to set up 512 char opera-
                                        tion
            mov     bl,04           ;use char gen #1 if attribute bit 3 = 1
            int     10h             ; & char gen #0 if attribute bit 3 = 0
            mov     ax,1000h        ;function code to change color plane
            mov     bl,12h          ; enable register in attribute controller
            mov     bh,07           ;disable color plane (attr. bit) 3
            int     10h
```

Here we have defined an 80h character font with an 8x14 character box for each character in the segment "font". For reasons of space, we've set all the characters in the font to be vertical bars except for ASCII codes 41h and 42h, which are the Greek letters alpha and beta. This font is loaded into RAM character generator 1 by setting the registers as shown in the code and using function code 1100h of INT 10. The default character generator is number 0. The new character generator is then activated using function code 1103h of INT 10. This allows you to select either character generator on a character-by-character basis by setting bit 3 of each character's attribute byte to 0 (for character generator 0) or 1 (for character generator 1). Thus, using the above example, if a character in the video memory area is a 41h and has 07 as the attribute, it will appear as an "A". Changing the attribute to 0fh changes the character to a Greek alpha.

The last portion of code above uses function code 1000h of INT 10 to disable color plane 3 of the attribute controller. If this is not done, setting bit 3 in the attribute byte would also turn on the intensify line going to the display and hence change the character's color as well as the font.

To remove the new font and restore the original mode of operation, you simply make character generator 1 inactive by using function code 1103h of INT 10 with BL = 0, and reactivate color plane 3 of the attribute controller using function code 1000h of INT 10 with BX = 120fh.

The EGA BIOS also provides support for an 80-character by 43-line display on the enhanced color monitor. In an excellent article on the EGA, Hoffman (*PC Tech Journal*, April 1985, pp. 58-77) gives a program that sets up the 43-line display mode. This article also gives concise descriptions of all the EGA BIOS function calls. One problem with the 43-line display mode is that it won't work properly if the ANSI.SYS screen driver provided with DOS is installed.

Consider next the EGA's 16-color high-resolution 640x350 graphics mode. To put the EGA in this mode, you put function code 0010h in AX, and do an INT 10. Unlike the text mode, where reasonable support is available through the BIOS and display memory manipulation is simple and direct, the graphics modes have very little BIOS support, and writing and reading the display memory efficiently is nontrivial. Thus you need to understand the structure of the EGA in more detail to do graphics programming.

Let's first examine the relationship between the bits in memory and the colored pixels that appear on the display. Figure 8-16 shows the memory organization for the 16-color 640x350 graphics mode. Notice that the 256K display memory is divided into 4 bit planes of 64K each. There is a one-to-

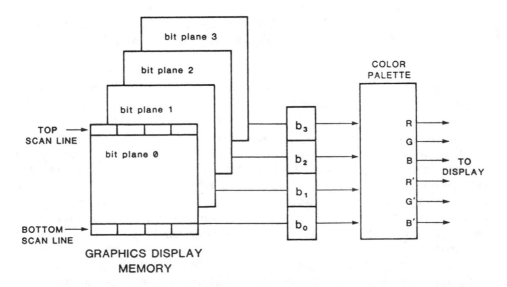

Fig. 8-16. Memory organization for the 640x350 graphics mode. Each pixel is produced by 4 bits, one from each bit plane, which are combined into a 4-bit value ($b_3b_2b_1b_0$) that determines which of 16 colors will appear on the screen for that pixel.

one correspondence between the bits in each bit plane and the pixels on the screen. For example, bit 7 of the first byte in each bit plane corresponds to the pixel in the upper left-hand corner of the screen. The color of each pixel is determined by the value of 4 bits, one coming from each bit plane as shown in the figure. The color palette is just a look-up table that translates the 4-bit numbers for each pixel into pixel colors. There are six output lines from the color palette to the enhanced color display (red, green, blue, red', green', and blue') and hence 64 possible colors. However, the palette input is 4 bits, giving just 16 distinct values. The programming of the palette determines which of the 64 colors each 4-bit value produces. For most purposes, the default setting of the palette provides a good selection of colors, but one can also program the palette using function code 1000h of INT 10. For details, see the article by Hoffman referred to earlier.

The display memory for the 640x350 graphics mode is mapped into memory as a 64K block starting at 0A0000h, with each 64K bit plane occupying the same address space. The CPU does reads or writes in the bit planes through a pair of graphics controller chips that provide several different ways of accessing the memory. In particular, there are nine registers plus a set of four 8-bit latches on the EGA that are relevant for the reading and writing of display memory by the CPU. Figure 8-17 gives an overview of these registers and latches. The latches provide a hardware assist to the CPU allowing 32-bit reads and writes. The basic idea is that whenever a read is done from the graphics memory address space, a byte is read from each bit plane into the four latches, and whenever a write is done, the contents of all four latches, possibly modified by the CPU data and/or the contents of several registers, is written into the bit planes. The details of this will become clearer as we consider the various write and read modes available. Since bits in the bit planes correspond one-to-one with the pixels on the screen, it's straightforward to calculate the address needed to access a particular pixel. There are 640 bits = 80 bytes per line on the screen. Thus if we let our coordinate origin be the upper left-hand corner of the screen, the byte address corresponding to a particular X,Y coordinate is given by $80*Y + X/8$. A desired pixel can then be picked out of the byte using the bit mask register as described below.

Three different modes, write modes 0, 1, and 2, can be used to write into the display memory. Write mode 2 is best suited for writing single pixels on the screen, and works as follows: First, write mode 2 is selected by writing a 2 into the mode register, and then the function select register is set to the desired method of writing the pixel onto the screen. You can specify that your data (a 4-bit color value) be written directly into the bit planes, or be ANDed, ORed, or XORed with the current color value of the pixel. A byte address is then calculated for the desired pixel as indicated above. The desired pixel within the byte is then specified by calculating (X modulo 8) and setting bit number (7 - (X mod 8)) in the bit mask register. For example, if X = 30, then (X mod 8) = 6 and you should set bit number 1 in the bit mask register. Assuming that the byte address is in BX and that

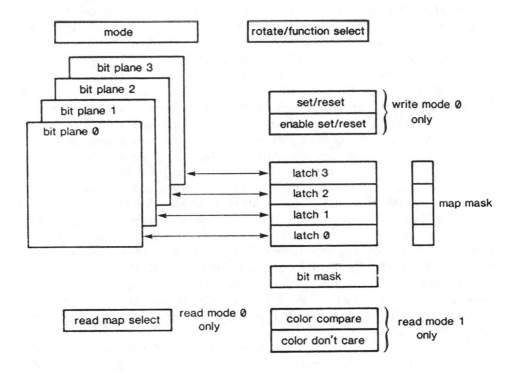

Fig. 8–17. The four 8–bit latches and associated control registers used to read and write the graphics display memory on the EGA.

ES is set to 0A000, you then execute the following read-modify-write sequence:

```
mov     al,es:[bx]
mov     al,color
mov     es:[bx],al
```

The mov al,es:[bx] instruction causes a byte to be read from each bit plane into the four latches, and the value returned in AL is ignored. Next, AL is loaded with the 4-bit color value. The final mov es:[bx],al causes two actions to take place. First, the low-order 4 bits in AL are written into the corresponding latches at the bit position(s) where the bit mask register contains a 1. This is either a direct write, or an AND, OR, or XOR with the existing latch bits, depending on the setting of the function select register. The resulting latch contents are then automatically written back into the bit planes. If you want, you can protect any bit plane from being changed by putting a 0 in the corresponding map mask bit, but normally the map mask contains 0Fh (all bit planes enabled for writing) when write mode 2 is used. An article on programming the EGA by Richard Wilton in *BYTE* magazine provides program examples of all of the EGA's write and read modes (*BYTE*, vol. 10, no. 11, pp. 209-220, 1985). The Hoffman article mentioned earlier also provides brief descriptions of all the EGA's programmable registers.

You set write mode 0 by writing a 0 into the mode register. This write mode can also be used to write single pixels, but it's not as efficient as write mode 2 for this purpose, because to write a color value you must first clear all the bits in the pixel and then set the desired bits to 1 with a second read-modify-write sequence. Wilton gives examples of writing single pixels with both modes. Write mode 0 is meant primarily for repetitive operations like graphics text output. The difference from mode 2 comes about in how the processor data is handled. In a mode 2 write, bits 0 through 3 of the processor data are put (using AND, OR, etc.) into latches 0 through 3 respectively in the bit positions specified by the bit mask. In mode 0, the 8 bits of processor data (except those bits that are masked off by the bit mask register) are duplicated in all four latches (except those masked off by the map mask register). The processor data is also automatically rotated by 0 to 7 bits as set in the data rotate/function select register before it is put in the latches. This makes write mode 0 useful for tasks that involve placing blocks of data on the screen at places other than byte boundaries. In addition, one can select memory planes with the enable set/reset register for which all the bits in the byte (except those protected by the bit mask) will be set to 0 or 1, as determined by the value of the corresponding bit in the set/reset register. Thus write mode 0 is very flexible and powerful for certain classes of graphics operations other than single pixel writes. Unfortunately, it would take an entire chapter to spell out in detail all the things that can be done with this mode. It's the default write mode used by the EGA BIOS code.

Write mode 1 uses the on-board latches to simply move graphics from one part of the screen to another. Thus it would be used for tasks like the scrolling of graphics text or for animation. The method of operation is very simple. You set write mode 1 by writing a 1 into the mode register, and then do a read of the desired source byte followed by a write to the desired destination. The read causes the 32 bits at the specified source address (one byte per bit plane) to be read into the on-board latches, and the write causes the contents of those latches to be written into all 4 bit planes at the destination address.

Two different modes are available for reading pixel values from the screen. Read mode 0 allows you to read a byte from one bit plane at a time. The mode is set by writing a 0 into the mode register and then a bit plane is selected by writing the bit plane number into the read map select register. The desired byte address is calculated as before, and you then do a mov al,es:[bx], which puts the byte from the selected bit plane into al. To read the complete color value for a pixel requires four memory reads, one from each bit plane. The byte article by Wilton gives a program that does this.

Read mode 1 allows you to rapidly find pixels of a given color. The mode is set by writing a 1 into the mode register, and then the desired color value to look for is set in the color compare register. When a read is done from the desired byte address (using, for example, mov al,es:[bx]), the byte returned in AL will contain a 1 in each bit position where the value in the four bit planes matches the value in the color compare register. Note that by setting the color compare register to the background color, one can rapidly search through memory to find all nonbackground pixels regardless of their color. Although normally not used in this graphics mode, you can also mask out bit planes using the color-don't-care register, so that specified planes always return a match during the color compare operation.

There are also hardware registers on the EGA, which make it easy to implement split screen operation and smooth (one pixel at a time) scrolling. If you want to investigate these features or do any significant EGA low-level graphics programming yourself, you'll probably need to get the IBM PC *Options and Adapters Technical Reference* manual set. Although expensive, it's the most complete source of hardware information about the board that's available.

We conclude this section with a few remarks on graphics software. In general, the state of affairs in this area is less than ideal. There are a number of graphics packages for the other high-level languages and assembly language, but none of them is compatible with the others and there is no agreed-on standard. The most widely used package is probably the HALO graphics primitives by Media Cybernetics. Part of the problem is that there is no single universal standard anywhere, although packages conforming to the GKS (Graphical Kernel System) standard from the German Standards Institute (DIN) are quite popular. However, the continuing development of powerful new graphics hardware is spawning considerable activity in the development of new graphics standards for microcomputers. We can hardly wait to see what develops!

If you want to write some graphics routines yourself, assembly language is essential for at least the lowest level routines, because you need all the speed you can get. The choice of algorithm for drawing lines, circles, and characters on the screen is crucial to good performance. Bresenham's algorithm is particularly good for drawing lines, and the concept of calculating the next point to output as a single pixel move relative to the current position works very well. Consult a good text on graphics such as Foley and Van Dam. You should also be forewarned that writing a good general set of graphics routines is a nontrivial programming project.

References

IBM PC Technical Reference, 1984, IBM Corporation, Boca Raton, FL. This manual contains authoritative descriptions of the PC's hardware, circuit diagrams for the IBM PC system board, and complete source code listings for the ROM BIOS routines.

IBM PC Options and Adapters Technical Reference, Vols. 1–3, 1984, IBM Corporation, Boca Raton, FL. This set of manuals contains complete hardware descriptions and schematics of all IBM-manufactured adapter boards for the PC.

D. Glasco and M. Sargent III, 1983, "Using IBM's Marvelous Keyboard," *BYTE* magazine, vol. 8, number 5, pp. 402—415. Presents an expanded discussion of how the IBM PC keyboard works and how it can be modified to suit your own purposes.

P. Norton, 1983, *Inside the IBM PC*, Robert J. Brady Company, Bowie, MD. Describes the PC hardware and system software, including the keyboard and video display.

D. C. Willen and J. I. Krantz, 1983, *8088 Assembler Language Programming: The IBM PC*, Howard W. Sams and Company, Indianapolis, IN. Contains introductory discussions on the hardware of the PC, including the keyboard and video display. Numerous example programs are also given.

Conrac Corporation, 1980, *Raster Graphics Handbook*, Van Nostrand-Rheinhold, New York. This book has excellent, detailed discussions of how video displays work and how to evaluate their quality. A discussion of video display signal standards and a glossary of video terminology are included.

J. D. Foley and A. Van Dam, 1982, *Fundamentals of Interactive Computer Graphics*, Addison-Wesley, Reading, MA. Another excellent book on computer graphics, containing many examples of graphics algorithms written in Pascal.

9
Controlling/Monitoring Devices

i/O, I/O, it's off to work we go. . . .
—The Seven Dwarfs

Chapters 5 through 7 showed you how to program and wire a microcomputer to read and write parallel I/O ports, including implementation of address decoding and data synchronization methods. The question now arises as to how the TTL level highs and lows interface to the real-world quantities of switch closures, threshold detectors, analog signals, and motor control. This chapter deals with the buffering and translation techniques required to interface the TTL world to the world we live in, providing the computer with the necessary isolation to operate reliably. Section 9-1 treats mechanical and solid-state switch closures. As outputs, switches are used to turn devices of all power levels on or off; as inputs, switch closures can be monitored to reveal the status of real-world situations. Switch circuits are often isolated from the computer either optically or by relays, and power control is implemented with relays, SCR's, and triacs. Section 9-2 treats digital-to-analog (D/A) conversion techniques. These allow display of data on oscilloscopes and control of devices whose operation depends on voltage levels. Section 9-3 discusses analog-to-digital (A/D) conversion methods, allowing the measurement of voltages. Section 9-4 illustrates the use of D/A and A/D methods with a discussion of signal averaging and lock-in detection, which enable you to pick signals out of noise. Section 9-5 describes waveform generation and measurement methods, including timed pulses, computer-generated music, and speech synthesis and recognition. Finally, Sec. 9-6 discusses computer-controlled motors, including stepper motors and servomotors. The techniques discussed in this chapter can be used to interface a computer to most devices in the home or in a scientific or engineering laboratory.

9-1. Switch Closures, Input and Output

This section treats the setting and monitoring of individual bits that are connected to switches, either for input or for output. Consider switch inputs first. If a switch is located in or near the computer and turns on a positive voltage of 2.5 to 5 volts, the computer can read it directly using 74LS244 buffers as discussed in Sec. 6-3. The switches on the IBM PC joysticks are read in this fashion. But if the switch uses other voltages, or is located some distance away, the input should probably be optically isolated from the computer. The 6-pin optoisolator shown in Fig. 9-1 is a convenient package that allows the computer to literally look at a bit of information (namely whether a switch is on or off), with typically 1500 volts or more of electrical isolation. The package contains an LED and a phototransistor and is available from many manufacturers. Currents of 10 to 20 mA through the LED cause it to emit light, and this light shining on the base of the phototransistor produces a base-emitter current, thus turning it on. This, in turn, pulls pin 5 of the optoisolator low if the phototransistor's emitter is tied to ground. Hence the computer can see whether the switch in Fig. 9-1 is closed. The big advantage of using the optoisolator is that the switch's circuit is electrically isolated from the computer's. It can involve AC or relatively high voltages and can handle discharges from static electricity, which may be as much as 1500 volts, without affecting the computer's circuit. Figure 9-2 shows how an optoisolator can be used to generate a 60-Hz signal from the line voltage.

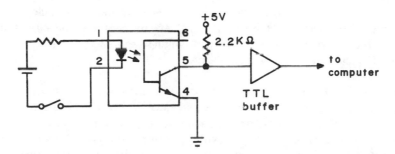

Fig. 9-1. An optoisolator chip is used to isolate a computer's circuit from that of a switch. The switch can involve AC or DC voltages totally outside the 5-volt world of TTL.

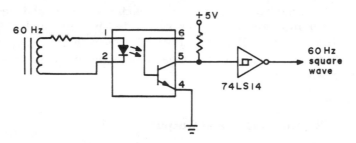

Fig. 9–2. Circuit to get a 60–Hz square wave from the powerline illustrates isolation of the computer from a non–TTL environment. Figure 5–25 provides an alternative circuit.

Many kinds of real-world information can be presented as switch closures. Doors and windows can be monitored, room lights can be detected (see Fig. 9-3), water levels can be reported, and temperature and humidity thresholds can be monitored. Burglar alarm devices like LED light beams also typically use switch closures to indicate intrusion.

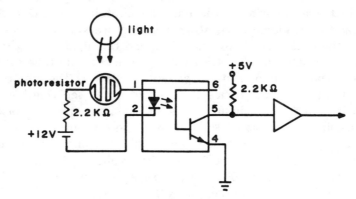

Fig. 9–3. The on/off status of a light can be monitored by using a photoresistor (a resistor whose resistance varies with the light falling on it) as the LED's current–limiting resistor. If the photoresistor circuit uses more than 5 volts, an extra current–limiting resistor may be needed so the LED current won't exceed 30 mA.

In addition to monitoring switches, you may want to turn on devices, like lights, motors, and sirens, or to open door latches. These things can be done by having the computer close switches, either relays or solid–state switches like transistors, SCR's (silicon-controlled rectifiers), and triacs (**triode AC's**). LED status lights can be driven directly from output latches like the 74LS374 (Fig. 5-23). Small speakers for audio output need more power, which can be supplied by a transistor as shown in Fig. 9-4. The 75452 peripheral driver shown in Fig. 9-5 can also be used instead of a

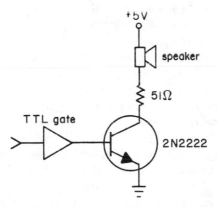

Fig. 9–4. A 2N2222 transistor can sink currents of up to 150 mA and can be used to drive a small speaker. TTL circuits can source the 3 mA required to turn the 2N2222 on. When driven by standard TTL gates, no current–limiting resistor in the transistor's base circuit is needed, but one is necessary when a 74LS244 is used to drive the 2N2222.

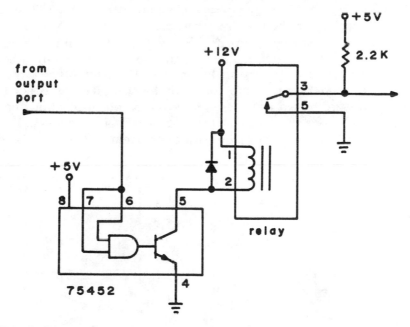

Fig. 9–5. A relay circuit allows the computer to turn on currents of several amperes at voltages outside those of the TTL world.

simple transistor. It can sink up to 300 mA and withstand collector voltages of up to 30 volts. The 7406 open collector hex inverter is another device that can withstand 30 volts, but it sinks a maximum of only 40 mA per gate.

Higher currents can be driven by using bigger transistors or by using relays. A simple relay circuit was shown in Fig. 9-5. Some relays work with 5 volts, and small relays requiring higher voltages can be operated with the 7406 (or with the 7407 noninverting open collector buffer). To protect the open collector output from seeing excessive voltages when the relay is turned off (the relay coil is an inductor, and inductors generate high voltages when a current suddenly stops flowing through them), a diode must be connected across the relay coil as shown in Fig. 9-5. This diode shorts out the voltage spike. Small relays are typically rated at 1 ampere, and can be used for driving bigger relays and other devices. Relays have no on-state voltage drop (as transistors do), and they physically isolate the output circuit from the computer's. On the negative side, they have slow response times (on the order of milliseconds), and can arc and wear out when turned on and off at high repetition rates.

In somewhat different applications, optoisolators coupled to SCR's and triac's play important roles. The SCR switches current on in one direction only, while the triac switches AC currents. Since the triac acts something like two opposed SCR's in parallel, we describe the SCR first. Figure 9-6 shows the SCR symbol, junction configuration, and equivalent circuit, and Fig. 9-7 shows the SCR's current-voltage characteristic. The SCR acts like a diode that can be switched on by momentarily raising the voltage of the gate relative to the cathode. once the SCR is on, it stays on as long as a minimum current flows from the anode to the cathode. This happens because the two effective transistors in the SCR keep each other turned on. When the lower (NPN) transistor is turned on by the gate, the upper (PNP) transistor is forward biased and therefore is turned on also. But once the upper transistor is on, the lower is forward biased and remains on. Thus once you turn the SCR on, it stays on until the current flow quits or tries to

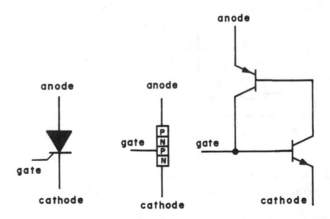

Fig. 9-6. Silicon-controlled rectifier (SCR) symbol, junction configuration, and equivalent circuit. Once turned on, the SCR stays on until the anode-to-cathode current falls below the holding value.

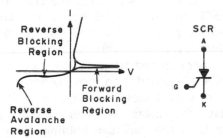

Fig. 9-7. SCR current/voltage characteristic. The SCR has two possible forward-biased outputs, unlike an ordinary diode. For anode-to-cathode currents above some minimum value, it offers very little resistance. But for smaller currents it has high resistance, blocking current flow unless a large voltage pulse is applied.

reverse direction. This is fine for DC currents if you want a latching switch, but there's no simple way to turn the SCR off (except manually!). The SCR is easier to use with AC voltages, which reverse polarity on a regular basis. If the gate is held at or above the anode voltage, the SCR provides a half-wave rectified signal as shown in Fig. 9-8a. By delaying the gate voltage relative to the AC voltage, the SCR turns on later in the cycle as shown in Fig. 9-8b. This is how room light dimmers work, and a computer could easily provide the desired gate delays. SCR's come in all sizes, from 300-mA varieties that include optoisolation of the gate (an optoSCR) to 500-ampere varieties used in mining equipment. They respond substantially faster than relays, don't arc, and can provide dimming capability. On the negative side, unlike relays, they're hard to turn off in DC applications and introduce a voltage drop.

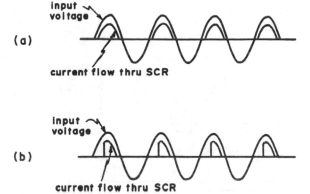

Fig. 9-8. (a) SCR response to AC input signal with the gate held positive. (b) Response with a gate voltage that lags the input signal (used in room light dimmers).

If a controllable AC switch is desired, the triac shown in Fig. 9-9 may suffice. While the SCR rectifies an AC signal, the triac passes current in both directions when its gate (G) has the same polarity as its MT2 (main terminal 2) pin. This device acts very much like two SCR's of opposing polarity connected in parallel and triggered by a common gate. A triac can be driven by the MOC3011 optotriac to provide optical isolation as shown in Fig. 9-10. A problem with triacs can occur in switching inductive loads, where the current lags the voltage in time. The triac is supposed to turn off for currents less than the minimum holding current, just like an SCR. With an inductive load, however, the voltage increases to its maximum value just as the current goes to zero, so that suddenly the triac must block a large voltage. Triacs cannot block instantaneously, and consequently the rate of change in voltage across the triac must be kept below the manufacturer's specification. Otherwise the triac may stay on once triggered, regardless of the gate voltage. The rate of change of the voltage can be reduced by "snubbing" the triac with an RC network as shown in Fig. 9-11. Alternatively, you can buy a circuit similar to that shown in Fig. 9-11, all potted neatly in a case about 0.5"x1.5"x1.2", and known as a *solid-state relay*. It can be plugged into a standard pc board that's UL approved for up to 220 volts AC. The convenience may well be worth the extra cost.

Fig. 9-9. Triac symbol and current/voltage characteristic. The triac acts as an AC switch.

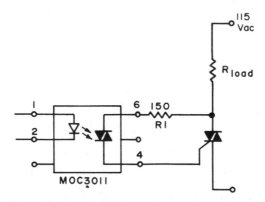

Fig. 9-10. An optocoupled triac circuit allows the computer to safely switch AC voltages.

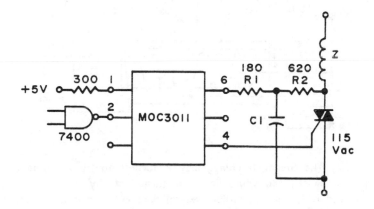

LOAD POWER FACTOR	C
1.0	O
0.75	0.22 μF
0.5	0.33 μF

Fig. 9-11. A "snubber" RC network is used to limit the time rate of change of voltage across a triac as it tries to turn off while driving an inductive load. The power factor is the cosine of the phase angle between the voltage and the current (for a resistor, this angle is zero (cosine = 1), but it can be 60° (cosine = 0.5) for significantly inductive loads. (From the Motorola MOC3011 Application Note)

Furthermore, solid-state relays can be driven by low-power CMOS circuits, which is ideal for battery-powered operation.

Many AC devices are controlled by 24 VAC rather than by the power-line's 110 VAC. This lower voltage doesn't develop fire danger and hence is hardly mentioned in the National Electrical Code (but don't run 24 VAC lines in the same conduit as 110 VAC). In particular, thermostats, sprinkler system valves, and low-voltage relays can all run on 24 VAC. So your computer can control a home using the circuit in Fig. 9-11. Another useful device is the low voltage latching relay shown in Fig. 9-12. This device turns on up to 20 amperes at 277 VAC. It acts just like an ordinary wall switch except that to turn it on you momentarily (0.1 second) apply 24 VAC between the white and red leads, and to turn it off, you momentarily apply the voltage between the white and blue leads. In practice, the white lead is always connected to one side of the 24 VAC line, and a pair of optotriac circuits (see Fig. 9-10) or small relays is used to turn the latching relay on and off. In addition, any number of local momentary contact switches can be used to turn the latching relay on and off—that is, it provides "n-way"

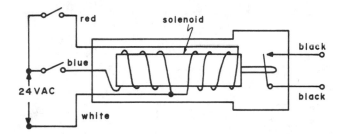

Fig. 9-12. The Sierra latching relay is turned on by a momentary 24 VAC across the red and white lines and turned off by the voltage across the blue and white lines. Inside the solenoid cylinder is a smaller metal cylinder that is pushed or pulled into one of two stable positions depending on the direction of the current through the solenoid.

switching. The relay fits readily into a standard junction box and passes the National Electrical Code. As such it's ideal for controlling 110 VAC lights, motors, and other fairly heavy duty equipment.

9-2. Digital-to-Analog Conversion

Reading and setting switch closures provides a computer with substantial I/O capability. However, some applications require more than a single bit of information, and for these we need to interface to the analog world of variable voltages. This section deals with the computer output of analog voltage levels (digital-to-analog conversion), while the following section handles computer input of analog voltages. One reason for this order of presentation is that many analog-to-digital (input) devices use digital-to-analog converters (DAC's) in their conversion. DAC's can be used to control motors and voltage-controlled oscillators, to generate waveforms, to display graphical data, to set rotor and galvanometer mirror positions, and to select temperature and pressure levels.

A DAC consists of four main parts: a voltage reference, a resistor network, a digitally controlled set of analog switches, and in most cases, an output buffer that converts a current to a voltage. The buffer is an operational amplifier (op amp). The op amp is so useful here and elsewhere that we will briefly review it first. Signals appearing at the inverting input (labeled -) are amplified and inverted by the op amp, while signals at the noninverting input (labeled +) are just amplified. Figure 9-13 shows an op amp used in a typical application: amplifying an input voltage V_i to give an output voltage $V_o = -R_o V_i / R_i$. This relationship can be understood quickly if you're willing to accept the characteristics of an ideal op amp. These are: infinite input impedance, infinite gain, and zero output impedance. If you're not familiar with the term impedance, don't worry. An impedance is

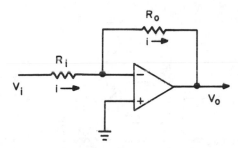

Fig. 9–13. A typical op amp circuit. The inverting input is held at ground potential and accepts neglegible current. Input current is pulled through the output resistor R_0 by the op amp's output voltage V_0, where $V_0 = -R_0 V_i / R_i$.

just a resistance generalized to include the resistance of inductors and capacitors to the flow of AC currents. It's measured in ohms, like ordinary DC resistance. The op amp's infinite input impedance means that no appreciable current can flow into the inputs, because the inputs look like a very large resistance to external signals, typically 10^6 to 10^{12} ohms in real devices. Infinite gain means that any voltage difference between the + and – inputs is amplified by a very large factor, so even the smallest voltage difference between the two inputs produces a very large output voltage. In real devices, this gain is typically 10^5 to 10^6. Zero output impedance means that the output can supply whatever amount of current is needed to maintain the output voltage. Real devices typically have output impedances of 10 to 100 ohms.

The properties of the ideal op amp allow us to derive the relationship between the input and output voltages for an op amp. The infinite gain property implies that the voltage difference between the + and – inputs is zero. If a difference tries to develop, an output voltage is produced that is fed back to the input through R_0 to make the difference zero. In Fig. 9-13, this means that the – input is at ground potential, since the + input is connected to ground. Thus the input current is $I = V_i / R_i$. Furthermore, since no current can flow into an infinite impedance, the input current must all flow through R_0. But the current through R_0 is $I = -V_0 / R_0$, with the minus sign appearing because the current is flowing toward V_0. Thus $V_i / R_i = -V_0 / R_0$, that is, $V_0 = -R_0 V_i / R_i$. Since R_0 can be bigger than R_i, the op amp can yield gain in a precise way. There's much more to op amps than this (for example their finite response times), but this is all you need to know for the moment. If you're interested in learning more about op amps, see the excellent introduction to the subject written by Hoenig and Payne.

Figure 9-14 shows the simplest kind of DAC, namely one based on a binary-weighted resistance ladder. An output latch is connected to the DAC inputs, and the data bits stored in the latch determine which switches are closed. Thus the computer can control the DAC output by writing

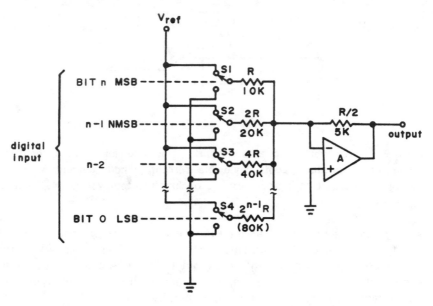

Fig. 9–14. A DAC built using a binary–weighted resistor network.

different numbers into the latch. By calculating the total resistance of the resistors switched to V_{ref}, we find the effective input resistance R_i to the op amp. Using this in the op amp voltage relation, we find

$$V_o = -V_{ref} \left(\frac{b_3}{2} + \frac{b_2}{4} + \frac{b_1}{8} + \frac{b_0}{16} \right),$$

where $b_i = 0$ or 1, b_0 is the least significant bit, and b_3 is the most significant bit. By adding more switches attached to increasingly higher resistances, one can make DAC's with higher resolution. Eight-bit DAC's are cheap and 12-bit DAC's are within reason. But few DAC's use a binary-weighted resistance ladder since it's hard to match the resistances accurately. Instead, the R-2R network illustrated in Fig. 9-15 is used.

In this network only two resistance values are used, which is relatively easy to manufacture. The R-2R network can be analyzed using Norton's theorem. To get a rough idea how the network works, consider the voltage source V_{ref} as having zero resistance to ground. Then the resistance to ground from the bottom node is 2R through either path, regardless of the corresponding switch position. Similarly the resistance to ground for the next-to-bottom node is 2R through either path, and so on, up the rest of the ladder. A current flowing into the top node thus sees two paths with equal resistance to ground and splits into two equal parts. At the next node it splits into equal parts again, and so on down the ladder. A switch n nodes from the op-amp's minus input gets $1/2^n$ of the current flowing through the output resistor. Hence it contributes $1/2^n$ of its voltage (V_{ref} or ground) to

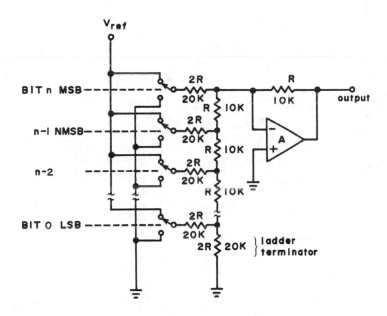

Fig. 9–15. A DAC built using an R–2R resistor network.

the output voltage. For the network shown, the voltage output is the same as that for the binary-weighted ladder in Fig. 9-14.

The heart of the DAC is a resistance ladder coupled to digitally controlled analog switches. Thus the DAC is primarily a current device whose output current can be converted to a voltage by use of an op amp. If the desired application requires an analog current proportional to a digital value, then the output op amp can be eliminated. Inexpensive op amps are limited in response time, and hence high-speed voltage DAC's have to use premium op amps. An advantage of the current mode versus the voltage mode is that currents are less susceptible to noise when traveling over long lengths of wire.

A critical part of a DAC is the analog reference, either current or voltage. If the DAC requires you to supply the reference yourself, it's called a multiplying DAC, since it multiplies the externally supplied reference voltage by a digital value. Normally you want a DAC that contains its own reference. Precision voltage references are usually based on zener diodes, connected up as discussed in Sec. 5-3.

Figure 9-16 shows both an inexpensive 8-bit DAC (Analog Devices AD558) and a higher performance 12-bit DAC (Burr Brown DAC80). Both DAC's include internal voltage references and output op amps. The AD558 settles to 8-bit accuracy within 1 microsecond and includes all the necessary latches and bus interface circuitry. This allows you to hook it up directly just like any other smart peripheral chip. The older DAC80 requires you to provide external latches, but it can be purchased with or without the

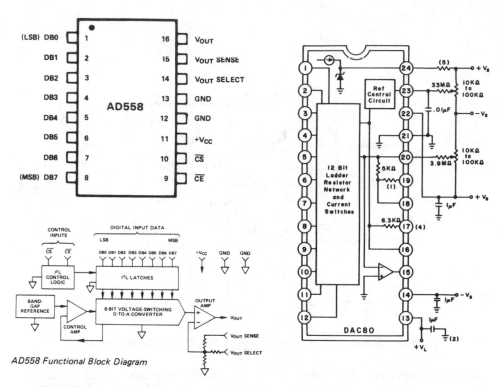

AD558 Functional Block Diagram

Fig. 9–16. Analog Devices AD558 8–bit DAC and Burr Brown DAC80 12–bit DAC. Courtesy Analog Devices and Burr Brown.

output op amp (the current mode version comes without), features user selectable output voltage ranges of -2.5 to 2.5, -5 to 5, -10 to 10, 0 to 5, or 0 to 10, settles to 12-bit accuracy within 5 microseconds, and will accept unsigned binary number inputs for the unipolar output ranges or signed binary numbers for the bipolar ranges.

When using a 12-bit DAC like the DAC80, you need to *double buffer* the input, that is, use two sets of latches. The problem is that you can't change all 12 bits simultaneously. You have to execute two OUT instructions to specify a 12-bit value, one for the low-order 8 bits and one for the high-order 4 bits. In between, the DAC output will be some unwanted value. To solve the problem, you output 8 bits and then 4 bits to the first set of latches, whose outputs are connected to the inputs of the second set of latches, and then transfer the data into the second set of latches with a strobe signal after the first set has the proper 12-bit number. Some of the newer 12-bit DAC's already have double buffering built into them.

To output several voltages, you can use several DAC's. Alternatively, you can multiplex the DAC output by using an analog switch IC and several sample and hold amplifiers. The sample-and-hold outputs will maintain the value of the output between the times that the DAC output refreshes the value.

One useful application of a DAC is to display waveforms on an oscilloscope or other vector CRT. For this, two DACs can be used to rapidly output the X and Y coordinates of each point in the waveform as voltages into the oscilloscope's X and Y inputs. If this is done repeatedly at a sufficiently rapid rate, the waveform can be seen as a steady image on the screen. An even simpler way of doing this is to use just one DAC that outputs Y values to the oscilloscope at equally spaced times, and let the oscilloscope's horizontal sweep provide the X axis. The approach is simple, requiring only a modest amount of software and a DAC. However, to free up the computer from continually having to redraw the oscilloscope screen, you might prefer the self-refreshing, versatile, bit-mapped raster displays discussed in Chap. 8.

9-3. Analog-to-Digital Conversion

This section describes five basic ways to convert analog signals to binary numbers, in order of increasing speed. A device that performs such a conversion is called an analog-to-digital converter, often abbreviated as A/D converter or just ADC. The first A/D converter discussed is an integrating ADC that is used primarily in digital voltmeters. The next three A/D methods employ DAC's and comparators in circuits that compare the DAC output with the input voltage to be measured, and the fifth method, called flash conversion, digitizes the input voltage directly in a flash! The first four methods are all capable of 12-bit or higher resolution, but flash conversion is seldom seen with more than 6 to 8 bits. The section concludes with a discussion of a convenient and inexpensive 8-bit analog data acquisition package boasting 100-microsecond conversion times and 16 analog input channels.

The *dual-slope integrating A/D converter* is illustrated in Fig. 9-17. This device utilizes an op amp wired up as an integrator. That is, the op amp output voltage is proportional to the integral of the current (the total charge) flowing in through the input resistor R. At the start of the conversion, the control unit zeroes the op amp output, V_o, switches the op amp input to the voltage to be measured, V_{in}, and starts the counter counting from zero. While the counter ticks away, the output voltage V_o gives the time integral of the input current (or voltage, since $V = IR$). Provided V_{in} is constant, $V_o = -V_{in} t/RC$, where t is the time from the start. The control unit lets the counter tick away for a fixed time t_1, then zeroes the counter and switches the input to the reference voltage V_{ref}. V_{ref} is chosen to have opposite sign from V_{in}, so that the integrating op amp then integrates V_o back to zero. The point at which V_o reaches zero is determined by a comparator. A *comparator* is just an op amp with no feedback resistor present, so it acts as a very high gain amplifier of any difference in voltage between its + and - inputs. Here the comparator output switches from a large negative voltage to a positive voltage at time t_2

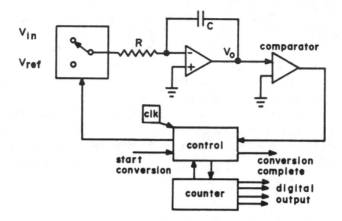

Fig. 9–17. The dual–slope integrating A/D converter integrates a positive input voltage V_{in} for a fixed time t_1 and then integrates a fixed negative reference voltage V_{ref}, until the op amp output voltage V_0 is driven back to zero. The time t_2 required to get the output back to zero is a measure of V_{in}.

when V_0 crosses zero. This causes the controller output to stop the counter and signal that the counter's output has the desired value, namely a number proportional to V_{in}. To see this, note that the maximum value of V_0 is given both by $-V_{in} t_1/RC$ and by $V_{ref} t_2/RC$. Equating these two expressions, we have $V_{in} = -(V_{ref}/t_1)t_2$. Since V_{ref} and t_1 are fixed, t_2, the time it takes the known reference voltage to integrate back to zero, is proportional to V_{in}. In particular, the proportionality constant can be chosen to give V_{in} in the desired units. The dual–slope integrating ADC is simple, can give 12-bit accuracy, and averages out noise fluctuations by virtue of the integrations. It's also slow, however, typically 100 milliseconds per conversion, so it's usually found in digital voltmeters, rather than in computer ADC's. Although the value of RC cancels out, these components should be stable, and the counter should be crystal controlled.

The *counter A/D converter* is another type of ADC that uses a counter, as illustrated in Fig. 9-18. At the start of a conversion, the control unit starts the counter counting from zero. The DAC converts the count into a reference voltage, which is compared to the input voltage V_{in}. When the reference voltage equals V_{in}, the comparator output changes sign, causing the control logic to freeze the count with the desired numerical output. The accuracy of this method is limited only by the DAC, and for V_{in}'s that remain constant during the count time, 12 bits is quite possible. The problem is, of course, that it can take a long time, perhaps 10 milliseconds, to match a voltage at the upper end of the conversion range. This method is certainly faster than the integrating method, but you immediately start to conjure up better search algorithms.

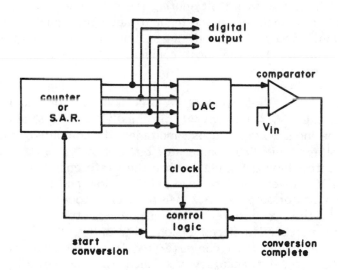

Fig. 9–18. The counter A/D employs a counter whose output drives the DAC output up from zero until it matches the input voltage and causes the comparator to flip its output. The counter's output is then proportional to V_{in}. Substitution of a successive approximation register (SAR) for the counter implements a binary search algorithm and is called an SAR A/D converter.

In particular, imagine a slightly more complicated system that has an up/down counter. Then, as V_{in} changes, the control logic can have the counter follow or "track" V_{in}. This is called a *tracking A/D converter*. The initial lock-on time is as long as with the counter ADC, but if V_{in} varies slowly compared to the rate at which the counter can change the DAC, the counter can continually give an up-to-date reading.

Neat, you say, but isn't there a better way than simple counting to have the DAC find a voltage that matches V_{in}? The answer is to use a binary search algorithm. It works the way you play that silly little number game against the computer. The computer says, "I've got a number between 0 and 100. Can you guess it?" Naturally you could start at 1 like the counter ADC, but why not start in the middle at 50? And when the computer says "Sorry, it's bigger," you respond with 75—that is, you always guess halfway between the limits established in the dialogue. That's a binary search algorithm, and it's exactly how the very popular *successive approximation A/D converter* works. The counter in Fig. 9-18 is replaced by an SAR (successive approximation register). At the start of the conversion, the SAR sets the MSB (most significant bit) and resets the rest of the bits. If the comparator indicates that the DAC output is too big, the SAR resets the MSB; otherwise it leaves it on. Then it sets the next bit below the MSB, and so on. Of course, if V_{in} changes in the middle of all this, the result is garbage. So for signals that may vary appreciably (more than 1 least significant bit) during the conversion time, you must use a sample and hold amplifier on the input to keep the signal constant during the conversion.   The SAR method can be both fast (10 microseconds) and accurate (12 bits).   It's the most common A/D conversion technique in computer applications.

Finally, consider the *flash A/D converter*.   Figure 9-19 shows a 3-bit version of a flash converter.   A precision resistor chain divides the reference voltage V_{ref} into a set of equally spaced smaller reference voltages.   The input voltage V_{in} is simultaneously compared to all of these reference voltages, yielding comparator outputs of 1 (a TTL high level) for those comparators having V_{in} higher than their reference voltages, and 0 for those having V_{in} lower.   A data read pulls $\overline{SEL}$ low and causes the 74273 to latch the comparator outputs.   A 74348 priority encoder then translates the bit pattern to the appropriate binary number—all this at speeds that can approach 10 nanoseconds per conversion!   The only problem with this technique is that an n-bit flash converter requires $2^n - 1$ comparators and 2^n resistors.   So for 7-bit accuracy you need 127 comparators, and 12-bit accuracy requires 4095 comparators.   Needless to say, 12-bit versions aren't commonplace!   You should also be aware that the high-speed flash

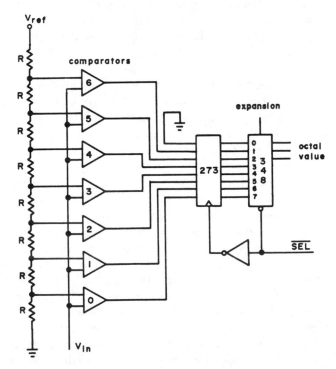

Fig. 9–19.   A flash A/D converter simultaneously compares the input voltage to a set of equally spaced reference voltages.   The priority encoder yields the digital value of the comparator with the closest reference voltage greater than V_{in}.

converters are by no means simple to use. It takes considerable experience in high-speed digital logic and proper grounding techniques to get one to work properly.

To get a better idea of the features available in commercial A/D converters, consider the popular ADC0816. Figure 9-20 is a block diagram of this single-chip data acquisition system. This 40-pin DIP uses an SAR A/D converter to convert any one of 16 inputs with 8-bit accuracy within 100 microseconds. The digital interface provides latched tristate outputs and a latched address (telling which of the 16 lines to convert) input, making microprocessor interfacing easy. You can simply connect the chip to the bus as you would any other smart peripheral chip. Note, however, that you must provide a clock signal of 500 to 1000 kHz for the chip.

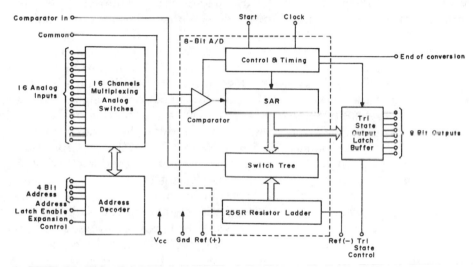

Fig. 9-20. Block diagram of the National Semiconductor ADC0816 single-chip data acquisition system. It provides 8-bit A/D conversion for 16 analog input channels, with latched tristate control, making micro-processor interfacing simple. It uses the SAR A/D method with conversion times of 100 microseconds. Courtesy of National Semiconductor.

Now let's turn to some applications of DAC's and ADC's. A/D converters together with the appropriate amplifiers can be used to record almost any analog signal you want. By combining an ADC with a DAC, you can both record and display the signal, effectively creating a multichannel storage oscilloscope capability. With a disk system, you can also store traces for later computation or retrieval. If you continually record an input signal, you have the flexibility of letting the computer "pretrigger" on any feature; that is, you can choose the feature of interest and have the computer display the signal preceding and following that feature. The 30 megasamples/second 8-bit TRW flash ADC's are very handy for high-speed data acquisition and are reasonably priced considering their bandwidth.

9-4. Signal Averaging and Lock-In Detection

You've seen how DAC's and ADC's can greatly broaden the scope of computer monitoring and control, even to the point of providing a multi-trace storage oscilloscope of sorts. In this section, you'll see how the computer can literally pull some kinds of signals out of noise in situations where you wouldn't be able to deduce a thing with an ordinary analog oscilloscope. Two methods are considered: signal averaging and lock-in detection. Both involve the repetitive addition of noisy signals in a fashion that is synchronized to the signal. Because the noise is not synchronized to the signal, it ultimately contributes only a uniform background level (in signal averaging), or it subtracts as often as it adds, preventing it from contributing appreciably to the sum (in lock-in detection). Meanwhile, the signal contributions are always in phase with one another, causing the signal summations to grow faster than the noise.

Signal averaging is nicely introduced with an example from medicine. Suppose a person is unconscious and it's important to know whether he can hear. Or suppose a leg is badly damaged and it's important to know whether the nerves in his feet are still functional. Signal averaging can answer these and similar questions rapidly and effectively. The brain produces electrical signals that can be monitored by electrodes attached to the skin. The analog signals that are picked up are the superposition of many responses. You might think of the brain as something like a CPU running many tasks at the same time. Consequently, the ears, eyes, nerves, and nose as well as thought are constantly influencing the brain wave signals. Now suppose that, at a specific time, you clap your hands near the patient and digitize the ensuing brain-wave response at 0.1-second intervals for 10 seconds in your computer. This gives 100 channels or time slots, with the digitized response for each time slot being stored in a 16-bit memory location. The curve so taken looks essentially random because of the large amount of noise present. Then clap and record again, adding each data value to the memory word for its time slot. After a large number of claps and data recordings, a characteristic curve emerges, revealing the brain wave due to the clap response alone, independent of everything else going on in the brain. That's signal averaging.

The technique is useful in other areas as well. In Fig. 9-21, you see a diagram of a source that produces a noisy square wave connected to a microcomputer set up to do signal averaging and thus to recover the original square wave without the noise. The curves in Fig. 9-22 show some results of signal averaging obtained with this apparatus. Curve (c) is the sum of 16 response curves (divided by an overall scale factor to make it fit nicely on the page), and curve (d) is the sum of 256 response curves. You see a well defined curve emerge with very little noise.

A program to do signal averaging is easy to write and provides another way to understand the technique. The following subroutine zeroes a 512-byte area reserved for the 256 time-slot data sums. A 16-bit word is

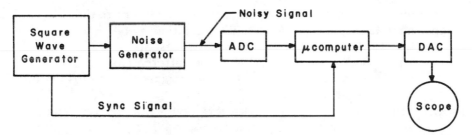

Fig. 9–21. Block diagram of a setup to produce a noisy square wave and then do signal averaging to extract the original noise–free square wave.

Fig. 9–22. Addition of 16 time responses like curves (a) and (b) yields curve (c). Addition of 256 responses yields curve (d). Although the individual response curves are noisy, the averaged curves show less and less noise as more curves are added.

used for each time slot. The ADC is read at regular time intervals following the trigger signal, and the value is added to the appropriate sum.

```
sigav:   xor    ax,ax              ;Zero curve summation memory
         mov    cx,256
         lea    di,curmem
```

```
rep     stosw
        mov     bx,nadd         ;bx counts # additions to do
avloop: mov     cx,256          ;Fill all 256 time slots
        lea     di,curmem       ;Start with first sum
        mov     al,1            ;Send out perturbation
        mov     dx,sync         ;This synchronizes CPU to response
        out     dx,al
rsloop: call    adc             ;Read response voltage (result in ax)
        add     [di],ax         ;Add it
        inc     di
        inc     di
        loop    rsloop          ;Do all the points
        dec     bx              ;Do NADD summations
        jnz     avloop
        ret


adc:    xor     ax,ax           ;Select ADC0816 channel 0
        mov     dx,channel
        out     dx,al
        mov     dx,adc          ;Start conversion
        out     dx,al
        mov     al,25
delay:  dec     al              ;Wait 100 microseconds
        jnz     delay
        in      al,adc          ;Get value
        ret
```

This code assumes that DS and ES already point at the data area labeled CURMEM and that the event you're measuring is produced by a trigger signal from the computer sent by the OUT SYNC,AL instruction. If an external trigger is available that is synchronous with the signal, you would replace this OUT instruction with a little loop that repeatedly tests the input signal until the appropriate rising or falling edge is detected. The constant NADD represents the number of 256-point response curves to average.

After executing the subroutine, you'd probably branch to a display routine to show the results. Alternatively, you could have the computer execute the display loop continuously, while running the RSLOOP routine under interrupt control. That way you can watch the signal emerge from the noise. Beautiful, eh?

A number of facts about signal averaging (actually signal summing in the routine just given) are worth mentioning. The signal-to-noise ratio (S/N) is proportional to the square root of the number of repetitions of the experiment. Thus, going from 1 to 256 repetitions increases the S/N ratio by a factor of 16. But to get another factor of 16, you have to go to 65,536 repetitions. Even such numbers can be dealt with, however, since you can go away and let the computer run overnight collecting data. Computers work much faster than human beings, and they can also work much longer, since they don't have to eat, sleep, or play. In this regard, digital signal averaging is better (and cheaper) than analog signal averaging. The analog version depends on integrating circuits that aren't accurate for long integration times because charge leaks off the capacitors. Finally, note that if you keep adding numbers to a 16-bit integer sum, it "wraps around" at 64K. To prevent this, the number of bytes used for the storage of each sum should be increased to handle the largest sum. The signal-averaging technique produces a background value equal to the sum of the noise. Part of this background may arise from the apparatus itself and can be measured by running the experiment without the signal. A final answer can then be obtained by subtracting this background average from the average obtained with the signal on.

An incredible example of signal averaging involves the 1-bit flash ADC, which just consists of a single comparator or a TTL gate. This works very well provided you have enough noise! Consider the case in which the signal-to-noise ratio (S/N) $\ll$ 1. You adjust the DC level of the input signal so that the average value of the signal plus noise matches the gate high-low transition threshold. Adding up many response curves yields the signal superimposed on top of a large constant background. To increase the data rate into the microcomputer, the comparator's output should be fed into a shift register like a 74LS164 to convert to byte format. Then eight 1-bit data samples can be read into the computer with one IN instruction.

When the S/N is small, you don't gain anything by using an A/D converter with more than 1-bit accuracy, and the high conversion speed of the 1-bit converter may be a major advantage. However, if the S/N starts to approach 1 or higher, a higher A/D conversion accuracy becomes necessary. The moral of this story is to use the 1-bit ADC for cases with S/N $\ll$ 1, but use the convenient ADC's for larger S/N's.

Two other names are given to signal averagers: multichannel analysers (MCA's) and transient digitizers. The MCA was the first device to become popular, specifically in nuclear physics. There, physicists need to plot the number of gamma rays impinging on a detector versus the energy of the rays to obtain a gamma-ray spectrum. The x-axis for these measurements is gamma ray energy, not time, but it's still signal averaging. MCA's can, of course, have any variable for the x-axis, and contemporary MCA's are just fancy microprocessor-based systems. Transient digitizers are simply high-speed dedicated signal averagers. Your own microcomputer can have substantially more flexibility than commercial MCA's or transient digitizers, but you'll have to go to considerable effort to compete with their elaborate (and convenient) ADC's, amplifiers, trigger circuitry, and other front-end equipment. For slow-speed work (100-kHz or less), you'll save a bundle by using a microcomputer and in addition have the convenience of general-purpose computing at your fingertips.

While signal averaging is particularly useful for distilling a time response curve out of the noise, *lock-in detection* is useful for pulling a constant or slowly varying signal out of noise. The basic idea here is to switch the signal on and off for equal periods of time. When the signal is on, you sum the input a number of times. When it is off, you subtract the input the same number of times. Any noise frequency present that differs from the on/off (chopping) frequency is added and subtracted equally, averaging its contribution to zero. The signal, on the other hand, adds and adds and adds. If the additions and subtractions are done a sufficient number of times, the result is a value that is proportional to the signal alone, with the noise removed. An example of a physics experiment using digital lock-in detection is diagrammed in Fig. 9-23. In the figure, a laser beam is turned on and off by a chopper (a device that can block or unblock a beam of light passing through it) running under control of the computer, but it's also possible to have the computer synchronized to a free-running chopper. When the beam is unblocked, the sample responds to the laser illumination

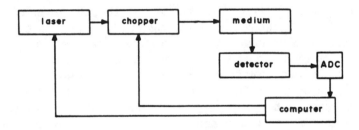

Fig. 9-23. An example of lock-in detection: The measurement of weak fluorescent emission by some medium (a gas, liquid, or solid). The computer controls a chopper that turns the laser beam passing through the sample on and off, and an optical detector monitors the light emitted by the sample at right angles to the laser beam.

by emitting light of own (typically at a longer wavelength). This fluorescent light is converted to an electrical signal by the detector, and then digitized and read by the computer. Note that (1) the signal must not be changing while the lock-in measurement of its amplitude is being made, and (2) no phase shift or time delay should exist between the on/off switching of the laser beam and the detection of the signal by the detector. For example, if a 90° phase shift is present, the signal itself would be averaged to zero along with the noise. Analog lock-in amplifiers include a phase shift control to compensate for phase shifts between the signal and the reference. In a computer, you can do the same thing by simply introducing a variable time delay between the on/off laser beam switching and the measurement of the detector's response. A subroutine that performs a digital lock-in operation goes as follows:

```
lockin:  mov   si,nav      ;Do NAV on/off measurement cycles
         xor   bx,bx       ;Zero sum (answer goes here)
avloop:  mov   al,1        ;Turn signal on
         mov   dx,sig
         out   dx,al
         mov   cx,10       ;Add 10 times (or whatever's good)
onloop:  call  adc         ;Get a value (answer returned in AX)
         add   bx,ax       ;Add since signal is on
         loop  onloop      ;Add a bunch of times
         mov   al,0        ;Turn signal off
         mov   dx,sig
         out   dx,al
         mov   cx,10       ;Subtract same number of times
ofloop:  call  adc
         sub   bx,ax       ;Subtract since signal is off
         loop  ofloop
         dec   si          ;Iterate NAV times (signal should
         jnz   avloop      ; remain constant during iteration)
         ret
```

In practice, the computer is usually programmed to vary some parameter in the experiment (for example, the laser's output wavelength in Fig. 9-23) and then to repeat the call to LOCKIN. By recording the signal for 100 parameter steps, you can generate a curve, ready for publication!

9-5. Waveform Generation and Recognition

One kind of data that can be manipulated by computers is an input or output voltage that is a function of time, i.e., a waveform. Data that can be regarded as waveforms include speech, music, digital data recordings, motor and relay control signals, and responses of various media to some stimulus. This section considers some of these waveforms, starting with binary varieties and concluding with the analog signals encountered in music and speech. Methods for generating and recognizing waveforms can be characterized by the degree to which programming is involved. Software-intensive methods are based on timing loops, while hardware methods use peripheral IC's that can internally produce or recognize complex waveforms. In general the software methods require dedicated operation of the CPU and are sensitive to variations in CPU execution speed, wait states, interrupts, and code changes, while hardware methods are more expensive, relatively insensitive to CPU timing, and less easily modified.

The IBM PC has three complications for methods that involve software timing loops: (1) every 72 clock cycles, the DMA controller takes over the bus and uses five clock cycles for refresh of the dynamic memory (see Sec. 6-4); (2) the time-of-day clock interrupts the program execution roughly 18.2 times per second; and (3) the published execution times for 8088 instructions usually neglect the fact that the maximum instruction fetch rate into the 8088 instruction queue is only 1 byte per 4 clock cycles, which can slow things down appreciably.   When programmed timing loops are critical, such as in decoding a waveform, you should turn off the time-of-day interrupt, and allow for the DMA memory refresh time and the time required to load the 8088 instruction queue.   Often a better solution is to use the PC's 8253 programmable interval timer to generate or time wave-forms as described below.

Timing loops can create one-shots and square waves like their hardware counterparts considered in Secs. 5-6 and 5-7.   Be sure to use the 8088 timings in Intel's *iAPX88 Book* when calculating execution times, not the timings for the 8086.   The simplest timing loop for the 8088 is:

```
           mov    cx,n              ;Load count value
here:      loop   here              ;Loop to here n times
```

In the absence of DMA refresh and timer interrupts, this loop lasts $17*n$ T states (clock cycles).   On a 4.77-MHz 8088 system, this gives a delay of 0.002 to 234 milliseconds in 3.6-microsecond steps, depending on the value in CX.   To compensate for the DMA refresh cycles on the IBM PC, multiply this number by $(72 + 5)/72$, to get a maximum value of 250 milliseconds, which agrees with what one measures with a stopwatch.   To perform this measurement, use DEBUG to fill memory with the HERE: LOOP HERE in-struction (the machine code is 0e2 0fe) and set a breakpoint after 128 instructions.   Run the code, and the breakpoint should be reached 32 seconds later, that is, 1/4 second per countdown.   Disabling the interrupts for this period has essentially no effect on the total time, but in a single loop it could cause a significant variation.   Hence interrupts should be disabled during critical timing loops.

In the code above, the 8088 fetch queue always had plenty of time to stay full.   This might be surprising, since a loop instruction jumping one byte further back empties the queue.   Now consider the loop

```
           mov    cx,n
back:      mov    ax,0
           loop   back
```

According to the timing charts, the loop instruction requires 17 T states and the mov ax,0 instruction requires 4 T states, but that neglects the time required to fill the instruction queue.   In this example, the queue is empty each time the mov ax,0 is executed, since a jump has just been performed. Since each byte requires 4 T states to be loaded into the queue, this 3-byte instruction actually requires about 12 T states to execute.   Hence the loop requires a little more than 12 + 17 T states per loop, which gives 0.43 second for 65536 loops (with the 77/72 factor), in good agreement with the observed value of 0.44 second. With this kind of thinking, you can estimate program-loop times, but to be more accurate, you should time any critical loop with a stopwatch. This is done by putting the loop inside some larger loop that executes a large number of times and then dividing the total time by that large number to get the answer. It's interesting to note that the similar Z80 instructions (BACK: LD HL,0   DJNZ BACK) require only 20 T states. In other words, where branching is involved, the queue makes the 8088 appreciably slower than a Z80. It also makes it very difficult to estimate precise timings for the 8088/8086, in contrast to the situation for the simpler 8-bit microcomputers.

To simulate a one-shot using some parallel port bit, you have to turn the bit on and then off. This leads to code like

```
        mov     cx,n
        mov     dx,port
        mov     al,1            ;Turn bit on
        out     dx,al
here:   loop    here
        mov     al,0            ;Turn bit off
        out     dx,al
```

Hence the one-shot code includes an extra 12 T states (one OUT instruction and the mov al,0). Queue filling adds very little to this loop's time.

Symmetric or nonsymmetric square waves can be generated with slight elaborations on this scheme. An example consists of a way to encode 1's and 0's on cassette tape. Each bit is represented by a low interval and a specific high interval. The high for a 1 is COUNT1 program loops long, while the high for a 0 is COUNT0 loops long. Specifically the code reads

```
one:    mov     bx,count1       ;Entry to output a 1's waveform
        jmp     either
zero:   mov     bx,count0       ;Entry to output a 0's waveform
either: mov     dx,casio
        mov     cx,18           ;Wait a low interval of 18 loops for
low:    loop    low             ; both 1's and 0's (noncritical)
        mov     al,1            ;Output appropriate high interval
        mov     cx,bx
        out     dx,al
high:   loop    high
        mov     al,0            ;Go back to low value
        out     dx,al
        ret
```

During the output of 1's and 0's this way, interrupts should be disabled. The high period count is important and has to be adjusted, taking into account the 77/72 DMA refresh factor. This approach can be used to provide recording rates of approximately 3000 bits/second on ordinary cassette recorders provided one defeats the automatic volume controls so that saturated recording can be obtained. This technique has been used on early Z80 computers with great success using inexpensive GE 3-5121 recorders. Nowadays, however, using a cassette recorder for computer data storage is nearly unthinkable except perhaps on inexpensive game computers.

Very similar loops can be written to recognize the duration of a single input pulse. For example, to measure the duration of a high value, use

```
        xor     bx,bx           ;Zero loop counter
        mov     dx,port
lowlp:  in      al,dx           ;Wait for bit to go low
        test    al,80h          ;Suppose data is on bit 7
        jz      lowlp
highlp: inc     bx              ;Loop while bit 7 is high
        in      al,dx
        test    al,80h
        jnz     highlp
```

The measured high time is then about (6 + 12 + 4 + 16)*bx T states or 8.5*bx microseconds (including queue fetch minimums and the 77/72 factor). Another popular way of storing 1's and 0's on tape consists of representing a 1 by 8 periods of a 2400-Hz square wave and a 0 by 4 periods of a 1200-Hz wave (the "Kansas City" format). This format has one tenth the data rate of the high-period modulated scheme but runs on any cassette recorder. This method is an example of frequency-shift keying (FSK). Other examples include representing a 1 simply by a high for a "baud rate" period and a 0 by a low for the baud rate period. This is the serial format used in connecting terminals to computers as discussed in Chap. 10. Single-density floppy-disk formats are similar but have data rates 40 times higher and require hardware bit-stream generation.

Two major problems with this kind of waveform generation and recognition are that a dedicated CPU is required, and that the timing is distorted by wait states, interrupts, and CPU clock changes. For long delay times, a viable alternative exists if you've implemented an interrupt-driven real-time clock. Suppose you want to wait n tenths of a second and that the real-time clock routine stores the current value in the location TENTHS. Then the following code works

```
        mov     cx,n
wait:   mov     al,tenths
        cmp     al,ah           ;Has TENTHS changed since last time
        jz      wait            ; thru loop?
        mov     ah,al           ;Yep.  Update current value
        loop    wait            ;Wait n tenths
```

The first time through the loop, the chances are that AH has something other than what's in TENTHS.   Consequently there's up to 0.1 second of error in this approach, but there would be if you preloaded the AH register too.   For more accuracy, a smaller time interval must be used.   Since the program timing is no longer important, code to do other things, such as polling, can be included in the WAIT loop.   Such an approach has been used in a controller designed by one of us that deposits adhesives on printed circuit boards for programmable lengths of time.   On the IBM, long durations can be timed in units of 1/18.2 second by comparing values of the timer_low and timer_high locations in the BIOS RAM memory area (see the BIOS listings in the IBM PC *Technical Reference* manual).

The IBM PC also offers a built-in timer of much higher resolution, namely the time-of-day counter using channel 0 of the System-Board 8253 programmable interval timer.   Its 16-bit count decrements every 4 I states (about 839 nanoseconds), and one can note its value at the beginning of a pulse and again at the end.   The period of the 16-bit channel 0 countdown is 1/18.2 second, at the end of which the clock interrupt occurs and increments a 32-bit count (timer_low and timer_high) in memory.   Hence arbitrarily long pulses can be timed with an accuracy of about 20 microseconds.   The primary source of error occurs when the pulse terminates while the timer interrupt is executing.   For pulse measurements less than 1/18.2 second, the timer interrupt can be turned off, and the accuracy improves to about 5 microseconds.   This technique automatically takes the 77/72 DMA refresh factor into account, since the 8253 timer operates independently of refresh.   Software is used only to mark the square-wave edge points.   An advantage of using the standard 65536 divisor for the channel 0 time-of-day count is that you can subtract the end count from the beginning count without paying attention to which is larger.   A carry is automatically provided.   The smaller divisor of 59659 suggested in Sec. 7-2 doesn't wrap around on the 16-bit boundary, meaning that you have to calculate the difference between end and beginning counts a little more carefully (about four more instructions).   On balance, the 59659 divisor, giving an accurate 20 interrupts/second, seems preferable.   What's an extra four instructions these days, especially since only advanced programmers would use the method?

The ability to time a pulse is used in the PC to measure the positions of joysticks attached to the IBM PC game adapter port.   Each joystick shaft is attached to two potentiometers, one for the right-left shaft position, and one for the forward-back position.   Hence the resistance of the potentiometers is proportional to the shaft positions.   The game adapter port puts these potentiometers into the charging circuits of two 555 timers (see Sec. 5-5) for each joystick.   Actually one 558 timer that has the equivalent of four 555's in one package is used.   By writing anything to port 201H, the timers are started, producing four high bits on the low-order input nibble of port 201H.   When the various capacitors have charged up enough through the potentiometers, the corresponding input bits go low.   Timing these high periods (IBM PC Cassette BASIC times all four at once using a program loop) gives a measure of the potentiometer resistances, and hence a measure of the joystick shaft positions. A program slightly better than the BASIC version is

```
timjoy: mov     dx,game         ;Point at game adapter port (201H)
        cli                     ;No interrupts while measuring
        out     dx,al           ;Start timers (24 microsec latency time)
        mov     cx,100H         ;Maximum count for timeout
        mov     bl,0FH          ;Initially all 4 pulse inputs are high

wait:   in      al,dx           ;Wait for a change
        and     al,bl           ;Only low nibble has pulses
        cmp     al,bl           ;Changes?
        loopz   wait
        jcxz    timout          ;Timeout due to resistances too high?
        xor     al,bl           ;No.  Set bits with changes
        mov     ah,cl           ;Save ah = count,
        push    ax              ; al = changes
        dec     cx              ;Allow for extra time here
        xor     bl,al           ;Update line statuses
        jnz     wait            ;All lines back low?
        jmp     done            ;Yep

timout: push    bx
done:   sti                     ;Got 'em.  Turn interrupts back on
        mov     dl,4            ;Decode change nibbles
decode: pop     ax              ;Get first count-change pair
        sub     ah,max-1
        neg     ah              ;Turn countdown value into countup
        mov     cx,4            ;Check four bits
decod1: shr     al,1            ;Next bit = 1, i.e., change?
        jnc     decod2
        mov     [di],ah         ;Yep.  Store count
        dec     dl              ;One more down, dl to go
decod2: inc     di
        loop    decod1
        sub     di,4            ;Point back at count vector start
        or      dl,dl           ;Four values stored?
        jnz     decode
        in      al,dx           ;Yep.  All done.
        ret                     ;Return push button values in al
```

Here the 4 angular position values are returned in the 4-byte array pointed to by the DI register, and the joystick pushbutton values are returned in bits 4—7 of AL.

The 8253 programmable interval timer is equally useful in generating waveforms. Each channel can interrupt on count completions, can generate symmetric square waves, and can produce one-shots with or without interrupting the CPU at count completion. The 16-bit counting resolution allows you to generate audio square waves with a frequency resolution finer than human ability to distinguish pitch, and baud rates for serial communications can be easily generated from any CPU clock speed. The IBM PC has a handy speaker attached to the 8253 channel 2 timer output ANDed with bit PB1 of the system board's 8255. Hence you can play tunes by changing the frequency of channel 2 as it counts in mode 3 and even modulate the output with PB1. Alternatively, you can let channel 2 go high (countdown in mode 0) and then modulate PB1 with a program. A program using the first method is given in App. C, where the keyboard is turned into a piano of sorts. The notes are produced accurate to 1 cent (100th of a half tone), 8 octaves can be played, and the tones last precisely as long as the corresponding key depressions. To obtain half volume, the PB1 bit is turned on and off in a tight program loop.

The ROM BASIC has a SOUND command, which uses the channel 2 facility to play square waves of desired frequency and duration. The disk BASICA.COM uses the SOUND facility, in turn, to play tunes using letters like A, B, C, that correspond to the musical note names A, B, C for the current octave. The tempo and octave can be changed easily (see BASIC manual), allowing you to play Beatles melodies or one voice of a Bach fugue. The IBM PC*jr* has an SN76496 Complex Sound Generator (described later in this section) in addition to the 8253 facility. The 76496 can superimpose three voices and noise with precise volume control.

The IBM PC uses a combination of software and hardware techniques to read and write cassette tapes. Channel 2 of the System Board 8253 is used to write the bits on the tape with four T-state counter resolution (much more accurately than the recorder can reproduce the bits), and a program loop is used to recognize the bit edges when reading. To write, the ROM BIOS routine cassette routines use the 8253's mode 3 (symmetric square wave) with a 1008-Hz frequency for 1's and a 2016-Hz frequency for 0's. The routine WRITE_BIT turns off time-of-day interrupts, waits for the current channel 2 output to go high and then low, and then loads the timer with the count for the next bit. To read the square-wave periods, the READ_HALF_BIT routine times a high or a low by subtracting the values in the channel 0 time-of-day counter at the beginning and end of the level, as described before. The time-of-day interrupt is turned off while cassette tapes are being read.

Another interesting smart peripheral is the Synertec 6522 PIO, which contains two counter/timers and a serial shift register in addition to two parallel I/O channels, all in a 40-pin DIP package. Serial I/O (see Sec. 10-2) involves the generation and recognition of a TTL waveform that is sent along a single wire. It can be done by dedicating the 8088 to monitoring and setting a parallel port bit or by using an 8253 channel. However, to relieve the CPU from translating to and from standard serial bit streams, special-purpose IC's called UART's and USART's were developed (see Sec. 10-3). Similarly, the NEC 765 floppy-disk controller in the PC handles the conversion of data bytes into a serial data stream and vice versa for floppy-disk writes and reads. Disk data rates are too high for 8088 software generation and recognition in any case (250,000 bits per second for 5-1/4-inch floppies).

Analog waveform generation and recognition use DAC's and ADC's respectively. Sections 9-3 and 9-4 discuss the measurement of analog waveforms. Computer recognition of waveforms goes a large step further in that a comparison of the waveform to some function must be made. This falls into the realm of numerical analysis and is outside the scope of this book. A large variety of analog waveforms can be generated easily on microcomputers and used to probe the response of media in the laboratory and to produce music. Only a few of these are discussed here. Note that the 8253 is great for generating square waves but is of little help for more complicated analog forms. You have to use program loops for them.

Some simple analog waveforms such as sawtooth and triangular waves (see Fig. 9-24) can be computed directly. For example, the following code generates a sawtooth wave on the output of a DAC:

```
          mov    al,0              ;Zero counter and value
          mov    dx,dac
loop:     out    dx,al
          add    al,n
          jmp    loop              ;AL wraps around at 255
```

A 4.77-MHz 8088 executes this loop about 500*n times per second. Delays can be incorporated to reduce the frequency. Similarly a triangular wave

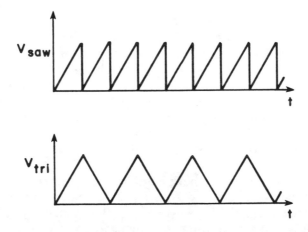

Fig. 9–24. Sawtooth and triangular waveforms can be easily generated by program loops.

can be produced by the code

```
        mov     ax,0
        mov     dx,dac
loop:   out     dx,al
        add     ah,n
        mov     al,ah
        jns     multwo
        neg     al              ;Take absolute value
multwo: add     al,al           ;Multiply by 2 to fill range
        jmp     loop
```

More generally, an arbitrary periodic waveform can be generated by sending numbers from a table to the DAC:

```
start:  mov     cx,tablen       ;Get periodic form length
        mov     si,offset tbl   ;Point at table
        mov     dx,dac
loop:   lodsb
        out     dx,al
        loop    loop            ;Output whole form
        jmp     start           ;Loop forever (or include a countdown)
```

In a fascinating article on music generated by microcomputers, Chamberlin (1980) has described how to generalize this concept to yield frequency (pitch) and envelope variations. The pitch variations come from skipping entries in the table, much as an increment greater than 1 is added in the sawtooth code. However, the increment must have a fractional part to sound reasonable, a feature that could be included in the sawtooth code too. Hence the pointer is 3 bytes long: high-byte, low-byte, and fractional part. Calling the latter two POINTR and the corresponding 16-bit increment INC, we have the following code:

```
dseg    segment                 ;Data map
buffer  db      100h dup(?)     ;Store waveform here
inc     dw      ?               ;Desired increment with fraction
pointr  dw      ?               ;Fraction and low byte of pointer
page    db      ?               ;High byte of pointer
dseg    ends

        mov     dx,dac
loop:   mov     ax,inc          ;Add inc to pointer L byte and fraction
        add     pointr,ax
        mov     bx,pointr+1     ;Make table pointer
        mov     al,[bx]         ;Get table value
        out     dx,al
        jmp     loop            ;The record ain't broke, the record . . .
```

This code can be repeated to add more voices to the DAC's output. For a single voice, the code can be shortened appreciably by using registers alone. Musical instruments are characterized by both the waveform and a slowly varying envelope. For example, a plucked instrument has a sharp attack and slow decay, while an organ has a mostly uniform amplitude. An envelope can be added by feeding the DAC output into a programmable amplifier and using a separate DAC-amplifier combination for each voice. Alternatively a more faithful reproduction can be obtained with a single DAC by using a set of waveforms for different points in time. This requires more memory (not much by PC standards) but allows the waveforms as well as amplitude to change shape as time proceeds. As Chamberlin explains, the various harmonics present in an instrument's sound have different envelopes, and consequently a set of waveforms can sound more realistic than a single waveform multiplied by an envelope. It adds a new dimension to waveform synthesis, and Chamberlin uses it to invent new instruments, such as the "blither"! Another feature of computer-generated sound is that a musician has potential access to infinitely many different instruments with a single kind of keyboard. This is a huge extension to the concept of the pipe organ.

For high fidelity, at least 12 bits must be used with a compander (compresser/expander) circuit to increase the dynamic range. On the order of 40,000 updates/second are needed. This rather high data rate is in principle possible with the IBM PC, provided a DMA channel is used. Every 25 microseconds, another 12-bit number must be output, which is somewhat faster than the 5-1/4 inch floppy disk rate. Unless you simply store this information and ship it without further processing, the 8088 has to have time to think about the next note. By having the DMA controller handle the output function, the 8088 gains crucial time to choose the next waveform. With the next generation of 8088's now upon us (a 6-MHz 80286 is three times as fast as the current PC's 8088), musicians should enter a completely new dimension in the world of music, with instruments of any audible tonality programmed to suit their individual tastes and abilities.

A much simpler way to produce computer generated music and other sounds is to add some special purpose hardware to the computer. A readily available example is Texas Instruments' SN76489 complex sound generator. This chip is a versatile sound source with three programmable 10-bit tone generators, a noise generator, four associated 4-bit attenuators, and an audio mixer—all housed in an inexpensive 16-pin DIP.

The SN76489 can be interfaced to a computer using one 8-bit parallel output port and 1 bit of a parallel input port. A standard Centronics printer interface (see Sec. 10-1) would be quite suitable. An audio amplifier connected to a speaker and a 2-MHz clock are also needed. The input port bit is used by the computer to monitor a READY line. When a byte is sent to the sound generator, it pulls the READY line low for about 32 microseconds while the chip reads the data and gets ready for the next byte. When READY goes back high, another byte can be sent. In one of his Circuit

Cellar articles, Steve Ciarcia gives a detailed description of how to wire up this chip and use it (see Byte Magazine, August 1982). The ill-fated PCjr used a variant of this chip (the SN76496) to provide its sound generation capabilities.

The 76489 contains eight programmable registers: three 10-bit registers that determine the frequency of the three internal tone generators, a noise control register that controls the internal noise generator, and four 4-bit attenuator registers that determine the volume of the output from the tone and noise generators.

You program the 76489 by outputting bytes to it as summarized in Fig. 9-25. Two kinds of bytes are used: the register/low-data byte, which has 1 for its most significant bit (MSB), and the high-data byte, whose MSB = 0. Before going further, note that the bit values in the Texas Instruments 76489 specifications are numbered backwards, with the MSB called bit 0 and the LSB called bit 7. Whoever made that choice apparently doesn't understand binary arithmetic! In keeping with the rest of this book (and the vast majority of the computer industry), we describe the byte contents by calling the MSB bit 7. Bits 4—6 then specify which of 8 registers the other bits and the high-data byte reference. Specifically, bits 6 and 5 give a binary number specifying which of the tone frequency registers (1, 2, or 3) or the noise-generator control register is to be used. If bit 4 = 0, a frequency value or noise parameter is stored. If bit 4 = 1, an attenuation value is stored. Bits 0—3 are the low-order data bits for a tone frequency or give a 4-bit attenuation value. The actual attenuation in decibels is twice the 4-bit value, with the exception that the value 0fh means "off." The high-data byte is used for tone frequencies alone. Its bits 0—5 give the high-order six bits of the tone frequency. This byte can be written consecutively, allowing rapid frequency sweeps for special effects. The

Bit numbers	b_7	b_6	b_5	b_4	b_3	b_2	b_1	b_0
Register byte	1	r_1	r_0	a/f	d_3	d_2	d_1	d_0
High-data byte	0	x	d_9	d_8	d_7	d_6	d_5	d_4

Fig. 9-25. Bit meanings for the SN76489 Complex Sound Generator. The binary number $r_1 r_0$ specifies tone frequency registers 1—3 and the noise-generator control register, respectively. a/f = 1 defines the binary number $d_3 d_2 d_1 d_0$ to be an attenuation value. a/f = 0 defines $d_3 d_2 d_1 d_0$ to be the low-order bits of the tone frequency divisor. $d_9 d_8 d_7 d_6 d_5 d_4$ are the high-order bits of the tone frequency divisor for the tone register most recently specified.

kind of noise generated is determined by bits 0—2 of the noise control byte ($1110xb_2b_1b_0$). Here $b_2 = 0$ gives periodic noise, while $b_2 = 1$ gives white noise. The binary number $b_1b_0 < 3$ provides noise with three different frequency spectra, while $b_1b_0 = 3$ lets the output from tone generator 3 determine the noise frequency spectrum.

This chip is great for special effects in games and can also play three-part chords in musical compositions. The latter application is somewhat marred by the low 10-bit frequency resolution, which can sound off-key to the musical ear, especially in the higher-frequency octaves. Better performance can be obtained with the General Instruments AY-3-8912 sound generator. Like the SN76489, it has three programmable tone generators with 4-bit amplitude control for each. However, the tone generators have 12-bit resolution instead of 10-bit, and there is an envelope generator that can produce a variety of different preprogrammed amplitude versus time outputs for the tone or noise generators.

The final kind of waveform we consider here is human speech. To digitize speech with an 8-bit ADC and play it back using a DAC requires around 8000 samples per second for reasonable fidelity. Such high data storage requirements make the direct digitization of speech relatively unattractive. By using a speech encoder/decoder such as the Oki MSM5218, this data rate can be reduced by a factor of 3 to 8, making this approach much more practical. Ciarcia has given a good description of how to hook up and use one of these devices (see Byte Magazine, June 1983). Another hardware approach to getting the computer to speak is to use a speech synthesizer chip. The most flexible of these are unlimited vocabulary allophone synthesizers such as the Votrax SC-01A, the Silicon Systems SSI263, or the General Instruments SPO256-AL2. Ciarcia has described the use of all of these chips in his Circuit Cellar columns (see Byte Magazine, September 1981, March 1984, and May 1985).

9-6. Motor Control

You have seen how computers can read and set switches and analog voltages. These capabilities already cover burglar alarm equipment, environmental control, soil humidity-controlled sprinkler systems, phone answering and dialing, laboratory control and monitoring, and so on. In addition, however, you might like to give the computer "hands." For this, motor control is needed. A basic tenet of motor control is that changes in position are monitored and used to control further change. An obvious example is a person driving a car. The person instructs the car to move along the road according to what he sees. If the car moves a bit too far to the right, the driver counteracts with a bit of a turn to the left. The concept being used here is called *feedback*. The system of car and driver is driven by inputs consisting of the difference between the actual position and the desired position as depicted in Fig. 9-26.

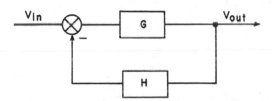

Fig. 9-26. Block diagram of a closed—loop control system. Part of the output is fed back into the input to generate an error signal. The control system tries to make the output follow the input in order to minimize this signal.

In this section, we consider two approaches to the problem of motor control. The first uses the stepper motor, a device whose output position can be determined simply by having the computer remember what pulses have been sent to it. Once the rotor position is calibrated and initialized, no feedback is necessary, unless the speed demanded is too high or the torque required is too great. Running a motor this way without feedback is called *open-loop* operation. The second method uses feedback, and is a *closed-loop* approach called a *servo system*. The servo system can respond more quickly and accurately than the open-loop stepper-motor system and is relatively insensitive to hardware variations. But it requires position sensors or transducers to tell where the motor has turned as well as relatively complicated drive electronics to ensure stability. Servo concepts are not limited to motor control; they also apply to systems like a thermostat and furnace.

The permanent-magnet stepper motor is pictured in Fig. 9-27. Like all motors, it consists of a rotor (the part that rotates) and a stator (the part that's stationary). In a stepper motor, the rotor features two gearlike cylinders that are turned one-half a tooth spacing with respect to one another. One gear is a permanent magnetic north (N) pole and the other is the south (S) pole. The stator is also gearlike and has a different number of teeth than the rotor poles. In the stator, however, each tooth is an electromagnet and can be made into a N or S pole by driving a current through a tiny coil of wire wound around it.

A simplified three-tooth rotor interacting with a four-tooth stator is illustrated in Fig. 9-28, adapted from an excellent introduction to stepper motors in *BYTE* (Giacomo 1979). In Fig. 9-28a, currents flow in the A and C stator coils, creating N and S poles, respectively. The rotor's upper S tooth is attracted to the stator N pole, while the rotor's lower N tooth is attracted to the stator S pole. Deenergizing the A and C stator teeth and turning on currents to make B and D into N and S poles, respectively, then causes the rotor to turn clockwise one position as shown in Fig. 9-28b. Alternatively, you could make B and D into S and N poles, respectively, and the rotor would turn counterclockwise one position. Similar combinations of

Fig. 9-27. Exploded view of a permanent magnet stepper motor. The rotor consists of two groups of gearlike teeth, one group being north poles and the other south. The stator consists of two groups of corresponding teeth that can individually be made north or south poles. (Photo courtesy of Superior Electric)

stator coil currents turn the rotor further around as shown in Figs. 9-28c and d.

Two methods of winding the coils are popular. The first assigns a single coil to each stator tooth. To reverse the polarity, you must reverse the current flowing through the coil, which requires a bipolar power supply. The other approach is the *bifilar* motor, which has two separate coils on each tooth, so that current flow through one coil creates an N pole, while flow through the other creates an S pole. The bifilar motor thus can be driven with a single-ended power supply. To fit both coils on a single stator tooth, thinner wire is used, which has higher resistance. The two coils are each part of separate electrical circuits called *phases*. Each phase contains many coils in series on a whole set of stator teeth. Typically the arrangement is such that the two coils on one stator tooth belong to different circuits from the coils on an adjacent tooth. The total number of circuits used is then four, and consequently the motor is called a *four-phase bifilar stepper motor*. Because of their permanent-magnet rotors, both two-phase and bifilar motors have a residual torque holding the rotor in a given position when no current flows. This torque is substantially less than that produced with current flow. You can feel the difference by manually advancing the paper on a Diablo daisy-wheel printer both with the power on and with the power off. (The paper-feed mechanism on such a printer uses a two-phase stepper motor with a bipolar power supply.)

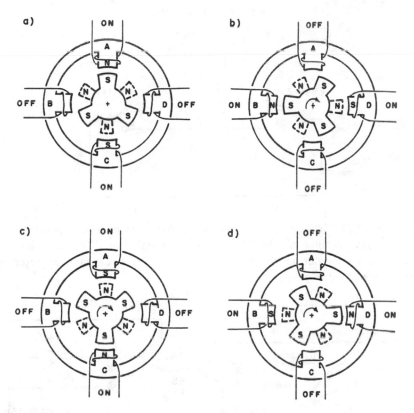

Fig. 9–28. Four–tooth permanent magnet stepper motor illustrates how a stepper motor can be turned to discrete positions. (Adapted from Giacomo, 1979)

Three-phase *variable reluctance* motors are also popular. These motors have an unmagnetized rotor and run from a single-ended power supply, since the unmagnetized rotor responds equally well to either magnetic polarity. Since it has no permanent magnet, a variable reluctance motor has no residual torque in the absence of current flow.

Figure 9-29 is a schematic diagram of a bifilar four-phase permanent-magnet stepper motor, and Fig. 9-30 shows a simple example of appropriate driver circuitry. Notice that a diode is connected across each phase of the stepper motor to protect the TIP35C power transistor used to drive that phase. The protection is needed because, as discussed in Sec. 9-1, a coil is an inductor, which tries to keep the same current flowing even after the transistor turns off. This can produce transient high voltages across the transistor and burn it out. A resistor is sometimes inserted between the coils and the positive supply terminal to decrease the inductance to resist-ance (L/R) ratio of each phase. Just as inductors don't want to turn off, neither do they want to turn on. A decrease in the L/R ratio allows the

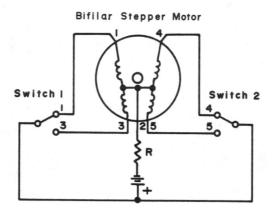

Fig. 9-29. Schematic diagram of a four-phase bifilar permanent-magnet stepper motor. Running current through the different windings makes sets of stator teeth into north or south poles, causing the rotor to move to particular positions.

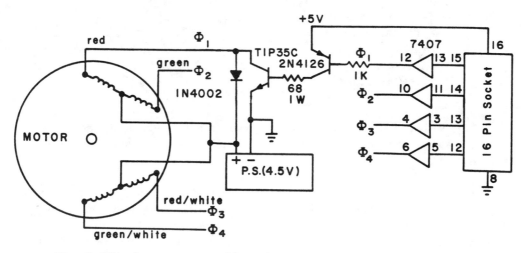

Fig. 9-30. Stepper-motor driver circuit. The complete circuit is shown only for phase 1. The other three phases use identical circuits. Integrated circuits can be obtained that condense nearly all of this circuitry into a single package.

current to start up faster, with a corresponding increase in performance as illustrated in Fig. 9-31. Adding the resistance increases the torque available at a given step rate but requires a larger power supply since a lot of energy is dissipated in the added resistor. The thin bifilar windings in a four-phase stepper have a fairly high built-in resistance, which improves its performance. More elegant methods use variable voltage power supplies that provide a large voltage to start the current flowing through the coils

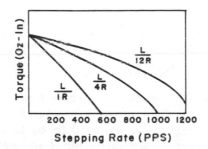

Fig. 9–31. Torque versus stepping rate (in pulses per second) for various L/R ratios in a stepper motor.

and then automatically reduce the voltage as the current flows more easily. You can implement these methods using microcomputers or in other ways, but the simple series-resistance method is most common.

To drive a four-phase stepper motor, you need to energize the four phases in the proper order for appropriate lengths of time. The simplest way to do this is to drive four bits of a parallel port connected to the drive circuitry shown in Fig. 9-30. Because their construction is somewhat more complicated than the 3-tooth motor of Fig. 9-28, real bifilar motors allow three distinct stepping methods: single-phase, dual-phase, and half-step. The method discussed in connection with Fig. 9-28 is single-phase. In dual-phase excitation, coils on two adjacent teeth are energized with the same polarity. This produces rotor positions halfway between the single-phase rotor positions. The half-step method capitalizes on this feature to rotate in half steps. First a single phase is energized, then two phases, then a single phase, and so on. Dual-phase excitation offers the most torque and the smoothest operation, but requires more power. All three methods can produce roughly equal motor speeds, provided their torque ranges are not exceeded.

The three stepping methods can all be implemented with the same program by using appropriate tables as follows:

```
steppr: cmp     cl,3            ;Make sure 0 < CL < 4
        ja      stpret
        mov     al,8            ;CL value legal.  Calculate table offset
        mul     cl
        and     ch,7            ;Keep count offset between 0 and 7
        add     al,ch           ;Add in counter offset
        inc     ch
        xchg    ax,si           ;Define table index
        mov     al,table[si]    ;Get next set of phase bits: a 0 value
        mov     dx,motor        ; turns on phase
        out     dx,al
        call    delay           ;Delay a bit or go do something else
```

```
stpret: ret

table:  db      7,0eh,0dh,0bh,7,0eh,0dh,0bh         ;Single-phase values
        db      6,0ch,9,3,6,0ch,9,3                 ;Dual-phase values
        db      6,0eh,0ch,0dh,9,0bh,3,7             ;Half-step values
```

On successive calls, the CH register is incremented to turn the rotor clockwise. A slight elaboration of the program could provide bidirectional operation. On entry, the CL register is assumed to contain the desired stepping method: 1 for single-phase, 2 for dual, and 3 for half-step. The routine outputs 4 bits to the port MOTOR, and assumes that a 0 value turns a phase on. Since the routine clobbers AX and SI, you may want to save them.

Clearly the stepping sequences can also be implemented in hardware that would respond to simple output strobe pulses, one for a clockwise step and one for a counterclockwise step. In fact, special LSI stepper-motor controllers are available that do this. Examples are the Cybernetic Micro Systems CY512 and the North American Phillips SAA1027 stepper motor controllers. Typically it's preferable to use one of these rather than the simple transistor drivers shown in Fig. 9-30. An LSI controller has the advantage of relieving the CPU from dedicated timing loops, and it's failsafe, should the CPU crash. Many of them can also implement dynamic acceleration and braking algorithms to improve performance. Complete stepper motor driver boards are also available from the stepper motor manufacturers. Some of these can implement a technique called *microstepping*, which provides up to 50,000 steps per revolution. This is accomplished by using variable current levels through the coils instead of just turning them on and off.

When just a knowledge of the rotor position is sufficient feedback information, the open-loop stepper-motor approach is ideal. For example, stepper motors can be used to turn knobs on predigital, but otherwise excellent, laboratory equipment that people throw away these days. The stepper-motor position can be calibrated to the desired equipment response through the use of appropriate conversion tables contained in a program. In many other situations, especially where high speed is required, the response achieved in this fashion is inadequate, and one must resort to a closed-loop method. The carriage and print-wheel circuits on Diablo daisy-wheel printers are examples. Very high performance is required, and the printer uses a combination of hardware and software to implement its servo loops.

The servo concept can be illustrated with a simpler example: automobile automatic cruise control. The cruise control matches a desired speed specified by a knob to the actual speed measured by a speedometer by driving the gasoline throttle with an output proportional to the difference between the desired and actual speed. In principle, the car speed stays essentially constant in spite of changes in the road grade. But the problem isn't completely trivial. Changing the gasoline flow to the engine changes the engine torque and hence accelerates or decelerates the car. The velocity is the integral of the acceleration, and hence the induced change in velocity may overshoot the desired value. The throttle is then cut back, but an overshoot in the opposite direction may occur. Unless designed carefully, the system can become unstable, with increasingly large oscillations about the desired speed, leading to a very jerky ride.

This potential problem in a cruise control circuit illustrates a major problem that must be dealt with in all servo system designs: instability. To counteract this problem, the feedback circuits have to be appropriately designed to damp out all incipient oscillations. When the output speed (in the case of a cruise control) is specified as a function of the desired input value, that function (called the transfer function) must always relax to the input value, regardless of road conditions. In mathematical terms, the Laplace transform of the transfer function can have no poles in the right-half complex plane, for such poles represent exponentially increasing deviations as time goes on. This observation forms the basis for an analytical approach to servo design called *root locus*. Such an approach is beyond the scope of this book, but note that it requires an analytic formula for the transfer function.

In cases where such analytic formulas prove to be elusive or impossible to write down, the designer can simulate the servo using a digital computer and vary parameters until the thing works. Experience with the analytically solvable problems is particularly helpful here in providing intuition about what changes to make in the simulations. The digital simulations are particularly interesting in today's world because part of the simulation may well become a final part of the servo loop, namely in the form of a micro-computer. The microcomputer not only can close a loop by controlling motors and monitoring position or velocity transducers, but also can provide information to other computers and to human beings as to what is going on. Furthermore, if instabilities in the final system do develop owing to inadequate simulation, there's a good chance that the system can be fixed simply by modifying the microcomputer's program, rather than by making relatively difficult hardware changes. Microcomputers win again! But in all honesty, sometimes it's incredibly hard to get those programs debugged. For an excellent discussion of servo systems involving microcomputers, see Bibbero (1977).

References

Optoelectronics Data Book, 1985, Motorola, Inc., Phoenix, AZ. Contains detailed specifications for all of Motorola's optocouplers and optotriacs.

Power Device Data Book, 1985, Motorola, Inc., Phoenix, AZ. Contains detailed specifications for Motorola's SCR's, triacs, and power transistors.

iAPX 88 Book, 1983, Intel Corporation, Santa Clara, CA. This book contains a one-page description of each of the 8088 instructions together with execution times for each.

H. Chamberlin, 1980, "Advanced Real-Time Music Synthesis Techniques," *BYTE* magazine, Vol. 5, No. 4, p. 70. Presents an excellent discussion of software techniques for computer music generation. See also his book *Musical Applications of Microprocessors*, 1980, Hayden Book Company, Rochelle Park, NJ.

S. Ciarcia, 1984, *Ciarcia's Circuit Cellar*, Vols. I through V, McGraw-Hill, New York. These five volumes, a collection of Steve's *BYTE* magazine columns, are full of interesting interfacing ideas.

P. Giacomo, 1979, "A Stepping Motor Primer," *BYTE* magazine, Vol. 4, No. 2, p. 90, and Vol. 4, No. 3, p. 142. Gives a good introduction to how stepper motors work and how to interface them to microcomputers.

C. C. Foster, 1981, *Real Time Programming—Neglected Topics*, Addison-Wesley, Reading, MA. This book discusses a variety of interfacing techniques, with special emphasis on digitally controlled servomechanisms.

R. Zaks and A. Lesea, 1979, *Microcomputer Interfacing Techniques*, Sybex, Berkeley, CA. Discusses a variety of microcomputer interfaces, including A/D and D/A converters.

R. J. Bibbero, 1977, *Microcomputers, Instrumentation, and Control*, Wiley, New York. This book contains high-level discussion of how to apply microprocessors in process controllers and servomechanisms.

S. A. Hoenig, 1980, *How to Build and Use Electronic Devices Without Frustration, Panic, Mountains of Money or an Engineering Degree*, Second Edition, Little-Brown, Boston, MA. Provides very clear discussions of op amps, op amp circuits, and a variety of other practical electronics topics.

P. Horowitz and W. Hill, 1980, *The Art of Electronics*, Cambridge University Press, Cambridge, England. This is our favorite general book on electronics. Contains a vast assortment of circuits, discussions of all kinds of electronic devices, and practical hints on circuit construction.

G. F. Franklen and J. D. Powell, 1980, *Digital Control of Dynamic Systems*, Addison-Wesley, Reading, MA. Contains in-depth discussions of hybrid analog-digital servo control systems.

10
Data Communications

Besides reading and writing data to devices like switches, analog-to-digital and digital-to-analog converters, and video displays, computers need to communicate with printers, terminals, and other computers. This kind of input/output is typically called *data communications*, since streams of digital data are transferred between sources and destinations. As with the other kinds of data transfer considered so far in this book, the flow must be synchronized, and this is typically done under the control of "handshaking" conventions that use either dedicated hardware lines or special character sequences. A simple example of handshaking involves a printer capable of printing only 120 characters/second, but receiving data at 10 times that rate. When the printer's input buffer is nearly filled, it sends a busy signal to the data source (by pulling high a line connecting the two), indicating that it cannot accept any more data for a while. Later it pulls the busy line back low, indicating that it can accept more data. The busy signal here is what is meant by a handshake signal.

Another example would be a data link between two computers, either or both of which have numerous responsibilities, such as servicing the keyboard, screen, and disk drives. At times data can be transferred between the two at the fastest speed of the communications hardware, but at other times the receiving computer is busy reading or writing the disk, screen, or keyboard. At this point, its communications input buffer fills up just like the printer's, and its communications interrupt handler must send a busy signal to the other computer.

In this chapter we consider three popular ways of transferring digital data between devices: (1) the Centronics printer interface, (2) the serial RS232 data link, and (3) the IEEE 488 interface bus, also called GPIB (general purpose interface bus). The Centronics interface is used for the parallel printer interface in the IBM PC and is primarily unidirectional; that is, data goes from the computer to the printer. Handshake lines are provided that go in both directions, and the IBM version can be programmed to provide up to eight input lines to the computer, as shown in Sec. 10-1. The Centronics interface is widely used for printer control and allows data transfer rates up to about 100 kilobytes/second, although printers print much more slowly than this, and the IBM (Epson) printer specifications list 1000 bytes/second as the fastest data transfer rate. Because of its simplicity, the Centronics interface is the easiest way to hook up a dot-matrix printer.

The Centronics interface and other interfaces considered in previous chapters all input or output 8 bits at a time in parallel at TTL voltage levels. This is convenient and in many cases straightforward. On the other hand, unless the lines are shielded (as the IBM Centronics cable is), the technique is susceptible to noise if many feet of cable are involved; eight data lines are required (sixteen for simultaneous input and output); and finally, simple as it is in concept, bidirectional parallel operation is nonstandard. Each implementation for bidirectional operation seems to have its own special set of handshake signals. Even the very flexible smart PIO's can't be programmed to handle some of these automatically. A standard way around the noise, multiplicity of lines, and lack of conventions is to use serial I/O. In fact serially coded ASCII (American Standard Code for Information Interchange) is the most generally applicable way of exchanging information between computers and is able to work over phone lines as well as in the same room. Serial I/O involves sending bytes 1 bit at a time, least significant byte first, with a few extra bits to keep everything synchronized. It's slower than parallel communications, but very general. The major drawback is that the serial communication definition allows many possible permutations and combinations, which can make the proper wiring of a cable between two devices difficult.

Because of its great importance, most of this chapter is devoted to serial I/O. Section 10-2 defines the serial ASCII encoding and describes the software and hardware of serial I/O. Section 10-3 defines the voltage and current conventions commonly used (RS-232C and current loop). Section 10-4 then describes modems (modulator/demodulators) used for sending serial data over phone lines, including the IBM PCjr internal modem. Section 10-5 shows how to connect any computer to any other using serial communications. Section 10-6 describes the more exotic serial transmission media of rf (radio), infrared (such as used by the IBM PCjr keyboard), fiber

optics, and powerlines. Serial I/O is the standard way to interface computers to terminals or to modems, and to transfer data between two
computers. It's especially valuable in connecting small computers up to
bigger machines to take advantage of big-machine data bases, number-
crunch power, and expensive peripherals.

The chapter closes with a discussion of the "byte-serial" IEEE 488 or
GPIB, which is used extensively in laboratory control. This bus was originally developed by Hewlett-Packard to allow flexible data transfer between
a number of laboratory instruments over a time-shared set of sixteen wires.
It features a special patented handshaking and addressing procedure,
whereby a master "controller" (usually a computer) instructs devices known
as "talkers" (transmitters) and "listeners" (receivers) to send or receive
data, respectively. A voltmeter is a typical talker, and when addressed it
sends a digital encoding of a voltage over the bus. A function generator is
a typical listener, and generates the function called for. Other computers
and storage devices can be both talkers and listeners. The IEEE 488 bus is
very convenient, works up to 1 megabyte/second, and involves only one
master computer interface. Hence a small computer box, such as the IBM
PC with an IEEE 488 card, can interface to many devices. Other kinds of
parallel interfacing are substantially less expensive for a single device, but
the computer must have a set of wires and an interface for each device,
which can lead to many wires and interface cards in the computer. On the
negative side, IEEE 488 interfaces require special bus-interface circuitry to
be present in the devices, which significantly increases their cost. Section
10-7 discusses the merits of the IEEE 488 further and defines the addressing
and handshaking conventions.

10-1. The Centronics Printer Interface

The Centronics printer interface allows data to be transmitted to a
printer 8 bits at a time. Since the computer can output up to 150
kilobytes/second, the printer needs some way to say "Wait!" It does this
by pulling the BUSY line high as described previously. In addition, there is
a second two-way handshake in the Centronics standard. When the computer sends a byte of data to the printer, it also sends a pulse down the
STROBE line. This tells the printer, "Hey, I've got another byte of data
here for you." When the printer has read the data byte and is ready to
accept another, it acknowledges that fact by sending back a pulse on the
ACKNLG line. This tells the computer, "OK, I've read what you sent." This
is a classic example of a two-way handshake. The first device says, "Here's
some data," and the second device replies, "I've got it." Figure 10-1 is a
timing diagram that shows the relationship of the various handshake signals.

The IBM PC typically uses the BUSY line for handshaking in a polled
mode. Polling means that the computer hangs in a little loop, testing the
line until the desired condition occurs. Thus a polling loop for the BUSY

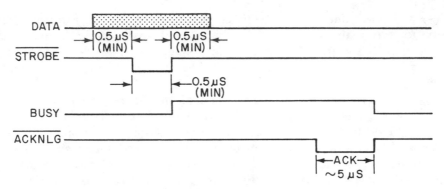

Fig. 10-1. Timing diagram for a Centronics parallel printer interface. The DATA and STROBE signals are sent by the computer and the BUSY and ACKNLG signals are sent by the printer.

line would be

```
        mov    dx,status
hang:   in     al,dx      ;Hang in loop till BUSY line goes low
        test   al,80H     ;BUSY line low if bit 7 = 1 in status port
        jz     hang
```

The ROM BIOS routine for the parallel printer port on IBM's parallel printer adapter (or the equivalent port on the monochrome adapter) works as follows: When a character is to be sent to the printer, the output routine sends the desired character to the data port (port address 3BCH on the monochrome display and printer adapter), where it's latched and held. The routine then polls the BUSY line (bit 7 of port 3BDH) until it goes low. Because such a loop could hang up forever on a nonexistent printer, the polling loop contains a countdown lasting about 16 seconds, which returns an error value if the BUSY line never goes low. This countdown has the disadvantage that it can time-out when you pause the printer (for example, to adjust the paper), leading to loss of characters. We use our own printer driver routine (see below), which can be interrupted by typing a control C, and therefore we don't need a timeout.

As soon as the BUSY line goes low, the PC's ROM BIOS routine pulses the STROBE line low (bit 0 of port 3BEH), telling the printer that a new byte is ready, and then the routine returns. Here as elsewhere on the IBM version of the printer interface, the high/low value of the BUSY and STROBE lines are inverted in the printer adapter registers. Hence the output routine looks for a 1 bit (bit 7 = 1 of 3BDH) to detect a low BUSY line value, and sets a bit high (bit 0 of 3BEH) momentarily to pulse the STROBE line low.

The ACKNLG handshake line is ideally suited to an interrupt-driven output routine. If printer interrupts on the 8259A interrupt controller's IR7 line are enabled (bit 4 = 1 on port 3BEH of the printer adapter and bit 7 = 0 in the 8259A's interrupt mask register), the inverted value of the $\overline{ACKNLG}$ line is gated onto the I/O channel's IR7 line.   Since the 8259A is programmed to produce an interrupt on a rising edge, the $\overline{ACKNLG}$ line can cause an interrupt.   For this approach, characters are typically stored in a FIFO buffer (see Sec. 6-1) until a printer-acknowledge interrupt indicates that another character can be transmitted. This output buffering technique is one kind of "print spooling."   This capability is built into the PRINT command of DOS 2.0, and is also available for DOS 1.1 from a number of the multifunction-board suppliers for the IBM PC (for example, AST Research).

The ROM BIOS printer routine (the default INT 17H) can handle up to four parallel printers.   The 16-bit port addresses for the corresponding printer adapters are stored in locations 40:8—40:0F and the number (0, 1, 2, or 3) of the desired adapter is passed to INT 17H in the DX register.   For printer 0, which is driven by the monochrome display and printer adapter, the port numbers given above are valid, but other adapters use different addresses.   The IBM PC BIOS routine is given in the IBM PC *Technical Reference* manual.   A simpler Centronics routine able to handle a single printer adapter goes as follows:

```
cenout:    push    dx              ;CENtronics OUTput routine
           mov     dx,data         ;Point at data output port
           out     dx,al           ;Output character to data latch
           inc     dx              ;Point dx at status port (data+1)

waitbs:    mov     ah,1            ;Keyboard character typed?
           int     16H
           jz      waitb2
           cmp     al,3            ;Yes. ©C?
           jz      cenret
waitb2:    in      al,dx           ;Wait for BUSY line to go low
           test    al,80H
           jz      waitbs          ;(BUSY low if bit 7 = 1 in status port)

           inc     dx              ;Point at control port (data+2)
           mov     al,0dh          ;Pulse STROBE low: Set bit 0 = 1
           out     dx,al           ; to pull STROBE low
           mov     al,0ch
           out     dx,al           ;Bring it back high
cenret:    pop     dx
           ret
```

To be compatible with the IBM PC conventions, the routine should load the appropriate port address into DX using the input value of DX and the port-address locations at 40:8—0F, and should return the status byte in AH.

Figure 10-2 summarizes the lines used for the IBM PC 25-pin Centronics interface. The standard Centronics convention uses a 36-pin connector, so IBM's pin numbers are nonstandard. Note that in addition to the BUSY, ACKNLG, DATA, STROBE, and ground lines, there are lines for PAPER END, SELECT, AUTO FEED, ERROR, INITIALIZE PRINTER, and SELECT INPUT. The SELECT INPUT line must be low in order for the printer to be selected. Thus by using individual SELECT INPUT lines for each of several printers, you could use the same interface to drive a number of printers, all sharing the same handshake and data lines. This idea is carried out in great generality in the IEEE 488 bus interface discussed in Sec. 10-7.

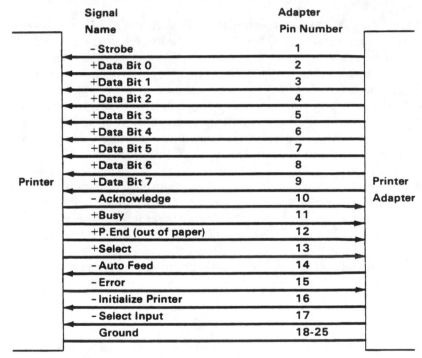

Signal Name	Adapter Pin Number
− Strobe	1
+Data Bit 0	2
+Data Bit 1	3
+Data Bit 2	4
+Data Bit 3	5
+Data Bit 4	6
+Data Bit 5	7
+Data Bit 6	8
+Data Bit 7	9
− Acknowledge	10
+Busy	11
+P.End (out of paper)	12
+Select	13
− Auto Feed	14
− Error	15
− Initialize Printer	16
− Select Input	17
Ground	18-25

Fig. 10–2. Centronics interface connector pinouts as they appear on the IBM PC's 25–pin D–shell connector. The pin connections on the printer end are the same for lines 1—14 and 19—25 but differ somewhat on the other lines, since a 36–pin connector is used there.

Now let's see how the interface is implemented on the IBM PC, and how it might be useful for other I/O purposes. The output byte on the IBM adapters is latched by a 74LS374, which can both source and sink current, and hence should not be driven externally. The output byte can also be read through a 74LS244 input buffer. If the 74LS374's tristate output enable pin had been connected to the extra bit on the adapter's command port (a 6-bit 74LS174 latch), the data port could have been programmed for external input as well as output, making the port substantially more useful. Five bits of the 74LS174 are used for command lines, one being the interrupt enable line and the other four being buffered through open-collector (three inverting) drivers onto the Centronics interface cable. Since these four lines are readable and as open collectors can be driven externally, they can be used for input as well as output lines. Together with the four standard input lines, this makes a total of eight lines that can be used for input in non-Centronics applications. Alternatively you can have twelve output lines and four input lines.

The port would have been useful for more than a printer interface if a smart port such as an 8255 had been used, and buffered by bidirectional 74LS245 drivers. Then files could be transferred between two computers at high data rates. It seems unfortunate that the Centronics convention is typically so unidirectional in character, since systems often end up with several interfaces that are not particularly useful for anything but printers with limited handshakes. One exception is the Victor 9000 implementation, which can be used bidirectionally and can be programmed to be an IEEE 488 port as well as a Centronics printer port.

10-2. Parallel/Serial Conversion: The 8250 UART

When extremely high data rates are not required, the number of wires required for data communications between two devices can be reduced substantially by converting the bytes to be transmitted into a serial bit stream. In fact, if the data rates are sufficiently slow, you need only two wires for bidirectional transmission, one for each direction, although usually you need a ground wire connecting the two devices as well. The information in a serial bit stream is contained in its time-dependent waveform: the bits are represented by codes having specific time durations. The standard asynchronous serial formats used in data communications all allocate a time interval known as a *baud period* to each bit. The word *baud* is used in honor of a Frenchman named Baudot, who studied various serial encoding schemes back in the 1800's. In the simplest form of encoding, a 1 is represented by a TTL high voltage for a baud period, and a 0 by a TTL low voltage for a baud period. To send information encoded this way, the transmitter and receiver clocks, which define the baud period, must be synchronized. You'll see later how this is done. The bits are transmitted as separate groups, typically 8 bits long, called *characters*. The name character is used because each group of bits represents one letter of the alphabet when text is being sent. In the standard asynchronous format, the time between characters when no data is being transmitted is indicated by a steady high voltage, called a *mark*. The transmitter tells the receiver that a character is about to start by sending a low bit known as the *start bit*, as shown in Fig. 10-3. The data bits follow, least significant bit first, with each bit lasting one baud-rate period. A 1 is transmitted as a high baud period and a 0 as a low baud period. Serial receivers and transmitters can be instructed to send or receive as few as 5 or as many as 8 bits per

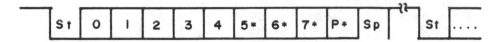

Fig. 10-3. Serial bit stream format. Each character is preceded by a low-level start bit, which synchronizes the receiver and transmitter clocks. The character (5, 6, 7, or 8 bits) follows, least significant bit first. The * indicates optional bits. An optional parity bit and one or more stop (high-level) bits terminate the character.

character (but they must both agree on how many!). In the figure, we indicate these optional bits by asterisks. Typically 8 bits are used so that a character contains an entire byte.

After the desired number of bits is sent out, an optional parity bit P may follow. The parity bit P is useful if the data line is suspected to be too noisy for accurate transmission. For even parity, P = 1 if the number of 1's in the character is odd and P = 0 if the number of 1's is even. That is, P is chosen so that the number of 1's including P is even. For odd parity, P is chosen so that the number of 1's including P is odd. The local receiver checks to make sure that the parity is still the same in spite of the noise incurred over the phone line. If the parity has changed, some bit has flipped its lid, and the receiver sets the parity-error flag in its status register (which the CPU can read if it wants to).

At the end of these bits, the transmitter inserts one or more high *stop* bits into the data stream. Basically the line must come high long enough to allow the receiver to ready itself for the next start bit. Typically one high baud rate period suffices for a stop bit, although transmitters can be instructed to insert 1, 1.5, or 2 stop bits under program control. Because any amount of time can elapse between characters (in addition to the time required for the stop bits) the serial data transmission method just described is called *asynchronous communications*. At least two (1 start and 1 stop) extra bits are required to transmit asynchronous data. So if you want to transmit whole bytes without parity (a very common choice), that's 10 bits. Just as in any business, you have to pay for overhead.

The way the receiving device stays synchronized to the transmitting device so that it can read the bits correctly deserves some comment. It's not obvious how this can be done, since the receiver and transmitter have independent clocks that may differ in frequency by several percent. Also, the voltage changes at the beginning of the baud periods can be shifted in time, owing to the limited bandwidth of the carrier medium. The standard solution to this problem is to have the receiver and transmitter use internal clocks whose frequencies are 16 times the baud rate. Then when the leading edge of the start bit is detected, the incoming serial waveform is sampled every 16 clock periods, starting with the eighth clock period after the leading edge of the start bit. This ensures that the waveform is always sampled near the middle of every baud period and is tolerant of small edge shifts and transmitter/receiver clock frequency differences.

The standard baud rates are: 50 (ham radio with 10-bit characters—some people can decode this speed by ear! Blame the ham radio operator's predicament on the FCC); 110 (yuck! it's an old teletype, better known as a clunk-clunk); 134.5 (ugh! it's an IBM 2741); 150 (too slow); 300 (also very slow, but standard for transmission over phone lines), 1200 (better, also goes over phone lines and is becoming very popular), 2400, 4800, 9600, and 19200 (now you're talking!). Most computer terminals can work at any of these baud rates, but printers and other hard copy devices usually are restricted to the lower rates. Using an 8-bit character with no parity and 1 stop bit, there is a total of 10 bits, so a transmission rate of 300 baud yields 30 characters/second. The general rule is to divide the baud rate by 10 to estimate the transmission rate in characters per second.

Section 9-5 showed that a computer can generate many kinds of waveforms. In particular it can convert a byte into an asynchronous serial bit stream, which it methodically outputs to some pin of a parallel port. The output bits are then buffered so the voltage and current levels conform to one of the conventions described in Sec. 10-3, and out they go to a terminal or modem. Early personal computer systems used this software method for serial communications. The trouble is that it really ties up the CPU and prevents the use of higher speed transmissions. Early in the days of LSI circuits, a special chip called a UART was developed to simultaneously transmit and receive serial data, performing the appropriate parallel/serial conversions and inserting or checking the extra bits used to keep the serial data synchronized. UART is an acronym for universal asynchronous receiver transmitter. A UART is typically configured as four I/O ports: an input status port, an output control port, an output data port, and an input data port. Bytes sent as 8-bit parallel data to the output data port by the computer are converted into a standard-format serial bit stream for transmission by a *transmitter* inside the UART. Similarly, an incoming serial bit stream is detected by a *receiver* inside the UART and converted into parallel data that can be read by the computer from the UART's input data port. Since a byte can start at any time, the serial transmission format is called *asynchronous*, and the name *universal* applies because the UART can work with all popular asynchronous serial formats.

Simultaneous conversion of an incoming and an outgoing serial data stream is called *full duplex*, and requires two data carriers. These carriers could be implemented with three wires: one for the outgoing stream, one for the incoming stream, and the third for a common ground line. Half duplex is sometimes used, which allows two-way communications, hence the name *duplex*, but only one direction is active at a time. It's similar to using walkie-talkies, for which you have to say, "Over," when you're finished talking and want to let the other person talk back. Half duplex has the advantage that only one data channel is required. Over ordinary phone lines, 1200 baud is quite common now using full duplex.

Running half duplex, 2400 baud should be equally reliable. A UART requires some extra circuitry to run in a half duplex mode, however, since the data stream direction has to be turned around electronically. The UART does provide for standard full duplex handshaking conventions.

National Semiconductor 8250 UART

Figure 10-4 shows the National Semiconductor 8250 UART used in the IBM PC family, which works with all popular asynchronous serial formats and internally generates all standard baud rates up to 9600 baud by dividing the crystal-controlled clock input frequency by a programmable 16-bit number. In addition it has an on-chip programmable interrupt controller to handle four kinds of interrupts. First we define the 8250 UART's pins, and then we explain how to program it.

The supply and CPU interface groups are similar to those seen in other smart peripheral IC's, but they provide for substantially more on-chip address decoding. The power/reset group contains the usual +5 volt power line, ground, and an active-high master reset line (MR in the figure).

The CPU interface group contains three chip-select lines (CS0, CS1, and $\overline{\text{CS2}}$), which have to be high, high, and low respectively, before the 8250 is selected. The three address lines (along with the DLAB bit discussed below) choose which internal register is to be read or written. The $\overline{\text{ADS}}$ address strobe line can be used to latch the chip-select and address lines by going low, or, if the address and chip-select lines are valid during CPU data transfers (as they are on the PC), $\overline{\text{ADS}}$ can be connected to ground. DISTR (data input strobe) going high and $\overline{\text{DISTR}}$ going low enables the CPU to read the 8250 (provided the 8250 is also selected with the chip select lines), and similarly DOSTR going high and $\overline{\text{DOSTR}}$ going low enables the CPU to write the 8250. Two buffer control lines for external devices are also provided: CSOUT, which goes high when the three chip-select lines are all active, and DDIS, which goes low whenever the CPU is reading the 8250. The last CPU interface line is INTRPT, which, if enabled, goes high whenever one or more of four kinds of interrupt conditions occur and are not masked off. Typically, several of the CPU interface lines are super-fluous in practice, and on the PC, only the $\overline{\text{CS2}}$, $\overline{\text{DISTR}}$, $\overline{\text{DOSTR}}$, and INTRPT lines are used. The rest of the interface lines are either ignored or dummied out (by connecting the lines to +5 volts or ground).

The clock group contains two inputs (XTAL1 and XTAL2), which can be connected to a crystal to control an internal clock oscillator, or an external clock can be connected to XTAL1. There is also a BAUDOUT line, which outputs a frequency equal to 16 times the baud rate, and a receiver clock input (RCLCK). On the PC (and in most serial port circuits), the 8250 receiver clock input is connected to the 8250 BAUDOUT line. UART's require the 16X factor in order to be able to sample bit values in the middle of each baud rate period as described previously.

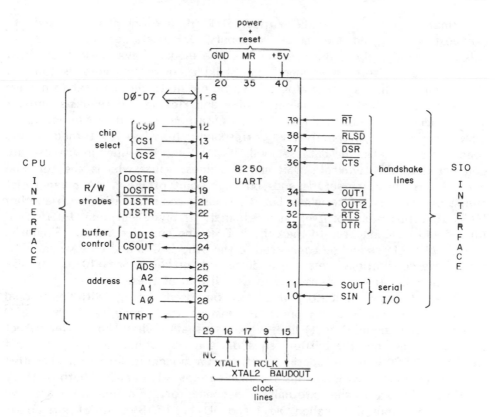

Fig. 10–4. Pinout of the National Semiconductor 8250 UART used in the IBM PC family. The pins are grouped into four main categories: power/reset, clock, serial I/O interface, and CPU interface. The serial I/O interface consists of handshake lines (4 inputs and 4 outputs) and the 2 serial data lines. The CPU interface consists of 8 bidirectional data lines, 2 read and 2 write strobes, 3 chip selects, 2 buffer control outputs, 2 address lines accompanied by an address–latch strobe, and 1 interrupt line. NC on pin 29 means no connection.

The serial interface group contains the receive data serial input line SIN and the transmit data serial output line SOUT. These lines carry the serial data in the format of Fig. 10-3. In addition there are four general purpose output pins and four general purpose input pins to be used for handshaking or anything else you'd like. The values on these pins do not affect the operation of the 8250 itself in any way, except that changes in the input lines can cause interrupts. Instead, the handshake lines can be read and written by the computer via the 8250's internal registers. The basic purpose of the lines is to allow a program to synchronize the data flow with the remote device.

Consider data transmission between a computer terminal and a modem (a device used to send serial data over telephone lines, see Sec. 10-4) coordinated by two handshake outputs, $\overline{DTR}$ (**d**ata **t**erminal **r**eady) and $\overline{RTS}$ (**r**equest **t**o **s**end), and two handshake inputs, DSR (**d**ata **s**et **r**eady) and $\overline{CTS}$ (**c**lear **t**o **s**end). Both the terminal and the modem have these four lines. The traditional "terminal-modem" handshaking convention goes as follows: the terminal pulls its $\overline{DTR}$ and $\overline{RTS}$ low, indicating to the data set (a modem or a computer), that the terminal is alive and kicking and requests permission to send. The terminal's $\overline{DTR}$ and $\overline{RTS}$ are connected to the data set's $\overline{DSR}$ and $\overline{CTS}$ lines, respectively. Correspondingly, when it's turned on and ready to send data, the data set pulls its $\overline{DTR}$ and $\overline{RTS}$ lines low; these are connected to the terminal's $\overline{DSR}$ and $\overline{CTS}$ lines. Just who is the terminal and who is the data set depends on your point of view. A given UART thinks of itself as the terminal, but it's usually communicating with another UART that also thinks of itself as a terminal. In any event, one UART's $\overline{DTR}$ line should be connected to the other's $\overline{DSR}$ line and vice versa. Similarly, one UART's $\overline{RTS}$ should be connected to the other's $\overline{CTS}$ and vice versa. The way these connections are made is discussed further in Sec. 10-3. As discussed in Sec. 10-4, modems tend to use all four of these lines.

The $\overline{RI}$ (**r**ing **i**ndicator) line can be used (along with additional hardware) to allow a computer to answer the phone, and the $\overline{RLSD}$ (**r**eceived **l**ine **s**ignal **d**etect) line, which is usually called the carrier detect line, indicates that the carrier (an audio tone on which serial signals sent over the phone lines are superimposed) from a modem is detected. The IBM serial port board (asynchronous communications adapter) has both of these lines brought out to the external serial connector. Finally, there are two unassigned output lines called $\overline{OUT1}$ and $\overline{OUT2}$. In IBM's serial port board, $\overline{OUT2}$ is used to enable interrupt requests on the INTRPT line, and $\overline{OUT1}$ is not used.

For computer-computer communications (see Sec. 10-5), the $\overline{DTR}$ and $\overline{DSR}$ lines can be very useful to synchronize data transmission. But they're all you need: you can usually forget about the $\overline{CTS}$ and $\overline{RTS}$ lines (although you may have to make sure they have the right voltage values). In fact, handshaking can be done with the serial lines SIN and SOUT themselves, using ©S and ©Q as discussed in Sec. 10-5, thereby avoiding the handshake line maze.

Programming the 8250 UART

That's all 40 pins. Now let's see how to program the 8250 UART to convert data according to the various asynchronous serial formats. The 8250 appears to the CPU as seven consecutive ports, accessing 10 registers as summarized in Fig. 10-5. You can receive and transmit serial data by simply executing IN and OUT instructions to the receive and transmit data registers, respectively. But before the 8250 can work, its control and baud-rate divisor registers have to be initialized. On the IBM PC, this can be accomplished painlessly by an INT 14H call with AH = 0 and with the bits in AL set as follows:

PORT	REGISTER SELECTED	DLAB BIT
3F8	Transmit data (output)	0
3F8	Receive data (input)	0
3F8	Baud rate divisor L byte	1
3F9	Baud rate divisor H byte	1
3F9	Interrupt enable	0
3FA	Interrupt ID	
3FB	Line control	
3FC	Modem control	
3FD	Line status	
3FE	Modem status	

Fig. 10-5. 8250 UART ports and associated registers. The port addresses here are for the first serial port (COM1) on the IBM PC. The ports for COM2 are 100H lower, starting at 2F8H. The address lines A0, A1, and A2 choose the port number relative to this offset. The DLAB bit is bit 7 of the line control register (3FB).

bits 1,0   = word length (10 gives 7 bits, 11 gives 8 bits)
bit 2   = number of stop bits (0 gives 1 SB, 1 gives 2 SB)
bit 3   = parity enabled (1) or disabled (0)
bit 4   = even (1) or odd (0) parity if bit 3 = 1
bits 7,6,5 = the values 000 through 111 give baud rates of 110, 150,
             300, 600, 1200, 2400, 4800, and 9600 baud respectively.

A popular choice is AL = 0E3H, for 9600 baud, no parity, 1 stop bit, and 8-bit words. To set this up you can just use:

```
mov    ax,0e3h     ;AH = 0 for serial port initialization call
int    14h         ;Use the BIOS routine
```

The alternative to doing this is to program the baud rate divisor latches and the line control register directly. See the IBM PC *Technical Reference* manual for a description of the individual bits in each 8250 register.

The IBM PC*jr* uses an input clock frequency of 1.7895 MHz instead of the PC's 1.8432 MHz. This clock frequency (with the appropriate values in the baud rate divisor latches) gives accurate baud rates up to 4800, but the 9600 baud divisor of 12 gives a baud rate with a 3% error. This generally works fine, but if you use the PC*jr*'s ROM BIOS to set this baud rate, it suppresses the possibility. Hence the code above produces 4800 baud. You can still run 9600 baud on a PC*jr* by writing the baud rate divisor latches yourself, but you'll lose serial data if you type anything on the keyboard while sending serial data at a rate faster than 1200 baud.

The ROM BIOS INT 14H call also allows you to send and receive serial data, and to check the serial port status. Unfortunately, you may not be able to use these routines for anything but modem communications. The problem is that the routines check the handshake lines with a countdown loop that times out too fast for most purposes. This causes characters to be lost if you're sending data to a device that must stop receiving data for anything more than a very brief time. To illustrate how you can write your own serial port drivers, we present some basic simple working routines (see also Sec. 4-6). Polling techniques are used rather than interrupts here (see Sec. 10-5 for more advanced routines) and the programs assume that the line-control parameters (stop bits, parity, and word length) and the baud rate have already been set by the INT 14H initialization call. To properly send or receive data from the 8250's data port (port 3F8), you need to know how to control the $\overline{DTR}$ and $\overline{RTS}$ output handshake lines, how to monitor the $\overline{DSR}$ and $\overline{CTS}$ input handshake lines, and how to detect when serial data has been received or more data can be transmitted.

Control of the output handshake lines is accomplished through the *modem control register* (port 3FC). To drive the $\overline{DTR}$ output low, indicating that the 8250 is operational, you must set bit 0 of this register to 1. Similarly, bit 1 = 1 forces $\overline{RTS}$ low, indicating that the 8250 is ready to receive data. You can pull both lines low with the code

```
mov    dx,3fch      ;Point at modem control register
mov    al,3         ;Force DTR and RTS low
out    dx,al
```

Section 10-5 discusses how to use the $\overline{DTR}$ line for handshaking; for now, we just make sure both $\overline{DTR}$ and $\overline{RTS}$ are low, since the remote device typically won't send or receive any data unless they are! Similarly the $\overline{OUT1}$ and $\overline{OUT2}$ are forced low by setting bits 2 and 3 high in the modem control register. $\overline{OUT2}$ must be low for 8250 interrupts to occur with the IBM PC serial adapters, although not on the PC*jr*. Setting bit 4 high causes the 8250's serial and handshake outputs to be looped back into the corresponding inputs for testing purposes. Bits 5—7 are always 0.

The state of the handshake input lines can be read as bits in the *modem status register* (port 3FE). As for the outputs, everything is inverted so that 1's correspond to low pin values and 0's to high values. Specifically bits 4—7 give the state of $\overline{CTS}$, $\overline{DSR}$, RI, and RLSD, respectively. Bits 0—3 give the corresponding delta or change signals. For example, if the $\overline{CTS}$ value has changed since the last time the modem status register was read, bit 0 is set to 1. Such changes can also be programmed to cause an interrupt. Section 10-4 shows how to use the $\overline{DSR}$ input for handshaking. For now, just ignore this register.

The *line status register* (port 3FD) is used to monitor the status of the serial lines. The DR bit, bit 0, tells whether data has been received, and the THRE bit, bit 5, tells whether the transmitter holding register is empty. If THRE = 1, the last character sent has been transmitted and you can send another character; if DR = 1, a character has been received and is ready to be read by the CPU. Other bits in the line status register are set to 1 if overrun (bit 1), parity (bit 2), or framing (bit 3) errors have occurred. Bit 4 = 1 announces that a break interrupt has occurred, that is, a space value for longer than a full-word transmission time has been received. Bit 6 = 1 says the transmit shift register is empty. Such a value implies that *two* characters can be sent, one that immediately goes into this shift register to be sent over the SOUT line, and one that waits its turn in the transmit holding register.

Summarizing the initialization, serial input, and serial output concepts, we have the following minimum serial port routines:

```
mctl    = 3fch               ;Modem control port for COM1 on PC
lstat   = mctl+1             ;Line status port

init:   mov    ax,0e3h       ;Set up for 9600 baud, 1 stop bit, no parity,
        int    14h           ; 8 bit words.  Use IBM PC ROM BIOS routine
        mov    dx,mctl       ;Point at modem control register
        mov    al,3          ;Force DTR and RTS low
        out    dx,al
        ret

serin:  push   dx            ;Input a character
        mov    dx,lstat      ;Point at the line status register
serin2: in     al,dx         ;Get status
        test   al,1          ;Character there?
        jz     serin2
        sub    dx,5          ;Yep.  Point at data register
        in     al,dx         ;Get character
        pop    dx
        ret

serout: push   dx            ;Output character in al
        push   ax            ;Save it
        mov    dx,lstat
serou2: in     al,dx         ;Get line status
        test   al,20h        ;Check THRE
        jz     serou2
        sub    dx,5          ;Holding reg empty; point at data port
        pop    ax
        out    dx,al         ;Output char
        pop    dx
        ret
```

As for the Centronics driver discussed in Sec. 10-1, a better routine checks the keyboard for input during the status wait loops. This allows you to quit trying to read data that isn't there or waiting for transmissions that are blocked by incorrect handshake signals. The keyboard status check is accomplished very nicely on the PC using an INT 16H call with AH = 1. This sets the zero flag to 1 if no character has been typed, and resets ZF if a character has been typed and returns that character in AX. The nice thing about this routine is that it leaves the character in the system input buffer, so you can peek at the keyboard input queue to see if a control C has been typed (a ©C means quit what you're doing, just as Ctrl Break does) without modifying the queue. The calling routine can read in the ©C if you want it to, or whatever. Such a routine for serial input reads as follows:

```
serin:    push    dx              ;Input a character
          mov     dx,lstat        ;Point at the line status register
serin2:   in      al,dx           ;Get status
          test    al,1            ;Character there?
          jnz     serin4
          mov     ah,1            ;Peek at keyboard input queue
          int     16
          jz      serin2
          cmp     al,3            ;Something typed. ©C?
          jnz     serin2
          pop     dx              ;©C typed.  Return to calling program,
          ret                     ; which should handle ©C appropriately

serin4:   sub     dx,5            ;Char present.  Point at data register
          in      al,dx           ;Get char
          pop     dx
          ret
```

See the IBM PC *Technical Reference* manual for further discussion of the 8250 pins and registers, and for the serial BIOS routines. See also Sec. 10-5 for interrupt-driven and handshaking serial routines. Section 4-6 and App. D contain complete serial drivers.

10-3. RS-232, Current-Loop, and Other Serial Conventions

You've now seen how a UART converts parallel data in the computer to and from serial bit streams. However, the TTL output of a UART like the 8250 cannot be transmitted error-free over any distance. The 8250's serial output doesn't have adequate drive power, and, in any event, TTL voltage levels don't have sufficient noise immunity to work reliably for distances longer than a few feet. To be sent over a distance, the TTL signals must be converted to another form. The two most popular forms are RS-232, which

is a voltage level convention, and current loop, which dates from early
telegraphy. For low data rates, current loop signals can go across the
country, which is why current loop was used for the telegraph. In addition,
current loop is easily implemented using optoisolators, which prevents wiring
mistakes from doing any damage. This is valuable in connecting microcomputers up to bigger computers. In contrast, RS-232 may cause hardware
damage if it is improperly connected. The RS-232 convention is rated for
distances only up to 50 feet but in practice can go at least 100 feet at 9600
baud (and farther at slower rates or with proper shielding). RS-232 is often
used for terminal-modem and terminal-computer connections and in general
is much more widely used than current loop.

   Since current loop is the simpler of the two conventions, we consider it
first. Figure 10-6 shows a circuit connecting the serial output (SOUT) line
of one UART to the serial input (SIN) line of a different UART some
distance away. both UART's are optoisolated from the current loop connecting path (see Sec. 9-1), which has its own power supply. The current
loop supply voltage and resistor are chosen to maintain about 20 mA flowing
in the loop when the transmitter (labelled TxD in the figure) is high. A low
value yields no current flow. So a 1 is represented by a baud period of
20-mA current flow and a 0 by a period of no current. Two loops of the
kind in Fig. 10-6 are needed for full duplex operation, so four wires are
required. To wire up a current loop, connect the UART's SOUT to the point
labelled TxD, and RxD on the other end of the circuit to SIN.

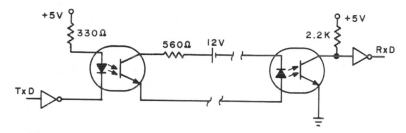

Fig. 10-6. A single-path optically isolated 20-mA current loop circuit.
A pair of these circuits makes a full duplex link, although the modem
control signals are missing. 1's are represented by a 20-mA current
flow; 0's by the absence of current flow.

   Ordinarily, current loop doesn't support the modem control signals $\overline{DTR}$,
$\overline{DSR}$, $\overline{RTS}$ and $\overline{CTS}$, so you just tie $\overline{CTS}$ and $\overline{DSR}$ low and keep the data rate
slow enough that no handshake is needed. If needed, a BUSY handshake
signal can be derived by NANDing SOUT with DTR on the end of the link
receiving high-speed data, and sending this signal back on the return link to
the data source, where it should be NORed with the Q output of a 74123
retriggerable one-shot clocked by the same signal. The one-shot is set to
time-out after one character time. Probably the best method of creating a
handshake, however, is to use the ©S/©Q protocol described in Sec. 10-5.

The most common serial communications method is a voltage level convention called *RS-232*. RS-232 is a standard set by the EIA (Electronic Industries Association) and represents 1's by -3 to -20 volts, and 0's by +3 to +20 volts. This gives a larger voltage swing as well as a zero crossing and is much more noise-immune than TTL levels. The RS-232 standard also defines a standard connector for serial communications, namely the 25-pin D-shell connector, also known as a DB-25 connector. Somehow the writers of the RS-232 convention also managed to define every pin on this 25-pin connector. The standard supports not only the DTR, DSR, RTS, and CTS handshake lines but a host of other signals as well. Fortunately a maximum of only nine pins are typically used, and if you're willing to cut a few corners you may be able to get by with only two!

Two IC's are normally used to handle the conversion of TTL-level signals to RS-232 level signals: the 1488 (Fig. 10-7a) has three NAND gates and one inverter that convert from TTL to RS-232, and the 1489 (Fig. 10-7b) has four inverters that go from RS-232 to TTL. We wish someone would make a single IC that has two transmitters and two receivers, since many applications need only one or two signal lines per direction. Table 10-1 defines the nine most commonly used pins of the RS-232 25-pin connector both from the point of view of a terminal and from that of a modem or computer. IBM likes to use the term DTE (data

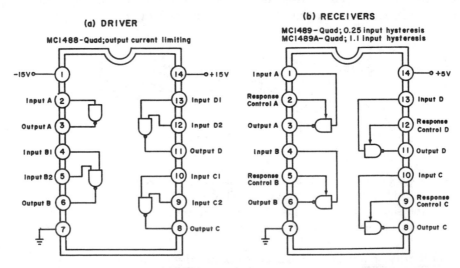

Fig. 10-7. (a) The 1488 TTL to RS-232 converter. (b) The 1489 RS-232 to TTL converter. Each package converts four signal lines. The 1489 receiver has a Schmitt trigger input and includes a response control pin, which can be used to set the switching threshold and frequency response of the gate. Normally the response control pin is left unconnected. The power supply voltages for the 1488 can range from +7 to +15 volts on the positive supply line, and -2.5 to -15 volts on the negative supply line.

RS-232 DEFINITION	I/O	TERMINAL DTE	MODEM DCE
Signal Ground		1	1
Transmit Data (SOUT)	O	2	3
Receive Data (SIN)	I	3	2
Request To Send (RTS)	O	4	5
Clear To Send (CTS)	I	5	4
Data Set Ready (DSR)	I	6	20
Chassis Ground		7	7
Carrier Detect (CD)		8 (input)	8 (output)
Data Terminal Ready (DTR)	O	20	6

Table 10-1. Pin numbers for the most commonly used RS-232 lines, from both the terminal and the modem (or computer) points of view. Devices wired like terminals are often called DTE's (**data terminal equipment**), and devices like modems or computers are called DCE's (**data communications equipment**). By connecting wires straight through, line 2 to line 2, line 3 to line 3, and so on, a terminal's transmitted data becomes the modem's received data, etc. To connect two devices of the same nature, such as two terminals, one device's line 2 must be connected to the other's line 3, and so forth. A cable wired this way is called a null modem.

terminal equipment) for anything that behaves like a terminal, and to use the term DCE (**data communications equipment**) for anything that behaves like a computer or a modem. Note that the meanings of six lines are interchanged between the two points of view, since, for example, the terminal's SOUT has to go to the computer's SIN. The convention assigns a male connector (the one with pins sticking out) to the terminal and a female connector (the one with holes for pins to fit into) to the modem or computer. If you don't want to use all the handshake lines in an RS-232 link (or the device on one end doesn't support the same handshake as the device on the other end), you can *dummy out* various control lines. Specifically, by connecting pin 4 to pin 5 you dummy out the RTS/CTS protocol, and by connecting pin 6 to pin 20 you dummy out the DTR/DSR protocol. You may also have to dummy out the carrier detect line 8 by connecting it to pin 21.

In any event, you should use a male connector (DB-25P) for terminals and a female connector (DB-25S) for modems or computers, and observe the corresponding definitions of pins 2 and 3. A minimal installation just connects up 2 and 3 appropriately and depends on the built-in chassis grounds to complete the circuits. In fact, we've run 9600-baud communications around a house that way, although the dedicated ground lines on pins 1 and 7 are highly recommended if noise is a problem (or if the building's wiring lacks the chassis ground wire required by the National Electrical Code).

The IBM PC is hooked up as a DTE with a male DB-25 plug instead of a DCE, so its designers must have thought it was more a terminal than a computer! In fact, the connectors on any piece of equipment can have either sex, so you'll often find a need for devices called gender changers, which consist of two male or two female DB-25 connectors connected by straight-through wires. Another useful piece of equipment is a *null modem*, which is an RS-232 cable with pin 2 on one end connected to pin 3 on the other end, 3 connected to 2, 4 to 5, 5 to 4, 6 to 20, 20 to 6, and 7 to 7. We've often found it useful to put null modem wiring into a female-female gender changer. This enables you to connect the IBM PC's serial port connector to other DTE devices like serial printers using a standard straight-through male-male cable. Because the number of possible ways of assigning and using RS-232 lines is so large, you may want to buy a device called an RS-232 *breakout box* to determine what signals go where. Ironically, RS-232 has earned the distinction of being the most nonstandard standard in electronics!

Figure 10-8 shows an RS-232 interface circuit that supports SOUT (labeled TxD), SIN (labeled RxD), DTR, DSR, RTS, and CTS. Note that the 1488 and 1489 invert the signals passing through them, so all signals on the RS-232 cables are inverted from their values at the UART. Thus the

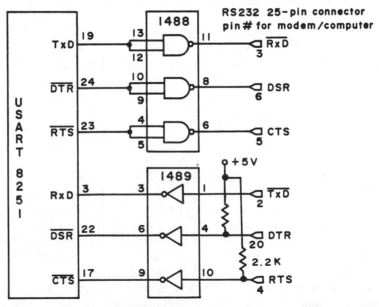

Fig. 10-8. Computer (or modem) RS-232 interface supporting the DTR, DSR, RTS, and CTS modem control lines. The 25-pin connector pins are labeled from the terminal's (DTE) point of view, while the inverted computer labels appear on the UART.

handshake lines are all active high when observed on the cable. Note also that this interface works with or without the control protocol, since the input handshake lines are pulled up. Many interfaces work this way, requiring you only to connect pins 2 and 3 (and one of the ground lines 1 or 7).

To initially check out the operation of a serial hookup, connect the serial output line on the serial connector to the serial input line. Your serial port should then act like a slow, expensive 1-byte memory. If not, try connecting the UART's SOUT directly to its SIN. If the UART still doesn't act like a memory byte, check your UART wiring and initialization code. Once you've gotten everything working this way, connect up your two devices and start worrying about the handshake lines if it doesn't work.

Useful trick: you can tell whether a given pin on an RS232 connector is being driven, by measuring its voltage with respect to the signal ground on pin 7 (sometimes you need to use pin 1). The output data line (2 or 3) will have about -12 volts and the input data line (3 or 2) will have nearly 0 volts. A driven handshake line (4, 5, 6, 20) will have about +12 volts.

10-4. Modems

When two devices are sufficiently close to one another, you can wire them together using the RS-232 or the current-loop convention. This approach allows the highest baud rates to be used. But for devices separated by substantial distances, a telephone line may be the only practical way to make a connection. This section describes how the phone can be used for low-speed data communications, typically at 300 or 1200 baud. Although these data rates are not very desirable for interactive programming, they're fine for shipping files between computers while you do something else.

The phone was designed by various telephone company wizards who discovered that a frequency bandwidth of 3000 Hz provides adequate fidelity to carry voice communications. They also invented an ingenious device called the *duplexer*, which allows two wires to carry voices in both directions at the same time. This duplexing is a special case of multiplexing, in which many signals are carried over the same line. At distances less than 100 miles or so, you can argue with a friend over the phone, both talking at once. This is full duplex. For longer distances, the finite speed of the electrical signals would lead to a returned echo somewhat after you said something, making it very hard to talk. Consequently, long distance communications use echo suppressors, which require the talkers to take turns talking. This is half-duplex operation. If you've ever fiddled with your phone wires, you've probably discovered that only two of the three or more wires are used for talking, ringing the bell, and dialing. In the four-conductor modular telephone cable, the middle pair, the red and green wires, do the job, when attached to the correct terminals. Taking the phone off the hook closes the phone circuit, drawing current and connecting you up with the local switching station. By touch tone, ordinary dialing, or rapidly pushing the hook button, you can dial a number.

More recent inventors figured out how to use this convenient facility to transmit low speed digital data in both directions simultaneously, that is, full duplex. Specifically, they allocated a frequency band from about 2025 to 2225 Hz to be used by the device that answers a phone call, and a band from about 1070 to 1270 Hz for the device that originated the phone call (see Fig. 10-9). The 1's level or "mark" is represented by 2225- and 1270-Hz tones for the answerer and originator, respectively. Tones of 2025 and 1070 Hz are used for the corresponding 0's level or "space." The device that translates an RS-232 serial bit stream into these frequencies is called a *modem*, short for **mo**dulator/**dem**odulator. The modulation technique is called **f**requency **s**hift **k**eying (FSK) because the modem shifts the transmitted frequency from one value to the other depending on whether a "1" or a "0" is being sent. To start up a connection, the modem answering the phone puts a steady 2225-Hz tone on the phone line, causing the modem on the originating end to reply with a steady 1270-Hz tone. When this handshake has occurred, both modems set their respective CTS lines high (as well as CD, carrier detect), allowing communications to proceed.

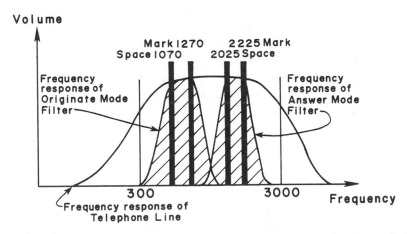

Fig. 10-9. Originate and answer mode frequency pass bands used for full-duplex, 300-baud data communication on phone lines.

Until a few years ago, people used *acoustic modems*, which utilize a cradle with rubber cups in which to lay the telephone receiver. The cradle has a microphone and a speaker, and you can even hear the data conversation if you listen carefully. To start the communication process, you dial the remote computer and wait until you hear the 2225-Hz signal. Then you press the phone receiver into the modem cradle. This method was particularly popular back when it was difficult or illegal to connect wires directly to the phone line; with the acoustic modem, the connection is electrically isolated by a sound link.

Today most modems can be plugged directly into modular phone plug jacks and are called *direct-connect modems*. To protect both the phone network from the modem and the modem from the phone network, the circuitry in this kind of connection must be approved by the Federal Communications Commission. Many modems include microprocessor-controlled circuitry that can both answer the phone and automatically dial phone calls. To take advantage of both facilities, such a modem must be able to transmit and receive as either an originator or an answerer. This type of device is advertised as an *originate/answer modem*. In general, the transmitter filters in a modem should be characterized by six or more poles, and the receiver filters by eight or more poles. This leads to quite reliable data communications over ordinary phone lines. The filters essentially prevent a modem from hearing an echo of the modem's own transmission, and consequently the echo suppressors used for long distance voice communications are not needed. The echo suppressors turn off automatically when modem frequencies are detected, allowing full duplex data communications to take place.

Modems operating at 1200 baud are also becoming popular. Although more expensive, it's usually worth it to get the factor of four increase in speed. The accepted standard for 1200-baud modems is known as Bell 212A. Make sure that what you buy is compatible with this standard.

Excellent smart 300/1200 baud, originate/answer/auto-dial direct-connect modems for computers are available from companies like Hayes Microcomputer Products, and a number of plug-in modem boards are available for the IBM PC. It may be worth the extra money to buy a separate modem instead of a plug-in board, because it doesn't use up a slot in the PC (although it does require a serial port) and it can be used with other computers as well. Also, 2400-baud modems work well on ordinary phone lines.

Many PC's are being used as smart terminals hooked to IBM mainframes. Serial RS232 communications provide one way to accomplish this, but many cards and programs are now available that emulate the IBM 3270 and later terminals. Although relatively expensive, this method operates at much higher data rates than typical RS232 rates and is the most natural way to communicate with IBM mainframes. Using a PC instead of a terminal allows you to record the time-sharing session on local disk for later perusal. You can also prepare files locally using a convenient high-speed screen editor and then ship them over the link.

10-5. Computer-Computer Communications

There are many software protocols for computer-computer communications, ranging from "hands on" to automatic. This section considers some very rudimentary approaches and summarizes some of the more elegant systems that are available for the IBM PC (and other) computers. If the computers in question are both PC's (or at least have compatible disk drives and the same disk format), often the best way to transfer data is to just take a diskette from one machine to the other. Taking a box of disks to a friend who lives 10 minutes away gives an effective data rate of about 50 kilobaud! If this is inconvenient or impossible, other methods must be used.

If the same communications program for both computers is commercially available, just get a serial communications link between the two computers running, run the communications program on both machines, and transfer files from one computer to the other using the program's commands. Many such programs exist for the IBM PC and other microcomputers. A good example is a program called CROSSTALK from MicroStuf, which runs on IBM PC's and compatibles as well as on other computers like the Victor 9000. To transfer files, run CROSSTALK on both the source and target computers. Then either computer can be used to transfer the files. With some loss of convenience, you can also transfer files using a variety of protocols by using CROSSTALK to make the computer emulate a terminal, a concept we turn to now.

All too often, you'll find that you want to transfer files between two different and incompatible computers, with no commercial file transfer program available to help you out. In this situation, the simplest and most general method is to program one of the computers (which we'll call the local computer) to act like a computer terminal. Then it's usually no trouble to get the other computer (which we'll call the remote computer) to accept its input from or send its output to the local computer "terminal." If the remote computer is a large mainframe, it will automatically expect to communicate with a terminal. The major disadvantage of this method is that a human being has to oversee the transfer. The concept is illustrated in Fig. 10-10 and can be implemented by a communication loop like the following code:

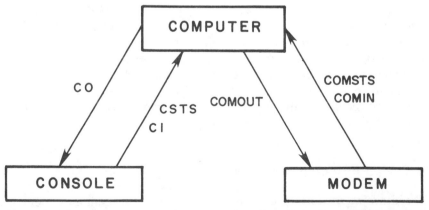

Fig. 10-10. Diagram showing how characters typed on local terminal are relayed by the local computer to the modem (or remote computer) and vice versa. One special local character such as control R (©R) is reserved and used to return to the local computer's operating system.

```
commprt  equ    3f8h            ;8250 data port addr for COM1 on IBM PC

commpg:  mov    dx,commprt      ;Point at communications base port
commlp:  call   comsts          ;Serial character received?
         jz     ctest
         call   comin           ;Yes.  Get it from serial port
         call   co              ;Output it to local console
ctest:   call   csts            ;Local character typed?
         jz     commlp
         call   ci              ;Yes.  Get it (call console input)
         cmp    al,"R"-40H      ;Was ©R typed?
         jnz    csend
         ret                    ;Yes: Return to local system
csend:   call   comout          ;No: Send character to serial device
         jmp    commlp


comsts:  add    dx,6            ;Modem input status routine
         in     al,dx           ;Get modem status in AH.  Has handshake
         mov    ah,al           ; information used by later routines
         nop                    ;Accesses to 8250 must be at least
         dec    dx              ; 2 microseconds apart
         in     al,dx           ;Get line status in AL
         sub    dx,5            ;Leave DX pointing at data port
         test   al,1            ;Return nonzero if character received
         ret

comin:   call   comsts          ;Serial input routine
         jz     comin
         in     al,dx
         ret


comout:  push   ax              ;Serial output routine
comou2:  call   comsts
         test   al,20h          ;Transmitter ready for another char?
         jz     comou2
         pop    ax              ;Yep, send it
         out    dx,al
         ret
```

The console input routine CI, the console output routine CO, and the console status routine CSTS can just be simple subroutines that make the appropriate DOS function call via INT 21H. This communication loop ships whatever you type on the local keyboard to the remote computer, and displays whatever the remote computer sends on the local CRT. To transfer a file to the remote computer, you first execute COMMLP to log onto the remote computer. You then tell the remote computer to copy input from the terminal into a disk file. On a Digital Equipment DEC10, for example, you would type:

.PIP filename=TTY: (cr)

The "." is inserted by the DEC10, and (cr) means carriage return.   On a
Data General Eclipse you would type:

) COPY filename @CONSOLE (cr)

where the ")" is inserted by the Eclipse. Each computer has its own copy-
from-terminal command. After typing the copy command, you type ©R to
return to your local system. You then type an appropriate local command
to transfer the file from memory or disk to the serial output (COMOUT).
When finished, you execute the communication loop again and type an end-
of-file character. This is ©Z for a DEC10 and ©D for an Eclipse.

   Transferring a file from the remote computer back to the local computer is slightly harder. You log on to the remote computer as before and
type

.TYPE filename

The trouble is that as soon as the carriage return for this command is typed,
the remote computer will start typing the file before you've had a chance
to instruct the local computer to read from the serial input into local
storage. There are several ways to get around this problem. The basic idea
is to have the input routine that is used to read in the file send the carriage
return for the TYPE command when the input routine starts to execute.

   A couple of practices are helpful or even necessary. To speed up data
transmission from the remote computer, tell it that your 'terminal' has
hardware tabs. That way it won't expand all tabs into spaces. Also turn
off page mode on the remote computer (if it has one). For local-to-remote
transfers, tell the remote computer not to echo (send back to you) the
characters you send it. Although mainframe computer systems usually can
accept data all day at 300 baud, they tend to get behind in echoing at this
rate, and you'll lose data. Higher baud rates require the use of a handshake
protocol. This can be done using either a software or a hardware handshake. The standard software handshake method is the ©S/©Q protocol,
also known as the *DC1/DC3* or *XON/XOF*F protocol. The way it works is
very simple. The remote computer sends a control S (©S) when it wants the
terminal to stop sending data and sends a ©Q when it's ready to receive
data again. You can implement this handshake on the local computer with
the output routine

```
comout: push    ax          ;Output routine with ©S/©Q handshake
comou2: call    comsts      ;Remote input available?
        jz      comou6
```

```
                call    comin           ;Yes.  Get it
                cmp     al,"S"-40H      ;©S?
                jnz     comou2
waitq:          call    comin           ;©S found.  Hang for a ©Q
                and     al,7fH
                cmp     al,"Q"-40H
                jnz     waitq
                jmp     comou2


comou6:         test    al,20h          ;Ready for transmission?
                jz      comou2
                pop     ax              ;Yes, get character
                out     dx,al           ;And send it
                ret
```

As with the earlier version, this routine assumes that DX is already pointing to the serial data port.

An older software handshake, the *ACK/NAK*, is the only handshake used by the early Diablo daisy-wheel printers and is still recognized by many machines. These printers have a 140-character input buffer. To prevent this buffer from overflowing, you send fewer than 140 characters followed by a ©C (ACK), and then wait for a ©F (NAK) to be returned. When the printer has processed the characters up to and including the ©C, it sends back a ©F, signaling that it can accept another buffer full of characters.

Alternatively, for hard-wired communications through UART's, you can use the DTR signal as a handshake to control data transmission. This approach is sometimes called *reverse channel*. For this method, the COMOUT routine requires both THRE and DSR to be active before shipping a character. By pulling its DTR bit low (recall that the handshake lines are active high on the serial cable), the destination computer can then deactivate the source computer's DSR to stop data transfer. The corresponding COMOUT routine becomes (bit meanings appropriate for UART)

```
comout:         push    ax              ;Serial output with handshaking
comou2:         call    comsts          ;Check UART status byte
                and     ax,2020h        ;Examine DSR and THRE bits
                xor     ax,2020h        ;Both high?
                jnz     comou2
                pop     ax              ;Yes
                out     dx,al           ;Send the character
                ret
```

You should be aware that some equipment has a hardware handshake that uses CTS instead of DTR. For these, you must replace the 2020H in the above code by 1020H.

If neither the ©S/©Q nor the DTR technique can be used, you can have the remote computer echo the characters it receives and wait for an echoed character to come back before sending another. For one reason or another, this approach never seems to work as reliably as the other techniques. Remote computers love to send out "helpful" additional characters.

The serial input and output routines can be run using interrupts along the lines discussed in Sec. 7-1. IR4 (interrupt request line 4) is reserved for COM1 serial interrupts. The skeleton for a serial-input interrupt routine reads as follows:

```
eoi      = 20h                ;End Of Interrupt command
pictrl   = 20h                ;8259A interrupt controller control port
picmsk   = 21h                ;Interrupt mask port
serdat   = 3f8h               ;Serial data port

;Set up serial input interrupts

         lea     dx,serint
         mov     ax,250ch     ;Use IRQ4 line for COM1
         int     21h          ;Take over interrupt vector
         in      al,picmsk
         and     al,0efh      ;Unmask serial interrupts
         out     picmsk,al
         mov     ax,0e3h      ;Set up 8250 for 9600 baud, 1 SB, no
         int     14h          ; parity, 8-bit words.  Use BIOS routine
         mov     dx,serdat+4  ;Point at modem control register
         mov     al,0bh       ;Force DTR, RTS, and OUT2 low
         out     dx,al
         mov     al,1
         mov     dx,serdat+1
         out     dx,al        ;Enable 8250 data ready interrupts
         ...                  ;Other code

;Serial interrupt handler

serint:  push    ax
         ...                  ;Code to do serial input goes here
         mov     al,eoi       ;Tell 8259A that interrupt's over
         out     pictrl,al
         pop     ax
         iret
```

The IBM PC BIOS uses a convention allowing up to four 8250's to be running together. Their port addresses are stored in RAM memory at locations 40:0—40:7. On entry to INT 14H, DX must contain the number (0—3) of the desired 8250. INT 14H uses this number to pick up the proper port addresses out of RAM.

A variety of terminal emulation packages are available for the IBM PC that support all the features discussed here and more. These are often worth the prices asked, because writing a really good, flexible terminal emulation program is no easy task.

Other more sophisticated serial communications methods can also be used on the PC to link a number of computers together. These are the various computer networking methods. The schemes commonly used to link many microcomputers together are called local area networks (LAN's), and those used to link PC's to IBM mainframes are called system network architectures (SNA's). Examples of LAN's are PCnet and OMNINET, which allow several PC's to communicate among each other, and the popular EtherNet, which allows all computers on the network to share resources. DOS 3.1 contains a fair amount of networking software that helps to standardize file transfer between personal computers. Networks are growing in popularity and in importance. AT&T has introduced StarLAN and IBM has introduced two PC networks, but no clear-cut winner among the competing schemes has yet emerged. The references at the end of the chapter discuss computer networking further.

10-6. Fiber Optic, RF, Powerline, and IR Carriers

Sections 10-2 through 10-5 discussed common serial communications techniques typically used to transmit ASCII codes between computers and terminals. The transmission media used are wires or phone lines. This section considers other kinds of transmission media and other kinds of codes. The media are optical fibers, radio waves, 110-volt AC powerlines, and infrared carrier. Each has special advantages and limitations. Codes other than ASCII are sometimes used in order to take advantage of the characteristics of some of these media. Optical fibers are useful primarily for high-speed data transfers and/or environments in which electric and magnetic fields would seriously impair wire links. The radio frequency (RF) and powerline methods are useful for remote control applications. The infrared carrier is used by the IBM PC*jr* cordless keyboard.

Light waves traveling down optical fibers have become an important communications medium. The lowest-loss fibers consist of a solid cylindrical glass core surrounded by a cylindrical glass cladding. The cladding has a lower index of refraction than the core, so light waves propagating down the fiber are trapped inside by total internal reflection. The best fibers have losses considerably less than 1 decibel/kilometer, that is, it takes about 2 miles to cut the light intensity in half! Optical fibers are used extensively in phone communications and wherever electrical noise is a problem. Since one end of the fiber system literally looks only at light, no electrical connection is made, and no electrical noise is picked up. The fibers can be run without problems in environments containing large ambient electric and magnetic fields. This is particularly handy on airplanes and ships, where the powerful motors present induce large voltage variations in wire systems. In addition, the data transmission capacity of fibers is substantially greater than that of coaxial cables, providing up to 100 times the data handling capability in the same volume. Around the home, you can run fibers on your wall: just paint over them, and no one will notice. Of course, you can also run 36-gauge wire (about the thickness of a hair) on the wall, and no one's likely to notice it either. The wire has the advantage that kinks where the wire goes around a corner are OK. Optical fibers shouldn't be bent in an arc of radius less than 1 inch, and even bends this small can cause large light losses if the fibers are painted over.

The major problem with optical fibers is in shining the light into them and detecting it coming out at the other end. Typically, infrared LED's or injection lasers and matched photodiodes are used to generate and detect the light. In some commercial systems, a short length of fiber is bonded directly onto the LED emitter surface, and a similar length of fiber is bonded onto the surface of a silicon photodiode detector. Optical fiber connectors are then used to connect the short fibers to the main fiber optic cable. Lenses can also be used to focus light down into a fiber (about 0.1 mm diameter) and to collect the transmitted light. Light coupling kits are available for less than $100 from Motorola and other companies. See in particular the TI 74LS462/463 encoder/decoder pair. These 20-pin IC's are all you need to interface TTL to the LED and photodiode. Bytes are input to the 74LS462 and delivered by the 74LS463 at the other end of the cable. Data can be transmitted serially at 1 megabit/second over the fiber in a phase-encoded format. The overall cost is still a lot more than the cost for an RS-232 wire link if the noise and distance limitations of the wire link are unimportant. But the technology is improving rapidly and costs are bound to decrease markedly. Commercially available single-fiber systems are simplex, that is, unidirectional. Two fibers are normally used for full-duplex operation, but it's also possible to transmit bidirectionally on a single fiber, using duplexing devices analogous to those used in two-wire phone communications.

One simple method of encoding data on an optical fiber is analogous to the 20-mA current loop technique, with light playing the role of current. Light on means a mark; light off means a space. With this approach, you modulate the LED current with TTL and transmit ASCII. At very high data rates, fancier encoding techniques are often used.

The second of our nonstandard communications media uses radio waves with codes impressed on a 360-MHz RF carrier wave. This approach is the same as used in garage-door opener systems, and works with up to 200 feet between the transmitter and receiver. A detailed description of circuits that can be used to implement this approach is given in Sargent and Shoemaker (1981). This radio wave method is not trivial to implement, however, since the test equipment necessary to check out the equipment has to have about 400-MHz bandwidth, and all sorts of little details (like leads that stick out too far) can change the operating characteristics of RF circuits.   If you want to build such devices, the 72- or 75-MHz radio control bands or the 27- or 49-MHz unlicensed bands might be better choices.   However, the FCC does have its rules, so even if you keep the power output under 100 milliwatts, you need a license to run such devices. In this connection, it's amusing to note that the remote smoke detectors that use 360-MHz radio waves are allowed to turn on the transmitters for only about 1 second.   It's okay to have your house burn down, but not to emit any extra RF!

A very different data transmission concept employs the AC powerline wiring present in all buildings.   In the United States, this wiring has 60-Hz 110-volt AC current flowing through it.   Since the middle of World War II, radio amateurs have known that the wiring can also be used for transmitting voice around a building and even to other buildings, provided the inductance in the outside power transformers doesn't provide too high an impedance (the impedance or AC resistance of an inductor is proportional to the frequency of the AC current).   Radio Shack and others market FM-intercom systems that modulate the powerlines, and you can transmit high-fidelity sound all over the house in this way.

In recent years, a British company, BSR, has developed and marketed a set of 110-volt AC triac modules that respond to serial codes impressed on a 120-kHz carrier wave.   This high frequency wave is then transmitted over the AC powerlines.   Three kinds of modules are available: 10-ampere appliance modules that plug into the wall and provide a socket for the appliance, 2-ampere lamp modules that plug in the same way and have light dimmer capability, and 2-ampere wall-switch dimmer modules that replace the usual wall switch.   Up to 256 modules can operate in the same system, and each can be selectively turned on or off.   They can be turned on or off in groups of 16 simultaneously, and dimmer modules can be dimmed or brightened. Each 16-module group is assigned a *house code*, so each module has both a house code ("A"—"P") and a unit code (1—16).   The idea is that the most any one home might need is 16 modules, and if you choose house codes different from your neighbor's, your home's control signals won't affect his in the situation where no power transformer blocks the 120-kHz signals.   The modules and controllers are marketed by both Sears and Radio Shack. Special computer-based controllers for the modules are marketed by a number of firms.   In particular, TecMar (Cleveland) makes a plug-in board for the IBM PC, and Bi-Comm Systems (St. Paul, MN) makes a smart controller that interfaces to any computer through an RS-232 serial port.

We now consider the codes used by BSR and show a way of putting them on the powerlines using a microcomputer and $20 worth of opto-isolated hardware.   We are indebted to Jim T. Fulton for his hardware schematic, a description of his system, which uses an Apple II computer, and several helpful discussions.   Since his technique makes it very easy to modulate the powerlines directly and to access all 256 module combinations, we have chosen his method for presentation. Steve Ciarcia (see references) describes an alternative method, which uses a remote-control sonar module marketed by Sears and others. This module can control only the 16 units corresponding to one house code.

Fulton's circuit is shown in Fig. 10-11. Two capacitors are connected to the 110-volt powerline, one for the 15-volt power supply and one to transfer the codes. Since one side of the power supply is connected to ground, you should use a three-pronged plug, which forces the wide blade to be the ground side of the AC power circuit. First consider the power supply, which is essentially the same as that used in the BSR controller. The 340-millihenry inductor is used to prevent the code frequencies from getting into the power supply. The two diodes form a full-wave unipolar bridge that charges up the 1000-microfarad capacitor, and the Zener diode limits the maximum voltage to 15 volts. The top optoisolator (see Sec. 4-1) converts the 60-Hz sine wave into a TTL level square wave, which the microcomputer uses to detect zero crossings of the powerline's AC voltage. The output circuit is driven by an optoisolator connected to one bit of an output port. When this bit is low, the optoisolator turns on, pulling pin 4 of the 555 oscillator (see Sec. 5-5) high. This turns the 555 on, and it gener- ates a 120-kHz square wave. The 555 output is amplified by a 2N2222 NPN

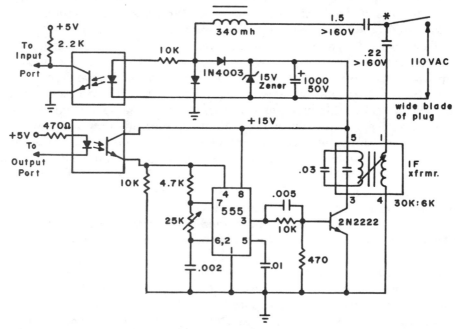

Fig. 10–11. Schematic of a simple 60–Hz powerline modulation circuit. It accepts a TTL serial output stream for delivery to the powerline on a 120–kHz carrier voltage. It also provides the computer with an optoiso- lated 60–Hz TTL square wave, which the computer can use to detect zero crossings on the powerline. Touching the point marked by the * is even more dangerous than reading this book! We cannot assume any lia- bility for doing either.

transistor, which drives the IF transformer T1. The transformer output is coupled to the powerlines by the 0.22-microfarad capacitor.

The codes are binary numbers that are translated into pulse groups, as illustrated in Fig. 10-12. A 1 bit is represented by three pulses of the 120-kHz carrier wave. Each pulse high lasts 1 millisecond, and each low lasts about 1.69 milliseconds. The last low is extended so that the sum of the three pulse times fits into a half cycle of the 60-Hz powerline period. This time is 1000/120 = 8.33 milliseconds. Similarly, a 0 bit is an 8.33-millisecond period that contains no pulses. The zero crossing input in Fig. 10-11 is used by the computer program that generates the pulse group to synchronize the pulse generation to the powerline zero crossings.

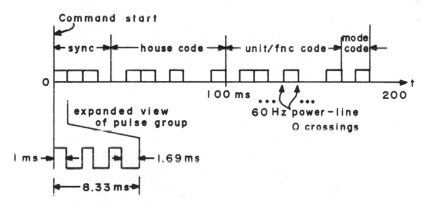

Fig. 10–12. BSR command sequence. The sequence consists of a sync code, a house code, a unit/function code, and a mode code. Each 1 bit is composed of three pulses with 1-millisecond highs and about 1.69-millisecond lows, yielding a total of about 8.1 milliseconds. The software extends the last low long enough to synchronize the bits to the powerline zero crossings, which occur every 8.33 milliseconds. A 0 bit is simply an 8.33-millisecond period synchronized to the zero crossings in which no pulses occur.

The codes are chosen to give nearly equal numbers of 1's and 0's, which helps transmission through the powerlines. A command sequence starts with a sync code, which contains three 1's (nine pulses) in a row, followed by a 0 bit. One of 16 possible house codes follows, represented by 8 bits. Actually these bits are all grouped into pairs of either 01 or 10. Hence only 16 combinations can occur. One can think of these bit pairs as being a form of bisync encoding, a method giving more reliable transmission. The 8-bit house code is followed by 8 bits giving either the unit number of one of the 16 modules or the desired function code. The 16 possible unit/function codes are encoded the same way as the house codes, as shown in Table 10-2. There are only six meaningful function codes: all of one house code off/on, individual units on/off, and dim/bright. The sync, house, and unit/function codes are followed by a 2-bit mode code: 01 specifies that

HOUSE	UNIT	FUNCTION	HEX	DECIMAL
A	1	—	69	105
B	2	—	A9	169
C	3	On	59	89
D	4	—	99	153
E	5	All on	56	86
F	6	—	96	150
G	7	Bright	66	102
H	8	—	A6	166
I	9	—	6A	106
J	10	—	AA	170
K	11	Off	5A	90
L	12	—	9A	154
M	13	All off	55	85
N	14	—	95	149
O	15	Dim	65	101
P	16	—	A5	165

Table 10–2. The 8–bit house, unit, and function codes for BSR powerline modules.

the preceding unit/function code was a function, and 10 specifies it was a unit number. The complete command sequence can be optionally followed by a second 4-bit sync sequence.

A program to generate the codes just presented and thus control the BSR modules is given in our earlier book (Sargent and Shoemaker, 1981). That program is for a Z80 computer, but it can easily be translated for use on an IBM PC.

One problem with both the RF and BSR approaches is that they can be "jammed." A persona non grata can come to the house with a strong RF noise generator to ruin the RF communications, or plug in a strong 120-kHz square wave to upset the BSR communications. Hard-wired (or fiber-optic) communication systems cannot be so jammed, unless the wires are accessible. Consequently, for security purposes the hard-wired approach may be preferable. With the relative ease of the radio and BSR methods, though, parallel wiring is unjustifiably expensive, except perhaps for new buildings or maximum security.

Another example of wireless data communications is the IBM PC*jr*'s cordless keyboard, which communicates with the processing unit via an infrared link. This approach gives freedom from a tangling cable, although you do have to point the keyboard approximately at the processor unit. The keyboard uses CMOS circuitry that runs on batteries. Since the keyboard is normally in a standby power-down mode, no on-off switch is needed. As discussed in Sec. 8-1, the keyboard's serial bit stream consists of biphase-encoded 440-microsecond bit cells. The infrared transmitter encodes a 1 as a 40-kHz burst lasting 62.5 microseconds at the start of the bit cell, and a 0 as a similar burst starting in the middle of the bit cell (see Fig. 8-6). The infrared receiver module contains a 74LS122 one-shot to convert the detected burst to a 220-microsecond pulse. A test LED can be enabled to send the output from 8253 channel 2 to the receiver by setting bit 6 = 1 in the NMI control port latch (0A0H). By monitoring the keyboard data-in bit PC6 of port 62H, you can see whether the receiver/test LED combination is working properly. Keyboard codes can be received from more than one cordless keyboard, and reception can be impaired by strong background light conditions or too-distant transmission. If you can't avoid these problems, you may want to use the keyboard cable option. The infrared input can also be used by devices other than a keyboard. Interrupt vector 49H has been reserved to process code values greater than those generated by the 62-key keyboard.

10-7. IEEE 488 Interface Bus

Section 10-4 showed how a dedicated serial communications link can be used to transfer data between two devices with handshaking so that no data is lost. The 16-wire IEEE 488 interface bus, popularly known as the GPIB (general purpose interface bus), allows data to be exchanged a byte at a time among up to fifteen devices at speeds up to 1 megabyte/second with full handshaking. One device has the responsibility to be the active bus controller (usually there's only one controller) that coordinates data transfers. It can assign itself and other devices to be either "talkers" or "listeners," with the restriction that only one device can talk at a time (very unhuman!). The bus was developed by Hewlett-Packard Corporation to connect their laboratory instruments and associated computers together. The method proved to be so successful that it was made into an IEEE standard in 1975 (revised in 1978) and is used by many companies today.

The general idea is depicted in Fig. 10-13, which has a computer for the controller, and various laboratory instruments and a printer all connected to the GPIB. The computer can assign any one device (including itself) to be the talker and one or more additional devices to be listeners. Suppose we want to read a number of voltages from a multimeter, print the values on the printer, and save them in computer memory for later computations. Before voltage readings take place, the computer assigns itself as the talker and the multimeter as the only listener and then transfers program control bytes to the multimeter specifying what kind, range, and number of voltage measurements it should make. The computer then assigns the multimeter to be the talker, and the printer and the

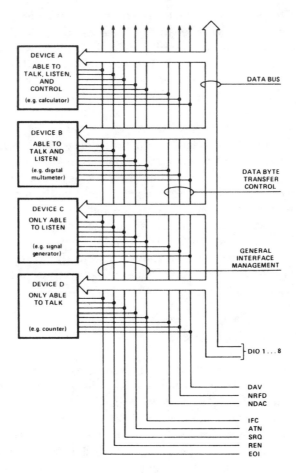

Fig. 10–13. Example of an IEEE 488 interface bus (GPIB) configuration. Reprinted by permission of Intel Corp., 1983.

computer to be listeners. Then the multimeter takes over the bus and asserts the digitized voltage values on the data bus. If the data were sent in ASCII to be directly printable on the printer, the computer would probably convert the data to binary for its internal use. When it's through transmitting data, the multimeter sends a finish code.

    This sounds great, but how are data transfers coordinated so that listeners having different speeds can all read messages accurately, and how do you program the devices to be talkers or listeners? To answer these questions, let's look at the various data and control lines to see what they do. The GPIB has eight bidirectional data lines, DIO1 through DIO8 (why didn't they use DIO0 through DIO7?), a controller **attention** line (ATN), and the three Hewlett-Packard patented handshake lines NRFD (**n**ot **r**eady **f**or **d**ata), DAV (**d**ata **v**alid), and NDAC (**n**ot **d**ata **ac**cepted). There are also four other special-purpose control lines, which we discuss later. To allow multidevice ORing capability, all bus outputs are active-low open-collector lines (see Sec. 5-3). Since the IEEE 488 standard does not use overscored names for active-low true values, we depart from our usual overscore notation for this section alone. Inputs are TTL-compatible Schmitt triggers. Note that DIOn low corresponds to a 1 and DIOn high to a 0. Thus the data on the DIO lines is inverted. The standard cable has 24 wires, including seven ground lines and a shield line in addition to the 16-line bus. The cable connector is a 24-pin ribbon connector. A very nice feature of this connector is that it's stackable, so several connectors can plug into a single socket.

When both the controller attention ATN and data valid DAV lines are low, the byte value given by DIO1 through DIO8 represents a command to one or more devices. Such commands assign devices to be talkers, listeners, controllers, etc. When ATN is high and DAV is low, the byte value on the data bus is data. Hence ATN is a switch that identifies whether the data bus value is a command or data, and DAV low means what its name says, namely that the data on DIO1 through DIO8 is valid for all listeners to read.

All bus transfers—both controller commands and talker-listener data transfers—take place using Hewlett-Packard's patented three-wire handshake. All devices must handshake when commands (ATN low) are being sent, but only listeners handshake for data transmission. This allows high-speed transmission between two fast devices, such as computers and hard-disk drives, even when slower devices are on the bus. To understand the GPIB handshake, see the timing diagram in Fig. 10-14 and the flowchart in Fig. 10-15). Initially the active controller takes over the bus by pulling ATN low and asserting a command on the data bus. This tells *all* devices to shut up and listen. They all pull both NRFD and NDAC low in anticipation of the command. When each device is ready to accept the command, it

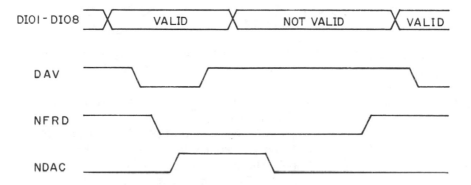

Fig. 10–14. GPIB three-wire handshake timing diagram. More than one listener can read data, each at its own rate.

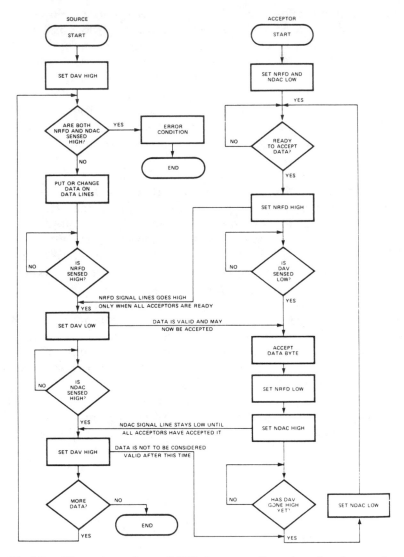

Fig. 10-15. Flow chart for a GPIB data transfer using the three-wire handshake. Reprinted by permission of Intel Corp., 1983.

releases NRFD (by turning off its open-collector output transistor). Thus NRFD goes high only when *all* devices have released NRFD. A bus termination resistor connected to +5 volts ensures that NRFD remains high unless some device pulls it low. When the controller sees that NRFD is high, it responds by pulling DAV low, thereby telling the devices to read the command. The devices then pull NRFD back low in preparation for the next transfer, and read the command, each device at its own rate. As each device finishes reading, it releases NDAC. The reading time delay can be quite long if the device is another computer that only occasionally polls

DAV to see if data is available. When the slowest device has released NDAC, NDAC goes high, after which the controller releases DAV. All devices then pull NDAC back low so long as ATN remains low. In this way, the controller can program one device to be a talker and others to be listeners. When the configuration is complete, the controller releases ATN.

Nonlisteners then release NRFD and NDAC since they're out of the picture until another command occurs. When the listeners are ready for data, they release NRFD, just as they do when they're ready to read a command. When all listeners are ready, NRFD goes high, and the active talker pulls DAV (as soon as it feels its data is valid). The listeners pull NRFD low and release NDAC as soon as they have read the data. When all listeners have released NDAC, the talker releases DAV, and the next transfer sequence starts.

When the talker is finished transferring the prescribed amount of data, it pulls one of the four remaining bus lines low, namely EOI (end or identify), here telling the controller that the transfer is complete. The controller then issues the next command. Note that listen-only devices only need to be connected to the data lines, the three handshake lines, and ATN. Talkers must have EOI connected as well. In addition, there are the SRQ (service request), REN (remote enable), and IFC (interface clear) lines. A talker uses SRQ to interrupt the controller either to indicate an error condition or to announce that it has data available. The active controller asserts REN to instruct a device to ignore its front panel controls in favor of programmed controls. The controller asserts IFC to return all devices to a known state. This signal terminates whatever is going on at the time and hence is used only for initialization or after something has gone wrong, such as a computer crash.

The controller commands consist of bytes whose meanings are divided into four general categories according the values of bits 5 and 6. Bit 7 (DIO8) is ignored. If both bits 5 and 6 of a GPIB command are zero, the low-order 5 bits specify various bus commands, such as "trigger the active talker" and "serial-poll" devices that might be requesting service. Nonzero values of bits 5 or 6 cause the low-order 5 bits to be used as a device address. These addresses are typically specified by DIP switches located on the devices. If bits 6 and 5 have the value 01, the device whose address matches the low-order 5 bits is assigned to be a listener. Similarly, if bits 6 and 5 have the value 10, the device whose address matches the low 5 bits is assigned to be a talker. A talker assignment automatically overrules any previous talker assignment, so only one talker can be active at a given time. The 5-bit address 11111 is reserved to mean that the talk or listen status specified by bits 6,5 is to be deactivated for all devices. Hence the command code 0111111 (3FH) deactivates all listeners. If bits 5 and 5 have the value 11, the low-order 5 bits specify a secondary address. This allows sub-units within an instrument "cluster" to be addressed. Note that even though there are 31 possible primary addresses, a maximum of 15 devices (including the controller) can be attached to the GPIB at a given time.

Since the service request line SRQ is shared by all devices, the controller has to figure out which device or devices are requesting service when that line goes low. This is accomplished by either a *serial poll* or a *parallel poll*. When eight or fewer noncontroller devices are attached to the bus, each can be assigned a unique DIOn line for parallel poll. The controller issues this poll by pulling ATN and EOI simultaneously low. Each device responds by pulling its assigned DIOn line low if and only if it has requested service by pulling SRQ low. This method is fast and efficient, and is similar to the single-line computer interrupt scheme discussed in Sec. 7-1. Alternatively, the controller can talk-address each device in turn and issue a serial-poll command. The device responds with an 8-bit status byte, 1 bit of which tells whether the device is pulling SRQ low. The controller grants service accordingly, issues a serial-poll disable command, and then continues the serial poll as long as SRQ remains low. Although slower, the serial poll provides the controller with more information about the status of each device.

A number of smart controller/listener/talker IC's are available that take care of the handshaking sequences so that the computer and other devices have more time for other purposes. For example, TecMar manufactures a GPIB board for the IBM PC that uses the Intel 8291 Talker/Listener and 8292 Controller IC's. Nevertheless it's useful to realize that a computer can run a GPIB using only an 8255 smart parallel port (see Sec. 6-3) connected to the GPIB through a pair of special octal buffer chips, the 75160 and 75161. The GPIB protocol is then created in software. The 75160 is a bidirectional inverting buffer chip with open-collector outputs and appropriate drive power on the GPIB side. It's used to buffer DIO1 to DIO8. The 75161 is properly configured to buffer the GPIB control lines. You can use port A of the 8255 for the bidirectional data bus DIO1 to DIO8, programming it in mode 0 to be an input port when listening and an output port otherwise. To keep from conflicting with other talkers on the bus, the output value is set to zero (releasing the open-collector data lines, since the 75160 inverts the signal) unless the computer is commanding or talking. Use port B as a mode 0 input port to monitor the handshake lines, EOI, and SRQ. Use port C as an output control port buffered by open-collector drivers to drive the three handshake lines, the ATN, REN, IFC lines, and a line that enables input from the bus buffers (for listening purposes). With this hardware and the conventions explained above, it's reasonably straightforward to write a program to control the desired data transfers. The program should include general talker and listener handshake subroutines. The Victor 9000 and Commodore Pet computers both use similar parallel port implementations of the GPIB. While the data rate is slowed down somewhat this way, it's very general and the ports can be used for other purposes, such as for a Centronics printer port. A specialized GPIB controller IC is not nearly so important for the GPIB as a UART is for serial communications, where without the UART one would have to use slow (less than 2400 baud), dedicated software encoding/decoding of the serial streams.

The question arises as to whether three handshake lines are really needed to synchronize the data flow between multiple devices on a single bus. It appears that DAV and NDAC alone should suffice if implemented as shown in Fig. 10-16. Here the controller or the active talker pulls DAV low when the command or data byte on DIO1 through DIO8 is valid. The active listeners, or all devices if ATN is low, then pull NDAC low within a specified time interval (say, 500 nanoseconds) both to acknowledge the presence of the data request and to prolong the data output until they are ready to read the data. When a device reads the data, it releases NDAC. When all devices have released NDAC, the controller or talker releases DAV in preparation for the next byte. The rising edge triggering of the flip-flop in Fig. 10-15 allows this method to work. Similar circuitry is required to drive the NRFD lines in the usual three-wire handshake.

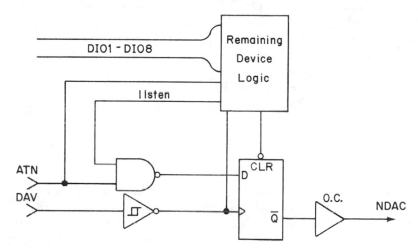

Fig. 10–16. Two–wire handshake circuitry that could synchronize data flow between multiple devices more simply than the GPIB three–wire handshake.

There's only one serious problem with this simple two-wire handshake: no one uses it! While standards, such as the GPIB, are never optimal, they can save you from continually reinventing the wheel. Note that the GPIB has substantially more features than are described here, and perhaps in other applications a three-wire handshake is necessary.

Before designing equipment based on the GPIB, you should read the IEEE-488-1978 standard, which includes complete state diagrams to define the outcome of every possible bus level combination. The standard also describes how tristate bus drivers can be used instead of open-collector drivers. Tristate drivers allow somewhat faster data transfer rates. Alternatively, the bus lines can be tristate, which gives somewhat faster response. Hopefully this section has prepared you to understand that formidable document.

Small Computer Systems Interface (SCSI)

Whereas the GPIB grew out of interfacing to laboratory instruments, another bidirectional parallel interface bus, the SCSI, was developed to interface to byte-oriented block-storage devices. Able to interface to eight devices with a byte-wide parity-checked data bus and a nine-line control bus, the SCSI has become very popular for connecting hard disks, tape backup, and even other microcomputers to a given microcomputer. In some sense it's like a small high-performance network. It is capable of 1.5-megabyte/second asynchronous transfers and up to 4-megabyte/second synchronous transfers. Its command structure is designed for 6, 10, and 12-byte commands, ideally suited to specifying a number of absolute sectors to read or write. Like the GPIB, it uses TTL-compatible open-collector drivers with bus termination resistors to obtain a wired OR, and it allows multiple "initiators" and "targets," but the roles are specified differently. Whereas a GPIB controller may assign one device as a talker and one or more devices as listeners, the SCSI initiator selects a target and then drives an IN/$\overline{\text{OUT}}$ line to specify the data/command transfer direction. The SCSI asynchronous transfer protocol is more like the two-line handshake shown in Fig. 10-16 than the three-line GPIB handshake, and the selection of one of eight devices is simplified by assigning each device its own bit in a select byte.

References

IBM Corporation, 1983, *Technical Reference*, IBM Corporation, Boca Raton, FL. This manual contains authoritative descriptions of the PC's hardware, circuit diagrams for the entire IBM PC and IBM manufactured adapter boards, and complete source code listings for the ROM BIOS routines. In particular, the 8250 UART and its programming are described.

IBM Corporation, 1985, *Adaptors*, IBM Corporation, Boca Raton, FL. This manual contains detailed descriptions of IBM PC cards, including video adaptors, 3278 emulators, and RAM cards, along with source code for some auxiliary ROM BIOS's.

PC magazine, Vol. 1, No. 9, is an issue devoted to serial communications, including reviews of available hardware and software.

S. Ciarcia, 1980, "Computerize a Home," *BYTE* magazine, Vol. 5, No. 1, p. 28. Describes the use of BSR modules and a method of controlling them with a computer.

S. Ciarcia, 1983, "Build a Power-Line Carrier-Current Modem," *BYTE* magazine, Vol. 8, No. 8, p. 36. This article describes the construction of a modem that permits serial communications within a building using the powerlines instead of the phone lines or dedicated cables.

E. Fisher and C. W. Jensen, 1982, *PET/CBM and the IEEE 488 Bus (GPIB)*, Osborne/McGraw-Hill Berkeley, CA. An excellent introduction to the IEEE 488 bus and how it works, with many references.

Jim T. Fulton, 1980, Letter to editor, *BYTE* magazine, Vol. 5, No. 6, p. 14. Explains how to build and use a simple BSR controller circuit.

A. Glossbrenner, 1983, *The Complete Handbook of Personal Computer Communications*, St. Martin's, New York. Describes using a modem to connect your computer into many information services.

L. E. Jorden and B. Churchill, 1983, *Communications and Networking for the IBM Personal Computer*, Robert J. Brady, Bowie, MD. Discusses computer networks and serial communications for the PC.

S. Leibson, 1982, "The Input/Output Primer. Part 3: The Parallel and HPIB (IEEE-488) Interfaces," *BYTE* magazine, Vol. 7, No. 4, p. 186. Provides an introductory explanation of the IEEE 488 interface bus.

H. Saal, 1983, "Local Area Networks," *BYTE* magazine, Vol. 8, No. 5, p. 60. Provides an introduction to local area networks, what they are, and what's available.

M. Sargent III and R. L. Shoemaker, 1981, *Interfacing Microcomputers to the Real World*, Addison-Wesley Publishing Company, Reading, MA. Contains more detailed discussions of serial communications using RF and powerline carriers.

D. C. Willen and J. I. Krantz, 1983, *8088 Assembler Language Programming: The IBM PC*, Howard W. Sams and Company, Indianapolis, IN. Contains introductory discussions on the hardware of the PC, including the asynchronous communications hardware and software. Numerous example programs are given.

I. H. Witten, 1983, "Welcome to the Standards Jungle," *BYTE* magazine, Vol. 8, No. 2, p. 146. Good discussion of the various serial communications standards including RS-232C, RS-449, and others.

11
The Bigger Picture

Inventions have long since reached their limit—and I see no hope for further developments.
  —Julius Frontinus, world famous engineer, Rome, 10 AD

William F. Buckley once referred to the Federal government as "that glorious cornucopia of self-generating dollars." As a conservative, he was of course being facetious. However, the IBM Personal Computer could well be likened to "a glorious cornucopia of self-generating add-ons!" Quantities of hardware and software modules are available to expand the IBM PC beyond the basic configuration sold by IBM. This chapter overviews the PC cornucopia with emphasis on the general types of products available, rather than on detailed reviews of any particular products. The number of products available is so large, in fact, that entire volumes are devoted to them, as listed in the references at the end of this chapter. Here we summarize some general ideas about what facilities are particularly worth adding to the basic IBM PC.

Chapters 2 through 10 covered many details of the IBM PC and how to interface it to various devices. They considered the way machine instructions cause devices to respond to the CPU, ways to measure and generate alien voltage and current requirements, ways to transfer data between peripheral devices and the CPU, and ways to program the computer in assembly language to support these hardware features. To carry out these concepts in practice, three ingredients must be added: (1) ways to store programs and data conveniently, (2) special purpose interface modules, and (3) programs to instruct the computer to carry out the desired tasks. Section 11-1 describes floppy- and hard-disk storage, without which the computer either is a controller (a special-purpose dedicated machine whose tasks never vary) or is severely limited! At least two double-sided 360-kilobyte floppies of this secondary storage (RAM memory is called primary storage) are required for efficient operation, and, for really convenient operation, a 10- to 20-megabyte hard disk is needed to provide on-line manuals, help files, and program and data storage. Section 11-2 describes some of the useful add-on boards available for the PC, notably the various "combo" boards that provide memory, clock/ calendar, and serial and parallel I/O capability on a single board. The Intel/Lotus/Microsoft Expanded Memory Specification allowing up to 8 megabytes of RAM is described and compared to the extended and virtual memory capabilities of the IBM PC AT. Chapter 12 explains how to make your own custom interface boards, in case the IBM PC cornucopia is lacking what you need.

The third ingredient, software, is every bit as important as the hardware itself. Without programs, the hardware is totally useless. The main purpose of computerizing laboratory experiments, devices, control applications, your house, or whatever, is to replace hardware logic by software, because software is relatively easy to design, modify, and pay for. The software is nevertheless often not trivial. There must be a new Peter principle, namely that whenever a discipline becomes easy, it will be expanded until it gets difficult again. So be it with software. Half to three quarters of the cost of computerization lies in software purchase and development. In this book, the programs are quite simple, because we only show how various facilities are programmed and how to interface devices, one at a time. But in most applications, many devices are involved, and usually less than 10% of the code deals with I/O.

To cope with the software task, it's essential to have development tools known as editors, assemblers, operating systems, interpreters, and compilers. Sections 11-3 through 11-5 explain the nature of these tools and describe some of the large repertoire of software available for the IBM PC. More detailed discussions of these tools and programming languages are given in the references. The basic principles of assembly language programming were discussed in detail in Chaps. 2 through 4. The hope is that this chapter gives some general perspectives and guides the reader to some excellent software.

In particular, Sec. 11-3 describes the tool you'll probably spend 60% to 80% of your time with: the editor. This is a program that allows you to enter, store, and change programs or other text, such as this book! To facilitate this important process, you should have a good *screen* editor. Microcomputers have major advantages here over their big brothers, since their screens are typically memory-mapped and therefore fast, and their CPU's are inexpensive and can be dedicated to one thing at a time, such as

you and your editing. A brief discussion of text formatting and word processing is also given, since it's so useful and microcomputers are so good at
it!

Section 11-4 discusses high-level language interpreters and compilers,
which, like assemblers, are translators, but deal with relatively machine-
independent languages like FORTRAN 77, BASIC, Pascal, FORTH, C, and so
on. Interpreters minimize program debugging time at the cost of slower
execution, while the reverse is true for compilers.

Section 11-5 discusses the programs called disk operating systems,
which allow you to store, access, and execute all other programs. The
standard IBM DOS version 2.0 and later (actually a form of MS-DOS from
Microsoft) is the primary focus of attention, but some comparison with
UNIX is made. The chapter ends with a discussion of computer hierarchies,
which shows where the IBM PC fits into the overall scheme of computing.

11-1. Floppy-Disk and Hard-Disk Storage

Mass storage has mass appeal! The primary storage consisting of RAM
and ROM plays an essential role in a microcomputer. Like the CPU itself,
nothing can be done without it. Lots of RAM helps considerably, and you
should have an absolute minimum of 256 kilobytes for an IBM PC. In fact,
since RAM is so inexpensive, you really ought to have the standard 640-
kilobyte maximum. Section 11-2 discusses how to get this RAM inexpen-
sively and reliably. In addition, you need some way of storing your data
when the power goes off. ROM and EPROM retain data with the power off,
but they're very limited in capacity and inconvenient to program. Various
other technologies are developing rapidly, such as optical memories, but for
now the most convenient large-scale memories are provided by floppy disks
and hard disks.

Floppy disk drives record data in serial bit streams on the coated
surfaces of thin plastic platters (called diskettes or disks) that look much
like phonograph records inside a paper envelope. The coating is the familiar
brown layer of metal oxide particles used on magnetic tapes for tape recorders. Data are recorded on the disk surface in a set of concentric
circles called tracks, and the data on each track are further divided into
equal-size pieces called sectors. To read or write data on the disk,
read/write heads like those used in tape recorders are pressed against the
magnetic surface as the disk spins underneath the heads. To move from one
track to another, the heads are moved closer to or farther from the center
of the spinning disk by a stepper motor.

On the IBM PC, the standard double-density floppy diskettes have 40
tracks on each side of a 5-1/4-inch diameter disk. Each track is divided
into nine sectors and each sector contains 512 bytes of data plus some
control information stored as a serial bit stream. Thus the disks can store
180 kilobytes per side, giving 360 kilobytes for two sides.

IBM invented the floppy-disk concept and introduced a special format (IBM 3740) for storing data in a reliable fashion on diskettes. In the original format (developed for 8-inch-diameter floppy disks), each sector has written in it (during the process called formatting) a 51-byte prologue field containing the track and sector number, a 128-byte data field, and a 28-byte postamble field, plus a delay gap between sectors. The track and sector numbers and the data field are followed by a CRC (cyclic redundancy check) checksum. Whenever data are read from the disk, a new checksum is calculated and compared to the one written on the disk. You get an error message if the two don't agree. If the two do agree, you can be quite confident that the data have been read correctly. A little hole near the center of the diskette identifies the start of sector 1, and is detected as it passes between an LED and a photodiode. This format scheme is called IBM soft-sectored. It's been modified for use on the IBM PC to use 512-byte data fields per sector.

The IBM PC AT also has a 1.2-megabyte 5-1/4-inch floppy disk drive known as "high density." These have 96 tracks per inch (96 TPI) instead of the 48 tracks per inch used in the 360-kilobyte drives, giving 80 tracks per side. Furthermore, each track has fifteen 512-byte sectors, for a total of 2400 sectors = 1,228,800 bytes per diskette. This capacity is much more useful for data storage and hard disk backup, especially with the various backup programs that use the PC's DMA capabilities for very efficient data transfer.

Both the 1.2-megabyte and 360-kilobyte floppy disk drives are inexpensive and readily available from mail-order houses in half-height size. One attractive arrangement is to put two half-height drives into one drive slot and a 20-megabyte half-height hard-disk drive into the other. This still leaves room for a half-height streaming tape drive for backup or a second hard-disk drive. On the older PC's this disk complement has to be accompanied with a boost in power supply.

A smaller floppy disk drive that is growing in popularity is the 3-1/2-inch microfloppy drive. This drive is used in Apple's Macintosh and in various IBM PC compatible portables including IBM's own Convertible. Typically these diskettes handle 720 kilobytes. Although they are floppy, they're housed in a special rigid cartridge that fits nicely in your shirt pocket. One principle has become clear: small is nice! The less room you must devote to anything, the better. If you could have a 10-megabyte computer in a corner of the kitchen counter, how much better you could prepare gourmet meals!

Floppy diskettes are great for most word-processing tasks and data storage. However, for more demanding requirements such as large data bases, frequent compilations (see Sec. 11-4), several users, or convenience in general, hard disks (also known as fixed disks) are desirable or even necessary. You can organize your programs and data on various floppies, but then you do the overall filing job. On a hard disk, you organize your programs and data according to subject into subdirectories and let DOS remember where they are. You don't have to hunt around for that floppy containing your spreadsheets on project X. You just tell DOS to change to the appropriate subdirectory, and there they are. This entire book, for example, is stored in one directory area of a hard disk, ready to be examined or modified at a moment's notice. Another directory area has compilers, a word processor, and other handy system utilities. This frees you to think logically about your data and programs, rather than remembering which box of floppies contains which utilities. As Charlie Brown would say, "Happiness is having your own hard disk!"

Hard-disk drives use rigid metal platters coated with a metal oxide layer and spinning at typically 3600 rpm—ten times faster than a floppy disk. Furthermore, the read/write heads don't touch the magnetic surface. They literally fly a few microinches above it. Even the tiniest particles of dirt on the disk platter can cause a read/write head to crash onto the disk surface, permanently ruining part of the disk. For this reason, the most popular hard-disk drives for microcomputers are *Winchester* drives, which are hermetically sealed to prevent dust particles from entering and causing a head crash onto the disk. Like the floppy disk, this hard-disk technology was also invented at IBM. The name "Winchester" comes from the fact that one of the earliest such devices had dual 30-megabyte disk platters. This reminded people of the Winchester 30-30 shotgun—hence the name. Winchester disks can be obtained with capacities of anywhere from 10 to 400 megabytes. We recommend having at least 10 megabytes per drive. The IBM PC-XT includes a 360K floppy disk plus a 10-megabyte hard disk. It runs the MS-DOS 2.0 or later disk operating system, which allows you to organize the files in a nice tree-structured way, as described in Sec. 11-4. One general point about all disks is that any important data should be "backed up"; that is, at least two copies should exist. In this connection, the major problem with the IBM PC-XT is that 360K floppies are too small for easy backup of a 10-megabyte Winchester. The IBM PC AT gets around this problem to a large extent with its 1.2-megabyte floppies. On a single-user basis, we recommend using the floppies to regularly back up any files you change on the hard disk.

DOS Disk Storage Format

DOS organizes diskettes and hard-disk drives in a fairly uniform way based on absolute sectors, directories, and groups of sectors called clusters. In this way, DOS doesn't have to know what track or side a given sector is on; the low level disk handler is responsible for that. This section summarizes how DOS organizes its disks in this abstract way and then describes how you can see the layout in action by using the SST debugger. Understanding this information could help you substantially one day when a program destroys your root directory for some unknown reason and you desperately need some files on the disk. The basic information as to how many bytes per sector, how many sectors per cluster, etc., can be found in a couple of ways for IBM format compatible media. We restrict our discussion to such media, and wish all other IBM PC "compatibles" would follow suit.

The basic unit of disk information besides the byte itself is the sector, which for IBM PC's is 512 bytes. In principle DOS could use physical sectors with other sizes, but typical disk controllers are limited to this size, and hence 512-byte physical sectors are used on all IBM PC disk systems as of this writing. On hard disks, the very first sector is called the master boot sector and contains information on how the hard disk is partitioned, perhaps with a DOS partition and a XENIX (Microsoft's version of UNIX) partition. We consider here only DOS partitions.

The first sector on a DOS partition and the very first sector on floppy diskettes is numbered sector 0 in DEBUG and SST and in the DOS interrupts INT 25H and INT 26H (absolute sector read and write). This sector is called the boot record and contains parameters on how the diskette is organized, along with an optional small boot program that loads a larger boot program elsewhere on disk. Each file consists of an integral number of clusters, and each cluster consists of one or more sectors as specified in the boot record and by DOS calls (INT 21H) ah = 1CH, 32H, and 36H. In principle, allowing multiple sectors per cluster allows higher capacity disk drives to be used. Unfortunately there's a limit to this approach since one of the basic disk parameters, the number of sectors on the disk, is only a 16-bit word. Hence as far as DOS is concerned, there can be only 65536 sectors, and 65536 x 512 = 33,554,432 bytes. Some systems get past this limit while still sticking with 512-byte physical sectors, by persuading DOS to use larger *logical* sectors. The sectors immediately following the boot sector generally contain two copies of the File Allocation Table (FAT), which identifies the clusters comprising each file. The FAT's are followed by the root directory, and then by the file clusters themselves, starting with cluster number 2 (0 and 1 don't exist).

The root directory and subdirectories consist of 32-byte entries that identify the files as follows:

Offset	Meaning
0	8-byte file name
8	3-byte extension
11	attribute byte
22	time created or last modified
24	date created or last modified
26	starting cluster
28	double-word byte count

The attribute byte has the following meanings for the value 1: bit 0, read only; bit 1, hidden file; bit 2, system file; bit 3, volume label entry (has no associated cluster); bit 4, subdirectory entry; bit 5, archive (used by backup programs). Not all of these bits can equal 1 simultaneously. In particular, if the attribute byte has the value 10H, the "file" is a subdirectory, consisting of these same kinds of entries, and if it has the value H, it's a label. The time is packed into a 16-bit word with format hhhhhmmmmmmxxxxx, where the h's give the hour, the m's the minutes, and the s's the seconds. Similarly the date is given by yyyyyyymmmmmdddddd, where the y's give the year minus 1980, the m's give the month (1 through 12), and the d's give the day (1 through 31). Offset 26 gives the starting cluster for the file. Subsequent clusters are specified by the corresponding cluster chain in the FAT.

The FAT consists of 12-bit entries for media with less than 4086 clusters and 16-bit entries for larger media (10 megabytes or more). Entry 0 identifies the kind of media being used such as 0FDH for a 360-kilobyte floppy, 0F9H for a 1.2-megabyte floppy, and 0F8H for a hard disk. Entry 1 is reserved. Starting with entry 2, each entry corresponds to a unique cluster on the disk. An entry value of (F)FFFH indicates that the corresponding cluster is the last cluster in a file. An entry (F)FF7H indicates that the cluster is unusable. An entry 0 indicates that the cluster is not being used. Other entries specify the number of the next cluster in the file. The directory entry identifies the first cluster in a file, and then a "chain" of FAT entries identifies the remaining clusters in the file, up to and including the cluster corresponding to the FAT entry (F)FFFH.

An easy way to understand this organization is to use SST's DISK command and then type Ctrl-F for FAT. As you move the cursor around with the cursor keys, the cluster chains will appear in reverse video. Then type Ctrl-P to see the root directory. Ctrl-L translates the 32-bit directory entries into English for you. You can use the Ctrl-D command to go look at the file clusters themselves. The alphanumeric format is usually the most useful display format for this, and shows both which sector and which cluster you're looking at. SST has other commands that let you overtype the disk and unerase files. Essentially the disk display/modify facility works like the memory display/modify facility except that you specify sectors instead of segments.

For more detailed information on the disk, refer to the IBM *DOS Technical Reference* manual and the discussions in Peter Norton's book *Inside the IBM PC*. Section 4-7 provides the information needed to control disk files from assembly language. You can also take over the NEC 765 floppy-disk controller chip from assembly language and make it do whatever you want, such as read and copy disks that are "copy protected." The IBM PC *Technical Reference* manual describes how to program this chip. However, if you're going to fool around with this sort of thing, you had better know what you're doing!

11-2. The Cornucopia of Add-Ons

Chapters 6 through 8 described what comes on the system board of the IBM PC: the 8088 microprocessor, 64 to 256 kilobytes of RAM, an eight-channel interrupt controller, a four-channel DMA controller, three counter/ timers, keyboard and cassette interface circuitry, and five slots for expansion boards on the usual PC, eight on the PC-XT (three of which are half length), and eight on the AT. The IBM PC is usually bought with the floppy-disk controller board, which is capable of controlling up to four floppy-disk drives, two within the main case and two external. One of the video boards described in Chap. 8 is also normally used, providing graphics and/or nice monochrome displays. On the five-slot PC, this leaves only three slots to handle all your remaining needs, such as serial and parallel ports, a battery-backed-up clock/calendar, additional RAM, modem/network cards, "faster" cards, mouse, extra video, laboratory interfacing cards, and so on. These can be important facilities for a useful computer and must be accommodated by expansion boards. More slots would require more desk space, and the PC is already big enough to cause problems in some cases. You can do very well with only three slots, provided you choose your boards carefully. If you nevertheless need more slots, consider buying an AT or AT compatible. In fact, once you've used an AT, it's hard to go back to an XT.

An excellent contender for one of the three slots is the popular multi-function board, which combines a substantial amount of parity-checked RAM with at least one serial port, one parallel port, and a battery-backed-up clock/calendar circuit. This ensures that you have the full 640 kilobytes of RAM in the PC low memory, perhaps with some "expanded" RAM discussed at the end of this section, plus a serial connection to the external world (for daisy-wheel printers, modems, or other computers), a parallel port for dot matrix printers or interfacing, and that great convenience, the clock/calendar, so you don't have to reenter the time and date each time you crash the computer or turn it on. Some people think it isn't very important for the computer to have the correct time and date, but they're wrong. MS-DOS stamps the time and date on each file when it's created or changed, and this can greatly reduce the confusion of recognizing the latest version of a given file (just as on the big machines). This can save you hours of frustration. Excellent multifunction cards are available from AST, QuadRAM, and others, including a large number of look-alikes from the Far East.

You can save money by buying multifunction cards with little or no RAM and then buying and installing the extra RAM yourself. Remember that nine RAM chips are needed for each block of memory. When you install the chips, the main danger is static electricity. A small static discharge, even one that you can't see or feel, can destroy a RAM chip. Using the installation procedure for MOS (metal oxide semiconductor) chips outlined near the end of Sec. 12-2 will allow safe installation of the RAM. You should also follow the procedures described there for finding pin 1 on an IC and for inserting IC's without bending the pins. Make sure that pin 1 on each RAM chip points in the same direction as pin 1 on the RAM already present. Finally, change the setting of switch 2 on the system board as indicated in the IBM *Guide to Operations* manual to reflect the new total amount of RAM present. On the AT, run the SETUP option of the AT diagnostics to tell the system the new amount of RAM. The PC power-on procedures check the RAM for you in a cursory fashion, and you can run the CHKDSK program to verify that the system knows about the new RAM you've installed. More definitive memory test programs are available from the multifunction board manufacturers.

A number of plug-in modem boards are available for the IBM PC, offering touch-tone and ordinary dial capability, answer and originate modes, an extra serial port, and possibly other features. The advantage of such a board is its compactness: no extra space is required beyond that for the PC. On the other hand, a modem board takes up a valuable slot, perhaps a half slot on the XT, and is dedicated to a single machine. Many smart external 300/1200/2400-baud modems exist, which add flexibility and conserve slots at the cost of extra space outside the PC. You have to decide what's best for your situation.

Thinking bigger and faster, you may want to include a 3278/3279 card to talk to IBM mainframes, or network cards to tie into a network. Many such cards exist; see the magazines mentioned in the references for the current offerings.

A hard-disk controller card is another desirable add-on. It typically controls up to four hard-disk drives. Boards that combine hard-disk controllers with a floppy controller or other features are also available. Typically, hard-disk drives have a substantial amount of intelligence, error detection and correction hardware, and buffering capability built in, so the interface card in the PC is fairly simple. The SCSI interface discussed at the end of Sec. 10-7 falls into this category. The AT disk controller also accepts many different hard disk drives ranging in size from 10 to 130 megabytes or more.

If you need a hard-disk controller and a modem board in addition to the combo board, you've filled up all five slots. But if you don't need one or the other, many other possibilities exist. One interesting choice is a second processor board offering greater speed. Many 80286 boards can be plugged into ordinary PC's, doubling or tripling the speed. Cards with the Motorola 68020, National Semiconductor 32032, and Intel 80386 32-bit microprocessors can be plugged into the AT, giving additional features and extra speed. Z80 cards are also available to run the old CP/M software, and the NEC V20 series of microprocessors is pin-for-pin compatible with the 8088 and allows direct emulation of the Intel 8080 microprocessor.

A variety of boards are available for applications requiring equipment control and data collection. The available functions include A/D, D/A, BSR AC outlet control, parallel I/O, voice synthesis, stepper-motor control, video camera digitization, EPROM programming, and more. A number of companies are now producing these boards, including Burr-Brown, Tecmar, Data

Translation, Apparat, and Datacube. Tecmar has the broadest line of data acquisition and control boards, although they currently don't provide board schematics. Having schematics for these kinds of interface boards is very important, both to answer questions that aren't covered in the manual and to allow custom modifications.

If the cornucopia lacks the special something you need, you can always wirewrap your design on one of the many prototype boards available. Vector Electronic Company, Apparat, and Tecmar all make such boards. Chapter 12 provides details on how to design and build your own boards for the PC.

The PC world is teaming with lookalikes, most of which are remarkably compatible and typically offer a lot of computer for the money. Nevertheless, don't let anyone try to tell you that any lookalike is 100 percent IBM PC compatible. Two areas are sure to be different: First, only the IBM PC has BASIC in ROM, and some programs like BASICA take advantage of this presence. Second, some "bad" programs directly use some of the ROM BIOS routines at points other than the standard entry points, and these routines cannot be copied by anyone else without violating IBM's copyrights.

One of the most interesting add-on areas for the PC is the Lotus/Intel/Microsoft (LIM) Expanded Memory Specification (EMS). This simple scheme and its AST/QuadRAM/Ashton-Tate (AQA) extension offer remarkably powerful ways to expand the PC's 1-megabyte RAM space. The technique is called "bank switching," an old idea but here with a standardized flexible format. According to the LIM EMS, four empty consecutive 16-kilobyte RAM areas in between 0C0000H and 0EFFFFH are used as a quartet of windows into a 2-megabyte RAM on an EMS card. Four such cards can be included in the specification. (With 1-megabit DRAM's, all 8 megabytes can fit on a single card.) The four 16KB pages windowed into the 8086 address space are determined by outputting the page numbers to the ports 02x8H, 42x8H, 82x8H, and 0C2x8H, where x is determined by dip switches. Notice that LIM have cleverly used high bits in the I/O ports to access 4 ports for what is usually considered a single I/O port. In fact, since the high-order 6 bits are usually ignored, each 10-bit I/O port actually corresponds to 64 possible ports! AQA took this idea to its logical conclusion: by outputting the remaining four bits to port 02x9H, you specify which of 16 page-register quartets you wish 2x8H, 42x8H, 82x8H, and 0C2x8H to address. In this way AQA EMS sprinkles 16KB pages all over unused RAM/ROM, unless you explicitly specify not to. For multitasking, having all this flexibility is very handy since each task can have its own quartet. Popular software such as Lotus 1-2-3 takes advantage of the LIM EMS to handle relatively large data bases with alacrity.

Consider the problem of generating a 300-dot/inch, 8-1/2 x 11-inch laser printer image in memory containing numerous different type fonts. With the EMS, you can store half a megabyte of fonts in expanded RAM, along with the 1 megabtye for the laser printer image. You access this RAM by windowing the pieces you want to modify into the EMS windows, perhaps two for the fonts and two for the page image. The scheme is almost as fast as using the segment registers themselves in real RAM space, since they too have to be changed every time you move outside the current "page," which is 64KB in size. Meanwhile you access up to a maximum of 8 megabytes on an ordinary PC. This similarity in speed vanishes relative to the 80386 protected mode, since the 80386 segments can be as large as 4 gigabtyes in length, but here we consider smaller machines.

Alternatively on the AT and other 80286-based machines, you could use the protected mode's extended memory to access up to 16 megabytes and up to 1 gigabyte/task of virtual memory. There are nice protection features associated with this approach, but it isn't significantly faster than using the EMS approach even given a protected-mode operating system. Using real-address mode DOS's, you periodically need to switch in and out of protected mode, which takes about 400 microseconds (see Sec. 6-6).

In addition to providing a flexible bank switching scheme, LIM contributed a standard software inferface specification accessed through INT 67H. With this, different programs including resident programs can all co-exist peacefully while using the expanded RAM.

In addition to high speed access to large data areas and RAM disks, the EMS is valuable for having many programs resident for overlapping use. You can have your word processor, spelling checker, compiler, spreadsheet, appointment calendar, and so on, all resident and ready to respond at a moment's notice.

11-3. Editors

An editor is a program that allows you to create, modify, store, and re-trieve text files. These files can be programs, letters, manuals, books, phone directories, or any other human-readable text. Many editor programs exist, since nearly every computer user needs an editor. Editors written in the 1960's and early 1970's were mostly *context* editors. You specified one-letter commands with optional numbers that moved an invisible cursor somewhere in a file. You could then use other commands to insert or delete characters at the cursor position as desired. Typically you could see and work on only one line at a time. It was also possible to write little text-processing programs, called macros, that could modify major portions of your file in a hurry. The most famous of these editors was probably TECO, developed for Digital Equipment computers and available in a similar form on many other computers including microcomputers.

With the advent of microcomputers and inexpensive CRT terminals, however, *screen editors* have become dominant. They allow you to look at a whole screenful of text at a time and use simple one-keystroke commands to move the cursor around by lines, words, or characters. When you're used to a screen editor, context editors make you feel blind. The first of the microcomputer screen editors was Michael Shrayer's Electric

Pencil, which also has substantial print formatting capability. For the most part, the screen editors haven't included the handy macro facility of the context editors. An exception is Michael Aronson's text editor, PMATE, which can be loosely described as a screen editor version of TECO (although the commands differ somewhat). This book was written using the PS word processor, which combines PMATE with a sophisticated output formatter and a set of user-friendly menus. It's really slick the way you can whiz around a file, moving paragraphs, deleting and inserting words, all with a few key-strokes. Since PMATE and PS are programmable, programs can be (and have been) written for it that produce many "personalized" letters rapidly, dial the phone, index books (PS was used to create the index for this book), renumber equations and references, and generate forms. One limitation of PS is that you still have to figure out what to write! Try as we might, we haven't been able to make the computer read our mind and correct our grammar. Come to think of it, we probably don't want it to: it might start to control us even more than it already does! However, some programs, like Borland's Turbo Lightning, check your spelling as you type words into your word processor.

In selecting an editor to purchase, do as much looking around and hands-on testing as you can. Also, beware of editors whose main claim to fame is that they're easy to learn, or that what you see on the screen is what you get on paper. Often what you see on a limited text-mode screen is not what you want to get. An editor with real power requires an exten-sive command set. In particular, look for an editor that has powerful text-formatting capabilities so that you can produce documents that look the way you intended them to look. Many editors are severely limited in this regard. Editors that allow you to move the cursor and insert or delete text using control-key commands (in addition to the cursor arrows) are by far the best. Although control-key commands are harder to learn initially, once learned, they can be touch-typed, making them much more efficient to use. Remember that it takes only a little while to learn to use any editor, but then you have to live with it forever afterward. Our philosophy is to use the most powerful and keystroke-efficient editor that we can find.

While display screens provide both text entry and display, you inevita-bly need hard copy (printed output). This is useful for looking over a pro-gram away from the computer or when the computer is doing something else, for providing the ultimate "backup" for your files, and for seeing more than one screenful of text at a time. Many dot matrix printers are avail-able for well under $500. Some of these, such as the C. Itoh 8510A and Epson FX-80, have graphics capability with resolutions that match the graphics screens. Other useful features to have in a dot matrix printer are a downloadable character set and a correspondence quality mode to pro-duce high quality text. This book was printed using a more elegant Diablo 630 daisy-wheel printer driven by PS. You just type in your text, include some control sequences, and presto!—out comes a book. With laser printers it's still easier, even if you use more fonts and insert graphical figures.

11-4. Interpreters and Compilers

Chapters 2 through 4 covered the writing and debugging of assembly-language programs in some detail. Later chapters used assembly language to encode various algorithms. However, assembly language has three serious disadvantages: it's obviously machine dependent; programs written in it require so much detail that it's often hard to see the forest for the trees; and it's difficult to learn. So while assembly language is very powerful and can be very efficient in run time and storage, it's typically not efficient in programmer time. One thing you can do to speed up assembly language programming is to use a fast, full-screen, symbolic debugger program like Scroll Systems' SST. With it you can fix bugs 10 to 100 times faster than with DOS's DEBUG.

To improve programmer productivity, software designers back in the 1950's decided they needed to have programs that translated relatively English-like languages, called *high-level languages*, into machine language. There is now a bewildering variety of high-level languages available, although only a few have large numbers of users. There are two basic types of high-level languages: interpreters and compilers (plus a few mixtures). Both approaches have their advantages, and the ideal is to have both types for any given high-level language. This section discusses these two language types and then considers five high-level languages that are popular on microcomputers (BASIC, FORTRAN 77, Pascal, C, and FORTH). As elsewhere in this chapter, only an overview is provided. The references for the chapter guide the reader to a more detailed understanding of the various languages. At the end of the section, a sample program is presented in seven versions: flowchart, assembly language, BASIC, FORTRAN 77, Pascal, C, and FORTH. With experience in one or more of these languages, you can get an idea of what it's like to program in the others. A few other important languages on the IBM PC are dBASE II for interactive data-base management; LOGO for teaching modern, structured computer programming to children; and SNOBOL4 for incredibly powerful string processing.

An *interpreter* runs programs by examining each byte of a program either exactly as it was typed or in a slightly compacted form. Consequently you can change a program and then run it again immediately. No initial translation into machine language (as with an assembler) needs to be performed, since interpreters continually translate as they execute. This "instantaneous" modification capability speeds up the debugging process. The drawback is that it also introduces substantial run-time overhead, slowing the execution speed way down compared to an assembly-language-coded routine (often by a factor of 100 or more). But if you're just debugging an algorithm, or if your program doesn't do much calculation, the interpreter may well get the job done the fastest. Furthermore, interpreters are interactive by nature. You can always interrupt the execution, perform a few calculations, examine and change variable values, and then resume execution where you interrupted it or somewhere else. Does that sound like a debugger program? It sure does, but with the difference that here a high-level language is used.

Compilers translate programs all the way into machine code. The speed of execution and the size of the machine code relative to optimally coded assembly language depend on the compiler. Some compilers are quick and dirty: good for debugging, but slow for execution and wasteful of memory. Others turn out optimized code at the cost of extra compile time and disk banging. For many computational purposes, compilers can produce code that is nearly as efficient as the assembly code produced by an average programmer. A disadvantage relative to interpreters is that compilers (like assemblers) require both compilation and link steps, which take substantial amounts of time on microcomputers. Furthermore, whatever screen or keyboard interactions you want to have with the program must be programmed explicitly; they are not there automatically as with interpreters. Hence it's nice to have both interpreters and compilers for a given language. Unfortunately, the only high-level language for which both are readily available is BASIC.

A major advantage of high-level languages is their portability. Code written on one computer can be transported over to another type of computer with only minor changes. An experienced assembly-language programmer can do the same with assembly language but at far greater effort per statement. One general rule is to beware the neat but nonstandard extensions that are often added to various high-level languages. Try to program using a subset of the language that runs on most machines. As time goes on, of course, the portable subset grows. Nobody uses the LET statement in BASIC anymore, and most people are using BASIC's IF-THEN-ELSE construction, which was absent in the original Dartmouth implementation. Similarly, quotation marks can be used in place of the Hollerith count in all contemporary FORTRAN's. Code that is definitely not portable should be confined to subroutines well labeled as troublemakers. Some operations aren't suited to high-level languages, because of speed, memory, I/O, or other reasons, and these can be coded in assembly language. A good high-level language compiler and linker allows you to link in assembly language subroutines with the high-level language program as described in Sec. 4-5. This mixture of languages can provide tremendous speed and power when used properly.

The most widespread high-level language on microcomputers is a modern, interpreted version of BASIC written by Microsoft. Microsoft's BASIC is used on the TRS-80, Apple II, IBM PC, and many other machines. Chances are there are more of these BASIC interpreters around than all other compilers and interpreters combined! Curiously enough, a number of the constructs in this BASIC are not supported by the version of BASIC on most big machines, whereas the latter often support array manipulations not present in Microsoft's implementation. Microsoft also markets a compiler version of its BASIC, which can be linked together with modules generated by other Microsoft compilers. The calling sequences tend to differ from one language to another (one language passes argument values, another near addresses, another far addresses), so you may have to use assembly-language interfaces to mix object files. Another popular implementation of BASIC is CBASIC-2, a compiled BASIC that differs substantially from Microsoft's BASIC in a number of ways, although it is possible to write in a portable subset. BASIC is easy to learn and use. The most common criticism is that it's hard to follow a BASIC program's logic, because of all the statement labels (each line gets a statement number in the interpreter versions), "unstructured" GOTO's, and BASIC's inability to call subroutines by name. The major versions of BASIC do have limited structures, including an IF-THEN-ELSE with the capability of including several statements after both the THEN and the ELSE. This helps to reveal the program flow.

The next most popular language around (excluding COBOL, which is very important on mainframe computers used for business) is FORTRAN. This language has been upgraded in several very useful ways in the FORTRAN 77 version. One interesting historical point is that the character-string data type, the IF-THEN-ELSE construct, and a number of other features of FORTRAN 77 *should* have been in the original IBM 1964 FORTRAN IV but were omitted for reasons known only to the designers. The features were well known from COBOL and ALGOL at the time, and shortly thereafter IBM released PL/I, which includes every construct but the kitchen sink! On big machines, carefully written FORTRAN IV is probably the most portable language around. Virtually every machine has optimizing compilers for it. It has the capability to handle huge problems, partly because subroutines can be separately compiled and can communicate with each other via labeled COMMON blocks. It also supports complex variables, which are required in many science and engineering applications. The only competitive language for these applications is PL/I, which is extensively used only on IBM mini and maxicomputers (although Intel does market a nice PL/M for its 8086-based computers). The new FORTRAN 77 is now supported on most machines, and removes a number of the annoying features of FORTRAN IV. Although FORTRAN isn't particularly beautiful, it combines widespread use with complex variables and labeled COMMON, giving it power and advantages that no other language has. Microsoft, Digital Research, IBM, and Lahey all sell full FORTRAN 77 compilers for the IBM PC that require a minimum of 256K RAM and a hard disk to run. They include support for the 8087 numeric coprocessor and arrays up to 64K in size, and allow programs to use all available memory. The Microsoft F77 can also interface directly to Microsoft C, which would actually be a better language for science and engineering if only it had complex numbers.

The third language is Pascal, which might be called an ALGOL derivative with powerful data-type capability. It has all the neat structures needed to write programs with few or no GOTO's, so your programs tend to have the clarity of flowcharts. It also provides extensive run-time error detection capability. It requires at least 128K of RAM and two disk drives.

It's an attractive language but is typically not run-time or code efficient. Pascal was developed by Niklaus Wirth to be a teaching language, and hence it didn't include a number of important features such as modular compilation and string manipulation functions. The result is that every implementation of Pascal has extensions added to it that are incompatible with other Pascal implementations. This severely compromises the portability of Pascal programs. Pascal programs also lack the flexibility of the C language, since certain things that a beginning student would never have to do are very necessary for operating systems code. In spite of these shortcomings, Pascal, especially Borland's Turbo Pascal, is very popular. Microsoft's Pascal is closely related to Microsoft Fortran, and the two compilers have the same second and third passes. A newer language, Modula-2 (also developed by Wirth), remedies most of Pascal's deficiencies and may become a more popular alternative.

A better high-level, structured programming language for many purposes is C, so named because it was a greatly enhanced version of an earlier language called B. C is a very popular compiler used by professional programmers for writing systems programs. There are more C compilers for the IBM than for any other language, 15 at last count! The machine language produced by these C compilers is compact and efficient (although we defy any compiler to compete with our assembly-language code). C code is also very portable, unlike assembly language, which must be changed for each machine you work on. In contrast to the other high-level languages considered here, C lets the programmer guide the use of machine registers to increase efficiency. It also has extraordinary flexibility, allowing you to do things that are very difficult or impossible in other high-level languages. In many ways it can be regarded as a language whose level falls somewhere in between assembly language and other high-level languages. C is intimately related to the UNIX operating system (UNIX is written in C) and is indispensable on computers that run UNIX. The major software houses like Microsoft and Digital Research are now writing their compilers for other high-level languages in C, in an effort to make them both efficient and portable.

The fifth language is FORTH. (The author of FORTH, considering it to be a "fourth-generation" computer language, wanted to call it FOURTH, but only five-letter words were permitted on the IBM 1130, the first FORTH machine.) This language is an extensible reverse-Polish language (operands first, and then the operation to be done, just as for Hewlett-Packard calculators), which lends itself admirably to control applications. Unlike the previous four languages, FORTH has the advantages of an interpreter with some of the speed of a compiler, and disk-driven versions can run with as little as 16K of memory. The language is heavily structured and lacks a GOTO altogether. It runs on virtually every computer known to man, and is used by Atari for many cartridge game programs. If you're interested in small (or not so small) control applications and prefer a high-level language, consider FORTH. After reading this book, you should have a healthy appreciation for the stack, which is the central data structure in FORTH. However, FORTH's data-handling capabilities have to be organized by the programmer, and the reverse-Polish notation takes some getting used to. Also, FORTH tends to be a world unto itself, and can't easily be mixed with code from other languages.

We conclude this section with seven ways of writing a simple lock-in detection algorithm (lock-in techniques were discussed in Sec. 9-4). The first method is a flowchart, as shown in Fig. 11-1. Flowcharts are not a programming language, but rather a tool for understanding the logical flow of a program. Flowcharting is not advisable for everything in sight, but

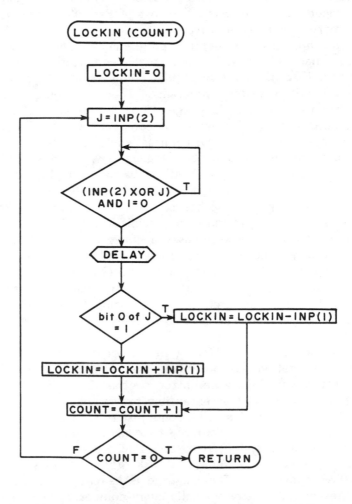

Fig. 11-1. Flowchart of a lock-in detection algorithm. This algorithm is implemented in six other forms in this section: assembly language, BASIC, FORTRAN 77, Pascal, C, and FORTH.

writing out a flowchart for a complicated algorithm may well be the only way to get a program using the algorithm to work. Although the lock-in algorithm here isn't really complicated enough to merit a flowchart, it provides a clear way to say what the program is supposed to do. In the flowchart of Fig. 11-1, INP(n) is a function that returns the value at input port n. DELAY is a user-coded phase delay routine, which plays the role of the "phase" knob on analog lock-in amplifiers (see Sec. 9-4).

The assembly-language version should be self-explanatory by now if you read the comments given along with the routine. It produces only 34 bytes of code, substantially less than any of the other methods. The BASIC program uses the WAIT function, which waits until the exclusive OR of the first and third arguments ANDed with the second argument is nonzero. The Pascal program looks just like ALGOL in this simple application. No fancy data structures are involved. To reveal the program logic, we've used indentation for all the high-level language versions. The FORTH program is the smallest of the five. Here, as in many controller applications, the limited data handling involved can be easily relegated to the program stack, making the FORTH algorithm very compact.

In the programs below, input ports 1 and 2 are connected to the signal to be averaged and to the reference, respectively.

ASSEMBLY LANGUAGE

```
;On entry CX has the desired count; on exit BX has the lock-in value

lockin: xor    bx,bx              ;BX accumulates the lock-in sum
        mov    ah,0
next:   in     al,ref             ;Get current reference flag: 1 for on,
        mov    dl,al              ; 0 for off
chglp:  in     al,ref             ;Wait for it to change
        xor    al,dl
        and    al,1               ;Check only bit 0
        jz     chglp
        call   delay
        test   dl,1               ;Was signal on?
        in     al,data
        mov    dl,al
        jnz    add
        sub    bx,ax              ;No: subtract input
        jmp    short inc
add:    add    bx,ax              ;Yes: add input
inc:    loop   next               ;CX has desired count on entry
        ret
```

BASIC

```
100 LOCKIN = 0
110 FOR I = 1 TO COUNT
120     J = INP(2)
130     WAIT INP(2),1,J
140     GOSUB 200
150     IF (J AND 1)>0 THEN LOCKIN = LOCKIN - INP(1)
        ELSE LOCKIN = LOCKIN + INP(1)
160     NEXT I
170 RETURN
200 'Delay subroutine goes here (if needed)
```

FORTRAN 77

```
        FUNCTION LOCKIN(COUNT)
        LOCKIN = 0

        DO 30 I = 1,COUNT
                J = INP(2)
10              IF(((J.XOR.INP(2)).AND.1).EQ.0) GO TO 10
                CALL DELAY
                IF((J.AND.1).EQ.0) LOCKIN = LOCKIN - INP(1)
                ELSE LOCKIN = LOCKIN + INP(1)
30      CONTINUE

        RETURN
        END
```

PASCAL

```
FUNCTION lockin(count: integer): integer;
    VAR i,j: integer;
    BEGIN
        lockin := 0;
        FOR i := 1 TO count DO
            BEGIN
                j := inp(2);
                WHILE (xor(j,inp(2)) AND 1) = 0 DO;
                delay;
                IF (j AND 1) THEN lockin := lockin - inp(1)
                ELSE lockin := lockin + inp(1);
            END;
    END;
```

C

```
lockin(count)        /* Lock-in detection function */
int count
{
    int i,j,lck;

    lck = 0;
    for (i = 0; i <= count; ++i) {
        j = inp(2);
        while ((j ^ inp(2)) & 1);        /* Wait for level change */
        delay();
        if (j & 1) lck -= inp(1);
        else lck += inp(1);
    }
    return(lck);
}
```

FORTH

(On entry, COUNT is on top of stack; on exit, lock-in value is there)

```
: LOCKIN 0 SWAP 0        ( Stack has: 0 lockin value, COUNT, 0)
  DO
    2 INP                ( Stack has: lockin value, INP(2))
    BEGIN  DUP  2 INP  XOR  1 AND  UNTIL
    DELAY
    1 INP  SWAP          ( Stack has: lockin value, INP(1), old INP(2))
    1 AND IF + ELSE - THEN
    LOOP;
```

Ordinarily, we comment more heavily than shown in these examples. Here the flowchart provides most of the commenting needed (we hope!).

With the exception of the interpreters, the high-level languages as well as assembly language need to have a linker program run after the compiler to bind the various program modules and system library routines together into an executable form. The ability to compile subroutines separately is very useful in program development, since then only routines with changes in them need to be recompiled. The compilers produce "object" modules that have various unresolved external references. The linker then resolves these references using corresponding internal pointers in other modules, or in the program libraries. Advanced linkers can also generate a linkable module from a number of input modules, thereby speeding up the linkage of commonly used routines such as a plotting package. The DOS for the IBM PC comes with a good linker. For more advanced applications, PLINK86 from Phoenix Software Associates is also available.

11-5. Disk Operating Systems

To develop software, run programs, or write papers, you need a *disk operating system* (DOS). This is just a program that handles I/O to and from the various devices attached to the computer and supervises the execution of other programs. Typically you just type in commands, and things happen. You can have the system type a file on the CRT console, or print it on the printer. You can display the names of files on the current disk directory. Or you can tell the operating system to load and execute another program such as an editor or a FORTRAN compiler. When that program has finished executing, control returns to the operating system.

This section first discusses the most popular disk operating system for 8086/8088-based microcomputers, namely Microsoft's MS-DOS, known on the IBM PC simply as DOS or PC-DOS. While some of the high-level language compilers and interpreters available on microcomputers are the equivalent of their mainframe counterparts, MS-DOS is not as powerful as mainframe operating systems like UNIX. But it's small and fast, has many UNIX features, and for most program development and word processing is all you need. If you like user-friendly, Apple Macintosh-like front ends, you have several possibilities. More software has been written to run under MS-DOS than for any other operating system. The important point is that MS-DOS has become a standard, much the way the less powerful CP/M-80 DOS (from Digital Research) is the standard for 8080/8085/Z80 microcomputers. The fact that so many people follow the MS-DOS conventions has made these conventions more useful than their betters. This chapter gives a selective overview of some useful MS-DOS features. We assume you'll read the manuals for actual usage, and the references provide further discussion. At the end of the section, we briefly describe MS-DOS front ends like Microsoft Windows and IBM's TopView, and compare MS-DOS to UNIX, which runs on hard disk PC's as well as on the Cray II supercomputer.

MS-DOS is a program on a diskette that "boots up" automatically in drive A (on drive C in most hard-disk systems) when the power is turned on or the computer is reset. The standard sign-on asks you to type in the date and time and then displays an "A>" on the console. The A> notifies you that disk drive A is initialized and that you can type further commands as desired. Alternatively, if a special **bat**ch file called AUTOEXEC.BAT is on the diskette, the commands it contains are **auto**matically **exec**uted before MS-DOS signs on with its "A>". We discuss this valuable feature in more detail later.

DOS 2.0 has 26 internal (built-in) commands and 19 external commands. When one of the internal commands such as ERASE (or its synonym DEL) is typed, DOS executes it instantly because the required code is already in memory. When an external command such as FORMAT is typed, DOS searches the current disk for a file with that command name and the extension .COM or .EXE, and then loads and executes that file. In fact, if you type the name of any .COM or .EXE file followed by a carriage return,

DOS will load and execute it. Thus the operating system is extensible in the sense that you can freely add any new commands to it that you want. The MS-DOS distribution disk includes a number of utility programs as standard external commands. These programs format diskettes, copy entire diskettes, compare files and diskettes, and provide many other services. The MS-DOS disk also includes a debugger, a linker, advanced BASIC (BASICA), and something that claims to be an editor, called EDLIN.COM. The first thing to do with your system is to quickly erase EDLIN from all your disks and buy a decent editor! In addition, you can buy all kinds of other .COM or .EXE files: editors, assemblers, compilers, games, and more. You can also make them yourself using the linker in combination with the Macro Assembler or a compiler. So it's easy to add new commands to the standard MS-DOS commands.

One useful but not well documented feature associated with output to the screen is that you can abort a command by typing control C (type a C while holding the Ctrl key down). Control C (Ctrl-C) is easier to type than Ctrl-Break as suggested in the DOS manual. Also, typing Ctrl-S pauses output to the screen, and typing Ctrl-Q or Ctrl-S again (Ctrl-S is a toggle) restarts the output. The more general (but harder to type) Ctrl-NumLock stops execution of anything until another character is typed. This facility is built into the ROM BIOS keyboard interrupt handler and thus is always present. Another very handy feature is that typing Ctrl-P toggles the echoing of screen output to the printer.

When a set of program object modules is linked together by the linker, a .EXE file is produced, which differs in some respects from a .COM file. As discussed in Sec. 4-6, both types of files are executable, but .EXE files allow larger programs and more intricate relocation features. Since they require some extra preprocessing, .EXE files take about 1 second longer to load from floppy and about 850H bytes extra to store on disk. For this reason, simple files are better converted to .COM files if possible. This conversion is performed by the program EXE2BIN.

Now let's look again at batch files, which can simplify the whole assembly and linking process. A batch file is a file with the extension .BAT that just contains a set of commands. Suppose you're debugging a program and have to go through many iterations of assemble, link, convert to .COM, and debug. You can write a batch file M.BAT that contains the following:

```
masm %1;
link %1;
exe2bin %1 %1.com
sst %1.com
```

Then, for example, typing "m piano" assembles, links, and converts the PIANO.ASM file to PIANO.COM, and runs it under SST. You don't have to debug this particular program, since we've already done that. Just play some Chopin! But you probably have many other ideas to check out. Batch files can have considerable decision power owing to the presence of replaceable parameters and the ECHO, FOR, GOTO, IF, and SHIFT commands.

The most important of all batch files is the AUTOEXEC.BAT file mentioned earlier. This file automatically brings up the system with your custom modifications. As an example, we give a simple AUTOEXEC.BAT for a hard disk system

```
prompt $p$g
path c:®;c:®ps;c:®bin
sst/r
hgc save
kb1
```

The prompt command tells DOS to output the full path name of the subdirectory you're currently working in. For example if you're in a subdirectory on drive C called LOTUS, instead of the DOS prompt C>, you see C:®LOTUS>, which is a great help if you use subdirectories (and you should!).

The PATH command sets up one or more path names to search whenever the system fails to find a file in the current (sub)directory. For example, it's useful to have a search path that points to a directory containing the system utilities, word processor, and compilers. In the example, the root directory, and the subdirectories PS and BIN are searched.

SST/R loads a resident copy of SST to catch DIVIDE OVERFLOWS in the act, to enable an NMI button (normally-open push button connected to the A1 and B1 lines on the I/O channel), to provide a scientific calculator, and to facilitate debugging in general. HGC SAVE runs a Hercules program that turns off the monochrome screen after 3 minutes with no keyboard action. KB1 speeds up the AT keyboard (see end of Sec. 8-1) to a 1/4-second auto-repeat delay and 30-cps autorepeat rate—one hot keyboard!

You can also make up your own diskettes to initialize the system in other ways. For example, a diskette could be dedicated to billing forms for sales of various computer boards and equipment. This diskette might have an AUTOEXEC.BAT file containing

```
astclock
mp
```

which defines the time and date using an AST multifunction-card option and then executes the Multiplan spreadsheet program. The nice thing about this usage is that Multiplan comes up running without requiring any effort (or knowledge) on the part of the user. In particular, messages can be displayed on the screen and the last command in the AUTOEXEC.BAT file can start the execution of any other program that you want. This makes it very easy to set up a floppy or hard disk for someone else that is easy to use and virtually self-documenting. You just say, "Insert this diskette, turn on the power, and do what the computer tells you.' The user doesn't have to know anything about MS-DOS!

Previous chapters explained how to assemble and link programs and how to generate interrupt-handling routines that are executed and then remain resident (see Sec. 4-6). The HGC.COM, SST.COM, and KB1.COM programs mentioned in the AUTOEXEC.BAT file above are examples of this kind of program. The idea is that you can extend the operating system with routines to suit your needs. These extensions do not require modifying MS-DOS itself or patching the BIOS program as you must do with CP/M on a Z80, for example. The extensions are introduced by simple system commands.

MS-DOS 2.0 and later versions also have a more general way of handling device drivers that is, in principle, independent of the underlying BIOS interrupt vector structure. As discussed in Sec. 4-6, one can define device drivers in a very general UNIX-compatible way. Although this method is typically more involved than simply taking over an interrupt vector, it can run on any MS-DOS computer provided appropriate changes are made to the low-level I/O interface calls. To load the device drivers automatically, include a line with 'device = ' followed by the driver filename in a special file call CONFIG.SYS. The CONFIG.SYS file can also overrule some special system parameters, such as the amount of RAM for file buffers.

MS-DOS 2.0 includes a number of other handy UNIX-like features, such as pipes, search paths, I/O redirection, and tree-structured directories. Hence even the small-computer user (one without a hard disk) has a DOS that is upward compatible with the high-powered UNIX operating system that requires a 10-megabyte (or larger) hard disk to run properly. To support these UNIX-like facilities, MS-DOS 2.0 has a number of new commands. The concept of I/O redirection, discussed in Chap. 4, allows any device to be treated like a disk file, and vice versa. In particular, one can redirect the standard I/O devices to arbitrary path names. A pipe is a method whereby the standard output from one process is fed into the input of another without any intervening console activity. For example, to display an alphabetized directory, you can type 'dir|sort'. This causes the output of the DIR command to be fed into the input of the SORT command, which then outputs the results to the screen. Hence you don't have to say anything about the intermediate disk file that's automatically created and later deleted (this works best on hard-disk systems, since floppies are annoyingly slow).

Tree-structured directories are very valuable for hard-disk systems, since they allow you to dynamically allocate logically meaningful directories. If you simply treat the hard disk like a single floppy disk, you'll end up with so many files on it that you can't find anything in the clutter of names printed out whenever you type a DIR command. With DOS 2.0 you can create subdirectories on any disk by using the MD (make directory) command. You can then go to the subdirectory (make that subdirectory active) with the CD (change directory) command. A file belonging to the active subdirectory can be accessed by its name alone. A file outside the active directory can be accessed (although not executed, as can be done in UNIX) by its *path name*. The path name consists of a backslash followed by a subdirectory name that appears in the main directory (usually called the *root* directory), followed by a backslash and the next subdirectory name, and so on, down to the subdirectory in which the file resides. The IBM *DOS* manual explains this in more detail.

A number of multitasking "shells" or front ends are available for DOS that add power and user friendliness. We mention here Microsoft *Windows* and IBM's *TopView*, or preferably Microsoft's high performance TopView look-alike, *Mondrian*. These programs give an attractive menu/mouse-driven screen to DOS and allow you to execute several programs apparently simultaneously, such as a compiler and a number crunch program, all while you edit away. Both programs require Program Information Files to tell them how much knowledge the programs to be run have about Windows or TopView. A major difference is that Mondrian runs in speedy text mode with a somewhat jumpy mouse cursor, while Windows runs in slow but elegant graphics mode with a well-behaved mouse cursor. On an AT, Mondrian is spectacular, boasting rapid switching between programs, while Windows runs at an acceptable speed. We don't recommend running either one on a 4.77-MHz PC. Compared to Mondrian, IBM's TopView (at least in June 1986) is a slow-running monster that needs an 80386-based PC to be useful. Ironically most people seem to be very happy with good old DOS plus an assortment of handy RAM-resident programs like Borland's *Sidekick*. This simpler approach runs fine on ordinary PC's and gives a useful measure of multitasking.

MS-DOS 2.0, 3.1, and later versions provide significant steps toward UNIX, while remaining relatively small and fast. UNIX lifts the microcomputer up into the multiuser, multitasking minicomputer world. The size of UNIX requires a hard disk and a full RAM complement. Microsoft's XENIX uses the AT's protected mode to access up to 15 megabytes of RAM. UNIX is very powerful, incorporating facilities such as forks (one program can branch out and spawn others) and pipes, spooling, tree-structured directories, an on-line manual, search paths, a huge number of system utilities, and concurrent processing in general. The original UNIX is a programmer's operating system: very user unfriendly initially, but very programmer efficient once you've become an expert. For example, to display a file on the screen you must type "CAT filename". CAT has nothing to do with your favorite pet; it's short for concatenate, and if the CAT command is given only one argument, then the standard output, namely the console screen, is assumed to be the destination. Further, try to find a BACKUP command to back up your hard disk files onto floppy disk. If you look long enough, you'll find that this function is named TAR, which stands for **t**ape **a**rchiver, and forces you to treat your floppy as if it were a magnetic tape drive. A system that works like this does not fare very well in the microcomputer world, which has many programming novices and nonprogrammers. To get around such obscurities, UNIX *shells* exist that present more user-friendly faces, complete with readable menus. As programmers, we realize that menus can slow a proficient programmer down. Nevertheless, they make the system much easier to learn, and substantially reduce the number of questions one has to answer. The user-friendly trend in computing is a delightful innovation spawned by the microcomputer community.

11-6. Computer Hierarchies

At this point you've seen how to use the IBM PC to interface to laboratory devices, to buildings, to various kinds of machinery, to printers, to other computers, and more. We've surveyed the large range of software available and various systems, putting the whole thing together. What remains is to glance at the position of the IBM PC and PC AT in the overall world of computing. When do you use an IBM PC? when a Cray II supercomputer? This particular comparison is extreme. Today at least, each has its place, and you'd probably seldom use one where you'd use the other.

Even within the IBM PC world, there is already a hierarchy, ranging from a small floppy-based PC to a 12-MHz AT with 15 megabytes of RAM and 300 megabytes of hard disk. The small IBM PC is a good machine to interface devices to, and to run experiments on. It's hard to beat for sophisticated word processing, although it's not fast enough for responsive bit-mapped screen editing. The AT adds the extra muscle to be good for simple to moderately complex calculations. There are several areas, however, where these microcomputers can't compete with their bigger brothers. They just compute too slowly. Even with an 8087 coprocessor, the PC takes about 20 microseconds to multiply two floating-point numbers. This is quite adequate for many kinds of calculations. However, a new multiplication of this accuracy can begin every 12.5 nanoseconds on a Cray I. That's more than three orders of magnitude faster. The Cray I compiles 5000 FORTRAN statements per second! So if you're number-crunch bound, you'll want to use the Cray I. Even with an 8087, the IBM PC would never finish a complicated weather calculation in time for a usable forecast. On the other hand, the Cray I can't be used to control an experiment directly, and it would be a waste of both the Cray I's and the programmer's time to use it for text editing. Of course, we anticipate having microcomputers with the power of a Cray I in our homes within ten years. But since the years go by so fast, we aren't rushing it. As the saying goes, "Every year things get better, so if you wait to buy your computer equipment until you die, it'll be fantastic!"

There's a whole spectrum of computing power in between the Cray I and the 8088. In addition to their raw computational power, big machines like the IBM mainframes and Cray supercomputers have big data bases and elegant peripherals. These are major advantages and are the primary reason that large computer centers are still, and probably will remain, useful. But using an elegant large time-shared computer 10 for teaching BASIC to students is ludicrous. An IBM PC can do this better, faster, and cheaper. On the other hand, a mainframe computer typically has the ability to handle very large data bases, useful in business and scientific applications. It has immediate access to a wide variety of software and has its programs and data bases securely backed up on magnetic tape. Big machines also offer large memories for big problems. But big machines are expensive.

Wouldn't it be nice to have the advantages of both when you want them? You can! That's where computer hierarchies come in. On the low level, running experiments, editing text, or doing simple calculations, you use one of your microcomputers. When you need the large machine facilities, you connect the microcomputer to the mainframe. For example, you could collect data from an experiment, perform preliminary processing, and then ship the data to the mainframe to number-crunch. When it's done, the mainframe ships the results back to the microcomputer for display on a screen or on paper. Alternatively, the big machine can plot the results on its fancy microfilm recorder, ready for the publisher! You pay for the big machine only when you need its power, not for the trivia of entering text, debugging programs, or taking data. Meanwhile, you don't personally have to maintain all that fancy equipment that makes the mainframes so powerful and expensive. If the micro and the mainframe are in the same building, the data rate between the two can be 9600 baud using a simple serial link. At worst it would be 1200 baud over an ordinary phone line. Alternatively, you might want to hook your PC into a computer network that includes a mainframe and get really fast data transfer rates.

In addition to providing paths up and down the hierarchy, networks can connect computers of similar power, leading to truly distributed processing systems. Imagine executing someone's program on a machine down the hall with data from a machine across the country, all from the machine in your own office. This sounds something like time sharing, but it's actually network computing and is already a reality in many places. Using networking software on an IBM PC, you can access files stored in other computers simply by typing the proper path name. Networks also provide access to the large data bases and expensive peripheral devices hitherto the sole domain of large time-shared computers. Computer networks have the potential to become very popular as the intensely competitive R&D efforts by Xerox, IBM, DEC, Intel, and others pay off in inexpensive network hardware and software.

A revolution continually brews in which today's minicomputers and smaller mainframes will be replaced by a new generation of microprocessors. Intel's 32-bit 80386 offers a stunning upward compatible route for the IBM PC and AT. You could have guessed that the eight 16-bit general registers of the 80286 (and 8088) would turn into 32 bits in a way that preserves the 8-bit and 16-bit capabilities. You could have guessed that the 80386 can run all the 80286 software with at most reassembly or recompilation. You could have guessed that it would run at least twice as fast, and have at least twice the physical memory space. But could you have guessed that it features a raw bus speed six times that of the 80286 (at 8 MHz, 24 megabytes/second vs the 80286's 4), that its physical address space is 4 gigabytes (vs the 80286's 16 megabytes), that its virtual address space is 64 terabytes (vs 1 gigabyte), that the maximum segment size is 4 gigabytes (vs 64 kilobytes), that it has special bit string insert and extract instructions that seem ideal for bit-mapped graphics applications, that index registers can be automatically scaled to give memory offsets in byte, word, double-word, or quad-word units, that while running UNIX in protected virtual address mode, a simple hardware task switch allows it to emulate an 8086 DOS enviroment, that it has on-chip hardware paging as well as virtual segments, and that the 80387 numeric coprocessor runs six times as fast as the 80287? This machine is substantially faster and bigger than a DEC VAX 11/780.

It looks like the ideal PS™ Technical Word Processor machine. People have been saying that word processing doesn't require high-speed comput-ers. True—if all you want is routine office correspondance looking as if it is typed on a typewriter. But more and more people want something better, something that looks typeset. Elegantly formatted text on bit-mapped screens carried out in real time so that the user cannot see screen redraw requires a machine like a 20-MHz 80386. On such a machine, we could edit proportionally-spaced multiple-font text with built-up mathematical formulas, line drawings, automatic hyphenation, figure insertion, compound headings/footings all displayed on 1000 x 1000 dot screens, and drive laser printers at three times that resolution in the background. For such word processing, what you see is what you want, rather than with today's what-you-see-is-what-you-get word processors. Actually to really have instan-taneous 1000 x 1000 bit-mapped screens even with optimized assembly language programs and all this elegant formatting requires about twice the speed of a 20-MHz 80386, but we're getting tantalizingly close to super word processing. In principle, specialized text processing hardware can be added to yield the desired response, but CPU's with large memories and sheer raw speed driving bit-mapped screens certainly offer greater flexibil-ity. The power of this computer illustrates a way in which many problems too big for today's microcomputers will be done with tomorrow's micro-computers, and the lines in the computer hierarchy will have to be redrawn.

But there's one infamous problem in sticking with familiar territory in computer circles: every 5 years brings a new computer generation. Unwill-ingness to learn new systems may save you time in the present but will make you obsolete in the near future. Of course, we never claimed that com-puting was a safe business. Computing is a two-edged sword: you can cut with it, but it can also cut you. It leads to one perilous adventure after another, with never a dull moment, and maybe after any number of humili-ating experiences you finally reach that pot of gold at the end of the rainbow. Then you breathe a sigh of relief and you're all ready for the next adventure!

References

The SST debugger and the PS™ Technical Word Processor are available from Scroll Systems, Tucson, AZ. The PMATE editor and PLINK86 linker are available from Phoenix Software Associates in Norwood, MA. Turbo Lightning, Turbo Pascal, and Sidekick are available from Borland International in Scotts Valley, CA.

The best source of information about the hardware and software products currently available for the IBM PC are the magazines devoted to the PC, especially *PC Tech Journal*, *PC World*, *PC* magazine, *PC Week*, and *BYTE* magazine.

In particular for a good discussion of DOS disk format, see Glen F. Roberts, 1986, "Finding Disk Parameters," *PC Tech Journal*, Vol. 4, No. 5, p. 112; for the Expanded Memory Specification, see Ted Mirecki, 1986, "Expandable Memory," *PC Tech Journal*, Vol. 4, No. 2, p. 66; and for data acquisition, see Eric. M. Miller, 1986, "Digitizing Analog Data," *PC Tech Journal*, Vol. 4, No. 5, p. 52.

P. Norton, 1983, *Inside the IBM PC*, Robert J. Brady Company, Bowie, MD. Provides an introductory overview of the IBM PC's hardware and system software. This book is at its best describing the operation of the floppy disks and the way the operating system stores data on them. See also P. Norton, 1984, *MS-DOS and PC-DOS User's Guide*, Robert J. Brady Company, Bowie, MD. This book describes how to use DOS and serves as a supplement to IBM's DOS manual.

IBM PC and AT *Technical Reference*s and *Adaptors*, 1983, IBM Corporation, Boca Raton, FL. This manual contains authoritative descriptions of the PC's hardware, complete schematics, and complete source code listings for the ROM BIOS routines. In particular, the NEC 765 disk controller chip and its programming are described.

J. Welsh and J. Elder, 1979, *Introduction to Pascal*, Prentice-Hall International, Englewood Cliffs, NJ. A good introductory book on Pascal. Many others are also available.

L. P. Meissner and E. I. Organik, 1980, *FORTRAN 77: Featuring Structured Programming*, Addison-Wesley Publishing Company, Reading, MA. One of many good books on FORTRAN 77.

B. W. Kernighan and D. M. Ritchie, 1978, *The C Programming Language*, Prentice-Hall Inc., Englewood Cliffs, NJ. This is the bible for the C language, and serves as the official language reference. At the same time it is a very well written tutorial book.

L. Brodie, 1981, *Starting FORTH*, Prentice-Hall Inc., Englewood Cliffs, NJ. This is widely regarded as the best book available on FORTH.

Disk Operating System, 1983, IBM Corporation, Boca Raton, FL. The DOS manual contains complete descriptions of all the DOS commands and utilities. Starting with DOS 2.1, this manual has been divided into two volumes. The second volume, called *DOS Technical Reference*, costs extra and contains what were formerly the appendices of the DOS 2.0 manual.

H. McGilton and R. Morgan, 1983, *Introducing the UNIX System*, McGraw-Hill Book Company, New York. One of the better introductory books describing the UNIX system for new users.

12
Building Your Own Interfaces

Experience is directly proportional to the amount of equipment ruined.
—Murphy

Many people reading this book will eventually want to build or troubleshoot an interface or a piece of digital circuitry of their own. When you're ready to do that, it's time to read this chapter. We try to walk you through the construction process, pointing out where the potential pitfalls are, some of the tools and equipment we've found useful, a bit of general construction philosophy, and the order in which to do things. This last point is all too often ignored, resulting in wails of "Why didn't I remember to do that first!" The importance of good documentation practices is also stressed, so that six months later when you want to change or repair something, you don't find that your schematic: (1) is unreadable, (2) doesn't correspond to the actual wiring on the board, or (3) is nonexistent. To keep the discussion down to earth, we illustrate the construction and debugging hints by a detailed discussion of the construction of a combination serial/parallel I/O board.

The construction of an interface circuit can be divided into three distinct phases: the circuit design, the actual wiring of the circuitry, and, all too often, the correction of errors (usually referred to as debugging). These three phases are covered in Secs. 12-1 through 12-3, respectively.

12-1. Designing Computer Interfaces

Unless you're an experienced digital designer, you'll probably be at a loss as to how to begin to design an interface. The starting point is to follow the golden rule of amateur design, namely, "See how someone else has done it." If you're building a circuit for your own use, the best way to do the design is to find a schematic of something that does roughly what you want and then copy it. However, if you're designing a piece of equipment to sell, this is a poor idea unless you enjoy defending yourself against lawsuits. In any event, you've first got to decide precisely what you need. Write out, in as much detail as you can, an answer to the question: Exactly what do I want this circuit to do?

Once you know what you want the interface to do, study schematics of similar circuits until you understand how they work, and then copy them, perhaps making some modifications to fit your particular application or the availability of parts. Usually you'll find that your circuit can be divided up into several fairly independent pieces such as address decoders, oscillators, data buffers, and high power drivers. Thus, even if you can't find an exist-ing circuit that does exactly what you want, you can usually find most or all of the various pieces from one source or another. There are many places to look for circuit ideas. The IBM PC *Options and Adapters Technical Reference* manuals give schematics for all of IBM's interface boards. Other good sources include the more technically oriented microcomputer magazines such as *BYTE* and *Ciarcia's Circuit Cellar* volumes, sche-matics of any boards your friends may have, other microcomputer interfac-ing books, and many of the examples given earlier in this book.

Often the heart of an interface is some LSI chip: a UART, an IEEE 488 chip, a stepper-motor controller chip, or a smart parallel port chip. When these chips are involved, make sure the chip you select is compatible with the general design philosophy of the IBM bus. For example, you don't want a serial port chip that expects the address and data bus to be multiplexed together, since the IBM has these brought out separately. Similarly, you wouldn't choose the Zilog PIO chip if you wanted to use it with interrupts, since this chip expects to read the instruction stream along with the CPU and will respond automatically when it sees certain Z80 op codes.

Once you have a tentative schematic, walk through it step by step, thinking through the logic of each gate, until you're convinced that the circuit will work properly and that it will respond if and only if it's given the proper commands by the bus. Don't forget about the "only if" part. When there are many small-scale logic parts on the board you should also think about minimizing the parts count. For example, extra NAND or NOR gates can be used as inverters, perhaps saving an extra package of 7404's. In addition, if your board choice is already determined, make sure all the IC's will fit on the board with a few additional spaces left over in case you need to add something later.

If you're not certain about whether a particular circuit idea will work, or what component values to use, you may want to test your ideas on a breadboard such as the Global Specialties PB-6 Proto-Board. Such boards (called *solderless breadboards*) contain a matrix of tiny contacts into which you can insert IC's, wires, and components. This allows you to very rapidly build, check, and modify a circuit with no soldering or wire-wrapping. When you're done, pull everything out and the breadboard is ready to use for something else. This preliminary step is particularly valuable for things like oscillators, audio amplifiers, and many other kinds of analog circuitry. To test these items you'll need a power supply for the breadboard (+5 volt and perhaps +15 and -15 volt supplies) and some test equipment such as a voltmeter, logic probe, or oscilloscope (see the debugging section below for a discussion of test equipment). Once you've gotten the particular subcircuit in question to work, you can go on to finish the design.

At this point you presumably have a rough sketch of the circuit you want to build. It's now very tempting to rush on and build the interface, but you'll be glad later if you first take the time to draw up a complete, well-laid-out schematic. It will be easier to read if you follow the standard conventions for digital logic schematics. The flow of the logic should be generally from left to right, with inputs on the left-hand side of the page and outputs on the right-hand side. If possible, group logically related sub-sections such as the decoding circuitry together. In the schematic, wires that simply cross each other are understood to have no connection. If they are to be connected, place a black dot on the intersection. When you draw the schematic, don't indicate any pin numbers where the wires connect to an IC. These will be filled in later as the actual wiring is done.

You can draw a perfectly adequate schematic freehand, but if you want the result to look professional, use a logic template (the Berol RapiDesign half-size or three-quarter-size logic symbol templates are excellent). We've found it helpful to draw the schematic on 11- by 17-inch graph paper with 0.1-inch grid lines. This makes it easy to keep the wires and components spaced evenly and squared up. To avoid smearing pencil lead all over the logic templates, use a Pentel mechanical pencil that has a thin metal sheath covering the lead.

To help make the these ideas concrete, let's consider the design of an interface board that has a serial port and two parallel ports with hand-shaking. More specifically, let's suppose you want a serial port that is compatible with the one IBM uses on its serial interface board, so that the ROM BIOS routines in the IBM can be used to initialize and drive it. In addition, suppose you want two parallel I/O ports with handshaking. These should be flexible so that they can be used for a variety of purposes. For example, you may want to use one port as a Centronics parallel output port for a printer and the other as an input port for a pair of Atari-type joy-sticks. Or you may want to use one as an output port to drive a Votrax speech synthesizer, and the other as an output port to control a stepper motor driver circuit. In other words, you don't want to commit yourself in hardware to any particular port configuration: you want a programmable parallel port.

To meet these specifications, you can follow IBM's choices by using the National Semiconductor 8250 UART (Sec. 10-2) as the heart of the serial port and the 8255 PPI (Sec. 6-3) for the parallel port. You can also use the same decoding circuit for the 8250 that IBM uses, and the same data-bus buffer (a 74LS245, Fig. 5-19). See the schematic of the asynchronous communications adapter in the IBM PC *Options and Adapters Technical Reference* manuals for further details. However, you also need address decoding for the 8255 to obtain a signal to drive its chip-select line, and the data bus buffer must be activated properly when either the 8250 or the 8255 is selected. A simple way to accomplish everything is to use a 7430 8-input NAND gate as an address decoder, just as IBM did for the asynchronous communications adapter. However, connect only the A3 and A5—A9 address lines plus AEN to the 7430's inputs as shown in Fig. 12-1.

The 7430 will then respond to addresses 3F8—3FF and 3E8—3EF, and its output can be used to enable the 74LS245 bus buffer. The 7430's output can also be ANDed with address line A4 to provide a chip enable for the 8250, and ANDed with $\overline{A4}$ to provide a chip enable for the 8255. The advantage of this choice is that the serial port is at its standard address of 3F8—3FF (the 8250 serial chip requires a block of 7 contiguous I/O ports). At the same time, the parallel port chip does not use any addresses that are reserved for use by other standard IBM adapter boards (see the I/O port address map given in Table 6-1).

As can be seen in the schematic of Fig. 12-1, OR gates with negative logic inputs are used to provide the two AND functions that generate the chip select signals from the 7430's output and address line A4. The two remaining OR gates in the 7432 are used to buffer the $\overline{IOR}$ and RESET lines so that all bus lines coming onto the board meet IBM's specification of no more than two TTL loads per bus line in each I/O slot. Note that $\overline{IOR}$ drives the direction line of the 74LS245 buffer so that the 74LS245 normally reads the data bus onto the board. It drives the data bus only when $\overline{IOR}$ is active. This is the way you should always wire up your data-bus buffers. The AEN line is wired into the 7430 decoder so that the board can never be accidentally selected during DMA transfers. This also is good practice, unless of course you want to use DMA on the board.

The necessary bus signals for the 8255 are just those already present for the 8250. It needs a bidirectional data bus, I/O read and write signals, a master reset signal, address lines A0 and A1, and a chip select. The only loose end is that the 8255 does not use A2, and it hasn't been decoded by the 7430. You could add another gate so that A2 along with A4 and the 7430 output would produce the chip select, but it's much easier to simply ignore A2. This means that the 8255 (which uses only four contiguous I/O ports) will respond to ports 3E8—3EB and 3EC—3EF. This causes no problem as long as you don't try to put some other I/O device at either of these

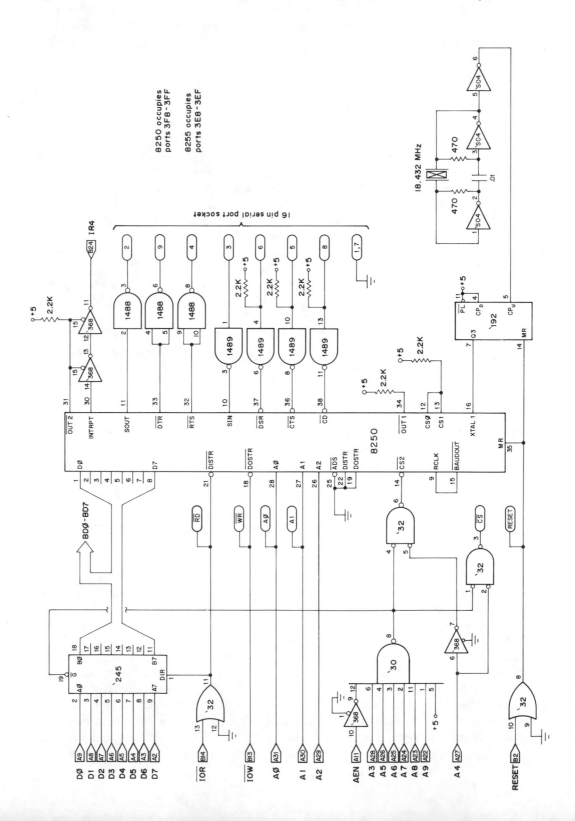

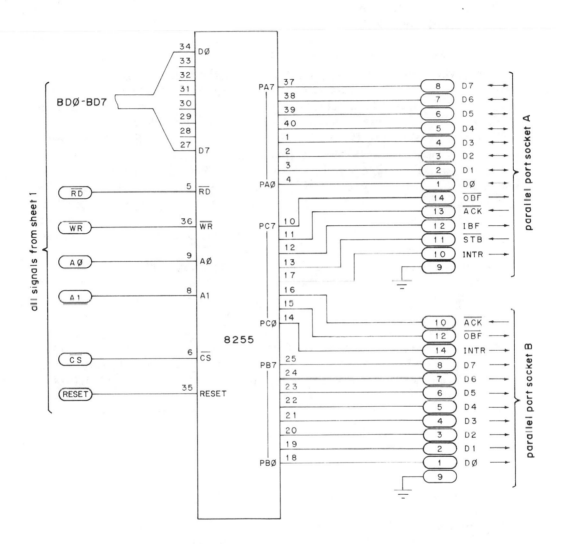

Fig. 12-1. Schematic diagram of a wire-wrapped serial/parallel interface board. One IBM-compatible serial port and two general-purpose parallel I/O ports are implemented.

locations. This redundant decoding wastes four I/O ports, but since there are still many possible port addresses left for other devices, this seems a small price to pay for simplifying the circuit.

The board must also have RS-232 line drivers and receivers. Instead of using the nonstandard parts chosen by IBM, you can use the familiar 1488 and 1489 line drivers and receivers (Sec. 10-3). To save an extra 1489 package, you can ignore the ring-indicator (RI) signal. This signal isn't used by IBM's serial port software drivers and would be useful only if you wanted the computer to automatically answer incoming phone calls using a modem. One improvement that can be made over the IBM design is to add pull-up resistors to the $\overline{DSR}$, $\overline{CTS}$, and $\overline{CD}$ (also called $\overline{RLSD}$) lines. With this arrangement, these handshake signals still work but are not required if you want to use a simple serial hookup with a 3-wire cable and no hardware handshaking. Following IBM's convention, the signal pinouts on the DB25 connector are connected to make the serial port behave like a terminal (a DTE device). The 8250 interrupt-request line is also wired up using two tristate gates from a 74LS368 buffer. This leaves four inverters for use in other parts of the circuit.

Finally a 1.8432-MHz clock is needed for the 8250. IBM uses a packaged oscillator chip, but these are not conveniently available. A 1.8432-MHz crystal together with the on-chip oscillator of the 8250 could be used, but crystals of this frequency are also not readily available. Instead, an oscillator can be made using a more common 18.432-MHz crystal and three 74S04 inverters. During its design, this circuit was first built on a solderless breadboard and tested using a variety of resistor and capacitor values. The capacitor value didn't matter much, and 470-ohm resistors gave the cleanest square-wave output. A 74LS192 counter is used to divide the oscillator output frequency by ten. With the complete design now in hand and neatly drawn up as shown in Fig. 12-1, the board is ready to build.

12-2. Construction Techniques

Computer interfaces can most easily be built on a prototype board. This is a piece of circuit board covered with a pattern of predrilled holes and having printed circuit traces for +5 volts and ground running to all parts of the board. Several varieties are available that are the right size to fit in the PC's I/O expansion channel slots and include the proper gold-plated edge connector. A number of companies sell such boards, most notably Vector Electronics. IBM also makes a prototype board that has bus buffering and some address decoding circuitry already present on the board.

Although there are a variety of usable wiring techniques, we greatly prefer the proven, reliable technique of wire-wrapping. Soldering is much too slow and messy, and we're not convinced of the long-term reliability of techniques such as slit-and-wrap. In wire-wrapping, a 1-inch length of

30-gauge stripped wire is wrapped about ten times around a square wire-wrap post. This may not sound so reliable, but the wire is stretched around the sharp post corners by the wire-wrap tool so that there are forty tight connections for each wire. This technique has been used to wire many mainframe computers, and we have never seen a reasonably done wire-wrapped connection fail. One cannot say the same about solder joints, which cause problems fairly often.

To do the wire-wrapping, you need a wire-wrap tool. The ones made by OK Machine and Tool Corporation are excellent and can be obtained at many electronics stores. Get the "modified wrap" variety, which puts a turn of insulated wire around the post before the stripped portion is wrapped. This strengthens the connection and helps prevent problems with shorts to adjacent circuitry. You also need a supply of wire-wrap wire. This can be bought in spools with a built-in wire stripper, or you can buy an assortment of prestripped wire in various lengths. The prestripped wire is more expensive but much more convenient. A variety of wire assortments can be obtained from Page Digital Electronics. Finally, you need to have wire-wrap sockets for your integrated circuits and some wire-wrap pins such as the Vector T46-4-9 pins. The latter are used to make connections to the card edge connector.

Other essential tools include a pair of wire cutters with very small jaws so that they can get into tight places (those sold by Radio Shack as 5-inch Nippy cutters are ideal), a small pair of needle-nose pliers for bending wires and component leads, and a good pair of fine-tip tweezers.

You also need a soldering iron to make connections to power and ground lines on the prototype card and to install miscellaneous discrete components. What is needed here is a small, light iron with a 25- to 40-watt heating element and a long thin tip. It's important that the tip be long and very narrow (about 1/16-inch diameter) so that you can get into the tight places often encountered on a wire-wrap board. In addition to some rosin-core solder, a clean-tip sponge to wipe off the soldering iron tip is handy, as is a spool of desoldering braid (both available from Radio Shack). The braid is placed over any connection you want to unsolder, and then heated with the soldering iron. The hot braid soaks up all the solder so that the connection can easily be taken apart. A bit of paintbrush cleaner on a Q-tip cotton swab can be used to clean off any solder flux deposits left behind, leaving the dismantled connection as good as new.

Installing Sockets and Discrete Components

Once you have a good circuit schematic and the proper tools, you're ready to start actual construction. The first items you should permanently install on any wire-wrap board are wire-wrap pins for all the card edge connector signals used in your design. There is a solder pad with a hole in the middle connected to each gold-plated finger on the card edge connector. You should insert a pin in the appropriate position for each bus signal used on the board (see Sec. 6-5 for a diagram showing where the various bus signals are located on the connector). A good way to insert the pins is to cut a short length of small diameter copper or brass tubing and hold it vertically in a clamp or vise. Insert a pin into the board by hand and then place the board on top of the tubing so that the pin extends through the board and into the tubing. You can now tap the pin all the way in with a hammer. The tubing supports the board around the pin area and prevents it from breaking. Insert the pins so they stick out on the *wiring* side of the board. When the pins have all been inserted, solder each pin in place.

Next, figure out how many sockets of each size (14-pin, 16-pin, etc.) you need, and try various arrangements of the sockets on the wire-wrap board to see which works best. Since there are many data and address lines, it's best to arrange the chips so that the lengths of these lines are as short as possible. The one restriction is that you should have pin 1 on every chip oriented in the same direction. Violation of this rule leads to almost certain disaster later when a chip is accidentally plugged in backward and goes up in smoke. Pin 1 on a socket is usually marked by a cut-off corner where pin 1 is, or by a small semicircular notch in one end of the socket. In the latter case, pin 1 is found as follows: Hold the socket with the wire-wrap pins facing down and the notch facing toward you. Pin 1 is the pin nearest you on the right-hand side of the socket.

Be sure you also leave room for any discrete components needed such as pull-up resistors and crystals. Make a sketch or mark on the board where you want the sockets, but don't permanently install them yet.

Before putting the sockets in permanently, it's wise to install a generous number of decoupling capacitors on the board. As discussed in Sec. 5-3, these are essential for reliable operation of digital logic circuitry. These capacitors should be soldered in place between the power and ground lines of the board. Most wire-wrap boards either have alternating rows of power (+5 volts) and ground lines or they have all the power lines on one side of the board and all the ground lines on the other side (these are usually called power and ground planes). In either case there are usually conveniently placed pairs of holes into which the capacitors can be soldered. The capacitors should be ceramic (not electrolytic or tantalum) with a capacitance of 0.01 to 0.1 microfarad. There should be about one capacitor for every two integrated circuit packages, and they should be distributed around the board so that no IC power supply pin is much more than 1 or 2 inches away from a capacitor. When installing the capacitors, keep the leads as short as possible. Failure to put in enough decoupling capacitors can result in a flaky board that is virtually impossible to debug. You should solder in these capacitors before installing the sockets to avoid the problem of having to cram a soldering iron in between the rows of wire-wrap pins on the sockets.

If the board needs -5, +12, or -12 volt power, you should also install extra capacitors near the socket pins where this power is used. These should have one lead soldered to ground and the other lead sticking through a free hole in the board (one not connected to +5 volts or ground). This lead can be cut off leaving about 0.5 inch sticking straight out of the wiring side of the board. Later, a wire-wrap connection can be made between this lead and the IC socket.

It's also a good idea to install a tantalum capacitor of 10 to 30 microfarads between +5 volts and ground on the board near the edge connector where the power and ground lines come on board. Most wire-wrap boards have positions marked for these capacitors. Make sure you put them in with the proper orientation since they are polarized. You may also want to install some discrete components such as crystals, pull-up resistors, or other capacitors and resistors at this time. Some ideas for ways to install these are discussed below. If you haven't used these types of electronic components before, you should familiarize yourself with how they're marked. Resistors are marked with four colored bands using a standard color code. You should either memorize this code or buy the little resistor color code card from Radio Shack. Capacitors are a little trickier to identify. Ceramic capacitors often come in the form of small flat disks with a number stamped on them that gives the capacitance in picofarads. Tantalum capacitors are often teardrop shaped, and the number stamped on them gives the capacitance in microfarads. Electrolytic capacitors are usually small cylinders and also have the capacitance given in microfarads. Both tantalum and electrolytic capacitors have one lead marked with a plus sign or sometimes a dot. This lead must always be connected to the positive side of any voltage difference to be applied to the capacitor. If the lead is reversed, the capacitor will be destroyed. Hi-Q ceramic capacitors are generally used for the capacitance range of 0.001 to 0.1 microfarad and come in many different shapes and markings. The best way to get acquainted with capacitor markings is to browse through the capacitors in an electronics store, observing the way the various types are marked.

To install the wire-wrap sockets, mix up a small batch of 5-minute epoxy and use it to glue *one* row of sockets in place on the component side of the board. Be careful not to slop any glue on the wire-wrap pins themselves, as this could cause trouble with the wire-wrap connections later. Toothpicks are very handy for mixing and handling the epoxy. Put the sockets in the desired positions, making sure you use a socket with the proper number of pins for each IC, and that all the pin 1's point in the same direction on the board. The advantage of using 5-minute epoxy is that it holds the sockets firmly in place and dries quickly, but is not so strong that you can't remove the sockets by prying them loose with a small screwdriver. Gluing in the sockets one row at a time instead of all at once makes it much easier to solder in the power and ground connections.

To make the power and ground connections to each socket, wire-wrap one end of a short piece of wire-wrap wire onto the proper socket pin and solder the other end to the nearest power or ground trace on the board. If the power or ground line is on the component side of the board, use an insulated length of wire and route the wire from the socket pin through the closest free hole to the other side of the board. Always keep the wire length as short as possible. If you've never wire-wrapped or soldered before, you may want to practice with a spare socket and a scrap of circuit board before you try the real thing. See the wire-wrapping hints below. To solder, you should tin the hot soldering iron tip with a bit of solder and then wipe it clean on a damp sponge just before you try to solder a connection. Touch the tip to both the wire and the printed circuit board trace so that both are heated simultaneously for a second or two, and then touch the end of a piece of solder to the intersection of the wire, the circuit board, and the soldering iron. As soon as the solder flows freely onto the printed circuit board trace and wets it without balling up, remove the iron and the piece of solder.

Repeat the gluing and power/ground connection steps for each row of sockets until all sockets are in place. At this point it's a good idea to put a label between the pins of each socket (on the wiring side of the board), identifying the IC that goes there. This simple step can save a lot of agony later, since otherwise it's all too easy to get confused as to which socket you are connecting wires to. The label must be thin to fit in between the pins. Try using Avery self-adhesive typewriter correction tape, which is 1/6 inch wide and comes in 600-inch rolls. Just cut off the length you need and use it on sockets, IC's, or anything else where a tiny label is needed. It's also nice to have pin numbers, or at least pin 1, indicated for each socket. This can be done with the correction tape, or with specially made labels called Wrap-ID's. The latter are little plastic rectangles with numbered holes for each socket pin. They just slip over the pins before you start wire wrapping. A disadvantage is that you need to buy Wrap-ID's for every size of socket used (this usually means having 14-, 16-, 20-, 24-, and 40-pin versions on hand).

Wire-Wrapping the Circuit

Once the sockets are all installed and labeled, you're ready to begin wiring up the circuitry. The key word here is *accuracy*. You can either double-check the accuracy of every connection as you make it, or spend hours later on trying to figure out which one of 500 wires was connected wrong. A good technique is to write down the IC pin numbers on the circuit diagram for every wire as you attach it, or to use a colored marker pen on a copy of the circuit diagram to show which wires you have attached. Alternatively, you can make a wire list showing every connection on the board, and then check off each connection as you make it. This is a method often used by professionals.

If you've never wire-wrapped before, here's how to do it. The most common wire-wrap tool has a thin rod at both ends. The longer of the two rods is used for wire-wrapping, and the shorter for unwrapping a connection when you've made a mistake. The wire-wrapping end has a center hole and a small side hole. To wrap a wire, first determine the length of wire required, strip off 1 inch of insulation on each end if you're not using pre-stripped wire, and insert one of the stripped ends as far as it can go into the small side hole. Prestripped wire of various lengths makes the wrapping much faster. It's best to choose a wire long enough that there's a bit of slack in the connection. That way you can wiggle the wires around with a tweezers later when you want to see which wire is which. Using random colors for the wire or using a color-coding scheme can also help you to distinguish one wire from another. With the wire inserted, slip the center hole of the tool over the post and turn the tool clockwise until all the wire in the tool is wrapped around the post (about 10 to 12 turns). When doing this, don't push down or pull up on the tool. The weight of the tool or very slight downward pressure is about the right force to apply. The first wrap on a post should start at board level, not higher, and the coils should be tight, forming an even single layer on the post with no gaps between the wires and no doubling up of one layer on top of another. Subsequent wires wrapped on the same post (up to two more) should follow with no intervening spaces. If you make a mistake, you can simply unwrap the wire using the short end of the wire-wrap tool. Slip it over the socket post and turn counter-clockwise until you see the wire begin to move. Then pull the tool off. If you've done it properly, the wire will come off with the tool. You may find it easiest to cut the wire near the post before unwrapping it. Just make sure you cut the right wire!

Discrete components such as pull-up resistors or capacitors can be mounted on a wire-wrap board in several different ways. It's simplest to mount the component right on the board with its leads going straight down through the holes in the board. Use a needle-nose pliers to bend the leads so that the component sits right on the board and the leads go cleanly through the holes. Make sure the leads don't touch any power or ground lines. Then cut the leads off so they extend out about 1/2 inch on the wiring side of the board, and make wire-wrap connections to them just as if they were wire-wrap posts. The contact won't be very good because the leads don't have sharp corners as wire-wrap posts do, but this can be remedied by soldering the wire-wrap connection after it's made. You can also buy special wire-wrap posts such as the Vector T49DP terminals. These have a wire-wrap post on one end and a tiny spring fork on the other. The terminals can be inserted into holes on the wire-wrap board and the component leads can be placed in the spring fork and soldered in place. Finally, if you have a number of small components, you can just solder them all into a DIP plug header. These plug directly into 14- or 16-pin IC sockets and have a double row of tiny forks onto which components can be soldered.

Checking Out the Board

When you've finished wiring up the board, it's tempting to plug all the IC's into their sockets immediately and put the board into the computer. This is called "smoke testing" the board, because problems with the board often make their presence known in the form of smoke coming from shorted components! To reduce the chances of this, it's wise to leave all the IC's off the board initially. Then take a voltmeter and check the resistance between the 5-volt power lines and ground. If it's not infinite, you may have a short or a bad capacitor somewhere. When you make this measurement, you may have to wait a second to get a true reading since it takes a little time for the capacitors to charge up. If you're using additional power-supply voltages, their resistances to ground should be checked also.

After the board passes the resistance check, plug it into the computer (still without IC's) and check that the proper voltages are present on all pins that should have power and not on any others. If all is okay, remove the board, plug in the IC's, and re-install the board in the computer. Whenever you install or remove computer boards, make sure the computer is turned *off*. Hot-socketing computer boards is an invitation to disaster.

When you install the IC's, make sure that pin 1 of each chip matches pin 1 on the socket. To find pin 1 on an IC, refer to the diagrams in Fig. 12-2, which show a top view (pins facing down) of typical pin 1 markings. Use both hands to insert each IC into its socket, being careful to apply even pressure to both ends so that they go in together. If the pins are spread too widely to go into the socket holes, place the IC on its side on a table, and, holding the body of the IC with your fingers, press downward so that the pins are not spread out so widely. To remove an IC from its socket, never use your fingers. One end almost always sticks in the socket, resulting in bent pins. After this happens a couple of times, the pins break off, giving you a collection of interesting but unusable 13- and 15-pin IC's. Instead, pry on alternate ends with a tweezers or a screwdriver, lifting the IC just a little each time so that both ends come out at once.

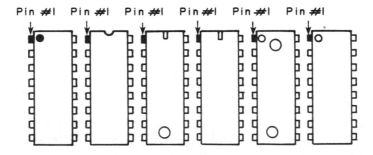

Fig. 12-2. Finding pin 1 on an integrated circuit DIP package.

Be especially careful when handling MOS (**m**etal **o**xide **s**emiconductor) chips, as these are easily damaged by static electricity. Almost all large-scale integrated circuits such as smart peripheral chips, memory chips, and almost anything else with 24 pins or more are MOS. Any chip that comes wrapped in aluminum foil or stuck in a piece of black foam is also MOS. An invisible static discharge of a few hundred volts can destroy MOS chips, and you can easily build up a charge of several thousand volts on your body just by walking across a carpet in a dry room. This static sensitivity makes MOS chips a bit of a pain to handle (especially here in the Arizona desert where the humidity is often 5% or less!).

The standard drill for handling MOS IC's is as follows: When not in a socket on a board, the chip should be stored in a piece of black conductive foam (not styrofoam!). Here it's safe from damage. Just before you insert the chip into a board, touch your hands and the foam to a ground such as the metal case on your computer (touch bare metal, not the paint). Then, without getting up or sliding around on your seat, remove the chip from the foam, and insert it into its socket on the board. If possible, keep the board on a grounded conductive foam pad or aluminum foil when it's not in the computer. To remove a MOS chip from a board, make sure you've grounded yourself before you touch it, use tweezers or a screwdriver to pry the chip out gently, and then put it back in a piece of conductive foam.

A problem facing all interface boards for the IBM is getting signals to external devices in and out of the machine. The wires have to come out the back of the computer, and there's only a 3.5- by 0.5-inch area per card available for connectors on the back of the machine. If you have only one I/O channel coming in or out of the board, a good choice is to mount a 25-pin D-type connector (DB-25, also known as an RS-232C connector) with right-angle leads on the rear edge of the interface board and then to screw it into a hole cut into the metal retaining bracket that attaches to the rear of the board. The prototype cards made by Vector Electronics have metal retaining brackets with precut holes for this. You can also fit two 9-pin (DB-9) or two 15-pin (DB-15) D-type connectors on the retaining bracket. If you have a large number of signals coming in or out, you could go to a 37- or 50-pin D-type connector, and have several cables coming out of the connector if the signals have to go to more than one external device.

Alternatively, you can use a simpler, though not as neat, method of getting signals in and out. The required I/O signals can be wired to 16-pin wire-wrap sockets, and DIP jumpers with ribbon cables attached can be plugged into the sockets. The ribbon cables may be routed directly to the desired external device.

Yet another cable connection method is to use a right-angle jumper header mounted on the prototype board. These connectors have two parallel rows of square posts on 0.1-inch centers sticking out, and are available in 10-, 20-, 26-, 34-, 40-, and 50-pin sizes. Use the wire-wrap version of the header so that you can wire-wrap directly to it. The mating socket connector connects to flat ribbon cable using an insulation displacement technique. The ribbon cable or cables are placed in the socket, which contains a set of posts having sharp-edged V's cut in their tops. The assembly is then placed in a vise and squeezed so that the posts cut through the ribbon cable insulation and make contact with the wires inside. This is a widely used method of making ribbon-cable connections. This method and the previous DIP jumper method are most appropriate when you don't have a metal retaining bracket to attach to the rear of the prototype card.

12-3. Hardware Debugging Tips

If you plug in your newly constructed board and it works just as you expected, you deserve congratulations. You've done everything perfectly and won't need the rest of this chapter. Unfortunately this is sometimes not the case. Some little detail has been overlooked, and the interface just lies there, dead as a doornail. Now what?

Before you sink into total depression, you should try a few simple tests that turn out to catch problems a surprising percentage of the time. The first thing to do is to pull the board out and inspect it *carefully*. Are *all* the IC's installed? Are they installed in the right sockets, or have two of them been interchanged by mistake? Have they all been installed in the right orientation with pin 1 where it's supposed to be? Were any IC pins bent underneath the chip when they were put in the sockets? Are any wire-wrap pins on the back side of the board bent and touching each other? Now put the board back in carefully and make sure any cables needed are really connected. Then if things still aren't right, remember that interfaces work only if both the hardware and the computer software that drives them are correct. Either one could be at fault. Make sure that the port numbers you wired up in hardware are the ones you're addressing with your software. Use the simplest software routine possible to make the interface do something. In many cases you can use BASIC or DEBUG to do a couple of input or output operations. The results will tell you whether at least some of the board is working properly.

It's always tempting to think that the problem lies in a bad chip. While such things do occur, they're really quite rare and it's probably not worthwhile to exchange chips until you've done considerably more checking of the circuit. One quick and worthwhile check is to touch your finger to each of the chips on the board while it's running in the computer. If any chip burns your finger, you've probably got a shorted chip and it should be swapped out. The fact that one chip is just hotter than the others doesn't necessarily mean there's a problem. Some chips, such as bus buffers or fast 74S series chips, just draw more current and normally run hot. Another situation where a chip swap might be considered is if you know that you've really mishandled a MOS chip by zapping it with static electricity. However, any time you swap a chip on a nonworking board, remember that the reason the chip is not working may be that it's been blown away by some other problem on the board. If this is the case, a swap only produces two dead chips instead of one. This is a good way to spend money very quickly if the chip in question is expensive.

If the above tests don't find the problem, you need to take a more structured and disciplined approach to the debugging job. Before discussing such methods, however, let's look at some of the tools necessary to do an efficient job of debugging an interface.

The most basic piece of equipment needed is a voltmeter. This need not be an expensive digital meter, since you generally need to know only whether +5 volts, a TTL logic high, or a TTL low is present, or whether there is a connection between two points. For this kind of work, Radio Shack's little $10 voltmeter is ideal. This meter is extremely small and light, and puts out only 1.5 volts when reading resistance, so there's no danger of damaging any circuitry. (Voltmeters measure resistance by applying a voltage difference between the two leads and then measuring the current that flows. In some voltmeters this voltage can be as high as 10 volts.) There are a few occasions when you may want an accurate digital volt-meter, but they are quite rare. We cut the ends off the test leads supplied with the voltmeter and replace them with XM Micro Hooks (made by E-Z-Hook Corporation). These have a tiny hooked wire that extends from the end when a small plunger is pushed, and are indispensable for making con-nections to closely spaced wire-wrap pins. It's also very useful to have several jumpers (12- to 24-inch pieces of wire) with Micro Hooks on both ends.

Another basic piece of equipment is a logic probe. This handy little device has three LED's on it. When you touch the tip of the probe to a circuit, one LED lights up if a TTL low level is present and another lights up if a TTL high is present. The third LED lights up when pulses are present, and then the relative brightness of the high and low LED's indicates whether the pulse train is mostly high or mostly low. Another feature is a pulse-catcher mode. You touch the probe to the pin you want to monitor, and then flip a switch on the probe. Once the switch is on, any TTL level change, either high to low or low to high, is latched, causing the pulse LED to light up. In this way even a single pulse a few nanoseconds long can be observed. Global Specialties makes several good logic probes, and other companies also have moderately priced models. Any probe you buy should have a pulse-catcher mode and should be capable of capturing pulses as short as 10 nanoseconds. Otherwise you run the risk of missing short pulses or glitches altogether. You can also buy logic monitor clips that clip onto a 14- or 16-pin IC and display the logic state of all 16 pins simultaneously. These are useful, but a logic probe is usually preferable since it can examine signals anywhere, not just at small IC chips, and it can capture single pulses.

A far more powerful, but much more expensive, debugging tool is the oscilloscope. You can do a lot of debugging without a scope, but certain problems require them. Examples include problems with oscillator circuits and measurements of their frequency, timing problems where two logic signals do not have the right time delay with respect to each other, and noise problems where logic signals may briefly switch to the opposite state at the wrong time. Even if you don't have a scope of your own, you should at least be able to borrow one occasionally if you plan to do any appreci-able amount of interfacing. A scope can also be used in any situation where the logic probe can be used, and provides much more information, such as pulse lengths, frequencies, and exact voltage levels. An oscilloscope for digital logic work should be a dual-trace scope (so two signals can be compared) and have at least 15-MHz bandwidth (so short pulses aren't missed).

If money is no object, buy the tool that professional computer engineers use: a logic analyzer. It can monitor and display logic signals on many lines simultaneously, and a trace can be triggered by complex logical combinations of many signals. Unfortunately, these devices cost thousands of dollars and require considerable skill to use effectively. However, they're usually not essential for logic debugging—they just speed it up.

Another very useful accessory is an extender board. You plug in the board under test on top of this card to raise it up above the top of the IBM's chassis. In many computers such a board is essential, but in the IBM you can always put the board in the leftmost card slot and have almost full access to the wiring side of the board. Nonetheless, an extender may be useful. When using an extender board, you should be aware of two potential problems. First, the board under test should be held straight up in the extender board so it doesn't flop to one side and hence not make good contact with all of the card edge connections. If the extender board doesn't provide good support, you may have to hold it up straight with some masking tape. A second problem is that on rare occasions cards can show flaky operation on an extender board due to the extra distance the bus signals have to travel, even though they operate properly when in their usual position down in the IBM chassis. We have not observed such problems ourselves, but the potential is there because problems have been reported in which memory boards have operated properly only when in the two or three rightmost slots of the PC (nearest to the bus drivers).

Suppose you've tried the simple tests above and found nothing. The board is still sitting lifelessly in the computer. What can be done next? While there's no universal step-by-step debugging procedure, the general philosophy is the same as discussed in Sec. 4-3 for software: divide and conquer. You want to mentally divide the circuitry into logical blocks and look at the inputs and outputs of each block rather than looking at the signals on every pin of every chip—an almost hopeless task. Here are the kinds of things you should look at:

1. If you have oscillators or clocks on the board, make sure they're running. An oscilloscope is invaluable here. A logic probe can tell you if pulses are being generated, but it can't provide information on wave shapes or frequencies.

2. Check the enable lines on buffers and the outputs of any address decoding circuitry. Use a scope or a logic probe together with a little assembly language program consisting of a loop that repeatedly accesses the ports or memory locations used by the board.

3. If a smart chip is involved, check its inputs to make sure it's being selected. If it is, you may only have a software problem. Make sure the chip is being properly initialized.

4. Remember that you can't tell anything by just looking at address or data lines because of the real-time-clock interrupts and the periodic refresh via DMA channel 0 that occurs every 15 microseconds. These activities activate the address and data lines as well as $\overline{IOR}$ and $\overline{IOW}$. You can turn off the interrupts, but don't stop the refresh or everything will come to a screeching halt.

Just as with software debugging, it's very important to spend time thinking about the problem. If you're looking at a board that you've designed, the problem may be a design error rather than a hardware malfunction. In any event, careful thought and a few well chosen measurements are usually the best way to proceed. Every debugging problem is solvable; some just take longer than others. This illustrates one of our basic mottos, as applicable to the design of a scientific theory as to the design of digital circuits: "Intuition is necessary, but not sufficient." Whenever you create something, experiment a bit to check your hypotheses.

References

IBM PC Options and Adapters Technical Reference, Vols. 1—3, 1984, IBM Corporation, Boca Raton, FL. This set of manuals contains complete schematics of the IBM PC and of all IBM-manufactured adapter boards. It's a prime source of ideas for interface board designs.

S. Ciarcia, 1984, *Ciarcia's Circuit Cellar*, Vols. I through V, McGraw-Hill, New York. These five volumes are a collection of Steve's *BYTE* magazine columns, and are full of interesting interfacing ideas complete with tested circuit diagrams that implement them.

P. Horowitz and W. Hill, 1980, *The Art of Electronics*, Cambridge University Press, New York. One of the best all around electronics reference books in existence. It covers all areas of electronics and includes many useful discussions of specific components and their uses.

D. Lancaster, 1976, *TTL Cookbook*, Howard W. Sams & Co., New York. This is the classic book on TTL circuitry and its applications. Although somewhat dated, it contains many valuable construction and design hints.

G. Young, 1980, *Digital Electronics: A Hands-On Learning Approach*, Hayden Book Company, Rochelle Park, NJ. A good self-teaching guide to digital electronics, with many practical construction hints and a chapter on troubleshooting.

Appendix A
ASCII Table

ASCII (American Standard Code for Information Interchange) is the standard method of encoding human-readable text for storage in computer memory or for transmission between computers and other devices. Since standard ASCII is a 7-bit code, having values of 0 through 7F hexadecimal, 128 different letters, numbers, and other characters are defined. However, because ASCII is typically stored in the computer as an 8-bit value, many manufacturers (including IBM) have defined an extended ASCII set having 256 characters. Unfortunately, the extended ASCII codes (80H through FFH) do not have standard definitions and their meanings vary from one machine to another. Only standard ASCII is discussed here.

The lowest 32 ASCII code values do not represent printable characters, but rather are *control codes* that are meant to provide control signals for the device receiving the ASCII data. The first table in this appendix shows two abbreviations for these control codes and their standard names. The first set of abbreviations names the control codes according to the way they're typed on a keyboard (the "©" means to type the key following the © while holding down the Control key), and the second set names the codes as contractions of the full control code names.

The second table presents the complete set of ASCII codes together with the code values in both hexadecimal and decimal. In the table, "SP" means the space or blank character, and "Del" is the "delete" character. The way the characters in the table are grouped reveals their relationship to one another. The basic grouping is in 32's, namely the four columns of 32 codes shown in the table. As the table shows, both the control codes and the lower case letters differ from the upper case letters by only one bit. Thus "©A" is the code for "A" with bit 6 set low ('©A' = 'A' - 40H), while "a" is the code for "A" with bit 5 set high ('a' = 'A' + 20H).

Code	Abbreviations		Name
00	©@	NULL	Null
01	©A	SOH	Start Of Heading
02	©B	STX	Start of Text
03	©C	ETX	End of Text
04	©D	EOT	End Of Transmit
05	©E	ENQ	Enquiry
06	©F	ACK	Acknowledge
07	©G	BEL	Bell
08	©H	BS	BackSpace
09	©I	HT	Horizontal Tab
0A	©J	LF	LineFeed
0B	©K	VT	Vertical Tab
0C	©L	FF	FormFeed
0D	©M	CR	Carriage Return
0E	©N	SO	Shift Out
0F	©O	SI	Shift In
10	©P	DLE	Data Line Escape
11	©Q	DC1	Device Control 1
12	©R	DC2	Device Control 2
13	©S	DC3	Device Control 3
14	©T	DC4	Device Control 4
15	©U	NAK	Negative Acknowledge
16	©V	SYN	Synchronous idle
17	©W	ETB	End of Transmit Block
18	©X	CAN	Cancel
19	©Y	EM	End of Medium
1A	©Z	SUB	Substitute
1B	©[	ESC	Escape
1C	©\	FS	File Separator
1D	©]	GS	Group Separator
1E	©^	RS	Record Separator
1F	©_	US	Unit Separator

	hex	dec		hex	dec		hex	dec		hex	dec
⌐@	00	00	SP	20	32	@	40	64	`	60	96
⌐A	01	01	!	21	33	A	41	65	a	61	97
⌐B	02	02	"	22	34	B	42	66	b	62	98
⌐C	03	03	#	23	35	C	43	67	c	63	99
⌐D	04	04	$	24	36	D	44	68	d	64	100
⌐E	05	05	%	25	37	E	45	69	e	65	101
⌐F	06	06	&	26	38	F	46	70	f	66	102
⌐G	07	07	'	27	39	G	47	71	g	67	103
⌐H	08	08	(	28	40	H	48	72	h	68	104
⌐I	09	09	)	29	41	I	49	73	i	69	105
⌐J	0A	10	*	2A	42	J	4A	74	j	6A	106
⌐K	0B	11	+	2B	43	K	4B	75	k	6B	107
⌐L	0C	12	,	2C	44	L	4C	76	l	6C	108
⌐M	0D	13	-	2D	45	M	4D	77	m	6D	109
⌐N	0E	14	.	2E	46	N	4E	78	n	6E	110
⌐O	0F	15	/	2F	47	O	4F	79	o	6F	111
⌐P	10	16	0	30	48	P	50	80	p	70	112
⌐Q	11	17	1	31	49	Q	51	81	q	71	113
⌐R	12	18	2	32	50	R	52	82	r	72	114
⌐S	13	19	3	33	51	S	53	83	s	73	115
⌐T	14	20	4	34	52	T	54	84	t	74	116
⌐U	15	21	5	35	53	U	55	85	u	75	117
⌐V	16	22	6	36	54	V	56	86	v	76	118
⌐W	17	23	7	37	55	W	57	87	w	77	119
⌐X	18	24	8	38	56	X	58	88	x	78	120
⌐Y	19	25	9	39	57	Y	59	89	y	79	121
⌐Z	1A	26	:	3A	58	Z	5A	90	z	7A	122
⌐[	1B	27	;	3B	59	[	5B	91	{	7B	123
⌐\	1C	28	<	3C	60	\	5C	92	¦	7C	124
⌐]	1D	29	=	3D	61	]	5D	93	}	7D	125
⌐^	1E	30	>	3E	62	^	5E	94	~	7E	126
⌐_	1F	31	?	3F	63	_	5F	95	Del	7F	127

Appendix B
Hexadecimal–Decimal
Conversion Table

Below is a table that is very useful for converting decimal number
hexadecimal and vice versa. On the facing page is a table showing pov
of 2. This is useful when working with the 8087 coprocessor.

HEXADECIMAL COLUMNS									
5		4		3		2		1	
hex	dec	hex	dec	hex	dec	hex	dec	hex	dec
0	0	0	0	0	0	0	0	0	0
1	65,536	1	4,096	1	256	1	16	1	1
2	131,072	2	8,192	2	512	2	32	2	2
3	196,608	3	12,288	3	768	3	48	3	3
4	262,144	4	16,384	4	1,024	4	64	4	4
5	327,680	5	20,480	5	1,280	5	80	5	5
6	393,216	6	24,576	6	1,536	6	96	6	6
7	458,752	7	28,672	7	1,792	7	112	7	7
8	524,288	8	32,768	8	2,048	8	128	8	8
9	589,824	9	36,864	9	2,304	9	144	9	9
A	655,360	A	40,960	A	2,560	A	160	A	10
B	720,896	B	45,056	B	2,816	B	176	B	11
C	786,432	C	49,152	C	3,072	C	192	C	12
D	851,968	D	53,248	D	3,328	D	208	D	13
E	917,504	E	57,344	E	3,584	E	224	E	14
F	983,040	F	61,440	F	3,840	F	240	F	15

POWERS OF TWO

2^n	n	2^{-n}
1	0	1.0
2	1	0.5
4	2	0.25
8	3	0.125
16	4	0.062 5
32	5	0.031 25
64	6	0.015 625
128	7	0.007 812 5
256	8	0.003 906 25
512	9	0.001 953 125
1 024	10	0.000 976 562 5
2 048	11	0.000 488 281 25
4 096	12	0.000 244 140 625
8 192	13	0.000 122 070 312 5
16 384	14	0.000 061 035 156 25
32 768	15	0.000 030 517 578 125
65 536	16	0.000 015 258 789 062 5
131 072	17	0.000 007 629 394 531 25
262 144	18	0.000 003 814 697 265 625
524 288	19	0.000 001 907 348 632 812 5
1 048 576	20	0.000 000 953 674 316 406 25

Appendix C
Piano Keyboard Routine

This program turns the IBM PC keyboard into a piano-like keyboard. See Sec. 8-1 for backgound information on the keyboard and Sec. 9-5 for more background on waveform generation. The *asdfghjkl;* row plays the key of C with some keys in the *qwertyuiop* row playing sharps and flats. The keys F and G play the notes f and g, respectively, with all other keys falling in place accordingly. Hence middle C (if the appropriate octave is chosen, see below) is the note a, Ctrl is b, S is d, and so on as shown in this table:

Key:		W	E		T	Y	U		O	P		]
Note:		c#	d#		f#	g#	a#		c#	d#		f#

Key:	Ctrl	A	S	D	F	G	H	J	K	L	;	' '
Note:	b	c	d	e	f	g	a	b	c	d	e	f g

To change octaves, type the function key Fn for the nth octave, where F4 gives middle C for key A. To change the volume, type the space bar to toggle half volume. Type either shift key to go up an octave, and Alt or Caps Lock to go down an octave. To quit, type Esc. Have fun!

The registers are used for storage as follows: BL returns the next code typed on the keyboard, BH saves the last tone code, CL contains the octave shift value, and CH contains the half-volume shift bit (2 if on). For speed in the volume chopping loop (see waitcd), the internal keyboard interrupt handler writes BL directly, which doesn't conflict with the system clock routine (but probably would with other interrupt routines).

```
title  PIANO KEYBOARD ROUTINE

eoi        = 20h                      ;End Of Interrupt command
pictrl     = 20h                      ;8259A interrupt controller control port
picmsk     = 21h                      ;Interrupt mask port
timer2     = 42h                      ;Timer channel 2 registers
portb      = 61h                      ;System 8255 PPI port B
kb_data    = 60h
kb_ctl     = portb


keynote    macro   key,note          ;Format of key-note table entries
           db      key               ;Key code from keyboard
           dw      note              ;Corresponding count value
           endm


kdata      segment at 0
           org     4*9
int9       dw      ?                  ;INT 9 vector
kdata      ends


cseg       segment
assume     cs:cseg,ds:cseg,es:kdata


           org     100h              ;Make this program into a .COM file
start:     xor     ax,ax             ;Setup return to system
           push    ax
           mov     es,ax
           push    int9              ;Save old keyboard interrupt routine
           push    int9+2
           cli                       ;No interrupts just now
           mov     int9+2,cs         ;Set up new keyboard interrupt routine
           mov     int9,offset keyint
           sti
           xor     cx,cx             ;Use middle octave (no shifts)
           in      al,portb          ;Turn off timer2 initially
           and     al,0feh
           out     portb,al

init:      in      al,portb          ;Be sure volume is on initially
           or      al,2
init1:     mov     bl,0              ;Zero new code (keyint updates this)
waitcd:    xor     al,ch             ;Toggle output bit for volume control
           out     portb,al
           or      bl,bl             ;New keycode? (keyint gets this)
           jz      waitcd
```

```
            or      al,ch           ;If half volume, be sure speaker is on now
            out     portb,al
            mov     al,bl
            cmp     al,1            ;Escape back to system?
            jnz     brktst
            in      al,picmsk
            and     al,0feh         ;Turn clock on (if off)
            out     picmsk,al
            cli                     ;Restore usual keyboard handler
            pop     int9+2
            pop     int9
            sti
            ret

brktst:     test    al,80h          ;Break code?
            jz      search
            and     al,7fh          ;Yep. Turn off break bit
            cmp     al,bh           ;Same as previous code?
            jnz     init            ;If not, ignore code
            in      al,portb        ;It is. Turn off speaker
            and     al,0fch
            out     portb,al
            jmp     init

search:     lea     si,table                ;Translate code
sloop:      test    byte ptr [si],0ffh ;End of table?
            jz      init
            cmp     al,[si]         ;No. Match?
            jz      outfrq
            add     si,3            ;No. Bypass count
            jmp     sloop

outfrq:     inc     si
            lodsw                   ;Get count (or special code)
            cmp     ax,5
            jl      stoctv
            jz      togvol
            cmp     ax,6
            jz      goup
            cmp     ax,7
            jz      godown
            test    cl,80h          ;Negative?
            jnz     shiftl
            shr     ax,cl           ;Divide count to increase frequency
            jmp     short outfr2
```

```
shiftl:    push    cx
           neg     cl
           shl     ax,cl        ;Multiply count to decrease frequency
           pop     cx
outfr2:    out     timer2,al
           mov     al,ah
           out     timer2,al
           in      al,portb
           or      al,3         ;Turn on speaker
           out     portb,al
           mov     bh,bl        ;Update old code
outfr5:    jmp     init

stoctv:    mov     cl,al        ;Update octave shift value
stoct2:    test    cl,80h       ;Negative?
           jnz     stoct3
           cmp     cl,4
           jbe     stoct4
           mov     cl,-3
           jmp     short stoct4
stoct3:    cmp     cl,-3
           jge     stoct4
           mov     cl,4
stoct4:    in      al,portb     ;Note on?
           test    al,1
           jz      outfr5
           mov     al,bh        ;Yep. Update frequency
           mov     bl,bh
           jmp     search
goup:      inc     cl           ;Go up an octave
           jmp     stoct2
godown:    dec     cl
           jmp     stoct2

togvol:    in      al,picmsk    ;Toggle volume
           xor     ch,2
           jz      setnvl
           or      al,1
           jmp     short setint
setnvl:    and     al,0feh      ;Turn clock on (if off)
setint:    out     picmsk,al
           jmp     init
```

```
keyint:   push    ax              ;Short keyboard interrupt routine
          in      al,kb_data      ;(to minimize effect on half volume)
          mov     bl,al           ;Set up BL for piano routine
          in      al,kb_ctl
          or      al,82h
          out     kb_ctl,al       ;Reset keyboard interrupt flip-flop
          and     al,7fh
          out     kb_ctl,al
          mov     al,eoi          ;Tell 8259A the interrupt's over
          out     pictrl,al
          pop     ax
          iret
```

;Key-to-note conversion table

```
table:    keynote 29,4832         ; Ctrl = b
          keynote 30,4561         ; A = c (262 Hz = middle C)
          keynote 17,4305         ; W = c#
          keynote 31,4063         ; S = d
          keynote 18,3835         ; E = d#
          keynote 32,3620         ; D = e
          keynote 33,3417         ; F = f
          keynote 20,3225         ; T = f#
          keynote 34,3044         ; G = g
          keynote 21,2873         ; Y = g#
          keynote 35,2712         ; H = a (440 Hz - concert A)
          keynote 22,2560         ; U = a#
          keynote 36,2416         ; J = b
          keynote 37,2280         ; K = c
          keynote 24,2152         ; O = c#
          keynote 38,2032         ; L = d
          keynote 25,1918         ; P = d#
          keynote 39,1810         ; ; = e
          keynote 40,1708         ; ' = f
          keynote 27,1612         ; ] = f#
          keynote 41,1522         ; ' = g
          keynote 28,1437         ; cr = g#
          keynote 75,1356         ; 4 = a
```

;Octave conversions

```
        keynote  59,-3        ; F1 = 55 Hz (A = 55 Hz)
        keynote  60,-2        ; F2 = 110 Hz
'       keynote  61,-1        ; F3 = 220 Hz
        keynote  62,0         ; F4 = 440 Hz
        keynote  63,1         ; F5 = 880 Hz
        keynote  64,2         ; F6 = 1760 Hz
        keynote  65,3         ; F7 = 3520 Hz
        keynote  66,4         ; F8 = 7040 Hz

        keynote  57,5         ;Space = toggle 1/2 volume
        keynote  42,6         ;Left shift key = up one octave
        keynote  54,6         ;Right shift key = up one octave
        keynote  56,7         ;Alt key = down one octave
        keynote  58,7         ;CapsLock key = down one octave
        db       0            ;End of table

cseg    ends

        end      start
```

Appendix D
Sample DOS 2.0
Installable Device Driver

This appendix gives the code for a DOS 2.0 installable device driver that controls a serial printer. For a discussion of how the program works, see Sec. 4-6. This is an example of a character I/O device driver. The IBM *DOS 2.0* manual gives an example of a block I/O device driver that creates and manages a simulated disk drive in RAM.

```
title          SIMPLE SERIAL PRINTER DRIVER

;Serial Port Parameters

pnum      equ     0          ;Serial port card number
sdata     equ     03f8h      ;Serial port transmitter register
mctrl     equ     sdata+4    ;Modem control register
status    equ     sdata+5    ;Serial port line status register
uparm     equ     0e3h       ;Baud rate, word length, and parity
                             ; Here the port is set for 9600 baud,
                             ; 8 bits, no parity (see INT 14 section
                             ; of Technical Reference App. A)
```

;REQUEST HEADER OFFSETS

```
len_fld        equ     0            ;Length field
ucd_fld        equ     1            ;Unit code field
ccd_fld        equ     2            ;Command code field
sta_fld        equ     3            ;Status field
res_fld        equ     5            ;Reserved area field
```

;Request header additions for initialization

```
units          equ     13           ;Number of units (block devices only)
end_addr       equ     14           ;End address for resident code
bpb_ptr        equ     18           ;BPB array pointer (block devices only)
```

;Request header additions for read or write

```
md             equ     13           ;Media descriptor byte (block devices only)
taddr          equ     14           ;Data transfer address
count          equ     18           ;Number of bytes in buffer
ssn            equ     20           ;Starting sector number (block devices only)

cseg           segment public  'code'
               assume cs:cseg,es:cseg,ds:cseg
```

;DEVICE HEADER -- must be the first item in an installable device driver

```
serial         proc  far
next_dev       dd      -1           ;Next device header field
attribute      dw      8000h        ;Attribute field (char device, no IOCTL)
strategy       dw      dev_strat    ;Device strategy routine pointer
interrupt      dw      dev_int      ;Device interrupt handler pointer
dev_name       db      'PRN     '   ;Eight byte device name field
```

;DEVICE STRATEGY ROUTINE

```
dev_strat:     mov     cs:rh_seg,es
               mov     cs:rh_off,bx
               ret

rh_off         dw      ?            ;Storage for the request header offset
rh_seg         dw      ?            ; and segment
```

```
;JUMP TABLE (for the 13 required device driver functions)

funtab     label     word
           dw        init            ;Code 0: initialize device
           dw        media_chk       ;Code 1: media changed?
           dw        build_bpb       ;Code 2: build BIOS parm block
           dw        ioctl_in        ;Code 3: input I/O control bytes
           dw        input           ;Code 4: input data from I/O device
           dw        nd_input        ;Code 5: nondestructive input, no wait
           dw        in_stat         ;Code 6: input device status
           dw        in_flush        ;Code 7: flush (clear) input queue
           dw        output          ;Code 8: output data to I/O device
           dw        out_verify      ;Code 9: output data w/verify
           dw        out_stat        ;Code 10: output device status
           dw        out_flush       ;Code 11: flush (clear) output queue
           dw        ioctl_out       ;Code 12: output I/O control bytes


;DEVICE INTERRUPT HANDLER

dev_int:   cld
           push      ds              ;Save everything in sight
           push      es
           push      ax
           push      bx
           push      cx
           push      dx
           push      di
           push      si
           mov       ax,cs:rh_seg    ;Point ES:BX at request header
           mov       es,ax
           mov       bx,cs:rh_off
           mov       al,es:[bx]+2    ;Get cmnd code from request header
           rol       al,1            ;Multiply code by 2
           xor       ah,ah
           lea       di,funtab       ;Point to start of jump table
           add       di,ax           ;Index into table
           jmp       word ptr [di]   ; and jump to requested function

;The following entries are not supported by this device:

media_chk:
build_bpb:
ioctl_in:
input:
nd_input:
```

```
in_stat:
in_flush:
ioctl_out:  or      es:word ptr [bx]+sta_fld,8103h
            jmp     exit              ;Unknown command, error & quit
```

;INITIALIZATION (command code 0) - initialize the I/O device

```
init:       lea     ax,e_o_p        ;Store end addr in request header
            mov     es:word ptr [bx]+end_addr,ax
            mov     es:word ptr [bx]+end_addr+2,cs
            mov     ax,uparm        ;Get UART parameters
            mov     dx,pnum         ;Get serial port card #
            int     14h             ;Initialize the UART
            mov     dx,mctrl        ;Set DTR and RTS low
            mov     al,3
            out     dx,al
            jmp     exit            ;Clean up and return
```

;OUTPUT (command code 8) - write data bytes to I/O device

```
output:     mov     si,es:[bx]+taddr ;Get data start address in DS:SI
            mov     ds,es:[bx]+taddr+2
            mov     cx,es:[bx]+count      ;Byte count in CX
nxtchr:     mov     ax,[si]              ;Get a char
            push    ax
print1:     mov     dx,status            ;Read xmitter status
            in      al,dx
            mov     ah,al                ;Save in AH
            inc     dx                   ;Accesses to 8250 must be at least
            nop                          ; 2 microseconds apart
            in      al,dx                ;Read handshake status
            and     ax,2020h
            xor     ax,2020h
            jnz     print1               ;Loop till xmitter and handshake clear
            sub     dx,6                 ;Then send char in AL
            pop     ax
            out     dx,al
            inc     si                   ;Point to next data byte
            loop    nxtchr               ; and repeat till no data left
            jmp     exit
```

```
;OUTPUT WITH VERIFY (command code 9) - write data to I/O device
;and verify by reading data back.  Make same as OUTPUT.

out_verify: jmp   output

;Just let the following two operations be NOP's for now

out_stat:                               ;Code 10: output device status
out_flush:                              ;Code 11: flush (clear) output queue

exit:         or      es:word ptr [bx]+sta_fld,0100H
              pop     si                ;Set return status
              pop     di                ; and restore all registers
              pop     dx
              pop     cx
              pop     bx
              pop     ax
              pop     es
              pop     ds
              ret


e_o_p:                                  ;End Of Program

serial        endp
cseg          ends
              end     serial
```

Appendix E
PC Keyboard
Redefinition Program

The KEYTRAN program takes over the PC's keyboard interrupt (INT 9), translating some input key codes to new values, and passing others onto the INT-9 handler active when KEYTRAN was run. Ctrl-Alt-D turns on a Dvorak keyboard layout; Ctrl-Alt-Q returns to qwerty. Alt and Shift-Alt aoe give corresponding umlauted characters needed for German text. Ctrl-Del turns off all translations, and Ctrl-+ (on numeric keypad) turns them back on. This feature is needed to allow KEYTRAN to be resident along with other keyboard handlers like communication programs that might assign different meanings to the keys. See Sec. 8-1 for further discussion of how the program works.

```
EOI          =        20h        ;End Of Interrupt command
kb_data      equ      60h        ;Keyboard data port
kb_ctl       equ      61h        ;Keyboard control port

data         segment at 40h      ;See PC Technical Reference BIOS
             org      17h        ; listing for definitions
kb_flag      label    byte       ;RAM keyboard flag byte with meanings

;bit 0 - right shift key pressed
;bit 1 - left shift key pressed
;bit 2 - Ctrl key pressed
;bit 3 - Alt key pressed
;bit 4 - Scroll-Lock state on
;bit 5 - Num-Lock state on
;bit 6 - Caps-Lock state on
;bit 7 - Insert state on
```

```
                org     1ah
buffer_head     dw      ?
buffer_tail     dw      ?
kb_buffer       dw      16 dup(?)  ;Only 16 entries, sigh!
kb_buffer_end label     word
data            ends


intpag          segment at 0
                org     4*9
int9            dw      ?
intpag          ends



cseg            segment
                assume  cs:cseg


dvorak          db      ?          ;Dvorak flag
newcod          db      ?          ;Unmodified key code for other programs


                org     58h
oint9           dd      ?          ;Old INT 9 address
prog            dw      ?
off             = 5ch - 103h       ;prog - offset table


                org     100h


start:          jmp     setup      ;Bypass tables and interrupt code


table           db      0,0,0      ;Unshift and Ctrl translation tables
ctable          db      0,0,0      ; put what you want
```

;**Dvorak keyboard** translation table

```
tabled          db      16,39,17,44,18,46,19,80,20,89,21,70,22,71,23,67,24,82
                db      25,76,26,47,30,65,31,79,32,69,33,85,34,73,35,68,36,72
                db      37,84,38,78,39,83,40,45,44,59,45,81,46,74,47,75,48,88
                db      49,66,50,77,51,87,52,86,53,90,0
```

;**Upper and lower case alternate** translation table for umlaut chars

```
altlc           db      30,132,24,148,22,129,48,225,0
altuc           db      30,142,24,153,22,154,0
```


;Keyboard interrupt routine

```
keybrd.         push    ax                      ;Save registers used
                push    bx
                push    cx
                push    dx
                push    si
                push    di
                push    ds
                push    es
                cld
                sti
                mov     ax,DATA                 ;ROM BIOS RAM segment
                mov     ds,ax
                assume  ds:DATA
                in      al,kb_data              ;Get and save key code
                mov     newcod,al
                cmp     dvorak,83               ;Transparent mode?
                jnz     keybr0
                test    kb_flag,4               ;Yes.  Check for Ctrl-+ only
                jz      keybr2
                cmp     al,78                   ;"+" key on numeric keypad?
                jnz     keybr2
                jmp     short keybr7            ;Yes. Reenable translations

keybr0:         test    al,80h                  ;Break code?
                jz      keybr3

keybr2:         pop     es                      ;Use INT-9 routine active
                pop     ds                      ; when symbol.com run
                pop     di
                pop     si
                pop     dx
                pop     cx
                pop     bx
                pop     ax
                jmp     [oint9]

keybr3:         test    kb_flag,4               ;Ctrl key pressed?
                jnz     keybr6
                test    kb_flag,8               ;No. Alt key pressed?
                jnz     altran

                mov     di,offset table + off   ;No. Translate key code
                cmp     dvorak,32               ;Use Dvorak table?
                jnz     keybr4
                mov     di,offset tabled + off  ;Yep
```

```
keybr4:        call      trans
               jnz       keybr2
               call      shfchk            ;Translation occurred; shift to
               jnz       keybr5            ; lower case?
               cmp       al,"A"            ;Yes if alphabetic
               jc        keybr5
               cmp       al,"Z"
               ja        keybr5
               or        al,20h            ;Convert to lower case
keybr5:        jmp       k61               ;Store code

keybr6:        test      kb_flag,8         ;Ctrl key. Alt key too?
               jz        keybr8
               cmp       al,16             ;Yes. Query control code?
               jz        keybr7
keyb62:        cmp       al,32             ;No. Dvorak?
               jnz       keybr2
keybr7:        mov       dvorak,al         ;Update keyboard control code
               jmp       k26               ;Restore regs and iret

keybr8:        cmp       al,83             ;Ctrl-Del?
               jz        keybr7
               mov       di,offset ctable + off
               jmp       short altra4

altran:        cmp       dvorak,83
               jz        altra2
               test      kb_flag,8         ;Alt key pressed?
altra2:        jnz       altra3
               jmp       keybr2
altra3:        mov       di,offset altlc + off
               call      shfchk
               jz        altra4
               mov       di,offset altuc + off
altra4:        call      trans
               jz        k61
               jmp       keybr2                 ;No xlation, use prev INT-9 routine

k61:           mov       bx,buffer_tail    ;Like IBM PC ROM code: store char
               mov       si,bx             ; in buffer
               add       bx,2
               cmp       bx,offset kb_buffer_end
               jne       k612
               mov       bx,offset kb_buffer
k612:          cmp       bx,buffer_head
```

```
            je      k26             ;Should give error beep: too much
            mov     [si],ax         ; code to dup
            mov     buffer_tail,bx


k26:        cli                     ;Restore keyboard and return
            in      al,kb_ctl
            mov     ah,al
            or      al,80h
            jmp     $+2             ;Slow down
            out     kb_ctl,al
            xchg    ah,al
            jmp     $+2
            out     kb_ctl,al
            mov     al,EOI          ;Send End Of Interrupt command to
            out     20h,al          ; 8259 interrupt controller
            pop     es
            pop     ds
            pop     di
            pop     si
            pop     dx
            pop     cx
            pop     bx
            pop     ax
            iret
```

comment ¶ SHFCHK - RZ iff Caps-Lock not active and neither Shift key is pressed. No regs changed
¶

```
shfchk:     test    kb_flag,40h     ;Caps-Lock state on?
            jz      shfch2
            test    kb_flag,3       ;Yes, either shift key pressed?
            jnz     shfch1
            or      sp,sp           ;No: RNZ
            ret
shfch1:     cmp     ax,ax           ;Yes: RZ
            ret

shfch2:     test    kb_flag,3       ;Caps-Lock not on; either Shift key
            ret                     ; pressed?
```

comment ¶ TRANS - Translate routine. Replaces byte in string cs:[di] by byte following matched byte. RZ iff match found.

¶

```
trans:          cmp     al,cs:[di]
                jz      trans2
                inc     di
                inc     di
                cmp     byte ptr cs:[di],0
                jnz     trans
                or      al,al
                ret                     ;RNZ
trans2:         mov     al,cs:[di+1]
                ret                     ;RZ

keyend:                                 ;End of resident code


setup:          xor     ax,ax           ;Get old int 9 vector
                mov     es,ax
                assume  es:intpag
                mov     ax,int9
                mov     word ptr oint9,ax
                mov     ax,int9+2
                mov     word ptr oint9+2,ax
                mov     di,offset prog  ;Move keybrd routine down to prog
                mov     si,offset table
                mov     cx,offset keyend - offset table
                push    ds
                pop     es
                rep     movsb           ;(Saves space)
                push    di
                mov     dx,offset keybrd+off  ;Set  DS:DX  to  target  INT 9
                                        addr
                mov     al,9            ;Set the keyboard interrupt (INT 9)
                mov     ah,25h          ; to DS:DX via DOS function call
                int     21h
                pop     dx              ;End prog but leave keybrd resident
                int     27h

cseg            ends

                end     start
```

Index